In Praise of Jerry Blavat and You Only Rock Once:

"To watch your growth from a young rebel to a now mature rebel has been phenomenal. Geator, you are one of a kind with a heart as big as all outdoors. I treasure these memories you write about in your book. Your friend, Dick Clark"
—Dick Clark

"Dear Geator,
I hear you wrote a book . . . that's impossible since you can't spell! Before I forget, please see that my pants are all on hangers. You were a great valet in the old days especially the way you folded my underwear. I know you will have great success with your book.
Luv ya. . . . Don"
—Don Rickles

"Jerry Blavat—the Geator—is one of the few guys in this business who has never been dictated to as far as the music he plays. His natural instinct for rhythm and blues, rock and roll, and other forms of music throughout the years has made him able to create careers for artists who otherwise never would have gotten play on radio. His love of the music, and his freedom to play his music, makes him unique and is why the Four Seasons are as popular today as we were in 1962, when he was first to play 'Sherry.'"
—Frankie Valli

"There will always be a place in my heart for Jerry. He is one of those pioneers who made personality radio an institution. When you read his book you will get a sense of the freedom he has had over the years to follow his dreams and help so many of us do the same. With fondness and gratitude for what he has contributed to my career, the ever-hopeful Mrs. Blavat."
—Connie Francis

"I love the Geator!"
—Aretha Franklin

"Whenever we were in Philly and the Geator was playing our music, we always knew we'd have a hit. It seems like yesterday, but Jerry was ahead of his time. He was the coolest guy in town. And now he's written the coolest book."
—Smokey Robinson

"There were very few white cats who knew the true sound of New Orleans. But my main man the Geator had it in his soul and knew where we were coming from. Whenever I did his TV show, it was a thrill."
—Fats Domino

"Jerry has always been a staunch supporter of my music. He was always on my side. He played an important part in East Coast radio and the music they were getting out. I have always appreciated Jerry for his taste and his judgment. Our music may not have been the most popular style of the day, but before others knew where we were going musically, Jerry understood it. He was in the middle of everything that was changing musical history. He always supported us. And because he had the freedom to play music that he believed in, he was one of the fellows responsible for our success."
—Burt Bacharach

"Wow! It's about time. Who better to write the book than someone who knows the anthology of our music from the '60s to the present day? The only one that comes to mind is the Boss with the Hot Sauce, the Geator with the Heator, Jerry Blavat. He played a big part in the very beginning of my recording career and has always supported my music. He is one that I am proud to call a friend."
—Dionne Warwick

"Jerry's mom cooked for Sinatra while the GEATOR cooked for the rest of us."
—Sid Mark, veteren DJ, WHPI, Philadelphia

"For a white boy the Geator's got too much soul. And can that boy dance! I remember doing his TV show and I'm doing 'Lucille' and he jumps up on the piano and starts to do the Slop. Yeah, there's only one Geator."
—Little Richard

"In our business, and in any business, people can only be happy when they stay who they are. I want to thank you, not only for me, but for all the artists and all the other people in the music business who either realize what you've done or don't realize what you've done. You knew me when. You defined me before I even defined myself. You have been so important to all of us throughout the years. I'm delighted that you've finally put your story down in writing."
—Berry Gordy, Founder, Motown Records

"It's too bad Jerry Blavat cannot be bottled, for he is the very essence of rock and roll. His enthusiasm and love for music is as strong as it was when he was a kid and later as a young man starting out in radio. His knowledge of doo-wop, rhythm and blues, rock and 20th-century pop is second to none. Mine is pretty good, but whenever I am stuck, Jerry is the first person I call,

He knew just about every major artist over the past 50 years. My introductions to Frank Sinatra, Sammy Davis Jr., Frankie Valli, Vic Damone, Al Martino all came from the 'Geator.'

I consider myself an expert, but no one knows more about doo-wop than Jerry. Jerry still experiences the same excitement when he hears classics like 'In the Still of the Night,' 'Why Do Fools Fall in Love,' and 'Earth Angel' that he did when he first heard them over 55 years ago. I do too, but the difference is that Jerry is in a position to pass these moments along to his radio audience instilling new memories and bringing 21st-century fans onboard.

Jerry's generosity to friends and strangers alike is a well documented fact. For all these reasons and more I am proud to call Jerry Blavat my first. I love him! Philadelphia, you are so lucky to have this man in your midst. Long may he reign."
—Seymour Stein, VP Warner Brothers Records, Cofounder Sire Records

"The Geator and I have been friends for nearly half a century. Why is that? Because he is a guy that puts friendship and loyalty above everything else. That's rare in our business. And that's what this book is about."
—Freddy DeMann, former manager of Madonna and Michael Jackson

"*You Only Rock Once* reads like compelling fiction, but every word is true. Jerry Blavat, 'The Geator with the Heator,' is living proof that anyone can achieve their dreams. From an against-all-odds beginning to multiple setbacks that few could overcome, Blavat amazes his supporters and confounds his adversaries with his tenacity and talent. Especially now in these trying economic times, the Geator is an inspiration to all of us trying to make a comeback or just get there in the first place. It's an enchanting must-read!"
—**Rollye James, radio personality and author of *What Am I Doing Here? (When Everything I Want Is Somewhere Else)***

"This riveting page-turner is an important slice of life in America and in the Philadelphia region. It is the story of an amazing man whose life has touched hundreds of thousands of people on the streets of the cities and suburbs, and some other people who he guided to fame and fortune in a journey that has more twists and turns than the greatest of Hollywood dramas. There is only one Jerry Blavat."
—**Larry Kane, veteran broadcast journalist**

"The Geator is the link in the rock 'n' roll chain, the bridge that spans several generations of the greatest music ever made. His timeless mastery of so many genres of superior sound connects the dots in a way few can. He's been there, done that, and is STILL doing that! In fact, listening to just an hour of Professor Blavat's show these days will enlighten even the most knowledgeable music historian. The house of rock that stands tall and thrives today is inhabited by the likes of bands ranging from Green Day to Pearl Jam and the Red Hot Chili Peppers among many others. However, this house was built on the solid gold foundation of the artists championed by the Geator over the years. From Ray Charles to Aretha Franklin, the Four Tops to the Four Seasons, Chuck Berry, Little Richard, Elvis, and more—it's all here—all nurtured by this soulful, passionate, musical genius. And, if that's not enough, he regularly hung out with the ORIGINAL rock star—Francis Albert Sinatra (who called him Matchstick)! I rest my case."
—**Pierre Robert, veteran DJ, WMMR Rock Radio, Philadelphia**

"Jerry was a huge influence on the Philadelphia music scene and continues to be a cornerstone of Philly culture. His unique voice has shaped the history of rock radio."
—**Kevin Bacon**

"It was the Geator who jump-started our career. When the record company was not going to release 'Twist and Shout,' he knew it was a hit. He took the demo back to Philly and busted it wide open. If it wasn't for the Geator, the Beatles never would have had a hit with it the second time around. We love you, Geator."
— **Ronnie Isley, The Isley Brothers**

"In the early days of my career, when I was in Philly, I had to listen to this guy, the Geator with the Heator. As I listened, I found out he wasn't just a disc jockey. He lived for the music, and I flipped when he would play 'My Hero' by the Blue Notes. At the end of the song, when the bagpipes would come in, he would go an octave higher and yell out, 'The Blue Notes, with bagpipes and all, are in the hall!'"
—**Patti Smith, performer, visual artist, and National Book Award-winning author of** *Just Kids*

"Long live the legend of the Geator!"
—**Davy Jones, The Monkees**

"The Geator is the last disc jockey."
—**Steve Van Zandt, Bruce Springsteen and the E Street Band,** *The Sopranos*

You Only Rock Once

You Only Rock Once

By Jerry Blavat

"The Geator with the Heator"

As told to Steve Oskie

Foreword by Dick Clark

RUNNING PRESS

PHILADELPHIA • LONDON

© 2011 by Jerry Blavat
Published by Running Press,
A Member of the Perseus Books Group

Books published by Running Press are available at special discounts for bulk purchases in the United States by corporations, institutions, and other organizations. For more information, please contact the Special Markets Department at the Perseus Books Group, 2300 Chestnut Street, Suite 200, Philadelphia, PA 19103, or call (800) 810-4145, ext. 5000, or e-mail special.markets@perseusbooks.com.

ISBN 978-0-7624-4215-7
Library of Congress Control Number: 2011925141

E-book ISBN 978-0-7624-4362-8

9 8 7 6 5 4 3 2 1
Digit on the right indicates the number of this printing

Cover and Interior Designer: Bill Jones
Editor: Greg Jones
Typography: Scala and Trade Gothic

Photography credits: back cover and bottom of page xxii; ©Michael Dress, Digital Warmth Recording. Page x, bottom, Photograph courtesy of Temple University Libraries, Urban Archives. Charles Myers/*Philadephia Daily News*. Used with permission of *Philadelphia Daily News* Copyright© 2011. All rights reserved.
Page xxix, bottom left, Photograph courtesy of Temple University Libraries, Urban Archives. Used with permission of *Philadelphia Inquirer* Permissions Copyright© 2011. All rights reserved.
All other photos courtesy of Celebrity Showcase

Running Press Book Publishers
A member of the Perseus Books Group
2300 Chestnut Street
Philadelphia, PA 19103-4371

Visit us on the web!
www.runningpress.com
www.geator.net

Dedication

I dedicate this book to all of the fans who have stood by me for all of these years, and to all of the people who have understood where I was coming from with my music. When others were knocking me, you were always there. You were the support that I needed, and you let me know that I was on the right path. The success that I have is because of you. Through it all, you have continued to support me and my family. I offer you a heartfelt thanks. We're growing old together, but we're doing it gracefully, with a youthful spirit, thanks to our music and our way of life.

Contents

Foreword by Dick Clark ∽ 13

Acknowledgments ∽ 14

Prologue ∽ 16

One: Trouble on the Home Front: Louis the Gimp ∽ 17

Two: Lifeline: Radio and TV ∽ 21

Three: The Bandstand *Years: Local Celebrity* ∽ 35

Four: The Street Was My Classroom ∽ 55

Five: Road Managing: Danny and the Juniors ∽ 76

Six: Breaking in as a Disc Jockey ∽ 101

Seven: The TV Years ∽ 167

Eight: Pied Piper: Going National ∽ 186

Nine: The Lean Years: Memories in Margate ∽ 223

Ten: Loyalty ∽ 265

Eleven: Trouble with the Law ∽ 271

Twelve: Beyond Teens ∽ 310

Index ∽ 348

Foreword

There are just not enough words to adequately describe Jerry Blavat, but let me give it a try.

I've known him since he was a teenager. Back in those days, he was a rebellious kid. I look at him today and all I see is a grown-up version of the kid I knew way back then.

Jerry has always had a magnificently wide taste in music, but he has built his reputation upon knowing everything about rhythm & blues and the rock & roll of yesteryear. This has not kept him from becoming an intimate friend of artists of all genres from Fats Domino to Frank Sinatra and beyond. He has an incredible memory for little bits of his extraordinary experiences!

The one thing you know for sure is that when he speaks, it's from the heart. He is incredibly generous, loyal and is always standing by when called upon for help. Some of his stories may sound unbelievable, but . . . you can count on his veracity.

Through the years, he has never been afraid to introduce his audiences to new and untested artists, who would eventually go on to stardom. He's always had the magic touch for finding music his audiences would love. Undoubtedly, his list of artists he introduced for the first time is unmatched.

In every respect, the Geator stands as a man who is truly one-of-a-kind!

—*Dick Clark, 2011*

Acknowledgments

I would like to acknowledge my four beautiful daughters—Kathi, Geraldine, Stacy, and Deserie. I hope as they read this book they understand why I might not have been there whenever they needed me. Although my career kept me away from home, I want them to know that my love for them was always paramount.

My gratitude also goes out to Keely Stahl, who transcribed my interviews with Steve Oskie, and who has graced my life with a sense of dignity, honesty, and love.

A special thanks to Greg Jones, my editor at Running Press. Greg is good at what he does, and the book is better because of it.

Assistance with *You Only Rock Once* came from George L. Frunzi, Ed.D.; WXPN-FM, which provided background material on Ben Vaughn; and David Auspitz for contributing recollections of the Angelo years and other incidents in the book. (Material on Pg. 131 is reprinted with Dr. Frunzi's permission. It originally appeared in his article, "Destination: Philadelphia," which was published in *Echoes of the Past*, Issue No. 84, 2008. Dr. Frunzi hosts Down on the Streetcorner every Sunday evening from 8 to 10 pm on Gold Radio at www.goldoldies.com.)

Thanks are due to countless others for their love, friendship and support over the course of my career, including Freddy DeMann, Frankie Valli, Bob Crewe, Bob Gaudio, Frankie Avalon, Dick Clark, Sidney and Caroline Kimmel, Victor Potamkin and Family, Dr. A. J. Di Marino, Eddie Jacobs, Carmen Nasuti, Richard Basciano, Joey Vento from Geno's Steaks (a man who speaks from the heart and whose generosity is well-documented), Seymour Stein, Congressman Bob Brady, Don Rickles, Larry Kane, Nicholas Pileggi, Nick Tosches, Bruce Jay Friedman, Susan Seidelman, Connie Francis, Rollye James, Larry Magid, Danny and the Juniors, my sister Roberta, Larry Platt, Stu Bykofsky, Dan Gross, Jason Fagone, Victor Fiorillo, Herb Lipson, David Lipson, Carl Poplar, Tim Whitaker, Dave Coskey, Sammy Davis Jr., Frank Sinatra, Jilly Rizzo, the Annenbergs, Bob Horn, Nat Segall, Bud

Hibbs, Jake Kossman, Morris Levy, Jocko Henderson, Bert Berns, Buzz Curtis, Allen Sussell, Harold Lipsius, Harry Finfer, George Burns, Dr. Norman Orentreich, Dr. Ronald Pennock, Father Nelson, the Sisters of the IHM, and so many others that would fill up more pages than you would be willing to read.

Finally, this book was written in loving memory of my parents, Louis Blavat and Lucille Rosa Capuano. Through it all, they loved each other in their own way and gave me the strength I needed to succeed.

Prologue

On January 17, 1996, when I was 55 years old, I sat at a table with Seymour Stein, Chairman of the Rock and Roll Hall of Fame, and Freddy DeMann at the Waldorf-Astoria in New York. Seymour and Freddy had been friends of mine for more than 30 years. Freddy's former client, the pop superstar Madonna, was also in attendance. At that moment, as we waited for the Rock and Roll Hall of Fame to begin its induction ceremony, Madonna was sitting directly across from me, dropping F-bombs. What she was going on about, I couldn't really say, because I was distracted by a thought that overpowered everything else, even Madonna's star power. "What the hell am I doing here? How did a little cockroach kid from South Philadelphia, with no formal education, overcome seemingly insurmountable odds to earn a place at this table?" That's when it hit me that my story might be worth telling—or more precisely, that's when I finally understood what my friends and associates had been talking about for all those years when they urged me to get everything down on paper.

I had always resisted the idea, fearing that my life might not seem significant to anyone other than me, and telling myself that I was too busy to sit still long enough to make the necessary investment of time. But sitting at that table, and staring at Madonna, one of the most recognizable entertainers in the world today, the sheer improbability of it all hit me. And shortly thereafter, I realized that I really might have something to say to the current generation of young people, and that maybe, in some small way, I could help them make sense of a world that seems to be growing more violent, more complex, and more troubling by the minute. The clincher, though, was the realization that Madonna wasn't the only celebrity that I've met over the years—far from it. I've truly been blessed that way. The "characters" that have populated my life read like a "Who's Who" in the entertainment industry in the 20th and 21st centuries. It's taken me a long time to complete this project, but I hope it was worth the wait. I hope my story will grab you like the songs of my youth grabbed me, and that you will enjoy the ride as much as I have on my trip down memory lane.

ONE: Trouble on the Home Front:
Louis the Gimp

For city kids, it starts with a neighborhood. Mine was at 17th and Mifflin in South Philadelphia. The year was 1945.

My father was a bookmaker—a Jewish one at that—and my mother was a Joan Crawford look-alike whose family originated in Abruzzi, Italy, making me half-Jewish and half-Italian, neither here nor there, a tough little outsider.

At seven in the morning, my mother would walk my sister and me to the day nursery at St. Monica's. The idea was to ship us off to a safe location so my father and his associates could make book, setting up shop in our living room to work the phones and take the action of degenerate and not-so-degenerate gamblers. My dad, known as Louis the Gimp, and his pals Moishe, Sammy, and Mickey, would take bets on anything people could wager on, including baseball, boxing, horseracing, and every other sport there was. If it was played with a bat or a ball or involved keeping score, they would take the action. The daily number, a presidential election, whether or not a pothole would get repaired, you name it, they had money riding. But of course I was none the wiser for it as I took my naps and ate my milk and cookies with the rest of the children at St. Monica's.

All day long our house was filled with colorful characters, but the gang cleared out by four in the afternoon when my mom retrieved me from the nursery. By the time I got back, all traces of their activities had been cleared away and the house looked normal again. Way before I listened to the Temptations—and the thousands of other groups that have infused me with the spirit of popular music for all these years—I got a rough introduction to the concept that "papa was a rolling stone."

I was eight years old when I realized that my father operated outside of the law, my first clue being when my mother gathered up the betting slips, put them in a baby carriage, and hauled them over to my grandparents when she was alerted that our little bookie joint was about to be raided. Not that the criminality was a bad thing. In that neighborhood, and in that era of the immigrant experience, it was a way of life for a significant portion of the population. There was never any shame associated with it for my father and there never was for me, not then and not now. Of course, my mother had a different perspective.

In keeping with the secrecy surrounding my father's routine, I saw very little of him until I graduated from the day nursery and entered St. Monica's elementary school; even then, sightings of my father were rare. More often than not, he was loan sharking, hanging out with numbers runners like himself, distilling gin in a dark basement set up for that purpose, or drinking and gambling elsewhere. Weeks would go by without my seeing him. To this day, I'm not even sure that my father lived with us at 1906 South Bancroft Street (a short "half-ball" throw from the corner of 17th and Mifflin), or that he ever spent the night there; that didn't stop my mother from turning the place over to him in the daytime.

Over the years, whenever my sister and I discussed the bond that developed between our parents, and the curious relationship that ensued, we looked for clues in the story of how they met.

When Louis Blavat made his way down the aisle of the Broadway movie theater in 1936, dragging his left leg after suffering from polio as a child, Lucille Rosa Capuano had never been kissed. More importantly, she had never seen anyone like Louis. At the time, she could not have known that trouble followed Louis around, that he caused a commotion wherever he went, and that he raised a racket in more ways than one. One minute she was watching a movie with her half-sister Philomena—a chaperone selected by their parents—and the next she was hearing shouts from the lobby. As Louis approached them— dressed to a T in his sharkskin suit from Sam's at 7th and Snyder—she couldn't have realized that he was being chased by the police, or that the shouts had anything to do with him. That's how calmly he went about his business.

Seconds before the policemen made their way into the theater, Louis slipped into the seat next to Lucille's, put his arm around her shoulder, and begged her to cooperate.

Too stunned to do anything, Lucille remained silent and sat rigidly in her chair when the policemen walked down the aisle and shined their flashlights. Emboldened by her silence, Louis took her hand, and for a moment they looked as though they had been sweethearts for a long time—until Philomena removed Louis's arm from Lucille's shoulder, reached across her lap, and forced their hands apart. This was just what Lucille needed to return to her senses, and she was able to take over from Philomena in defending her own honor. Just as the policemen gave up the chase, turned on their heels, and walked out of the theater, Lucille slapped Louis's face.

Louis burst out laughing, which shocked Lucille all over again. While Philomena demanded that he get up from the seat, Lucille stared at Louis in fascination. Whatever else could be said about him, Louis loved life, and Lucille must have felt that in his laughter. As a result, she probably wasn't thinking straight, and seeing the policemen might not have fully registered in her mind. More than anything, she felt shock and confusion, and that prevented her from putting two and two together and realizing that Louis was bad news. Perhaps it was pride on her part, but from that day forward, she insisted that things would have been different if the police had succeeded in arresting him. Just the thought of it would have prevented her from getting involved with him in the first place—or so she claimed.

"Get outta here!" Philomena demanded.

As Louis rose from his seat, started up the aisle, and made his way to the lobby, Lucille couldn't help but turn around, crane her neck, and gaze after him as he withdrew, drawing Philomena's wrath once more. "Watch the movie!" she cried, and Lucille did as she was told. But by the time Louis walked out of the darkness of the movie theater and into the sunshine at Broad and Snyder, my mother was already smitten.

She was immediately aware of the stark contrast between the men she lived with and the sharply dressed stranger who had forced his way into her consciousness that day. What struck her most was the quality of his clothing, the glitter of his wristwatch, and the luxurious scent of his cologne. Each of these elements distinguished him from her father, her brothers, and other members of the Capuano family, whose daily attire consisted of heavy, steel-toed work boots; rugged overalls made of a coarse material; and the healthy perspiration that arose from physical labor.

In the weeks that followed, they conducted their courtship secretly, sneaking around behind everyone's back. Every Saturday or Sunday they would meet at the Broadway movie theater, and now they were holding hands for real. My mother was perfectly aware that her parents would have been appalled by my father's presence in her life, and she did whatever she had to do to keep them in the dark. Our family history is a little hazy on Philomena's role in all of this. Was she aware of the courtship? Did she cooperate in keeping my mother's secret? In years past, some members of the family believed that Philomena understood my mother's attraction to my father, and though she may have disapproved of the relationship, she made a deliberate decision not to interfere.

Falling in love with my father caused an unbearable tension in my mother. If she continued to live at home in her present circumstances, her status as the youngest female child consigned her to doing the bulk of the household chores, and though she never intended to hurt her parents, her relationship with my father offered an alternative. He was showering her with jewelry, fine clothing, and other expensive gifts, giving every indication that he could rescue her from a grim existence. More importantly, she was 16 years old and he was 20, and their physical attraction was strong. As a result, the feelings of guilt and shame must have oppressed my mother badly.

After six weeks of courtship, they married, ushering in the cold reality of their life together. In those days, marrying outside of one's religion was considered a sin, and my mother's family disowned her.

TWO: Lifeline:
Radio and TV

They began their married life in a one-bedroom apartment at 7th and McKean. The neighborhood was mixed, as opposed to exclusively Italian, and though her childhood home was only blocks away, my mother must have felt as though she were in another world. Within a few weeks, however, my father began to behave as though he weren't married at all. He came and went as he pleased, and my mother began to see less and less of him. It is impossible to say whether she questioned her decision to marry my father within days of their elopement, or if it happened later, but it couldn't have pleased her to realize that he had no intention of changing his ways.

From the very beginning, their marriage had a drama of its own, played out against the backdrop of her family's disapproval. Before he even opened his mouth, my father had two strikes against him. For one thing, he was a Christ-killer (a *matsa Cristo*), a "Jew bastard." For another, he wasn't an honest workingman like the Capuanos. To look at him—with his fancy suits, his Stetson hat, and his expensive watch—he had rejected their values, their way of life, the cherished immigrant ideal of making an honest living in America. While they made their money slowly, a dollar at a time, getting up at an ungodly hour to trek to the coal regions of Northeastern Pennsylvania, loading their truck with anthracite coal, making the long trip back to South Philadelphia, and peddling the coal door to door, Louis the Gimp preferred to make his money extravagantly, in fits and starts, going for a bigger score whenever possible, even if it meant being short of cash on a regular basis.

Although the uncles and grandparents on my mother's side refused to acknowledge it, it would be incorrect to say that all of my father's activities were illegal. There were stretches of time in which he worked in the baggage room at the Pennsylvania Railroad and as a bail bondsman with his partner, Benny Glickstein. After he married my mother, there was even an occasional ceasefire in the hostilities with the

Capuanos—or a temporary de-escalation of the war—and when that happened he was known to collect money for their coal deliveries. When the Capuanos switched to delivering ice in the summertime, Louis sometimes lent a hand with that as well. After taking bets for years—and writing numbers—he knew how to lean on delinquent customers and collect payments more effectively than the Capuanos, who were much more inclined to take pity on a family and let them slide until the following week.

Although my father occasionally assisted the Capuanos, most of his activities ran afoul of the law, and he spent a lot more time violating local ordinances than abiding by them, which sometimes resulted in his spending a day or two in jail. Still, any fair-minded person would recognize that his particular combination of lawful and unlawful activities was extremely rigorous, and could not have been maintained without a certain work ethic. My father worked hard all right, but on things that his in-laws disapproved of, and for the most part, they based their low opinion of him on that.

In addition to the aforementioned activities of numbers writing and bookmaking, my father supplied homemade booze to speakeasies that would stay open on Sundays in defiance of Pennsylvania's "Blue Laws." Most of his ventures were aided, abetted, and sponsored by the local Jewish mob, which in turn had an alliance with the Italian mob, and though these affiliations won my father a certain amount of respect with a segment of the population, they deprived him of the respect and acceptance of my mother's family.

Throughout her first few months of marriage, my mother's impasse with her parents continued, but the birth of my sister Roberta caused a thawing in their relations. Fearing for the safety of her newborn, and with my father seldom around, my mother reached out to her parents. They responded by urging her to leave her husband and move back in with them. Missing her daughter terribly, my grandmother was desperate for this to happen, and my mother soon agreed.

Despite his indifference to being married, the idea of his wife leaving him was a blow to my father's pride, and he came to realize that he loved my mother more than he had known. Like most of his associates, my father was less than respectful to women, and he paid a heavy price for taking my mother for granted. Though she refused to succumb to his pleading for the first few months of their separation—a period in which my father vacated the apartment on McKean Street—she eventually agreed to take my father back on the condition that they have a place of their own. She realized, of course, that she would never live this down with her parents, who had already forgiven her once. Moving in with my father a second time was beyond their comprehension, and the only thing that saved my mother was the fact that she was the only daughter from the Capuanos' marriage. As for their son-in-law, the fact that he had won their daughter back was as infuriating as you would expect, and he could hardly have done more damage to his relationship with them if he had assaulted my mother physically.

For most of my adult life, I believed that my father purchased the property at 1906 South Bancroft Street with the money he had earned through his various illegal enterprises. Instead, it was my maternal grandmother who bought it, despite her distaste for my father. Whether he ever intended to pay my grandmother back is unclear, but the fact remains that he acted like he owned the place when he initiated the practice of turning my mother's home into a bookie joint in the daytime.

Although his underworld affiliations provided a certain amount of protection, the Philadelphia Police Department had to keep up appearances by making the occasional raid, but the Department never seemed too upset if word on the street alerted my father beforehand. Thus, my sister Roberta's baby carriage was pressed into service both before and after she learned to walk, and my mother developed the habit of transporting the betting slips to a neutral location. (For obvious reasons, she preferred to avoid my grandparents' home, but because my father was something of a black sheep with his own family as well, she didn't always succeed in coming up with a viable alternative.)

Although living like this continued to upset my mother—and she gave serious consideration to returning to her parents—she decided that it would be better for everyone if things remained as they were. As a result, she became pregnant with me in October of 1939, and I was born at Mt. Sinai Hospital in July of the following year. By that time, my father's hold on my mother was shakier than it had ever been, but he succeeded in persuading her to have me circumcised by a *mohel*. As it turned out, my *bris* came and went with very little fanfare—and none of the extravagance that you sometimes see today—and it generated only a meager gathering that consisted of my parents, my sister, and only one of my paternal grandparents—my *bubba*, bless her soul—since my paternal grandfather had passed away before I was born. Needless to say, my mother would have been insane to invite the Italian side of my family to the *bris*, and she prudently refrained from doing so.

The Jews have a word for foolishness of an exceedingly high order—*meshugas* (phonetically pronounced muh-SHU-gas)—and by any measurement, the battles that took place between the two sides of my family rose to that level. But the interdenominational madness didn't end there. Instead, it took an even more bizarre turn when it was discovered that I was born with rheumatic fever and an atrial septal defect, otherwise known as a hole in the heart. Learning that I was gravely ill, fearing that I might not survive, and responding to my mother's threat to leave him once and for all, my father consented to having me baptized in the Roman Catholic Church.

If having a second child had any effect on my father at all, it was only a marginal one, but he did put in a few more hours at the Pennsylvania Railroad, which offered the kind of benefits package that a more conventional family man would appreciate.

In my early years, my mother was out of the house a lot also, working at the Navy Yard (where they nicknamed her "Lucy the Riveter") and setting diamonds at Eskin's jewelry store downtown. Often, my sister and I were looked after by "Skinny Annie," who weighed less than a hundred pounds and made my mother's acquaintance at Eskin's. Eventually, "Skinny Annie" moved in with us for a time during my father's extended absence. But even when Annie was around I had a certain amount of freedom.

In my case, the flip side of freedom was a loneliness that never went away, making me susceptible later on to the generosity of Bob Horn, Nat Segall, and a number of other men who became like second fathers to me. Watched over by people in the neighborhood—who provided a kind of safety net—I began exploring my surroundings and developing the independent spirit that people have recognized in me throughout my adult life. Just as importantly, the situation with my father provided me with a strong sense of empathy whenever I encountered similar feelings in the thousands of young people I've met over the course of my career.

When I wasn't exploring the neighborhood on my own, I was shuttling back and forth to my grandparents at 1534 McKean, which is the address we used to establish our residency for the day nursery at St. Monica's. As it turned out, our actual address at 1906 South Bancroft was in the St. Thomas Aquinas parish, which did not have a day nursery or grammar school. Without our grandparents' address, my sister and I would not have been admitted into St. Monica's and my father might have been forced to take his bookmaking elsewhere.

I've always felt that I've had a guardian angel watching over me, ever since I survived an encounter with a moving car at the age of five or six. After a pimple ball got away from me in front of my grandparents' house, I ran into the street without looking both ways like I had been taught. Just then, a DeSoto sedan came barreling down McKean Street, and I had no chance of getting out of the way. Instead of freezing in my tracks, I dove under the car as it passed over me. Lying face down on the street, all I could hear was the roar of the engine and the screams of my playmates. When the sedan cleared my body I realized that the car had missed me. Once the danger passed, the only real challenge was to survive my mother's tearful embrace when she squeezed the breath out of me afterward.

As harsh as they were to my father, my maternal grandparents were exceedingly sweet to me, although I never felt entirely accepted by them because of my Jewish blood and the fact that I was my father's son. All along, I sensed a certain resentment toward Roberta and me—particularly after the Capuanos let down their guard and allowed my father to become involved with their coal and ice businesses with predictable results. Although my father succeeded in collecting a great deal of money for them, he gambled most of it away, just as he had hocked a piece of my mother's jewelry to cover gambling debts a day or two after buying it for her.

One day, my sister and I were sitting in our grandparents' living room when we heard a commotion outside. When we opened the front door, we saw that a fistfight had broken out between my father and several of my uncles. I ran to the corner of 16th and McKean, where Vito, Joe, and Jimmy were working my father over in front of the Paradise Cafe. I remember that it was three against one, and that I threw myself at Jimmy and started punching him. My uncle Carmen held me back while his brothers finished the job. When it was over, my father lay bleeding in the street.

As a member of a Jewish gang, my father had every right to expect an act of retaliation, but fortunately for the Capuanos, a man named Angelo Bruno interceded on their behalf. At the time, Angelo owned a grocery store in the neighborhood, but more importantly, he was a rising star in the local Italian mob and he persuaded my father's associates to turn the other cheek. "Don't get involved," he told them. "This is a family matter. It has nothing to do with the business we conduct on the street." If Angelo's wife, Sue, had not been a *paisan* of my mother, with their parents originating in the same region of Italy—and if Angelo himself had not been a lifelong friend—the beating of my father would have had serious repercussions for the Capuanos.

Shortly after the fistfight, my parents were divorced, but the official decree did very little to alter their relationship. My mother always said that he was the only man she ever loved—even after she remarried—and they went on seeing each other throughout the rest of my childhood. After the fight, my father never had another direct confrontation with the Capuanos, but the bitter feelings persisted.

Because I spent so much time with my grandparents—and they only spoke Italian—I began to pick up their native language; before long I was able to detect the disparaging remarks that my uncles were making about my father. My uncle Joe in particular—who I was extremely fond of otherwise—had a habit of underestimating me that way, and it was at that point that I probably heard the *matsa Cristo* phrase for the first time. Remarks like this were frequent, and whenever Joe or one of my other uncles talked that way in front of my sister and me, our grandparents would say "*stai zitto*," which means "shut up" in Italian. Though they disliked my father as much as their sons did, they had no desire to hurt innocent children who happened to be caught in the crossfire. And so, if there was resentment, it was tolerable for us as long as my father stayed away from the Capuanos and kept a low profile.

Because we lived so close to my grandparents, we got into the routine of eating dinner there every night. In fact, I can never remember eating dinner on South Bancroft Street at all; as long as we avoided the subject of my father, there was an abundance of love and laughter at my grandparents' table. While we ate, there was always music playing in the background. The Four Aces, Tony Bennett, Sinatra, Patti Page, Joni James—one of their records always seemed to be playing, and I believe that I first began to develop an appreciation for music at approximately that time.

Because of my health issues, my mother was strict with me, insisting that I go right home after having dinner at my grandparents and get in bed by 7:30. We had no air conditioning in the summertime—and slept with our windows open—and the old familiar loneliness would always come over me whenever I heard the kids playing in the street. In the end, though, not being allowed to join them turned out to be a blessing as I found my way to the radio as a form of entertainment. Eventually, I began to console myself more and more with the radio shows I discovered, until the radio became a lifeline to the bigger world outside. For a long time, my personal favorites included *The Lone Ranger*, *Hopalong Cassidy*, *The Shadow*, *Nick Carter*, and a program called *Private Eye*. But that was before I discovered the radio serial, *Straight Arrow*.

Sponsored by Nabisco Shredded Wheat—which was manufactured in Northeast Philadelphia—*Straight Arrow* told the story of a Comanche Indian who operated a ranch out west. Whenever he learned of an injustice, he transformed himself into the warrior that gave the show its name, leaving his ranch, entering a cave, and trading his cowboy garb for war paint and other accoutrements of the trade. Straight Arrow had a magnificent Palomino horse, which he would mount with a specific cry that I recall to this day, sixty years after the fact, shouting "Kaneewah, Fury!" and taking on the world as only superheroes can. That particular radio show had a profound influence on many areas of my life, ranging from my interest in horseback riding as a teenager to my life-long fascination with the history, culture, and spirituality of Native Americans.

Later, when Nabisco began to grace their cereal boxes with trading cards about the Indian way of life, I attempted to eat Shredded Wheat morning, noon, and night until my mother interceded. At the time, there was absolutely no chance that I could have gotten away with it—my mother watched me like a hawk when it came to what I was eating. Constantly worried about my health, she would force me to consume a raw egg every day before she walked my sister and me to the nursery, following it up with a bowl of the dreaded Wheatena. Not surprisingly, I hated the ritual, but I never questioned or disobeyed my mother. She was the best, a giver not a taker, and even at a young age I knew how hard things were for her with my father coming and going from her life. (To this day, I rarely eat a full breakfast. By comparison, my grandfather had a more enjoyable routine. I can remember seeing him in the early morning in an undershirt and suspenders, a stogie stuck in his mouth, sitting at his breakfast table with a glass of red wine, a piece of Italian bread, and a hard-boiled egg, dunking the bread in the wine.)

Although my mother was able to regulate my diet once again, she had less success in moderating my interest in Native Americans and preventing it from growing into an obsession. Shortly after I became infatuated with the radio program *Straight Arrow*, I discovered that comic books were an excellent outlet as well—particularly the old Classic Comics versions of *Deerslayer* and *The Last of the Mohicans*. To that point, I hadn't been much of a reader, but now I read everything I could get my hands on about cowboys and Indians, becoming a regular at the South Philadelphia branch of the public library on Broad Street, where I checked out books about Sequoia, Black Hawk, Pontiac, Red Cloud, and some of my other heroes. The more I read about Native Americans, the more I admired the nomadic lifestyle they led until the white man took it away. In retrospect, I can easily see that my adult behavior has been shaped by this admiration, and that whenever possible, I have insisted on having the freedom to come and go as I please.

In those days, there was a candy store at the corner of 16th and McKean—half a block from my grandparents—and the proprietor was referred to as "Jew Sarah" by the Italian people she sold to. No one thought anything of the term in that era, and if Sarah had any problems with it, she never let on. I remember that I used to go into her store for the Classic Comics—which also included non–Native American titles like *Sir Lancelot* and *Robison Crusoe*—and Sarah would let me sit at her counter and read for hours on end without buying. At the time, her generosity represented a great break for me because the Classic Comics cost ten cents more than regular comics, and their ornate, beautifully crafted illustrations were much to be cherished.

Although we owned a television on South Bancroft Street, we rarely had a chance to watch it, since we spent the majority of our time at our grandparents'. Somehow, I discovered a program called *Barr's Diamond Theater*, which came on at 10:30 on Tuesday nights and ran old movies from the 30s and 40s, including *The Adventures of Robin Hood*, *The Three Musketeers*, *Captain Kidd*, and the film version of *The Last of the Mohicans*. Eventually, I took to checking the television listings in the newspaper to select the movies I wanted to see, and I would plead with my mother or Skinny Annie to let me stay up to watch them. Because it was obvious that I had my heart set on this—and I always took care of business when it came to getting good grades—my mother agreed to a compromise on a trial basis. If I went to bed at seven o'clock, she would wake me at 10:30 to see the movie, but only if I went back to bed immediately after and had no trouble getting up for school the next day. (When it came to watching cowboys and Indians, I was the only kid I knew who actually rooted for the Indians.)

Because of my reverence for my mother, I always did my best to keep up with my schoolwork. Very often, I studied for the sole purpose of being allowed to stay up later.

Movies became an even bigger part of my life when my father started meeting my sister and me downtown. Every Friday after school, Roberta and I would leave St. Monica's and catch the trolley to 16th and Market. My father would be standing in front of a local bar that had a large plate glass window in front. On the other side of the glass—while my father talked shop with bookmakers and numbers runners like himself—we could see chickens spinning on rotisseries behind him. As we hopped off the trolley, he would greet us, lead us into the bar, and buy a barbecued chicken for the three of us to share. One week, Roberta would select the movie and the next week I would, and we would tell my father which theater he was taking us to and what time the movie was playing. Predictably, I would select cowboys and Indians, and Roberta would select Abbott and Costello, Laurel and Hardy, or another comedy of that era. The Fox, the Stanley, and the Goldman theaters were all within walking distance of the bar, and within minutes of finishing our supper, we were settling into our seats with popcorn and candy. After the movie, my father would put us in a cab and pay the fare to South Bancroft Street. (To this day, barbecued chicken is one of my favorite foods.)

One Friday night, we had some extra time before the movie was scheduled to begin, and we stopped into a small novelty shop across the street from the bar. Their merchandise seemed run-of-the-mill until I happened down the center aisle and discovered an Indian war bonnet, built to scale for a child like myself. As soon as I saw it, I stopped in my tracks so suddenly that my father bumped into me. Without saying a word, he lifted the war bonnet off the mannequin it was displayed on and placed it on my head. He just carried it to the front of the store and bought it for me.

The next night, when I was supposed to be asleep, with my mother working and Skinny Annie watching us, I was jumping up and down on my mother's bed, wearing the headdress and simulating an Indian war cry. I had a hammer in my hand and I was pretending it was a tomahawk, swinging it around like I was being attacked.

Despite the ruckus I was raising, Annie indulged me for a few minutes, remaining in the living room and letting me have my fun. At the time, neither one of us suspected that the top of the hammer would come lose from the wooden handle and fly across the room, which is exactly what it did before it shattered a six-foot mirror.

Skinny Annie came running up the stairs. "Oh, my God, what did you do? Wait till your mother comes home!"

I'm not sure who was more frightened about my mother's reaction—Annie or me. I had never broken anything important, and I was scared to death when I went to bed. When my mother finally arrived home after work and opened my bedroom door, I was crying uncontrollably and begging her to forgive me. But she was too exhausted to be angry.

"Don't worry about it," she said. "We'll get a new mirror. Go to bed."

During the week, when we ate dinner at our grandparents, Roberta and I would wait for our father to call. He would call at the same time every night—often the call would come when he got out of work at the railroad—and we would run to the phone to prevent one of the Capuanos from picking it up. My mother would never talk to him in front of her family, and that made the calls awkward for all of us. Despite the fact that the phone calls left something to be desired, I never wanted them to end—that's how starved I was for his affection. In order to get me to hang up, my father would say, "I have to go, the train's coming," and he would imitate a train whistle.

It was always an empty feeling to leave my grandparents' house and go home to South Bancroft Street, particularly on holidays when my cousins would join us at the Capuanos. These were all-day affairs from 12 noon till seven or eight at night—often punctuated by afternoon trips to the Broadway Theator or the Savoy, which were close enough to McKean Street for our mothers to feel comfortable about it. Although the holidays were exciting, my cousins would always talk about the things they had done with their fathers, and on those occasions, Roberta and I had less to brag about. We were the oldest, but our younger cousins always had an advantage because their fathers were a daily part of their lives. To counteract this, my uncles often included us in their outings with their children, but it wasn't the same as having a father of our own. (If our father hadn't been such a vagabond—and a phantom that we rarely saw—we would have felt differently, but it was years before he finally settled down and became a real part of our lives.)

When we were growing up, Roberta was something of a tomboy. Athletic and sturdily built, she would play football and half-ball with the guys in the neighborhood. Often, she was the only girl playing. Like me, she was getting more and more streetwise by the day. For those and other reasons, my mother was comfortable with the idea of our taking the trolley by ourselves and moving freely throughout the neighborhood. It is also true that times were simpler back then, and parents had less to worry about.

For ten cents on a Saturday afternoon, Roberta and I could go to the Venice Theater on Snyder Avenue and be entertained from noon to six, watching a series of cartoons, short features, and full-length movies. These included up to 15 cartoons; several *Three Stooges* shorts; a chapter from *Rocketman*, *Flash Gordon*, or *Bullets Durham*; and the feature presentation, which was usually a comedy, a horror movie, or a shoot-'em-up. Hollywood was churning out B movies faster than you could watch them in those days, and the kids of my generation were the primary consumers.

Every summer, my mother would send Roberta and me to a YMCA camp in Downingtown, a rural community thirty miles from Philadelphia. The YMCA operated three camps: Camp Castle for children between the ages of six and eight; Camp Dwight for kids from nine to fifteen; and Camp Hilltop for young people between sixteen and twenty.

Imagine my delight when I discovered archery and horseback riding among the activities at Camp Dwight! For a nine-year-old—and for someone who loved Native Americans like I did—the discovery was incomparable. This was the first time that I had ever been closer to a horse than a television set or movie screen, and it was all I could do not to cry "Kaneewah, Fury!" when they lifted me onto a horse for the first time. Although I won several awards in baseball, I lived for the archery and horseback riding and spent that first summer fantasizing about being Sequoia, Red Cloud, Crazy Horse, or one of my other Indian heroes. (Because she loved sports, Roberta enjoyed the YMCA camp also. Just as she did back home, she excelled in all of the athletic activities.)

During my second summer at Camp Dwight, my counselors selected me as a riding instructor for the younger kids, despite the fact that I was still short and skinny myself. My nickname at the camp was "Shorts" and I still have pictures of myself riding one of the horses. More than anything else, I resembled a piece of uncooked spaghetti.

As a riding instructor, I would get up early, muck out the stables, and lead the horses over to Camp Castle, where I would help the younger kids overcome their fear and enjoy the experience.

Summer camp ended the second week in August, and I was only home a few days when I had an idea to sell pony rides in the neighborhood. As soon as I mentioned it to my father, he helped to make it happen. There used to be a stable at 5th and Bainbridge in South Philadelphia, near the Famous Deli, one of the best Jewish delis in town. My father rented me a pony for the day, paying $5 for the privilege, and I was able to convert it into $8 or $10 by charging fifty cents for a ride around the block.

My father never raised a hand to me when I was a kid, and he never hit my sister, except for one occasion. It happened on a Friday night, after we had left the movie theater.

"Let's call your mother and let her know I'm sending you home in a cab," he said.

At the time, my mother was at the Capuanos, and when Roberta spoke with her, she heard my uncle Jimmy in the background. "Are they with that Jew bastard?" Roberta began to cry and could not continue the conversation. After she hung up, my father asked if someone had said something, and Roberta lied to him in an attempt to keep the peace. He asked her again, and again she lied, insisting that no one had said anything. My father slapped her face. Years later, Roberta would remark, "It was the only time daddy ever smacked me."

When I think back to that incident—and the fact that my father never hit me as a child—I realize that my health problems and my scrawny physique might have been a factor. At a certain point, I discovered an ad for a Charles Atlas bodybuilding kit in the back of a comic book, and my father was only too happy to buy it for me. Every night, I would go up to my room and follow Charles Atlas's regimen, doing twenty-five sit-ups, lifting weights, and working out with a series of ropes and pulleys. To this day, I am still devoted to an exercise routine that consists of riding my bike, making daily visits to the gym, and other physical activities.

Although I was half-Jewish, my religious education was exclusively Catholic. The sisters of the Immaculate Heart of Mary had a strong influence on me at St. Monica's. Judging by the holy pictures, no other order of nuns resembled the Blessed Mother more closely than the sisters of the IHM, and for some reason, that impressed me. Ever since then, I have always felt that nuns sometimes get a bad rap when people look back on their parochial school days. I'm sure my knuckles must have been struck by a nun or two, but the only form of corporal punishment I can clearly recollect was administered by the only lay teacher in the school, and not one of the sisters at all. There was a Mrs. Neill at St. Monica's, a woman who wore her hair in a bun, played the organ in church, and taught second grade. On more than one occasion, she called a student to the front of the room, instructed him to hold out his hand, and used a wooden pointer to rap him on the knuckles.

For the most part, the IHM sisters were good to us at St. Monica's. One of them in particular, a sixth grade teacher named Sister Benedictine, took a fancy to me. Because the seating chart was alphabetized, I always sat with the As and Bs at the front of the classroom, and Sister Benedictine approved of the way I sat up straight, paid strict attention, and completed my homework. One day, without the other children seeing, she slipped me a Captain Midnight ring from a jar of Ovaltine at the convent. Perhaps I was looking for affection wherever I could find it in those days, due to the deprivation I felt with my father, but whatever the reason, I basked in Sister Benedictine's kindness for an entire school year.

During the 3rd grade school year, my uncle Jimmy sponsored me for my Confirmation, and we began to spend time together. A few years later, knowing that I was fascinated with Native Americans, he took me to see *Broken Arrow* at a movie theater uptown. As I knew perfectly well before we even reached the theater, the film starred James Stewart and Jeff Chandler, and told the story of Cochise and the Indian scout Tom Jeffords, who negotiated a peace treaty with the Apaches. By the time my uncle returned me to South Bancroft Street, I had gone into minute detail about every aspect of the movie and the actual incident it was based on, causing my uncle to shake his head in amazement. He took me to see a number of other films, including *The Savage* starring Charlton Heston. (Years later, when I was hosting my television show *Jerry's Place* in 1968, I had an opportunity to interview Heston at the Fontainebleau Hotel in Miami Beach.)

As my childhood unfolded, the ubiquitous row houses of South Philadelphia were virtually indistinguishable from one another, except for the seasonal decorations that sometimes hung in the windows or were pinned to the front doors. Just as our parents could allow us a certain amount of freedom in those days, it was safe to hang the decorations outside without fear of vandalism or theft, and so you saw your fair share of American flags on the 4th of July, Indian corn at Halloween, and Christmas lights during the holiday season. This was my neighborhood, my Philadelphia, and my America as I knew it in the mid-1940s. It shaped me, it schooled me, it opened my eyes to the ways of the world; by the time I was a teenager I had enough energy and ambition for a lifetime.

THREE:
The Bandstand Years:
Local Celebrity

I learned to jitterbug at the Capuanos', watching my mother, my aunt, and my uncles. Whenever they played an Artie Shaw record—or Tommy Dorsey and His Orchestra—they would clear a space in the living room and get right down to it. I would do my best to imitate the grown-ups. If my sister Roberta was around, I would practice with her. (After bathing in the same bathwater at the age of three or four, Roberta going first and then me before the water was emptied from the tub, there was certainly no shame in dancing with her later on.)

I can't claim that I had an extraordinary gift for dancing as a six- or seven-year-old, but by the time I was tall enough to jitterbug with my mother (without tripping her or getting tangled in her steps), I was showing signs of actual coordination. Shortly after that, I began to notice whether or not specific records were "good to dance to." Either the song was good to dance to, or it wasn't. Before I reached my tenth birthday, I had become a good little dancer, and it was at approximately the same time that the early appreciation I had for phonograph records began to develop into something more—an ear for music that would eventually fuel my career.

Every New Year's Day, we would walk three blocks to Broad Street and watch the Mummers' Parade, a Philadelphia tradition that is roughly equivalent to Mardi Gras in New Orleans, at least in terms of its public drunkenness and general loosening of inhibitions. Broad Street would be lined with people eight or ten deep. Even from 17th and Mifflin, we could hear air horns, fireworks, and the unmistakable sound of banjo music from the "string bands." These bands had classic Philadelphia names like "Ferko," "Fralinger," and "Two Street," and had been practicing their routines since the middle of the summer in anticipation of performing them in front of the judging stands at City Hall. The prizes they were competing for were modest, but it was all about pride.

Over the years, a specific form of dancing developed—the "Mummers' Strut" danced to the tune of "Oh, Dem Golden Slippers"—and apparently I took to that as well, showing off for my mother, my sister, and the Capuanos on our way home every year.

When he wasn't delivering coal, my Uncle Jimmy was singing with a group of neighborhood guys that he had grown up with. After serving in the army together, they formed a group called the Four Chimes, cut a record, and appeared on a local television show called Bob Horn's *Bandstand*. One afternoon, my mother, sister, and I joined the Capuanos in my grandmother's living room, and we watched in amazement as Uncle Jimmy and his fellow bandmates performed. This show was the precursor of Dick Clark's *American Bandstand*, and like its successor, the Bob Horn version featured teenagers between the ages of fourteen and sixteen dancing to popular records.

After I got over the initial shock of seeing my uncle on television, I stared in outright amazement at the dancers. Their energy, their vitality, the pure joy that presented itself in their movements made them immediately recognizable to me. Seeing myself in them so clearly, I felt as though a bolt of lightning had hit me, and the words came pouring out of me as if they had a mind of their own. "I want to dance like that!" I declared, and everyone in the room stopped what they were doing and looked over at me.

"You're not old enough," my Uncle Carmen said. I kept my mouth shut.

By that time, my mother had already introduced one of her coworkers at Eskin's jewelry store to Jimmy—a beautiful Irish woman named Mim—and the two of them had married a year or two before. When I said I wanted to dance, everyone laughed it off except Aunt Mim, who looked over at me and smiled. I think she knew that I would dance on *Bandstand* one day.

If it weren't for the fact that the average 45-RPM record lasted less than three minutes in those days, I would say that Uncle Jimmy had his "fifteen minutes of fame" on *Bandstand* that afternoon. But in any case, the record never took off and it was back to delivering coal for Uncle Jimmy. My own prospects, however, were about to improve dramatically.

The next day, after asking around in the neighborhood, I found out that one of the older kids, a guy named Johnny Panvini, had a possible "in" for us at *Bandstand*. Johnny knew a girl named Jo Mazzu who lived a few blocks from me at 2108 South Bancroft, and Jo was a "regular" on the show. At that time, the regulars were issued membership cards, and Jo Mazzu had one. After Johnny introduced me to Jo, she and I started jitterbugging together at her house. By that time, I had gone to a lot of school dances at St. Monica's, St. Richard's, and the Epiphany, but I had never met a girl who danced as well as Jo. For some reason, our styles clicked in a certain way and the hours passed quickly when we danced together after school. Eventually, Jo invited Johnny Panvini and me to check out *Bandstand* for ourselves.

A day or two later, Johnny and I met in the neighborhood after school, caught the subway uptown, transferred to the elevated train (known in every neighborhood of the city as "the El"), and got off at 46th and Market, half a block from our destination. As we stepped onto the platform, we knew we had an issue to deal with—the fact that I was 13. Because he was 14, Johnny met the minimum requirement, but I didn't, so we knew we would have to pull a fast one for me to get in.

When we arrived, there was a line of teenagers waiting to get into the studio. Sticking to our game plan, we waited patiently in line until Big Jack, the doorkeeper, was a few feet away. Big Jack was a college football player with a brush haircut. Right on cue, I made my move, slipping out of the line while Johnny greeted Big Jack, made a wise-crack, and doubled him over with laughter, giving me just enough time to slip into an entrance that the technicians used. As I waited for Johnny to make his way inside, I had no way of knowing that a world unlike anything I had ever seen was waiting for me a few feet away.

During that period of my life, I used to hang with older guys because the kids my age didn't interest me. In years past, the street had been our playground, and we had played half-ball between parked cars, a bottle cap game called "dead box," and 115-pound football at the Chadmore Athletic Club, but I was starting to outgrow my old play-mates. We still got along and I still liked them, but sports didn't grab me like music and dancing did. (Even when a bunch of us were together at Chadmore, which was a half a block away on Bancroft Street, I would listen to the radio and shoot pool with the older guys and spend very little time with kids my own age.)

I remember one kid who went to Connie Mack Stadium with his

father. The stadium was at 21st and Lehigh in North Philadelphia. When he came back to the neighborhood, he was starry-eyed and couldn't stop talking about it. He described walking up the concourse behind home plate and seeing the field for the first time—how big it was and how green and how the infield dirt changed colors when the groundskeepers watered it down. He mentioned looking at the huge light tower in right field and seeing the scoreboard lit up in different colors. Well, that's how I felt when I saw the *Bandstand* studio for the first time.

The set they built had pennants hanging on the walls, and hundreds of local high schools were represented, including Roxborough, Frankford, and Cardinal Dougherty. As soon as my eyes adjusted to the light, I looked for Southeast Catholic—the school I would attend the following year—and sure enough, there it was. Bob Horn had come up with a magic formula that was perfect for the times, and every element of it was designed to make the kids feel as though they belonged to something, from the membership cards that said "WFIL TV *Bandstand* Club" to the formation of a committee so that kids could select the records they danced to. The show was designed to be teenager-friendly in every possible way, and it succeeded magnificently. Looking back on it, a sense of belonging is one of the hardest things to come by for a teenager, and *Bandstand* gave us that and more.

I had never seen a television studio in person, or cameras, or the kind of microphone that Bob Horn used on his podium, and that first day I took it all in hungrily.

Jo Mazzu and I did our thing that afternoon, jitterbugging like nobody's business, and I had never felt more alive. Soon, some of the older girls were asking me to dance, and the excitement of it all began to feed on itself until I could think of nothing else. By the second or third week, the show's producer, Tony Mammarella, started to notice me on the dance floor, as did Bob Horn.

"Who's the kid?" Bob asked.

"Jerry Blavat," Tony said.

"He can really dance. There's something about him."

Whatever that indefinable something was, apparently I had it going on, because a minute later, I was talking to Bob Horn himself, the host of the show.

"Are you 14?" he asked.

"I'm 13," I said, "but I'll be 14 in less than a year."

Horn laughed at my joke. "At least you didn't lie to me."

"I wouldn't do that."

Horn turned to Mammarella, who had listened to the entire conversation. "Put him on the committee."

As a member of the committee, I now had access to Horn, and I started to make the most of it simply by being myself. I wasn't trying to squeeze anybody out or make the other committee members jealous, but that is exactly what happened. Within a week or two, there were undertones of jealousy coming from the kids who had been regulars before I came on the scene. Before long, *Bandstand* became my life, and I started going every day and staying up later and later to get my school work done. For my mother, my interest in *Bandstand* was a runaway train she couldn't stop, but even if she wanted to slow me down, she couldn't say anything when she saw my next report card. Fifty-five years later, I still have the report card in my office, and like all of the report cards before it, I got nothing but As and Bs.

Not only was I jitterbugging at Jo Mazzu's—and dancing at Chadmore A.C. and three different parishes—but I had taken to practicing by myself. Waiting for the trolley to take me uptown—so that I could transfer to "the El" and get to the *Bandstand* studio—I developed the habit of latching onto telephone poles and pretending they were dance partners. Snapping my fingers to create a beat, putting beats together to produce a rhythm, and keeping one hand on the telephone pole at all times, I would practice my steps in advance until I had them down cold. By the time I got to *Bandstand*, I had gone through a process of trial and error.

Depending upon the steps you move to, the rhythm that comes to you naturally, and the way the music fills your heart, you can create your own style of jitterbugging; I believe that I did that. Because my moves were well-rehearsed, I brought a certain professionalism to it as well.

All of my early experiences—dancing in my grandparents' living room, doing the Mummers' strut, practicing with Roberta as a child and Jo Mazzu as a teenager, attending dances every weekend—combined to give me a unique style, and by the time I started dancing on *Bandstand*, my steps were different than most kids'.

Another part of the *Bandstand* formula was to do a roll call, giving each of the kids a chance to say his or her name on television. A few days after I identified myself on the air, I received my first piece of fan mail. Addressed to the station as all of the fan mail was, Bob Horn handed it over to me one day, and I couldn't stop looking at it. My first admirer informed me that she loved the way I danced.

"How many times are you gonna read it?" Bob smiled.

I looked up from the letter. "Sorry," I mumbled.

It was at about that time that I started to win all of the dance contests on the show, until Bob Horn took me aside.

"Look," he said, "you can't enter the contests any more. You're winning all of them. We've gotta give the other kids a chance!"

"No problem," I said.

"How would you like to be the head of the committee?"

Committee members didn't get paid, but Bob gave me $15 a week to serve as the leader. Between that and the fan mail, I felt like I was important. Although I allowed myself to enjoy the attention, I continued to take my job seriously, and to have a deep and abiding love for music. Being a committee member at first, and the head of the committee later, I felt a responsibility not only to the kids who danced on *Bandstand*, but also to the ones who watched the show at home. This sense of responsibility coincided with my increasing ease and comfort with Bob. If I had misgivings about a record that he intended to play on the air, I wouldn't hesitate to tell him, and he welcomed my feedback. By listening to the radio at night—particularly the black stations—I heard music that was absolutely authentic, and very early in our relationship, Bob realized that I had a better handle on what the kids would like to dance to than he did as a forty-year-old man.

"What's that?" I would ask.

"'Tutti Frutti,'" he would say.

"By who?"

"Pat Boone."

Almost immediately, I would make a face. "You gotta be kiddin'."

"What's the matter?" Bob would say, looking puzzled.

"Don't play that one. Play the original by Little Richard."

Bob would make some phone calls to promotion men, and within a day or two he would get his hands on a copy of the original. The next time he saw me, he would shake his head in amazement.

"Where did you hear that record?"

"Jocko, man! He plays it all the time."

Appearing on WDAS in Philadelphia, Jocko Henderson was one of several black disc jockeys that I tuned in to regularly to hear the real sounds and not the pale imitations. The same with Georgie Woods who appeared on WDAS also, and Mitch Thomas who later created a black version of *Bandstand* on a Wilmington, Delaware station. I would hear "Sh-boom" by the Chords on the radio, and then the promotion guys would bring it in by the Crew Cuts and I would say, "Bob, you should hear the real song on this," meaning the original by the Chords. The promotion guys would give Bob "Church Bells May Ring" by the Crew Cuts, but before he played it on the air, I would turn him on to the original version by the Willows, and that's what made it onto the show.

The promotion guys would give Bob the cover versions because they had national distribution and would immediately cover the local hits on the little independent labels. I would say, "Why don't you play the real thing?" So Bob would ask the promotion men to get him the original versions of the songs. In addition to the original versions of "Tutti Frutti," "Sh-boom," and "Church Bells May Ring," I told Bob that he should play "Ain't That a Shame" by Fats Domino, not the Pat Boone version, which many radio stations were playing. Pat Boone was a nice guy, but his version just didn't make it.

Eventually, we got into a routine in which I would get to *Bandstand* early, listen to the latest batch of records, pick out five or six that I liked, and Bob would use them on his "Rate the Record" segment without listening to them himself, trusting my ear.

In addition to getting fan mail, I was sometimes recognized on the street by strangers who saw me on *Bandstand*, and eventually my status as a local celebrity enabled me to become precocious sexually. Until then, I wasn't ahead of the curve or behind it; I was where most guys were when it came to masturbation, necking in movie theaters (where the girls who were interested would make sure to leave an empty seat next to them), and fumbling with bra straps later on. But the first sexual experience that went beyond "petting" for me probably would not have happened if I hadn't appeared on television. I was fourteen years old at the time.

At the corner of 17th and Mifflin, there was a place called Pat's Luncheonette, and we used to hang out there after shooting pool at Chadmore A.C., drinking fountain sodas, eating Tastykakes, playing pinball, and listening to music on the jukebox. One day, Pat called me over to the cash register.

"Do me a favor," he said. "I got a delivery."

The delivery was going across the street to the Fulton Manor Apartments, which was heavily populated by service men and their wives or girlfriends. Tenants of the building were mostly transient because of their service commitments.

Pat gave me the delivery, and I walked it across the street and rang the buzzer. A second or two later, a female voice came over the intercom.

"I've got a delivery," I said.

After Pat's customer buzzed me into the lobby, I walked up the steps to the third floor and knocked on the door of her apartment. A second or two later, she opened the door and let me in. Although I typically acted older than my age—and did a pretty good job of keeping my cool in most situations—she was not what I was expecting. A spectacular blonde in her early twenties, she was like nothing I had ever seen. Most of the girls in my neighborhood were dark-haired Italians, and none of the blondes on *Bandstand* looked anything like this one.

"I know you," she said. "I see you on *Bandstand*."

I smiled.

"I think you're terrific," she said.

I thanked her, handed over the sandwich, and left as soon as she paid me. But a week or so later, Pat came out of the luncheonette and walked over to me at the corner.

"That delivery you made? She wants another one. She wants you to bring it up to her."

As casual as I was with Pat, I have to say I was laboring under some serious expectations, but nothing happened on that second visit either, except a little longer conversation about *Bandstand* and some of the songs she liked.

A week or two later, she saw me on the corner and invited me up to her apartment. No delivery this time, just the invite. She told me to wait five minutes and ring her buzzer.

When she opened the door that day, she was wearing a kimono, and I could see the outlines of her breasts. But as sure as I was that something was going to happen, she seemed to hesitate ever so slightly. At that moment, the look on her face was new to me, and I was too young to figure it out. Looking back on it, it could have been shame or sorrow or a loneliness that was similar to mine; whatever it was, she worked through it soon enough. Without a word, she went down on me, allowing the kimono to open.

Afterward, when I walked out of her building, I thought to myself, "Man, I just got blowed!" and I flashed back to an incident that had happened two years before.

After playing basketball one day with some older kids in the schoolyard, I went over to the house of one of the kids. His nickname was Big Ron. There were five or six of us, and he took us up to his room, opened a drawer, and pulled out something called a "two-by-four"—not the wooden kind, but a small comic book two inches by four inches with comic book characters having sex. He said, "Come on, let's all jerk off." Ronnie and the others were fifteen. I was twelve.

After Ronnie pulled out his cock, some of the other kids did, too, and I panicked. I had never masturbated, let alone been involved with a circle jerk. "I'll see you guys later," I said, and I tore out of the there.

As soon as I got back on my bike, I started to think about what they were doing, and instead of returning to the schoolyard, I went home, closed the door to my room, and started playing with myself. And now, as I left the Fulton Manor Apartments, I remembered the earlier experience of learning how to masturbate, and the shock I felt the first time I came. This time, the physical sensation was even stronger, and I was shocked all over again. As it would have with anyone, that first taste of sex caused me to become eager for more.

Despite the fact that I had been in her apartment a total of three times, I never did learn the woman's name, and when I didn't see her in the neighborhood for a few weeks, I asked Pat about her and he told me that she moved out.

A month or two later, I was shooting pool at Chadmore A.C. when one of the older guys walked in. His name was Eddie Cadumo.

"Yo, Ed."

"Go ahead," he said. "Take your shot."

Eddie waited for me to miss—it wasn't a long wait, as I recall—and then he said, "You want a job?"

I looked at him. "What kinda job?"

It turned out that Eddie was a delivery driver for the Buccelli Bakery in South Philadelphia, and he needed someone to ride along with him as he delivered dinner rolls to restaurants and grocery stores. Once again, I would be making deliveries, but they wouldn't be as exciting as the ones I had made for Pat.

There were about twenty stops on our route, including Ralph's, Dante and Luigi's, and Palumbo's Supper Club. Eddie would pull over as close to the stop as possible or double-park and wait for me to run the rolls up to the front door.

Because Eddie and I got along, I enjoyed riding in the truck with him, but I liked the pocket money even more. If I remember correctly, he paid me $5 a day. But the greatest fringe benefit was watching Eddie in action. Whenever traffic backed up behind us—and the cars started beeping their horns—Eddie would lean out of the window and curse the drivers out. "Up yours!" he would yell, causing five more cars to join in the beeping.

Christmas night was always dead when it came to hanging on the corner, and 1954 was no exception. After I left my grandparents' house, I walked to 17th and Mifflin, but no one was there. I was standing under the sign at Pat's Luncheonette.

A couple minutes later, an older guy named Bobby Rucci drove up to the corner and rolled down his window.

"What are you doin'?" he asked.

"Nothin'. Nobody's out."

"Come on, I'm gonna take you somewhere."

When I got in his car, I said, "Turn up the heat; I'm freezin'."

Bobby made a right at 18th Street and headed uptown. He made another right at Bainbridge, then a left on 11th Street and parked in front of a luncheonette called Pie's Place. "Let's go in," he said.

I followed him into the luncheonette, where three or four sad-looking guys were smoking cigarettes, drinking coffee, and nursing slices of pie. I had no idea why Bobby had brought me there.

"Wait over here," Bobby said, directing me to a booth along the wall. There was a curtain that separated the counter from the back room, and I sat down at a booth while Bobby disappeared behind it. One of the guys at the counter looked up at me. He was my father's age, and he looked rundown.

"Hey, you're that kid on *Bandstand.*"

"Yeah," I said. "You watch the show?"

"My niece watches it," he said and went back to his piece of pie. Just then, Bobby stuck his head out from behind the curtain.

"Come back here," he said.

I walked into the back room, where a younger crowd had taken up residence. They were older than me, but younger than the guys at the counter. Some of them were playing cards; others were shooting craps with piles of money next to them on the floor. They were listening to the jukebox, and I'll never forget what was playing. It was "White Christmas" by the Drifters. That was the first time I ever heard it, but when I stopped to listen, Bobby said, "Come upstairs. I wanna introduce you to somebody."

He led me up a rickety staircase and walked me down the hall to a bedroom. When I looked inside, there was a beautiful African-American woman sitting on a bed in her robe. She was about thirty and had a light complexion.

"Have you ever gotten laid?" Bobby asked.

He was looking at me, and waiting for me to answer. The woman was looking at me, too.

"Yeah," I lied.

The woman glanced over at Bobby. It was obvious that she didn't believe me.

"All right," Bobby said. "I'll see you later."

After Bobby walked away, the woman removed her robe. Her body was spectacular, and she allowed me to stare at her for a long time before she moved the proceedings along.

"Take your clothes off," she said. "I'm going to get into bed, and I want you to get on top of me."

She got into bed and pulled the sheet up until it covered her breasts. I removed my clothes, trying my best to look experienced; then I got on top of her.

After a few seconds, she said, "I'm gonna open up my legs. Get comfortable—that's all you gotta do. I'm gonna guide you."

She did exactly as she said, and a few minutes later, I came, allowing myself to rest in her arms.

"How was it?"

"Great," I mumbled, and she laughed.

After a minute, she crossed the room, filled a basin with water, and washed me off. She did it gently, but when she was finished, she made it clear that my time was up. "Tell your friend he owes me three dollars."

By now, my interest in sex was off the charts, and between that, my preoccupation with *Bandstand,* and my delivery job with Eddie Cadumo, it was getting more difficult to keep up with my schoolwork, but somehow I developed the self-discipline to do it. I had no choice, because giving up *Bandstand* was never an option.

Bandstand was my introduction to show business. Besides rotating the dancers, one of my duties as the head of the committee was to take care of the entertainers. I met hundreds of stars that way—Sammy Davis Jr., Bill Haley and His Comets, Tony Bennett, Joni James, Patti Page, and others. When I met Sammy, he saw me jitterbugging and said, "Man, where'd you learn how to dance like that?" I said, "Everybody in South Philly dances like that." He said, "No, man, you're like a little white me!" I turned around and said, "No, I don't know think so." Sammy laughed, and it was the start of a lifelong friendship.

After the performers lip-synched to their records, the kids had an opportunity to dance with them. I would select the dancers. The kids would cut in on each other, and I would dance with some of the guests myself, including Jaye P. Morgan, one of the sexiest women I had ever seen.

One day, Johnnie Ray was scheduled to appear. At that time, he was the only performer who was hotter than Sinatra. He had one of the first double-sided hits with "Cry" and "The Little White Cloud That Cried." When he walked into Bob's office before the show, he was wearing a magnificent Chesterfield coat.

A month before—when the Philadelphia Zoo was promoting the opening of its season—WFIL had purchased a lion cub to appear on *Bandstand.* Bob had a contest for the viewers to name the lion cub. Eventually, he would donate the lion cub to the zoo; in the meantime, he kept it in a cage in his office. The cage had a blanket over it.

"What's in the cage?" Ray asked.

"It's a lion cub," Bob said.

"Can I see him?"

"You can take a peek at him, but don't try to pet him."

The lion cub was sleeping, but he woke up when Ray pulled off the blanket. "Look how beautiful he is!" Ray said. Ignoring Bob's advice, he reached into the cage to pet the lion cub. The second his arm entered the cage, the lion cub swiped at him, slashing the Chesterfield coat. Ray screamed. He was terrified. He fell backward, and Tony Mammarella caught him. I thought that Ray was going to pass out, but fortunately, the only thing that was injured was the coat. The arm of it was torn to shreds.

I also met the promotion guys who plugged their records to Bob, and pretty soon, they were including me in the dinners they were treating him to. It was obvious that they were trying to ingratiate themselves to me by giving me copies of their records and urging me to listen to them, because they knew that I was selecting the music and influencing Bob's tastes.

One of the promotion guys was a fella by the name of Allen Sussell. Like my father and his associates, Allen was a sharp dresser, but he was more conservative than they were, and my idea of wearing the right kind of clothing began to gather steam. I had always admired sharp dressers, but I had no concept of dressing appropriately for specific occasions until I started paying attention to Bob Horn, Allen Sussell, and Harry Finfer, another promotion guy.

Because I had learned to speak only when spoken to at my grandparents'—and had gotten smacked on the few occasions that I violated the rule—I was smart enough to keep my eyes open and my mouth shut in order to absorb whatever knowledge I could from the adults around me. In addition, I always had an inquisitive eye and was observant about life itself, and now I was learning as I went along.

Before long, Bob Horn introduced me to his family and started inviting me to his house on the weekends. The Horns lived on Sweetgum Road in Levittown, and Bob would either drive me up there after the show on Friday or pick me up on South Bancroft Street. In the summertime, he would invite me to his place in Stone Harbor, and I would help him with the dances he ran at the Starlight Ballroom in Wildwood and work as a cabin boy on his boat, *The Bandstand*. As a cabin boy, I served drinks to Nat Segall, a booking agent who always seemed to be down there; Ray Jackson, who ran the Starlight with Bob; and some of the entertainers who appeared on *Bandstand*, including Johnnie Ray, Patti Page, Don Cornell, and Tony Bennett way before he left his heart in San Francisco. Bob's wife was Ann, a former entertainer herself, and their kids were Marianne, Pinkie, and their son, Peter, who at that time was in the air force. Peter would come home from the base on weekends and tool around in a souped-up MG. Later, he became the brother I never had.

Eventually, Harry Finfer started a distributorship with Allen Sussell and an attorney named Harold Lipsius. It was called Universal Records, and they would let me hang out at their office on Girard Avenue, listen to their new releases, and take home any of the records I liked. Professionally, there was something in it for all of us. They knew that some of the records would find their way onto *Bandstand,* and I knew that the private research I was conducting on Girard Avenue (as well as the hours I spent listening to the black disc jockeys on the radio) would keep me ahead of the curve and preserve my status for close to three years as the most powerful kid on the show. During the same time period, I was also frequenting the record bins at the Sun Ray drug store, which was across the street from the Broadway movie theater. This store was different because you could listen to the records before you bought them and find absolute gems at a discounted price of three for a dollar. Other than the promotion men themselves, it was the only place I knew where you could find obscure labels like Atlantic, King, Federal, Vee-Jay, and Chess-Checker.

Harry took a liking to me and started inviting me to his house for dinner. Although I never spent the weekend like I did with the Horn family, I ate with the Finfers a lot, including a Passover seder or two. Once I got to know Harry's wife, Sylvia, and their children, I realized that they reminded me of my Uncle Sam's family in Silver Spring, Maryland, where Roberta and I had gone with our father. Although Uncle Sam was a highly successful businessman and found my father's lifestyle distasteful, he treated our father with respect in front of Roberta and me. His refinement always impressed me, and I came to see many of the same qualities in Harry Finfer and his family. These were the kind of people I hoped to emulate some day, but as I would find out later, a part of me would always be drawn to the street smarts, the hustling, and the wheeler-dealer tendencies of my father. Eventually, I came to see that my best bet would be to dress well, respect others, and balance the various influences on my life as effectively as possible.

By the time I was 15, transportation became an issue, and two important events occurred that resulted in my having my own set of wheels. Occasionally, our family would go to a neighborhood taproom on a Friday night. Located at the corner of Hicks and Moore, this taproom featured a Friday night special of spaghetti and hard shell crabs. The crabs were delivered fresh from the Eastern Shore of Maryland, and were perfectly seasoned with paprika, hot pepper flakes, and a number of other spices that were a closely guarded secret. After we entered via the Ladies' Entrance at the side of the building (every neighborhood taproom had one back then), a waitress named Millie handed out bibs to those who wanted them, small metal hammers, and nutcrackers to break open the shells. Once she did that, we would get busy on the crabs, piling the shells on the paper tablecloth as we ate.

One night, a neighborhood guy named Sammy Aquaroli—better known as "Sammy La La"—called me over to his table. Sammy was thirty years old. He was a degenerate gambler who went to the racetrack every day and hung out at the taproom every night. Like everyone else in the neighborhood, he knew me from *Bandstand*.

"I got a proposition."

"What's that?"

"You know my mom."

"Adeline? Sure."

"She's got some properties down in Wildwood. If you help me paint one of them, you can spend the weekend for nothing."

Having a place to stay in Wildwood sounded good to me, so I said to my mother, "Yo, mom, can I do that?" She knew Sammy, so she let me go.

Sammy's mother was a sweet lady, and whenever I went to Wildwood, she let me stay as long as I wanted if I fixed up her properties before I went to the beach. Once we got down there, Sammy would let me drive his big Buick LeSabre. Once in a while, Sammy would stretch out in the back seat and doze off, or else he would read the *Daily Racing Form*, making only cursory attempts to check on my driving, saying "You doin' okay, Chief?" I'd say, "I'm fine," and Sammy would go back to picking out horses to bet on. That was how I learned to drive—by driving Sammy La La around Wildwood.

At about the same time, my father needed a driver, someone to chauffer him around as he went from place to place writing numbers, loan sharking, collecting gambling debts, and doing the handful of other things he did to supplement his income. Thinking nothing of it, my father shrugged off the minor inconvenience of my date of birth, fudged it by one year, and lied to an unsuspecting clerk at Southern Auto Tags at Broad and Snyder, producing my first-ever driver's license. To this day—55 years after the fact—the driver's license that is renewed by the Commonwealth biennially indicates that I was born in 1939 instead of 1940.

Once I started driving my father around, his life became an open book for me, and some of the mystery that surrounded him during my childhood began to fall away. I saw him in all his fallibility as a father, sometime-husband, and racket guy—and that kind of thing can't help but affect a young person. I was fifteen years old, but I felt a lot older because of the closeness he granted me and my clear-eyed look at the way that he and his friends behaved. In the long run, I'm not sure it was any healthier for me than the long absences of my childhood.

In the fall of 1955, just as the new models came out, Allen Sussell bought a cream colored '56 Thunderbird. The first time I laid eyes on it, I flipped. The car was parked in front of Universal Records on Girard Avenue. It looked like a rocket ship to me. I had never seen anything like it. The closest thing I could think of was the kind of spaceships I used to see on *Flash Gordon* and *Buck Rogers*.

When I walked into Universal, Harold Lipsius was on the phone with Georgie Woods.

"Harold, whose car is that?" I asked, when Lipsius hung up the phone.

"It's Allen's."

Just then, Allen Sussell walked up the hall wiping his hands.

"You like that car, kid?"

"It's amazing!"

"How would you like to drive it?"

"Are you kiddin'? Can I take it to my neighborhood?"

"Here are the keys. Be back in a half hour."

I felt like a million bucks driving down Girard Avenue, and I couldn't wait to see people's faces when they saw me behind the wheel. Unfortunately, it was the middle of the afternoon, and when I got back to the neighborhood, none of the people I wanted to show off for were around. I used up every minute of my half hour looking for a girl to impress or one of my friends, driving to every intersection I could think of that was likely to have someone worthwhile. I even drove to the Paradise Café, where my uncles had roughed up my father; in the end, a couple people I barely knew stopped to admire the car. Other than that, nothing. (Now that I think about it, it was a little like exiting the Fulton Manor Apartments after my first blow job, looking around for someone to tell, and realizing that the corner was empty.)

From that moment on, I was dying to have a car of my own, and I started talking up the idea to my father. Although he had never been the demonstrative type with his children—someone who hugged or kissed—he never hesitated when Roberta or I told him we needed money. But this was by far the biggest thing I had ever asked for, and he told me he needed to think about it. (Before I got the bakery job, our usual transactions began with my saying something like, "Dad, I wanna go to a dance," and he would invariably reach into his pocket and peel off a few bills. "What do you need?" he would say, handing me five dollars. "Here's a fin.")

Now that he had succeeded in obtaining my license—and I was bugging him about a car—my father took me to Harold B. Robinson, a car dealer at 6600 North Broad Street, where they sold a variety of Dodges, Plymouths, and Chryslers.

"Pick out a car you like," my father said.

Robinson was connected to the Jewish racket guys in an unspecified way, and I picked out a Plymouth Fury that looked as good as new without asking any questions. On that particular model, the driver pushed a series of buttons to change gears.

"Okay," my father said, "you like that one?"

"It's great!" ("Fury" was the name of Straight Arrow's horse. How could I not like it?)

For the next few minutes, my father conferred with Robinson in his office. To this day, I have no idea what kind of agreement they came to, but I drove the Fury off of Robinson's lot.

Within a day or two, my father showed up at our house on South Bancroft Street when Roberta and I were in school. At the time, he was paying my mother $50 a month for child support.

"Instead of paying the $50 a month," he told her, "I wanna pay the monthly fees for the car. It comes out to the same amount."

Although she should have known better, my mother agreed to his proposition, and I didn't waste any time enjoying the privileges of having a car, making regular visits to the drive-in movie theatre at Broad and Pattison. Now that I had graduated from blow jobs to intercourse, the idea of going backward—or "repeating a grade" in my sexual education—didn't interest me, but I was meeting with opposition at every turn. There was a lot of panting at the drive-in—and moaning and groaning from both of us—but I got my hand slapped on a regular basis by a series of teenage girls who were just as determined as I was. In every case, my determination to "go all the way" was met in the back seat by an equal determination to draw the line at fondling, copping feels, and—if I was lucky—finger-fucking. (If you had told me when I was a kid that I would be sitting in front of a large movie screen for close to two hours without watching the movie for a single second, I would have told you that you were crazy. But the only people who actually watched the feature presentation at the South Philadelphia Drive-In were middle-aged couples.)

That period of my life was exciting because of the people I surrounded myself with. They were going places—the places that I wanted to go—and because they were older than me, some of them had either made it in the entertainment industry already or had gotten a significant amount of recognition. If I had stayed in my neighborhood—and had never cultivated aspirations of my own—I would never have met ambitious people like these, and it was fascinating to watch them climb the ladder to success, as I hoped to do myself. Allen Sussell, for instance, started a record label a year or two later with Bob and Gene Schwartz, naming it after one of his daughters. Laurie Records went on to produce the work of Dion and the Belmonts, the Passions, and the Chiffons.

At the time, my father always got a kick out of it when one of his friends saw me on television, but his mind worked a certain way. As a street guy looking for an edge—or another angle to play—he got an idea. He thought nothing of expanding his bookmaking, number writing, and loan sharking operations to include Bob Horn, Nat Segall, and some of the promotion men from *Bandstand*, and he took to frequenting the Little Brown Jug, a hole-in-the-wall bar that was up the street from the *Bandstand* studio, where Bob and the others hung out after the show. A couple doors down from the Little Brown Jug was a place called Pop Singer's, where the *Bandstand* kids would drink cherry cokes at the soda fountain. Inevitably, my two worlds collided when Bob Horn and my father became friends at the Little Brown Jug, and Bob and some of the others started to place bets with my father without my knowledge.

One day, my dad called me in the middle of the afternoon. It was a Sunday in November.

"Where are you?" I asked.

"I'm at the Energetic Club. Come around."

The Energetic Club was at Broad and Moore. It operated without a liquor license, and all of the Jewish racket guys hung out there. When I got there, he said, "I want to talk about the Army-Navy game."

"What about it?"

Now that I had a car, my father cooked up a scheme in which three of us would shuttle the cadets and midshipmen back and forth between the Sylvania Hotel on Locust Street and the stadium in South Philadelphia. As we waited at the curb, we could hear my father as he approached the servicemen in the lobby. "You going to the stadium?" he would say. The servicemen would present themselves to him, and he would walk them out to us.

By charging each of the servicemen five dollars, and cramming six of them into each of the three cars, he would make ninety dollars before the game even began. And then we would wait outside of the stadium and drive them back to the Sylvania after the game was over. By the time they were finished tipping him, my father made a couple hundred dollars, gave me thirty-five, and paid the other two drivers twenty-five.

Something important was happening inside me, and it took me a while to figure it out. But as the days wore on, I got a handle on the fact that it had to do with my family, my neighborhood, and the way they looked to me after I was exposed to Bob Horn and *Bandstand*.

When I compared my father to my grandparents and my uncles, I saw what my mother saw originally. He had a way about him that was different, but it was more than that. Although you couldn't always explain the strange hold that he had over you, it was there just the same. When my father took Roberta and me to the movies on a Friday night or a stage show at the Two-Four Club on a Sunday afternoon, where I saw all of the Jewish racket guys wearing pinkie rings and fancy suits like my dad, it was obvious that the racket guys were more interesting than anything I saw in the neighborhood. It wasn't even close. But then I met Bob Horn and he introduced me to professional entertainers and managers and promotion men, and it blew my mind completely. It became a whole different life. As glamorous as my dad had seemed to me previously, the *Bandstand* thing blew it away. There was nothing the old neighborhood could offer me except the sentimental connection I felt and the love I had for my family.

I remember looking up Bancroft Street and seeing the high-rise buildings uptown and knowing that my father's world was where I wanted to be, with its night clubs, speakeasies, and after-hours joints; compared to that, the old neighborhood was nowhere. I was outgrowing my neighborhood like I had outgrown my younger friends. And once the world of *Bandstand* opened up to me, the feeling was even more pronounced. No matter how hard I tried to ignore it, there was always a certain emptiness when I got back to Bancroft Street from *Bandstand*, or from hanging out with my father at the Energetic Club on a Sunday afternoon. I felt like I was straddling two different worlds—the anonymous world and the world in which people became famous; the drab, workaday world of the Capuanos and the other people in the neighborhood and a world with big buildings and even bigger personalities. Seeing them up close, I respected the people in the neighborhood a great deal, but I knew that I wanted something more.

FOUR: The Street Was My Classroom

In addition to the Army-Navy Game, my father found a number of other ways to use my car to his advantage.

One day, he asked me to pick him up at Benny Glickstein's bar, the 9M. He had some stops to make. We had only gone a block or two when we saw a fat woman waiting for a trolley, and my father recognized her. She was about forty years old.

"Stop the car," he said.

After I pulled over to the curb, he got out of the car, walked over to the woman, and started talking to her. The next thing I knew, she was sitting in the back seat.

"Drive down to where they're building the Walt Whitman Bridge," my father said. I looked at the woman in the rearview mirror and her face was expressionless, as though it was just another day in her life.

"Okay, park over here," he said, when we reached a secluded area of the construction site.

"Take a walk," he said. "Come back in ten minutes."

When I came back, my father was in the passenger seat. "Now I'm gonna take a walk." As soon as he disappeared, the woman said, "Come here." I got in the back seat with her, and she blew me.

When my father returned to the car, the fat woman was still in the back seat and I was behind the wheel.

"Come on," my father said. "Drop her off."

We ended up dropping her off at the same trolley stop that she had been waiting at in the first place, and we drove away.

Even though some of these things were shocking to me at first, that was life with my father; the older I got, the more I learned to accept it. There was no use moralizing about it—then or now. The bottom line is, that was his way of life.

I did run into trouble, however, when I took my mother into account. When I was a kid, the street had been my playground; now it was more like a classroom, and the lessons were getting more and more interesting. I was getting into things that a mother could never approve of, especially mine, and I was forced to conceal most of it from her. Just as she had been forced to keep her parents in the dark when my father was courting her, I was forced to obscure my true self, with similar results. The cost for my mother had been a horrible burden of guilt, and now I was feeling it myself. I got my street sense from my father, but I got my strength from my mother, and there was no one in the world that I respected more than her. The need to hide things from my mother was extremely distasteful to me, but I felt I had no other choice; later that night, when she asked if everything was all right, I said "Everything's fine, mom. Don't worry." But I kept picturing the fat woman's face as she waited for the trolley afterward.

The idea of sharing a woman with my father took on a whole new meaning a few weeks later, when I met a hat-check girl named Gloria. Gloria was nineteen and worked at Palumbo's. She lived in a small apartment above Nat Segall's office at Juniper and Locust, and I ran into her one day when she was leaving for work. As soon as she saw me, she recognized me from *Bandstand*. We talked whenever I saw her.

Because Gloria worked at night, I started cutting school to see her in the middle of the afternoon, and eventually I fell into a relationship with her. I would meet her at her apartment. There was hardly any furniture: a kitchen table, a couple of chairs, and a bed—but of course the bed was all that I was interested in.

One afternoon when Gloria and I were going at it, I thought I heard the door of the apartment open. For a moment or two, I did my best to ignore it, but seconds later, I heard the door close. I didn't say anything to Gloria.

The next day, when I went to her apartment, I stopped by Nat's office first. He had a funny look on his face, but I didn't think about it until later, when I knocked on Gloria's door.

"It's open," she said.

When I walked into the room, Gloria was sitting there with a black eye.

"What happened?" I asked.

"I can't see you no more."

"Why not?"

"Your father's paying my bills."

For the next few seconds, I was dazed and slow on the uptake. But then it all hit me at once. My father had been paying for Gloria's apartment, and had walked in on us the day before, catching me in bed with his girl. That ended that.

After my father gave her a black eye, they settled back into their relationship and continued to see each other for another few months. And because she lived in Nat's building, I continued to run into Gloria myself, although I was never tempted to sleep with her again. As for my father, he never said a word to me about it, and I could only imagine what was going through his mind.

Taking a cue from my father, I found another way to make money with the car. I started to drive some of my classmates to school for fifty cents per person, and then I got my mother into the act by having her make sandwiches for the kids. Although some of the kids were cheapskates and tried to bargain with me, I could usually get a dollar for one of my mother's meatball or sausage sandwiches. After a while, it added up, and when you factored in the $15 a week I was making on *Bandstand* and the $25 I was earning with Eddie Cadumo, I was one of the few kids in the neighborhood that had serious money in his pocket.

On Wednesday nights, Bob Horn ran dances at the Carmen Roller Skating Rink, which was right across the street from the Carmen Burlesque Theater at Germantown and Allegheny. The dances would end around nine o'clock at night, and afterward Bob would usually unwind at a bar called Funzie's. The bar was next to the skating rink, and more often than not, some of the promotion men would be there as well.

Although Bob placed bets with my father at the Little Brown Jug, I don't think he ever had a gambling problem; his drinking was another story. During my *Bandstand* days, he wasn't a hard-core drinker that would sit at a bar alone, but he was gregarious enough to enjoy unwinding with the promotion guys in a casual setting. It certainly didn't help that the promotion men were picking up his tab.

Bob was fond of imported beer and Old Granddad, and once in a while, he would combine the two by drinking a "boilermaker," otherwise known as "a shot and a beer." At times like that, his fondness for booze was something to keep an eye on, and by the time I was fifteen, I started to do just that.

Whenever we sat in a bar or restaurant together, I would watch what Bob was drinking and how much he had put away, and I came to know what to look for when he was approaching the danger zone.

For the most part, I was a clean-cut kid, and my only "vice" was rock and roll, but eventually, I took to drinking Bob's shots for him in order to keep him out of trouble. Once or twice, Bob took on a confused expression when he looked down at the empty shot glass, but it only lasted for a second before he shook it off and signaled to the bartender for another one.

On one particular occasion at Funzie's, I was looking out for Bob in exactly that way and waiting for his son Peter to arrive. The plan was for Peter to meet him there, and for the two of them to drive back to Levittown together. As soon as Peter arrived that night, I drove back to South Philadelphia, and I didn't think anything of it until the next day.

After my mother wrapped the last of the sandwiches the next morning, I hopped into the Fury to pick my classmates up. I had everybody in the car when 'DAS interrupted Kay Williams' *Daddy Kay in the Morning* show to announce that Bob Horn had been arrested for DWI the night before.

That day, 2:15 couldn't come fast enough, and after classes were dismissed, I raced over to the *Bandstand* studio to find out what happened from Tony Mammarella.

Tony explained that the reports were accurate. Bob had been arrested, and he wouldn't be hosting the show that day, but as soon as the heat died down, he would be back. In the meantime, Tony would be hosting the show. I carried out my usual duties as the head of the committee and danced like I always did that day. At the same time, though, I was eager to talk to Bob.

Now that he had been removed from *Bandstand*, Bob started to use Nat Segall's office, and I was able to find him there after the show. Bob said that he was pulled over for running a red light at Erie Avenue and Rising Sun. Peter was in the car with him, but both of them felt that Bob was all right to drive. He went on to reiterate what Tony Mammarella had told me that he would just have to wait it out. I didn't know it at the time, but Bob would be in and out of court for the next two years, enduring multiple trials for DWI and morals charges, and I would stand behind him every step of the way.

I had no idea what was going on behind the scenes. Bob's arrest was a blessing in disguise for Triangle Publications, which not only operated WFIL-TV and WFIL-Radio but several newspapers and magazines, including the *Philadelphia Inquirer, TV Guide*, and Sammy La La's personal favorite, the *Daily Racing Form*. Walter Annenberg owned Triangle and called all of the shots.

Despite Bob's enormous success with *Bandstand*, there were those within the organization who wanted to replace him with a younger host in the hope of pitching the show to ABC, the network they were affiliated with. Entire books have been devoted to the subject—and chapters of Dick Clark's autobiography have dealt with it—but the important thing as I retrace my own history is the fact that a number of lives were irrevocably altered when Bob was removed from *Bandstand*, including mine.

Bob was enormously popular with the kids who danced on *Bandstand*, and without an unexpected occurrence—or some form of divine intervention—WFIL-TV would have a public relations nightmare on its hands if they removed him without just cause. Bob's first arrest for DWI gave that to them, and they did everything they could to take advantage of the break. As it turned out, Dick Clark had already been hand picked as the next host of *Bandstand* as soon as the changeover could be accomplished. Clark had been working as a disc jockey on WFIL-Radio, and he had all of the qualities they were looking for. It took the big-shots at WFIL-TV less than three weeks to install Clark as the new host of the show.

In that interim period between Bob Horn's arrest and the installation of Dick Clark, Tony Mammarella continued to host the show. I had nothing against Tony, but when I became aware that Bob Horn would not be coming back, I did everything I could to rally to Bob's side. When it came to Dick Clark, it was nothing personal for me. I didn't know Dick as anything other than a voice on the radio. He just wasn't Bob Horn. I was still dancing on the show, but when Tony Mammarella told us that Dick Clark would soon be taking over, I knew that I had to do something. A day or two before Clark took over, I got an idea. If the kids refused to dance on *Bandstand*, WFIL wouldn't have a show.

On July 9, 1956, I led a group of protesters in picketing *Bandstand*. At my urging, hundreds of kids gathered in front of the studio and began to block the entrance. Now, WFIL had the public relations nightmare it was dreading, and it would only get worse if any of the kids were injured. As our numbers swelled, George Koehler, the general manager of WFIL, came out of the building to speak with me. He was accompanied by Dick Clark.

"We would like to talk to you," Koehler said.

I turned to one of the regulars—Frankie Spagnola—and said, "I'll be right back. Don't let anybody cross the picket line."

Koehler and Clark took me up to the executive office. For the first few minutes, Koehler did most of the talking.

"Bob isn't going to do the show. Dick is, but nothing's going to change. You're going to get what Bob was giving you, and you're going to have the same duties as the head of the committee."

"I'm not interested in the money. We want Bob back."

Koehler and Clark looked at each other. They were expecting a confrontation, but they had no idea how determined I was.

By now, Dick Clark's face is recognizable to millions of people—and an indelible part of American pop culture—but at the time, he looked nondescript to me, handsome maybe, in a Pat Boone kind of way. I had no idea that he would go on to become one of my strongest supporters later in my career.

When their attempts to reason with me began to show signs of failing—and as the hour approached to let kids into the building to prepare for a broadcast that was now in jeopardy—Dick Clark spoke up for the first time.

"You were getting fifteen dollars a week. How about if we double it to thirty?"

Offering to double my "salary" had the unintended effect of doubling my resolve. "I'm not interested. We want Bob Horn back."

That was it. I walked out. I went back to the street and rejoined the picket line. We continued to block the entrance, and the next thing I knew, the police pulled up in front of the building. I glanced up at Koehler's window, knowing that he had made the call to the precinct. He and Clark had a Plan B, and Plan B showed up in the form of several squad cars.

As the squad cars emptied, two policemen headed toward me, and the others dispersed the crowd. All of the kids that I had led in picketing started to move away from the building, looking at each other. They had no idea what to do.

"Keep picketing!" I shouted, as the two cops led me to their squad car, but it was obvious that the protest would fall apart in my absence.

As it turned out, the cops took me to their station at 55th and Pine, but word on the street got to my father right away, and I spent less than a half hour there. As soon as my father showed up, he worked his magic with the desk sergeant.

"I want him out of here."

Meanwhile, the cops had dispersed all of the picketers. Their mission was accomplished, and they had no interest in holding me. They released me to my father, and we drove back to the *Bandstand* studio. As we made our way back to 46th and Market, he actually seemed amused by what I had done, and proud of me in his own way.

The picket signs were leaning against the side of the building, and the picketers were enjoying the show. Dick Clark was the new host, Bob Horn was officially "suspended," and I was on the outside looking in.

In addition to hosting *Bandstand*, Bob had been doing a morning show on WFIL-Radio, and after his first arrest for DWI, Koehler informed him that he would only be doing his *Bandstand* radio show until the heat died down, but he would continue to be paid his full salary. In the meantime, if he chose to do so, he could serve as the radio station's music director. Because Bob found the offer insulting, he decided to consider his options. At that point, Bob began to divide his time between Levittown and Stone Harbor and continued to host *Bandstand* dances throughout the region. For my part, I had already decided that I would never dance on *Bandstand* again. And so, I continued to assist with his appearances at the Starlight Ballroom in Wildwood, the Carmen Roller Skating Rink in Philadelphia, and a number of other venues.

I even tagged along with Bob when he drove to New York City to see his friend Lee Vines, who at the time was the announcer for the *Hallmark Hall of Fame* television show. We met Vines at a place called Hector's. It was on Broadway, and it had a bar in the front and a cafeteria in the back. The place was nothing at all like the cafeterias I was used to. Back home, my experience was limited to Linton's cafeteria and an old-fashioned "automat" named Horn and Hardart's—but neither one of them served alcoholic beverages.

Bob had vacation time coming to him, and for several weeks he and his family lived on the station's money; with the legal system closing in on him, though, he knew that he would have to make some difficult decisions. Free on bail since his June 21 arrest, Bob was indicted by a grand jury a month later, and predictably enough, the station used that to its advantage.

In the weeks that preceded his arrest, Bob had signed a contract for three more years as the host of *Bandstand*, but the contract contained a morals clause that precluded him from getting involved with any unseemly activity that would reflect unfavorably on the station. Sure enough, WFIL-TV reneged on their promise to reinstate his contract, and instead voided it. Bob responded by initiating a lawsuit against WFIL and Triangle Publications.

One morning, I couldn't find my car. I walked around the neighborhood, but it wasn't there. I went back into the house and called my father.

"Yo, dad. Where's the car?"

"Gloria's got it."

"Why didn't you tell me?"

"Relax. She'll bring it back tomorrow."

Gloria returned the car as promised, and everything was fine until a week or two later, when I came out of the house and saw that the car was missing. I figured, okay, Gloria's got the car.

I called my father and said, "Your girlfriend has my car."

"Gloria don't have the car."

"Where is it then?"

It turned out that the car had been repossessed. In the four months that I "owned" it, he hadn't made a single payment, despite his promise to my mother. No car payments and no child support, until we found him out. And that was the end of my car.

There was nothing I could do about it, except scrape together a few bucks and buy an old junker from someone else.

As it turned out, it took me a while to get the money together, and during that time, Sammy La La would let me borrow his Buick for a few hours and take a date to the South Philadelphia Drive-In.

Bob Horn's first arrest for DWI was tied up in the legal system for months, and before it could even be tried in the courts, another charge emerged that was even more serious. I was getting a haircut at Orlando Puppo's barbershop when I heard about it for the first time. Orlando's son Ralph was married to Angelo Bruno's daughter, Jeannie, and his barbershop was located in his home at Broad and Snyder.

Although he was an old-school barber, Orlando had known me my entire life, and had reluctantly agreed to provide my first "duck's ass" haircut when I was in the 8th grade. This style—which was commonly known as a "D.A."—was all the rage at the time, but it went against every instinct that Orlando possessed. It also fell into disfavor at St. Monica'a when I forgot to tone it down one day and the Mother Superior made an unscheduled visit to our classroom. Little did Orlando know that he would play a part in my getting sent home from St. Monica's for the day. "I told you it was a bad idea," he said on my next visit to the shop, and whenever I got a haircut over the next few years, he would mention the incident to anyone who would listen.

"Did you hear about your friend?" Orlando asked. We were halfway through my haircut.

"What friend?"

"The guy that hosted *Bandstand*. It's all over the news. He got arrested for statutory rape."

"That's crazy!" I said.

Orlando pointed across the room. "Look at the paper."

As soon as I spotted the *Daily News*, I jumped up from the chair.

"I gotta go!"

"I'm not finished!"

After Orlando finished my haircut, I sat in his barbershop and read the newspaper accounts of Bob Horn's latest arrest. Months before, when he was still hosting *Bandstand*, Bob had met a young girl who I'll call "Lori" to protect her identity. Lori had danced on *Bandstand* a handful of times, but I knew her from the neighborhood. Now, in the fall of 1956, Lori accused him of having improper relations with her prior to his removal from the show. On November 8, a grand jury indicted Bob on a charge of statutory rape.

The charge was leveled at a time when the local newspapers were publishing articles about call girls at the Wharton Estates, and the names of local celebrities and prominent Philadelphians were being dragged through the mud. These celebrities included Steve Allison, who had a nighttime talk show on WPEN, and Larry Brown, a disc jockey who eventually played a major role in changing a local group's name from the Juvenaires to Danny and the Juniors. The prostitution charges eventually evolved into accusations that local disc jockeys were getting involved with teenage girls, and before you knew it, Bob Horn's name was associated with Lori's. (Needless to say, these newspapers included the *Philadelphia Inquirer* and the *Philadelphia Daily News*, which were owned by Walter Annenberg, who would have profited greatly from Bob Horn embarrassing himself, since Annenberg was still defending himself against Bob's breach of contract lawsuit. In addition, the local papers might have had an axe to grind against Steve Allison, who was consistently critical of them on his talk show.)

When describing Lori, no one could say that she was just another teenage girl. For one thing, she had the face and body of a woman. Although her birth certificate said she was fourteen, you would have started with eighteen and worked your way up if you were asked to guess her age. For another, her home life was fractured. While her father, who I'll call "Mack," drove a truck for Frank's Beverages (which manufactured Frank's Wishniak soft drink), her mother, who I'll call "Betty," turned tricks out of their house on Sheridan Street. Lori watched all of this at a young age—just as I had watched my father— and her attitudes toward sex were advanced and uninhibited. Although there was a sexual element to my interest in Lori, I believe that I would have been drawn to her anyway, because of the outlaw nature of her mother. After all, I had lived something similar with my dad.

Not surprisingly, then, I turned my nose up at Lori as a dance partner on *Bandstand*—she was a mediocre dancer at best—but I took to cutting classes and visiting her on Sheridan Street in the middle of the day. The first time I did this, I was talking with Lori in the living room when a client showed up at the door. To that point, I had no idea that she and her mother were conducting business.

When Lori went upstairs with the client and Betty followed, I had suspicions about what was happening, but I never could have predicted the next experience that would come to me. At the time, Lori was friendly with a young man named Rickie. I found out later that Rickie was one of three drag queens in the neighborhood—the others were named Victor and Francine. When Rickie wore makeup and women's clothing, he looked just like a girl; if you closed your eyes, he sounded like one, too. His father sold a cleaning product out of a cart—it was called "javelle water" and worked like a bleach—and it came to be known throughout the neighborhood that you could always tell if Rickie's father was home if the cart was parked in front of their house at 7th and Jackson. If the cart wasn't there, it meant that it was safe to knock on Rickie's door, and you could fully expect Rickie to blow you. Instead of paying Rickie for the privilege, however, Rickie paid you five dollars. The guys uptown called him Rickie the Queer, but that didn't stop them from knocking on his door.

One day, when I was waiting for Lori to come downstairs—and Betty was otherwise occupied with a client—Rickie let himself in the front door.

I was sitting at the kitchen table when Rickie saw me. "I know you," he said suddenly. "I watched you on *Bandstand*." And he walked into the kitchen. At the time, of course, I thought he was a "she."

"Stand up," he said. "Let me take a look at you."

Rickie did more than look at me—he blew me—and later, when I found out that he was a transvestite, I was embarrassed. I was street-wise, but at the time I had no idea.

When Lori came down the steps from the second floor, she knew what was going on, but she didn't say a word.

Because my father hung around 7th and Jackson—which was a predominantly Jewish neighborhood—he got wind of what had happened and pounded on Lori and Betty's door.

"You keep my son out of here!" he shouted. Apparently, he had no objection to my frequenting a house of prostitution, but when I got involved with a drag queen, he took great offense. It was clear that Betty respected my father's ties to the local Jewish mob and would honor his wishes. The next time I knocked on the door, she said, "You can't come around anymore. Your father don't want you here."

From the minute I learned about Lori's accusations—and the fact that the District Attorney's office was pressing charges against Bob Horn—I knew that the case was bullshit. But given the personalities involved, I also knew that Bob was in for the fight of his life. His reputation was hanging by a thread, but now his freedom was at stake as well.

Before it was all over, Bob would be forced to endure two trials on the same charge of statutory rape, with the first trial ending in a hung jury and the second ending in acquittal. But before he was finally exonerated, the legal system made his life a living hell. During both trials, I testified on Bob's behalf, telling the court that I had been Lori's lover, and that Bob had not been involved with her at all. But my involvement in the trial went beyond providing testimony.

When the attorneys were preparing their cases for the first trial, I got a phone call from Johnny Christian. Christian tended bar in the neighborhood and went by the nickname "Mahoody."

"I wanna see you," he said.

"What about?"

"I can't tell you on the phone."

The next day, I went to Mahoody's taproom, and while he poured drinks for customers at the other end of the bar, he kept walking back and forth to me.

"For $2,500," he said. "Lori will refuse to testify in court."

"What did you say?"

"You tell Bob Horn that we want $2,500. If he comes up with it, she won't testify against him."

What I didn't know at the time was that the DA's office had put Lori up to testifying against Bob in the first place. They had arrested Lori's mother for prostitution charges, and now they were proposing a deal.

"We won't prosecute your mother if you testify that you were involved with Bob Horn."

Whether the DA's office believed Lori's initial accusation and was simply doing what it always did to persuade a witness to testify, or it intended to frame Bob Horn for reasons of its own (including the power wielded by Walter Annenberg), it was impossible to say at the time. But certainly there was a hint of impropriety in the DA's behavior and in Lori.

Surprisingly, however, when Lori agreed to serve as a witness, the DA's office made the mistake of dropping their charges against her mother before the situation had played itself out. Now that they had done that prematurely, Mahoody saw an opportunity to make a play for $2,500, and it couldn't have been difficult for him to sell the idea to Lori. With her mother off the hook, Lori okayed Mahoody to make the

After Mahoody made the offer, I went over to Nat Segall's office, where Bob had set up shop for his defense. Bob called his attorney, Louis Lipschutz, and told him about the bribe. At the time, Lipschutz was a prominent defense attorney in Philadelphia—the best that money could buy.

When Bob hung up the phone, he said, "We've gotta meet with Louis tomorrow at three o'clock."

Lipschutz's office was at the Lewis Tower Building at 15th and Locust. Bob and I were there fifteen minutes early. After ushering us in to his swank inner sanctum, Lipschutz turned to me. "We're going to give you the $2,500. You set up the meet."

As I sat there listening to him, I realized that there was very little difference between the language that he was using as a distinguished, highly respected attorney on the right side of the law, and the kind of language that my father and his friends used on a regular basis. "Setting up a meet" was something my father would do. Nevertheless, I kept my mouth shut like I had learned to do as a kid.

"We're going to call the DA's office," Lipschutz continued, "and let them know that Bob is being blackmailed." And he proceeded to do just that, reaching Emmitt Fitzpatrick, the Assistant DA, seconds later.

"Your whole case would have fallen apart," he told Fitzpatrick, "if we kept quiet about the bribe. Instead we're putting it out there in good faith."

"We don't see it that way," Fitzpatrick responded.

"I'm sure you don't. Your witness is selling her testimony."

"Our witness is a little confused. She'll come to her senses eventually."

"It just goes to show you, this was a bullshit case from day one."

Fitzpatrick told Lipschutz to await further instructions, and after conferring with his boss—the District Attorney, Victor Blanc—he called Lipschutz back the next day. The DA's office decided to bust Mahoody for the bribe attempt, and on the following Saturday, at ten o'clock in the morning, I showed up at Betty and Lori's front door with $2,500 in my pocket. A huge, overstuffed detective named John O'Brien was sitting in an unmarked police car, calling the shots while three or four underlings waited around the corner.

The front door was open. When I walked up the steps, I could see

The front door was open. When I walked up the steps, I could see into their living room. Mahoody was sitting on the sofa in a tee-shirt, looking awfully cozy. The fact that he had been sleeping with Lori was obvious.

"Do you have the money?" Mahoody asked.

"I have it," I said, and just as I reached into my pocket, John O'Brien burst through the doorway. Mahoody was shocked. The look on his face was priceless.

"They're trying to bribe us!" Mahoody yelled, as four more detectives poured into the room.

"Sure they are," O'Brien answered.

"They want us to throw the case!" Mahoody continued desperately.

O'Brien handcuffed him, not even bothering to answer. But before I could enjoy the spectacle of Mahoody being led to the unmarked car, one of the other detectives collared me and led me in the opposite direction.

Fifty years after the fact, I'm still not sure if the police and the DA's office miscommunicated about the nature of my involvement, or they were just trying to make it look good to Lori and Mahoody, or they fully intended to implicate me in the bribe. But my father had to straighten things out again. This time, he seemed a little less amused than the day I picketed *Bandstand*.

When my father arrived at the jail, Emmitt Fitzpatrick and John O'Brien were talking to each other in a hallway. My father sought them out immediately. I could hear him shouting from my cell.

"What the fuck? You can't hold my kid! He didn't do anything wrong!"

The next thing I knew, my father was driving me home.

"What the fuck did you do?" my father said, when he had me alone in the car. "Why didn't you tell me you had the money? I woulda grabbed it!"

"Dad, come on!"

"I'm serious!"

At that point, all I could do was shake my head. My father was a piece of work, and he never ceased to amaze me.

Because they were so intent on gaining a conviction, the DA's office swept Mahoody's bribery attempt under the rug and pretended that it didn't happen, just as they ignored the fact that Lori had attempted to sell her testimony. Instead of prosecuting Mahoody, they dropped the charges against him.

There are those who would say that the DA's office indulged in legalized extortion when it promised to let Betty off the hook for the prostitution charge if Lori cooperated. Or maybe the prosecutors figured that Lori's double dealing was par for the course and were therefore undeterred. But as I mentioned earlier, Bob Horn had to survive two trials before he was exonerated.

With his career in tatters, Bob continued to drink heavily, and on the night of January 22, 1957, he drove the wrong way down a one-way street in North Philadelphia and collided with another car, injuring five people, including a little girl who was close to death for several weeks. Although the girl eventually recovered, her life was never the same, and the accident resulted in Bob's second DWI charge in seven months.

After he beat the statutory rape charges, Bob Horn decided to relocate to Houston, Texas, where he had a number of industry contacts. He had a job waiting for him as a disc jockey on KILT—the first format radio station in America—and while his wife and kids remained in Levittown, he made plans to pack his bags and go. The two DWI cases would eventually be heard in October, and Bob would return to Philadelphia to defend himself.

"How would you like to come down to Texas with me? There's a record distributor down there. I think I can get you a job."

For the past few months, I had been doing a lot of the driving for Bob in his '56 Cadillac convertible, so we would certainly be going in style. My only question was whether my mother would allow me to go. To that point, she had been comfortable with my spending weekends with Bob during the school year, and days at a time during the summer; going to Texas with him was something else entirely.

By that time, my mother had remarried, having succumbed to the constant pressure that her parents were exerting on her. My grandparents felt that it was improper for an Italian woman of a certain age to be single, particularly when she was raising two children. My mother was working as a riveter at Boeing Helicopter at the time, and one of her supervisors, a guy named Matty Gunnella, had taken an interest in her outside of work. Despite the fact that she wasn't in love with Matty, she accepted his marriage proposal and invited him to move into the house on South Bancroft Street. Matty had only been living with us for a few weeks, but already there was tension between us. He strongly disapproved of my interest in show business and the company I was keeping, and he never hesitated to make snide remarks. For that reason, my mother was more receptive to the idea of my going to Texas with Bob for the summer. In addition, I had never let her down after asking her to trust me; in the end, she allowed me to go. (One other factor may have been the timing of my request. My 17th birthday was on July 3, and when my mother allowed me to go, it felt like an extra birthday present.)

"There's only one thing you have to remember," Bob said, after I obtained my mother's permission. "You can't call me Bob Horn. From now on, I'm Bob Adams."

While spending time with Bob, I continued to experience new things, but not all of them were pleasant. At a roadside stand in Louisiana, I made the mistake of ordering a cup of coffee, not realizing that they were using chicory, a coffee substitute. Without thinking, I spat the chicory out as soon as I tasted it, drawing stares from the next table. Instead of being embarrassed, however, Bob got a kick out of my reaction.

"You just proved my point," he said. "You can take the kid out of South Philadelphia, but you can't take South Philadelphia out of the kid."

"I guess not, but you could have warned me about the coffee."

Since Bob was in a good mood, I decided to turn his Caddy into a confession booth by telling him that I had downed his shots of whiskey on the sly. I didn't know how he would take the fact that I had looked out for him that way, but we ended up having a good laugh about it while barreling down the road.

Although the taste of the chicory stayed with me, the ledger balanced out on Southern cooking when we went to another cafeteria after arriving in Houston a few days later. Like Hector's in New York, I had never seen anything like it, but the real highlight was tasting pecan pie. From the first bite, I was hooked, and I've had a taste for it ever since.

As Bob had promised, he was able to call on some of his industry contacts to get me a job in Houston. From his years on *Bandstand*, he knew all of the record companies and most of the distributors, and within days of our arrival, I landed a job with a large record distributor called Poppa Daly's. The job was perfect for me. I stood behind a counter and waited on individual customers that came in to buy records off the street, and I placed orders for large record stores in the back. Once again, I was in heaven, because I was listening to music all day, and the music was completely authentic. I heard songs that I hadn't even heard on Jocko's show or Georgie Woods' in Philadelphia. I discovered too many songs to mention them all—one example was "Ain't Got No Home" by Clarence "Frogman" Henry—but what KILT was playing was definitely the real deal, just like 'DAS and 'HAT had been the real deal back home. As you can imagine, Poppa Daly's was teeming with records, and as long as I did my job, they had no problem with my taking the occasional record home.

As good as it was to work at a record distributor for a kid like me, my life outside of work was even better. Back then, it was safe to hitchhike, and when Bob was on the air at KILT and unable to give me a ride, I could stick out my thumb by the side of the road and get around without a problem.

At the time, Bob and I were staying at a place called the Bama Apartments, which had a large swimming pool that was unlike anything I had seen in Philadelphia. I had seen rec center pools, of course, and had driven past the occasional country club, but I had never been to an apartment building that had a pool of its own.

On my very first afternoon of lounging around the pool after work, I made another discovery that was even better. Due to its proximity to the Houston airport, the Bama was extremely popular with flight attendants, and a disproportionate number of them lived there. After getting paid in the daytime for listening to music, I would come home to feast my eyes on the stewardesses by the side of the pool.

Although I can't recall if I approached her first or it was the other way around, a flight attendant named Wanda May started coming on to me early on. Wanda was in her mid-twenties and worked for a different airline than her roommates, which meant that she often had the apartment to herself. If my sex life had stalled in Philadelphia—as I continued to lose my wrestling matches at the South Philadelphia Drive-In—it picked up again in Texas, and I went on to regain some of the momentum I had established at the Fulton Manor Apartments and

Pie's Place. In terms of the sex itself, it was positively thrilling, and I couldn't wait to answer the perennial question that fall of how I had spent my summer vacation.

All in all, the summer of '57 would have been flawless if Bob hadn't taken a turn for the worse. At a certain point, he read in the newspaper that Dick Clark was thriving in his absence, and that *Bandstand* was going national, and his drinking increased. As he became more and more despondent, I did what I could to rally him, alternating between "Bob, you can't do this," and "You're going to be okay," but there wasn't a platitude in the world that was going to help. He had it all and lost it, and no one knew it better than him. Unfortunately, his troubles were far from over.

As September approached, I began to feel guilty about returning to Philadelphia for high school and leaving Bob alone; in the end, feeling guilty was a reality check for me. As fortunate as I had been to experience fantastic things at a young age, I was still just a kid, and at the very least, I had a high school education to complete. My senior year was fast approaching, and as incredible as the summer had been, I was level-headed enough to realize that I couldn't drop out of school. In addition, I had my mother's feelings to consider—and the trust she had shown in me—and I knew that I would return to Philadelphia when the time came. As depressed as Bob had become, however, he never stopped being a friend to me, and he always had my best interests at heart. At the end of the summer, he did whatever he could to send me back to Philadelphia with a clear conscience.

After I brought it up, we briefly discussed the possibility of Bob calling his wife in Levittown and asking her to rejoin him; however, Bob rejected the idea so forcefully that I couldn't even consider going behind his back and calling Ann myself.

Because he worked for the railroad, my father sent me a one-way train ticket from Houston to Philadelphia, but in those days, there was no such thing as an express train. The ticket I had was for a milk train that stopped in every small town you could think of, and some of the towns weren't even on the map. One night, when we were traveling through the south, I got off the train to stretch my legs, and there were crickets jumping all over the platform. These were not your normal insects. To a city kid, they almost looked like birds; that's how big they were. I changed my mind in a hurry about stretching my legs. I got back on the train and slept in my seat, waking up with a stiff neck. I can remember that I was the only long-distance passenger. All of the other passengers got on and off within fifty or a hundred miles of their original stop. It took me three days to get home, and I missed the beginning of school.

After I returned to Philadelphia, I started hanging out with Nat Segall, going from one mentor to another without pausing in between. Despite the fact that I had grown up quite a bit, I still felt a void where my dad was concerned and had yet to outgrow seeking out father figures to fill it as best I could. Because of his close ties to Bob Horn, it made sense that I gravitated toward Nat. Ever since the 40s, the two men had been partners in one venture or another. Nat had owned a club called Downbeat around the corner from the Earle Theator, where Billie Holiday, Charlie Parker, and other giants of jazz performed. After Holiday was busted for narcotics one night, the police started raiding the place on a regular basis, and Nat was forced to close it down—but not before he and Bob produced a series of jazz shows at the Academy of Music. Later, Bob and Nat were partners with Bernie Lowenthal in a record label called Sound and Teen. (By the time I met him, Lowenthal had shortened his name to Lowe to make it sound less Jewish.)

Nat's office was on top of Bill Rodstein's club, Big Bill's, at Juniper and Locust, a short subway ride from my high school, and every afternoon I would spend a few hours there. Operating under the names Keystone Music and Keystone Amusement Agency, Nat was doing a little bit of everything—booking club dates, managing groups, and promoting Sound and Teen—and by the time he was in his mid- to late-thirties, he had a vast network of contacts within the entertainment industry.

Nat had a piano in his office, where he would audition new talent with the possibility of their being recorded. During my *Bandstand* days, he had gotten a call from Don Costa, who was bringing Jaye P. Morgan in to record at Reco Arts Studios. Don was her producer and needed a piano to go over her parts before they went in to the actual session. Nat knew that I was smitten with Morgan, and he said, "After the show, why don't you come up to my office?" When I went up there, I was blown away. There was Jaye P. Morgan standing by the piano with Costa, rehearsing "Just a Gigolo." Watching her rehearse cemented the love I had for her as a kid. Besides Joni James, Patti Page, and the DeCastro Sisters, Jaye P. Morgan was one of my all-time favorite females.

One day, Nat and Bernie disappeared behind closed doors and formally dissolved Sound and Teen, now that Bob Horn, their third partner, was indisposed. But Nat and Bernie continued to remain friendly and do business with each other. Eventually, I would have further dealings with Bernie myself after he formed Cameo-Parkway Records.

For hours on end, I would sit and listen to Nat as he wheeled and dealed on the phone, booking his clients at places like the Celebrity Room, Scioli's, and Chubby's. His clients included both comedians and musical acts.

At the time, Nat was managing a group called Doc Stark and the Night Riders. They had appeared on *Bandstand* once or twice, but I hadn't run into them since.

"Come on," Nat said. "Let's go to the 20th Century. Doc's performing."

We caught the last set of the night, and afterward, Nat re-introduced me to Doc as he was having a drink at the bar.

"You remember Jerry Blavat," Nat said.

"Sure I do!" Doc answered. "How you doing, young man?"

"I'm doing great, Doc. I dug your set."

"Thanks. I'd like you to meet my wife."

He turned to the woman sitting next to him. To that point, she had been talking to someone else. When she turned around, we immediately recognized each other. She was the prostitute from Pie's Place—the first woman that I had ever slept with.

"Jerry, this is my wife, Beverly."

Beverly didn't crack—not even for a second—and I kept it together also.

"Hi, Beverly. Howya doin'?"

Back on Christmas night, I hadn't asked Beverly her name, and she hadn't asked me mine.

"Honey, I'd like you to meet Jerry Blavat."

"Hello, Jerry. It's nice to meet you."

Beverly offered her hand and we shook. Doc turned back to Nat.

"Nat, what did you wanna see me about?"

"The schedule for next week," Nat said.

In the weeks that followed, I cut school once or twice to visit Beverly at Pie's Place, but not surprisingly, it was impossible to recapture the excitement of the first time I made it with her, and I never went back there again.

Just as I had gravitated to people like Bob Horn and Nat Segall, they were naturally inclined toward treating me like a son. Even in the earliest days of my relationship with Nat—seeing him at the *Bandstand* studio or serving him drinks on Bob's boat—the tone he took was paternal.

Three or four years before, when I first appeared on *Bandstand*, Nat and I had been talking one day at the Little Brown Jug. Bob Horn was across the bar, placing a bet with my father, and Nat stepped into the breach with some fatherly advice.

"I wanna be a singer," I said.

"No, you're a dancer," Nat said. "Just be a dancer."

I must have looked a little hurt, because Nat picked up on it right away.

"Don't worry about it," he said. "You've got plenty of time to decide."

The final tally on Bob Horn's court cases included the acquittal on the statutory rape charge (a judgment that was handed down on June 26, 1957); a DWI conviction with a $300 fine and one year's probation on October 2, 1957 for the initial incident on Erie Avenue; and a second DWI conviction five days later on October 7, 1957 in the case involving the auto accident that severely injured the little girl. After Bob unsuccessfully appealed the second DWI conviction, he served six months in a Pennsylvania jail, and that was the end of Bob Horn in the radio business.

FIVE: Road Managing:
Danny and the Juniors

By the time Bob Horn went to prison, I was a senior in high school. I had a car, I had money in my pocket, and I was getting laid. Most of my classmates would have been happy to trade places with me. But the thought of Bob wasting away in a jail cell was hard for me to take. He had his share of weaknesses—I could see that now—but I would always be grateful for the influence he had on my life.

While the Bob Horn situation played itself out, Nat Segall brought me along slowly, grooming me to work for him. As Nat's professional network expanded, so did mine, and I began to make valuable contacts that would pay off down the road. Looking back on it, I realize that Bob Horn had introduced me to the entertainment industry and "handed me off" to Nat Segall, just as teachers in a lower grade hand students off to the instructor who is next in line for the following school year.

One of Nat's clients was the comedian, Don Rickles. Nat booked Rickles at the Celebrity Room on a regular basis, and Rickles became popular with the crowd. Because of the "Blue Laws," Philadelphia was dry on Sunday, and a number of private clubs had proliferated in the city, including a place called the Erie Social Club at Tulip and Harbison. The existence of these social clubs provided me with another opportunity to make my way in the world.

Typically, Nat would book his comedians for an entire week at the Celebrity Room, from Tuesday to Saturday. But because Sundays were dry, Nat would book Rickles at both the Celebrity Room and the Erie Social Club on weekends, and it was my job to drive Rickles back and forth between the two locations. After Don's second show at the Celebrity Room, which was located on Juniper Street uptown, I would drive him to the Erie Social. On Saturdays, the Erie Social had an early show, which meant that I was driving Don back and forth not once, but twice, and he did two shows at each location for a total of four shows. At the time, of course, I was full of energy, and instead of feeling like Nat was running me ragged, I loved every minute of it.

Because Don had a tendency to perspire—or *schvitz*, as he would say—I took to carrying a small suitcase for him with changes of under-wear and fresh shirts; as long as I remembered to do that, the schedule was never a problem.

On Sundays, I would pick Don up at the Sylvania Hotel, which was a few feet away from Nat's office, and would drive him to the Erie Social Club for an early show at four o'clock in the afternoon. With all of our driving around, Don and I were spending a lot of time together, and we developed a lifelong friendship. Don would call me a "little *pisher*" in those days (another Yiddish word) and take me out after the show to the "Sinatrama Room" at the Latimer Club, and to the Two-Four Club, where Roberta and I had gone with our father. (The Latimer was another one of Bill Rodstein's clubs, and the "Sinatrama Room" was a tribute to the life and music of Frank Sinatra.)

During that period, Nat Segall lived on Sartain Street uptown, and I took to eating dinner with him on a regular basis. One of our favorite spots was Tad's at 16th and Market, not far from the place that my father took Roberta and me to when we shared the barbecued chicken. At Tad's you could get a steak for a $1.69, a piece of garlic bread, and the biggest baked potato you had ever seen in your life. Later, when I became suc-cessful, I would experience a different class of restaurant, and I would come to recognize the steaks at Tad's as being of an inferior quality, tough as nails and full of gristle. But at the time, they tasted great.

After dinner, Nat and I would go to the Celebrity Room, where he would introduce me to all of the entertainers he booked. I had met most of the singers as a committee member at *Bandstand*—and some of them remembered me—but the comedians were a different story. All in all, I remember watching performances by singers like Patti Page and Joni James, and comedians like Henny Youngman, Jack E. Leonard, Dick Shawn, Myron Cohen, and Don Adams, who later went on to star in the hit television show *Get Smart.*

After drinking with Rickles at the Vesper, the Alpha, and other pri-vate clubs, I developed a taste for nightlife, and began to dress older in order to sneak in to the bars by myself. By that point, I had graduated from the humble clothing stores of my youth and started shopping at better places, spending a lot of my pocket money at Edwin Barry Shoes, Slax n' Jax, and Irving's, where you could pay $5 a week on the layaway plan. Not only did I feel better about myself when I dressed well, but the investment paid off by enabling me to make my way past nightclub bouncers without getting stopped. That was how I got into places like the Thirteen Club, the Hideaway, and the S.A. Club until I became a regular and the bouncers started greeting me by name. Along with the 20th Century, these clubs were located in the heart of Philadelphia's nightclub district at 13th and Locust, half a block from Nat's office—and they were all owned by Frank Palumbo. Palumbo operated all of his nightclubs with a single liquor license, constructing a series of doors that led from one club to the other. The solution he arrived at was ingenious, but it wouldn't have worked if he didn't have friends on the Liquor Control Board.

One block away, at Broad and Locust, the former prizefighter, Lou Tendler, had a restaurant, and at the same intersection, you could get waffles and eggs at four in the morning at the Harvey House. Right around the corner, you could go to the Walton Gardens, which was managed by Lou Walters, whose daughter is famous television personality Barbara Walters.

Dave Shore's was another favorite of mine during that time period. It was a kosher restaurant where all of the Jewish racket guys ate, and if I ever walked in there, the manager, Rose Linchek, would recognize me as the Gimp's son and call me *boychik* as she led me to my table.

On Saturday and Sunday nights, I would go out with some of the older guys from the neighborhood, guys who didn't have to go to the great lengths that I did to prove they were old enough to get in. We would meet at Club Dahlia (which was one step up from Chadmore A.C. in terms of the age group that hung out there) and go to one of the clubs I just mentioned or drive over to Jersey and drink at Aljo's or LaMania's.

Every year, some of the older guys from Dahlia would chip in and rent a house in Wildwood for the summer, and though I knew they genuinely liked me, I had no illusions about why they were inviting me down so often. Once I became recognizable from *Bandstand*, they started to use me as a "chick magnet" before the term even existed, and it sure looked like they had better luck meeting girls when I was hanging out with them. The hot clubs at that time were the Hurricane, the Beachcomber, the Rainbow Room, and the Stardust. National recording artists performed at some of these clubs, and I saw live performances by Little Richard, Fats Domino, the Flamingos, the Treniers, and others.

Even though the drinking age was twenty-one, it was easy for me to get into the clubs by disappearing into a group of older guys as we entered; we would usually stay until closing time and talk four or five of the girls we met into coming back to the house. In the morning, you would wake up to signs of debauchery everywhere, with naked bodies draped all over each other, empty beer bottles, and overflowing ashtrays.

With all the carousing I did, my senior year got off to a fast start, but sometime that fall, Rickles left Philadelphia for Los Angeles. He was booked at a club called the Slate Brothers, and though he didn't know it at the time, that booking turned out to be the break he was waiting for. Most comedians get heckled at one time or another, but Rickles had perfected the art of heckling the audience, and no one was sacred when they attended one of his shows. One night, Frank Sinatra caught Rickles' act at the Slate Brothers, and Rickles let him have it, doubling Sinatra over with laughter. Over the course of the next few nights, Sinatra brought all of his show business friends to the Slate Brothers so that Rickles could give them the same treatment. From that point on, there was no stopping Rickles, and to this day, he acknowledges Sinatra as a major reason for his success.

Before he left town that year, Rickles gave me a magnificent cashmere sweater from Morville's, one of the best clothing stores in Philadelphia. Morville's was out of my price range, and Rickles had spared no expense.

"Thanks," I mumbled, uncomfortable with the show of emotion.

"You're welcome, kid. Wear it in good health."

All these years later, I can't tell you why I did it, but I ended up selling the sweater to one of the guys at the Thirteen Club, using the money to hustle a couple of marks in pool, and doubling my initial investment with a game called "Harrigan."

When I look back at this episode, I don't think it was ingratitude, and I'm not sure I even asked myself what would happen if Rickles inquired about the sweater in the days ahead. I just think I was so into having my own look that the sweater didn't make it for me. Plus, I was extremely practical and knew that I just wouldn't wear that sweater.

At that point in his career, Nat also managed Mickey Marlowe,

Sandy Stewart, and Freddie Bell and the Bellboys. These were up-and-coming names in the industry, and Nat was doing well with them. Because the management side of his operation was thriving, people were seeking him out, including Artie Singer, who was involved with Danny and the Juniors. Not only was Artie serving as their vocal coach, he was cowriting songs for them. Along with Johnny Madara and Dave White (a member of the Juniors), Artie had written a song called "Do the Bop" and played the demo for Dick Clark.

Naturally, when Bob Horn lost *Bandstand*, all of the record companies and promotion men turned their attention to Clark, and their efforts were rewarded when the show went national and became a huge success. By then, Clark was more influential than Bob Horn had ever been. Whatever else could be said about him, he was a brilliant and instinctive businessman, and by the time Singer walked into his office, Clark had the record business in the palm of his hand. If you were touting an up-and-coming group—and hoping for a break—Clark was the man to see.

Tony Mammarella was in Clark's office when Singer played him the demo of "Do the Bop." Anyone else would have been nodding his head in time to the music, but Clark sat still and didn't say a word. Singer waited for Clark to respond, hoping that the song would be his meal ticket.

"I like it," Clark said finally. "But it's the wrong title."

"What would you suggest?" Singer followed.

Clark thought it over for a moment, and said, "'At the Hop.'"

Dick Clark may not have had an ear for music—or even a passion for it—but he had his finger on the pulse of the younger generation. As soon as he said "At the Hop," Mammarella knew that he was on to something.

"Dick's right," Mammarella said. "These kids are going to record hops when they're not dancing on *Bandstand*."

"I'll change the lyrics," Singer said.

"I think you should consider publishing this with Dick's company. You won't be sorry."

As Nat explained it to me later, Singer wasn't aware that Mammarella had a piece of Clark's action.

"If we call it 'At the Hop,'" Clark said, "the kids will relate to it."

"I follow you," Singer said, and the rest was history.

Shortly after its release, "At the Hop" was well on its way to becoming the #1 record in America. As it started to climb the charts, Artie Singer asked Nat Segall to manage Danny and the Juniors. Dick Clark had all of the publishing rights, but there was plenty of money to go around.

Nat could detect the scent of money as well as the next guy, so he readily agreed to manage Artie's group, but he would have some juggling to do. Gloria Mann was looking for a follow-up to "Teenage Prayer," her hit record of the year before, and Sandy Stewart was about to perform "My Coloring Book" on the *Perry Como Show*. Both of their careers were on the rise, and the same could be said for many of Nat's other clients. Now, in addition to everything else, Danny and the Juniors would require delicate handling. I was halfway through my senior year when Nat asked me to serve as their road manager.

"You'll go on the road with them," he said. "But first, you'll do the *Alan Freed Christmas Show* in New York."

This was it—my first big break in the industry—and my face told the entire story.

"You don't have to thank me," Nat said, dead serious now. "You're ready for it, and you're the right person for the job."

"What do you need me to do?"

"I need you to be their mother, their father, their priest, and their accountant. Can you handle it?

"Yeah!"

"You'll wake them up in the morning and make sure they're dressed properly, and you'll get them to the show on time. If they screw up, it's your fault. That's the job. Do you want it?"

"Do you have to ask?"

"Not really. And you'll make sure the money is right, you understand?"

"Definitely, Nat."

"I'm serious about being their mother. You'll give them an allowance, and you'll say no to them when they ask for more. And they *will* ask, trust me."

Nat's offer to go on the road with Danny and the Juniors couldn't have come at a better time. I had learned a lot hanging around his office—and prowling the streets of Philadelphia—but I was beginning to experience diminishing returns. I needed something to challenge me, and to usher in the next phase of my development.

In addition, my relationship with Matty Gunnella was deteriorating badly. Ever since I had returned from Houston, my new stepfather had been on me about the way I was dressing, my habit of staying out until all hours of the night, and my refusal to get a "real" job. He simply couldn't accept the fact that I had no intention of living the kind of life he had, and that I had other options available to me. A few days before Nat asked me to go on tour with Danny and the Juniors, Matty and I had nearly come to blows when I declined his offer of a part-time job at Boeing. The only saving grace for me was that my mother hadn't been home to see the confrontation.

Just as I had taken my job seriously as the head of the committee on *Bandstand*, I was ready to jump into road managing the same way. "When do I start?" I asked.

"You'll go up there on Monday," Nat said. "I'll be up there, too, but I can't stay the whole week."

As I mentioned, I had been to New York with Bob Horn, and I had even gone with some of the neighborhood guys from Dahlia. After a dance on a Saturday night, four or five of us piled into a car for something to do, and got to Manhattan by three in the morning. One of the guys knew a pool hall on the Lower East Side, and we parked right in front, played a couple of games, and came right back to Philadelphia. But my next trip to New York would be nothing like the previous ones.

Before he even offered me the job, Nat had bought me a train ticket and made a reservation at the Forrest Hotel at 49th and Broadway; that's how certain he was that I would accept. The last time I had been on a train, I had needed my father to get me a free ticket from Houston to Philadelphia, and the best he could do was a milk train that took forever. Now I would be riding in style, and the money would come out of the Danny and the Juniors account.

When I walked to the subway at Broad and Snyder the following Monday morning, it would be the last time that I would see the light of day until the middle of the afternoon. After transferring from the subway to the El, walking underground at 30th Street, and boarding my train to New York, I arrived at Penn Station. Even in an "off-peak" hour, this was the busiest train station I had ever seen.

The last leg of my journey was to take the 7th Avenue subway to 42nd Street, and as I looked for the entrance under Penn Station, I saw a sign for Madison Square Garden. Throughout my childhood, a series of championship fights had been held there, and my father had taken the action on all of them, working the phones on South Bancroft Street. If I had been there to hear him—instead of at the day nursery—the names of the boxers would have rolled off his tongue—Marciano, Robinson, LaMotta. Although I had only come 100 miles, it felt like a much longer journey when I thought of the life I was leaving behind.

Nothing before or since has compared to the feeling I had when I stepped out into the sunlight at Times Square. New York was right in my face from the start, hitting me like a ton of bricks with glittering neon signs, thousands of tourists, eight lanes of traffic, buses belching smoke, and taxis beeping their horns furiously. When I wasn't breathing exhaust fumes, I was smelling Sabrett's hot dogs as they bobbed up and down in their lukewarm water; chestnuts being roasted by their vendors; and the unmistakable smell of corned beef from one of a thousand delis. As I walked to my hotel, the combination of sights, sounds, and smells was loud, angry, and exhilarating—and unlike anything I had ever experienced. The very idea of staying at a hotel was thrilling in its own right. Although I could never have articulated it at the time, I knew from that moment on that this was the life for me, and that somehow I had to become what I am today.

If I thought that Times Square was exciting in the daytime, I had to see it at night to feel the full impact of the neon lights flashing against the sky, the hordes of people moving in and out of the theatres on Broadway, and the famous "news ticker" that sent the headlines of the day dancing across the side of a building. As I explored New York City for the first time, I'm not ashamed to admit that I was one of those people who craned my neck to marvel at the skyscrapers. Even though I brought a certain amount of street smarts with me, I wasn't much different than a hayseed from Iowa when it came to experiencing Manhattan; the thing about it was, I didn't care. I was having a blast, just like Nat said I would, and the road managing hadn't even begun.

After Danny and the Juniors checked into the hotel, Nat took us to the Turf Restaurant, which was a short distance away. Although he told us that we could order anything we wanted, he recommended the hamburgers; as soon as they arrived at our table, I could see why. Each one of them was as thick as two or three hamburgers from Dewey's or the White Tower back home.

Danny and the Juniors consisted of Danny Rapp, Frankie Maffei, Dave White, and Joe Terranova, whose stage name was Joe Terry. As we said good night to each other in the lobby, Nat waited for the others to disappear into the elevator before prepping me for my duties one final time.

"You won't see me in the morning," Nat said.

"How come?"

"I'm catching an early train back. Just use your smarts. You'll be fine."

"Don't worry. I'll take care of everything."

"By the way, since you haven't asked me, I'm paying you fifty bucks a week."

Danny and the Juniors' first appearance was on Patti Page's TV show, *The Big Record*, and after that, we immediately went into rehearsals for the *Alan Freed Christmas Show*, which was scheduled to run for ten days.

Over the next few days, I must have passed ten or twelve Broadway theaters, and I couldn't help thinking that Philadelphia only had two theaters that featured Broadway shows, the Forrest and the Shubert. Because of my love of old movies, and my encyclopedic knowledge of actors' names, I made it a point to look at each of the theater marquees, staring up at the large block letters that announced the presence of Gwen Verdon in *Damn Yankees*, Rex Harrison in *My Fair Lady*, and Paul Muni in *Inherit the Wind*.

I was really looking forward to meeting Alan Freed. Not only was he one of the first white disc jockeys to play our music on the radio, but he also was credited with inventing the term "rock and roll." Between the performers, the production personnel, and the technicians, however, the Christmas show was a huge endeavor for Freed, and he had very little time to spend with the likes of me, or with Danny and the Juniors for that matter. Because he had a thousand pieces to put in place before the show opened, he spoke with us only in passing and allowed his assistants to work out the details. As it turned out, Freed wasn't as hip as I expected him to be, but it was still a positive experience.

Needless to say, New York is always exciting—particularly with the holidays coming up—but for the ten days we were there, it was fascinating musically as well. In addition to Danny and the Juniors, the *Alan Freed Christmas Show* featured Little Richard, Frankie Lymon and the Teenagers, Paul Anka, LaVern Baker, Buddy Knox, and the Mello-Kings, who had a song called "Tonite, Tonite, Tonite." And right across the street from the Paramount Theatre, where Alan Freed's show was taking place, Jocko Henderson, the disc jockey from Philadelphia, was hosting a show of his own. Working out of the Loew's State Theatre, Jocko was presenting many of the top R&B artists and doing big business in his own right.

After one of the shows at the Paramount, Freed's managers, Jack Hook and Morris Levy, asked Jocko to meet with them. When Jocko walked backstage, he was dressed impeccably in a black suit, pinstriped shirt, white tie, and camel hair topcoat, looking every bit as prosperous as he was. The minute we saw him, everyone called his name, and I shouted, "Yo, Jocko! The Ace From Space!" All my years of listening to Jocko on WDAS and WHAT had put that phrase on the tip of my tongue, since that was the nickname he had given himself in developing his radio persona. At the sound of it, Jocko looked my way, and his eyes lit up when he saw me. He knew me from my *Bandstand* days.

"Jerry Blavat!" Jocko said. "What are you doin' up here?"

"I'm with Danny and the Juniors" I answered.

Jocko broke into a smile. "Good for you, Blavat," and disappeared into a back office, where Hook and Levy were waiting for him.

The next day, when we arrived at the Paramount, I looked across the street and saw that the marquee had changed at the Loew's State Theatre. I could hardly believe my eyes. The night before, there were lines around the block for both shows—Jocko's and Freed's—but now Jocko's show was gone. A few minutes later, I found Jack Hook backstage.

"What happened to Jocko's show?"

Hook knew that Nat Segall had taken me under his wing, but he had no way of knowing if Nat had schooled me on how business was conducted.

"We thought a change of venue was in order, and all it took was $50,000."

If Hook was trying to shock me, I wasn't going to give him the satisfaction of thinking that he had succeeded. I nodded my head and walked away.

By the next night, Jocko had reopened at the famous Apollo Theator in Harlem, and for the rest of the week, both holiday shows flourished. I had no idea how much revenue the shows produced, but judging by the $50,000 payoff, Hook and Levy had made it worth everyone's while. And Freed had no competition next door.

By our third or fourth day in New York, I discovered a small Roman Catholic church within walking distance of the hotel. It was more of a chapel really, and was called St. Malachy's. It had religious frescos that were beautiful to look at, and votive candles flickering in the shadows. Many of the worshippers were actors from Broadway shows, and the amazing thing was, the chapel was open all night, just like many of the bars and restaurants in the neighborhood. Every night for the rest of the week, I would visit St. Malachy's to say a few prayers.

Before I went to the Paramount one night, I saw a young Indian woman entering an apartment building next door—not the Native American kind but a woman from South Asia. With her light brown complexion and long black hair, she could have been a Native American, but I recognized her traditional *sari* as something I had seen in a geography book at school. I stared at her as she disappeared into her building.

One morning as I was leaving the hotel, I saw her carrying a bag of groceries, and we struck up a conversation. Although she seemed hesitant at first, she became more comfortable when I asked about the *sari*. After she explained the tradition to me, she paused for a moment and smiled.

"I have a confession to make. I've noticed you these last few days."

"Oh, yeah?" I said. "Thank you." (Answering that way had worked for me at the Fulton Manor Apartments, so I figured I would try it again.)

It turned out that she was a college student, living in an apartment that her parents were paying for. Her parents—and the rest of her family—had remained in their native country. When I tried to draw her out, she was reluctant to talk about herself, and I couldn't tell if her humility was a cultural thing or part of her personality. Eventually, she asked me what I was doing in New York, and I told her about Danny and the Juniors. By her reaction, I could tell that she knew nothing about rock and roll, but she seemed to be intrigued by what I was doing at a young age. After we talked for an hour or so, she invited me up to her apartment.

While she brewed a pot of tea, she lit candles, burned incense, and played Eastern music on her turntable. As I waited for her in the living room, I noticed a series of finely crafted, full-color drawings mounted on the wall. Some of the drawings depicted a series of Indian women in poses that could only be called saintly. In my limited experience, the closest thing that I had ever seen to these drawings were the Madonnas in a Catholic church. But clearly, the drawings in the young woman's apartment did not depict the Blessed Virgin Mary.

As I continued to look around, however, I noticed drawings of an erotic nature. A few minutes before, when we talked in front of her building, she had carried herself with a certain modesty, but there was nothing modest about these. Although I wanted to examine them more closely, I walked over to the more spiritual drawings before she returned to the living room.

"What are they?" I asked, when she returned with the pot of tea.

"The drawings? Those are Hindu goddesses."

She put the tea down and walked over to me. "This is Indra," she said. "And this is Durga."

As she named each of the goddesses, she pointed to them one at a time. "Come over here," she said finally. "You'll appreciate this."

I walked over to her. As I drew near, I realized that she was wearing a fragrance that I had never experienced before. It was extremely feminine, but in an understated way.

"This is Saraswati," she said, "the goddess of knowledge, music, and all of the creative arts."

Although I immediately understood the significance of the drawing—and why she wanted me to see it—I was having trouble concentrating.

"And these?" I asked, turning toward the other wall.

"Those are from the *Kama Sutra*," she said calmly. As she answered, her upper lip moved ever so slightly. It wasn't a smile—or even an invitation—but I could tell that she was pleased with the suggestion.

From the first moment I had seen her two or three days before, I had been impressed with her beauty, but to that point, it was her hair, her skin, and the shape of her face that had gotten to me. Now, as we stood in front of the drawings together, I became aware that her body was remarkable as well. Although the *sari* was a modest garment, it was revealing in its own way.

"Are you familiar with the *Kama Sutra?*" she asked.

As I turned toward her, all of her modesty was gone, and before I knew it, I was fumbling with her *sari.* Unfortunately, I had no idea where to start with that kind of clothing, or how to get where I wanted to go.

"Wait," she said.

Girls had told me to "wait" before, and to "stop" for that matter, and I always respected their wishes, even though it usually meant that the party was over. But this time, it only meant that she would disrobe without my help. Although I never saw her bedroom, we made it on the carpet, doing our best to emulate the drawings before the sun came up the next day. Somehow, when we were lying together afterward, we both realized that we would never see each other again.

As it turned out, New York had another surprise in store for me before we left town. While walking down Broadway one day, I ran into Frankie Avalon. I knew him from my neighborhood in South Philadelphia.

"Yo, Frank. What are you doing here?"

"I'm getting my publicity shots," he explained.

Frankie was on his way to Kreigman's, a photography studio that specialized in headshots for actors, musicians, and other entertainers. "Come with me," he said. "You got time?"

I didn't have to be at the Paramount for another hour, so I went to Kreigman's with him while he picked up his photos. Later, he took me to a place called Howard's, where he picked up his wardrobe for an appearance that was scheduled for that night. Although I didn't need any other evidence that New York was the show business capital of the world—or that I wanted to spend the rest of my life being a part of the entertainment industry—running into Frankie was a helpful reminder. Over the next few days, I went out of my way to walk down Broadway, and sure enough I ran into Jimmy Darren (another friend from the neighborhood), as well as Bobby Darin and Connie Francis.

The *Alan Freed Christmas Show* got great reviews, and Danny and the Juniors were singled out for praise in nearly all of the daily newspapers. (At the time, New York and its surrounding counties had more than a dozen newspapers, and most of them sent a reporter to cover the show.) Now, after ten days in Manhattan—and more than thirty performances—we were scheduled to begin the next phase of the tour, a series of one-nighters in Raleigh, Charlotte, Minneapolis, Buffalo, and north of the border in Canada.

Prior to my sophomore year in high school, Southeast Catholic had been renamed Bishop Neumann, and in the two years since then my visibility at the school had increased. In addition to serving on the Student Council, performing in the Drama Club, and working at the Neumann bookstore, I served as secretary of the senior class. More importantly, though, I used my contacts in the entertainment industry to get national recording artists to appear at school dances. Joni James, Joe Valino, and Danny and the Juniors all had hit records when I arranged for them to appear at Neumann. These appearances enhanced my reputation as a mover and shaker, but now—with Danny and the Juniors scheduled to go on tour—I would need permission to miss three weeks of school. (Joe Valino had a record called "Learnin' the Blues," which he performed in the Neumann gymnasium. Unfortunately for him, Frank Sinatra did a cover version a year or two later that blew Valino out of the water and effectively ended his career.)

Since my junior year, I had developed a relationship with the priests who ran Neumann, and they would usually allow me to leave school early if I had a valid reason. There were limits to this, of course. If I wanted to cut classes to visit Lori on Sheridan Street, I had to do it on the sly. But as long as I asked permission—and the request wasn't too outrageous—I could count on them to cooperate. Missing three weeks of school was another story, however.

By my senior year, I had already established the fact that the Norbertine Fathers were partial to the Yachtsman, a private Republican club at the corner of 13th and Walnut, next to the Latin Casino. Whenever I took them out to dinner there, my guests included Father Pollini, Father Cox, and Father Burke. But as much as they liked the

Yachtsman, I would have to come up with something better if I wanted to gain their cooperation this time.

As the *Alan Freed Christmas Show* was winding down, I invited the priests up to New York, paying their train fare, putting them up at the Statler Hilton Hotel, and taking them to a restaurant called the Headquarters, which was operated by the former chef of General Douglas MacArthur. Father Koob, the principal of Bishop Neumann, joined us in New York, and once he settled into our booth, every component of the Bishop Neumann hierarchy was represented, including the athletic director and the head of the Student Council. Despite my frequent absences, I was still an officer on the Student Council, and one of the more influential ones at that.

As we ate dinner that night, I explained that I had an opportunity to go on the road with Danny and the Juniors, emphasizing the more educational aspects of the assignment.

"I may be away from school in the beginning of January," I said.

Father Koob spoke for the others. "For how long?"

"Probably three weeks."

Father Koob made a face. The three other priests waited for Father Koob to respond.

"Is there any way you can shorten that?" he asked.

"I can't, Father. The tour is already booked. But you know," I said, "I need a hernia operation."

All four of the priests blinked at me in confusion, not quite making the connection.

"This is what I'd like to do," I continued. "I'm going to get my hernia repaired."

"When exactly?"

"I'm not sure, Father. But could I get a leave of absence for that, instead of being on tour?"

"I don't think that's a problem," Father Koob replied, turning to the others. "Fathers, what do you think?" and the other priests nodded in agreement.

Father Koob smiled benevolently. "Well, it's settled. Anyone for dessert?"

In January, 1958—with Father Koob's blessing—I served as a road manager on a tour that was produced by Irvin Feld. In addition to

Danny and the Juniors, the performers included Paul Anka, the Everly Brothers, Buddy Holly and the Crickets, Margie Rayburn, and a group called the Poni-Tails who had a song called "Born Too Late." The band-leader for the tour was Sam Donahue, who fronted the Glenn Miller Orchestra. Donahue and the band members rode on one bus while the performers rode on the other.

I used to give Danny and the Juniors an allowance of $20 per day, which came out to $5 per person; just as Nat predicted, they pissed it away almost immediately and were constantly asking me for an advance. I never caved in to their requests and eventually they stopped asking. Instead of rebelling openly, they chose to make snide remarks and complain among themselves. I think they realized that I was simply carrying out Nat's wishes. My other duties consisted of breaking up fights between White and Danny Rapp, investigating the disappearance of White's watch, and choreographing some of their dance steps. (When his watch was stolen, White argued persuasively that a replacement should come out of petty cash, "since you're so worried about us getting to the show on time." He said it with such a classic teenage sneer that I almost agreed, but at the last minute, I told him that we would take it up with Nat when we got back.)

Once we returned to Philadelphia, Danny Rapp complained to Nat that I was too strict with them on the road, and Nat listened to him patiently. Encouraged by Nat's demeanor—and under the mistaken impression that Nat actually cared about his complaint—Rapp requested that Nat replace me with his brother, Billy. Billy was a certifiable alcoholic and Danny was well on his way to becoming one, so there was no chance of Nat honoring the request. Instead, Nat reached into his drawer, removed his general ledger, and demonstrated exactly how much money the group had made over the course of the three-week tour. This ended the argument immediately, and with the money that Nat had deposited into their accounts, each of them bought a brand new Chevy Impala.

In the weeks that followed, Nat booked local club dates for Danny and the Juniors, a return trip to New York, and a second tour of one-nighters that was scheduled for the summer. The way things worked out, I spent enough time in Philadelphia to remain in Father Koob's good graces and graduate with the rest of my class, but not before Nat

Segall and I collaborated to produce Bishop Neumann's senior prom. Held at the Randolph Social Club on Roosevelt Boulevard, and head-lined by Cozy Morley, Fisher and Marks, and the singer Gloria Mann, the event was talked about for years. When you consider the long his-tory of Southeast Catholic High School—and later Bishop Neumann—I can honestly say that no one had seen anything like the prom that Nat and I produced in June, 1958.

That summer, the tour included Wheeling, West Virginia; Nashville, Tennessee; and other southern cities. One night, after a show in Wheeling, Joe Terranova and Frankie Maffei were determined to get laid. The simplest solution, of course, was to take them to a whore-house. Wheeling was wide open at that time—like Galveston had been when I visited it with Bob Horn—and any bellhop could point you in the right direction.

Later that night, I took Joe and Frankie to a brothel. It was located back in the woods.

After Joe and Frankie picked out the girls they wanted, I waited for them downstairs. After fifteen or twenty minutes, Frankie came down the steps. The girl was walking alongside of him, counting her money. As soon as the happy couple got back to where I was sitting, I realized that Joe was still on the second floor. Just then, the madam appeared in the doorway.

"That other guy?" she said. "Get him outta here."

"Why? What did he do?"

"He shot his load already. He won't leave!"

I walked upstairs and found Joe in one of the bedrooms. The girl was sitting in bed topless.

"Can you give us a minute?" I said. The girl got up and walked away.

"Yo, Joe. Come on."

"I wanna fuck her again."

"You're not gonna get a hard-on. You just fucked her!"

"Yes, I will. Watch me."

I had no desire to watch him. Instead, I walked downstairs and handed the madam another seven dollars. After the madam went upstairs to tell the girl, Frankie reached into his pants pocket. He had one dollar left from his five-dollar allowance.

"I got five dollars that says he won't get it up again."

"You don't have five dollars," I said, "you have one dollar, and I already said he wouldn't get it up."

Frankie stuck the dollar bill back into his pocket.

Twenty minutes later, the madam came down from the second floor. Joe was still up there. "Get him the fuck outta here! I'm calling the cops."

I went back to the second floor. "Listen," I said, "she's calling the cops."

Joe shrugged. He got up from the bed and put his pants back on, and we bolted out of there.

The next stop on the tour was Nashville. We stayed at the Hermitage Hotel while Danny and the Juniors completed their engagement at the Tennessee State Fair.

I can't speak for Johnny McBrown or the Rockettes—the other headliners on the show—but Danny and the Juniors enjoyed a unique brand of Southern hospitality in Nashville. The governor of Tennessee was in attendance at the opening night ceremonies, and we met his driver, Bo Bozanic, who was also the head of the Tennessee State Police. Bo was a large man with a thick Southern accent. He liked rock and roll more than country, and for the next three days, he showed us around Nashville, starting with radio station WSM, where Ralph Emery was broadcasting his all-night show.

As the highest-ranking officer in the State Police, Bo headed a large organization that was responsible for controlling the "down-and-dirty" Nashville, but at night, he took pride in revealing it to us in all of its tainted glory.

Although Nashville wasn't entirely dry at that time, the selling of alcohol was strictly curtailed. If you went into a bar, you could only buy beer or wine; if you wanted a cocktail, you would have to supply the liquor yourself and pay for a "setup," which consisted of the ice and the tonic or water. But as the head of the State Police was only too happy to point out, Nashville had a two-block area called the Alley where almost every form of vice existed. You had to know someone to get into the Alley, and thanks to our tour guide, we were able to join the politicians, show business people, and other bigshots who frequented its speakeasies, strip joints, and whorehouses on a nightly basis. (These were the kinds of places where you would knock on a door, a slot would open, and you'd have to give them a password or drop somebody's name to get in.)

As we finished a late-night meal at Jimmy Kelly's steakhouse on Louise Avenue, we watched country music superstar Red Foley sign autographs while his porterhouse got cold, and I couldn't help but be impressed by how gracious Foley was to his fans. When I tried to point this out to Danny and the Juniors, however—in a failed attempt to enhance their sense of professionalism—only Joe Terranova showed a spark of recognition. The other three band members were too busy chowing down to even consider what I was saying—either that or they were anticipating the excitement to follow. Because our initial perform- ance at the fairgrounds had gone over well with the crowd—and we were advised by the highest law enforcement authority in the state that it was the best place to go to celebrate—we had decided to visit the Rainbow Room. (Our other choices were the Black Poodle, the Voodoo Room, and the Carousel Club, which was owned by the horn player, Homer "Boots" Randolph, who was best known for his 1963 hit, "Yakety Sax.")

Although it had more than its share of competition, the Rainbow Room easily qualified as the Alley's most notorious strip club, where every one of the dancers was more outrageous than the one before. With or without the use of props, the performers at the Rainbow Room defied the laws of gravity and physics in executing their contortions, and gave the laws of anatomy and physiology a run for their money as well.

Predictably enough, we got horny as hell at the strip club, and Rapp insisted that we make our obligatory trip to a whorehouse.

"There's no need for that," I said.

"What are you talking about?"

Even with the brand new Impala waiting for him back home— which I helped to make possible—Rapp was holding a grudge over the fact that I was still their road manager instead of his brother.

"Relax," I said. "I took care of it."

"What do you mean you took care if it?"

"Wait till we get back to the hotel."

The night before, a crafty-looking brunette had approached me at the hotel bar and asked if I wanted some company. At the time, I didn't know that the bell captain doubled as her pimp. I called her from the fairgrounds and made the arrangements, and as soon as we arrived back at the Hermitage, I sent the guys up to their rooms and told them to wait. Rapp groused about this for another minute or two, but the rest of the guys told him to relax.

At the appointed time, the hooker met me at the hotel bar, and I paid her thirty-two dollars in advance. (Seven dollars per person was the going rate in Wheeling, but in Nashville it was a dollar more. At the time, I had no intention of sleeping with the hooker myself.)

After visiting each of the four rooms, the brunette knocked on my door unexpectedly, and before I even answered, I suspected that something was wrong. Was she going to shake me down for more money? Had Rapp given her a hard time?

"Is there a problem?" I asked, as the brunette entered my room.

Without saying a word, she started to unbutton my shirt.

"Hold on a second. This wasn't included in. . . ."

"This one's on the house," she said.

An hour later, the phone rang in my room. It was the bell captain tracking her down.

"Where the fuck are you?" he shouted.

"I'm just getting done," she said.

"Come down to the lobby! Now!" And he slammed down the phone.

Somehow, she must have taken a liking to me, because she stayed for another go-round and didn't charge me a cent.

During that period, we would go on the road for weeks at a time and then return to Philadelphia to play club dates until the next tour was scheduled to begin. After we got back from Nashville, we had a week or two to relax before we packed our bags for our second trip to New York. This time, Danny and the Juniors were scheduled to appear on the *Dick Clark Saturday Night Beechnut Show*.

In those days, I was always on the lookout for a better set of wheels. With the fifty dollars a week that Nat was paying me, I wasn't ready to buy myself a new car, but I did find a '54 Pontiac on a used car lot on Essington Avenue. After finding the Native American connection irresistible with the Plymouth Fury—since "Fury" was the name of Straight Arrow's horse—I fell in love with the Pontiac as soon as I noticed its hood ornament, which depicted Chief Pontiac. Once I took a spin around the block to satisfy myself that the car was mechanically sound,

I traded in the broken-down Nash I'd been driving, tossed in another $100, and drove the Pontiac off the lot. (Buying a new car would have to wait until I became a performer myself, but I would become one soon enough.)

In addition to being lightning-quick with a putdown, Don Rickles studied acting and appeared in a movie. He had a bit part in a film called *Run Silent, Run Deep* with Burt Lancaster and Clark Gable. One day, with less than a week to go before Dick Clark's show in New York, Rickles called Nat Segall and invited us to the world premier at the Globe Theater in Atlantic City. Frank Sinatra was appearing in Atlantic City at the same time.

After the premiere of *Run Silent, Run Deep*, Nat and I were walking out of the lobby when Rickles caught up with us.

"I'm going to the 500 to see Frank. Why don't you come with me?" And that's how I met Frank Sinatra for the first time, walking through the kitchen of the 500 Club and getting introduced to him in a cluttered little room that served as his dressing area.

"Howya doin', kid?" Sinatra said, allowing me to shake his hand, but before I could even answer, he turned back to Rickles and exchanged a raunchy remark. Later, I would become much more to Sinatra than a throwaway handshake, but at the time, that was all I got.

After we left the 500 Club, Rickles turned to me and said, "You know who that was, you little *pisher*?" It was a rhetorical question, since Sinatra had been a headliner for years.

"Of course I do!"

"How come you weren't in awe?"

Nat looked over at me like a proud papa. He could have answered Rickles' question, but he was confident that I could handle it.

"He's great and all, but it was no big deal. I met a bunch of stars on *Bandstand*."

The only thing I can add is, Sinatra's music wasn't my thing. I respected it, and I enjoyed it to some extent, but I was all about rock and roll. Now, when I had seen Sammy Davis Jr. dance on *Bandstand*, that was another story. Sammy's talent blew my mind, and I was a lot less casual about it.

Because of his enormous popularity on *Bandstand*, ABC had created the *Dick Clark Saturday Night Beechnut Show*, which broadcast live from the Little Theater on West 44th Street. The network had entrusted Clark with a Saturday night timeslot, and he was going up against two of television's heavyweights at 7:30 p.m.—*Perry Mason* and *People Are Funny*, a highly popular game show. ABC wouldn't have made the investment it did—or taken the risk—if Dick Clark's drawing power hadn't increased dramatically in the last year, and if teenagers hadn't emerged as a major player in the demographic studies of the day.

Although a rehearsal was scheduled for 1:00 p.m., the performers had been instructed to arrive before that so that *Photoplay Magazine* could get the shots it needed for a spread. Along with Joe Terranova, Dave White was usually one of the more reliable members of the group, but on February 22, 1958—the day of the *Beechnut* show—he showed up late, and I had to stand in for him. The photographer placed me right next to Dick Clark.

Fortunately for all of us, Dave White arrived in time for their live performance of "Rock and Roll Is Here To Stay," and Danny and the Juniors took its place in a lineup that also included Chuck Berry ("Sweet Little 16"), Bill Justis ("Raunchy"), Billy and Lillie ("La Dee Dah"), and the Chordettes ("Lollipop"). These were heady times indeed—for me and for Danny and the Juniors.

After staying overnight at the Forrest Hotel, I arrived at Penn Station early the next morning. Danny and the Juniors were traveling separately (and no doubt sleeping late), and I was alone on the platform when Dick Clark walked over to me. The night before, we had exchanged a cordial handshake, but that was our only contact. I hadn't exactly been avoiding Dick, but I wasn't looking forward to any extended discussion with him either. At the time, I had no way of knowing how he felt about me after I had picketed him on *Bandstand*.

"Jerry, why don't you sit with me on the ride back?"

From the way he said it, I couldn't tell if he was going to lay into me or hold a normal conversation.

Once we sat down, Clark got right to the point. "I gotta tell you, I didn't like Bob Horn. As far as I'm concerned, he wasn't very nice. But I owe him a debt of gratitude."

I didn't say anything. I just listened.

"You know that I have the publishing for 'At the Hop,' right?"

I shook my head. "I didn't really know."

"And I'm involved with Swan Records and Cameo-Parkway."

"I didn't know that either," I said.

"The point is, I wouldn't have any of it if it weren't for Bob Horn."

As soon as he made that admission to me, I started to relax. But I still didn't know where he was going with it.

"You tried to stop me. You even picketed the show. And if you remember, we offered to double what you were making. You wanted Bob Horn, but that wasn't going to happen."

"Look, Dick, I wasn't picketing against you. I would have picketed against anyone. Bob was my friend."

"I've got no hard feelings about that, and that's exactly my point. I know if I lose *Bandstand* tomorrow, the same thing'll happen to me. Everybody'll jump ship and someone else will take over."

"I don't see you losing *Bandstand*."

"You're not listening to me. I have great respect for the loyalty you had for Bob. That's hard to find in this industry."

I looked at him. The admission he had made to me—and the genuine humility he had shown—made all the difference in the world.

"Dick, you've got my loyalty. It was never personal."

"I'm glad," he said.

We shook hands, and I could tell that he respected me.

In 1959, after I'd been on the road with them for almost two years, Danny and the Juniors made another trip to New York. While we were in town, Nat Segall and I went to the Copacabana, which was owned by Jules Podell. If New York was the show business capital of the world, the Copacabana was the epicenter of show business, but the club was undergoing a change. Until then, Podell had always resisted rock and roll, preferring to book major stars of a more conventional variety. These stars fell into two general categories—singers of popular music like Frank Sinatra, and comedians like Sophie Tucker, Dean Martin, and Jerry Lewis. But after ascending through the ranks with "Splish Splash" and "Queen of the Hop," Bobby Darin had crossed into the mainstream with "Mack the Knife," which was on its way to becoming the biggest song of the year. Weary of resisting the inevitable, Podell made Darin the first rock and roll singer to ever play the Copa.

For me, the Copa represented everything that was exciting about New York. I couldn't wait to see it, but I was also curious about how things would go with Darin. The last time I had seen him, he was asked to leave Club Dahlia because he acted like a jerk, deliberately throwing darts at the wall instead of aiming at the target. I had met Darin at the *Buddy Deane Show* in Baltimore, and he was at Dahlia as my guest, simply to hang out and relax. I hadn't even asked him to perform. But after he had too much to drink and refused to leave, I had to step in or there would have been a problem. I wasn't even sure Darin would remember the incident, that's how drunk he was, but I remembered it like it happened the day before. (Later, the *Buddy Deane Show* served as the inspiration for the movie *Hairspray*.)

Unlike other nightclubs, the Copa didn't have a stage. Its showgirls and headliners performed in a space that was cleared on the floor, with the paying customers a few feet away.

As the audience waited for Darin to appear, the house band struck up a tune, and a group of Copa showgirls came bounding onto the floor. The girls were stunning, and if you weren't a "leg man" already, you were soon to be a convert. The girls did two or three numbers, and then the announcer took the microphone and introduced Darin.

Because there was no coatroom at the Copa, the men's and ladies' rooms were used for that purpose; so it was possible to check out the women as they came and went by positioning yourself halfway between the two. I fell in love with the Copa that week, and on one of my later visits, I learned that you could drink in the lounge without paying a cover charge for the main showroom. The Copa showgirls seemed to prefer the lounge, and that's where they would relax after their last performance of the night. Their legs seemed to go on forever, and none of the barstools seemed tall enough to accommodate them.

One night, I introduced myself to a Copa showgirl, and we had a pleasant conversation. She told me that the dancers came from all over the United States, drawn to New York by the lure of show business. Some of them were sophisticated types from major cities, while others had come to New York from small towns in the Midwest. She herself was a New Yorker, born and raised, and there were hints of cynicism in her manner.

In the end, I suppose I should have paid more attention to the glimpses she gave of her true self, but I couldn't see past her legs. The next night, after she changed out of her costume in the dressing room,

I met her in the lounge and she invited me to stop by her apartment at 72nd Street and First Avenue. Because the Copa girls weren't allowed to go home with a customer, I ended up taking a cab and ringing her buzzer outside. As I waited for her to admit me into the building, I couldn't help thinking about my first sexual experience at the Fulton Manor Apartments. A lot had happened in the five years since then— sexually and otherwise—and I felt like I was ready for anything.

After I rang the buzzer, she must have unlocked the door to her apartment and opened it by several inches, because I was able to enter the living room immediately. As soon as she heard me, she said "I'm in here," and I walked a few more steps and found her in bed.

"Why don't you get undressed?" she continued. "I'll be right back."

She threw off the covers and walked toward the bathroom in the nude. As spectacular as her legs were, her ass had nothing to be ashamed of, but only the legs were part of the cost of admission at the Copa. I only had a second or two to admire her before she entered the bathroom and closed the door.

After a few minutes, I realized that she was taking too long in the bathroom. And then I became aware of noises out in the hall. I heard footsteps and male voices coming toward her apartment. Then suddenly the footsteps stopped. Something wasn't right, so I scrambled to put my clothes back on. Just then, the showgirl emerged from the bathroom.

"Where are you going?" she asked. I ignored her and ran to the door of her apartment.

As I opened the door, I saw two men coming toward me. Fortunately, the showgirl's apartment was on the second floor with a window a few feet away, and I was able to jump from the window onto the street below. I was still holding my shoes as I landed on the side-walk, and as I looked up at the second floor, I saw three faces peering down at me. The showgirl was flanked by her two accomplices. They weren't surprised or upset—they just turned away as though it was all in a day's work. It was a shame really. I had such high hopes when the showgirl buzzed me in, but I left with a sprained ankle.

SIX: Breaking in as a Disc Jockey

The next time Danny and the Juniors went on tour, Billy Rapp was their road manager, and they paid a heavy price for it. With no one to stand up to them, they blew most of their money, and eventually three of their cars were repossessed.

When you're on tour, you're like a family, and squabbles never bother you. But I had to admit that Danny and the Juniors had become more difficult to control. I wasn't sorry to see the road managing come to an end, but at the same time, I felt badly for them. After having hits like "At the Hop" and "Rock and Roll Is Here to Stay," their follow-up efforts were only mildly successful, and within a year, their popularity would fade nationally. (After "Rock and Roll Is Here to Stay," they released a song called "Dottie," and it never rose higher than #39 on the charts. Locally at least, the "B" side of "Dottie" turned out to be a bigger hit. Its "B" side was "In the Meantime.")

More than anything else, Nat Segall was tired of listening to Danny Rapp's complaints, but whatever his reasons may have been, I was completely on board with his decision to replace me. When it came right down to it, I wasn't the least bit concerned. In fact, Danny Rapp probably did me a favor by pushing so hard for his brother to take over.

Because the road managing was never a fifty-two week proposition in any given year, and the tours typically lasted only a week or two, I had always had plenty of time to come up with additional ways to make money.

By that point, I was hooked on New York City, and I had already started to take the train there every chance I got. I started to knock on doors in New York, focusing my efforts on the Brill Building and 1650 Broadway. These two buildings were located near each other, and people tended to confuse them. 1650 Broadway was the home to many rock and roll and independent labels. Eventually, it became as influential in the development of the "new" music (especially R&B) as the Brill Building had been to pop music and Tin Pan Alley. The Brill Building housed ASCAP publishers and composers from Broadway and Hollywood, while 1650 Broadway housed BMI, which was founded by radio broadcasters to make it easy for writers of all genres to get their music published.

Because this section of Manhattan was a hotbed of songwriters, record labels, and music publishing companies, I focused my efforts there, and within a month, I had made deals with several of them to promote their records in Philadelphia. At the same time, I continued to develop opportunities through my network of contacts back home; before I knew it, I was affiliated with companies in both cities. These companies included Swan Records, Laurie Records, Co-Ed, Del-Fi, Hill and Range Publishers, George Goldner's Gone and End label, and ten or twelve other independent labels that Universal Distributors handled. Looking back on it, I realize that I was flying by the seat of my pants, and going where the music took me.

I had a wealth of companies to represent, but there were only a limited number of stations that played that kind of music in Philadelphia. These included WIBG, WHAT, WDAS, and a smaller station in Camden, New Jersey whose call letters were WCAM. When it came to record promotion, each of these stations had a different set of rules to play by.

In 1958, when I first started to promote records, the music industry was less than a year away from a major upheaval that would change the way that business was conducted. That upheaval would come in the form of a congressional investigation into the deeply entrenched, industry-wide practice of "play-for-pay" or "payola." Over the next several years, the payola investigation—spearheaded by the Oren Harris Committee—would bring down some of the most prominent figures in the industry, including Alan Freed, and would dramatically affect many others, including Dick Clark. But for the first few months that I was promoting, it was business as usual with one major difference: Unlike the other promoters, I didn't have any money to pay the disc jockeys.

If you didn't have any money on a record, it didn't get played, unless the disc jockeys liked you or the music you were representing or both. If nothing else, however, the disc jockeys knew me from my *Bandstand* days, and they respected my ear for music.

In terms of sheer wattage, WIBG was the largest station that I promoted records to. It had a predominantly white audience, and once the payola investigation started, promotion men were not allowed to have direct contact with the disc jockeys. In order to get airplay, we had to deal with Roy Schwartz, the program director. Schwartz gave you fifteen minutes of his time, but only after you sat in the reception area with other promotion men until he was ready to see you. Conversely, WHAT and WDAS were much smaller stations, and they had no program director. Instead, the record promoters dealt directly with the on-air personalities. (To an extent, the payola investigation left the black guys alone, and I gravitated toward WHAT and WDAS, where the disc jockeys could play what they wanted.)

In my early days as a record promoter, I touted songs like "Teenager in Love" by Dion and the Belmonts, "Shimmy, Shimmy, Ko-Ko-Bop" by Little Anthony and the Imperials, "Those Oldies But Goodies" by Little Caesar and the Romans, and many others. (Later, I would use the Little Caesar and the Romans song as an intro to one of my radio shows.)

For the entire time I was on *Bandstand*, I got a first-hand look at how the promotion men ingratiated themselves to Bob Horn and me in order to get their records on the air. Now, I was seeing how the other half lived. Mitch Thomas, for instance, used to take the train up from Wilmington, Delaware to do his show on WDAS, and I got into the habit of picking him up at 30th Street and driving him over to the station. But I never did it without stopping at Mayo's Chocolates at 17th and Snyder to pick up a frozen banana beforehand. By the second time I brought him one, Thomas was hooked on frozen bananas and playing most of the songs I promoted.

At 'DAS, the disc jockeys would allow the promotion men to sit in with them on their shows, and this would afford me an up-close and personal look at how a DJ operated on a station that had an engineer. At WCAM in Camden, on the other hand, Jack Lamar, Sam Scott, and the other disc jockeys played their own records on a turntable and operated a control board. Before I ever went on the air myself, I got a sense of how it was done. I also came to understand how the successful black jocks created their own personas. Although I admired all of the 'DAS disc jockeys, Jocko Henderson was the one I respected the most, and he went on to have the greatest influence on my career.

I promoted records to every one of the WDAS disc jockeys. In addition to Jocko Henderson (the aforementioned "Ace From Space") and Mitch Thomas (whose catch phrase was "Promise Mr. Thomas"), these DJs included Kay Williams ("Daddy Kay"), John Bandy ("Little Lord Fauntleroy"), and Georgie Woods ("The Man With the Goods"). Watching these guys in action was a privilege and a pleasure, and though it hadn't occurred to me to become a disc jockey myself, I never forgot the lessons they taught me.

Getting into nightclubs wasn't the only benefit of dressing more fashionably. It came into play with record promotion. Whenever I dropped in, Georgie Woods and Jocko never failed to admire my clothing, checking me out from head to toe. "I like your kicks," they would say, referring to my shoes, or "Nice threads. Where'd you get those?" I came from the old school, and the way I dressed had evolved from the flashy clothes of my father to the classier threads of guys like Harold Lipsius, Allen Sussell, Bob Horn, Harry Finfer, and Matty "the Humdinger" Singer, another promotion man. Whenever Georgie or Jocko complimented me that way, I knew that I was doing something right.

Of course, there is a naysayer in almost every crowd, and Roy Schwartz, the program director at WIBG, referred to me derisively as "Mr. Lucky," noting the stark contrast between my clothing and that of the other promotion men who showed up at his office. The other promotion men were good guys, but I considered them *schleppers* with their open collars, short-sleeved shirts, and scuffed shoes. That didn't stop Schwartz from trying to belittle me behind my back, however. The other three stations that I was promoting records to were playing the songs I offered, but Schwartz wasn't responding, and I couldn't help feeling that there was something personal about it, as though he enjoyed turning me down. There were a number of occasions when I could have said, "Listen, I came to you with this record three weeks ago and you wouldn't play it. Look how well it's doing on 'DAS and 'HAT." But when I shared my frustration with Jocko, he told me that a reminder like that was unnecessary.

"Believe me," Jocko said, "he knows."

Sure enough, Schwartz was keeping tabs on the record-buying public by checking with his sources in the industry. All he had to do was pick up the phone or visit a record store or a "one-stop," which was a wholesale location that carried the records of multiple distributors. The one-stops saved the record stores the trouble of going from one distribu-tor to another, and there were a number of them locally. Schwartz checked in with one-stop owners like Herb Slotkin and Sid Williams, and they gave him the lowdown. I used to get a kick out of it whenever I imag-ined someone reporting to Schwartz that a record he had turned down was selling like gangbusters. This was particularly true whenever I intro-duced a song to WHAT or WDAS and they had been playing it for weeks.

I also hung around Cameo-Parkway, where Bernie Lowe paid me $25 a week to run errands and listen to demos. They were always cut-ting records during that period and deciding which artists to sign. It was nothing new for me after I had done essentially the same thing in help-ing Bob Horn select the music for his "Rate the Record" segment on *Bandstand.* If a solo artist or group was worthy of being signed imme-diately, before another label signed them, I would tell Bernie that. If I uncovered the occasional gem that had what it took to become a hit record right away, so much the better.

A guy named Henry Coltabianco was running a place called Sonny's Cut Up Chickens at 9th and Washington, and one of his employees was a kid named Ernest Evans. Evans was quite a "cut up" himself. He used to entertain the customers with wisecracks, but when he broke into song one day, Coltabianco took notice. Coltabianco started to manage Evans, and they both got stage names. Coltabianco called himself "Henry Colt" and Dick Clark's wife, Barbara, gave Evans the name "Chubby Checker." She thought he resembled Fats Domino and was playing off of that, creating an inside joke that never became com-mon knowledge.

Before Chubby became an international star with "The Twist"—a song that would figure prominently in my life less than a year later—he cut a record called "The Class," and I was able to use my connections to get him his first professional booking, persuading Chuck Mayo to pay Chubby $50 a night to perform at Mayo's Lounge at Broad and Wharton.

Artie Singer had his own record company. It was called Singular Records. "At the Hop" was originally cut on Singular, but when Dick Clark suggested that Artie allow ABC Paramount to pick up the master, buy the song from him, and distribute it nationally, most of the profits went elsewhere. It was no coincidence, of course, that Clark suggested

ABC Paramount since he was on the ABC network with *Bandstand*. From that point on, Danny and the Juniors recorded on ABC Paramount, and Artie had a contract to produce them. But that didn't prevent him from developing other artists for his own label.

Artie and I were friendly at that point, and one day I told him to come over to a house at 13th and Dickinson. I had found a 13-year-old who played the guitar like nobody's business, and I wanted Artie to hear him. The kid's name was Pat Martino, and he went on to sign with Singular Records under the name Ricky Taino, which I came up with in his living room. Martino went on to become one of the best musicians that Philadelphia ever produced, and to this day, he remains one of the foremost jazz guitarists of this or any era. I'm proud of the fact that I discovered him and helped with his first recording, a guitar solo called "Sometimes," which was based on the flip side to "At the Hop." But it wouldn't have been possible without the immense talent that God gave him.

Around the same time, I heard from Father Cox at Bishop Neumann. "Jerry," he said, "can you come down to the school? I have a tape I'd like you to hear."

I went down to Neumann and listened to the tape. A kid named Robert Ridarelli had recorded it. He wasn't particularly original, but he definitely had the pipes.

Frankie Day was managing Ridarelli. Frankie played bass with Billy Duke's band, and I knew him from *Bandstand*. After meeting for a drink at Aljo's, I hooked Frankie up with Bernie Bennick, a former shoe salesman who was currently a partner at Swan Records. Swan shared an office with Cameo-Parkway at 1420 Locust Street. (Once again, there was a Dick Clark connection. Clark had dealings with both of these labels, but later, as the payola scandal continued to destroy careers, Clark divested himself of these and other interests.)

Although Bennick liked what he heard, he wasn't really a music guy, so he let Bernie Lowe listen to the tape. Lowe told Bennick that he wasn't impressed with it, and that was the last Bennick heard about it until Ridarelli recorded his debut hit, "Kissin' Time," on Bernie Lowe's Cameo-Parkway label in the summer of 1959, going by the name of Bobby Rydell.

In addition to finding talent for the labels I was affiliated with, I helped to "break" records for them. One day, I dropped in on a guy named Felix Valdera who owned the Paramount record store on Ridge Avenue and the Paramount one-stop on South Street. Felix was touting a local singer named Fay Simmons, who had recorded a cover version of "And the Angels Sing." Ziggy Elman and Johnny Mercer had written the original for Benny Goodman and His Orchestra in the 40s, and Martha Tilton had done the vocals.

As soon as Felix played the demo for me, I flipped. It had a distinctive rhythm, and after the first few bars, I knew that it had a chance to sell a lot of records. I asked Felix for a copy of the demo and took it to Mitch Thomas at 'DAS. Thomas played it while I was sitting in with him, and the switchboard lit up with calls.

Later that day, I picked up the phone and called Allen Sussell in New York.

"Allen," I said, "I think you should make a deal to pick up this record."

After one listen, Allen released the song on Seneca Records and distributed it nationally on Laurie, and it became a huge hit in Philadelphia. Along with the Chubby Checker, Pat Martino, and Bobby Ridarelli situations, this marked the beginning of an important phase of my career. For the first time, I could use my contacts to help other people professionally, not just myself, and I discovered how gratifying it is to do that.

Several months before, when I was still involved with Danny and the Juniors, I had met a girl named Pattie Scotese. Pattie lived on 9th Street between Oregon and Shunk. She had four sisters: Rita, Phyllis, Rosemary, and Annette.

Rita was the oldest of the Scotese girls. She was part of a dance team at the RDA Supper Club, an after-hours club owned by Don Battles. Before he bought the RDA at Juniper and Vine, Battles had worked for Frank Palumbo at the CR Club. Battles knew me through Nat Segall, so I didn't have to sneak in to the RDA as long as I came in with older guys like Sammy La La. One night, when Rita was dancing to Latin music with her partners, a husband and wife named Ray and Essie, I saw her for the first time. Like the Copa showgirl in New York, Rita had great legs and a beautiful figure.

Everybody knew everybody in South Philadelphia—or so it

seemed—and when I started talking to Rita, she told me that I knew her sister, Annette. Annette went by the nickname of "Nanny."

"You met her through Frankie Avalon," Rita said. "He used to go out with one of Nanny's friends."

"Which friend?"

"Angela DiCiurcio," Rita answered. "And I know *you* from *Bandstand*."

As soon as Rita said it, I remembered Nanny. She was the same age as me, but I had no idea she was Rita's sister.

Just then, I remembered Angela DiCiurcio's sister. Her name was Connie, but everybody called her "Blue Eyes." As it turned out, both of the DiCiurcio girls "married well." Angela ended up with Joe Scarpati, a football player from the Philadelphia Eagles, and Connie married Bob DeFano, who recorded on Chancellor Records, the same label as Frankie.

"Why don't you and your friend come over for coffee?" Rita said, referring to Sammy La La.

Later that night, Sammy and I went over to the Scoteses'. It was two in the morning, but the place was crowded. Rita's sister, Phyllis, was sitting on the couch with her boyfriend, Alex Martinelli, and another sister, Rosemary, had a date there also. Rosemary—whose nickname was "Scottie"—was in the kitchen with her date, a guy named Tucker. She was pouring coffee and placing Italian pastries on a plate. Nanny was helping her.

After I sat down, I started to look around. There was a huge mirror in the living room. It was even bigger than the one I had broken when I swung my "tomahawk" on Bancroft Street.

When Nanny came out of the kitchen, we recognized each other.

"You're Frankie's friend! Howya doin'?"

"Great."

"Who's that?" Nanny said.

"That's my friend, Sammy La La."

A moment later, I heard someone coming down the steps from the second floor. From where I was sitting, I couldn't see the stairway unless I looked in the mirror. I couldn't see the person's face, but whoever it was stopped halfway down the steps. Judging by her voice, it was a girl in her late teens or early twenties.

"Who's that you're with?" she asked.

"Nobody," Nanny said. "Go back to bed."

I turned to Rita. "Who's that?"

"That's my sister Pattie."

Pattie leaned over the railing, and that's how we laid eyes on each other for the first time—looking at each other in the mirror.

"Can you keep it down?" Pattie said. "I'm trying to sleep!"

Alex shook his head. "Kathi's trying to sleep, too. Did you ever think of that?"

I looked over at him. I had no idea who Kathi was, but before I could ask, Pattie made a U-turn and went back to bed.

For the next half hour, we continued to socialize in the Scoteses' living room, ignoring Pattie's request. Every few minutes, laughter would break out in the room, usually when Rita and Phyllis went at it, or when Scottie got into the action.

A few minutes later, I heard footsteps on the stairs again. All of a sudden, an adorable three-year-old girl wandered into the living room. She was rubbing the sleep from her eyes and wincing at the bright lights.

"Kathi!" Rita said.

The little girl walked over to Rita. She was still half-asleep when Rita hugged her and kissed her on top of her head. Kathi nestled into Rita's arms and looked around the room shyly.

I turned to Alex. "Whose baby is that?"

"Pattie's," Alex said.

I lowered my voice. "She lets her stay up this late?"

Alex shook his head. "I said the same thing. Didn't I, Phyl?"

"I keep telling her it ain't right," Phyllis said.

Rita must have overheard, because she said, "Come on, Kathi. It's time to go up," and walked Kathi up the steps.

A couple days later, I dropped by the Scoteses' to see Rita. I happened to have two girls with me. They were just girls I liked to dance with—I wasn't interested in them romantically—but Pattie stared at me when she opened the door.

"Rita's not here," Pattie said.

"Where's she at?"

"She got called in to work."

Rita was stunning from the minute you laid eyes on her, but Pattie had a different look entirely. She was cute in a shy kind of way.

"We're going to Dahlia," I said. "You want to come?"

"There's two girls with you already. What do you need me for?"

The other girls cracked up when she said it, and so did I. That was my introduction to Pattie's sense of humor.

"Come on—we'll have fun."

"I'll take a raincheck," Pattie said.

I never found out if it was intentional or purely a coincidence, but the next time I saw Pattie, she showed up at Dahlia with Scottie.

"Where are your girlfriends?" Pattie asked, referring to my "entourage."

"They took a raincheck," I said, and she laughed.

After a while, I asked the Scotese girls if they wanted to go to the Venus Lounge.

"I gotta meet Tucker," Scottie said. "He's getting out of work."

"How 'bout *you*, Pattie?"

"I'll think about it," Pattie said.

That first night, I took Pattie to the Venus Lounge, a club at Broad and Reed. Although she was reluctant to talk about herself, Pattie mentioned that she washed hair and provided manicures at Don's, a beauty salon around the corner from her house.

Over the next few weeks, I started taking Pattie to the Venus. I was nineteen and she was twenty-three. We had a good time together, but I could tell that she was holding back. After three or four dates, I still didn't know much about her, other than the fact that I liked her. Something about her intrigued me. She wasn't like her sisters. She was almost standoffish. But it was more than that. The way Pattie looked was getting to me, and I appreciated her sense of humor. When I got to the point where I wanted to see her more often, though, Pattie wasn't always available, but she wouldn't come out and tell me that she had a boyfriend. She would just say, "No, I can't," and leave it go at that.

Once I switched my attention from Rita to Pattie, word got around, and I found out that Pattie's boyfriend was Charles Caputo. Caputo went by the nickname of "Chubby." I assumed that he was Kathi's father, but it turned out that Pattie had met a guy named Mino Barone who worked at Jim's Steaks at 9th and Wharton. Pattie had eloped with Barone, but the relationship was short-lived, and she had met Chubby when she was on the rebound from that. That explained some of her reluctance to get involved with me.

One night, Pattie told me to pick her up in an hour, but when I went to her house, Scottie answered the door.

"She's not here," Scottie said. "She wants you to pick her up at 12th and Jackson."

I went to the address that Scottie gave me. At that very moment, Chubby's mother was giving Pattie a tour of her son's bedroom, saying, "This is where you and Chubby are going to live." As soon as she heard that, Pattie ran out of the house and jumped into my car. "Hurry up," she said, "Let's go." And that was the end of her boyfriend, Chubby.

In order for us to go out together, somebody had to watch Kathi— either Pattie's father or one of her sisters. But just as often, no one else was available, and Pattie and I stayed home and necked on the couch or floor. For the first few months of our relationship, that's all Pattie would let me do. As frustrating as the relationship was physically, there was something about being around the house with her that strengthened my feelings. With Kathi part of the picture—along with Pattie's sisters—I experienced a kind of domestic harmony that was new to me, and together with the way Pattie looked, the way we made each other laugh, and how turned on I was by her physically, I started to fall in love for the first time.

Although I took the sexual frustration in stride, I had a harder time accepting the way that Pattie was raising her daughter. Alex Martinelli and I were in complete agreement about that. Kathi was so adorable that, whenever Pattie's sisters brought one of their dates back to the house for coffee at two in the morning, the sister would wake Kathi up, bring her down to the living room, and show her off. Rita and Nanny did it all the time, and so did Scottie; unfortunately, Pattie didn't do much to stop it. The only one of the Scotese girls that had the sense not to wake Kathi up like that was Phyllis, so the poor kid's sleep was constantly getting interrupted.

At one point, Pattie and I came in at ten o'clock at night, and her father Pat was eating dinner with Kathi. I pulled Pattie aside and said, "Pattie, that's not right! Kathi's too little to be eating this late. She should be in bed!" When we walked back to the dining room, Pat gave me a dirty look.

Whenever I said something about the way that she was raising Kathi, things would improve for a week or two, but eventually, they would fall back into the same pattern until I spoke up again. I knew that Kathi wasn't my kid, and that I could only say so much, but I had a sense of right and wrong, and it bothered me to see her in an environment like that. That was about the only thing that Pattie and I disagreed about in the first few months I knew her. (I had been brought up in a highly regimented way, knowing exactly what time we ate dinner at my grandparents' and what time I was expected to be in bed. I even knew what we were having for dinner on specific days of the week. Monday was soup. Tuesday was spaghetti. Wednesday was pasta fagiole, and so on.)

One day, Harold Lipsius called me on the phone. He and his wife, Clara, belonged to the Har Zion synagogue at 54th and Wynnefield Avenue. One of the kids was getting bar mitzvah'd, and they needed somebody to play records at the reception. Harold thought I might enjoy doing it. I took Pattie with me and brought the records that I used to dance to, including "Long Tall Sally" by Little Richard, "Shake, Rattle, and Roll" by Joe Turner, and "Little Darlin'" by the Diamonds. I had those kids rockin' and rollin' like they never had before, and right in the middle of it, Harold tapped me on the shoulder.

"This is terrific," he said, "Nobody's playing this kind of music any more. Have you ever considered running your own dances?"

I hadn't considered it, but it made a lot of sense.

"You're better at it than most of the disc jockeys that are doing it," Harold continued.

As Pattie and I drove home that night, I kept thinking about what Harold had said. I had a blast at the bar mitzvah. It came easy to me, and I certainly had the record collection. More importantly, though, I was as qualified as anyone else to do a record hop, and maybe more qualified than some of the older disc jockeys who had been doing them for years. I was a dancer and knew what kind of music to play. This was something that Bob Horn recognized when I was fifteen years old, when he had allowed me to substitute for him two or three times when a scheduling conflict prevented him from running a dance at the Avalon Pier or Dorney Park in Allentown.

Whenever Harry Finfer took one of his artists to a local dance, I would tag along with him. The WIBG disc jockey, Joe Niagara, was running dances at the Levittown fire hall with Steve Van Buren (another football player who had retired from the Philadelphia Eagles). As I watched Niagara, I felt as though something was missing. It was like he wasn't really into it. WAEB, a local radio station in Allentown, sponsored record hops also, and the same thing happened. With few exceptions, the older generation of disc jockeys didn't seem to be passionate about it like I was. They would just stand up there and play records. They were great disc jockeys, but they had no affinity for the music, and they didn't relate to their audience. If it were me, I would have been down on the dance floor with the kids. When I considered Harold's suggestion, I realized that I had a feel for it, and I was confident that I could bring something to the table. When it came to running a dance myself, there was no reason that I couldn't pull it off, particularly in my neighborhood, and that gave me an idea.

Directly across from my house on Bancroft Street, there was a church hall called St. Elizabeth's. One morning, I knocked on the door and talked to the Episcopalian priest who ran it. Aside from saying hello, we hadn't really talked to each other, but he knew me well enough. I told him that I wanted to run some neighborhood dances, and that if he let me use the hall, I would make a small contribution to his parish. Once I said that, the priest quickly agreed.

In order to spread the word about my dances, I made up some posters and the kids in the neighborhood helped me put them up. Between that and the word of mouth, we had about 40 kids the first week, twice as many the second week, and between 100 and 150 the week after that. Within a month, we were packing the hall, and the priest came to see me.

"You're doing well, I see."

"Thanks, father. We're doing great."

"There's only one problem. This is an Episcopalian parish."

At first, I had no idea where he was going with it.

"You're Roman Catholic," he said, "aren't you?"

"I belong to St. Monica's parish," I answered.

"I'd like you to become an Episcopalian."

I stared at him. Not only had the dances outgrown St. Elizabeth's, but the priest also wanted me to convert in order to stay there! Knowing that this would never happen, I politely declined, and by the next day, I started to look for another hall.

Around that time, Pattie's mother remarried. Her husband was a guy named Johnny Gentile, whose nickname was "Shammy." They were living a block away from Alex Martinelli and his family. Once they found out that I was looking for a place to hold my dances, both Shammy and Alex told me about the Dixon House at 20th and Mifflin. The Dixon House was a "community red feather" facility, which meant that it did charitable work and depended on the neighborhood for financial support. The building had a gymnasium where kids played basketball. It was twice the size of St. Elizabeth's.

The lady who ran the Dixon House was Mrs. Murphy, and though she drove a harder bargain than the Episcopalian priest, we cut a deal for a 60-40 split. If we took in $100, I would keep $60 and give the other $40 to the Dixon House. (This kind of arrangement would play a major role later in my career.)

I asked Pattie to help me by collecting the money at the door, and she got a kick out of doing it. We charged fifty cents per person and attracted close to two hundred kids every Saturday night.

Although I had no interest in going to college (despite a two-year scholarship offer from Temple University), I got a real education by running those dances. Still a teenager myself, I was able to apply everything I knew about being young, including the lessons I had learned on *Bandstand*. The dances were orderly, and if anyone started trouble, we kicked them out and banned them from coming back. To make the kids feel as though it was their dance, I started a committee to select the music, pull the bleachers out from the wall, and get everything ready. To keep the peace, I hired my father to work as a bouncer. The kids were happy because they were dancing; the parents were happy because the kids were off the street; and Mrs. Murphy was happy because the Dixon House was making money. She also appreciated the fact that we cleaned up afterward and put everything back where we found it.

I used to take some of the kids to Cameo-Parkway with me. Four or five of them would pile into my car, and they would help me create dance steps for the songs that Bernie Lowe was releasing. Bernie would play us a song and leave the rest to me. Although the kids weren't able to choreograph dance steps on their own, they built on the ideas that I introduced. More often than not, we came up with something that the

Cameo-Parkway artists could use. Chubby Checker's song "The Fly" was an example of a song that we choreographed. Although it didn't do anything nationally, the kids did "The Fly" on *Bandstand* for a short period of time.

The Dixon House had a yard in back of the building, and in the summertime, we took the dances outside. The kids enjoyed dancing in the open air, and the crowds continued to grow. Although a large cyclone fence separated the Dixon House from the adjoining properties—and the neighbors could see us from their backyards—we didn't think anything of it at the time.

In 1958, Hank Ballard and the Midnighters recorded a song called "The Twist." A year later, Chubby Checker had a huge hit when he covered it. When the neighbors saw the kids doing "The Twist," they took it into their heads that the kids were dancing in an obscene manner. This was the same thing that happened when the older generation saw Elvis gyrating his hips on television. The next day, the neighbors took their complaints to Mrs. Murphy, and she called me in for a talk.

"We gotta stop the dances," she said.

I was taken aback. "Why? Everybody's happy with them."

"Not the neighbors. What's this dance they're doing?"

"You mean 'The Twist'? It's the number one record on *Bandstand*."

"The neighbors are up in arms. They think it's vulgar."

I thought for a moment. "It's the biggest dance in Philadelphia, but that's all it is—a dance! How 'bout if I talk to the neighbors? I'll take some of the kids."

"If you can convince them, it's fine with me."

The neighbors were making it sound like "The Twist" was a horrible influence on the kids, but it wasn't like that at all.

"I'll have them sign a piece of paper that says the dances are okay."

Later that day, I took four or five of the committee members and went door-to-door. The kids were polite and did a great job of stating their case. They let the parents know how much they enjoyed the dances and what a loss it would be if the dances were taken away. By the time we were finished, we collected more than fifty signatures, and Mrs. Murphy agreed to keep the dances going.

While we were collecting signatures, one of the neighbor ladies said that she had always loved to dance, and that she was sorry she had stopped. "Can you teach me to do some of those dances? I have some friends that would be interested, too."

"Sure I can!"

The Dixon House had a conference room above the gym, and on Sunday nights I gave dance lessons for five dollars per person. I'd fill up a coffee urn, bring donuts, and set up my record player, and that was all I really needed. At first, we had about ten women from the neighborhood, but then they started to tell their friends, and we ended up with around thirty-five women on a regular basis. Mrs. Murphy and I used the same 60-40 split that we had established for the Saturday night dances. (The irony of the whole thing was, I had met these women when they complained about the kids doing "The Twist," but by the following year, Jackie Kennedy and other members of high society made that dance fashionable by doing it at places like the Peppermint Lounge in New York City. The ladies from 20th and Mifflin were shaking their hips just like everyone else. The other dances I taught them were "The Cha-Cha," "The Stroll," "The Stomp," and "The Boogaloo," but they really went crazy when I got Chubby Checker to do "The Twist" at the Dixon House. Both generations attended that performance—the kids *and* their parents.)

Pattie and I were spending a lot of time together. She was collecting money at the dances, and we were seeing each other on a regular basis. Unfortunately, my mother disapproved of her from the very beginning. She had a problem with the age difference and the fact that Pattie had a child.

"It's not right," my mother said. "You're too young. You don't need that responsibility. That's not your child."

We were in the kitchen on Bancroft Street, and I was helping her with the dishes.

"Mom, I like this girl."

"You don't even know who the father is."

I stared at her. It wasn't like her to say things like that, but she was adamant.

"You better wise up. That's all I'm gonna say."

On the day before Easter in 1959, I took Pattie to New York. To that point, we still hadn't slept together, but for the moment, it wasn't important. Everything was better when Pattie was with me, and I couldn't wait to show her some of the things that had excited me when I had gone to New York by myself.

Before we left, I assured Pattie that the sleeping arrangements would be up to her, and when we arrived, I checked us into adjoining rooms at the Edison Hotel. As soon as I unpacked, I went into her room and we started to make out, winding up in bed. This time she didn't stop me, and I finally made love to her. After we finished, Pattie started to cry. This had never happened to me before, and I had no idea why she was upset. I had been waiting for more than a year to make love with her, and now she was sobbing uncontrollably. I had no idea what to do.

"I'm going back to my room," I said. "Why don't we go home?"

"It isn't you," she managed. "It's me."

After I packed my suitcase, I went into Pattie's room. She was still in bed.

"Let's stay," she said.

We made love for the rest of the day, stopping only for room service at two in the morning. Pattie made me hide in the closet until the waiter left. That's how determined she was to keep up appearances.

After we finished eating, we made love all night and got up around eight in the morning. When we were lying there, Pattie never explained why she had cried the day before. I realized that she hadn't been intimate with anyone since Kathi had been born nearly four years before, and that it was an emotional time for her.

It was raining at that point, and Pattie told me she was hungry.

"Come on," I said, "let's get breakfast."

"Great, but I want a hot roast beef sandwich."

"At nine in the morning?"

"Yeah, I've got a craving."

"Okay, let's go."

Despite all of the time we had spent together, Pattie was still a mystery to me, and I was surprised that her mood had changed so quickly. I was even more surprised that she wanted a roast beef sandwich at nine in the morning.

By nine o'clock, we were sitting in a booth at Lindy's. While Pattie was eating, I took a bite of her sandwich. I wanted to compare it with Nick's Roast Beef at 20th and Jackson. I laughed, but Pattie had no idea why. There was no comparison: Nick's had Lindy's beat.

After we shared a piece of Lindy's cheesecake, Pattie and I walked to St. Patrick's Cathedral, where an Easter Mass was in progress. They were playing hymns on a pipe organ, and we could hear them from the street. Then I showed her the Forrest Hotel, where I had stayed with Danny and the Juniors. As we made our way past the apartment building where the young Indian woman lived, I realized how much my life had changed, and that I had no desire to get involved with anyone else.

We took a ferry to the Statue of Liberty, where I had to talk Pattie into climbing to the observation deck. It was raining harder now, and we really couldn't see much, so we made our way back to Penn Station and caught the next train home.

Pattie's father started out as a tailor and worked his way up in life. Now he and his brothers owned Scotty Togs, a company that manufactured children's clothing. Like many self-made men, Pat had an inordinately high opinion of himself, and that was a major factor in our relationship. In his youth, Pat had run around like I had, and he still enjoyed being a man about town, which may have been the cause of his divorce from Pattie's mother, Mary. Pat immediately assumed that I was "on the make" with Pattie.

If all I was interested in was sleeping with her, why had I stayed in the relationship for more than a year without getting anywhere sexually? And why was I so concerned about Kathi's well-being? Pat couldn't see any of that, and ironically enough, my concern for Kathi turned out to be the biggest problem we had.

When Pattie and I walked up 9th Street with her suitcase, Pat was waiting for us on his front step.

"They're finally home," he sneered. "The honeymooners!"

I stared at him and looked at Pattie.

"You went away all weekend, heh? Don't come around here no more. I don't want you seeing my daughter."

All of my street sense told me to avoid a confrontation, particularly in the state Pat was in.

"Pattie, look, I'm not gonna start an argument here. I'll call you later."

As soon as I got around the corner, I called Pattie from a pay phone. I could tell that she was upset.

"You can't come over here," she said. "He won't let you."

"Don't worry, we'll figure something out."

Whenever I wanted to see Pattie, I would call her from a pay phone on Shunk Street and pick her up around the corner from her house. When Pat wasn't home, I would pick her up at her front door. This went on for a few weeks, but once Pat realized that Pattie wasn't seeing anyone else—and that she was serious about me—he accepted our relationship to some extent.

Even though I was still living with my mother, I continued to be secretive with her, and it didn't occur to me that I was doing the same thing that she had done when she met my father a generation before. When she found out that Pattie and I rented a place at 1645 South 23rd Street and started to fix it up, my relationship with my mother deteriorated even further.

"What are you doing?" she asked. "Are you thinking of marrying this woman? If you do, I'll disown you."

"Mom, you don't mean that."

I couldn't believe that my mother would say something like that. Like me, she failed to realize that history was repeating itself.

Pattie and I continued to fix up the house at 23rd and Morris, working on it whenever we could. I was still promoting records, evaluating artists for Cameo-Parkway, looking for talent, and doing the occasional errand for Bernie Lowe, including day trips to New York. Pattie was still working at the salon and helping me with the record hops. At the rate we were going, the house would be livable in another two or three months. When we weren't painting, putting up wallpaper, or getting Kathi's room ready, we were making love on the floor.

Pattie and I got married on Valentine's Day in 1960 by a magistrate named Louis Vignola. The ceremony took place in Vignola's office at 9th and South, and the only witness was my father. To put it plainly, my father didn't give a shit who I married, as long as it didn't interfere with his lifestyle. Although we invited her to our home afterward, my mother refused to come over.

Whenever Pattie and I went out, Rita Perry and Felice Pandola would babysit Kathi. Rita and Felice were on my committee, and I knew that we could trust them. Kathi was five years old, and we had gotten her into a regular routine. She was eating dinner by six o'clock, getting to bed early, and sleeping through the night without anyone waking her.

In the morning, she ate a good breakfast, and I walked her to McDaniels Day Nursery, bringing back memories of my mother walking Roberta and me to St. Monica's. One night, the girls from the committee were unavailable, and Pattie's father came over instead.

The next morning, Kathi had trouble getting up. When I asked her what time she had gone to bed, she told me that she had stayed up late. "What about dinner?" I asked. It turned out that six o'clock had come and gone, and Kathi still hadn't eaten. When she told her grandfather that she had to eat at her regular time—and that I insisted on it—Pat said, "You don't have to listen to him. He's not your real father."

After I walked Kathi to McDaniel's Day Nursery, I called Pattie's father at Scotty Togs, telling Pattie to go upstairs and listen in on the phone in our bedroom.

"Pat, this is my home, and you're invited any time. But I live by certain rules, and when you're here, I want you to respect them. I've assumed the responsibility of raising a child that's not mine and building a life for her."

"What are you talking about?" Pat said.

"She ate her dinner late, and she stayed up past her bedtime. And when she told you I would get mad, you said she didn't have to worry about me, I'm not her real father. Don't ever say that again, and don't ever come into my home if you're not gonna go by my rules. And Pattie, you're listening to this, if you don't like what I'm saying, you can pack your bags, and you and Kathi can move back to Ninth Street."

There was silence. Pat wanted no part of taking Kathi back. Looking after her cut into his nightlife.

"I apologize," Pat said. "I didn't mean to do anything wrong." And that was it. I hung up the phone, and I never had any further problems with Pat over the way that I was raising Kathi.

The popularity of the dances continued to increase. I would bring some of the kids over to the house on Saturday afternoons and play a stack of records to see if they could dance to them. Then we would pick up the speakers and sound system and set them up at the Dixon House. We started to get kids from other neighborhoods, and my father would have to break up the occasional fight. Once he dealt with the troublemakers, they never caused problems again.

The kids also helped me get airplay for the records I was promoting; I would have the members of the committee call Georgie Woods and dedicate a record "from the kids at the Dixon House." Woods was the most popular disc jockey in town, and when the kids requested a song, Woods would play it on the air. After that, it was just a matter of time before the record stores would get calls.

One day, when I was driving home, I decided to take Mifflin Street instead of Morris. I had been married for about six months, and I still felt badly about the situation with my mother. I adored my mother and missed her very badly, and when I got to 16th and Mifflin, something told me to stop at 1906 South Bancroft Street to see her. I knew that deep down inside she wasn't happy with Matty Gunnella, and that she was having a difficult time with Lou Anne, my half-sister, who was born with "craniostenosis," a deformity of the skull. Not only was my mother in anguish over that, but her father, Alfonso Capuano, was in poor health as well.

Even though she refused to acknowledge my marriage, I wanted my mother to know that I loved her deeply, and that I regretted the chill that had come over our relationship. I was there to break the ice, and to let her know that I understood her feelings. I knew that I had disobeyed her in marrying Pattie, and that I had gone against her wishes. At first, she was a little cold, giving me a look that said, "What are you doing here?" But after I hugged her and said, "Mom, I miss you," she invited me in.

After I sat down, I asked her how she was doing, and she told me about Lou Anne and my grandfather. I could tell that it was a relief for her to talk about it, and that she was happy to see me. (By that time, my sister Roberta was married and living in Reading, Pennsylvania, and my mother was lonely without us.)

Although it didn't solve all of our problems, my mother and I went on to have a good visit. By the time I left, I could tell things would eventually work out between us.

As I walked down Mifflin Street, it was like a weight had been lifted from my shoulders, and I decided to stop into Pat's Luncheonette. I noticed that no one was on the corner, and I asked where everyone was. Pat told me that a bunch of guys were shooting craps behind the Fulton Manor Apartments.

When I went into the alley behind the Fulton Manor, I saw the craps game right away. It was some of the older guys that I knew from Dahlia. I hadn't seen them since I had been going out with Pattie. They included Richie DiPietro, Joe Sabatini, Vito Egg, Mikey "Golf" Geofreddo, Joe "JoJo Boy" Ferrigno, and Rocco Bene. Dom Pina was there also. He was a part-owner of the Venus Lounge, and he knew me from the times I had gone there with Pattie.

My father had done all of the gambling in our family; I never gambled after seeing how destructive it was. After all, he had bought pieces of jewelry for my mother and hocked them days later to cover gambling debts. But after the visit with my mother, I felt lucky, and I thought I would throw a couple of "passes" in the craps game.

As I walked over to them, Dom was saying that Thursdays were a dead night for him at the Venus, and that he wanted to do something about it. It was the usual street talk.

"Why don't you do a radio show?" I said.

"A radio show?"

"Yeah. Do a live remote."

"Who would do it?" Dom asked.

"I would."

"What do you know about doing a radio show?"

"I'm telling you—I can do it."

"He knows everything there is to know," one of the other guys said sarcastically.

"You can't get that done," Dom said. He and the other guy were smirking.

I had the dice in my hand. I said, "This is my lucky day. If I make my point, you'll give me the opportunity to do a radio show."

"You're never gonna make your point," Dom followed.

I tossed the dice against the side of the Fulton Manor. I needed to roll a six without crapping out. I threw the dice once, then twice, then a third time, until a six finally came up.

"Holy shit!" Pina exclaimed. "All right, if you're that lucky, go get a radio show."

Something told me to turn down Mifflin that day instead of Morris, and to visit my mother. And if the visit hadn't gone as well as it did, I probably wouldn't have gone into Pat's and found out about the craps game. It turned out to be the luckiest day of my life.

The next morning, I called Bud Hibbs, the general manager of WCAM. The station was owned by the city of Camden, and anybody could buy airtime. Sam Scott and Jack Lamar were two of the disc jockeys, and Lamar was also calling horseraces. There was a Gospel show, an Italian show, and a three-hour show that featured Latin music. All you needed to go on the air was a third class FCC license, which the station provided.

Bud Hibbs was a straight shooter, and we came to an agreement very quickly. Every week, I would pay WCAM $125 for an hour of airtime, and I would assume the 10:30 to 11:30 p.m. time slot on Thursday nights. I was twenty years old, and I was about to have a radio show.

When I swung by the Venus Lounge, I told Dom Pina that I would charge him $160 a week. The show would consist of interviews with guests that I lined up and other celebrities. Dom didn't balk at the figure, and he never asked what I was paying the station. He was a gambler and wanted to take a shot.

Now that I owned the hour, I realized that I could make money by getting advertisers. I would sell fifteen-minute blocks for $60. I went around South Philadelphia, calling on old friends and other people I knew, and sold all four of the blocks of time. My advertisers included John P. Crisconi, who owned Crisconi Oldsmobile; Tony Ambese, who ran a Seven-Up bottling plant; Freihoffer's Bread; and Dale Dance Studios, which had a location on Walnut Street in Center City. (Years before, I had won a dance contest on *Bandstand,* and the prize had been tango lessons at the Dale Dance Studio. Although the tango never caught on with the *Bandstand* kids [because the steps were too intricate to master], the owner remembered me, and getting him to buy a block of time was an "easy sell." Being a dancer myself, he was confident that I could persuade people to use his services.)

While hanging at Nat Segall's office, I observed him closely as he conducted his negotiations. He was constantly working the phones, wheeling and dealing, and looking for an edge, but he was always reasonable with the agents, managers, and club owners that he dealt with. In Nat's world, you had to split hairs profitably in order to survive, and that's exactly what he did when he negotiated a "half-commission." (I had never heard that term before Nat took me under his wing, but it was part of my vocabulary now.)

Nat cut hundreds of deals in my presence, and every one of them prepared me for the world I was about to enter. By the time I entered into discussions with Bud Hibbs and Dom Pina, I knew the golden rule of creating any kind of proposal: everybody had to wet their beak, and if they did, they would be happy with the deal.

Once the pieces fell into place, my only real expense was the $125 that I would owe WCAM each week, but the plus side of the ledger already totaled $400 ($160 from Pina and $240 from the advertisers), yielding a profit of $275. And this was on top of the money I was making promoting records, running record hops, and teaching the ladies to dance. Not bad for a kid with no formal education since high school.

The whole venture depended on my ability to draw a crowd to the Venus Lounge, and to put money in Dom Pina's pocket. Though I was nervous when I first went on the air, I got more comfortable as I went along. At the time, Ricardo Munez was broadcasting in Spanish on WCAM, and my show came on right after his. By the second or third week, my show took off, and Dom Pina was pleased with the results. As the crowds got bigger, my confidence increased. Before long, the place was packed, and Thursday nights became one of the best nights of the week for the Venus Lounge.

Just as I suspected, I had no trouble lining up guests like Frankie Avalon, Jimmy Darren, Danny and the Juniors, and other local celebrities. And a fair share of people came to me and asked to be put on the air. If I ever had to replace someone at the last minute, all I had to do was call Nat Segall, Harry Finfer, or Harold Lipsius and they would come up with a singer or a comedian they were handling. By the very nature of the Venus Lounge—where connected guys mingled with the celebrities—anybody who was anybody would stop in when they were in town. In other cases, managers and publicists would line up appearances so their clients could plug a song, an album, or a movie. I even got into the act with prizefighters.

The list of people I interviewed in my first three or four months on the air included Tallulah Bankhead, Rocky Marciano, Rocky Graziano, Connie Francis, Don Adams, and Annette Funicello, who came in with Frankie Avalon. I interviewed Brian Hyland after he released "Itsy Bitsy Teenie Weenie Yellow Polka-Dot Bikini" and Savannah Churchill when she came out with "Time Out for Tears" on Philadelphia's Jamie label.

I even dipped my toes in the water of local politics with Paul D'Ortona, a member of Philadelphia's City Council. (Later, when D'Ortona became the president of City Council, I introduced him to the actress Joan Crawford, and the results were interesting to say the least.)

Some of the interviews were more surprising than others. Annette Funicello told me that she hated to wear the "mouse ears" on the *Mickey Mouse Club* television show. They were uncomfortable, and she could never get used to them. "Plus they ruined my hair," she laughed. Her solution was to take them off every chance she got and slip them back on right before the director yelled "Action!" The director was annoyed with her on a regular basis.

Rocky Graziano appeared on the show two or three times, and whenever he did, he insisted that we interview the Philadelphia middleweight, Joey Giardello. Drinks were free for guests who appeared on the show, and as soon as the interview was over, the two boxers would sit at the bar and get shit-faced, swapping war stories from their battles in the ring. (Years later, I would hang with them at P.J. Clark's in New York.)

Now that I was officially an "on-air personality," I needed a professional headshot, and I ended up going to a photography studio operated by a guy named Michael Denny. Several years before, Denny had been involved in the situation at the Wharton Estates. This was the same scandal that had ensnared Bob Horn, but because Denny wasn't a public figure, he managed to survive. His studio happened to be in the same building as the Dale Dance Studio. Once Denny was finished with the headshot, they posted it at the Venus Lounge, and I felt like a card-carrying member of the media. (Philadelphia didn't have a place like Kreigman's, where Frankie Avalon had gone for his publicity photo in New York, but Denny did a competent job.)

By the time I arrived at the Venus Lounge at nine or nine-thirty on the night of a show, the on-site engineer had wired the microphone, connected the phone lines, and conducted a sound check for sending "the feed" back to WCAM (another technical term that I rolled past Dom Pina occasionally, for the sole purpose of stroking his ego). After a while, my preparation for the show became practically nonexistent, and all I had to do was show up at the appointed time and do my thing. I went on the air in September of 1960, and by the time the New Year rolled around in January of '61, I had enough money to buy the latest Chevy Impala—the first time that I had ever bought a new car.

On January 14, 1961, a light snow started to fall in the late afternoon. Kathi and I were standing in front of the house. Kathi was bundled up against the cold.

"Every snowflake is different," I said. "Did you know that?" By way of reply, Kathi tilted her head upward and caught a snowflake on the tip of her tongue.

By the time Pattie and I went to bed that night, the snow was coming down harder, and the forecast was calling for three or four inches by morning. But when we woke up, we were dealing with a full-scale blizzard. Now I was worried. Schools were closed, and I had a radio show scheduled for 10:30 that night. I owed WCAM for the airtime, and my advertisers were expecting a show.

By noon on Thursday the 15th, eight inches of snow had collected on the parked cars, and there was no end in sight. People were slipping and sliding on the sidewalks, and buses were skidding through stop signs. Restaurants, dry cleaners, clothing stores—they had all closed for the day. The business district was a ghost town, and the public transportation system was barely able to function. Kids were riding sleds, throwing snowballs, and building snowmen on the street corners. The entire city was shut down.

I knew that the Venus Lounge wasn't going to open, and that I had to come up with an alternative. The first thing that came to mind was to broadcast from WCAM, and to play music instead of conducting interviews. By mid-afternoon, I was calling some of the committee members from the Dixon House and asking for help. I knew that the schools were closed, and that they would probably be closed the next day.

As it turned out, four of the kids helped me dig my car out of the snow and load my records into the trunk. After we finished, I asked if they wanted to come with me. I had no idea what I would find when we arrived at WCAM, and I thought they would come in handy. The kids who came with me were Michael Iperi, Petey DeLuliis, Little Danny Bartolomeo, and a kid named "Yonnie."

When we got to the station, the only one there was Ricardo Munez, who gave me a crash course in operating the turntable and control board. I had seen Jack Lamar do it, but I had never done it myself, and

Ricardo spent a few minutes with me during the last half hour of his show. Whenever he cut to a commercial or station break, he would pass along another piece of information, but the minute he signed off the air, I was on my own.

In those days, a studio was just a glorified glass booth, and I put the four Dixon House kids in the next studio over so they could watch me through the glass. They had never been in a studio before and had no idea how I was going to do it. I'm an optimist by nature, and I knew I could pull it off.

Once I got the neighborhood kids situated, I put on my headphones and went to work. I had been thinking about this moment ever since I realized that I couldn't do my show from the Venus Lounge, and I had a clear idea of what I wanted to do.

I opened with "Those Oldies But Goodies" by Little Caesar and the Romans and "Rock and Roll Music" by Chuck Berry. After that, I played "Why Do Fools Fall in Love?" by Frankie Lymon and the Teenagers, "Little Girl of Mine" by the Cleftones, and "Slippin' and Slidin'" by Little Richard. I was off and running, playing one song after another in quick succession. I played "Come Go with Me" by the Vikings and two more songs by Frankie Lymon—"I Promise to Remember" and "The ABCs of Love." When I kicked, it was all fast stuff, but then I altered my pacing, bringing it down with "Earth Angel" by the Penguins and "In the Still of the Night" and "To the Aisle" by the Five Satins. Then I changed the pace again with "Teenager in Love" by Dion and the Belmonts. (The Crew-Cuts had a square version of "Earth Angel," but I played the original.)

I can't explain the way I feel when I'm playing my music, other than to say that I'm in my own world. I've been spinning records for more than fifty years, and the excitement has never worn off.

By the time I played "Teenager in Love," the phones were ringing off the hook, and I was gesturing frantically for the Dixon House kids to answer them. Like Munez had done with me, I could only talk to them while the records were playing. The first chance I got, I went to a record and rushed into the other studio, asking them to write the dedications down as they came in. Before long, all four of them were scribbling at once, putting the dedications in a pile and tossing the phone back and forth like it was a hot potato. As soon as one of them hung up, the phone would ring again and one of the other three would get in the act. (WCAM had two lines for incoming phone calls—one for Pennsylvania and one for New Jersey—and they both went crazy that night.)

The adrenaline was rushing through my veins, and I didn't want it to stop. When the next record was playing, I rushed back into the other studio for more dedications, but when I finally looked at the names that the kids had written down, I was shocked to see that most of them were impossible to read. It was like an episode of *The Dead End Kids*. The handwriting was okay, but the spelling was horrible, and I had to make up some of the names as I went along. Even though it slowed my rhythm, I was able to get it done.

By now, the snowstorm was working in my favor. The jock who normally held down the 11:30 to 12:30 time slot didn't make it in, and neither did the guy after him, and I just kept playing music until I was finally replaced at 2:30 in the morning. The guy who replaced me was an engineer, not a disc jockey, and he played canned music the rest of the way. Instead of having sixty minutes of airtime like I did at the Venus Lounge, I was on for four hours. Throughout the listening area, kids were surfing the radio dial for news about school closings, and I benefitted from that as well.

The listeners who tuned in that night didn't realize that the music was from my own record collection. Many of them were hearing these records for the first time. In other instances, when they were familiar with the artists, I was playing flip sides that they had never heard.

At that time, WIBG was firmly entrenched as the dominant force in Philadelphia radio with guys like Bill Wright, Sr., Jerry Stevens, Harvey Miller, Frank X. Feller, and Joe Niagara. WIBG was working from a Top 40 format, but I was offering a clear alternative. To me, music is timeless, and it was having the same effect on my listeners as it had on me when I first heard it; many of the kids who tuned in that night are still with me to this day.

After that first group of songs, I played records by the Paragons, the Jesters, the Chantels, the Shirelles, the Channels, and many others. When I pulled off the headphones for the last time that night, I was exhilarated like I had never been before, and the kids were feeling the excitement also. By the time I dropped them off, it was three-thirty in the morning. Fortunately, none of their parents objected. They knew

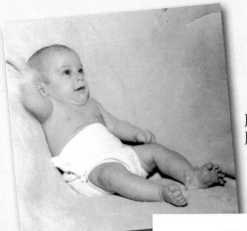

Jerry Blavat,
July 3, 1940.

Mom and Dad after
they ran away and
married.

My Mother and
Grandmother.

The Capuanos—my cousins, Skinny Annie (center),
my Mom (in hat), and my Grandmother.

My Aunt Mim and
Uncle Jimmy at a
picnic.

With my Aunt Mim and
cousins at camp.

Mom and me at
summer camp.

My cousin David, me at age 9, and my Mom.

At a birthday party with my cousins.

Born to dance. I must be about 10.

My Mother made sure that I ate a raw egg and Wheatena
every morning.

Me at 12 years old.

My sister Roberta, me, Skinny Annie, and my Mom at Palumbos.

Two years later, at age 14.

My Mom and Dad out on the town.

(l-r) Skinny Annie, my Mom, and my aunt Philomena
on my Mom's second wedding day.

My 7th grade graduation. That's me third from right in the front row.

All dressed up
for *Bandstand*
in 1954.

A shot from the 1955 *Bandstand Yearbook*. That's me on the right.

I (center) am leading the protest outside the *Bandstand* studio
after the firing of Bob Horn.

To quote JERRY BLAVAT, a sophomore at Southeast Catholic, "one of the nicest things that ever happened to me at 'BANDSTAND' was meeting JO MAZZU." (So there you are!)

My first featured close-up from the *Bandstand Yearbook*.

My high school gradua-tion picture, Bishop Newman, 1958.

My first broadcast as a radio talk-show host at the Venus Lounge.
My first guest was Annette Funicello.

The Supremes on *The Discophonic Scene*, the only local TV show
they ever appeared on.

Closing the deal to nationally syndicate *The Discophonic Scene*.

Hamming it up at the syndication party for *The Discophonic Scene* with (l-r) Lou Marks, Dodie Goodman, and Al Martino.

Chubby Checker and I clowning around backstage at *The Discophonic Scene*.

Broadcasting from the Geator's Den along with some fans.

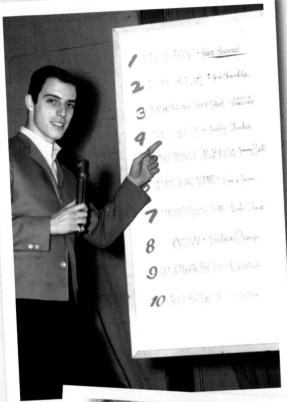

When I started
to play my music
as "The Geator."

Me with yon teens on my WFIL-TV show.

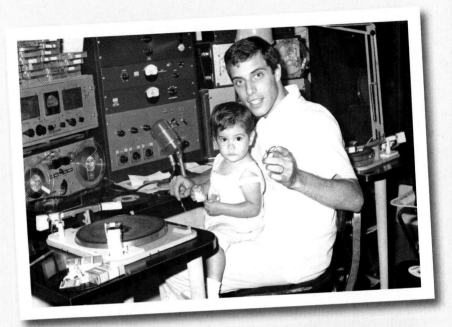

In the home studio I built in my garage, with my assistant deejay, my daughter Gerri.

Listening to music at home with Pattie and our daughters.

that schools would be closed the next day.

When I finally got home, I was totally exhausted. I got to bed around four-thirty, and the next thing I knew, Pattie was waking me up. Bud Hibbs was on the phone. I was still half-asleep.

"Tell him I'll call him back."

I fell asleep again and Pattie came back into the room.

"He has to talk to you," she said. "It's important."

I thought to myself, "I better get this," and I picked up the phone.

"What did you do last night?" Bud asked.

"What do you mean?"

"You were at the station."

"I had to come in—the Venus was closed."

"Did you do interviews?"

"No. I played music."

"What kind of music?"

"My own records."

"Whatever you did, we've never had a reaction like this to any of the shows we carry. We've been getting calls all morning."

The phones were ringing off the hook the night before, but I couldn't believe that it would carry over to the next day. I thought to myself, if the reaction was that strong, there was no telling what would happen if I played music from the Venus Lounge.

When the following Thursday rolled around, I showed up at the Venus Lounge. I had my records with me and the turntable I used at the Dixon House. A few minutes later—when I was setting up my turntable with the engineer—Dom Pina walked in.

"What's this?" he asked.

"I wanna play records."

"This isn't like Mayo's up the street. This is a lounge. You can't do that here."

Pina was the boss. Once he refused, there was no point forcing the issue. I knew that we couldn't go any further.

"After next week's show," I said, "why don't we call it quits?"

Pina gave me a look. "Let's call it quits tonight." He was a little testy about it, and Pattie and I never went back to the Venus Lounge until it was under new management a few years later.

With the phone calls pouring into WCAM—and the sponsors in the palm of my hand—I knew that I was in a good position with Bud Hibbs. The next day, I met with Hibbs at the station and told him that I wanted to play music five nights a week.

"You saw the reaction when we did the show from the studio," I said. "What I would like to do is hand over all of my sponsors to you. It adds up to $240. I don't want to get paid. I would like you to gamble on me."

"Gamble on you how?"

"I can sell the time for you, but I don't want you to charge me for the hours I'm on the air."

Hibbs knew that I always paid the station on time, and that I was reliable with the money.

"Just a minute," he said. "Let me get Emmitt in here."

Emmitt Mara was the sales manager, and he was good at what he did. But more importantly, he was a fan of mine from the *Bandstand* days. When Emmitt joined the meeting, he liked my idea.

"It's dead time anyway," he said. "We're playing canned music. I think we can make this happen."

Over the next few days, Mara and I met with potential sponsors in Jersey, and I picked up a few of my own on the Philadelphia side, including Edward Barrie Shoes, Slax n' Jax, Krass Brothers, and Rual's on Frankford Avenue. By the time we were finished, we sold enough advertising to support an expanded schedule.

Once I started playing music from 10:00 to 11:30 five nights a week, the show absolutely exploded, and my life changed. After listening to my heroes all of those years—Jocko and Georgie in particular—I knew that I had to come up with a persona to use on the air. The guys I admired had nicknames like "the Ace From Space," "the Man With the Goods," and "Little Lord Fauntleroy," and I needed a nickname, too.

If I was going to create a radio persona—and a catch phrase that would set me apart—I had to rhyme like Jocko; when I was shaving one morning, my radio persona took shape. By the time I put the razor down and patted my face with the towel, I had become "the Geator." My thought process had a logic of its own, an internal architecture that arose out of A.M. radio, and a cadence that came from the black disc jockeys. They were my true radio fathers. People like Jocko, Georgie, Mitch Thomas, and Kay Williams had taught me well.

While shaving, I thought about an alligator lying in the mud. He won't bother you unless you get too close. When you do, he'll snatch you right up. That was me. WCAM was located at 1310 on the A.M. dial. The big boys were at the other end of the dial (like WFIL) or more toward the middle (like WPEN and WIBG), and that's where the alligator came in. I was at the wrong end of the dial on a 250-watt station, but my phones were ringing off the hook. Why? Because as soon as those kids ventured to my end of the dial, I had them from that moment on— just like that alligator snatches you up in the swamp.

I could remember cruising South Philly in the dead of winter. As soon as you hopped into somebody's car, you asked them to turn up the heat. But after a while, you said, "Yo, it's too hot! Turn it down!" My music was like that. Kids came up to me all the time and said the same thing. When they blasted my music, their parents told them to lower the volume. The more I thought about it, the more sense it made to incorporate a car heater into my rap.

On those same winter nights, we would go to the Melrose, the Aramingo Diner, or Bea Bea's Lawnside Barbecue on South Street. And that's when it hit me. My music was almost too hot—like the barbecue sauce at Bea Bea's. I thought about all of that and put it together from there, trying different combinations until the pieces fell into place. "Alligator" got shortened to "gator," and "gator" became "Geator" to create the right kind of rhyme. And that's how I became "the Geator with the Heator, the Boss with the Hot Sauce."

I wasn't just creating a persona. I was creating a world that had a language of its own, and I was inviting the kids to join me. I couldn't see their faces when they called in with a dedication, but I knew that they were out there. They were "over yonder," like in Western movies, and like "yon Cassius" in Shakespeare's *Julius Caesar*. My listeners were special, too. I needed to set them apart, and it was only a matter of time before they became "my yon teenagers."

I didn't stop there. I needed nicknames for everybody—not just me, but for the kids who were calling in regularly and the person who answered the phones. That person turned out to be Nat Segall.

Nat was at Chubby's one night, a nightclub over in Jersey. He was checking on one of his acts. Since he was less than a mile away, he stopped in when I was on the air. He sat in the next studio over, just like the neighborhood kids the week before, and the phones went crazy again. Even though we never planned it, Nat got caught up in the excitement and started to answer the phones. Not only could he handle himself with the listeners, but he could also actually spell, so the dedications got through on the air, and they eventually took on a life of their own.

As I watched Nat through the glass, I could tell that he was having a great time. He was usually very reserved, but now he was animated, and I got a kick out of it. Nat reminded me of "Dathan," the character that Edward G. Robinson played in *The Ten Commandments* (one of the most miscast movies of all time) and I started to call him that on the air. (When you said it out loud, it sounded like "day-tahn.")

"Yon teenagers," I would say, "call my main man Dathan with your requests!"

Once I gave Nat a nickname, it all came together. "Dathan" became a sidekick that my "yon teens" could identify with, just as I had identified with the Lone Ranger, the Green Hornet, and the Cisco Kid in my youth.

As I got into the swing of things, my approach to playing music changed. It happened by chance. One Sunday, I went to a 12:15 Mass at St. Gabriel's. The priest who officiated was a little man with white hair. When he delivered the Mass, he spoke in a regular voice, but when he started his sermon, he lowered the microphone and altered his tone. It was almost as though the microphone was an extension of himself, and for the next three to five minutes, he would not only mesmerize me but also the entire congregation with his delivery. At the conclusion of the sermon, he would go back to his regular voice. I later found out that his name was Father Nelson, and that he was the principal of Archbishop Prendergast High School. He later became a Monsignor.

Most priests took too long to deliver their message, but Father Nelson was different, and I would go back every Sunday to watch him. I was intrigued by the way he altered his approach during the sermon. I started to use a similar technique on my radio show, talking over the "intro" of a record until the lyrics started, falling silent, and then talking over the instrumental break. Like Father Nelson, I would alter my pacing depending on the mood and rhythm of the song. (Over the years, a number of other influences found their way into my radio persona. I was a big fan of Burt Lancaster. I used to love the way he delivered his lines. One of my favorite movies was *Elmer Gantry*, and whenever I said, "This is the Geator, the Big Boss with the Hot Sauce," I used the same rhythm that Lancaster used when he said, "Repent, you sinners!")

As soon as the radio show took off, the record hops exploded. The dances were packed, and we were turning kids away. I didn't have a big ego about it. All I knew was that I was doing what I loved. I never realized how remarkable my success had become until I got a call from Harvey Miller at WIBG. Harvey had been doing record hops at the Ice House in Cherry Hill.

"Do you have any idea how hot you are?" he asked. "Why don't you make a guest appearance at the Ice House? You'll see for yourself."

"Humble Harv" had a reason. His attendance had been dwindling. It was March of 1961, and I had been playing music on the air for less than two months.

Harvey's attendance was down to about 300 kids, but after we promoted my appearance on our respective shows, more than a thousand showed up, and I was shocked by the reaction. I didn't realize that they looked at me like a performer. Years later, I realized that's exactly what I was, but at the time, I never took myself too seriously. All I wanted to do was reach people with my music and communicate the excitement and passion I felt.

After the hop, the promoter asked if I wanted to do Friday nights at the Ice House. I would have to work around the Jersey Devils hockey games whenever the team was in town. I immediately agreed.

Even when I did the dances after a hockey game from 10 p.m. to midnight, the Ice House was packed, and my listening audience continued to grow on WCAM. Emmitt Mara was happy because I was making his job easier, and the station was happy because we were able to sell spots. Eventually, Emmitt suggested that we add a show on Saturday afternoons from the Ice House, and that is exactly what we did. We called the show *The Geator's Den*, and it took off. By now, the radio shows and record hops were fueling each other, and the success I was having went beyond anything I could have anticipated. In addition to answering the phones when I was on the air, Nat Segall was handling the money.

In the daytime, I would visit the record distributors, looking for newer releases that fit in with my show. I started to mix the newer releases with my oldies. All of a sudden, the distributors started to get calls on whatever I was playing. Now, the promotion men recognized the importance of my show and started coming around. They knew that I had the ear of the kids.

Because of the payola investigation, most disc jockeys were no longer able to select their own music. That job went to a program director. The record companies had a way of getting around that, but word on the street was that Blavat could not be influenced. If I didn't like the record, and if it didn't fit in with my show, it wouldn't matter—the promotion men had no shot. It was none of my business how the other guys operated, but I never wanted to compromise my integrity or the ability to select the music that I wanted to play. In my entire career, I've always had the freedom to do that, and I've never been dictated to by anyone. All along, I've been able to rely on my instincts for reaching an audience. (My own mother came to me at one point with a record that my Uncle Jimmy made. I listened to it, but it wasn't for me. When I told my mother, she was taken aback, but she respected the way I felt.)

Years later, I realized how I touched my listeners. One of them was a "yon teen" named George Frunzi, who went on to earn a doctorate degree in education. Frunzi has distinct recollections from that period and writes for a magazine called *Echoes of the Past*. In a recent article, he described my early success this way:

"Blavat took us a bit further by introducing Philadelphia to 'Shadows' by the Five Satins and 'Please Don't Ask Me to Be Lonely' by the Dubs. He introduced us to the Paragons, the Six Teens, the Cuff-Links, the Metallics, the Students, the Collegians, Dino and the Diplomats, 'Long Tall Girl' by the Carnations, and an almost unending list of vocal groups and songs never before heard by his following. As his play list expanded, so did his audience, and so did his popularity. Word of mouth was his best form of advertising, and the word was beginning to spread, fast and furious. He would feature killer records like 'Need Your Love' by the Metallics, 'To Make a Long Story Short' by Eddie and the Starlites, 'The Fire Burns No More' by the Chesters, and 'Love No One But You' by the Jesters, and the next day that 25% [of the listening audience] that wanted more went scrambling wildly around the city trying to find the records that Blavat played the night before."

Eventually, the phenomenon that Frunzi described led to my

involvement with the Record Museum, a chain of record stores in Pennsylvania, New Jersey, and Delaware. Before it did, though, it caused a WCAM disc jockey, Hy Lit, to receive a flood of telephone calls from my listeners. Lit had been let go from WIBG in the wake of the payola scandal and had surfaced at WCAM, assuming the 6:00 to 8:15 p.m. time slot that immediately preceded Ricardo Munez. I'm sure that my overwhelming popularity—coupled with the fact that my record hops were bigger than his—made phone calls like these a source of annoyance to him. My listeners would call the station three or four hours before my shift began and start requesting songs. (Although WCAM was only a 250-watt station, its radio tower was located on the Cooper River in Camden, which meant that its signal reached approximately 500,000 teenagers within a fifteen-square-mile radius.)

In September of 1961—after I had been playing music on WCAM for close to eight months—Al Pierce, the mayor of Camden, called me into his office with Bud Hibbs.

"Have you ever taken money to play records?"

I stared at him. "Absolutely not, Mayor."

"How about Hy Lit?"

"I don't know anything about Hy Lit."

"Well, we have a problem. There've been accusations."

"What kind of accusations?"

"You two are the only ones playing records. We have to be careful about our license."

"I play oldies. Nobody offers money for that. Ask Bud. He'll tell you."

"He's always been on the up-and-up with us," Bud said.

It turned out that Hy Lit was accused of accepting money for playing records, and when Pierce threatened to take him off the air, Lit said, "Wait a minute. What about the other guy?"

Needless to say, "the other guy" was me. His accusation was completely false, but it didn't matter. Within a week, Bud Hibbs called me into his office. I could see that he was troubled.

"I know you don't take money," he said, "but unfortunately, the station is city-owned. The mayor has decided to take all of our music shows off the air. He doesn't want to get into a legal battle."

I was stunned. One minute, I was on top of the world, and the next it was all going to collapse. My record hops were dependent upon the exposure I was giving them on the air. The station didn't pay me, so the dances represented a significant portion of my income. Pattie was pregnant with our first child, and for the first time in my life, I was scared.

Sure enough, when I lost the show, attendance at the Ice House dwindled, and a couple weeks later it was over. I started to promote records again, but in a limited way, and the only thing I had going for me was a record hop at the Alhambra Roller Skating Rink on Passyunk Avenue and another one at Strange Hall in Frankford.

There were many sleepless nights as I wrestled with it over and over again in my mind. I knew that I had done nothing wrong, and I tossed and turned, unable to fall asleep for hours. I would wake up at four or five in the morning. For some reason, I decided to go to Mass one morning, driving over to St. Thomas Aquinas church at 17th and Morris. I sat in the back pew and watched the older women pray. They were wearing veils and holding their rosary beads.

When I left the church that day, I felt much better, and going to Mass became a ritual for me over the next few months. Back in grade school, the IHM sisters had said, "If you pray for your intentions, God will hear you." The same old women would be at St. Thomas every morning, praying for their special intentions.

Things were difficult as Pattie's due date approached, and the only thing that comforted me was going to church. I would sit in the back of the church and pray. "Please, direct me," I said. "Tell me which way to go. I want to get back on the air. I want to play my music. I have a positive effect on the teenagers. They trust me. If you give me an opportunity to go back on the air, I promise I'll use whatever success I have to keep them straight."

Ever since I had survived my encounter with a moving car at the age of six, I had felt as though I had a guardian angel, and I had faith that things would work out in the end. Going to church every day—and putting myself in God's hands—gave me the serenity I needed, and I was no longer angry about what had happened. (I always had a special fondness for the Blessed Mother, and I would never leave the church without visiting the side altar and praying to her, and one day that would save my life.)

After Mass one morning, I visited my mother on Bancroft Street.

We sat in the kitchen and talked, and although it was a short visit, it lifted my spirits. When I got back home, Pattie told me that Bud Hibbs had called. It was December, and I had been off the radio for three months. It turned out that I *did* have a guardian angel.

"Jerry, do you wanna go back on the air?"

I was shocked. "Are you kidding? Of course I do!"

It turned out that Hy Lit had gotten a job at WDAS, and that the mayor of Camden was no longer afraid of a lawsuit. Hibbs explained that WCAM had lost all of the sponsors that I had gotten them, and that the listeners had been calling from day one to ask what happened to me. It was like all of my prayers had been answered.

"Get with Emmitt," Bud said.

It took a month or so for Emmitt Mara and me to line up the sponsors we needed, but on January 15, 1962—four days before my daughter Geraldine was born—I was back on the air five nights a week.

Within days of my return to WCAM, my audience was bigger than ever, and "Dathan" was back on the scene. He was not just answering the phones—now he was my manager. As successful as I had been earlier, it was nothing like the success I experienced after that.

Despite the fact that he had divested himself of Swan Records, Cameo-Parkway, and other interests in the wake of the payola investigation, Dick Clark had a lot going on. He had a film production company called Drexel Productions, a Dr. Pepper franchise, and a drive-in restaurant called the Steer Inn on Admiral Wilson Boulevard in Camden. He invited me to make an appearance at the Grand Opening of the Steer Inn. It was a Friday night in February.

Clark talked it up on the local portion of *American Bandstand*, and I mentioned it on WCAM. (From 3:30 to 4 p.m., *Bandstand* was broadcast locally on Channel 6, an ABC affiliate, and from 4 to 5 p.m. it was seen on the entire ABC network.) Although we expected a good turnout, we were unprepared for the mayhem we caused. Teenagers from all over the area descended on the Steer Inn, clogging traffic on Route 130 and the Ben Franklin Bridge. Before we even went on the air, the Camden Police Department had to shut down the Admiral Wilson Boulevard and divert traffic elsewhere. Although I set attendance records at many of my record hops, I had never closed down a highway before.

Ed McAdams, one of Dick Clark's assistants, was on hand at the

Grand Opening, and the show went off without a hitch, with one exception. As part of the promotion, Dick was giving away bottles of Dr. Pepper. There was a tractor-trailer full of them, and in the excitement, McAdams forgot to bring the bottles inside. In the sub-freezing temperatures, hundreds of bottles broke, but nobody knew it at the time. Clark called me the next morning, and we laughed about it over the phone.

Early in 1962, Pattie and I rented a bigger place at 2724 Mifflin Street. We had two little ones now—Kathi and Geraldine, with Stacy on the way. The place we rented was modest. We had a little bit of grass in the front and a small backyard that doubled as our driveway. Every Sunday, I would make the 12:15 Mass to watch Father Nelson do his thing.

For the next several years, the popularity of the record hops increased, and we took them to nearly every neighborhood of the city, and to other cities as well. In the Philadelphia area alone, our venues included the L&M Ballroom, Wagner's Ballroom, the Drexelbrook Country Club, Chez Vous in Upper Darby, and MEPRI Hall in Mt. Ephraim, New Jersey. (MEPRI stood for Mt. Ephraim Police Reserves, Inc.)

In the summertime, kids went to the shore for the weekend, so we shifted the dances to the weeknights. We started doing dances on Fridays and Saturdays at the shore and contacted Dave Friedman, who owned WMID in Atlantic City. Friedman agreed to carry my radio show on his station and tie it in to local record hops. He paid the cost of the show, which was $100 per week, and we became partners on the record hops. Friedman got us the Lyric, the Jefferson Hotel, and the Ocean City Convention Hall. It turned out to be a profitable arrangement for all.

By now, having my own recording studio was long overdue. It seemed like I was always running from the radio station to a record hop, and once the commitments started to overlap, I had to do what Jocko Henderson did when he divided his time between WDAS in Philadelphia and WADO in New York. Jocko had a recording studio in his home on Wissahickon Avenue in Germantown, and it enabled him to do some of his radio shows live and tape some of the others. For the past few months, Jocko had allowed me to use the studio at his house until I built one of my own.

The only way this would work is if I built a first-class recording studio with state-of-the-art equipment. In order to get the job done properly, I enlisted the help of Norman Burke, an audiology technician at Hahnemann Hospital, and Joe Tarsia, a recording engineer who worked at Reco Arts before establishing the famed Sigma Sound Studio, where the Philadelphia Sound first came into being when Kenny Gamble and Leon Huff recorded their legendary hits with the O'Jays, the Stylistics, Patti LaBelle, and others.

Once I got the studio built in my garage at 2724 Mifflin Street, I did the first half of my Friday night radio show live and popped in a tape for the second half, freeing me up to get to the record hops. This worked out fine until I got even busier, and eventually we made a deal to use the Arco Atlantic Go-Patrol helicopter to get from one record hop to the other.

When I first went on the air, the other disc jockeys were knocking the shit out of me. "Why would you listen to him? He's talking over the music!" Their style was to announce the record before it played, disappear while it was playing, and repeat the name of the record afterward. For me, it's always been about my passion for the uniquely American art form of early rock and roll. That was the difference between me and the other disc jockeys of my era. And the more my competitors knocked me, the bigger I became, because they made people aware of the differences between us and called attention to me. When they knocked me like that, it had the opposite effect of what they intended.

The black jocks accepted me for doing my thing. After all, they had been doing theirs for a long time. But the guys on WIBG resented me for breaking the rules and defying the conventions of the day. Sure, I "talked over" the music, but I picked my spots carefully and was methodical about it, "talking over" the instrumental sections of a song but never the lyrics. As my popularity increased, the jealousy and backstabbing intensified. They would say, "Blavat's insignificant. He's on an obscure radio station in Camden." Meanwhile, I was tearing them up. They were getting two hundred kids at their record hops. I was getting two thousand.

Knowing the kind of ear I had for music, Dick Clark called me one day and said, "Bobby Marcucci has a record I want you to hear. Tell me what you think." The record was "Party Lights" by Claudine Clark, and it was released on Chancellor Records, the same label that had Frankie Avalon. I listened to it and said, "Dick, this record's a smash." Clark went on *Bandstand* and said, "Jerry Blavat is playing this record—you have to hear it." By now, Clark was mentioning me on *Bandstand* all the time, and the kids who were appearing on the show—Arlene Sullivan, Arlene DiPietro, Kenny Rossi, and others—started to come to my dances. The exposure that Clark gave me on television contributed to my success as well.

The L&M Ballroom was located at 5th and Rockland in North Philadelphia, and one day Nat Segall got a call from the owners. In previous years, Hy Lit had been successful with his Friday night dances there, but his numbers had started to decline. After getting as many as 700 kids to his earlier shows, Lit was down to about 100, and he left the L&M Ballroom to find a new location. My very first dance packed the L&M with more than 1,000 kids. The place was so crowded that kids were turned away at the door. By now, I had become a thorn in Hy Lit's side. Not only was I back on WCAM—which amounted to a rejection of Lit's claim that I had taken money also—but now WIBG faced the fact that I was becoming a major power not only in Camden, but also in the Philadelphia market.

The record promoters were bringing me their new releases before going to WIBG. If I liked a record, I played it immediately; with WIBG, the promotion men had to go through Roy Schwartz, the program director. If Schwartz didn't like it, the disc jockeys wouldn't be able to play it, and because WIBG worked from a format, there was a strong possibility that the record would never get on the air. As a result, I was playing records that no other stations were playing, including "He's So Fine" by the Chiffons, "Tossin' and Turnin'" by Bobby Lewis, "So Young" by the Students, "I'm So Happy" by the Teenchords, and two by Jimmy Soul—"Twistin' Matilda" and "If You Wanna Be Happy." Just as Hy Lit had gotten calls from my listeners when we were on WCAM together, other radio stations started to get calls, including WIBG. In addition to busting records, I was influencing the playlists of other stations.

One of my biggest fans was a young producer who was about to start his own label. His name was Phil Spector. Phil heard me play the Teenchords and the Students, and the Students had such an impact on him that he came to see me at WCAM. Afterward, Phil went back into the studio and re-recorded "I'm So Happy" with a group called the Ducanes. After I played it on my show, it became a major hit in

Philadelphia. Eventually, Phil took his wife (the former Ronnie Bennett, who sang with the Ronettes and later as a solo artist) and recorded "So Young." Shortly after that, the Beach Boys recorded a cover version of the same song.

After starting Philles Records with seed money from Lester Sills, Harold Lipsius, Harry Finfer, and Helen Noga, who was Johnny Mathis' manager, Phil sent me the first release of a girl group called the Crystals. The demo was called "Oh, Yeah, Maybe Baby." When I listened to it, it didn't knock me out. Later, however, when Phil sent me the record, I liked the "B" side a lot more. It was called "There's No Other Like My Baby," and I said, "Phil, that's the hit."

"There's No Other Like My Baby" had a "talking intro" that started before the actual beat was introduced. But when I played it on my show, I skipped the intro altogether and started the song with the percussion. When Phil heard what I had done, he went back and re-pressed the record without the introduction, and that became Phil Spector's first national hit. He would eventually buy out his partners and create the now-famous "Wall of Sound."

Unlike other disc jockeys, I would listen to both sides of a record when I got a new release, and many times, I would play the "B" side, and it would become a gigantic hit. "Good-bye to Love" by the Marcels was another example of this. It was the flip side to "Blue Moon."

By that time, word had gotten around that Dick Clark thought highly of me and respected my ear, and I started to hear from other producers and executives. Like Phil Spector, the other record guys were listening to my show, getting ideas for their records, and using me as a barometer. Although my influence on the music industry was growing, I never really looked at it in those terms. I was just turning people on to the records I loved.

Next, the president of the Drexelbrook Country Club called Nat. They were interested in doing a dance on Sunday afternoons, and had a large banquet hall to accommodate us. Their intention was to have something exciting for the members' kids to do. By our fourth week at Drexelbrook, all hell broke loose. The dance was originally intended for the members' kids and their guests, but now kids from all over were trying to get in. The kids were spilling out of the banquet hall onto the lawn outside, making all kinds of noise and disturbing the members.

Finally, the president of the country club canceled the dances.

On my way to and from the Drexelbrook Country Club, I used to drive past Chez Vous, a roller skating rink on the second floor of an Acme supermarket in Upper Darby. Roller skating rinks were becoming passé. It was getting harder for them to make a go of it, so I told Nat that we should contact Chez Vous and work something out. The woman who owned the place was Mrs. Kelly. She was a wonderful woman—as sweet as could be—and she was aware of our success at Drexelbrook. Without missing a beat, we switched from Drexelbrook to Chez Vous on Sunday afternoons and enjoyed the same kind of success.

By that time, Dick Clark and I had become even closer, and we started to hang out together at the Vesper Club. One night, he mentioned a show he was doing at the Steel Pier in Atlantic City.

"Why don't you and Pattie come down for the weekend?" Dick asked. "I've got Jerry Lee Lewis booked. You can introduce him."

Jerry Lee Lewis had gotten in trouble with the press by marrying his thirteen-year-old cousin, Myra, and bringing her to England, making headlines all over the world. Disc jockeys had stopped playing his records for a few years, and Dick Clark was one of them. Now, Lewis was attempting a comeback.

"I'm bringing him back for a show," Dick said. "I don't know how he'll react."

That same weekend, I was scheduled to do a record hop in Atlantic City, and the timing worked out perfectly.

Dick had just married Loretta, his second wife, and they were staying at the Mount Royal Hotel in Atlantic City. I reserved a double room right next to his. When the night of the show rolled around, Dick brought me on stage. "I want to present someone that all of you know from *Bandstand*. He's the hottest young disc jockey around. Here he is, ladies and gentleman, 'the Geator with the Heator, the Boss with the Hot Sauce,' Jerry Blavat!"

The crowd erupted in applause. I danced my way onto the stage, and without missing a beat, I said, "Ladies and gentlemen, the killer, the thriller, Jerry Lee Lewis!" Out came Jerry Lee, pounding away on the piano, back in business again. I got so excited when he did "Whole Lotta Shakin' Goin' On" that I jumped on top of his piano and started dancing. Not only did we bring the house down, but Jerry Lee couldn't believe that somebody could dance on his piano as fast as he played. The crowd went crazy.

That same weekend, Frank Sinatra was appearing at the 500 Club. Dick said that he had never seen Sinatra in person.

"How would you like to go to the show?" I asked.

"It's sold out."

"Don't worry about it. When I'm done my hop tonight, meet me in front of the 500 Club."

I called Paul "Skinny" D'Amato, the manager of the 500 Club. I first met him through Don Rickles, and Nat Segall had been booking acts at the 500 for years. I told Skinny whom I was coming down with, and he said, "I'll see you tonight."

When my record hop ended, Pattie and I looked for Dick and Loretta at the 500 Club. There was a line around the corner, and I couldn't see them at first. There were at least a hundred people ahead of them. Even though people recognized Dick, no one approached him. They were so into Sinatra that nothing else mattered.

When I saw Dick and Loretta, I said, "Why are you standing in line? Come with me." And I took them to the alley next to the club, where Skinny's brother, Willy, was waiting. As we made our way through the kitchen, Sinatra came out of his dressing room in a tuxedo. Skinny had told him that I was coming.

"Hey, kid, howya doin'?"

"Okay, Mr. Sinatra."

Dick looked at me in amazement, and Sinatra walked away without acknowledging him. I knew that Frank was never a fan of rock and roll.

"How do you know Sinatra?" Dick asked.

"Through Don Rickles."

After Willy seated us at a "ringside" table—another sign of respect—I sensed that Dick was upset that Sinatra hadn't said anything to him.

After Lionel Hampton performed a set on his vibraphone, the comedian Pat Henry came out to warm up the crowd. All of a sudden, in the middle of Pat's act, Sinatra walked onstage. The place went crazy. They gave Sinatra a standing ovation. Their reaction put my recent success in perspective, and it was a healthy experience for me to see it.

Sinatra turned to Pat and said, "You're over." Sinatra's line got a bigger laugh than anything Pat had said. Pat had been Sinatra's open-ing act for years and knew the routine.

During his act, Sinatra acknowledged some of the celebrities in the audience, including the comedian Guy Marks, Jack E. Leonard, Phyllis McGuire of the McGuire Sisters, Leo Durocher (a coach with the Los Angeles Dodgers), and Durocher's wife, the actress Laraine Day. Even though Dick Clark was a national star, Sinatra didn't acknowledge him. I could tell that Dick was crushed.

When the show was over, Skinny D'Amato walked over to our table. "How did you like the show?"

"It was fantastic," I said. "By the way, there's no check."

"Mr. Sinatra picked it up."

When Skinny walked away, I realized that we were sitting at Frank's table. Dick couldn't believe that we were sitting there, and that Sinatra picked up the check.

"Well, he must like you."

Clark's mouth fell open. "I'll be damned."

After the L&M Ballroom was sold, it was strictly a catering opera-tion for weddings and other events, but Nat received a call from Joe Smith, whose family owned Wagner's Ballroom near Broad and Olney. During the latter part of the 40s and 50s, ballroom dancing was the rage, and Wagner's did very well; now that rock and roll had come in, they were struggling to survive. We made the same arrangement with Joe and ran our dances on Sunday afternoons at Wagner's. In order to accommodate that, we switched our dances at Chez Vous from Sunday afternoons to Friday nights.

Joe's mom, the matriarch of the family, was from the old school, and when the kids slow-danced too close, she would walk around the dance floor and poke them with her cane. When the kids started to "grind," Mrs. Smith would actually step between them, but when the dances got too crowded, it was impossible for her to make her way around, paving the way for the kids to "grind" to their heart's content.

In addition to my weeknight shows on WCAM, I did a Saturday afternoon street corner harmony show. Today they call it "doo-wop." That show featured Earl Lewis and the Channels, the Chanters, the Kodaks, the El Dorados, the Magnificents, the Chantels, Frankie Lymon and the Teenagers, the Cleftones, and Lewis Lymon and the Teenchords. (Lewis was Frankie Lymon's brother.) The Saturday afternoon show became as hot as my show on the weeknights.

We got a call from Lou DiLuca, who managed MEPRI Hall in Mt. Ephraim, and started to do dances there. Occasionally, the record companies would send in recording artists to promote their product. This wasn't unique to my dances; the other disc jockeys would have the same guest artists. The difference between our dances and theirs was that we were jam-packed whether we had a guest artist or not, while the other disc jockeys depended on the companies sending a guest artist for promotion. These guest artists included the Contours, the Orlons, the Marvelettes, Martha and the Vandellas, and Smokey Robinson and the Miracles.

One day, when I was doing the radio show on WCAM, Barney Ales called me on the phone. Ales was running Motown for Berry Gordy.

"Berry wanted me to send you a demo," Ales said. "We got a new artist, Stevie Wonder. Berry wants to know what you think of the demo. It's from an album called *The Jazz Soul of Little Stevie Wonder*. Berry thinks this demo can be a single."

The demo arrived two days later. It was a song called "Fingertips," and it started out with the line "Everybody say yeah!" As soon as I heard it, I thought of "Shout!" by the Isley Brothers. I called Barney Ales.

"The kids'll love it," I said.

"We're releasing it," he said.

"I think it's a hit."

"How would you like him to do one of your record hops?"

"I've got a hop coming up in Atlantic City," I said.

"That's perfect. We're doing a show with Teddy Powell."

Powell was a promoter who featured black artists at the Atlantic City Coliseum. His upcoming show included the Temptations.

"When's your hop?" Ales asked.

"Friday night at the Jefferson Hotel."

"Our show is Saturday. We'll be there."

Stevie Wonder's real name was Steveland Morris. I knew how old he was, but Ales never bothered to tell me that Stevie was blind. I was dancing onstage with some of the kids when Nat Segall signaled me. Stevie Wonder had arrived and was ready to go on. "Now here he is," I said, "with the hottest sound in town, Little Stevie Wonder!"

The next thing I knew, Stevie's assistant walked him on stage. This was Stevie's first public appearance. He was wearing sunglasses. As soon as he started to play his harmonica, I realized that he was blind. The place went wild.

After my return to WCAM, I never took my success for granted or got a big head. I felt incredibly fortunate to live the life I was living, and to succeed in what was fast becoming an increasingly competitive industry.

Kal Mann, who wrote songs with Bernie Lowe and Dave Apple for Cameo-Parkway Records, came to Chez Vous. I used to play an oldie called "Every Day of the Week" by the Students. That night, the kids did a dance called "The Stomp" to "Every Day of the Week." Kal saw this and asked Nat whose record it was. Nat told him it was a mediocre hit years before on the Chess label out of Chicago. The next thing I knew, Kal took the same beat as "Every Day of the Week," changed the lyrics, and called it "The Bristol Stomp." The song became a huge hit for the Dovells, a group that Nat would manage. It was a complete rip-off, and that happened again when Cameo-Parkway released "Mashed Potato Time" by Dee Dee Sharp. That was a rip-off of the Marvelettes' version of "Please, Mr. Postman." Same beat, different lyric. (Another time, when 2,000 kids did "The Stomp" at Chez Vous, the floor shook so much that all of the windows were knocked out at the Acme supermarket down below. The cops put barricades around the place and we had to pay for the windows to be replaced.)

On my radio show, I continued to play a mixture of oldies and newer releases that had the same feel, including songs like "Quarter to Three" by Gary U.S. Bonds, "Don't You Know" by Rico and the Ravens, "Bila" by the Versatones, "La La" by the Cobras, and "Bongo Stomp" by Little Joey and the Flips. The promoters continued to come to me with their product, and I ended up playing records before stations like WIBG, WHAT, and WDAS. As I became more comfortable as the Geator, I felt like an actor playing a part. The music was my script, but I ad-libbed and improvised. (Later on, when I did my TV shows and appeared in films, I would use a similar technique.)

My popularity also arose from the fact that I was only a few years older than the kids who listened to me on the radio. I looked like them, I dressed like them, and I related to them in a way that set me apart from the other disc jockeys. I didn't have the classic pipes of a disc jockey—or the perfect radio voice—but when I played my records, the kids felt the energy, honesty, and excitement. At the hops, I got down on the floor and danced with the kids, and when they dedicated a song to that special person, they knew that I understood where they were coming from. Maybe it all went back to the loneliness I felt as a kid. Later, when I created *The Lovers Hour*, it was with exactly that in mind—being able to help kids with some of the emotions they were experiencing for the first time. (Most of my listeners were blue-collar, working-class kids that attended either public or Catholic school. They weren't high-brow, private school kids at all. I would have welcomed the private school kids, but they were into a different sound. WIBG, a format radio station with 50,000 watts, was able to reach that audience. I was always on 1,000-watt stations, but again, once you found me, I hooked you.)

When I prayed to get back on the air, I had pledged to use my microphone in a good way, and now I was a part of the community, making appearances at school assemblies, talking to kids about the danger of drugs, and making sure they didn't step out of line at the dances.

One day, when I was driving back to 27th and Mifflin, I got to within six or seven blocks of my house when I saw a group of kids in the middle of the street. I realized that I had driven right into a gang fight. The kids all went to Bishop Neumann, but they were from two different neighborhoods—Schuylkill and Grays Ferry—and tension had escalated between them. I jumped out of my car and walked over before punches were thrown. As soon as I got in the middle, they recognized me. Most of them were my listeners and knew me from the neighborhood.

"Are you guys crazy? If the cops come, you'll get arrested, and you're three blocks from the school. If they find out, you're gonna get kicked out!"

They looked at each other and didn't say anything.

"If you got a beef, go one-on-one up the alley, settle it, and shake hands." They agreed, and it was all over.

As far back as the Dixon House in 1959, I had been getting involved with kids' problems. One kid was high when he showed up at the dance. It turned out that he was taking Benzedrine, a form of speed that was known on the street as "bennies."

After the dance, I said, "Come on, let me take you home." I knocked on his door and his mother answered. She took one look at him and fell apart. Apparently, she wasn't aware of what the kid was doing.

"You better watch your son," I said. "I think he's got a problem. You may need to get some help." About a month later, I saw her on the street. She thanked me for opening up her eyes, and said that her son was getting help.

Situations like that started to happen more frequently. One of the most effective measures we took when a kid was causing trouble was to bar him from the dances. That happened with a kid named Mikey Dugan. Once Mikey realized that all of his friends were at the dance and he was on the outside looking in, he cleaned up his act. I don't know how many times a kid said, "Please, Geator, give me another chance. I promise I won't cause any trouble." More often than not, the same kid would give us a heads-up when trouble was brewing. Even though we had 2,000 kids at some of the dances, we almost never had an incident inside the building. The kids knew my policy and respected it, and if I ever found out that there was a problem on the subway or the El, those kids would be banned.

In a way, I had come full circle. After Bob Horn, Harry Finfer, and Nat Segall had become "second fathers" to me, I found myself assuming the same role with some of the kids who came to my dances and listened to me on the radio. (The guys were "Geator Guys" and "coyotes"; the girls were "Geatorettes" and "Amazons.") I had grown up fast and was a father now myself, and the role came naturally to me.

Very often, a disc jockey occupied a special place in a teenager's life, provided that the jock was accessible and took the responsibility seriously. In many cases, talking to someone like me was a lot easier than talking to their parents. And because I was closer in age to them than their parents were, the bond was even stronger.

After we did the radio show, Nat and I would go to Chubby's to eat. Now that the Latin Casino had moved to Jersey, Chubby's wasn't a nightclub any more; it was an open-hearth restaurant. One night, we got a call from Donnie Kirshner.

"Geator, how come you didn't come to the show? Darin's asking for you."

Before he became a solo artist, Bobby Darin had written songs for Nevins and Kirshner. Now, he was performing at the Latin.

"Donnie, I didn't even know he was in town."

"We've been here all week! Why don't you come over?"

"We just sat down to eat."

"I'll tell you what. We're staying at the Warwick. Come over when you're done."

When we got to Darin's suite, it was after one in the morning. Darin was wearing a silk dinner jacket and an ascot. Kirshner was sitting a few feet away, talking to Lou Adler, who managed Kirshner's West Coast office. A skinny blonde was lying on the couch in a robe. It was Sandra Dee.

Dee stayed up with us for a while, but she was struggling to keep her eyes open. Finally, she said, "Bobby, I'm going to bed."

A few minutes later, I needed to use the bathroom, and when I closed the door behind me, I saw three of Darin's hairpieces. Each one of them was resting on a mannequin. As long as I had known Bobby, I never realized that he wore a toupee.

We stayed up until four in the morning, trading stories about Connie Francis, Danny and the Juniors, and other people we had worked with.

The next day, Darin came over for some of my mother's ravioli. After we ate, we went our separate ways. Darin did his show at the Latin, and I did mine on WCAM.

Having a manager paid off in more ways than one. Nat and I were tighter than ever. In his eyes, I wasn't a kid any more, I was an equal, and the money we were making had a lot to do with it. (Nat was driving a Cadillac now, after trading in his Volkswagen Beetle.)

Whenever I had an idea, Nat was able to carry it out, and that's exactly what happened after we syndicated my radio show in Atlantic City. If we could do it there, there was no reason that we couldn't do it elsewhere, and in a matter of weeks, Nat and I negotiated deals to place my show in other cities and tie it in to local record hops. In addition to WMID, we worked out similar arrangements with Herb Scott at WPAZ in Pottstown and Ray McFadden at WTTM in Trenton. (McFadden was involved with WAAT in New Brunswick also, and we cut a deal with that station as well.)

Plugging my local dances on WCAM served as a business model, and we used it to establish a regional presence in the summer of 1962. We had a tie-in to local record hops in Atlantic City, Pottstown, and Trenton, and just like before, one part of the "machine" continued to fuel the other. (The whole key was being on the radio, and the same thing happened when I bought my own nightclub years later.)

Now that we were in other markets, I bought three more tape machines to accommodate the different radio shows I was doing. I didn't want to do five different shows, so we needed a way to handle the station identifications and commercials. Having that many machines enabled me to start and stop the recording as needed, and to insert the material that was unique to each of the stations I was appearing on.

In order to help me with this, I hired Bill Willis, one of the kids from the record hops, and nicknamed him "Kilocycle Pete," telling the listeners "Kilocycle Pete is going to the phones right now!" and urging them to call with dedications. By then, Nat was too busy handling our business affairs to continue answering the phones. (Another kid took dedications for us also, and I dubbed him "Electronic Al.")

Looking back on it, I realize that I was doing things differently than the guys at the other stations. Although they had 50,000 watts working for them, they were only drawing two or three hundred kids to their record hops, while I was drawing in the thousands. The other guys were earning salaries at their stations and making money on the side with the dances. I wasn't getting paid for radio at all. Instead, I was making all of my money on the dances.

As soon as you got a paycheck from a radio station, program directors and management dictated what to play. I refused to do it that way. I traded dollars for freedom. Throughout my entire career, it's always been about the music. After fifty years, I've never gotten paid for doing radio or taken money to play a record. If I had done either one, it would have compromised not only my integrity but also my ability to create my music and share it with the audience.

The record companies would send their national promotion men into the major markets, where they would entertain the local disc jockeys. They would usually book rooms at the Marriott on City Line Avenue or the Franklin Motor Inn. If you attended a major convention, it was common to see hookers at the hotel, and when local promoters came to the Franklin Motor Inn, it was no different. There would be a time later in my marriage when I would get laid by hookers, but in the early years with Pattie, I was faithful.

Songwriters would approach me for my input and advice. One time, I found myself in the middle of a situation with Florence Greenberg of Scepter Records. Florence asked me to come to New York to hear the Shirelles' new release, "Foolish Little Girl," which was produced by her son, Stan Green. Green was blind and had shortened his name from Stanley Greenburg. (I had been one of the first guys to play the Shirelles' song, "Soldier Boy," whose original producer was my old friend Luther Dixon. Dixon was responsible for the Shirelles' early hits.)

Before I got to Florence's office, Burt Bacharach approached me. Bacharach was writing and producing for Scepter with his partner, Hal David, and working with other artists. He and David had first collaborated on Perry Como's hit, "Magic Moments," in 1958. David's older brother, Mack, cowrote songs for the Disney film, *Cinderella*.

"I want you to hear something before you see Florence," Burt said.

He played me a song called "Don't Make Me Over" by a new artist named Dionne Warwick. It was completely different than anything I had heard. I said, "Burt, this song is amazing."

"Florence doesn't like Dionne's voice. She wants to use the same track with the vocal by Tommy Hunt."

Tommy had just left the Flamingos and was pursuing a solo career, and even though he was magnificent, Burt knew that Dionne Warwick's voice was the one he wanted for the track he produced. He knew Dionne and her sister Dee Dee from when he produced some of the Drifters' sessions and they did backup vocals. The Warwick girls were cousins of Cissy Houston, Whitney Houston's mother.

"Give me the demo," I told him.

When I went into her office, Florence Greenberg played me "Foolish Little Girl," which didn't knock me out. She had no idea that the Dionne Warwick demo was in my pocket. (This was before the world knew the musical genius of Burt Bacharach and Hal David, and that Dionne would fit them like a glove in the music they would later create.)

On my way out, I bumped into my pal, Bert Berns. Berns also went by the names of Bert Russell and Russell Byrd and was doing independent production for other companies. He was eventually responsible for songs like "I Want Candy" by the Strangeloves, "Hang on Sloopy" by the McCoys, and "Piece of My Heart" by Janis Joplin. (Later, I would run into Janis Joplin at the Atlanta International Airport. She was whacked out on drugs and invited me to join her band, simply because she liked the coat I was wearing. She didn't even know who I was.)

Berns told me he was writing and producing for Scepter. At the end of a session with Chuck Jackson, they had ten minutes of studio time left. Berns rushed the Isley Brothers in to do a song he wrote called "Twist and Shout." Florence had just signed the Isleys to her subsidiary label, Wand. Berns played the demo, and just like "Don't Make Me Over," I flipped for it.

I left Scepter that day with two demos, "Don't Make Me Over" and "Twist and Shout." I went on the air that night and played both of them. The "Twist" craze was the biggest thing in the country, and the phones lit up immediately. The same thing happened with Dionne Warwick. "Don't Make Me Over" started off with 16 bars of heavenly music, and then Dionne's amazing voice came in and the audience heard it for the first time. Then there was a bridge musically, and when Dionne came back in a second time, she sang an octave higher: "Accept me for what I am. . . ." As the music went to a higher octave, my voice would go to a higher octave, and I would say, "Daughter of the moon, sister of the stars, soul sister, Dionne Warwick!" I had learned my lessons well from Father Nelson, and by altering my voice at just the right time, I was able to create an interplay that enhanced the record. And that's how I busted "Don't Make Me Over."

The kids went bananas for "Twist and Shout" and "Don't Make Me Over" every time I played them, and as the dedications poured in, the record stores started to get calls and so did Scepter's distributor, Main Line. The stores couldn't find the product, and the next thing I knew, Florence called me up in a panic.

"You're playing two songs that we didn't intend to release!"

"Florence, a hit's a hit."

"I'll tell you what. I'd like to send Dionne Warwick in to do one of your record hops with Wally Roker." Roker was a promotion man at Scepter. He wanted to see the reaction that this record was getting to make sure that it wasn't "hype."

"No problem," I said. "As a matter of fact, do me a favor, send the Isley Brothers, too."

"They don't even have a 'B' side for 'Twist and Shout.'"

The second side of "Twist and Shout" was just the track of the song without the Isley Brothers' vocal. It was called "Latino Twist and Shout." Later, Ronnie Isley told me that they had been rushed into the studio, his voice cracked, and he thought it was the worst thing they had ever recorded. He couldn't believe that it became a Top Ten record.

Florence sent Dionne Warwick and the Isley Brothers to my record hop at MEPRI Hall. Just like Stevie Wonder, it was Dionne's first public appearance and the first time that the Isleys ever appeared at my hop. When the records busted in Philadelphia, Florence got a lot of heat from the jocks at WIBG. They were pissed off that she had sent Dionne and the Isleys to my hop and not theirs. Because of that, Florence sent them to some of the other dances in the area.

That's how strong my audience was. They could bust a record overnight. The next day, the kids would go into the record stores, tell them what I played, and ask if the stores had it. Then the record stores would contact the distributors and one-stops. (Although I've gotten plenty of accolades, it was my audience that bought the records and made them hits. All I did was expose them to the music.)

Burt Bacharach had another situation with Florence Greenberg, and it involved Dionne Warwick again. He had cut a song called "Make It Easy on Yourself," and just as she had with "Don't Make Me Over," Florence felt that the Bacharach-David composition didn't fit into the mold of rock and roll. Florence kept it "in the can," but Burt knew it was a hit and believed in what he was doing. He called Calvin Carter, whose sister, Vivian, had formed Vee-Jay Records with her husband Jimmy Bracken. Vee-Jay was one of the first independent black labels, and I had first discovered it in the discount racks at the Sun Ray Drug Store when I was a kid.

Burt sent the demo for "Make It Easy on Yourself" to Calvin Carter, and Carter immediately realized that it was perfect for Jerry Butler. "This is the crossover hit we need," Carter said. Burt flew out to Chicago, recorded the song with Butler, and sent it to me. I loved it, and as soon as I played it on the air, it busted wide open.

Somehow, everything I played ended up on WIBG, and "Make It Easy on Yourself" was no exception. It became a national hit, and when Ewart Abner came into town to take care of the disc jockeys, he invited me to his room at the Marriott. Abner ran Vee-Jay Records for Carter and Bracken. When Nat and I went to see him, he said, "You busted the record for us. What can I do for you?"

I said, "Ab, I don't really need anything."

"Listen, there's a record convention in Florida. I want to fly you and Nat down to the Fontainebleau. You'll be my guest."

The next thing I knew, Abner sent us two first-class tickets to Miami.

"I think we should go," Nat said. "All of the record guys are gonna be there. It's important that they see you."

At the time, a kid named Joe Wissert became close to me. He came to our record hops and hung around when I did my radio show, and when his dad passed away, I became like a second father to him. Joe was fascinated with the music business and did his best to learn whatever he could from being around me. Eventually, I agreed to go to the music convention in Florida, but knowing Wissert's love for the industry, I told Nat that I wanted to take Wissert along. "We'll pay his way," I said.

"Where's he gonna stay?" Nat asked.

"We have a suite. He'll sleep on the couch."

When we got to the convention, owners and executives from every record company were there, along with promotion men and disc jockeys from all over the country. I ran into Bob Crewe at the Poodle Lounge. I had known him for years, beginning with "Silhouettes," a song he produced for the Rays with his partner Frank Slay. Slay was with Swan Records now, producing Freddie Cannon. I had danced to one of Crewe's songs on *Bandstand*, a single called "Certainly Baby" by Charlie and Ray. Now, Crewe was cowriting songs and producing a group called the Four Seasons, which featured a falsetto singer named Frankie Valli. Crewe had a demo with him and a portable record player. The record player was a battery-operated turntable made by Philips Electronics.

"Let me hear it," I said.

Crewe was on his way to see Morris Levy of Roulette Records. He played me the demo of "Sherry," and as soon as I heard it, I said, "When you see Morris, tell him he can't go wrong. It's a smash."

When Nat and I left the bar, there were hookers everywhere. The ones who weren't doing business up in the suites were sitting by the pool. All of the record executives and promotion men had cabanas, and that's where you went to hear their product.

Whenever the major players recognized me, they would wave me into their cabanas, saying, "Geator, I want you to listen to something." But before they played me anything, they would offer me a drink from a fully-stocked bar. It was the first time that I ever tasted Crown Royal. As a kid sneaking into bars, I always ordered Seven and Sevens. That's what the older guys in South Philly would order.

For the next few hours, I sampled new releases. Whenever I liked something, the promotion men would give me the demo, knowing that I would play it as soon as I got home.

Two records stick in my mind from that convention: "Oh, My Angel" by Bertha Tillman and "This Is My Prayer" by Theola Kilgore. "This Is My Prayer" was distributed by Florence Greenberg's Scepter label and produced by another old friend, Ed Townsend, who had a gigantic hit in 1958 with "For Your Love" and later wrote and coproduced "Sexual Healing" with Marvin Gaye.

When Nat and I got back to our suite, Joe Wissert wanted to hear the demos, so we went to dinner without him. After dinner, I saw Crewe getting drunk at the Poodle Lounge. I thought he was celebrating.

"Yo, Bob, congratulations!"

"I'm fucked," Crewe said.

"What do you mean you're fucked?"

"Morris hates the record. He said you lost your fucking ear."

"Hold on for a second."

I went to the phone at the end of the bar and called Ewart Abner's suite. "Ab, I want you to hear something."

"Come up."

When we got to Abner's suite, he hugged us and invited us in. He had known Crewe for years. I said, "Ab, you gotta hear this record. It's a fucking smash."

Abner had gigantic speakers in his suite, and as soon as "Sherry" came blasting out of them, he knew I was right. He turned to Crewe and said. "Tell me about this group."

"It's a combination of Bob Gaudio and Frankie Valli," Crewe said. "They're outta Newark."

Gaudio had a couple of hit records with the Royal Teens—"Short Shorts" and "Believe Me"—and Frankie had performed with the Four Lovers. When Danny and the Juniors had appeared on the *Clay Cole Show* in New York, Gaudio had told me that the Royal Teens were breaking up and that he was going to form a group with Frankie.

I could see that Abner was a little hesitant. He turned to me and said, "Geator, this is a white group. We're a black label. We don't have any white artists."

I said, "What the fuck does color have to do with a hit record?"

"As much as I like the song," Abner said. "I don't know if we can break it. The black stations might not play it."

"Ab, it's a hit record. I'll tell you what. I'll take it back to Philly and prove it to you."

It was around midnight when we left Abner's suite. Crewe was still down in the dumps. I said, "Bob, don't worry about it. It's a hit."

When I got back to my suite, there was a party going on. It was a combination of hookers and industry types. It was so crowded that I couldn't even see Wissert when I first walked in. When I found him, he was sitting on the edge of my bed with a sheet wrapped around him. He was swapping spits with a hooker. I couldn't believe what I saw.

"Yo, Joe, come here." I had a drink in my hand.

Joe rose from the bed unsteadily. I was standing on the other side of the bed, and he made his way over to me.

"Joe, I hate to break it to you, but that broad you're swapping spits with has been blowing people all day."

"No!" Joe said. "Don't say that. I love her!" He looked absolutely heartbroken.

"Joe, she's a fucking hooker."

With that, Joe lurched forward, burying his head in my shoulder. Before I could react, he knocked me over backwards and fell on top of me, pinning me to the bed. The second we landed, the glass I was holding shattered into pieces, opening a cut over my eye.

Blood was pouring all over, and I couldn't see out of my eye. The entire suite cleared out, except for Nat, who pulled Joe off me and held a towel over my eye. The next thing I knew, I was on my way to Mount Sinai Hospital, ten minutes from the Fontainebleau.

When we got to Mount Sinai, there was a young surgeon on call who patched me up with fourteen stitches. I never found out his name, but I owe him a debt of gratitude. To this day, you can barely see a scar.

We were supposed to go back to Philadelphia the next day, but Pattie was pregnant with our second child and I didn't want her to see me like that. I told her that I had to stay a few more days, and when she asked about it, I said that I might have an opportunity to syndicate my radio show in Florida. It was a total fabrication, and I could tell that she didn't believe me. "I'm gonna stay," I said, "but Nat's coming back."

Within a few days, the swelling had gone down, and I flew back to Philadelphia. When Pattie saw me, she asked how many stitches I had gotten.

"How did you find out?" I asked.

"Nat told me."

Nat thought it was better to break it to Pattie gently, and it turned out to be the right thing to do. It was easier on her in the long run, and she understood why I had made up a story about syndicating my show in Florida.

As soon as I got back on the air, I played "Sherry," "Oh, My Angel," and "This Is My Prayer." The phones rang off the hook. "Sherry" was the most requested of the three. I wound up playing it two or three times a night. By the end of the week, the distributor, Main Line Records, was getting calls left and right, and Ewart Abner was calling me from Chicago.

"Geator, you're right," Abner said. "It's a hit. Tell Crewe to call me. I want to make a deal."

The rest was music history. Frankie Valli, Bob Gaudio, Nick Massi, and Tommy DeVito were on their way to stardom as the Four Seasons. "Sherry" reached #1 on all the charts, and the Four Seasons became the first white group to record on Vee-Jay Records. (When I was offered "points" for "Sherry," which is generally regarded as a completely legitimate form of compensation—even by the government—I turned them down. It wasn't about the money; it was about the music.)

When the listeners couldn't find the oldies that I played, they would tell us when they called in a dedication. "We can't find 'Lost Love' by the Superiors, 'Long Lonely Nights' by Lee Andrews and the Hearts, 'Paper Castles' by Frankie Lymon, 'Guided Missiles' by the Cuff Links, or 'They Say' by the Rainbows."

The reason was simple: there wasn't a single record store in Philadelphia that stocked the oldies that I was playing. Nat and I discussed the situation with Jerry Greene and Jared Weinstein. After working for "Slim" Rose at Time Square Records in New York, they had approached me when I first played oldies on WCAM. They wanted to open up a record store just like Slim's in Philadelphia. At that time, I was the only guy playing strictly oldies in the Philadelphia market. While looking for a commercial property and commuting back and forth from New York, Jerry and Jared would sleep on my living room floor at 23rd and Morris. They had become sponsors for my show on WCAM. They weren't familiar with Philadelphia, so I helped them find a retail location at 1005 Chestnut Street. The store was called the Record Museum.

Now that I was back on WCAM, it was obvious that the Record Museum could provide my listening audience with the perfect place to buy the records I was playing. From that point on, Nat and I had a financial interest in the store, and on Saturdays, I would make an appearance. The kids started to congregate there, and sales went through the roof. Eventually, the Record Museum grew into a chain of more than twenty locations.

Jerry and Jared also owned Lost Nite Records, a reissue label that specialized in hard-to-find doo-wop and R&B titles like "There's a Moon Out Tonight" by the Capris. Nat and I formed a business relationship with them on that, too, and Lost Nite went on to become an important part of my career.

Promotion men and independent producers from all over the country were coming to see me at 2724 Mifflin Street. They wanted to play their new product for me and knew they could catch me when I was taping my show. I loved to watch their reactions. I could tell whether or not they were sincere about the music I was playing just from the look on their face.

One of the producers was Huey Meaux. He had just cut a record called "You'll Lose a Good Thing" with Barbara Lynn, a singer from New Orleans. When I heard the demo, I flipped and called Harry

Finfer, who was still involved with Harold Lipsius at Jamie-Guyden. Jamie-Guyden picked it up and it became a national hit.

Another time, an independent promotion guy named Danny Driscoll came over. He was promoting for three or four different labels and played me a song on Co-Ed Records by the Duprees, a new group out of Jersey City. They had re-cut "You Belong to Me" by Jo Stafford with a Glenn Miller-type arrangement and street corner harmony. I could remember lying in my bunk at summer camp in 1952 and listening to the original on my transistor radio. It knocked me out to hear what the Duprees did with it, and from the moment I played it, it became an instant hit. (The Duprees had a couple of "B" sides that I popularized in the Philadelphia area—"Take Me As I Am," which was the "B" side of "You Belong to Me," and "Love Eyes," which was the "B" side of "Have You Heard," a song that Joni James also recorded. These two songs—and many others—added to my reputation as a disc jockey who consistently played the flip sides.)

It was at about the same time that a young record promoter named Freddy DeMann knocked on my door. He was working for Jerry Blaine, the owner of Jubilee Records. Blaine had been a musician and bandleader and went into the record business in the late 1940s. He also had a number of subsidiary labels, including Josie, which had hits with the Cadillacs. When Freddy came to see me, he played three or four songs that I didn't like. One of them was okay—"Snap Your Fingers" by Joe Henderson. And then he pulled out "I Love You" by the Volumes. Blaine had released it on the Chex label, and it was Freddy's last shot.

"Freddy," I said, "this is a hit."

"Yeah, but I don't have any money on this record."

"I don't take money."

"If I don't get any of these records played, I'm gonna lose my job."

"Freddy," I said, "go back to New York."

After Freddy left, I played his record, and just like "Don't Make Me Over," "Twist and Shout," "He's So Fine," and all of the others, it busted wide open. Again, the kids were calling the stores, and the stores were calling the distributors.

A week later, Freddy called me and said, "You made me a hero. That was the last record in the world they thought I could promote. They thought I might be able to get some airplay for Joe Henderson or one of the other artists, but the Volumes were a lost cause."

Blaine had called Freddy into his office and said, "How the fuck did you get Blavat to play the record without any money?"

"Geator loved the fucking record," Freddy told him.

From that moment on, Freddy and I became close friends. Even if he didn't have any records that I liked, we would have dinner together whenever he was in town, and we would stay in touch throughout the various stages of our careers. (Later, Freddy moved to the West Coast, married a wonderful girl named Candy, and went on to manage some of the greatest names in show business, including Michael Jackson, Madonna, and Lionel Richie.)

As the summer wound down, Dick Clark suggested that I cut a record with Kal Mann and Bernie Lowe. Dick remembered a song called "Back to School" by Timmy Rogers. Bernie and Kal had written it. After changing the title to "Back to School (One More Time)," I released my first single on the Favor label, and it was distributed by Cameo-Parkway. The label was aptly named, since Bernie released the record as a favor to Dick Clark.

In September 1962, I appeared on *Bandstand*, and "Back to School (One More Time)" became a local hit with national recognition. As it climbed the local charts, I thought back to my conversation with Nat Segall years before, when I told him that I wanted to be a singer. My version of "Back to School" started like this:

"Yon teenagers gather round
Hark to the sound I'm puttin' down
I got real sad news for you
Your vacation days are through."

One night, I was taping a show at 2724 Mifflin Street when Alex Martinelli came down to my studio. Alex had become my brother-in-law by marrying Phyllis Scotese, and I had just left him hours before when we did a record hop. I was shocked to see him.

"Yo, Alex. What's up? It's after midnight!"

He looked worried, and I could tell that he didn't want to interrupt my taping. I stopped what I was doing and said, "What's the problem?"

"It's your father."

"What do you mean my father?"

"He got shot in the leg."

"Where's he at?"

"Mount Sinai Hospital."

That was the hospital I was born in at 5th and Reed.

I turned the equipment off and said, "Let's go."

On the way to the hospital, I asked Alex which leg my father got shot in—the good one or the bad one.

"The bad one," Alex said.

When we arrived in the emergency room, one of the orderlies had my father on a stretcher. He was wheeling him up the hall. When the orderly saw me, he stopped. As usual, my father had a stogie in his mouth, and he winked at me.

"Are you okay?"

"I'm fine."

I turned to the orderly. "Where are you taking him?"

"He's being admitted."

I walked alongside as the orderly wheeled my father up the hall. Before we got to the elevator, an old man came toward us. He had a hospital gown flapping open in the back, and he was carrying a urine bag on a metal pole. Suddenly, the old man saw my father and they started talking to each other in Yiddish. Whatever they were saying caused the old man to become overjoyed and to stare at me as though I was a long lost son.

"*Boychikluh!*" he cried, as he lurched forward to embrace me. He didn't realize it, but he dropped the urine bag, spreading a yellow puddle on the floor. The old man wrapped his arms around me, and before I knew it, he kissed me on the cheek, shook his head in amazement, and walked away, muttering to himself in Yiddish.

"Dad, what was that all about?"

My father laughed. "That's the *mohel* who circumcised you when you were born."

My father had been at the 9M Bar when someone tried to rob his friend, Fibbles, the bartender. Before Fibbles could react, my father jumped over the bar and wrestled the guy to the floor. That's when the gun went off and shot my father in the leg. As they got my father situated in the hospital room, he said, "At least they didn't shoot me in my good leg!" and we broke out laughing.

After they arrested the guy for armed robbery, the case never went to trial. I found out later that he paid my father a large sum of money not to testify. The guy never showed up in the neighborhood again.

As popular as I was, the backstabbers were right about one thing: I was appearing on small radio stations. In order to be accepted in the world of radio, you had to be in a major market, and as close as they were geographically, Philadelphia and Camden were worlds apart. Adding four stations by way of syndication—Trenton, Pottstown, Atlantic City, and New Brunswick—didn't change my status. Even Dick Clark, one of my biggest supporters, said the same thing: "You know, you've got to get into the Philadelphia market. Then you'll be considered major."

A day or two later, Nat and I decided to make our move. WIBG was out of the question, leaving WDAS and WHAT as the only two possibilities. WDAS was out because they were already successful with the disc jockeys they had.

"Billy Banks lives in my building," Nat said.

Together with his sister, Dolly, Billy Banks owned WHAT. He had earned a small fortune as a radio salesman for WIP, and now he was a man about town. He lived at the Park Towne Place apartments, and he liked to go out at night. Banks was a scotch drinker, and one night, I met him at Lou Mayo's joint, the Bellevue Court.

Although the meeting went well, Banks explained that he was leery of bringing me on. All of WHAT's disc jockeys were black, and their audience was predominantly black as well. Banks knew how hot I was, but he was afraid to take a shot.

When I told Dick Clark what happened, he said, "Let me call Dolly." Although Billy was older than Dolly, Dolly ran the station. Once Dick Clark got involved, Dolly agreed to meet with us.

"I'm impressed," she said. "Dick Clark called me personally. He said you'd be an asset to the station. We're gonna think about it."

Meanwhile, Nat and I started a full-court press on Billy. We took him out to dinner and drank with him at Mitchell's Steak House, Lou Tendler's, Arthur's, and the RDA Club, where everybody made a fuss over me because I was the Gimp's son. This impressed Billy. Just as I did with the priests, I picked up the tab. Billy enjoyed the way we were "schmoozing" him, but he and I genuinely hit it off. He started calling me in the afternoon and saying, "What are you doin' later?" At one point, I introduced Billy to Nick's Roast Beef at 20th and Jackson, and he wanted to go back. I called Nick DiSipio and said, "Look, I'm bringing Billy Banks down. I want you to make him feel like a star." Nick made Banks feel like the most important person in the bar, and Banks finally said to his sister, "Let's give Blavat a shot."

Although it was almost unheard of to be on two radio stations within a few miles of each other, I held that distinction when WHAT put me on the air in November, 1962. I was on from 8 to 10 p.m. on WHAT and 10 p.m. to midnight on WCAM. In order for me to make the drive from Philly to Camden for my 'CAM show, I would tape the first half-hour.

A curious thing happened after I was on WHAT for a couple of months. The station's ratings had gone way up, and for the first time, WHAT was competitive with WDAS at night. WDAS had owned the market, but now I was as popular as Georgie Woods. All of a sudden, WHAT was getting flak from the black community about having a white disc jockey, and some of the listeners threatened to picket the station. The next thing we knew, there were picketers outside, and Dolly and Billy suspected that 'DAS had organized them.

WHAT was planning an outdoor event in their parking lot—part picnic and part carnival—and they were expecting a large turnout among the black community. All of WHAT's disc jockeys were going to attend, and I told Dolly and Billy that I wanted to dance with the kids and mingle with as many of the protesters as possible. From the moment the block party began at 12 noon until it ended at six o'clock at night, I was doing my thing, introducing the other disc jockeys, dancing on stage, and circulating among the crowd. When it was over, I was drenched with sweat, and my problems with the black community were over. They embraced me as one of their own.

At the same time that I was on WHAT-AM, Sid Mark had a jazz show on WHAT-FM from Monday through Friday. On Fridays, he did a Sinatra show called *Fridays with Frank*. Sid was highly respected as one of radio's foremost experts on jazz. In order to get to his FM studio at night, you had to walk through the AM studio, which had a glass partition. Mark and his guests—who included Stan Kenton, Dizzy Gillespie, Thelonius Monk, and the comedian Lenny Bruce—used to watch me as I did my show. They couldn't get over how much I got into it. Nat Segall, who formerly owned the Downbeat jazz club, knew all of these artists. They had worked for him at one time or another. For a short period of time, besides managing me, Nat would become Sid Mark's manager, negotiating the deal for Sid to do his TV show, *The Mark of Jazz*.

Sid, who was one of the most gracious men in the business, became a lifelong friend. Years later, he asked if I could get tickets for a Madonna concert for his daughter. After I got the tickets from Freddy DeMann, I asked him why his daughter liked Madonna so much. He said, "When you first came on radio, there was nobody like you. It's the same with Madonna. The kids love her." I don't know about the Madonna comparison, but I certainly was different from other DJs.

Nat also handled bookings for Lenny Bruce, and I'd hang out with Bruce whenever he was in town. He was out of his mind, and one time he turned to me and said, "You know, man, you're just as crazy as I am." I really didn't know where he was coming from, but maybe he was right.

Seeing the success she was having with my show, Dolly Banks decided to challenge WDAS across the board, bringing in Maurice "Hot Rod" Hulbert from Baltimore. (Years before, Hulbert was the original "Ace from Outer Space," but lost his claim when Jocko Henderson improved upon the original.) Dolly installed Hot Rod in the 6 to 8 p.m. time slot. The results were disappointing. Not only was Hot Rod an older disc jockey, but he also had a drinking problem and lost his rhythm on the air. Many times he would slur his words. Unfortunately, Dolly fired him, and once he was gone, she expanded my show from 6 to 10 and gave me an additional hour from 10 to 11. As soon as the ratings came in, it was obvious that she had made the right move. We were now head to head with 'DAS and, from 6 to 8, two points ahead of them.

When one of their sisters died—and they were "sitting *shiva*" at Billy's apartment—Dolly asked if my mother would cook Italian food for them. My mother was happy to do it. After that, they didn't treat me like an employee—they treated me like a member of the family. Of course, my success had something to do with it.

Their nephew was Len Stevens. He had an ad agency, and like Dolly and Billy, he appreciated what I was doing for the station. Later, Stevens would go on to create the local television station Channel 17 and buy one of the first restaurant-discos, the Library on City Line Avenue. Dolly's husband was Shep Shapiro, a shoe salesman from Chicago who looked exactly like Prince Rainier, and that's what I called him.

I never got the connection of how Nat knew Billy so well, but it hit me when the family was sitting *shiva*. Billy's apartment, Dolly and Shep's apartment, and Nat's apartment were all designed by Dorothy Lerner. Dorothy's husband, Sam, owned the Celebrity Room. Nat booked acts for the Celebrity Room, and he introduced Billy and Dolly to Dorothy.

Now that I was fully established on WHAT, I realized that I didn't really need WCAM anymore. I requested a meeting with Bud Hibbs. He had always been honorable with me, and we had a great relationship. Bud wished me well. At that time, neither one of us realized that I would be back on WCAM years later, and that we would work together on WVLT Cruisin' 92.1.

Knowing the kids were about to go to bed during my extra hour from 10 to 11, I decided to do a different type of show than from 6 to 10. It would be an hour where I would play nothing but slow songs with a story line, with instrumental music in between. I would tell stories that related to my own experiences growing up, speaking directly to their hearts. I remembered what it was like to fall in love for the first time, and while playing an instrumental, I would tell the story and create the mood. I would enhance the story line of the song by sharing my own experiences, and by assuring them that, as painful as some of their experiences might be, it was all a part of growing up. It was about teenage love, and I called it *The Lovers Hour*. To heighten the effect, I again borrowed Father Nelson's technique, speaking in a tone that was different from the rest of my show.

By 10 o'clock, the kids were lying in bed listening to *The Lovers Hour*. It became the hottest portion of my show with songs like "Lover's Prayer" by the Clickettes, "Just Suppose" by Lee Andrews, "This Could Be the Night" by the Velours, "Heart's Desire" by the Avalons, "Let It Please Be You" by the Desires, and "In My Diary" by the Moonglows. When the kids fell asleep, their parents would come into their rooms and turn the radios off, and when they woke up the next morning, the radios were tuned to WHAT. For the first time in the station's history,

WHAT was ahead of WDAS in ratings.

The year 1962 was the most important year of my career. While radio was becoming homogenized, I played music that bucked all of the trends, and my "yon teens" proved that there was an audience for it. If it were up to the program directors who formatted Top 40 radio, black artists like Smokey Robinson and the Miracles, the Temptations, the Four Tops, James Brown, the Supremes, Stevie Wonder, and countless others would never have gotten a shot. Over the years, I have been recognized as one of the people who wouldn't allow a Top 40 mentality to destroy the record business; however, if I deserve any recognition at all for changing AM radio or altering the course of popular music, I didn't do it deliberately. The music came from my heart, not a research chart.

SEVEN: The TV Years

B illy Banks had a bar in his office. He would open it at the end of the day on Friday, and Dolly and the salespeople would join him. Sid Mark would be there also.

After taping the second half of my show at home, I would get to the station early and join them in Billy's office. Then I would go live from 6 to 8, pop in the tape, and get to Chez Vous by 9.

Everything changed on November 22, 1963. I was taping my show when Kilocycle Pete ran downstairs and told me that President Kennedy had been shot. I couldn't believe it.

I finished taping my show and headed to 'HAT. All of the radio stations had interrupted their programming. When I arrived, everyone was watching the events unfold on TV. You could hear a pin drop in Billy's office. Walter Cronkite was crying as he announced that President Kennedy had died in the hospital. The news coverage continued as Kennedy's body was taken back to Washington on Air Force One.

I went on at 6 o'clock and played music that I would ordinarily play on *The Lovers Hour*. I spoke as calmly as I could, informing the "yon teens" that we were canceling all of our record hops that weekend out of respect for a nation in mourning.

I left the station at 8 o'clock to meet Nat at 69th and Market. We stood outside Chez Vous as the kids arrived, informing the ones who hadn't heard my radio show that there wouldn't be a dance. I could see that they were disappointed, but I'm sure they understood. We stayed there till 10:30. That's how many kids we had to turn away.

That entire weekend, America watched the events leading up to President Kennedy's burial and the swearing in of Lyndon Baines Johnson as the 36th President of the United States. I never got into politics on the radio, and I would stay out of the political debate throughout the next decade as the Vietnam War raged on and college kids started to protest. My message came through in my music, and I believed, as I do today, that the most important thing for young people is education, along with respecting the American way of life and working hard to accomplish your goals.

The music world would also change drastically in 1963. When the "British Invasion" occurred, it altered radio play and popular music forever. At that time, I couldn't foresee what was about to take place, least of all the emergence of a drug culture.

When the Beatles arrived, they had an unmistakable gift for popular music. But when it came to rock and roll, they were lightweights. Even though they made an album called *Rubber Soul*, soul was exactly what they were missing. On the other hand, the Rolling Stones had a harder edge to them and a blacker sound, especially when they played the blues. It was no surprise that they weren't as popular as the Beatles.

The Beatles dominated radio play. Even WDAS was playing them. One day, Dolly came into my studio and said, "How come you don't play the Beatles?"

"Dolly, that's bubblegum music."

"What about your audience?"

"My kids are hip. They don't want the Beatles. They want the real deal."

My kids didn't want Herman's Hermits or Freddie and the Dreamers or the Dave Clark Five. Their music was superficial, and the kids saw through it. They wanted to hear "I Do" by the Marvelos, "She Tried to Kiss Me" by the Butlers, "Ladies' Man" by the Volcanoes, "Mixed Up, Shook Up Girl" by Patty and the Emblems, and "Heat Wave" by Martha and the Vandellas, a song that is associated with me to this day.

"I'll prove it to you." And I opened up my mike. "Yon teens, as you know, everybody's playing the Beatles. I'm going to play you one of their songs. If you like it, let me know."

When I played "I Want to Hold Your Hand," it was a shock to my audience. The phones lit up, and the decision was unanimous: "Don't play the Beatles!" Dolly was sitting with me. That was the end of the conversation.

For a long time, the British Invasion dominated the airwaves. Only the Beach Boys, the Four Seasons, and Motown held their own when the climate changed for American artists, but I refused to worry about it. I had the music I loved; I had my own following; and I was as confident as ever that my music was timeless. But when the British Invasion gave way to a counterculture—and more teenagers were getting high—that's when I took it personally. I knew how impressionable kids were, and what a disastrous effect it would have if their heroes glorified drugs.

I believed that a performer had an obligation to set the right example for his audience, and that music should entertain, not exploit. Because I had the same responsibility to my listeners, I continued to use the forum I had on the radio in the best way I knew how, and to reinforce my message in the personal contact I had with the kids at the record hops. I never "preached" to them, but I couldn't ignore what was happening around me, and I would never play a song that encouraged mindless rebellion or the use of drugs.

In the 50s, you had no astronauts, no Vietnam, and no need for the Geator. Wholesome types like Pat Boone and Dick Clark were fine then. But the 1960s were a hip teenage time. When a father bought his son a $95 suit, and the kid said, "I'm sorry, dad, it's not hip enough," I understood where the kid was coming from.

Around that time, Nat got a call from Morris Levy. We had known Morris from the days of the *Alan Freed Christmas Show*, when he and Jack Hook had persuaded Jocko to move his show to the Apollo Theator. Morris was aware of my popularity in the Philadelphia market and asked to meet with us. He had recently acquired the Rama, Gee, and Gone labels from George Goldner, after bailing Goldner out of gambling debts.

When Nat and I got to New York, Levy said, "You're the only guy in the country who's still playing Frankie Lymon."

Lymon's voice had gotten deeper, and his last few records had flopped, but my listeners loved his oldies. It just so happened that Morris owned all of the "masters." (George Goldner was one of the great innovators when it came to discovering and promoting artists. He had produced the Chantels, the Clefftones, Little Anthony and the Imperials, and Frankie Lymon and the Teenagers, and they were among the assets that changed hands when Goldner had to turn over his record labels to Morris.)

Morris said, "I want to come out with an album—*Jerry Blavat Presents Frankie Lymon's Greatest Hits*. Look over my catalog and pick out twelve songs that you can promote. I'm gonna give you a flat fee of

$2,500. I'll make the check to whoever you want."

After I picked the songs, the album went on to become one of the biggest sellers in the Philadelphia area. The cover had a picture of me getting into the Arco Go Patrol helicopter with Eddie Nixon, one of my dancers. (Levy released the album in other markets as well, dropping my name from the title. He was afraid that the other disc jockeys would-n't play it if my name were still attached.)

The success of *Jerry Blavat Presents Frankie Lymon's Greatest Hits* gave us the idea to create compilation albums of our own, release them on Lost Nite Records, and sell them exclusively at the Record Museum.

One night when I couldn't sleep, I went down to my studio and lis-tened to records. As I listened to slow songs, a thought came to me. *The Lovers Hour* is so big on radio, why don't I tape it as an album? Instead of speaking continuously like I did when I was on the air, I started and stopped the tape, collecting my thoughts in a deliberate way. I taped until four in the morning, and finally I was wiped out and went to bed.

When I woke up the next day, I listened to what I had done, and I couldn't believe how soulful it was. I called Nat, Jerry, and Jared and told them to come over. I played the tape for them, and they flipped. No one had ever done an album like that. The closest thing was Jackie Gleason's *Music for Young Lovers* on Capital Records, which had strictly instrumentals.

I released *For Lovers Only* in two volumes. In Volume I, I included a little-known instrumental by the Wendell Tracy Orchestra called "Who's to Know?" and in Volume II, I used the Clebanoff Strings' ver-sion of "By Love Possessed," which was the theme song for the *Late Late Show* in Philadelphia. ("By Love Possessed" was also used in a motion picture of the same name starring Lana Turner.)

Jerry and Jared took the actual tape that I made in my studio and mastered it to create Volume I. As a result, when you listen to "Just Suppose" and "Love Me Always," you can hear when I stopped and started the tape to adjust my story line. Despite the imperfections in the finished product, the album sold more than 25,000 copies.

Interestingly enough, when I played "By Love Possessed," the song became so popular that Joe Wissert brought it to Harold Lipsius' atten-tion. I had gotten Wissert a job with Harold at the Jamie-Guyden label. Needing a new release for a South Philadelphia group called the Four

J's, Harold recorded a version of "By Love Possessed" with lyrics by Elmer Bernstein, and it became a national hit. Later, we went on to produce *For Dancers Only* and *For Collectors Only*.

After we released *For Lovers Only*, the armed forces contacted us about entertaining the troops in Vietnam. A lot of the soldiers from Philadelphia had taken the album with them, and now servicemen from all over the United States were hearing it in their barracks and rec halls. I immediately agreed, and the United Service Organization (USO) started to put together a tour.

After the compilation albums took off, Nat and I approached other disc jockeys and did the same thing with them. We paid a flat fee of $2,500; they selected their favorite oldies; we obtained the rights. Because of my success, oldies shows were popping up in Philadelphia and other cities; eventually, Lost Nite released compilations by Georgie Woods, Joe Niagara, Jerry Stevens, Bill Wright, Sr., a Pittsburgh disc jockey named Terry Lee, and jocks in other markets. Like we did with the other albums, we sold these compilations exclusively at the Record Museum.

I would also call the record companies to find the oldies that I played on the air. One example was "Drinkin' Wine-Spo-Dee-O-Dee" by Larry Dale. It was released on Atlantic, so I called Jerry Wexler.

"Jerry, I wanna buy 'Drinkin' Wine.'"

Wexler said, "I don't even know if we have that. I'd have to check the warehouse. That was years ago. . . ." He called me back and said. "We have three hundred pieces in stock."

"Okay, I'll buy them for five cents a piece."

"They're collectin' dust," he said. "We'll send them to you."

After they pressed a certain amount of records, the companies would get the ones that didn't sell back from the record stores. But there wasn't really a market for them. I was able to get on the phone when the Record Museum needed an oldie and talk to Atlantic, Vee-Jay, Fire/Fury, and other labels and buy some of their "returns." We were buying up a lot of their oldest merchandise for pennies on a dollar, and the kids would go into the Record Museum and find oldies that no one else had.

Due to my success on radio, Ed Hurst invited me to bring some of my dancers and cohost a segment of *Summertime on the Pier*, which was televised from the Steel Pier in Atlantic City. We would do some of the latest dances—the Boogaloo, the South Street, the Stomp, and the Wagner Walk—and I would introduce some of the artists I featured on the radio. Ed's partner, Joe Grady, was no longer doing the show.

It was Dick Clark's sidekick, Charlie O'Donnell, who planted the seed for me to do my own TV show. Charlie was Dick's announcer and a big fan who used to join me when I did *The Geator's Den* at the Ice House. Dick was moving *Bandstand* to L.A., and Charlie was going with him. Dick invited his close friends and associates to a going-away party at the Venus Lounge, which was no longer a club but a catering operation with new ownership; I was there with Pattie and Nat, along with Dick and his wife, Loretta. In addition to Charlie and Jane O'Donnell, the other guests included Bernie and Roz Lowe, Kal and Esther Mann, Lew and Janice Klein, Bernie Bennick, and Harry Chipitz, who ran Cameo-Parkway for Lowe along with Dave Apple. (One of the new owners of the Venus Lounge was Pete Ierardi, who was married to Frankie Avalon's cousin.)

Charlie suggested that WFIL might be looking for a local show to replace *Bandstand*. Dick thought it was a great idea and called Lew Klein over. Lew was Dick's executive producer, but he wasn't moving to L.A. Dick suggested that Lew should go to one of my hops and see how popular I was first-hand. Lew agreed, and one night he showed up at Chez Vous. He couldn't believe the crowd and the way I danced on stage with the kids, and he told Nat to make a pilot.

Nat reached out to some people at Channel 10—Debbie Miller, who was a producer for some of their shows, along with Matt Robinson and Peter Duncan, who were writers for the *Gene London* and *Pixanne* shows, and a director named Bob Orlander, who also appeared as an actor on *Action in the Afternoon*, a local show that WCAU produced for the network. Debbie put it all together, and we picked up the tab, shooting the pilot at Channel 12, the same channel that Mitch Thomas had appeared on when he did a black version of *Bandstand*. (Channel 12 was based in Wilmington, but it had additional studios near Germantown Avenue in Philadelphia.)

In the original script, they had me going through a tunnel with the kids and coming out the other side to find a recording artist or a record. To me, it was square, but that's what they had written. Even though I didn't like the script, we made the pilot, and the only good thing about it was the dancing and how I identified with the kids.

We gave the pilot to Lew Klein during the holidays, and he sat on it for more than a month. By mid-January, we still hadn't heard anything, and I thought it was a dead issue. I wasn't taking it seriously because I knew that I was already on television with *Summertime on the Pier* and Ed Hurst's *Aquarama* show from South Philadelphia, which had replaced *Summertime on the Pier* after Labor Day. More importantly, I wasn't that impressed with the pilot. When it came right down to it, the delay didn't really bother me, but Nat kept saying that I needed my own TV show. He saw it as the next step in my career. As it turned out, he was right.

All of a sudden, at the beginning of February, Debbie Miller called Nat. The call surprised us. Word had gotten around Channel 10 that they had shot a pilot for Jerry Blavat. Bruce Bryant, the general manager, and Al Hollander, the program director, wanted to see it, and Debbie and her people showed it to them. "WCAU is interested in doing a Saturday afternoon show," Debbie said. "They'd like to set up a meeting." Although I didn't realize it, Bryant and Hollander were aware of my appearances on Ed Hurst's TV shows.

Nat called Harold Lipsius, who was handling all of my legal matters, and they met with 'CAU. Bryant and Hollander weren't really impressed with the pilot, but they liked Jerry Blavat. Once the general manager made the decision to develop a show around me, it was up to the program director to create the vehicle, so I was brought into a second meeting with Hollander. Bryant wasn't there.

Hollander was very respectful to me and attentive to my ideas about a dance show. I told him I didn't want to be behind a podium. I wanted to be able to dance on a riser with the kids around me. I wanted to have the artists on risers with the kids dancing around them. The artists would be on for the whole show, even when they were not performing, giving it the feel of a live house party. Hollander liked the idea.

There was really no need for a set to be made other than risers and lighting. I got with their lighting guy, Al Vanaman, who was terrific. We decided to use "cyc" lighting so the lights could stream down on the risers. When I would introduce an act, the lights would open up on them and then go dim, until they were dancing in silhouette.

Hollander liked everything I proposed. This was the first time that WCAU, a CBS-owned station, was going to do a rock and roll dance party. CBS was considered the upper echelon of the networks because of Bill Paley, and they really didn't have any teenage shows. They had Ed Sullivan, Jackie Gleason, and most of the other heavyweights, but they never really focused on teenagers. I believe that's why Al Hollander allowed me to produce the show. We signed a 13-week deal, and as far as 'CAU was concerned, if it worked, fine, if it didn't, they took a shot.

Al asked me, "What should we call this show?"

"Well, the kids are gonna be dancing to discs. The thing that excites them and motivates me is the beat and the music and the sound. Everything about this show has to revolve around the sound—the music, the guest stars, the mood that we create. Let's call it *The Discophonic Scene*. It's the world of the yon teen."

"*The Discophonic Scene*," Hollander said. "I like it."

Now I needed a theme song. There were hundreds of possibilities, but as soon as I remembered "Jam Up" by Tommy Ridgley, I knew that it was the perfect song to kick off the show. I had won a jitterbug contest by dancing to it at the Epiphany on Jackson Street in 1953. (Ridgley was one of the greatest musicians who ever came out of New Orleans. He had discovered Irma Thomas, who was seventeen at the time. Her hits included "Time Is on My Side," which the Rolling Stones covered a few years later.)

We opened up the show in silhouettes, with kids dancing on risers. After the first 16 bars, you heard, "Freeze! Don't dare leave that screen!" Then the music kicked in again and the announcer said, "This is *The Discophonic Scene*, the world of the yon teen. And here's the teenage leader, the teenage greeter, 'the Geator with the Heator, the Boss with the Hot Sauce,' Jerry Blavat!" And then the camera would zoom in on me, dancing on my podium, dressed not in a suit and tie but in a V-neck sweater, khaki pants, and chukka boots. Just like my radio show, the pacing never let up, and the music never stopped. (Our announcer was Gene Crane, a great talent on staff at WCAU and the voice of *The Late Late Show*. Crane had first appeared when WCAU produced the *Sealtest Big Top* show for the CBS network. Ed McMahon appeared on that show also.)

The Discophonic Scene was an instant success in March, 1965. It went on the air as a half-hour show from 2:30 to 3:00 on Saturday afternoons. WCAU picked up the cost of the talent. I coproduced it with them and was paid $500 a show. Even before I went on television, the hops were so crowded that kids were turned away, but now my following was bigger than ever. (The only thing I regretted about my deal with Channel 10 was the fact that I couldn't entertain the troops in Vietnam. When we went into production, I had to cancel the USO trip, and I arranged for Georgie Woods to go instead of me. When Georgie got back, he said, "I can't believe how many of those kids are listening to your album over there.")

From the very beginning, my experience on radio had taught me the importance of keeping advertisers happy. They fueled the entire machine, and when the advertisers were happy, the station was happy. In addition to recognizing the importance of producing effective spots, I found out that I was good at it, and it wasn't long before the advertisers started to gravitate toward me as a spokesman for their products.

On live television, most people read a teleprompter to do their commercials. All I ever asked for was a fact sheet with the main bullet points they wanted me to cover. The production assistant would give me a ten-second countdown and over the next sixty seconds I would ad-lib my way through every one of the bullet points and nail it every time. It was like I had a sixty-second timer in my head to go along with my instincts for advertising. I was uncomfortable with teleprompters in the first place. It felt dishonest to me to read someone else's words, and I wanted to look directly into the camera like I was looking my audience in the eye.

By the second week, I got a call from Frank Beasley, the general sales manager of 'CAU. "J.M. Korn and Son would like to set up a meeting," he said. "They want to discuss the possibility of sponsoring the show. They handle a new soft drink for Pepsi-Cola. It's called Mountain Dew." (Later, Beasley would go on to marry Jane Norman, the star of *Pixanne*.)

The president of the agency was Mel Korn. Frank Beasley and I met him in his office. Before talking about Mountain Dew, he said, "You know, I used to be in the record business. I put up the money for Al Alberts' first song, 'Tell Me Why.'" Not only had he backed Al Alberts, but he also loved to play the drums, and he had a drum set in his office.

"I love your show," he said.

Korn had cans of Pepsi-Cola and Mountain Dew on his desk. Mountain Dew was so new that it hadn't come out in bottles yet.

"I'm having a problem with Mountain Dew," he continued. "Other than Harold Honickman, none of the bottlers want to carry it." Honickman was a friend of Korn's, and he was carrying Mountain Dew as a favor.

"How would you introduce it into this market?" Korn asked. "It's completely unknown."

"Let me taste it."

"It's got a lot of sugar."

He wasn't kidding about the sugar. As soon as I tasted it, I made a face. "Whoa! It's too sweet!" But something clicked in my mind. "I got it. The kids will be up in the stands. I'll sit with them and we'll all have cans of Mountain Dew. We'll give 'em straw hats and corncob pipes, and we'll taste the Mountain Dew together. As soon as we taste it, we'll all react at the same time. 'Yahoooo, Mountain Dew, it's good for *you*!'"

Korn was staring at me. He was already excited. "Then what?"

"I'll say, 'Kids, make sure you go out and get your Mountain Dew. It's a brand-new soft drink, and yahoooo, it's just for you!'"

That was all it took. Korn took the idea to Pepsi, and they bought a 15-minute block of the show. They agreed to sponsor us for six weeks, but as soon as we put it on the air, every candy store in the tri-state area was getting calls for Mountain Dew. When they saw what happened, the other bottlers picked up the product, and Pepsi signed a one-year contract. The response was amazing, and we produced a compilation album called *For Yon Teenagers Only* exclusively for Mountain Dew.

Two weeks later, Frank Beasley called me again. "Harry Egbert wants to meet with you. He saw what you did for Mountain Dew."

Egbert was the account executive that handled Lit Brothers, a chain of eleven department stores in Philadelphia, Morrisville, Willow Grove, and other locations. Lit Brothers was known as a lower-priced alternative to Gimbels, John Wanamaker, and Strawbridge and Clothier. Their shoppers tended to be older, and the agency wanted help in tapping into a younger market. Beasley and I met with them, and I said, "Why should my yon teens go to a department store like Lit Brothers when they can shop in the neighborhood? Germantown Avenue, Frankford

Avenue, Passyunk Avenue. . . . The kids can stay in the neighborhood and still get the latest styles. You have to motivate 'em to go to a depart-ment store."

The agency set up a meeting with Lit Brothers at 8th and Market. Mountain Dew had a 15-minute block of our show, and the station only had 15 more minutes to sell.

I met with Bernard Litvak, the president of Lit Brothers, and we walked around the store together. The buyers were doing a good job, but the clothing was all spread out. They had suits on the third floor, T-shirts on the fourth, and dungarees on the seventh.

I said, "I like what you have. Why don't you create a style shop with all the merchandise in one place? You can call it the Discophonic Style Shop of Lit Brothers, where an entire floor is devoted to the latest styles. You can divide the floor in half—one side for the guys and one for the girls. I can say, 'Yon teens, if you're going to buy, take a tip from Geator and go to the Discophonic Style Shop at Lit's, where they handle all your clothing needs.'"

Litvak seemed impressed. We left the meeting, and a day or two later, Beasley said, "They love your idea. They're gonna try it at three of their stores—8th and Market, South Philly, and the Northeast. They're gonna buy 15 minutes of the show. They'll have opening and closing billboards, just like Mountain Dew. We'll build a set that will resemble the Discophonic Style Shops, and that's where you'll do the commer-cials."

Eventually, Lit Brothers converted all eleven of their stores to Discophonic Style Shops. I supported the conversions with personal appearances, and the concept grew from there. Before long, young Lit Brothers customers were getting membership cards, "Lit-Teen" charge accounts, Geator pins, Geator book covers, and something called a "Geator Guide" that called attention to weekly specials. Not only did the Discophonic Style Shops take off, but Mountain Dew was the #1 soft drink in Philadelphia during the summer of 1965. (During the same time period, we recorded a song called "The Discophonic Walk," which was one of the dances we did on the show. It became a local hit.)

The ad agency came up with another tie-in to what I was doing on radio and television, starting a modeling school at Lit Brothers. During some of my personal appearances, I served as a judge in the selection of the "Discophonic models." The majority of my personal appearances were mobbed, and the police were often called in for crowd control. The whole thing happened in a matter of two months, a period in which we changed the entire image of Lit Brothers. (A woman named Pat Canfield headed the modeling school at Lit Brothers, and years later, I was shocked to learn that she had become a secretary for Hosni Mubarek, the president of Egypt.)

Because we were riding high with the personal appearances, the agency came up with the idea of my writing a weekly column in the *Philadelphia Daily News*. I called it *Teen Notes* and took to writing it in the afternoon before I taped the TV show. The Marriott was right across the street from Channel 10 on City Line Avenue. They had a patio, and in nicer weather, I would sit outside and write. I enjoyed doing the column because it was something different for me, it fit right in with the Geator persona, and it gave me another forum to influence kids in a positive way.

Although the *Teen Notes* column was actually a paid advertisement for Lit Brothers—and I devoted a certain amount of space to their lines of clothing and my personal appearances—they gave me all the leeway I needed to speak to the kids directly, spread the word about the charities I was involved with, and encourage kids to volunteer. The charitable efforts included Unicef, the Rock Jamboree, "Fifty Days of Fun," the Hero Scholarship Thrill Show, and the "Happiness Edition" of the *Philadelphia Inquirer* on "Old Newsboys Day," which benefitted handicapped children. A lot of my teenage readers donated their time and energy to the charities, became candy stripers at local hospitals, or found other ways to volunteer. (As host of a segment of the Thrill Show, I would bring in the Four Tops, the Orlons, the Intruders, and other artists.)

Based on our success with Mountain Dew, Pepsi decided to buy an entire half hour of our show as we entered our second year. Their new advertising campaign was aimed at "The Now Generation." At the time, a guy named Warren Weiner was working for Mel Korn, and he was assigned to the Pepsi account.

In order to support the campaign, they wanted me to do a promotion with the actress Joan Crawford, who was married to Alfred Steele, the president of Pepsi. Crawford was 61 at that point, but I remembered the crush I had on her as a child. She looked so much like my mother.

The filming took place at the Chalfont Haddon Hotel in Atlantic City, which is now the Resorts International Casino. When I walked into the room, I joined a small camera crew, a director, and the people from the ad agency, including Mel Korn and Warren Weiner. Joan Crawford arrived a few minutes later. Korn made the introductions.

"Ms. Crawford, this is Jerry Blavat. He does a television show in Philadelphia. He's our new spokesman for Pepsi-Cola."

Crawford extended her hand. "Hello, young man."

Before she could say another word, I said, "Miss Crawford, I love you."

She looked up in amazement. "You do?"

"Yep. I know everything about you."

"A young man like you?"

"You were a Ziegfeld dancer, you worked with Clark Gable, and you were married to Franchot Tone," I said. "And I remember that you won an Academy Award for *Mildred Pierce*. You were too sick to make it to the ceremony, so they gave you the award in bed."

She laughed. "But you forgot that my first husband was Douglas Fairbanks Jr."

She was right. I had forgotten about that, and later, I found out that she had married Fairbanks at St. Malachy's Catholic Church, the actors' chapel that I had visited when I was road managing Danny and the Juniors.

"How do you know all that?" she asked.

"You were always one of my mother's favorite actresses, and my mother looked so much like you."

While Crawford and I were talking, the director was getting impatient. "Miss Crawford," he said, "we have to do the spot." He was polite about it, but it didn't do any good.

"No," she said, "we'll get to the spot later. We're talking."

After Crawford and I talked for more than an hour, we taped the spot in less than ten minutes. Later, Korn, Weiner, and I had dinner with Crawford and her personal assistant, a large Hungarian woman who Crawford affectionately called "Mama."

Even though television was exciting to me, radio was my first love, and nothing could replace the feeling of being behind a microphone, playing music, and forging a connection with my listeners. The listeners were faceless, but I knew they were there. .

The radio shows also gave me an opportunity to take more chances than television, and to play a lot more music. After all, I was on television for one hour per week, I was on radio for 25 or 30. (Pepsi's decision to buy an entire half-hour had enabled us to expand the show.)

On a typical Friday, I would write the column for the *Daily News* at lunchtime, tape the television show in the afternoon, do a record hop at night, and return to WCAU to edit the show at three in the morning. There was no other way to do it since the show was aired on Saturdays. Occasionally, I would have more than one record hop on a Friday night, and that's where the Go Patrol helicopter came in. It would take me from Chez Vous on 69th Street to the Concord Ballroom in the Far Northeast. In addition, I had to make sure that all of my taping was done for WHAT and the other stations I was appearing on. Although Dolly Banks didn't like it when I taped my show, my ratings kept the advertisers happy.

The Friday night editing sessions turned into a good time because I would bring a case of beer for the guys in the editing room and take them out for breakfast at the Marriott afterward. A television show is only as good as the talent associated with it, and I worked with some of the best people around. In addition to Al Vanaman, I had a sound guy named Dave Bova, a cameraman named Phil Carrol, and a number of technicians who brought a high level of professionalism to the show.

Writing the television show was a labor of love, and so was booking the guests, although both of these tasks were time-consuming. My guests included a mixture of local performers and national recording artists like Sammy Davis Jr., Little Richard, Fats Domino, the Ronettes, the Clara Ward Singers, the Supremes, the Four Tops, and James Brown, who blew the kids away by doing a routine with his cape. (He threw off the cape at just the right moment in "Please, Please, Please," and one of the Fabulous Flames put it back on his shoulders, only to have him throw it off again.)

Stevie Wonder made an appearance on my show, and this time, I was ready for the fact that he was blind. When I offered to take him back to his dressing room, he was too proud to accept, and he ended up bumping into one of the cameras. Fortunately, he wasn't hurt.

By now, Nat and I had taken an office together at 1920 Chestnut Street. In addition to handling my money, scheduling my record hops, and coordinating my personal appearances, he was still booking his other clients. At that point, we were busier than ever, and we hired a girl named Trish Laden to work for us part-time. Trish was into the British thing, but also my thing, and she and her girlfriend Cheryl went to my dances. They were magnificent-looking, extremely bright, and wise beyond their years. They almost looked like sisters, and it was hard to believe they were only eighteen.

When the Rolling Stones came out with "Satisfaction" in May 1965, I heard from their distributor. "How would you like to interview them from London?" Whether I liked the Stones or not, Dolly Banks would have had a fit if I turned the interview down, so I immediately agreed. As soon as she heard about it, Trish Laden insisted on accompanying me to the station; though I have no idea how she did it, she ended up going to England and having an affair with Mick Jagger. Not to be out-done, Cheryl accompanied Trish and had a brief relationship with George Harrison.

Family, friends, and people in the industry were always stopping by, including Lou Rawls, Dionne Warwick, Marvin Gaye, and Berry Gordy; for the past few years, we would host an open house party that started on Christmas Eve and lasted until New Year's Day. I would order Italian pastries from 9th Street and ribs from Bea Bea's Lawnside Barbecue on South. One year, on Christmas Eve, we had so many people at the party that we were running out of food.

I sent my father over to Bea Bea's to pick up more ribs. He took one of his friends with him. After an hour and a half, they still weren't back, and we hardly had any food left. By now, I was worried about my father. When I called Bea Bea's to see if he had picked up the food, no one answered the phone. The next thing I knew, my father walked in the door with his friend. They had the ribs, but my father's shirt was cov-ered with barbecue sauce. As it turned out, there was a shootout in front of the restaurant and my father got caught in the crossfire. He ran down South Street—limping on his bad leg—and he tripped before he got to his car.

Our last party had gone off without a hitch, but instead of running out of food, we ran out of room. The first floor of our house was as crowded as one of my record hops. Now that Pattie was pregnant with Deserie, the house at 2724 Mifflin Street was definitely too small.

Not only was Nat moving up in the world by getting a bigger office, but Pattie and I were also making changes, too.

Harold Lipsius lived on Sherwood Road, a beautiful street that was right off City Line Avenue. This was known as the Overbook section of Philadelphia. One day, he told me that he had seen a house that we might like. It was at 5859 Overbrook Avenue, and a lawyer named Ben Abrams was looking to sell it.

In those days, Pattie usually went along with my thinking, but when we pulled into the driveway, it was love at first sight for both of us. The house was enormous. It had 22 rooms, and every one of them was over-sized, including the foyer, kitchen, and dining room. The backyard was huge also. A fence separated it from the other properties. The front lawn had magnificent shrubbery and a Japanese cherry blossom tree that changed colors with the season. The bark on that tree was incredible. It reminded me of the kind of bark that Native Americans used to make their canoes.

When I found out that Cardinal Krol—the highest-ranking official in the Archdiocese of Philadelphia—lived next door, it was almost like the man upstairs was giving his blessing. It made me realize how far I had come from my humble origins, my Catholic School education, and my father's dubious influence. I called Harold Lipsius and said that we wanted the house.

I don't know how he did it, but Harold talked Ben Abrams into selling the house for $50,000. I would have paid $100,000, that's how much we loved it. After the sale was completed, I installed a bar and swimming pool in the back, and a friend named Lenny Paisano helped me build cabanas like I had seen at the Fontainebleau. Little by little, the house on Overbrook Avenue became my castle, my palace, and the place I went to when I had to get away from it all.

As it turned out, Cardinal Krol was a golfer, and he had an eight-hole golf course on his property. One morning, I noticed four or five golf balls floating in my pool, so I rang his buzzer. The Cardinal's residence was even larger than mine, and a group of cloistered nuns was assigned to him. One of the nuns answered the door, asked me to wait in the foyer, and brought Cardinal Krol to me.

"Hello, Your Eminence."

"You're Jerry Blavat!"

"Yes, I'm your neighbor." And I showed him the golf balls. "I think these belong to you."

Cardinal Krol laughed. "Would you like to come in?"

"I can't, Your Eminence. But I'm honored to meet you."

Cardinal Krol and I became friendly, and one day he called on the phone. "You have a pool over there, don't you? Would you mind if the sisters come over for a swim?"

"I don't mind at all."

"Bear in mind that they're cloistered."

That meant that no one could lay eyes on them in their bathing suits—not even Pattie.

"Nobody is to be there," he continued.

"I understand completely. They can change in one of the cabanas."

By the time the nuns arrived, Pattie and the girls had cleared out of the house, and I had laid out a meal for the sisters on our dining room table. I ordered sandwiches from Lenny's on 54th Street and Jim's Steaks on Haverford Avenue, and had bottles of Pepsi for the sisters as well. When Pattie got back to the house at three o'clock, all of the sandwiches had been eaten, the sodas were gone, and the place was—you guessed it—immaculate.

By the time we moved to Overbrook Avenue, my mother accepted Pattie to some extent. She never treated her warmly, but she wasn't disrespectful either. Although she and Matty Gunnella visited us frequently, they never came over when Pattie's family was around. Something about them rubbed my mother the wrong way, and that's where she drew the line.

Our house was always open to family and friends, and my mother did a lot of the cooking when she was there. I loved to cook, also. Our kitchen and dining room were big enough, and it felt good to see people enjoying themselves. That's the way my grandparents did it in South Philadelphia. We often gathered in my basement, which my father nicknamed "the rathskeller." (He got the name from an old Jewish haunt that the racket guys hung out at on Spruce Street.)

One day, I invited some of my coworkers from Channel 10 over for crabs and spaghetti, including my director, some of the camera guys,

Tom Brooksheir, John Facenda, and others. Brooksheir was a retired football player who did the sports on 'CAU, and Facenda was the dean of late-night broadcasters on Philadelphia radio, one of the city's most trusted television news anchors for more than two decades, and the so-called "Voice of God" on NFL Films. Unlike Bobby Darin, it was obvious that Facenda wore a hairpiece.

That night, a WIBG disc jockey named Frank X. Feller crashed the party. Feller had been drinking, and when he saw Facenda, he walked over to him unsteadily. Instead of shaking hands with Facenda, Feller placed his hand on top of Facenda's head and started to babble. Facenda, in that magnificent voice, said, "Would you kindly remove your hand from my head?" His voice had never sounded better, and you could hear a pin drop. At that point, I escorted Feller out of the party and never invited him back.

Whenever I wrote the *Daily News* column on the patio of the Marriott, people would come up to me and say hello. They recognized me from the television show and knew me from around town. One day, a guy in a suit approached me.

"How come everybody knows you?" he asked.

"I do a TV show called *The Discophonic Scene*. My name's Jerry Blavat." And I snapped my fingers and did a few seconds of my rap. "I'm the Geator with the Heator, the Boss with the Hot Sauce, the rebel jock who rocks the ol' tick tock."

"I've got a meeting at Channel 10," he said. "I'm a sales rep for Warner Brothers Seven Arts. I represent their syndicated shows." He extended his hand and we shook. "My name's Al Silverman."

"I'm taping this afternoon. Why don't you stop by?"

Channel 10 had set me up with an office on the balcony. It had a desk, a chair, and a phone, which was all I really needed to work on the scripts and book the acts. Before the guests would arrive, I would go down to the set, rehearse, and do a sound check. The songs were performed without lip-synching, so the sound check was important.

Unbeknownst to me, Silverman was up in the booth when I taped the show that day, and he flipped over what he saw. When I was finished taping, Al Hollander called me into his office. Bob Orlander, the director, was sitting with him. I could tell that they were excited.

"Silverman asked for a copy of the show," Hollander said. "He wants to take it back to New York."

"They're interested in syndicating the show," Orlander followed.

A few days later, Silverman set up a meeting at Warner Brothers Seven Arts, and I took the train up to New York, bringing a copy of the show with me. When I arrived, they took me into a room with a huge conference table and leather chairs. Silverman was there with six or seven other reps. Their boss, Robert Rich, was sitting at the head of the table. He was the executive vice president of the syndication division.

"Before we watch this," Rich said, "why don't you tell us about the show?"

For some reason, I wasn't nervous, even though a lot was riding on my answer. I treated it like I was doing a commercial for one of my advertisers, only this time, the product was me.

"This isn't like any other show in America, because the host doesn't stand on a platform. He's all over the place, dancing with the kids and talking to them. And the artists aren't lip-synching like they do on Dick Clark's show. It's a live show."

By then, Rich was excited. He directed his assistant to start the tape. I sat back to watch it with them, and within seven or eight minutes, Rich said, "Turn it off. We want the show."

His assistant turned off the tape.

"We want to make a deal with you," Rich continued.

"I can't make a deal," I said. "You gotta talk to WCAU."

Things moved quickly after that. Nat Segall and Harold Lipsius worked things out with WCAU, and WCAU came to an agreement with Warner Brothers Seven Arts. Other than the below the line costs— which referred to the production expenses associated with each episode—Warner Brothers Seven Arts took care of everything, picking up the cost of syndication. Channel 10 owned the show, and it would continue to originate in Philadelphia. The syndication was scheduled to begin on April 1, 1966. At that point, *The Discophonic Scene* would appear in 42 markets throughout the United States, including New York, Chicago, and Los Angeles. The Geator was going national.

EIGHT: Pied Piper:
Going National

At first, the disc jockeys at WIBG tried to ignore me. Then they downplayed my impact. But once I went on television, they couldn't ignore me any more. They got 70% of the radio audience, but I was a major power with the kids.

It was a classic case of denial. The WIBG jocks got 200 kids at their record hops; I went around the corner and got 2,000. But even though the numbers didn't lie, they would never admit that I had a bigger following.

The RDA Club was jammed on Sunday nights. Their specialty was "sizzling steaks," and people brought their families. I used to see Joe Conway there, the general manager of WIBG. He was always cordial to me, but somewhat distant, because he knew how his disc jockeys felt about me. At bottom, though, he was a businessman.

One night, Conway walked over to my table. He was with Jim Crumlish, the District Attorney, whose kids attended my dances. "How would you like an air shift on WIBG?"

"It sounds great."

"Call me tomorrow."

You didn't talk business at the RDA, so I wasn't surprised that he cut the conversation short. When I called the next day, his secretary put me through right away. That was surprising. Usually, you could never get through to the general manager of a top-rated station.

"We would like to put you on at night after Hy Lit," he said.

Lit had switched from WDAS to WIBG. He was on from 7 to 11 p.m. Conway was offering me an 11 p.m. to 1 a.m. shift. Moving from WHAT to WIBG would have been a step up in terms of prestige, and I would reach a bigger audience.

"We'll give you $35,000 a year," Conway said. "And then we'll see how it goes. We might be able to switch you to a different time slot."

Normally, that would have been a generous offer, but I was already earning $135,000 a year.

"There's only one thing," Conway added. "We don't want the Geator. We want you to be Jerry Blavat."

"Joe, you gotta understand, I've been successful with that persona."

"How much do you make?"

"No disrespect, but I made over $135,000 last year. You want me to change all that and become a format jockey. Thank you for your offer. It was very kind of you, but I have to turn it down."

"But we're the number one station."

"That doesn't matter to me. The freedom to play my music and speak to my audience is more important. I'm already on television, and I'm syndicated. Being on WIBG isn't gonna enhance my career." And that was the end of my brief flirtation with a 50,000-watt, format radio station.

Needless to say, preparing for a television show takes a lot of time, and even though I was only on for an hour a week, I was going in to WCAU almost every day, listening to music, booking the guests, and making sure the guests got paid. This caused problems at WHAT. Dolly had always been irritated by the fact that I taped part of my show, and now I was taping even more. Once that happened, she started to give me some flak about being away from the station.

I was on the air from 6 to 11 p.m. on WHAT, but traffic was horrendous in the late afternoon. I had to get to the station by 4:30 in order to be on the air at 6:00, and that gave me even less time to plan the TV show. Still, I knew that the 6 to 8 time slot was important to Dolly, since it encompassed "drive time."

"Dolly," I said, "why don't I continue to do the show live from 6 to 8? You can put Sonny Hobson on after that."

Hobson was a young kid who hung around the studio and watched me work. He wanted to be a disc jockey, and I gave him the nickname "the Mighty Burner" and made him part of the show. After he developed a rap of his own, he was ready to be on the air by himself. I was still taping *The Lovers Hour* in my garage, and my entire shift would have been covered if Dolly agreed to let Hobson replace me for two hours a night.

As it turned out, Dolly tried it for a while, and Hobson held his own from 8 to 10; but when the syndication of my TV show picked up steam, I had to go to other markets to promote it. When we reached the point where I couldn't do 6 to 8 at all, it added fuel to the fire. (One of my trips included a convention in Chicago, where I appeared with Gypsy Rose Lee and Bob Eubanks, the host of *The Newlywed Game*. Warner Brothers Seven Arts was also syndicating their shows.)

In her quest to challenge WIBG and go after white advertisers, Dolly brought in a program director, George Wilson. It never made sense to me. Her competition was WDAS, not WIBG. Plus, Wilson was from the Midwest and didn't know the Philadelphia market.

Dolly told Wilson to leave me alone, but he still tried to tell me what to play, and that didn't work. Once he found out that he couldn't change me, he started to complain to Dolly. "Blavat's got the ratings," Dolly would say. "He knows what to play."

Wilson also had a problem with the fact that I wasn't coming in on Fridays. That was the day that I taped the TV show. He told Dolly that I was "ruining the station."

I told Dolly, "You're trying to format a black radio station with a white program director. Wilson's telling the black guys what to say and what to play. They know the market better than he does!"

I knew that the ratings were going to drop, and sure enough, they did. The WDAS disc jockeys had the freedom to play what they wanted; the WHAT jocks didn't. Wilson was changing a station that had already been successful, and Dolly didn't realize it until it was too late.

Finally, Dolly called me into her office and said, "Look, I'm not gonna suck hind tit to WCAU-TV. We gotta do something about the radio show."

I understood where Dolly was coming from, but by that point, WHAT was more trouble than it was worth. Now that she had given me an ultimatum, I called Nat Segall.

"Nat, do we really need WHAT?"

"I really don't think so."

I appreciated the opportunity that Dolly gave me. We had both benefitted from it, and it wasn't like I was leaving her high and dry. She still had my advertisers.

The next day, I sat down with Dolly and told her that it wasn't going to work. "We've been together a long time," I said. "We're like family.

But maybe we should go our separate ways." Dolly was shocked. She never thought that I would leave radio. While WHAT's ratings continued to decline, George Wilson started to make all kinds of side deals with the record companies. The jocks knew it, but Dolly didn't, and eventually she had to fire him.

Now that it was syndicated nationally, *The Discophonic Scene* was so hot that Nat got a call from Ken Greengrass, who managed Steve Lawrence and Eydie Gormé. Steve and Eydie had a national show on CBS, but they weren't getting the ratings. Ken was aware of my success, and he came up with an idea for me to do a portion of Steve and Eydie's show that featured the latest dances and hottest rock stars of the day. Ken had already proposed the idea to the network, and they loved it.

When I met with Ken in New York, he laid out the whole package and said, "There's one thing you have to understand. In order for me to get this done, I have to represent you."

I said, "Kenny, what am I gonna do with Nat?"

"This is network," he said. "Nat can handle you locally."

"I really don't know how to present this to Nat. We've been together a long time. We're making a lot of money. I don't know if I want to do that."

Greengrass was well-respected nationally. In addition to Steve and Eydie, he managed Florence Henderson, the New Christy Minstrels, Simon and Garfunkel, and many others. He was presenting me with a great opportunity, but the more I thought about it, the more uncomfortable I was. I had been with Nat since I was a kid; I was already syndicated; and I didn't really need it. More importantly, I didn't want to hurt Nat. So I passed on Ken Greengrass, Steve Lawrence, and Eydie Gormé.

Four months after ABC came out with a rock and roll show called *Shindig*, NBC countered with *Hullabaloo* and cut into ABC's ratings. Once that happened, Nat got a call from Lee Salomon, the head of the William Morris Agency in New York. For a short time, Salomon had been married to Mickey Marlowe, a local singer that Nat had managed in the 50s. One of Salomon's clients was Jack Good, the producer of *Shindig*. Good wanted to talk to me about hosting the show. After requesting a copy of *The Discophonic Scene*, Salomon set up a meeting at William Morris.

Nat attended the meeting, and from the outset, he rubbed Good the wrong way. Good was British. He was an Oxford or Cambridge kind of guy, and he thought that Nat was crude. After the meeting, Salomon asked Nat's permission for Good to follow up with me directly. Nat agreed.

When I followed up with Jack Good, he said, "You have a lot of potential here. We think we could work you into the show, and even though you're syndicated, this could be an important step in your career. But I don't think that's going to happen with your current representation. I found it very difficult to work with him." Essentially, he was echoing what Ken Greengrass had said, namely, "Nat can handle you locally."

As a former musician, old-time booking agent, and manager of artists in the 50s, Nat was more than capable of handling my record hops and personal appearances, but he lacked the savvy and sophistication to advise me on the kinds of national opportunities that were being presented to me. To a certain extent, I had started to look to Mel Korn for guidance in these matters, and Mel agreed that Nat was limited.

Because we were only discussing a six-minute segment, the *Steve and Eydie* show wouldn't have been that big of a deal, but the *Shindig* opportunity was huge and I didn't want to pass it up. At the same time, I had been with Nat forever; he had given me my first break in show business, and we had built an empire together. In the end, I just couldn't bring myself to hurt him, and I discontinued my talks with *Shindig*. I was content with Nat financially, and if I had become the host of Good's show I would have had to fly to Los Angeles once a week. Truthfully though, it was the representation issue that put a capper on *Shindig*.

I never really told Nat that Ken Greengrass wanted to represent me, and that Jack Good had been critical of him also. More and more, our relationship was strictly business. I wasn't seeing him as often socially, and he must have sensed that I was outgrowing him. In addition, Nat started to behave a little strangely. Even though he was friendly with his former wife Sherry, Nat had been divorced for a long time, and he was showing a lot of interest in teenage girls. He was taking them to the record hops and giving them money to get home. I was never sure how innocent it was, and to be honest, I didn't want to know. Nat was from an old show business world—not the teenage world that I had introduced him to. It was almost like "Dathan"—the name I had given him—gave him a new life.

Now that Warner Brothers Seven Arts was syndicating my show, it was broadcast in Houston, Texas, where my old friend Bob Horn was living. Bob was still going by the name of Bob Adams, but he was no longer in radio. He had started an advertising agency that covered the entire southwest. "Bob," I said, "I can finally repay you for what you did for me. I'm going to give you $500 a week to represent the show in Texas."

Bob was ecstatic about my offer. The $500 came out of my end, not Warner Brothers Seven Arts', and over the next four weeks—while Bob represented the show in Houston, Beaumont, Galveston, and Austin—I sent him a total of $2,000. I loved the man and was eternally grateful for what he had done.

Every week, I did a record hop at the Ritz Convention Hall in Chelsea, which was a section of Atlantic City. One week, we decided to televise the dance as part of my syndicated show. Frankie Valli and the Four Seasons were at Steel Pier and the Four Tops were at the Harlem Club, so both of these acts were able to appear with me at the Ritz.

As we were getting ready to tape, Nat walked over to me, and I could tell that he was upset.

"What's wrong?"

"I just got a call from Ann. Bob died."

Bob Horn was mowing the lawn when Ann and the kids went out to dinner without him. When they came back, he was slumped over with his head on the kitchen table. He had suffered a massive heart attack, brought on by heat stroke, and he died at the age of 50.

I was stunned. My show was starting in less than an hour, and there was no way I could cancel it and fly to Texas. "Nat, you gotta go down there. Take some money. Whatever they need, give it to them."

While Nat made his travel arrangements, I did the show as planned, calling Ann Horn the next day. Bob's finances had never recovered from the *Bandstand* fiasco and the lawsuits that followed. We sent $2,500 and helped give Bob a proper burial.

Next, Channel 6 made a play for my television show. Once they saw how successful the syndication was, they wanted to talk with us, and Mel Korn set up a meeting. We met with George Koehler, who was still the general manager of WFIL, and Tom Jones, the head of their TV syndication.

Channel 6 wanted to move my show to prime time on Saturday nights, opposite Jackie Gleason. Although I wouldn't move right away, it was going to happen eventually. The other advantage of switching to Channel 6 was the opportunity to broadcast in color. My show on Channel 10 was still in black and white. I liked the idea.

I went back to Bryant and Hollander, and said, "You guys have been great to me, but I have an opportunity to go prime time on Saturday nights. Triangle wants to pick up my syndication." Our original deal with Warner Brothers Seven Arts was about to expire.

Hollander told me that they were happy where the show was, and that they had no intention of changing it. "It's profitable the way it is. You've been supportive of the station from the very beginning, and we understand that this is an opportunity to further your career. We won't stand in your way."

I left Channel 10 on good terms, and went across the street to Channel 6. Instead of using "risers" like I had on Channel 10, Channel 6 built a brand-new set for my show, designing it like a teenage nightclub. For several weeks, they continued to broadcast it on Saturday afternoons, but after that, I was on from 7:30 to 8:30 on Saturday nights, opposite Jackie Gleason. The program was called *The Jerry Blavat Show*. (My producer was Joe Novenson, a former opera singer who was also a producer for *Bandstand*.)

Triangle Publications, which owned WFIL, the *Philadelphia Inquirer*, and the *Philadelphia Daily News*, promoted the show heavily, running full-page ads in both newspapers. They also used billboards. When it was all said and done, *The Jerry Blavat Show* got 70% of the television audience locally, soundly defeating *Jackie Gleason*. In Los Angeles, the show appeared on Sunday nights on KTLA and more than held its own, just like it did in New York, Kansas City, and the smaller stations in the outlying areas.

Dick Clark had started a tradition called the "Mother's Club." A group of guys would get together one night a month. Every month, we would go to a different house, throw in five dollars a piece, eat takeout food, and play blackjack. When Dick went to the West Coast, I continued the tradition at 5859 Overbrook Avenue. The only difference was that I had access to WFIL's film library, and we would watch a movie before we played cards. It wasn't always the same group of people, but the regulars included Nat, my father, Alex Martinelli, Jerry Green, Jared Weinstein, and Electronic Al; people from the record business like Kenny Gamble, Howie Michaels, Harry Chipitz, and Bernie Lowe; and promotion men like Buzz Curtis, Larry Cohen, Matty Singer, and others. We usually got together on Monday nights, and I would get steaks and hoagies from Jim's or Larry's. We had a pool table that Pattie had given me for one of my birthdays and I bought two "one-arm bandits" from Stan Harris Vending, so we always had something to do when we got together.

Howie Michaels was a friend from way back. He had danced at the RDA Club when Rita Scotese performed with the husband and wife team, Ray and Essie. Later, Howie was instrumental in getting an article written about me in *Philadelphia* magazine. More recently, he had discovered a "blue-eyed soul" group called the Soul Survivors and started to manage them. One night, I went to see them at a club at 13th and Locust. I thought they were amazing.

A week later, at a meeting of the "Mother's Club," Howie Michaels told Kenny Gamble about the Soul Survivors. Kenny was writing and producing with his partner, Leon Huff. "You should see this group," Michaels told him, and after Gamble went to see the Soul Survivors, he and Huff wrote a song called "Expressway to Your Heart." He recorded them on a new label we formed called Crimson Records, which was a subsidiary of Lost Nite.

When the Soul Survivors appeared on my TV show, "Expressway to Your Heart" busted wide open. Disc jockeys started to lay on the record. Orders came in from all over the region, and right off the get-go, we had a smash. I had the same arrangement with Crimson that I had with Lost Nite and the Record Museum, and I was getting royalties from the compilation albums. Nat was still handling the money.

Once management saw how well our Saturday night show was doing, Tom Jones sat down with George Koehler and Lew Klein. "You know," Jones said, "we should really consider putting him on five days a week." Koehler and Klein agreed with him, but their boss, Roger Clipp, the manager of the radio and TV division of Triangle Publications, resisted the idea, saying, "Yeah, it's popular, but if we put

Custer's Last Stand on, that would be popular, too." At the time, there was a lot of back-room politics going on at Channel 6. Clipp was getting up in years, and three people wanted his job: Jones, Koehler, and another guy named Bud Vaden, who was Clipp's second-in-command. Out of those three, Jones and Koehler were pushing the hardest for a five-day-a-week show, and they brought it up at every one of their staff meetings. Finally, Clipp gave them an opening.

As soon as their meeting ended, Jones called me and asked, "How fast can you do a pilot for a five-day-a-week show?"

"I don't know," I said. "Get me a cameraman."

"He doesn't want a *Bandstand* show. It's gotta be different."

"No problem."

I called Patti LaBelle of the Bluebells, and said, "I want you to meet me at the station tomorrow. I'm gonna make a presentation for a five-day-a-week show. It's not gonna be a *Bandstand* show. It's gonna have live performances with a house band, a rhythm section, and maybe some horns. It's gonna be like a teenage Johnny Carson show in the afternoon."

Nobody was doing anything like that. Patti loved the idea, and so did the Tymes, another local group, and they agreed to come to the station the next day. Once the guests were lined up, I spoke with the lighting guy and told him what I had in mind. When we shot the pilot for Roger Clipp, they brought the lights down low and I walked into an empty studio. Then a spotlight came up and I addressed Clipp directly. "Mr. Clipp, Jerry Blavat here. Let me tell you my idea for a five-day-a-week show, which I think would be sensational. As you know, we no longer have *Bandstand* in Philadelphia. I envision having kids in the audience and recording artists not just as guests, but also as cohosts for an entire week. Some dancing will be featured, just like it is on my Saturday night show. After the guests perform with my house band, the cohost and I will interview them. There isn't a show on television that gives the kids an up-close-and-personal look at their favorite stars, but this show will do that and more. It's gonna create excitement."

At that point in the pilot, I had Patti LaBelle and the Tymes perform, and Roger Clipp liked what he saw. Instead of *The Jerry Blavat Show* on Saturday nights, I went on the air with *Jerry's Place* in the 5:00 to 5:30 p.m. time slot Monday through Friday, right after the soap opera

Dark Shadows. Channel 6 built a ramp for me, and I would dance up the ramp on one foot while the kids chanted, "Go, Jerry, go!" The house band consisted of some of the best musicians in the city—guys like Buddy Savitt, Roy Straigis, Roland Chambers, and George Young—and the kids were writing in for tickets from all of the high schools, YMCAs, and every other youth group you could think of in the area.

In addition to Patti LaBelle, my cohosts included Jimmy Clanton, Bobby Vinton, Frankie Valli, Connie Francis, and many others. My guests were a "Who's Who" of the music industry, with names like James Brown, Aretha Franklin, Marvin Gaye, Sonny and Cher, Dion, the Everly Brothers, Chuck Berry, Little Richard, Jackie Wilson, and Gene Pitney, to name just a few. At least once in every show, I would go into the audience with a microphone, and the kids would ask the guest or cohost a question. Nobody else had done that, and the kids loved it.

At that time, Donnie Kirshner was working for Screen Gems-Columbia. He was putting together the music for *The Monkees*, a prime time show on ABC. My show was on Channel 6, an ABC affiliate. After the producers of *The Monkees* saw me on KTLA in Los Angeles, Kirshner called me.

"They want you to do an episode of *The Monkees*," he said.

The Monkees consisted of Peter Tork, Michael Nesmith, Micky Dolenz, and Davy Jones. Doing their TV show would be another step in my career, and I was excited about it. "Donnie, get me the script."

Columbia sent me the script, along with a first-class, round-trip ticket to L.A. They reserved a room for me at the Beverly Hills Hotel and sent a limo to pick me up at the airport. When I arrived, the driver said, "I gotta take you to wardrobe right away. They screwed up the shooting schedule. They're already in production, and they need you on the set."

When I got to wardrobe, they fitted me with the outfits that I was going to wear over the course of the day's shooting. While I was there, I fell in love with a magnificent tweed overcoat. It had a matching cape that unbuttoned from the rest of the coat. It looked like something the British would wear for horseback riding or a foxhunt. I tried it on, and it fit perfectly. I asked if the coat was part of my wardrobe, but I already knew the answer. It wasn't right for the part I was playing.

As soon as they took me to the sound stage, I heard the director yelling at his assistant. The director was Jim Frawley. A stand-in was on my "mark"—the spot on the sound stage where I was supposed to be—but they needed me to shoot the scene.

"Where's the disc jockey?" Frawley shouted.

"He's here," the assistant answered, hustling me over to Frawley.

"You know your lines?" Frawley asked.

"Yeah," I said. I had studied my lines on the plane—enough to ad-lib them anyway. The script called for me to play a disc jockey named Mr. Arnold.

"All right, let's run through the scene."

In my first scene, Davy Jones was dressed like a girl. "She" was supposed to be the disc jockey's love interest. Instead of following the script, I ad-libbed, but everything I did was consistent with the story line. At first, Frawley didn't know that I was ad-libbing, but when someone pointed it out to him, it didn't matter. He realized that the line I had ad-libbed was better than the one in the script.

I ended up improvising most of my lines. At one point, when Jones tried to keep up with an improvisation of his own, he called me "Mr. Blavat," and I said, "Don't call me Mr. Blavat. Call me Geator, Jerry to you. Never in my life have I, the Geator with the Heator, the Boss with the Hot Sauce, snapped over a fox like you!"

The episode was called "Some Like It Lukewarm," a takeoff on the old Marilyn Monroe comedy with Jack Lemmon and Tony Curtis. Dean Martin's daughter, Deana, appeared in the episode also, and it was shot in two days. When we were finished, Frawley told me that I was a natural. "You should think about getting an agent."

As I was about to leave the set, the wardrobe assistant walked over to me. She was holding the overcoat that I had admired the day before. Before I knew it, she gave it to me, and said, "It's a gift from the director." That's what I was wearing when I ran into Janis Joplin in the Atlanta airport on my way home. "I love that coat," Joplin said, so stoned she could barely stand up.

Whenever a movie studio produced a big-budget picture, they would contact the top-rated television hosts in all of the major markets and fly them out to interview the stars. The interviews would be taped on-site and shown locally to generate interest in the new release. MGM, Warner Brothers, and Columbia did this routinely, and the segments went something like this: "Hi, this is Jerry Blavat. I'm speaking to you from Las Vegas, where I'm about to say hello to Clint Eastwood, the star of *Where Eagles Dare.*" You would sit with the star for three or four minutes and tailor the interview to your local market, and then another television personality would replace you and do the same thing.

Richard Burton costarred in *Where Eagles Dare,* and I was supposed to interview him as well. When Sammy Davis Jr. found out, he said, "I'll meet you in Vegas." Sammy was friendly with Burton and Elizabeth Taylor, and arranged for the four of us to have dinner together. At the last minute, Sammy called and said that Burton hadn't made it to Vegas. "Meet me in L.A. instead. We'll have dinner with them there." Sammy was doing an episode of *The Mod Squad,* and he said, "Come on. I'll get you a guest appearance." The producer of *The Mod Squad* was Aaron Spelling, who was married to Carolyn Jones. Jones had starred with Frank Sinatra in *A Hole in the Head* and was a close friend of Sammy, but she is probably best known for playing Morticia in *The Addams Family.* (The other connection was Quincy Jones. Jones had produced albums for Sammy and Frank on Reprise Records, and was married to Peggy Lipton, the female lead on *The Mod Squad.*)

Within a month or two of appearing on *The Monkees,* I did a brief walk-on on *The Mod Squad.* Afterward, Sammy and I had dinner with Richard Burton and Elizabeth Taylor at the Beverly Hills Hotel. Burton and Taylor drank too much, and although it wasn't as intense as the fight they had in *Who's Afraid of Virginia Woolf?* they were both pretty soused and ornery. Burton left the table in the middle of the meal, and Taylor went back to her bungalow as soon as we were finished. I ended up spending the night at Sammy's home on Summit Drive before returning to Philadelphia.

When MGM re-released *Ben-Hur,* Channel 6 flew me to Miami to cover the world premiere at the Criterion Theater. The press party was held at the Fontainebleau—my old stomping grounds—and I was scheduled to interview Charlton Heston, Stephen Boyd, and the director William Wyler. The interviews took place by the pool, and this time, the TV hosts were allowed six minutes with each of the people they were interviewing.

I did my six minutes with William Wyler and Stephen Boyd, but by the time I interviewed Charlton Heston, I ran out of questions about

Ben-Hur.

"Mr. Heston," I said, "I know we're all here for *Ben-Hur*, but I've got to tell you, one of my all-time favorite pictures is *The Savage*." My uncle Jimmy had taken me to see *The Savage* when it first came out after my Confirmation.

Heston couldn't believe it. "I've got to tell you a story about that. It was the first time I ever rode bareback. The director was William Marshall."

I told him that I remembered the scene. "You were being chased by the Crow Indians."

Heston was amazed. "I was scared to death," he said. "I fell off the horse six times." He went on and on, and the director kept signaling me to end the interview. Just like I had with Joan Crawford, I had exceeded my time limit. Heston had the same reaction as Crawford. "I want to keep going with this young man!"

We wound up talking about his early days in Hollywood, and how he met Cecil B. DeMille, who directed him in *The Greatest Show on Earth* and *The Ten Commandments*. And then he told me about Orson Welles, who directed him and costarred in *A Touch of Evil*. We went on for half an hour, and when it was over, Heston said, "That's it for the day."

As he got up to leave, Heston turned to me and said, "What are you doing tonight?"

"Nothing. I'm here at the hotel."

"I'm having dinner with Wyler. Why don't you join us?"

We had dinner at the Fontainebleau. Heston drank Heineken, and when we were finished eating, he asked if I played tennis. I had never played tennis in my life, but I told him that I had.

"Meet me at the courts tomorrow morning at seven o'clock."

When I went down the next morning, I wasn't dressed in a tennis outfit. I was wearing shorts, a tee-shirt, and sandals. Heston, of course, was dressed for the part. His shirt, shorts, sneakers, and racket were all of professional quality, and he had a couple of tennis pros with him. WFIL provided a TV crew to record our "match."

The truth is, I was no match for Heston at all and failed to return a single one of his serves. He had me running back and forth from one side of the court to the other, with absolutely no chance of reaching the ball and hitting it over the net. After five or ten minutes, I never got one ball to him, and Heston broke up laughing and said, "Get some sleep. I'll see you at the premiere."

Since most of the interview had nothing to do with *Ben-Hur*, we only used a small portion of it on *Jerry's Place*, but our tennis match was one of the funniest things I ever saw, and we ran it in its entirety. Fortunately, MGM sent along clips of the press party, and we used them to promote the opening.

Occasionally, whenever I could, I would fly down to Puerto Rico to get away for a couple of days. One time, when I was at the Caribe Hilton, Donnie Kirshner reached out for me. He had left Screen Gems and was starting his own label. Kirshner had a distribution deal with RCA.

"'Expressway to Your Heart' is a smash in Philadelphia," he said. "I would like to put it out on my label. I'll give you twenty-five cents per royalty and $10,000 up front."

Twenty-five cents was a lot of money for a royalty, and the up front money was more than fair; however, the most attractive part of the proposition was getting national distribution from a giant like RCA. Crimson was a little cockamamie label without national distribution. Accepting Kirshner's proposal was a no-brainer—or so I thought.

"Don't worry about it," I said. "Let me talk to the guys."

When I got back, I met with Jerry, Jared, and Nat. I told them about Kirshner's offer, and said, "I think we should go with it." I couldn't believe it when they hesitated.

Jerry spoke up. "We don't need Kirshner. We're going to get our own distributors nationally."

I stared at him and turned to Nat. "Nat, you were in the record business with Sound and Teen. If you don't have a follow-up, you're not gonna get paid by the distributors. This is guaranteed money!"

Even though "Expressway" was a smash, it was impossible to know if there would ever be a follow-up hit. Without a follow-up, they would be a "one-hit wonder," and they wouldn't have any leverage. The whole idea was to tell the distributor, "If you don't pay me, I'm not gonna give you the next release. I'm gonna give it to your competitor."

"No," Nat said. "We're gonna build a label with these kids."

I called Kirshner and said, "Donnie, I'm sorry. I can't deliver. They want to distribute themselves."

"That's crazy!" he said. "You're not gonna get paid!"

"I'll tell you what. Keep it on Crimson, but let me distribute it nationally. I want to get involved producing the group."

When I brought that idea back to the guys, they passed on it, putting me in a bad position. Nat and I almost always agreed, but this was different. Looking back on it, this was the first time that cracks started to show in our relationship, and there would be a lot more in the days ahead.

At that point, I decided to give up my interest in Crimson, Lost Nite, and the Record Museum. "Guys," I said, "I think it's time for you to buy out my end."

"Are you crazy?" Jerry said. "You're making money!"

"It's not about that. I don't know if it's ego or what, but walking away from Kirshner's deal doesn't make any sense."

I kept waiting for Nat to say something, but he never did. He was siding with Jerry and Jared.

"Let's call David," I said, referring to David Steinberg, the attorney who represented us. "Give me $25,000 for my end. You don't have to pay me right away."

Until then, Nat had always shared my vision of the future, and we had been extremely successful together; the situation with Donnie Kirshner convinced me that I had to make a change. As a result, that was the end of my involvement with Crimson, Lost Nite Records, and the Record Museum. Over time, I got my $25,000. Nat stayed in, but it turned out to be a bad decision. Crimson came out with another record or two, including "Explosion," the Soul Survivors' follow-up to "Expressway to Your Heart," but the records were never hits. Like Kirshner and I had predicted, Crimson had trouble getting paid by their distributors. Eventually, Crimson, Lost Nite, and the Record Museum all went out of business in one way or another. (After her brief relationship with George Harrison, Trish Laden's girlfriend, Cheryl, was back in the states. Later, she would marry Richie Ingui of the Soul Survivors.)

After my show one day, Lew Klein told me that Leonore Annenberg wanted to meet with me. I knew that she was the boss's wife, but as a street kid from South Philadelphia, I had no idea how huge the Annenberg dynasty was. When I walked into the conference room, Mrs. Annenberg was sitting with her daughter, Libby.

After Klein introduced me to Mrs. Annenberg, she said, "Libby is going to graduate from high school this year. We would like you to host her coming-out party and help us hire a band."

Mrs. Annenberg was prim and proper. I was impressed with her, but I talked to her casually, like I would anyone else. I turned to Libby and said, "Do you have any groups that you like?"

Libby was ready for my question. She handed me a list of five or six groups. "But I really like the Critters."

The Critters were a lot like the Lovin' Spoonful. In fact, they had done a cover version of the John Sebastian song, "Younger Girl." Needless to say, soul was a foreign concept to them, and they weren't my cup of tea. But at least the billionaire's daughter hadn't asked me to book the Beatles or Stones. I called Buddy Howe at GAC. He spoke to the Critters' manager and they agreed to do it at a reduced price as long as I put them on my TV show.

The party was scheduled for a Sunday night in May. It was held at the Annenberg's estate on Montgomery Avenue. When I woke up on the day of the party, it was pouring rain, and the forecast was calling for the rain to continue.

Whenever I do a gig, I make it a point to get to the venue two or three hours ahead of time, especially when I've never been there. Libby's coming-out party was no different, and I arrived at the estate at five o'clock, two hours early. Two gigantic tents had been set up adjacent to the house. I walked into one of them, and it was leaking. The Critters were going to perform in that tent, and the adults were going to have a formal dinner in the other one.

When I walked into the house, everyone was scurrying around. I checked the pantry, the kitchen, and two or three other rooms, but I couldn't find Mrs. Annenberg.

Finally, I discovered a room that had bookcases from floor to ceiling. It was either a den or a library; I couldn't tell which. I had never seen anything like it.

A fire was burning in the fireplace, and a man was sitting with his back to me in a leather chair. I could hear him talking to himself.

"Goddamn weather!"

"My man!" I said. "Don't worry about a thing."

He turned and said, "Who are you?"

"I'm the Geator with the Heator, the Boss with the Hot Sauce, and I'm doing the party for the Annenbergs' daughter."

"Is that right? Can you stop the rain?"

"Don't worry. When the Geator gets up and starts to finger pop, rain or shine, it's a party."

"We'll see about that."

By seven o'clock, the rain stopped and the party was a huge success. I played records in between the Critters' sets, and the kids had a ball. Slowly but surely, as they heard the excitement, the adults came in from the other tent and joined in on the dancing.

The party was supposed to end at 1 a.m., but it was still going strong when Mrs. Annenberg walked over to me. "You were wonderful," she said. "Mr. Annenberg would like to thank you."

When I walked into the house, I was shocked to see the man I had spoken to earlier. I didn't realize that I had been talking to Walter Annenberg all along. I apologized for being rude.

"I'm sorry, Mr. Annenberg. I thought you were one of the guests!"

"Not at all. What do I owe you?"

"You don't owe me anything. It's a pleasure to finally meet you."

"That's very generous of you. Have you eaten yet?"

"Yes, I have. Thank you."

Just then, his assistant whispered in his ear. "Maybe you know how to solve this one," Annenberg said. "The kids are swimming in my pool. How do I get them to leave? It's one-thirty in the morning."

"Simple. Is the pool lit? All you have to do is turn out the lights. They'll get the message."

"Good idea," he said. His assistant turned out the lights and the kids started to leave.

When I went in to Channel 6 the next day, Lew Klein took me aside. "They were thrilled with what you did."

The next thing I knew, the Annenbergs sent me a cigarette case from Caldwell's. The inscription read, "With deep appreciation, Lee and Walter Annenberg."

When I told my mother about the Annenbergs, she baked them a ricotta pie, and I took it over to their house. As soon as they tasted it, they flipped, and from that moment on, they couldn't stop talking about my mother's cooking. A day or two later, Walter called me on the phone. "Mrs. Annenberg and I love the way your mother cooks. Do you think she would cook for us sometime?"

For some reason, I felt very comfortable with him. "Absolutely, Walt-a-phonic Walt!" And he laughed when I called him that.

"You'll come over for dinner," I said.

Even though they invited themselves to dinner, they did it in style, showing up at our house with a Cadillac full of toys. I had four little ones now—Kathi, Geraldine, Stacy, and Deserie—and the Annenbergs brought something for all of them.

Technically, three of the daughters were "mine," but I never made a distinction between Kathi and the others.

Walter's car was several years old, but that was one of the most interesting things about him. He was frugal, but he spared no expense when it came to giving gifts. This was true whether he was giving them to friends, family, or a public institution. In fact, he was one of the greatest philanthropists that ever lived.

When I gave him a tour of my house, Walter was impressed that Cardinal Krol was my neighbor, and this was the first of many occasions that the Annenbergs joined us for dinner. Whenever they did, my mother would do the cooking, and I would hire a group of servers. The Annenbergs were classy people, and I wanted everything to be just right.

The house on Overbrook Avenue continued to be a gathering place for friends, family members, prominent Philadelphians, and people in the entertainment business, especially during the holidays. Sammy Davis Jr., Frankie Valli, Trini Lopez, Gary U.S. Bonds, Chubby Checker, Berry Gordy, Bob Crewe, Phil Spector, Jerry Wexler, Ahmet Ertegun, and future U.S. Senator Arlen Specter and his wife, Joan, either had dinner with us or stayed over. When Frankie Valli slept over, he came down to breakfast the next morning and asked if I had come into his room in the middle of the night.

"No," I said, "Why?"

"'Cause—I heard doors opening and closing and saw lights going on and off."

Pattie was on the other side of the kitchen when he said it, and she just looked at me. She'd been convinced since the day we moved in that the house was haunted, although she conceded that the ghosts were friendly.

Although he was dubious about *The Jerry Blavat Show* at first, Roger Clipp was behind me 100% as the summer of 1968 approached, and he decided to pitch the show to the network. I brought in the Supremes, Sonny and Cher, Lou' Rawls, and Bobby Rydell, and taped a special show. When we finished taping, Clipp set up a meeting with Oliver Treyz in New York. Treyz was the head of programming for ABC and had been responsible for *Bandstand* going national. Treyz was looking for a summer replacement, but my show wasn't the only one he was considering. Dick Clark was producing a show on the West Coast, and his idea was similar to mine. Instead of doing the show in studio, they would film it in different locations, including the beach.

Roger Clipp, Bud Vaden, and I flew to New York in Clipp's private plane. It was my first opportunity to sit down with Clipp for an extended period of time, and we got along well. I happened to mention my interest in Native Americans, and Clipp was intrigued by it. Later, he told me that he admired the rapport I had with kids. "I like your honesty," he said.

Dick Clark was already established on the network, and even though they used his show instead of mine, I was glad that I had given it a shot. Clark's show was called *Happening '68*, and it ran throughout the summer. My old friend Charlie O'Donnell was the announcer, and Mark Lindsay and Paul Revere—the frontmen of Paul Revere and the Raiders—were cohosts. The show ran on Saturday afternoons after *Bandstand*.

From 1965 to 1968, I had the hottest teenage dance show in the United States, and my popularity continued to increase. After Channel 6 expanded *Jerry's Place* to one hour in the summer of '68, I did the first rock and roll show at the Robin Hood Dell in Fairmount Park, drawing 40,000 kids. The Dell only seated 8,000, but the kids were sitting in the trees, on the lawn, and anywhere else they could see or hear. A writer referred to it as "Beatlemania on a small scale," and I couldn't really argue with him.

I also made appearances at the Thrill Show, which drew as many as 90,000 people to John F. Kennedy Stadium in South Philadelphia, which had been renamed from Philadelphia Municipal Stadium after President Kennedy's assassination.

Bob Hope was the master of ceremonies, and I produced a ten-minute segment, featuring guests like the Four Tops and the Intruders. (This was the same stadium where the annual Army-Navy Game was played from the 1930s until 1980.)

It was amazing to think back to the remark that Harold Lipsius had made at the Har Zion synagogue years before, when he said, "You might be able to make a few bucks by doing dances on the side." It turned out to be the understatement of the century, but as good as the money was, I felt even better about the fact that I was making a difference in people's lives. Whenever I received a proclamation from the mayor's office, a congressman, or a senator, I felt like I was rewarding the man upstairs for the faith he had shown in me.

One day, Walter Annenberg called me and said, "Do you think your mom could have a small dinner party for us? I would like to invite Commissioner Rizzo."

I knew most of the people in city government, including James Tate, the mayor; Fred Corletto, the managing director; Abe Rosen, the city representative; and Bob Crawford, the commissioner of the Department of Recreation, which organized my show at the Robin Hood Dell. I had known Frank Rizzo since he was a police captain at 12th and Pine.

"That's my man," I said. "Absolutely!"

On the night of the dinner party, Frank arrived before the Annenbergs. I gave him a tour of the house.

"Why don't you have an alarm system here?"

"I don't need an alarm system."

"I'm gonna put one in for you. Al Pearlman's gonna call you." Pearlman was a member of City Council. He owned Tracy American Air Conditioning and Refrigeration, a company that also sold alarm systems. With Frank Rizzo, there was no use arguing.

When we got to the dining room, Frank noticed my "beer meister," a refrigerated device that dispensed draft beer. He asked what it was doing there, and I told him that I usually kept it in one of the cabanas by the pool, but that Walter Annenberg had gotten such a kick out of it on his last visit that I brought it into the house.

"You can do *me* a favor," Frank said. "Put in a good word for me with Mr. Annenberg."

"What are you talking about? The guy loves you!"

"Yeah, but he listens to you."

Mayor Tate would leave office four years later, but unofficial candidates were already jockeying for position. Tate didn't want Rizzo to become the mayor, even though he thought highly enough of him to make him the police commissioner. Tate favored two candidates—Paul D'Ortona and Fred Corletto—and that's why Rizzo wanted me to put in a good word for him with Annenberg. The election wasn't for another four years, but he was already lining up support.

In addition to seeing each other at my house, Rizzo and Annenberg were getting together occasionally, something that Annenberg got a kick out of. One night, when the Annenbergs were having dinner with us on Overbrook Avenue, Walter joked about having lunch with Frank at Dante and Luigi's and seeing Angelo Bruno at the next table. He couldn't get over the fact that the police commissioner was sitting a few feet away from a reputed member of the Mafia. Knowing all three of them—Rizzo, Annenberg, and Bruno—I knew that Annenberg was the only one who was surprised. Although they couldn't acknowledge it in public, Rizzo and Bruno respected each other and would have taken a chance encounter like that in stride, without betraying any emotion at all. I also knew that Walter would have been even more surprised if I had told him that I had known Angelo Bruno my entire life, and that our families were very close. In addition, he never knew that I had picketed his television station in 1956, when Dick Clark replaced Bob Horn.

When one of Annenberg's columnists at the *Philadelphia Inquirer* wrote an unflattering column about Rizzo, Annenberg had him reassigned. The columnist, Joe McGinnis, left the newspaper, and eventually, Rizzo's bid to become mayor gathered steam.

Around the same time, Nat and I put a group of investors together and started "The Jerry Blavat School of Radio and Television." The board of directors included John Facenda, Sid Mark, Frank Ford, Edie Huggins, Les Keiter, and Georgie Woods. Some of the board members taught classes at the school, along with a guy named Richard Bartlett, a film and television director who was known for his work on *Wagon Train*. Many of the kids were interested in broadcasting, so opening the school seemed like a constructive thing to do.

Early in 1969—about a year after "Some Like It Lukewarm"—the Monkees appeared on my television show. Donnie Kirshner came to

Philadelphia with them, along with a young actor named Jack Nicholson. Nicholson had just shot *Easy Rider* and was about to become a star. After the show, Nicholson couldn't stop talking about it. "I've never seen anybody dance on one leg like that! You were amazing!"

At one point, I put together a band called Geator and the Geatormen. It had an eight-piece horn section consisting of young musicians from Wilmington, Delaware. We performed oldies and popular songs of the day, including "Sweet Soul Music" by Arthur Conley, "Girl Watcher" by the O'Kaysions, and "Ain't Nothin' But a House Party" by the Showstoppers. The audience loved it. In addition to performing on *Jerry's Place*, we appeared at the 500 Club, Dick Lee's, Aljo's, Skeet's, the Anvil Inn, the Erlton Lounge, and other clubs in the area. This club band would become extremely important to me later on.

Just when things were going well, Channel 6 decided to change the format of my show. Joey Bishop was on the ABC network at night, and Pat Boone had a syndicated show. WFIL was carrying both of them. They wanted to group those shows with mine to create "the three Bs" (Bishop, Boone, and Blavat). Their objective was to compete with Westinghouse Broadcasting, which had the *Mike Douglas* and *Merv Griffin* shows, and to sell blocks of advertising. If a sponsor bought a segment of Pat Boone's show, they got a segment of mine, and so on. Unfortunately, the format they were proposing would do away with my "yon teens" entirely, and there wouldn't be any audience at all. I would do an opening monologue (similar to Johnny Carson's), sing a song, introduce my cohost, and interview the guests.

From the very beginning, I was uncomfortable with the format. Channel 6 wanted me to appeal to an older audience, but doing a show without any teenagers, rock and roll, or dancing took away my greatest strengths. In addition, I was concerned about the effect it would have on the kids. I didn't want to disappoint them, or make them feel that I was forgetting about them; as Nat pointed out, though, I had a contract with Channel 6, and it ran till the end of the year. In the end, I went against my own instincts and paid a heavy price—attendance at my record hops started to decline.

One night, Sammy Davis Jr. was appearing at the Latin. I was wearing the overcoat that I had gotten from the director of *The Monkees*. When I walked into Sammy's dressing room, he flipped.

"Where'd you get that?"

"Jim Frawley gave it to me."

"Let me try it on."

Sammy was into the "mod" look. He wore Nehru jackets and beads. I took off the coat, and Sammy tried it on.

"I gotta get one of these!" he said.

When he appeared on *Jerry's Place* a few days later, I presented him with a complete wardrobe on the air, finding the look that he was into at Ward's Folly and the Apple on Sansom Street. At the end of the show, I surprised him with an overcoat like the one he had admired.

The only good thing about the new format was that I started booking more guests from outside the music business, and that's when Joan Crawford appeared with me for the second time.

By now, Paul D'Ortona was the president of City Council. He was a South Philly guy, and I had interviewed him on my radio show from the Venus Lounge. One day, he came on *Jerry's Place* to present Joan Crawford with a proclamation. After the show, Crawford said, "Why don't you join me for dinner tonight and bring Mr. D'Ortona?"

At the time, both Crawford and D'Ortona were in their 60s, but Crawford still had an aura about her, and D'Ortona was completely smitten. "Come to my suite at seven o'clock," she said.

Crawford was staying in the President's Suite at the Bellevue. When we arrived, her valet answered the door. "Miss Crawford will be out momentarily. Can I fix you a drink?" Twenty minutes later, Crawford came out of her bedroom in a leotard. She had been drinking, and she wasn't wearing any makeup. Her wig was in the other room, and her hair was cropped close to her head. There were freckles on her face and shoulders, and she was a far cry from the movie star the world adored. To put it politely, she wasn't looking very glamorous.

D'Ortona was half-crocked also. He was all over her and Crawford loved the attention. "You know, Geator, I was a Ziegfeld girl," she said, forgetting that I had mentioned it when I met her for the first time. She put her glass down—Pepsi and vodka—and started to dance for us. D'Ortona couldn't take his eyes off her.

By the time we sat down for dinner, Crawford and D'Ortona were drunk, and it was obvious that I was in the way. "I'm going down to the bar," I said, and neither one of them tried to stop me. I had a drink at the bar and drove home to Overbrook Avenue. The next day, D'Ortona said, "I never had a night like that in my life."

By that point in our marriage, things began to change with Pattie. Even though she loved me, I believe that she was uncomfortable with the success we were having, and that she had mixed feelings about our new environment. As a result, she developed friendships of her own.

I've always thought of South Philadelphia as a small town inside of a big city, and if that's the case, Pattie was a small town girl at heart. She loved our house on Overbrook Avenue, but she would have been just as content to live in the old neighborhood. Pattie was less ambitious than I was, and living anonymously without any famous friends wouldn't have bothered her at all. Sammy loved Pattie, and so did Frankie Valli and the other show business people who visited us at the house; more and more, though, when I entertained other guests downstairs, Pattie hung out with her own friends in another part of the house. Another kind of person might have been thrilled to have the kind of houseguests we had, or at least curious about what made them tick; Pattie wasn't like that.

We were growing apart in other ways as well. When I talked to her about it, it was clear that she didn't want any more children; more importantly, she was treating it like a duty. It was at that point that I began to stray.

It wasn't like I was cheating on Pattie every night, but I felt guilty whenever I gave in to temptation. I had opportunities with some of the guests on my show, and with some of the actresses who were appearing in town. Even though Pattie and I had issues, I still loved her as the mother of my children, and I won't make any excuses for being unfaithful.

As it turned out, Joan Crawford wasn't the only actress I met. I also met the actress who was playing Dulcinea in *Man of La Mancha*. After the show, I took "Dulcinea" to the Variety Club, a private club on the second floor of the Bellevue; when the bartender, Benny, announced last call, Dulcinea was just getting started. We wound up at the Two-Four, the after-hours club that my father had introduced me to.

Dulcinea had a magnificent body, and she drew stares wherever she went, even when she was sitting quietly. But when I came out of the men's room, she was arguing with a couple of guys at the bar. As I got closer, the shouting got louder, and she took a swing at one of them. When another guy jumped in, I ended up punching him, and a full-scale brawl broke out with Dulcinea in the middle of it. It was like she was reliving the part of Dulcinea!

Everyone at the Two-Four Club knew me, but no one recognized Dulcinea, except for the owner, Lefty Katz. Just then, Katz ran over.

"You gotta get outta here," he said. "The cops are gonna come. You're gonna get arrested." I grabbed Dulcinea's hand and ran out of there, as the free-for-all emptied into the street. The next day, the *Daily News* ran a story on the front page, but kept my name out of it. The headline said, "Brawl at the Two-Four Club." (Dulcinea and I were hot and heavy for a day or two, but neither one of us took it seriously.)

Judi West appeared on my show also. She was in town with the Arthur Miller play, *After the Fall*, which was based on Miller's relationship with Marilyn Monroe. West flirted with me all day, and when I dropped her off at her hotel, she invited me up to her room. When we got upstairs, I saw that she had put up pictures of Monroe. Her room almost looked like a shrine, and I realized that she was imitating Monroe in the way that she walked and talked.

When we were making out, I said, "Why don't you relax?"

"Marilyn would never relax."

Unlike Dulcinea, she didn't know what she wanted, and it looked like we would never get it on. When I realized that it wasn't going to work, I made an excuse and left. (Eventually, Judi West starred in *The Fortune Cookie*, a Billy Wilder movie with Jack Lemmon and Walter Matthau.)

Other guests included Phyllis Diller, Robert Goulet, José Ferrer, and Adam West, who played Batman on television. After the show, I usually took them out to dinner or had them over to the house. In nicer weather, I took some of them to the Belmont Mansion, which was owned by my old friend, Don Battles.

As she explained it to me on *Jerry's Place*, Phyllis Diller wanted to be a classical pianist originally, but she was discovered as a comedienne by Bob Hope, and her career took off from there. Diller and I went on to become close friends. At one point, she invited Nat and me to attend one of her performances at the Americana Hotel in New York. This was the final performance of a weeklong engagement, and the great Shirley Bassey was in the audience. Bassey was taking over as the headliner the next night. As was the custom, Diller acknowledged her from the stage, and Bassey got a round of applause.

Later that night, when we were having drinks in Diller's suite, there was a knock on the door. Diller's husband was Ward Donovan, and as soon as he opened the door, the comedian Shecky Greene fell face-first into the room, obnoxiously drunk, and he started insulting everyone before passing out on the couch. Diller hadn't invited him, and eventually, she had to call security to have him removed.

The ABC network asked if I would do a satellite interview with the singer, Tom Jones. Jones was the hottest thing in England, and his show, *This Is Tom Jones*, was about to be seen in the States. ABC had scheduled the show in prime time and selected me to promote it on WFIL, which was their top-rated station. When I did the interview, I asked Jones about the material he intended to perform, and he told me that it would feature soul music. American artists had influenced Jones heavily, and he devoted a five- to eight-minute portion of every show to soul, R&B, and rock and roll, performing "Soul Man" by Sam and Dave, "Without Love" by Clyde McPhatter, "Stagger Lee" by Lloyd Price, "Send Me Some Lovin'" by Little Richard, and "Sweet Little Sixteen" by Chuck Berry. As soon as I saw *This Is Tom Jones*, I knew that ABC had a hit.

At a time when his contemporaries were churning out one bubblegum hit after another, Tom Jones was one of the first British performers to feature soul music, and I always respected him for it. Shortly after our interview, my friend Peter DePaul booked Jones at the Spectrum (home of the 76ers and Flyers). His July 1969 show was one of his first appearances in the United States.

Even though we appeared on different channels, I was often a guest on *The Mike Douglas Show*. Technically, we were competing with each other, but his show was on in the morning and mine was on in the afternoon, so we never looked at it like that. Once in a while, a guest would cancel on Douglas, and his producer would call me at the last minute and ask me to fill in. Whenever I did, they would introduce me as an authority on the teenage thing, and I would appear with groups like Martha and the Vandellas.

Because he couldn't ad-lib to save his ass, Douglas's producers wrote the questions down for him on cue cards, and he was particularly helpless when he had a guest that he didn't know. People from the world of rock and roll threw him for a loop, and he never varied from the questions that were written down. A guest could have said something outrageous like, "I just killed your mother," and I'm not sure that Douglas would have reacted. He was too busy sneaking a peek at his next question. I used to sit there and think, "God bless him, if the public only knew what a dunce this guy is, he'd be dead in the water."

One Saturday, I got a call from Walter Annenberg. "Geator, can you stop by the house?" Like always, Annenberg asked how my mother was doing before he got down to business. "You're at the station a lot. What do you think of George Koehler?"

"I think he's a terrific guy."

"Well, you know, Roger's retiring."

"George has always been fair with me. I respect him a lot."

"I think we share the same opinion," Annenberg said.

When I got to WFIL on Monday, I walked into Koehler's office. "George, I think you're gonna take Roger's place."

"I don't think so," he said.

Lo and behold, Koehler won the battle for Clipp's job. He became the manager of Triangle's radio and TV division. Tom Jones and Bud Vaden were out, and Lew Klein replaced Jones as the head of TV syndication. Koehler brought in Gene McCurdy as the General Manager of WFIL-TV and named George Walsh as my program director. Walsh was a former cameraman, and I had no problem working with him.

In addition to the $500 a week they paid me to host the show, I got $2,000 a week to produce it. We could only afford to pay some of the guests. The majority of them did the show for promotional consideration only. Bernie Webber, one of the kids from my dances, handled the paperwork, while Nat helped with the booking.

When President Nixon appointed Walter Annenberg as an ambassador to the Court of St. James, Annenberg held a news conference at Channel 6. It took place in the executive conference room, and both the electronic and print media were present. As he answered their questions, Annenberg spoke into a bank of microphones and stared into the television cameras. Flash bulbs were going off, and reporters were scribbling furiously. The Annenbergs were leaving for England a few days later.

As I made my way into the conference room, I shouted, "Walt-a-phonic Walt! My man!" The entire room fell silent, shocked that I would address Annenberg so casually. Annenberg looked up from the microphones and smiled. "Geator! We'll get together before I leave."

"I'm gonna miss you," I said, and walked out of the room.

The next time I heard from Walter Annenberg, it was four in the morning on the East Coast. He was calling from London, where they were five hours ahead. After his secretary put me through, he said, "Geator, I've got a situation here. I think you can help me."

The British press was knocking Annenberg something awful, even though he was spending a small fortune to redesign the American Embassy. They looked down on him for being a newspaper publisher, and felt that he didn't meet the high standards of the diplomats that had preceded him, including Joseph Kennedy. Annenberg's father, Mo, had gone to jail while building the original Annenberg empire, and the British press was all over it, treating it like a skeleton in Annenberg's closet.

Knowing how much the British people loved American entertainers, Annenberg got an idea that would eventually turn things around. "Your friend, Sammy, is here," he said. "He's making a movie with Peter Lawford and Jerry Lewis. If Leonore and I throw a dinner party, do you think you could get them to attend? We'll invite the entire cast and crew."

This was a shrewd political move on Annenberg's part. Lawford was a Democrat; he was married to a Kennedy. At the same time that Annenberg was appealing to the masses in England, he was reaching out to the other political party in the United States.

"That's a great idea," I said. "Let me call Sammy."

"It's too bad your mother can't do the cooking," Annenberg said. "She'd win all of them over."

I laughed, and said. "I'll call you as soon as I talk to Sam."

I reached Sammy at his hotel. "Yo, Sam!"

"Geator, where you at? London?"

"No, I'm in Philly. Listen, I got a call from Walter Annenberg."

"Who?"

"Walter Annenberg. He's the ambassador to England. He would like to invite your entire cast and crew to a formal dinner at the embassy."

"I got no problem with that. Let me call Peter."

The dinner party made headlines in all of the American and British tabloids, pronouncing Ambassador Annenberg the darling of the show business world.

Weeks later, the Annenbergs were back in the States, honoring Lord Mountbatten at the Variety Club International. The event took place at the Bellevue, and I was invited to attend. The Annenbergs told me that Lord Mountbatten was quite a dancer, and they asked if I would dance on one leg up the red carpet. I told them, "No problem."

Lord Mountbatten sat on the dais with Mr. and Mrs. Annenberg, Governor Milton Shapp, Mayor Tate, the actress Maureen O'Hara, and several other dignitaries; when I danced up the red carpet, Lord Mountbatten rose to his feet and applauded. As I joined them on the dais, he said, "My, my! You're very spry, young man—very spry indeed." I didn't find out until later that Lord Mountbatten was a British war hero. He had been a favorite of Winston Churchill, and Churchill had made him the Supreme Allied Commander in World War II.

Richard Bartlett was still teaching at the Jerry Blavat School of Radio and Television when he showed up with a movie script called *Cycad*. He was going to direct the film, and some of the talent was already assembled. Gary Merrill, a Hollywood actor who had married and divorced Bette Davis (his costar in *All About Eve*) was attached to the project, along with a producer named H.G. Peters. Peters operated a studio in Primos, a Philadelphia suburb, and the film was going to be shot there. Bartlett thought that I would be perfect for the role of the drifter, a Pal Joey type with a girl in every port.

Gary Merrill's character operated a general store. His brother left all of his money to Merrill's son, but the will stipulated that his son had to provide the family with an heir. Unfortunately, the son was impotent. No one knew if he was gay or straight, and he raised exotic plants in a greenhouse—including the "cycad" of the title, which was an Egyptian fern capable of living for a thousand years. Merrill's character got a hooker to marry his son and hired the drifter to get her pregnant.

This was the first time that I was forced to stick to a script, and when I read for the part, I struggled from the very beginning. Merrill hated me and complained to Bartlett. "He can't act!" Merrill said. "What does he know about acting? All he knows is music!" But Bartlett liked my look and wanted to give it more time. He offered me the role whether Merrill liked it or not. The filming was scheduled for May, 1969, in Primos, Pennsylvania.

Once we went into rehearsal for *Cycad*, Merrill did everything he could to sabotage my performance. He even chewed on a clove of garlic to throw me off, but somehow I got through it. Everyone else seemed to like what I was doing, including Bartlett and Peters.

One night, when we were halfway through the filming, I visited Don Rickles at the Latin. Merrill and some of the other cast members were in the audience. Afterward, they all went backstage. Merrill was surprised to see me with Rickles, and from that moment on, he and I became friends.

Although it never interfered with his work, Merrill used to drink, and one night, after a party for the cast members at my house, he got drunk and drove his car into a fire truck. I didn't know anything about it until he posted bail and showed up on my doorstep.

One day, when I was on the set, one of the assistant directors told me that Sammy Davis was trying to reach me. Sammy saw a video camera that Sony had just come out with and knew that I was friendly with the people at the Hi-Fi House, a local Sony distributor. Sammy wanted me to get the camera for him "at cost."

When Bartlett and Peters found out that I was close to Sammy, they wanted him to appear in *Cycad*. Their idea was to create a flashback scene in which Sammy appeared as himself. After making love on the beach, the hooker would ask the drifter about his background, and the drifter would mention the fact that he had been in show business and was friends with Sammy Davis Jr.

Sammy was appearing at Hugh Hefner's Playboy Club in Lake Geneva, Wisconsin, and when I asked him if he would do it, he said, "I'm not gonna fly into Philly, but if you come out here with a film crew, I will."

While he was in Lake Geneva, Sammy stayed at the Hefner mansion, a mile or so up the road. On the day I arrived, I joined him there after his performance. It was a magnificent property with acres of land, horses, and every luxury you could imagine. When I had flown in, a driver had picked me up in a Mercedes limo, which I had never seen before, and the place was teeming with Playboy bunnies.

I knew that Sammy wouldn't take any money for doing the scene, so I decided to surprise him with some Italian food, making arrangements with Vince Marra to fly out the day after I arrived with the film crew. Marra's family had been in the restaurant business for years, and I asked him to bring sausage, meatballs, and gravy on the plane. Like my father, Marra was a degenerate gambler and the black sheep of his family, but he always had a good heart. Little did I know that he had never flown on an airplane.

Marra was deathly afraid of flying. Instead of packing the food securely and checking it with his luggage, he insisted on bringing it on board with him, and he was holding on to it for dear life before the plane even took off. By the time the captain taxied onto the runway, Marra was terrified, and he started drinking as soon as they served the alcohol.

To make matters worse, Marra was a heavyset guy who could barely fit in his seat, and whenever he got up to use the bathroom, he spilled a little more gravy on himself. By the time he landed, there were just as many meatballs rolling around on the floor as there were in the containers.

Sammy sent a driver for Marra, and when he arrived at the hotel, his shirt was covered with gravy. Only a few of the meatballs and sausages had survived, and Marra's suit reeked of garlic. Although they didn't look all that presentable, Sammy enjoyed them just the same, and he appreciated what Marra had done.

Sammy was usually very jovial, but after dinner that night, his mood took a turn for the worse. He kept playing a demo of Frank Sinatra's new album over and over again, which featured a song called "What Are You Doing the Rest of Your Life?" and when I asked him what was wrong, he wouldn't tell me. I had never seen him so quiet, and on my way back to the hotel, I realized that he and Sinatra were on the outs, mostly because Sinatra disapproved of Sammy's lifestyle.

When the shooting of *Cycad* was finished, we had a "wrap" party at my house. Everybody felt that the movie would be a smash and Bartlett swore that I was "the next Dustin Hoffman." Instead of just mentioning me in the credits, they were going to feature me with the phrase "Introducing Jerry Blavat." That was the phrase they used to launch an actor's career, although I tried not to think about the fact that they used it when Paul Newman made *The Silver Chalice*, a complete bomb that almost ruined his career before it got started. That picture was so bad that Newman took out a full-page ad in the trades to apologize for his performance. It wasn't until he made *Somebody Up There Likes Me*—the story of Rocky Graziano—that Newman's career got back on track.

Peters and Bartlett were going to do another movie called *Calliope*. They offered me a part, along with Phyllis Diller, Lorne Greene, Dan Blocker, and a baseball player named Dick Allen, a friend of mine who played for the Phillies. They had scheduled a screening of *Cycad* for September in Los Angeles, where film distributors would see it for the first time.

Before I returned to WFIL, Gary Merrill invited Pattie and me to sail with him on a 125-foot yacht that he rented. Merrill was interested in Janet Rose, a friend of Pattie's that he had met at one of our parties. Janet joined us on the trip, and one of the ports we docked at was Newport, Rhode Island, where we ran into Frank Sinatra. Despite the fact that one of his crew members had drowned on a previous trip four years before, Sinatra had rented a yacht also. The actress Rosalind Russell and her husband, a film producer named Frederick Brisson, were sailing with him.

After Sinatra and Merrill exchanged pleasantries, Sinatra saw me and said, "How are you, Matchstick?" For some reason, he had started to call me that at Jilly Rizzo's place a few years before. I laughed and said, "Fine, Mr. S."

During the five weeks that I was away, Channel 6 got a series of guest hosts to fill in for me, including Al Alberts, Bobby Rydell, Connie Francis, and Mickey Rooney, and my weekly Arbitron ratings started to nosedive. Channel 6 wasn't happy about it, and when I got back to the station in July, George Koehler called me into his office. Now that I had put in a good word for him with Walter Annenberg, Koehler was in charge. George Walsh and Gene McCurdy were sitting with him when I got there.

"Look," he said, "we've gotta do something about the ratings. Doing the movie will help your career, and the notoriety you've gotten is good for the station. But in the future, we have to ask you not to be away for more than a week."

As soon as he said it, I knew I had a problem.

"I have an offer to do another movie. They're going to pay me $25,000."

Koehler frowned. "You have a decision to make. If you don't want to do TV, we'll have to discontinue the five-day-a-week show. Starting in September, we'll do an hour version on Sunday afternoons, and we won't renew your contract at the end of the year."

If I decided to do the second movie, WFIL would honor my contract but phase me out of their programming. Instead of being on the air every day, I would be on once a week, opposite football. It would be the kiss of death for my show.

I discussed the matter with Nat. I had never intended to be a disc jockey, or to limit myself that way. Instead, I had always seen myself as a performer. I wanted to branch out and grow, and to that point, I had never had second thoughts. I had always done things instinctively, even if it meant bucking the establishment, and I was never afraid to take a shot.

"You did *The Monkees*," Nat said. "That was a huge success. And the buzz is out there for *Cycad*."

We hadn't seen *Cycad* yet; they were still editing it. But based on what we were hearing, it was going to be a major motion picture. Because of that, it made sense to do a follow-up.

"You've done TV for five years," Nat said. "I think it's the right move. Besides, they already gave us a half-deposit."

Peters had cut a check for $12,500 for *Calliope*. He was dealing with us in good faith, and there was no reason to think that would change.

WFIL had invested a lot of money in my show, but George Koehler understood my decision. He was honorable about it, and we got along well in my last few months with the station. I could tell that Koehler genuinely liked me.

Instead of doing the Sunday afternoon show from Channel 6, I taped it at H.G. Peters' studio. Peters tried to syndicate it, but he was a filmmaker and knew nothing about television syndication. At one time, I was going from city to city with one of his sales reps. I felt like I was back on WCAM in the old days, selling with Emmitt Mara. This time it wasn't working, and I started to think of my new time slot as my "rugged cross." (One of the executives that we pitched the show to thought that I would be terrific as a game show host, but I wasn't interested because of *Calliope*.)

When Peters flew me out to L.A. for the screening of *Cycad*, I didn't realize that my entire career was on the line. Peters put me up at the Beverly Wilshire Hotel and introduced me to Lorne Greene and Dan

Blocker, the stars of the next movie. It was first class all the way. Although I invited Sammy to the screening, he was out of town and couldn't make it. I sat in the first row with Peters, Bartlett, and their people. Bullets Durgom, Jackie Gleason's former manager, sat directly behind me. I had met Bullets through Sammy years before. He was sitting next to Abby Greshler, a friend of Nat's who had managed Martin and Lewis, Burt Lancaster, and Vince Edwards, the star of *Ben Casey*. Distributors and exhibitors filled up the rest of the screening room, and I could hear them talking behind me. Peters and Bartlett introduced *Cycad*, making it sound like the greatest movie in the world; the distributors were waiting for the proof.

Peters and Bartlett had been true to their word about featuring me in the opening credits, and a surge of excitement ran through me when I saw my name on the big screen.

When I appeared for the first time, I liked the way I looked, but that was all I could really say. It was up to everyone else to evaluate my acting. Unfortunately, it was all downhill from there. In the first five or ten minutes, I got the feeling that *Cycad* wasn't very good, and I turned to Abby Greshler.

"What do you think so far?" I whispered.

"The only good thing about this picture is you," Greshler replied. "Nothing else works."

By now, I could hear whispering behind me, and the sound of distributors leaving. I looked over at Peters and Bartlett. They still thought they were going to win an Academy Award. When the lights came up, I turned around. All of the distributors were gone.

"You better hope this picture never comes out," Abby said. "It's that bad."

"Holy shit," I thought. "These guys aren't gonna produce another movie. They won't have any backing!"

Just like the record business, if you don't have a hit, the distributors won't pay you. How were these guys going to raise money for another picture if *Cycad* bombed?

Peters and Bartlett talked for a minute, then walked over to me.

"Don't worry about them," Peters said. "We'll distribute it ourselves."

The minute he said it, I knew it would never happen. If he couldn't syndicate a television show that he was producing, he would never be able to compete in the film industry, where the stakes were much higher. As I walked out of the screening room, I knew my career was in trouble.

That night—while I stared at the four walls of my hotel room—reality set in, and the pressure started to get to me. I'm not proud of it, but I ended up sleeping with a $300-a-night hooker named Elaine.

Cycad had a handful of screenings in the suburbs of Philadelphia, but it was never distributed. The movie died, and for all intents and purposes, so did my film career. I often wondered what ever happened to the print of *Cycad*, but no one could track it down.

Going back on the plane, I realized that I wouldn't be able to negotiate another contract with Channel 6. Television schedules were devised months in advance in order to line up advertisers, and it was too late for me to bring it up. My Sunday afternoon show would continue until the end of December, but without ratings, it was already dead in the water.

The record hops were on their last legs also. I wasn't on radio to promote them, but the problem was deeper than that. The kids stopped accepting the Geator because I was no longer doing my dance show, and the music itself had changed. Underground radio had taken over, and everything was psychedelic. Hardly anyone was doing record hops. If they did, they were lucky to get 100 kids.

When I took stock of where I was, all I had going for me was my club act with the Geatormen, the Jerry Blavat School of Radio and Television, and the money I had in the bank. The club dates depended on the popularity of my TV show, just like the record hops did. Once I was off television for good, it would be more difficult to attract an audience. For the second time in my career, I was unsure of where I was going, just like I was when the mayor of Camden took me off WCAM originally.

The music scene had changed, and I didn't fit in with FM radio. The listeners had shifted toward acid rock. The Woodstock Generation had arrived, and the drug culture had taken over. I could see it when I walked down Sansom Street, where one "head shop" after another had opened. I couldn't believe the things they were selling—rolling paper, hash pipes, and the kind of "hookahs" you used to see in *The Arabian*

Nights. I was running into kids who had come to my record hops and *The Discophonic Scene.* They were the same ones that we had given the corncob pipes to in order to advertise Mountain Dew. Now they were buying pipes of their own and using them to get stoned.

Over the next few months, I found myself flying back and forth to the Coast as often as I could, hanging with Sammy and trying to get a part in a film. I read a few scripts, talked to some agents who had seen me in *The Monkees*, and met with Joe Pasternak, the famous movie producer at MGM. Pasternak was responsible for Vic Damone's film career and also produced *Where the Boys Are* with Connie Francis. Currently, he was producing Elvis Presley's movies. Whenever the talks progressed, the agents and producers advised me to move to L.A. My family was back in Philadelphia, and I knew that Pattie would never go for that.

While I was there, however, I fell into a relationship with Elaine, the high-priced call girl. When I got back in touch with her, she gave me a freebie, just like the hooker in Nashville had when I was road managing Danny and the Juniors. For some reason, hookers liked me, and I ended up shacking up with Elaine for days at a time. I would wait for her to come back from turning a trick and then cook for her late at night. This went on for a couple of weeks, until she caught me in bed with one of her girlfriends, a redhead who shared the same profession.

When I read in the paper that *Man of La Mancha* was in town, I looked up my friend Dulcinea. She was appearing at a theater in Pasadena, and after I left a message for her, she invited me to meet her at her hotel after the performance. I didn't realize how far away Pasadena was from Beverly Hills, or how long it would take on the freeway, and when I got there it was late. It turned out that Dulcinea wasn't staying in a hotel at all; it was a cheap motel. She had been drinking and was waiting for me in bed. To be honest, it was one of the worst fucks I ever had, and I was pretty disgusted by the time I drove back to Sammy's. That was the last time I saw Dulcinea.

The night manager of the Beverly Hills Hotel was a guy named Nick Pappas, and once in a while, he got me a good rate on the kind of bungalow that Burton and Taylor had stayed in. It was fun to stay there, but as far as my career was concerned, time was passing, and I wasn't getting anything done.

One day, Sammy and I had lunch at the hotel. When we walked into the Polo Garden, Gary Merrill was sitting at a table with Bette Davis. I hadn't seen him since the yacht in Newport, Rhode Island. When I said hello to him, Merrill told me that he was having problems with his career also, and that he was going to run for office in Maine.

A few minutes later, when Sammy and I were waiting for our food, we heard a commotion a few feet away. We looked up and saw Merrill and Davis arguing. Just then, Davis hit Merrill over the head with a bottle of champagne, got up from the table, and walked out of the restaurant.

Sammy and I went to the clubs at night—Bumbles, the Factory, and the Candy Store—and we hung out with some of the actors and show business types, including Joey Bishop, Buddy Greco, Steve and Eydie, Don Costa, Dionne Warwick, Robert Blake, Tony Curtis, and even Fred Astaire. But L.A. was too laid back for me, and I knew that I had to get back to Philadelphia to start all over again. It was obvious that I had made the biggest mistake of my life.

NINE: The Lean Years:
Memories in Margate

I trusted Nat implicitly. At the end of the night, he would take the money from a record hop and deposit it into our bank accounts. He had one for our office expenses on Chestnut Street, one for me, and one for his commissions. Once a week, he would send Pattie a check for household expenses. The same thing happened with our other business ventures, including the broadcasting school, the compilation albums, the songs I recorded, and the money I was paid for the television shows. Nat gave me an "allowance" every week and deposited the rest into my account as savings. He had been handling my money since 1960 when the records hops first took off.

Once in a while, when my father served as a doorman at the hops, Nat would catch him stuffing some of the cash in his pocket, and he would look at my father and say, "That's your son you're stealing from." My father would justify it by saying, "If it wasn't for me, he wouldn't be here." I was making money hand over fist, and the small amounts he was taking didn't really bother me. Now that the hops had died, however, there was less money coming in.

One night, we were booked at Carlo's Satellite Lounge in Trenton. Carlo was a shady guy with a reputation for stiffing the performers. Sometimes he paid you, and sometimes he didn't. The first time we played there, we packed the place, and Carlo paid me in cash. This allowed me to pay the Geatormen right away, dividing up the money in the parking lot outside. They were young kids who needed money for college, so cash was their preferred method of payment.

I had a problem on our second gig. When it was time for Carlo to pay us, he was nowhere to be found. I walked over to the manager.

"Where's Carlo?"

"He'll be back."

We waited around for a while, but Carlo didn't come in. By now, it was after 2 a.m. and the place was closed. Finally, the manager handed me an envelope. "Here's your money," he said.

When I counted the money, it was a thousand dollars short.

"Where's the rest of it?" I asked.

"Carlo said that's all you're getting."

"We agreed on two thousand dollars."

"You'll have to talk to him tomorrow."

"Where's he at?"

"I don't know where he's at."

The manager had a cocky attitude, and that pissed me off even more. It was three in the morning, and the band decided to go home. I assured them that they would get paid.

Carlo lived in an apartment above the club. I rang the bell, but no one answered, so I walked around the back. There weren't any lights on upstairs. I got in my car and drove around for a few minutes, then I went back to Carlo's, parking a block away. I rang the buzzer a second time. A light came on and Carlo stuck his head out of the window.

I said, "Carlo, you owe me a thousand dollars."

"You ain't gonna get the fuckin' money."

"Give me what you owe me."

"You ain't gettin' shit."

Because I often got paid in cash, I kept a gun in the glove compartment of my car, along with a permit to carry it. It was a .38 caliber, snubnosed revolver. I took out the gun and fired into the air.

"Jesus Christ!" he said. "You're packin'?"

I waited for him to do something. "Hold on," he said, disappearing into his apartment and coming back with another envelope. He threw the envelope out of the window. It had two thousand dollars in it—a thousand more than he owed. Everybody got paid a little extra, and that was the last time we played Carlo's Satellite Lounge.

As it turned out, Carlo's was the exception to the rule. We also performed at the Erie Social Club, the 400 Lounge at Frankford and Pratt, and Lou Turk's joint in Chester; we never had a problem with any of them.

In May 1970, Sammy was in town to do *The Mike Douglas Show* for a week, and to appear at the Latin Casino. One Saturday, he called me and said, "My mother's coming in tomorrow. Can your mom cook something?" Sammy's mother was Elvera "Babe" Sanchez, a former chorus line dancer who had worked as a barmaid at Grace's Little

One of my first 8 x 10 glossy promotional photos that I would sign and give to fans.

A thank-you note to me from Walter Annenberg.

WALTER H. ANNENBERG

June 27, 1967

Mr. Jerry Blavat
WFIL-TV

Dear Jerry:

I am greatly impressed not only with your dynamic personality, but the sincerity with which you conduct yourself. This is all the more remarkable because of your comparative youth.

Again, may I thank you for your tremendous help at my stepdaughter's affair.

With all good wishes,

Cordially,

Walter Annenberg

WHA:G

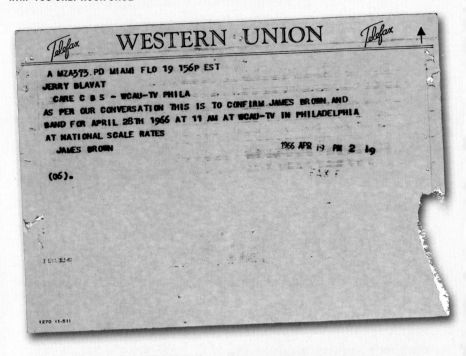

Telegrams from James Brown and Frankie Valli confirming their appearance on *The Discophonic Scene*.

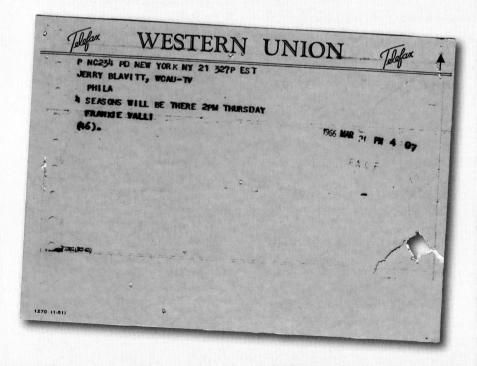

My sponsors, the Lit Brothers department store, set up Discophonic Shops in their stores.

Rockin' with James Brown on *The Discophonic Scene.*

Little Richard on my show.

Talking to the kids was one of the best parts of *The Discophonic Scene*.

Jamming with Sammy Davis Jr.

Doing a big show at the Robin Hood Del East in 1966
with 40,000 fans.

Swamped by fans at an event promoting *The Discophonic Scene*.

Ike and Tina Turner on my show.

Pattie and I with Phillies star Richie Allen.

Joan Crawford, the city council president, and yours truly.

Do you remember *The Singing Nuns*?

With Sammy
and Liza
Minnelli.

What a group! Julio Iglesias, me, Jilly Rizzo, Mickey Rourke and Frank Sinatra.

Mayor Frank Rizzo presenting awards to me, Sammy
and Bobby Rydell.

Dick Clark,
Dick's wife Kari
and I at an event
in 1987.

Sammy on my show in the '70s.

My Dad and my Riviera, "The Black Phantom."

My Mom and I in her
later years.

Here I am with Richie Allen (left) and director Richard Bartlett at
the wrap party for the movie *Cycad* at my home.

With Angelo Bruno and his family, which became my second
family after Pattie and I broke up.

Talking with Distict Attorney
Emmitt Fitzpatrick during the
Bruno investigation.

Here I am, at the Bruno
family's request, keeping
the press away at Angelo
Bruno's funeral.

My Dad and I catching some rays on my boat.

At a black-tie event with Sidney and Caroline Kimmel.

With Freddy DeMann and Olga at Freddy's 50th birthday party.

Love at first sight. Keely and me.

One of my proudest moments: my induction into the
Rock and Roll Hall of Fame in 1998.

Another memorable moment: getting the 50-Year Service Award from
Philadelphia Mayor Michael Nutter (center) and Congressman Bob Brady (left).

Belmont on Kentucky Avenue in Atlantic City.

The Latin Casino had an early show on Sunday nights. It started at seven, and Sammy got to my house around 11. With him, he had his mother; his dancers, including Altovise Gore; Brian Dellow, who did security for Sammy; Murphy Bennett, Sammy's valet; George Rhodes, his music conductor; Rhodes' wife, Shirley; Joe Grant, his lighting guy; and Karl Barrie, a comedian who opened for Sammy in Puerto Rico. My mother made ravioli and sausage. (Years later, Dellow worked for Quincy Jones, and Joe Grant would manage Dionne Warwick.)

Everybody was having a great time. Sammy turned to me and said, "What are you doing tomorrow?"

"What do you want to do?"

"You know any judges?"

The table fell silent.

"What do you need a judge for, Sam?"

Before he could answer, his mother shook her head and whispered to me, "What the fuck did he do now?"

Sammy said, "I wanna marry Altovise tomorrow."

Everyone was in shock, including Altovise. He turned to her and said, "You will marry me, right?"

"Sammy, you know I will." And she broke out in tears.

His mother kicked me under the table. "What the fuck is that crazy little bastard doing?"

The next morning, I made arrangements for Judge Joseph Gold to conduct the wedding ceremony in his chambers. Karl Barrie and I acted as "best men."

Afterward, Sammy said, "Let's have a dinner party at Cinelli's." Cinelli's was in Jersey, not far from the Country Squire, where Sammy was staying.

"I'll take care of it."

"Why don't you call Mike Douglas and invite him?"

Pattie and I met Sammy, Altovise, and the rest of the party in front of the motel. We drove over to Cinelli's in a limousine, and when we arrived, Mike Douglas was standing in front of the restaurant with his wife, Genevieve. They congratulated Sammy and Altovise, and we walked into the dining room. I made sure that there weren't any photographers.

As we approached our table, Sammy turned to me and said, "Sit next to me." I ended up sitting on one side of Sammy while Altovise sat on the other. Pattie sat next to Altovise, and Mike and Genevieve sat a few feet away. Everyone seemed to enjoy the dinner at Cinelli's, and Sammy and Altovise left for L.A. the next day.

When my television contract expired, I booked as many one-nighters as I could with Geator and the Geatormen. As long as I had a hit TV show, it was easy for us to stay busy, but now that I was off the air, I faced some uncertainty where the club dates were concerned because I didn't have a vehicle to promote them. Meanwhile, Nat was approached by the Esko Brothers, who wanted me to record a song they had written called "Tasty to Me."

One of the most glaring examples of "bubblegum" music was a song called "Yummy Yummy Yummy, I've Got Love in My Tummy" by the 1910 Fruitgum Company. "Tasty to Me" had a similar sound. Even though bubblegum wasn't my cup of tea, I went into the studio in June 1970 and recorded the Esko Brothers' song. "Tasty to Me" became a local hit on the Bond label, and my friend Morris Levy bought the master and distributed it nationally on Roulette Records. Although it didn't do much—topping off at #97—it increased my visibility. I performed the song in Nashville, then flew out to L.A. to do Dick Clark's show.

I stayed with Sammy in L.A., and when he heard the song for the first time, he broke up. Sy Marsh was with us at the time. Sy was Sammy's manager. Sammy turned to him and said, "The Geator's got a record. He should do *The Mike Douglas Show*."

"I'll call 'em tomorrow."

While I was in L.A., I called Al Martino, whose string of hits dated back to the 50s. Martino's real name was Alfred Cini, and I knew him from South Philadelphia.

"What are you doing in L.A.?" he asked.

"I'm doing *The Dick Clark Show*."

"Why don't you come over to my house?"

Martino lived at 927 North Rexford Drive, right around the corner from the Beverly Hills Hotel. The houses on the drive were huge, and it was hard to see some of the addresses. Some of the house numbers were visible from the street, and others were not. In other cases, the sign was posted between the two houses, and you couldn't tell which house the sign was referring to. When I got to the house that I thought was Martino's, I rang the doorbell, but no one answered. I thought to myself, "What's goin' on here? I just talked to Al on the phone."

A moment later, a bearded man in a smoking jacket came to the door. He was close to eighty years old. I thought he was Al's butler or houseboy.

"Yeah? What do you want?" he said.

There was something familiar about his voice. It reminded me of a gangster in the movies. I thought he was putting me on, and for some reason, I started to imitate him.

"What do I want? Listen, where's Al Martino?"

"Al?" he said in the same gangster voice as before.

"Yeah, Al Martino, see." I drew out the word "see" to make sure he got the point.

Just then, Al came out of the house next door, and yelled, "Yo! Geator!"

I looked over at Martino, and when I turned back to the old man, he slammed the door in my face.

"Who was that guy?" I asked, as Martino led me into his house.

"Who—him? That's my neighbor, Edward G. Robinson."

My mouth fell open. I had just met "Dathan" in the flesh!

After we visited for a while, Martino walked me out to my car. Just then, a limousine pulled out of Edward G. Robinson's driveway and paused when it got to the street. Robinson was sitting in the backseat. He rolled down the window. "You finally found Al, didn't you?"

"I'm sorry, Mr. Robinson. I didn't recognize you at first."

"That's quite all right," he said, putting the window back up as the limousine drove away.

When I got back to Philadelphia, I waited for the *Douglas* show to call. After a week or two, I still hadn't heard from them, and I called Sy Marsh. "Douglas is being a prick," he said.

"What do you mean?"

"He's pissed off that you sat next to Sammy at Cinelli's."

Douglas felt slighted. He thought that he was a bigger star than me, and that he should have been the one to sit next to Sammy.

"Fuck him," I said. I never appeared on *The Mike Douglas Show* again, and neither did Sammy.

The next time I was on the West Coast, Pattie called me and said,

"Nat hasn't sent a check over."

"For how long?"

"Going on three weeks. He says it's on the way."

I called Nat from L.A. "Nat, what's going on with the check?"

"Don't worry. I'll get it right out."

Pattie got the check, but it happened again a few weeks later. To make a long story short, Nat was playing games with the money. He took $45,000 at a time when I was struggling, too. I was his meal ticket, and for the past few years, his income had become even more dependent on mine. Gloria Mann was over for Nat, and so were Danny and the Juniors; without the record hops, both of us were hurting. Nat used my money to take care of the office, pay his rent at Park Towne Place, and support his lifestyle. When I confronted him about it, he broke down.

"Nat," I said, "we've been together since I was a kid. If you needed the money, you should have said something."

"I didn't know how to tell you."

"You shouldn't have lied to Pattie. You should have told me the truth. We would have worked something out."

"I thought I could make it up from my commissions."

Although he told me that he would "make good on it," we both knew that he didn't have a way to do it. While I was out on the West Coast hustling to revive my career, we had no money coming in, other than advance bookings from my club dates.

Nat had very little money of his own. More importantly, his business methods were outdated.

Nat was ashamed of what he did, and eventually, he closed our office, borrowed money from his sister, and opened a liquor store in Ventnor, New Jersey. After he moved to Ventnor, I no longer had a manager, and I took care of things myself.

Nat had gotten us our accountant, an old Jewish guy named Manny Eskin. Manny was in poor health, but his sons worked with him, and they had always been completely legit.

"Manny," I said. "Did you know that Nat was taking the money?"

"We knew, but we thought you were aware of it."

After that remark, I decided to find another accountant. My sister-in-law, Nanny, was a bookkeeper, and she recommended a guy named Bruno Fedele. Bruno has been with me ever since.

When Fred Corletto, Philadelphia's managing director, invited me to a party at the shore, another possibility presented itself. His guests included Harry Jay Katz; John Crisconi and his daughter, Jeannette; and John Achione, a big contributor to St. Agnes Hospital. Achione directed an annual ball for St. Agnes, and one year I brought Frankie Laine, who appeared on my television show. Jim Tate, the mayor of Philadelphia, and Joe Nardi, the newly-elected mayor of Camden, were at the party also. Nardi had danced at my record hops in his youth, and was aware of my early success at WCAM. Corletto's party wasn't the time or place to talk business, so I told Nardi that I wanted to meet with him.

I had known Harry Jay Katz for years. A man about town, he was just as well known for being a playboy as he was for being a businessman; make no mistake, though, he was smart. It turned out that he was trying to get one of the sports teams involved with the city of Camden, but to that point, the project hadn't gotten any traction. WCAM was still city-owned, but it was losing money, and I came up with the idea of putting together a group of investors to buy the station, including Katz and Mel Korn. I wanted to program the station and do an air shift at night; when I told Nardi what I had in mind, he was receptive to it. I knew the strength of WCAM's signal, and I felt the station could become a powerhouse. The mayor asked me to sit down with the general manager, a civil servant who I will call "Jack Aaron." He had taken over from Bud Hibbs, but he knew nothing about radio.

In order to capture a share of the market, I came up with a nickname for the station, calling it "the little giant between two cities" and distributing posters in Philadelphia and Camden. Our slogan was "the Geator's back in town," and sure enough, the "little giant" came alive. The press picked up on it right away, and suddenly, the station was newsworthy. I even got a letter from Ambassador Annenberg congratulating me.

By then, WFIL had overtaken WIBG as the most powerful station in the city, and though we barely made a dent in their ratings, they knew that we were there. Like in the early days, the promotion men started to come around, and I realized how much I had missed radio. I was back in my groove, playing the rock and roll I loved; more importantly, my plan to build the station back up before buying it appeared to be working.

Not surprisingly, my radio show struggled to some extent. With groups like Steppenwolf, Led Zeppelin, Vanilla Fudge, and Grand Funk Railroad taking over the airwaves, I couldn't expect it to take off like it had in the past, but some of my oldest listeners rediscovered me, and a younger audience tuned in as well. I didn't take a salary, but I started to do dances, adding them to my schedule of one-nighters. By working the clubs late at night and running the dances, I was earning money again. (Some of the most successful record hops were at Paul VI High School in Haddon Township and Bishop Eustace in Cherry Hill.)

Because I had Joe Nardi's backing, Jack Aaron moved some of the programs around to accommodate what I wanted to do, and I had to compromise also. WCAM had block programming. People were still buying time, and they were still broadcasting horseraces from Garden State Park, so I only programmed the station from noon to 6 p.m. My shift ran from 6 to 8:45, and then Ricardo Munez did his show, *The Spanish Hour*, from 8:45 to midnight. Gene Arnold, a guy that Jack Aaron had made a deal with before I took over, played underground music from midnight to 1 a.m. I couldn't stand his music, but I didn't object to him being on at that time of night.

As time went on, Jack Aaron resented the fact that I had creative control over WCAM and was turning the station around, but we established an uneasy truce that lasted a couple of months.

One night, Aaron invited me to his home. He had always seemed a little strange to me, and that night I found out why.

When I arrived at his home, he said, "Do you smoke?"

"No. I used to, but I don't any more."

"That's not what I'm talkin' about. Come here. I wanna show you something."

Aaron led me down to his basement, and when we got there, it was like we had entered another world. He had oscillating fans, high intensity lamps, and a series of timers that controlled the environment—in short, everything he needed to grow marijuana. Before I could stop him, he started to explain the techniques he used to grow the plants "hydroponically," going on and on about it like it was the proudest achievement of his life. Finally, he reached into his shirt pocket, pulled out a joint, and offered it to me. I said, "I don't do that," walked up the steps, and left the house.

When we saw each other at the station, neither one of us said anything about the incident; it took a while for his resentment to boil over.

One day, I turned on the radio expecting to hear Pat Delsey, but he wasn't on the air. Delsey had the mid-day shift. He had been around since the infancy of rock and roll, along with two of the other WCAM jocks, Sam Scott and Jack Lamar. Delsey, Scott, and Lamar loved the way I was programming the station. All of a sudden, instead of Pat doing his shift, I heard Gene Arnold playing music that wasn't on my play list. Arnold shouldn't have been on the air at all, and I raced to 'CAM. When I arrived, Pat Delsey was sitting in the lobby.

"Pat, why aren't you on the air?"

"Jack Aaron took me off."

"What do you mean?"

"He doesn't like the music."

"Aaron's not the program director. Go back and do your show."

I went into the studio with Delsey and took Arnold off the air. "This isn't your shift," I said. "Pat, get back on."

Arnold didn't say anything. He left the studio, and Delsey started his show. Ten minutes later, Jack Aaron came running into my office.

"I'm the general manager here," he said, "not you. I don't like the music you're playing."

"You got a problem, talk to the mayor."

The mayor's office was right below us on the 17th floor.

"I don't have to talk to the mayor," he said. "I'm taking the station off the air."

No one in his right mind would take a station off the air, but when I followed him out of my office, Aaron walked into the studio. Before he could break the connection to our transmitter, I grabbed him. After we wrestled for a few seconds, Aaron got up and walked away. A few minutes later, he came back with two policemen.

"Did you attack him?" one of the cops asked me.

"Fellas," I said, "let's go the mayor's office. I'll explain it to you there."

When we got to Nardi's office, one of the policemen said, "This gentleman says that Jerry Blavat attacked him."

"Mayor," I said, "that's not so."

Nardi turned to the policemen. "I'll handle this."

After the policemen left, I explained that Aaron was going to take the station off the air. The mayor turned to Aaron. "Is that true?"

"I don't like the music he's playing."

"You shouldn't have started a fight with him, Jerry."

"That was the only way I could stop him!"

"All right," he said. "Let me talk to Jack alone."

I left. After I did my shift, I tuned in to the station at midnight, but Gene Arnold wasn't on the air. We were playing canned music, and the next day, Jack Aaron didn't show up for work. It was a Friday, and the mayor asked me to see him. He told me that Aaron resigned. When I got to the station for my Saturday show, Aaron was cleaning out his office.

"I don't have any hard feelings," he said. "Come to my office. I wanna talk to you."

I had to go on the air in fifteen minutes, but I went into his office. When I sat down, he locked the door. As soon as I turned around, he lunged at me, knocking me off the chair. I got up and cracked him two or three times, and that was the end of the fight. I unlocked the door, walked out of his office, went into the studio, and did my show as Aaron left the building.

The mayor appointed Joe Scardilli as the general manager, but he wasn't a radio guy either. He had operated Family Shoes in Stratford, New Jersey. It was a political appointment, plain and simple—the kind that still goes on to this day. I got along well with Scardilli, but the station continued to have problems. Shortly after Scardilli arrived, some of the advertisers stopped paying. With everything else that happened, I realized that buying WCAM was no longer a good idea.

Once I dropped out as a potential buyer, Nardi stepped up his efforts to unload the station. It was costing the city too much money. Eventually, Leonard and Phil Chess approached Nardi with an offer to buy. In addition to operating their record label in Chicago, they owned a number of radio stations. The Chess Brothers knew what I was doing for WCAM and saw it as an opportunity to compete with WDAS and WHAT in the Philadelphia market.

"They put down a deposit," Nardi said.

In a way, I was relieved to hear about the offer. I hadn't had time to put together a group of investors, and as a result, I didn't have the real money. The Chess Brothers, on the other hand, had more than enough to get it done. Not only was I happy for Nardi, but I also thought that the Chess Brothers might retain me as the program director.

In the long run, the deal with the Chess Brothers fell through. Once WDAS learned that they were going to convert 'CAM into a black station, they blocked the Chess Brothers' attempt to obtain an FCC license. But it didn't change anything for me. There was too much turmoil at the station, and as the collection problems increased, I left WCAM voluntarily and turned my attention elsewhere. (At the time, I had no idea that Pat Delsey, the WCAM disc jockey, would put a group together and buy the station years later.)

Although I was scuffling, I turned down a lucrative offer from Marty Fields to get back on the radio. Fields, a friend of Mel Korn, had bought WPEN with the intention of starting an underground station. FM had been around since the 60s, but it had never taken off until a handful of disc jockeys, including Tom Donahue and Bob Mitchell, emerged in San Francisco and called it underground radio. Now, it had overtaken AM as the place to be on the radio dial. At the same time, the drug culture had grown dramatically across the United States—and I wanted no part of it. I would rather have cut off my arm than play "Purple Haze," "In-A-Gadda-Da-Vida," or "Magic Carpet Ride," and just as I had done with WIBG, I politely declined.

After I declined Fields' offer, a guy named Donald Dunleavy came to see me at the 400 Lounge. Dunleavy had married Annette Borrelli, who I knew from South Philadelphia. He and his partner, Tony Capuccio, wanted to book me at the Elbow Room, a club they ran in Margate, New Jersey. The Elbow Room was right next to the Margate Mariner motel. Dunleavy and Capuccio offered me $1,000 for two nights, plus a room at the motel. It was the fall of 1970.

Together with my group, I packed the Elbow Room through the fall and winter, playing there every weekend. The Elbow Room was the only game in town, but after St. Patrick's Day, they were in competition with places like Merrill's, the Old Tavern, the Beacon Inn, and Gables. Because Pennsylvania's "Blue Laws" were still in effect, Philadelphia was dry on Sundays, and the clubs in Margate had a tradition of Sunday afternoon jam sessions that featured live music. From St. Patty's Day to Labor Day, people would drive down from Philadelphia or charter buses to get there.

After St. Patty's Day in the spring of '71, Dunleavy and Capuccio asked me to book additional acts. Using my friendships, I got Hank Ballard, Chubby Checker, the Drifters, the Ronettes, Mary Wells, and other artists to appear. They would work for us well below their normal rate, and we would put them up at the Margate Mariner. After the club closed at four in the morning, we would go up to my double-suite, and I would make breakfast for everyone.

A number of bar bands were playing the other clubs—the Exceptions, Joanne and the Night People, the Rockets, and Johnny Caswell and the Crystal Mansion. Everything worked until the beginning of the summer, when Dunleavy and Capuccio gave checks that bounced.

"Yo," I said. "You can't do that. These are my friends."

"What do you care?" Capuccio said. "You're still gettin' your end."

My reputation was more important than the money.

"Listen," I said, "you either make good or I'm pullin' out."

They made good, but I knew that I didn't want to work for those guys. A skunk is a skunk. Once I pulled out, their business went downhill, mostly because they didn't have the money to place ads and book the right acts. After I left, they changed the name to the Oar Room, and the club died.

It wasn't hard for me to find another club. I got a call from Phil Matalucci in Avalon. He was opening a place called Phil's Rock Room, and he offered me the same money as Dunleavy and Capuccio—$1,000 for the weekend and a room at the Avalon Hotel. The difference was, Phil wanted me to spin records; he didn't want me to perform with the Geatormen.

I didn't want to do it, but I had to break up the band—at least temporarily.

"Guys," I said, "can you get work?"

"It's summertime. We'll be fine."

These guys were great musicians, and I knew they could get work. That summer, I packed Phil's Rock Room every weekend.

In September 1971, I did the Thrill Show at JFK Stadium for the last time. Abe Rosen, the city representative, took me aside and said, "Don't mention Commissioner Rizzo's name."

I usually acknowledged the police and fire commissioners and asked the audience to give them a hand. This time, however, with the mayoral campaign in full swing and the election coming up in November, Mayor Tate was still smarting over the fact that Rizzo had gotten the nomination instead of Fred Corletto or Paul D'Ortona. Sure enough, Rizzo would defeat Thacher Longstreth to become the mayor of Philadelphia a few months later.

Also, I heard from the lawyer that Dunleavy and Capuccio had been dealing with. His name was Mike DelColla. He and his partners, Don Dagway and Mike DelBona, owned the property that Dunleavy and Capuccio had been leasing. DelColla and his partners also owned the Martinique Motel in Philadelphia and leased the Margate Mariner to a guy who acted as manager of the property.

By the time I got the call, Dunleavy and Capuccio were history, and the manager had run off with the money from the summer rentals. He had loaded all of his belongings into his station wagon and driven off with his wife and kids, never to be heard from again.

"We're not club operators," DelColla told me, "and we don't have anybody to run the motel. You were successful down there. Why don't you buy them?"

I knew the problems the Margate Mariner was having first-hand, even before the manager ran off with the money. When you operated a motel, you had to worry about the upkeep of the rooms, the pool, the grounds, the linens, and everything else. That wasn't my gig. But knowing what I had done at the clubs, I liked the idea of buying the Oar Room. I could spin records, perform with the group, and book additional acts myself. In the right hands, the club had a lot of potential.

"How much do you want for it?"

"$250,000."

"Guys, I don't have that kind of money."

"Can you come up with $200,000?"

"Let me think about it."

The more I thought about it, the more sense it made, and we eventually agreed on a sale price of $200,000. I had enough in my account at Central Penn Bank to pay $80,000 up front, and made a deal to pay interest every month on the rest. At the end of each summer, I would give them additional money until it was paid off. Once I took over, it was no longer the Oar Room; it became "Memories," and I have owned it ever since. One of the first things I did after renovating the place and decorating it to my liking was negotiate a deal to do a live radio broadcast. My radio shows had enabled the record hops to explode. If I could do a live radio show from Memories on the weekends in the fall and winter, it would be a home run.

A former Philadelphia disc jockey named Eddie Newman had just sold WAYV to Tom Donatucci and Bob McMurtry in Atlantic City. Newman had done a show from the Roosevelt Hotel on Walnut Street years before. The station was playing the right music for my audience, and three weeks after we opened, I did my first live broadcast on WAYV from Memories.

My father worked the door. He would collect the money and check IDs, and some of the guys that worked with us at the record hops would assist him, including Spanish Pete, Lou the Cop, and Pepsi from Downtown. (All of his former associates seemed to have a nickname. Even my brother-in-law, Alex Martinelli, had one—Uncle Doo-Doo.)

Memories was open seven days a week all summer long, and in the off-season, it was open on Fridays and Saturdays. When the summer was over, I wouldn't book any acts; I would spin records and do my live radio broadcast. During the week, I would work clubs like Yesterdays in Pennsauken, Charley's Other Brother in Mount Holly, Steak and Brew in Willow Grove, and the Downtown Tavern in Conshohocken.

When I booked an act, my budget was usually $600 to $1,500. Hank Ballard, Mary Wells, the Drifters, the Righteous Brothers, the Clovers, Lee Andrews and the Hearts, and Little Anthony and the Imperials were among the artists who appeared at Memories. The reality was, they were no longer in demand, and they were scuffling for engagements. A promoter named Richard Nader was doing rock and roll revivals at larger venues in New York, but other than that, Memories was probably the first club that exclusively booked oldies acts. The other clubs at the shore were booking rock bands. Because they weren't getting booked on a regular basis, the acts I brought in were happy with what I was paying—particularly when I cooked for them and put them up at the Margate Mariner.

There were exceptions to the rule, depending on the success of the artist and his or her drawing power. I paid the Platters $1,250, Ronnie Spector a little more, and Frankie Valli $2,500. Frankie was doing me a favor. He usually got a lot more, but he was breaking in some new guys and wanted to test the show before he took it on the road.

In March 1973, Chuck Berry was doing a Richard Nader concert at Madison Square Garden, and I told him that I would give him an additional $7,500 if he would come down to Memories and do one show. Chuck agreed, but wanted the money up front. "No problem," I said.

When I booked an act, I used my own musicians as a backup band, instead of the artists having to bring their own in. This brought the cost of the act down. I also would perform with the backup band. My drummer was Mike McCourt. Mike was scheduled to back up Ronnie Spector at the same concert that Chuck was doing, so I sent him up to New York with the $7,500 and my .38 snub-nosed revolver.

"What's this for?" he asked.

"You're carrying a lot of money. Make sure it gets there."

After the show at Madison Square Garden, Mike went into Chuck's dressing room and introduced himself. "You have it?" Chuck asked. The dressing room was crowded, but Chuck wanted his money. Mike took out the $7,500 and handed it over.

Chuck put the money in his pocket. "Thanks. I'll see you down there."

Mike stared at him. "I'd like a receipt please."

"No receipts."

"Can you just write something on a napkin?"

"No."

I love Chuck, but he's always been a pain in the ass to work with.

"How are you getting down there?" Mike asked.

"I'm driving," Chuck said.

"Do you want me to drive you? I know the way."

"No."

"Look, I can't go back without you."

"Ok. I'm staying at the Woodard at 55th and Broadway. Be at my door at nine o'clock in the morning. If you're not there, I'm going back to St. Louis with the $7,500."

"What's your room number?"

"You'll find it."

After he left the dressing room, Mike went to the Woodard to make sure that Chuck was staying there. They didn't want to tell him Berry's room number at first, but he finally convinced them. Mike ended up staying in a flophouse on 42nd Street to make sure he woke up in time to meet Chuck in the morning.

When Mike got to the hotel in the morning, Chuck took him to the car he rented—a bright red Cadillac. The first thing Chuck did was drive to a gas station and buy a map. He flattened it out on the hood of the car and started to read it.

"Chuck, what are you doing?" Mike said. "I know the way."

"Don't bother me," Chuck said, getting back in the car.

For the next forty-five minutes, Chuck Berry drove all over Manhattan in an unsuccessful attempt to find one of the tunnels. Finally, Mike said, "Chuck, you want to make a right here. The Holland Tunnel's right over there."

"If you don't stop talking, you can get out of the car right now."

For the next two hours, Mike didn't say another word. It was freezing cold, and Chuck was blasting the heat. To hear Mike tell it, the interior of the Cadillac was at least ninety degrees, and Chuck was smelling "ripe." The only fresh air Mike got was when Chuck rolled down the window to pay the toll on the Garden State Parkway.

By the time they got to Atlantic City, Chuck was hungry, so they stopped into a restaurant. Just as the food was delivered, a fire broke out in the kitchen, and smoke began to make its way into the dining room. While the employees and customers scrambled to leave the building, Chuck Berry sat there eating his food. He didn't give a shit. Fire or no fire, he was hungry.

While Chuck finished his breakfast, Mike McCourt called me in Margate. "I can't do it any more. You've got to come get him." Fortunately, the fire was contained before Chuck or anyone else was injured, and I was able to drive to the restaurant and retrieve him. Mike McCourt drove back to Margate with me, and Chuck followed in the Cadillac.

When Chuck walked into Memories for the first time, he said, "You know, Geator, I would like some company while I'm here. It's gotta be a fan. I'm not lookin' for a hooker."

Other than a hooker, I didn't know where I would find someone. After all, he wasn't Mick Jagger. At the same time, though, I knew how difficult he could be. If I didn't find him the right kind of "female companionship," he might not do the gig.

"I'll handle it," I said.

The only way to handle it was to call Skinny D'Amato.

"I've got a problem. Chuck Berry's coming in, and he's looking for a girl in her early twenties."

"Yeah? So what's the problem?"

"She's gotta be a fan, and I don't know of any fan that wants to spend the night with Chuck Berry."

Skinny laughed. "I'll call you right back."

A half hour later, he called and said, "I got a girl for you."

The girl he got for me had been coming in to Memories, but I didn't know that she was hooking on the side. She was a nineteen-year-old blonde. When I explained the situation to her over the phone, she agreed, and I promised her $200 to spend the night with Chuck Berry. At that time, $200 was a lot of money for a small-time hooker, but the girl wanted more.

"For an extra hundred," she said. "I'll even do you."

"That's not gonna happen. It's not negotiable."

Around four in the afternoon, Mike said, "Chuck, let's rehearse."

"Why? Don't you know my songs?"

"Of course. But in case you want to do them a certain way. . . ."

"No. You do them just like the record."

"What key do you do the songs in?"

"Just follow me."

The club was packed that night, and when Chuck came in, the blonde was with him. He walked on stage and started to play. The crowd went crazy. Unfortunately, even though some of the band members knew "Maybellene," "School Days," "Sweet Little Rock and Roller," and the other major hits, they were lost when it came to the B sides. I had been playing the B sides for years, and the audience wanted to hear them; but when Chuck played "Little Queenie," "Almost Grown," and "Let It Rock," the guys had a hard time following him. They did the best they could, but Chuck made things difficult by yelling out the chord changes as he went along. (To this day, Chuck Berry travels without a band, and without a musical conductor. It's just Chuck and his guitar. If there is a house band, he walks in and expects them to know his music.)

McCourt and the others were excellent musicians, but without a rehearsal, it just didn't sound like Chuck's records. The audience was in good spirits, however, and didn't seem to mind. They were happy to see Chuck in person, but I felt that his performance was off.

If anyone in the audience was upset, Chuck's last song won them over. It was "My Ding-A-Ling," and the audience sang along with him.

As Memorial Day weekend approached, I needed a headliner to kick off the new season, and I decided to call Little Richard. I had worked with Richard a number of times over the years, booking him at my record hops in Wildwood. When I got him on the phone, I told him that I had a budget of $10,000. Richard had some other bookings in the region, and he told me that he would do it. "I need a half-deposit," he said, and gave me the name of his agent at the Dean Agency in Nashville.

I wired $5,000 from my personal account, asking the agent to send a contract as soon as possible. In the meantime, I documented it by writing "Richard Penniman, Memories, Memorial Day Weekend." Three weeks before his scheduled appearance, I still didn't have the contract, so I called Richard. I had already started talking about his appearance, and now I had to advertise it.

"Don't worry about it, Geator. I'm gonna be there."

Another week went by, and I still didn't have a commitment from him in writing. I called him again and said, "I need the contract."

"I got a problem," he answered. "All my other dates canceled on me. I'm on the West Coast. I'm gonna need an additional $5,000 to come on in with my band."

"Richard, we made a deal for $10,000. You already got the half-deposit from the agent."

"I'm gonna do the date, but I need an additional $5,000."

"Richard, it's not gonna happen. You got me in a bind. You either do the date or I want my deposit back."

"I already spent it."

"That's not my problem, my man."

"If you pay for the air fare, I'll come in."

"I'm not gonna fly you in. That's not my responsibility. Just get me back my deposit."

"I don't know where I'm gonna get it."

"Richard, get me the fuckin' money," I said, and hung up the phone.

Meanwhile, I was in a panic. Memorial Day weekend was right around the corner. I needed a headliner as big as Richard so the public wouldn't think I was jiving them. In my mind, there was only one guy on the same level, and that was Chuck Berry. Even though he was a pain in the ass, I called him again, reaching him at "Berry Park," his property outside of St. Louis.

"Chuck, I got a problem," I said, explaining the situation.

"I'll do it for $10,000, but I need somebody to bring me half of the money in cash before I get on the plane."

"No problem," I said, and hung up the phone.

Like before, I sent Mike McCourt with the money. When Mike landed in St. Louis, Chuck was waiting for him at the gate.

"Where do you want to do this?" Mike asked.

"Follow me."

Chuck led Mike into the men's room. There was a shoeshine stand over in the corner, and Chuck climbed into the chair.

Mike handed over the $5,000 and Chuck counted it before putting it into his pocket. "Come on," he said, "let's go."

"Chuck, please, can you give me a receipt?"

Chuck made a face, then pulled out a business card from his wallet. He scribbled on it and handed it to Mike. It said, "Jerry, I'll see you in Margate. Chuck."

As soon as Chuck finished his set on Memorial Day weekend, he wanted to get paid. He left his guitar on stage and came looking for me. I took him back to the office and gave him the money in cash. He took his time counting it. After we went back into the club, Chuck had another drink. When he was ready to leave, he walked over to the stage to get his guitar. It was missing.

Chuck went ballistic. I grabbed my bouncers and told them to lock the doors; then I got up on stage and said, "Chuck Berry's guitar is missing. Nobody's gettin' outta here until it's recovered. I don't wanna know who took it. Just put it in the men's room."

Chuck went back to the Mariner while we looked for his guitar. We were panicking. We even went to some of the other clubs in the area and talked to the bands to see if anyone had a Gibson guitar that we could buy. Fortunately, when Mike McCourt checked the men's room an hour or two later, Chuck's guitar was leaning against the wall, and that was the last time Chuck played Memories.

Mike DelColla was aware that I had originally booked Little Richard, and wanted to know what happened. When I explained the situation, he asked if I got my deposit back.

"No. He spent it."

"We should sue him," Mike said. "I'll take the case on consignment."

Mike went into Federal Court and got an injunction. Richard got some cockamamie lawyer to represent him and lost. His lawyer argued that we didn't have a contract, but the judge agreed that the paper trail we had after I wired Richard the money was sufficient. On top of the original $5,000 that he ordered Richard to repay, the judge granted an injunction against him for $50,000 in damages, the amount I would have lost if I hadn't gotten Chuck Berry to replace him.

For the next several years, Richard avoided Philadelphia, Atlantic City, and every other town that fell in our judicial district, and we weren't able to collect until 1980 when one of the casinos offered him $75,000 to headline a show. This was big money. Richard accepted the offer.

Every year since 1973, DelColla had reinstated the injunction, and as soon as we heard about Richard's upcoming appearance, I called Dave Zann at Banner Talent, the agency that booked him. Because I had worked with them in the past, they were willing to cooperate. As a formality, we served the legal papers to both Richard and his agency, and when it was time for him to get paid, Zann told him, "Richard, there's a constable here. He has a court order. We have to give him the money." Without batting an eye, Richard said, "I understand." The truth is, this wasn't the first time that Richard had been sued, and he knew the routine. In fact, it had probably happened to him so often that he might not have made the connection to Memories and the incident from seven years before. To this day, Richard and I are still friends, but business is business.

It was at that time that Nat and I became close again. He lived alone at the Margate Towers and would come to see me at the club. Occasionally, when the Margate Mariner was oversold, I would spend the night at Nat's apartment. At one point, I didn't see him for a couple of weeks. His brother, Sam, ran a jewelry store in Atlantic City, and I was shocked and deeply saddened when he told me that Nat had passed away.

One night, Jim Keating came to see me at Memories. He had replaced Jack Downey as the general manager of WCAU in Philadelphia. Keating was aware that I had done a compilation album for WCAM called *The Little Giant Presents Golden Oldies*, and that Downey and I had talked about my doing a compilation for WCAU prior to Downey's departure. Downey had fallen out of favor with CBS for endorsing Frank Rizzo as a mayoral candidate and had gone to work for Frank as Deputy Commissioner of Public Works. Keating told me that WCAU was changing its format to oldies and asked if I would like to do a Sunday night show.

Now that I was no longer involved with WCAM, there was no reason for me to turn down Keating's offer. I did the show live from the WCAU studio and had a blast playing the music I loved. Our ratings in the 7 to 11 p.m. time slot were solid if not spectacular, but the show fit in nicely with my schedule.

In addition to my Sunday night show, we made a deal to take over the ballroom at a new Holiday Inn at 4th and Arch on Thursday nights. WCAU would promote it on the air as an oldies dance party, and I would put up the money to book the acts. The Holiday Inn would get free radio spots to promote the hotel. They would also get the revenue from the bar. I would get "the door." Little by little, I was putting the pieces back together again.

Because of what we were doing, oldies enjoyed a resurgence in Philadelphia, and I was asked to put together some bigger shows. One of them was for Larry Magid at the Spectrum. The artists included Screamin' Jay Hawkins, Jackie Wilson, Bo Diddley, Hank Ballard and the Midnighters, and again, I would work with my old friend, Chuck Berry.

Around the same time, I emceed an oldies show for Larry Marshak at the Academy of Music in New York. Marshak and I went on to co-produce *The Greatest Rock and Roll Reunion of Them All* at the Civic Center in Philadelphia, headlined by Fats Domino. The Four Seasons were on the bill, and we brought back a number of artists to perform with their original groups, including Dion (the Belmonts), Ronnie Spector (the Ronettes), Ben E. King (the Drifters), and Jimmy Beaumont (the Skyliners). The engineer who produced my radio spots for the show was a young kid named Howard Eskin, who would become the "king of sports talk radio" in Philadelphia.

Larry Magid also produced a benefit show at the Spectrum with Sammy Davis Jr. I shared the "master of ceremonies" duties with Henry Winkler, the actor who played "the Fonz" on *Happy Days*. All of the musical acts were accompanied by a complete orchestra, and before I introduced Sammy, I did two or three songs myself, including "Lucille" and "Shake, Rattle, and Roll." The show was produced by Al O'Neal, who also handled the money—unfortunately, the money never got to the charity.

When I came home late at night after the gigs, Pattie would be entertaining her friends. They would be out by the pool in nicer weather, or downstairs. I didn't have much in common with them. Instead of going home right away, I would stay out later, and if Pattie's friends were still there when I got back, I would have a drink at my bar downstairs before I went to bed. I would always kiss my girls while they were sleeping.

Pattie and I were growing farther apart. In happier days, we would take the kids to Puerto Rico, and I started to go there by myself just to get away. A friend of mine, Barry Sinkow, was now the entertainment director at the Americana. Barry would get me a special rate whenever I came down. One President's Weekend, the Americana was packed, and I ran into a couple of girls in the lobby. I knew one of them from back home. Her name was Diane. She lived around the corner from WHAT and was a big fan. Her friend was Bobbi. When they told me that they didn't have a place to stay, I invited them to stay with me. We spent the night together, and I ended up with Bobbi.

When I got back home, I continued seeing Bobbi and even got it on with her at her mother's house on Brown Street when no one was there. At one of the shows at the Holiday Inn, when I had the Drifters performing with me, she showed up with a friend of hers. Her friend was tall, and she was wearing a bandanna. Something about her reminded me of Ruby Tuesday, the girl in the Rolling Stones song, and I started calling her that. She loved the Stones and immediately adopted the nickname, "Ruby."

That night after the show, we went to Harlow's on Bank Street. Bobbi knew that I disapproved of drugs, but that didn't stop her and

Ruby from ducking into the ladies' room and smoking a joint. A year or two before, I wouldn't have been caught dead with someone who was smoking a joint; now it seemed to be an acceptable thing to do.

Before we left Harlow's, Ruby picked up a guy in his early twenties, and the four of us went back to Ruby's place in South Jersey. The guy that Ruby picked up was ten years younger than she was, and as soon as we arrived, she pulled him into her bedroom while Bobbi and I went at it on the sofa. Bobbi was usually energetic, but she had smoked too much pot and ended up falling asleep.

I made my way to Ruby's bedroom. When I looked in, I could see that the guy was too stoned to get it on. As soon as Ruby saw me, she gave me a look that said she wanted me to replace the guy, and that's exactly what I did. Before I even got into bed, the guy fell asleep, and I started to get it on with Ruby. Right in the middle of it, Bobbi came into the bedroom and started screaming, "Take me home right now!" That was the end of Bobbi and the beginning of "Ruby Tuesday."

Instead of going right home after my gigs, I would drive over to Ruby's and cook for her. Ruby was one of the most sensual lovers I ever had, but as good as the sex was, I felt guilty about it. I wasn't happy with the way my sex life was going with Pattie, but I couldn't justify what I was doing.

When I got to Ruby's one night, she was talking to someone on the phone. It turned out to be a psychic, and Ruby insisted that I speak with the woman before she hung up. The psychic told me that I was going to be rich beyond my imagination, and asked if I had ever had stomach problems. Psychics weren't really my thing, and I wasn't overly impressed with what she said, but she intrigued me. I had undergone an operation for the hernia that was first diagnosed in high school, and later would be operated on four more times. Strangely enough, a few years later, I would speak to another psychic and have a more powerful experience.

One Thursday, Jilly Rizzo called me. He said that Frank was going to be at the Civic Center and wanted to invite me to the show. I said, "Jill, I gotta be in New York to meet with Larry Marshak."

When I was in New York, I bumped into Fabian in front of the Brill Building. He told me that he was in for a couple of days. "Listen," I said, "I'm gonna have a drink with Frankie Valli at Jilly's. Why don't you come over?" Mike McCourt had driven me to New York, and Ruby was with us also.

We got to Jilly's around midnight. The place was empty, but an hour later, there was a commotion at the front door. Who came in with an entourage of people but Sinatra, Alan King, and Jilly. They had flown from Philly to New York in Frank's plane. When Frank saw us at the bar, we exchanged pleasantries before he went to his private table in the back. Once Frank got there, the place was jam-packed.

A few minutes later, Jilly walked over and whispered in my ear. "The old man would like you, Frankie, and your lady friend to join him, but not the other guys." Mike McCourt was smart enough to know the protocol, but I couldn't embarrass Fabian like that. Ruby, Frankie, and I went back to Sinatra's table, but when he invited us to sit down, I said, "Thanks, Mr. S., but we have to get back to Philly." Frankie stayed at Sinatra's table, and Ruby and I went back to the bar and left with Fabian. He never knew what went down.

When I was seeing Ruby, I never realized that Pattie's sister, Rita Scotese, lived in the same apartment complex. One night, Rita saw my car parked outside of Ruby's building and called Pattie.

"Do you know where your husband is at two o'clock in the morning?"

"He's working," Pattie said.

"He is? How 'bout if I tell you that his car's at the Village of Pine Run?"

When I got home at three in the morning, Pattie's car wasn't in the driveway. Like always, I gave each of the girls a kiss, and then I went to bed. The next thing I knew, Pattie came in and said, "Where were you?"

"I just got home from work."

"Yeah? I went to the Village of Pine Run looking for your fucking car."

"I don't know what you're talking about."

After that incident, I rarely went to Ruby's apartment, but we got it on elsewhere. I even employed her as a bartender at Memories, and she would stay at the Margate Mariner.

Even though I was sexually involved with Ruby, I wasn't in love with her. It was pure sex, and I always told her that if word ever got out, the affair would be over. Unfortunately, it came to an end on a Sunday night in September 1976, when I came home from Memories to find that Pattie had changed the lock on the front door. When I walked around the house, I couldn't get in the back door either, and all of my clothes were in the swimming pool. A lot had happened in ten years. Instead of Cardinal Krol's golf balls, my own suits and ties were floating on the surface of the water.

It was early in the morning, and I didn't know where to go. I didn't want to check into a hotel where people would recognize me, so I went to the RDA Club. By then, Don Battles had moved the RDA to the Drake Hotel, which was owned by another friend of mine, Stanton Miller. Don gave me a key to one of the rooms, and as I got into bed, I felt the kind of loneliness I had experienced as a kid. I couldn't sleep. I felt like my world had been turned upside down. I had gone from a palatial home to a single room in a hotel, and the next morning, I woke up with an emptiness that I had never felt before.

When Pattie changed the locks, she took away my sanctuary from the outside world, but more importantly, I missed my daughters something awful. Not being able to go into their room and kiss them good night was devastating to me. Strangely enough, however, throwing me out might have been the best thing that Pattie ever did for me in terms of my career. In order to fill the void, I started to work more, spinning records at the Center City Club at Broad and Locust and the Parkway House at 22nd and the Parkway, where I eventually got an apartment. (Coincidentally, this was the same building that Dick Clark lived in when he was going through a divorce.)

People like Sammy Davis and Frankie Valli gave me emotional support in the earliest days of the breakup, once they got over the shock. The two of them—and other show business friends—had always thought that Pattie and I were the perfect couple. When I told them what happened, they couldn't believe it.

Eventually, I adjusted to my new life. At night, rather than go back to an empty hotel room after work, I hung out at the clubs until two or three in the morning like I had when I was a kid. My instincts told me to go back to the streets to resurrect my career, and to have faith that things would work out.

Over the years, people have asked me why I haven't divorced Pattie. I'm not sure I understand it myself. All I can tell you is that I never wanted my kids to feel the kind of loneliness that I had felt growing up. There were too many times when my father wasn't around when I needed him to be a dad, and when I needed to talk to him about my problems. As a result, my answers came from living in the streets. I wanted to be there for my kids every step of the way, and getting divorced would have made that impossible.

In addition, I wanted to preserve a sense of unity. I may not have been in love with Pattie, but I loved her as the mother of my children; even though we were separated, I wanted our kids to feel that we were working together to provide them with a home. (There was another reason as well. Even though I strayed, I was still deeply thankful for what God had given me in my success, and I knew that divorce was a matter of excommunication in the Roman Catholic Church. At the time, divorce was never an option.)

I was determined that my separation from Pattie wouldn't change the way that my kids were being raised. I talked to them every morning before they went to school at Merion Mercy Academy and saw them whenever I could. Every night, I would call them before they went to bed, but it wasn't the same as being there for them. It was always painful for us when it was time to hang up the phone.

When Pattie and I were together, we would take the girls out to dinner every Sunday night. We would go to Frankie Bradley's on Chancellor Street, along with my in-laws and their kids. In happier days on Overbrook Avenue, I would cook dinner for the girls and take them on long walks on the grounds of St. Joseph's University. Now, that part of my life was over, and there was a void that could never be filled.

I was still getting my hair cut at Orlando Puppo's barbershop at Broad and Snyder. Once in a while, I would see Angelo Bruno there, whose wife, Sue, was a *paisan* of my mother. Their parents had originated in the Abruzzi region of Italy, and I had known the Brunos my entire life. When I was a kid, they owned a grocery store where my mom would shop. To the law enforcement community, Angelo Bruno was the head of organized crime in Philadelphia; to the people I grew up with, he was a neighbor who never bothered anyone, and if you had a problem, you could talk to him about it.

The Brunos have been a part of my life for as long as I can remember. Whenever Pattie and I had a party on Overbook Avenue, we would invite their daughter, Jean Angela, and her husband, Ralph Puppo, Orlando's son. The Brunos' grandchildren would swim in our pool and go out to dinner with us. (I had known Ralph Puppo since we were kids. When I was dancing on *Bandstand,* he was singing on Stan Lee Broza's *Children's Hour,* a talent show on Channel 10 sponsored by Horn and Hardart's.)

When Sue found out that Pattie and I had split up, she would invite me over for dinner during the week, and eating with them gave me a sense of family all over again. That was the thing that I missed the most after the separation, and the Brunos opened their hearts to me and treated me like one of their own. Because they didn't want me to be alone, they would invite me to join them on the holidays, and I was happy to accept the invitation. Every so often, on a Sunday afternoon, Sue would call me and say, "We're going to Jean Angela's. Why don't you take a ride with us?" And I would drive them to Jean Angela's house in Radnor. I would also hear from Angelo's sister, Lena, who was married to Peter Maggio. She was always raising money for worthy causes, and she would ask me to serve as an emcee at fundraisers.

After Pattie and I split up, I continued to take the girls out to dinner on Sunday nights, and I often took the Brunos' grandchildren with us. In addition to Frankie Bradley's, I would take the kids to Di Medici's on 8th Street or Fisher's Seafood House at 54th and City Line. One night, when I was dropping her grandchildren off, Sue invited me over for coffee in the morning, and I started going over to the Brunos' two or three mornings a week. Not only did it get me out of my apartment, but it also kept my spirits up through some of the darkest days I had ever experienced. (The Brunos opened their home to the people they loved, just like I had done on Overbook Avenue.)

After I moved into the Parkway House, I would spin records in the Parkway Room, a night club they had on the first floor, and take women up to my apartment afterward. I started to live my life like I was on the road with Danny and the Juniors; more often than not, though, it turned out to be an emptier form of consolation than the support I got from my friends.

In November, Pattie asked me what I was doing on Thanksgiving. I had a standing invitation from the Brunos, but other than that, I didn't have any plans.

"Why don't you have dinner with us?" Pattie asked.

Even though it would feel a little strange to have a family dinner, I accepted the invitation. "Okay," I said, "I'll cook something."

After Thanksgiving dinner, I took the kids for a walk like I used to. Before I left, Pattie said to me, "I want you to come back." I had no idea that she was even considering it. I knew that if I accepted, the kids would be happy, but in my heart I knew it wouldn't work. I was already adjusted to my new life. Kathi was already married, Gerry soon would be going to college, and Stacy and Deserie would soon be out of Merion Mercy. I realized that with the kids away, Pattie and I really didn't have anything in common. I didn't want to hurt her, so I said, "Let me think about it." After that, she never asked me again.

During the summer, in addition to my regular customers, Memories was jam-packed with Philly people who would hang out at Jimmy's Milan, the Saloon, Elan, Artemis, and other hot spots in town. A lot of them were friends with Irv Fisher, who owned a beach house on Vendome Avenue in Margate. Al DeEva would stay with Fisher, along with his girlfriend, Lorraine; Bobby Santore, one of the owners of the Saloon; and a local personality, Jackie Edelstein. I would hang out with them during the day, before I rented a house for an entire year at the shore. That's where my father would live. So did my mom on weekends. Matty Gunnella, my mother's second husband, had died by that time, and my parents were able to get along.

When Frank Sinatra was scheduled to appear at the Latin Casino, I heard from his publicist, Lee Salters. "Frank's comin'. Would you like to see him?"

Knowing that Sinatra was friendly with Walter Annenberg, I decided to invite Walter and other local dignitaries. Salters was all for it. "Great idea. Tell me how many people. We'll give you Frank's table."

Although the Annenbergs were unable to attend, our group included the district attorney, Emmitt Fitzpatrick; the deputy mayor, Mike Wallace; Judge Thomas Shomus; Vince Verrelli, the owner of Yellow Cab; Angelo Bruno's granddaughter, Sue; and Larry Fields, a columnist at the *Philadelphia Daily News*. (Emmitt Fitzpatrick had tried to scare me by putting me in jail during the Bob Horn trial in the 50s, but now we were friends. His daughter attended Merion Mercy Academy with two of my girls.)

Everyone met at my building, and after a small cocktail party that I hosted in the Parkway Room, a limousine picked us up and took us to the Latin. Salters met us at the backstage entrance and led us to Sinatra's table. Like always, Pat Henry warmed up the crowd until Sinatra interrupted him.

Larry Fields had been drinking heavily from the minute he arrived at the cocktail party, and by the time Sinatra began to sing, Fields was drunk. The next thing we knew, he was sleeping with his head on the table.

When the show was over, Salters invited us backstage, but Fields was in no condition for us to accept the invitation. Instead, four of us grabbed his arms and legs, carried him out to the limousine, and piled in after him. Before the limo pulled away, we asked Salters to thank Sinatra for us.

Despite the fact that he had slept through the entire concert, Larry Fields reviewed it in the *Daily News* the next day, calling it one of the most amazing shows that he had seen in his entire life. His ghostwriter, Sam Bushman, wrote the review for him. When we read it, Mike Wallace and I broke up laughing.

One morning, when I was having coffee with the Brunos, Raymond "Long John" Martorano walked in. Martorano was an associate of Angelo's. One of their ventures was John's Vending, which had candy, cigarette, and pinball machines, as well as jukeboxes.

"Sam just bought Torello's," Martorano said, referring to a friend of mine, Sam Rappaport, who used to come to the clubs I worked. Sam owned a significant amount of Center City property, including the building that the Center City Club was in.

Torello's—one of the first upscale Italian restaurants in Center City—had gone bankrupt on Chestnut Street. With the coming of new restaurants in Philly, they couldn't keep up with the competition. Plus, Chestnut Street from Broad to 20th was now a walkway with no cars. It was full of fast-food joints, penny arcades, and movie theaters that showed "blaxploitation" and X-rated films. They were not Torello's customers, and after eight o'clock at night, it was deadsville.

"What does he intend to do with the property?" Angelo asked. Raymond didn't know, other than the fact that they had their cigarette machines in there. I didn't know it at the time, but Angelo had an idea. The stop had been very successful for them. He called Sam Rappaport.

Sam called me and said, "I got a call from Angelo. He thinks it might be a good idea for you to come out with a Memories concept for Center City. Why don't you meet me at Torello's?"

When I walked in, I immediately knew what I wanted to do. By day, Chestnut Street was packed with local business people going to lunch, and there wasn't a place in the area that had great Italian sandwiches like in South Philly—sausage and meatballs, roast pork, and roast beef the way Nick's did it (cutting it right in front of you).

The space was great. One of the problems, though, was that Torello's had one of the longest bars around. It was along the right-hand side as you walked toward the back, and it seemed to go on forever. The thing I didn't like was that the bar faced the wall. The wall itself had a huge piece of artwork that depicted a bullfighter in action. It was a mosaic that must have cost $10,000. But from my experiences working clubs and bars, people would rather look at each other across the bar than at a mosaic. I had to change the whole look and concept—thus Torello's, the famous Italian restaurant, would now be called Memories West, at 1734 Chestnut Street.

The first thing I did was have workers change the look, decorating the restaurant with gigantic posters of old movies and movie stars. I got a sculptor to make miniature statues of Bogart, Charlie Chaplin, the Three Stooges, and other Hollywood personalities. I then placed them into cutout shelves on the walls over the booths. For the bar, we kept the mosaic, but we added a "Wall of Fame." Whenever celebrities were in town and came in for lunch, they would sign their autograph on the wall. Sammy, Dinah Shore, Joey Bishop, Andy Griffith, Jim Nabors, and many others were on the "Wall of Fame." My friend, Joe Scrappy—Joe Letizia—who had been one of Sinatra's bodyguards and had dated Julie Newmar, brought in a young actor who had written a screenplay called *Rocky*. It was Sylvester Stallone, and he autographed the wall also.

Now I had to come up with a menu. I realized that the office workers had a limited amount of time for lunch, and that we had to get them in and out of there quickly. The menu itself was art deco, and everything on it came out to a "round number" when we included the tax. The soups, salads, and sandwiches were two bucks, and the daily specials were five. The soups included lentil, escarole, and pasta fagiole, and the daily specials featured lasagna, stuffed eggplant, veal scaloppini, and other Italian specialties. The roast beef, roast pork, sausage, and meatball sandwiches became an everyday thing, and so did the hoagies. Terry Ianelli, a baker on Passyunk Avenue, created four different rolls for me, and I brought my Aunt Millie in to work with my mother. The two of them had a ball creating the menu and doing all of the cooking themselves. (I was still friendly with Pattie, and once in a while—when my cashier didn't show—I would get her to fill in. You could feel the tension between her and my mother, but they never made a scene.)

"That's a great idea," Sam said, when I described the concept to him. "You got the first six months no charge. After that, I'll charge you $3,000 a month."

Sam owned the liquor license, and though I didn't sell a lot of alcohol at lunchtime, it enabled me to do a "Happy Hour" with special drink prices from 4:30 to 7 p.m. My mother would take the rolls that were left over from lunch, create a homemade gravy, and make miniature pizzas that were complimentary.

The next thing I did was install a sound system throughout the entire restaurant and create a series of tapes that played music continuously. At lunchtime from 11 to 2, I played music from the 40s and 50s, featuring Patti Page, Rosemary Clooney, the Four Aces, Sinatra, Tony Bennett, and the popular big bands. During the Happy Hour, the tapes consisted of rhythm and blues, rock and roll, and the hits of the latter 50s and 60s.

At night, it was different. By 8:30, the clientele on Chestnut Street changed. The office workers deserted the area, and the arcades and movie theaters took over. There was nothing more depressing than sitting at the bar at 9 or 10 p.m. without a single customer in the place, knowing that you were losing money, particularly when the bars and restaurants were thriving a block away on Walnut Street. The city had planned to make Chestnut Street an exciting place to be, but it never experienced the resurgence that everyone was hoping for.

I never realized the hours I would have to put in at Memories West. By comparison, Memories in Margate was a breeze. We didn't open until nine o'clock at night at the shore, and eight hours later, we were gone. With Memories West, however, someone had to open the place early in the morning and close it late at night. In a way, it was good that our business fell off after Happy Hour, because I was getting in by eleven in the morning and staying until ten or eleven two or three nights a week. I don't know what time I would have gotten out if the place were busier. In addition, I was still at the Downtown Tavern on Thursday nights and the Center City Club on Fridays.

Fortunately, Chuckie Weir helped me. Weir was one of the kids who had watched me tape my radio show on Overbrook Avenue, and now—after his wife kicked him out of the house—he would often sleep on my couch. By then, I had moved to the Society Hill Towers. I wanted a bigger place so my kids could visit whenever they wanted.

Weir would get up early and go into Memories West, opening up the place, making sure it was clean, letting my mother and Aunt Millie in, and getting the rolls when the delivery guy pulled up to the back door. Once he got his life straightened out, Weir was a hard worker. He worked all day and closed the place at night. Occasionally, he would drive me to New York.

At lunchtime, Memories West became a meeting place for lawyers, politicians, and celebrities, including Frank Rizzo; Al Pearlman; Emmitt Fitzpatrick; Tom Gola; the city solicitor, Shelly Albert; and the Deputy Police Commissioner, Morton Solomon. Chestnut Street was dead at night, and I continued to lose money when Memories West emptied out after Happy Hour. But eventually, fate was on my side. A development in local radio provided me with the opportunity I needed. After acquiring WIBG from Storer Communications, Buckley Broadcasting decided to convert the station to a religious format, but the week before the format change took place, they wanted to have a big blowout on the air to commemorate the heyday of WIBG. Their idea was to bring back some of the older disc jockeys like Hy Lit, Joe Niagara, and Bill Wright, Sr., and to have me do a 7 p.m. to midnight shift from Monday to Saturday. Hy Lit's show would be right before mine.

The people from Buckley Broadcasting came to see me at the restaurant. I told them that I would love to do it, but not from the studio. I would take all of the tables and chairs out of the back room at Memories West, convert it into a dance floor, and do a live remote. I also invited them to bring their advertisers and promised complimentary drinks. Knowing how successful I was at Memories in Margate, I was sure that it would be a home run.

Buckley Broadcasting loved the idea, and things went according to plan during the week that I broadcast from Memories West. By Tuesday night, you couldn't get into the place, and I had to call Morton Solomon to request extra policemen. The line stretched around the block, and the city used police officers on horseback to control the crowds. Memories West went from "dead" to bursting at the seams in a matter of twenty-four hours. Originally, I figured that we would gross around $10,000 for the week, as opposed to the $5,000-$6,500 that we had been averaging. Instead, we grossed more than $16,000.

Instead of acknowledging me as I went on the air, Hy Lit ended his Friday night show by saying, "Now you can turn your radios off, because WIBG is no longer broadcasting." I heard it when I was getting ready for the broadcast, and so did the customers.

After playing my theme song—"Work Out" by Rickie D—I responded by saying, "Hy, you're such a professional. I don't know if that really becomes you informing the listeners that we're off the air. When they hear the voice of the Geator, that doesn't make you too classy."

Some of the people from WPEN were regulars at Memories West, including the general manager, Larry Wexler. The station had recently converted to oldies, and I planted the idea of continuing my live broadcasts. When he saw what we were doing for WIBG—and the excitement we were creating—Wexler wanted the show. Two weeks after the WIBG gig ended, I was back on the air on Friday and Saturday nights on WPEN. On Friday nights, we did about $6,000; on Saturday nights, we doubled it. Once again, the secret was being on the radio.

Things went smoothly until WPEN brought in a new program director, Julian Breen. Breen objected to the live broadcasts. He wanted me to do my show from their studio and stop promoting Memories West on the air. More importantly, though, he didn't like the music I was playing. Like always, I was playing the hottest local oldies, including a lot of "B" sides, while Breen preferred to format the station with songs that made the Billboard charts. I told him that I wasn't interested in doing a formatted show from the studio. It didn't sit well with him, but Larry Wexler was in my corner.

Because we opened Memories West in November 1977, I had a couple months before Memories in Margate started back up for the season. But as soon as St. Patty's Day rolled around, I had to operate both businesses at the same time. One morning, when I was having coffee with the Brunos, Sue told me that I looked tired.

"He's running back and forth to the shore," Angelo said.

Sue looked at me and said, "You better take care of yourself. I'm worried about you."

Operating the two businesses continued to take a toll on me physically, and finally I asked for some time off from WPEN. I was still doing the live remotes from Memories in Margate on Friday nights, and I couldn't have done the WPEN show on Fridays anyway. Larry Wexler was disappointed in my decision to take a hiatus, but Julian Breen was happy about it, and he took the opportunity to hire another disc jockey to play formatted oldies from the studio. Ironically enough, my replacement was Hy Lit. Unfortunately, the station never got the ratings and had to change its format. WPEN became "The Station of the Stars," playing pre-rock and roll hits from the 40s and 50s.

Because of my schedule that summer, I saw the Brunos less frequently, but the next time I came over for coffee, Angelo told me that Teddy Pagano might be interested in buying Memories West. The Paganos operated a family-style restaurant in Southwest Philadelphia, and Angelo went back a long way with them.

"Teddy's interested in buying it," Angelo said. "What do you think?"

"Ange, that would be terrific."

"Why don't you show him the operation?"

When I walked Teddy around the restaurant, he said, "I don't want another Memories. I want to open a crab house."

In addition to crabs, Teddy wanted to serve shrimp, flounder, French fries, and cole slaw. He was going to call it Pagano's Crab House. I didn't like the concept, but I didn't want to say anything and blow the deal. I just couldn't see the businessmen eating hardshell crabs at lunchtime.

To make a long story short, Teddy Pagano offered me $80,000 for Memories West. He wanted the liquor license, which was owned by Sam Rappaport, and an assurance that the rent wouldn't be increased. I ended up buying the license from Sam for $7,500, and Sam agreed to freeze the rent at $3,000 per month. I had never signed a lease with him—we had a handshake agreement—and Sam helped me out by putting everything in writing for Teddy. Teddy gave me $40,000 up front and started to make monthly payments. I held the liquor license until

Teddy was paid up and then turned it over to him. (The sale couldn't have come at a better time. The summer months were traditionally slow for restaurants in Center City, and I knew that I couldn't keep up the pace of driving back and forth to the shore.)

When I look back on that chapter of my life, I realize what an amazing friend Angelo Bruno was. He had suggested a moneymaking opportunity to me, put the right people together to make it happen, and then helped me unload the business when it was getting to be too much.

In 1978, Resorts International was the first casino to open up in Atlantic City. Most people think that Sinatra was the first act booked, but it was actually Steve and Eydie. Frank was the second artist to perform there. I was invited to Frank's performance. Sammy, who was scheduled to open up Caesar's several weeks later, was also there. We all had a great reunion together.

With the arrival of the casinos, I no longer was booking acts at Memories. You couldn't compete with what the casinos were offering them. The casinos also brought the eventual demise of the Latin Casino, which would become a disco named Emerald City. I then concentrated on just spinning and doing my live broadcasts. In the fall and winter, Memories was only open on weekends. I supplemented my income with appearances in Philadelphia.

In addition to the Center City Club and the Downtown Tavern, I made appearances at the Library on City Line Avenue. Len Stevens, Dolly Banks' nephew, had opened the Library several months before. By now, the disco thing had taken over, and Len's idea was to turn the Library into a combination restaurant and disco like Studio 54 in New York. Len's concept took off, and whenever I played the Library, I spun a combination of disco songs and oldies. The disco artists included Donna Summer, the Village People, KC and the Sunshine Band, and the Bee Gees of *Saturday Night Fever*.

Prior to disco, one of the hottest jocks on WDAS was "The Good Doctor," Perry Johnson. WCAU was converting from oldies to disco and lured Johnson away from WDAS by doubling his salary. Unfortunately, they saddled him with a format and changed his persona. The audience didn't buy it, and eventually he lost his job.

I realize now that disc jockeys are some of the most insecure people you will ever meet, and the constant format changes are a major reason for that. I was one of the lucky ones. I never changed my persona no matter what was happening in the industry, and I never let anyone dictate the music I played.

I started to do one-nighters at a place called the Winner's Circle in Cherry Hill. They were doing great business until a disco named Valentino's opened a half a mile away. Before long, Valentino's was the hottest disco around, and Danny Prestillo, the owner of the Winner's Circle, took me aside.

"I gotta do something to compete with these guys."

"Let's do a TV show."

Gene McCurdy, who had replaced George Koehler at WFIL years before, was the new station manager of Channel 17. I knew he would be interested. The result was a half-hour show on Saturday nights called *The Discophonic Scene '79*. We taped the show on Thursday nights, and the Winner's Circle was packed with young people in their early to mid-twenties. The show aired during prime time from 7 to 7:30 and became one of the hottest shows on the station. Naturally, the record companies sent artists in. Our guests included Rick James, Gloria Gaynor, Teddy Pendergrass, Donna Summer, Peaches and Herb, Tavares, and other disco stars. Danny Prestillo and I coproduced the show.

Every other week, we would tape three shows at a time to control costs. It was the same principle as booking a recording studio. If you booked six hours of recording time, you had to utilize that, which is what happened years before when Bert Berns rushed the Isley Brothers in to record "Twist and Shout" at the end of a Chuck Jackson session. The program director of Channel 17 was Zvi Shubin, who loved *The Discophonic Scene '79* and was looking to develop a five-day-a-week dance show with me.

New Jersey had traffic circles in those days. Hardly anyone knew the rules on who was supposed to yield. It typically became a matter of who was first to make the turn. The Winner's Circle was located on a traffic circle on Route 38. After we taped the shows, the TV crew would usually have breakfast at the Diamond Diner, which was directly across the circle from the club. By the time all of the remote equipment was taken away in the truck, it was two or three in the morning.

One night, it was raining when I drove out of the Winner's Circle parking lot to go to the Diamond Diner. The crew members followed me in their cars. A small work crew was paving a section of the road. There were no roadblocks or barriers of any kind. It had been raining earlier and visibility was poor. Without realizing it, I drove onto a patch of road that had just been paved. A guy came running over to me with a flashlight. He was screaming.

"Listen, you dumb motherfucker, can't you see we're paving here?"

"Yo! Wait a minute. How am I supposed to know you're paving? Nobody's directing traffic."

"Get outta the car," he said.

"Get outta the car? Who the hell are you?"

With that, he reached in my car and grabbed my keys. The guys who were behind me saw that there was a confrontation. Some of them blew their horns to let the asshole know they were there. Some of the others got out of their cars.

I got out of my car and said, "Give me my fucking keys. If not, you're gonna have a problem."

He gave me my keys back and said, "Pull over there." I figured, "Fuck this guy." I didn't know who he was, and as far as I was concerned, he was out of line. I got in my car and drove away. Instead of using the traffic circle where they were paving, I took Route 38 to the first cut off and came back around. All of a sudden, the asshole from the road crew came running after my car and threw his flashlight at me. It went right into the open window and landed on my seat. Instead of going to the diner, I was so pissed off that I drove back to my place in Philly.

As soon as I got home, I called Danny Prestillo at the Diamond Diner.

He said, "Where are you?"

"Dan, I don't know if you realize this, but I had a confrontation with a fresh guy outside the club. They were paving."

"Yeah, I saw that, but I went around the back."

Prestillo knew a back way to the diner. He avoided all the bullshit.

"Maybe you should call the cops," I said, "and let them know that there's a problem out there."

"Don't worry about it."

I also did a show at the Coliseum in Voorhees Township every

Sunday night. It was just twenty minutes from the Winner's Circle. Two weeks after the incident with the road crew, I got a call from Al Zurzolo, who operated the club at the Coliseum. He told me that the cops had been looking for me.

I said, "What are you talking about?"

"I don't know. They have a warrant for your arrest. Maybe you better not come in tonight."

I called Sal Avena, a big attorney in Jersey. He represented Angelo Bruno on some of his legal matters. "Sal, I don't know what this is about, but apparently there is a warrant for my arrest in New Jersey."

"For what?"

"I have no idea."

"Well, it's probably some kind of misdemeanor," he said. "Maybe you failed to pay a traffic ticket or something."

"I don't think so."

"How much do you make at the Coliseum?"

"I make a gee whiz at night—a thousand dollars."

"Well, you don't want to lose it. Go in, and if you have any problems, call me and I'll straighten it out."

I got to the club at nine o'clock. An hour later, the police were all over the place. The next thing I knew, the police chief of Voorhees came up to the stage and motioned me off. When I got off the stage, they took me to the office. Two Cherry Hill policemen were with them, and they said, "You're under arrest." They started to put cuffs on me when the police chief said, "He's not going anywhere. You don't have to embarrass him."

They put me in the back of a police car and took me to their station in Cherry Hill.

"Officers, what's this about?" I asked.

One of them said, "You tried to run down a police officer."

"What are you talking about? What police officer?"

"Me."

As he turned around, I couldn't believe it. It was the guy from the road crew that gave me bullshit at the Winner's Circle.

"You're a policeman?"

"Yeah. And you tried to run me down."

His name was Larry Leaf. I didn't say another word as he and his partner took me to the station. When we got there, they asked if I would like to make a statement. I said, "No. I want to talk to my lawyer."

I called Sal Avena and told him what happened. He said, "Put the captain on the phone."

When he got back on the phone with me, he said, "They're taking you to Camden County. They're gonna book you for an aggravated assault on a police officer, which is an indictable offense."

"Sal, that's crazy."

"There's nothing I can do right now. You'll have to wait till tomorrow morning when I get a judge to set bail."

"Sal, I thought you would take care of this."

"I didn't realize it was aggravated assault."

"I never knew anything about that!"

They took me to the Camden County Jail. It was in City Hall—the same building that I used to broadcast from on WCAM. WCAM was on the 18th floor, and the holding cells were on the 16th. The Cherry Hill cops were going to turn me over to Camden County, and as soon as we got off the elevator, a female police sergeant recognized me. When the cops left, she said, "Geator, what are *you* doing here?"

"I have no idea, but they said that I tried to run over a cop."

"Let me look at the paperwork," she said. "You gotta make bail."

After she glanced at the paperwork, she said, "You don't belong here."

The sergeant picked up the phone and called Judge James Greenburg, a municipal judge in Cherry Hill, and I heard her say, "Your honor, I've got Jerry Blavat here."

"What's the charge?"

"He's been booked for assaulting a police officer. The bail is $5,000."

She continued to talk with him, then hung up the phone. "The bail is set for $5,000. You need five hundred. Do you have it on you?"

I called Al Zurzolo and told him what I needed. He drove over from the Coliseum and put up the bail money.

The next day, at 7:30 in the morning, my daughter, Geraldine, called me at my apartment. "Daddy, are you okay?"

"Why, Gerry?"

"We're listening to the news. They say you're in jail."

"Ger, I'm not in jail. You got me at my apartment. Go to school."

"Yeah, but it's on KYW that you spent the night in Camden County Jail for assaulting a police officer."

"Ger, everything's fine."

When I hung up the phone, I called KYW, the all-news radio station, and reached someone at the editor's desk. I said, "What's going on with Jerry Blavat?"

"He's in Camden County for assaulting a police officer."

"Where'd you get the story?"

"It was reported by the Cherry Hill police."

"Yeah? Well, that's not the case."

"What do you mean?"

"You're talking to Jerry Blavat. I'm not in jail."

The guy hesitated. "Hold on, give me your number. I'll call you right back."

I gave him my number. A few seconds later, he called.

"You're not in jail."

"No. I made bail last night."

When the preliminary hearing rolled around, I didn't want to use Sal Avena. I called my friend Sam Rappaport, who was involved with Lewis Katz at People's Bank of New Jersey. Lou was the head of the Democratic Party in Cherry Hill. Lou represented me.

When we went to the preliminary hearing, they didn't dismiss the case but referred it to the grand jury. Katz said, "Don't worry about it. It's all bullshit. We'll put you in a pre-intervention program. If you don't get in trouble for six months, it's blown out. The case will be expunged from the record."

Meanwhile, because of the incident, I didn't want to do my TV show from Winner's Circle any more. I knew that the Cherry Hill cops would have a hot nut for me and would look to break my balls.

One of the guys that I knew from around town was Kenny Shapiro. Kenny owned an after-hours club on Market Street called the 22 Karat Club and was looking to promote it. He offered to do the show from there. Kenny also owned Yellow Cab Limos. Because it was an after-hours club, we would start to tape at eight o'clock.

One of the hottest nightclubs in Philadelphia at that time was Elan in the Warwick Hotel. It was Philadelphia's version of Regine's in New

York. You would have dinner early, and it would turn into a disco at ten o'clock. It was where Philly's elite would congregate to meet and greet. One night, I stopped by for a drink. One of the fashion models who used to hang there told me that Monti Rock was coming to town. Rock was a former hairdresser whose flamboyant style got him on the talk-show circuit. He had appeared on my television show in 1968, and now—going by the name of Disco Tex and His Sex-O-Lettes—he had one of the hottest disco records. His real name was Joseph Montanez and he was from a Puerto Rican family in the Bronx.

The girl said, "Hey, Monti wants to do your show."

When Rock came in town to do my show, he stayed at the Warwick. He had a friend with him, a blonde named Olga. Olga was a Castilian beauty from Puerto Rico. Not only was she stunning to look at, she had a lot of things going for her. She had her own line of cosmetics and a modeling agency based in Willow Grove. Olga reminded me more of a New York chick. She had her own limo and, unlike any other woman I had seen, was always picking up checks.

Olga knew about my TV show, and I said to her, "Listen, how would you like to have some of your models integrated with my dancers? I'll give you a credit at the end of the show saying 'Models supplied by Olga's International Modeling Studio.'" She liked the idea. Whenever we taped, she came over with some amazing ladies.

Although I wasn't immediately attracted to Olga, I found her exciting. Men were flocking to her, but from what I could tell, she wasn't encouraging any of them. She drank nothing but Tattinger's, one of my favorite champagnes.

Once we taped the show, we would have drinks in a private room above the 22 Karat Club. One night, I said to Olga, "Why don't you come back to my apartment?" She laughed and said, "No. This is strictly business."

As the weeks went by, I was more determined than ever to sleep with her. We taped earlier than usual one night, and instead of going to the private room upstairs, Olga went to Elan. After I finished with the crew, I went to Elan to see her. Like always, she was entertaining a group of people. She was surprised to see me.

"What are you doing here?" she asked.

"Looking for you."

I had a drink and danced with her to Syreeta's version of "He's Gone," which was produced by Syreeta's husband at the time, Stevie Wonder. It originally was one of the first songs that the Chantels ever recorded.

After I danced with her, I said, "Why don't you come back to my apartment?"

"I don't know," she said. "I'll call you when I'm finished."

I gave Olga my number and went home. When I was in bed around two in the morning, she called and said, "I'm coming over." That night, we started an affair that was strictly sexual.

I found myself seeing Olga more often. I would go up to Willow Grove, and one day, she introduced me to her daughter. I was shocked to learn that she had a daughter. When I asked her about it, she told me that her daughter was from a previous marriage.

Occasionally, if I had to go to New York and she had to visit a cosmetic factory that created private labels for her, I would hook up a ride in her limo. She had it all—even her own photographer on staff. He took promo pictures for me, and I used one of them for the cover of *For Lovers Only: Volume Three.* My daughter, Stacy, was on the cover with me. Olga and I had no way of knowing it at the time, but something would happen that would change the way I felt about her.

TEN: Loyalty

I was preparing for my radio show the evening of March 21, 1980, when Angelo Bruno got assassinated.

Early that morning, Sue Bruno had called me on the phone. "Are you coming over for coffee?"

Ever since Pattie kicked me out of the house, changed the locks, and prevented me from seeing the girls more than once a week, coffee at the Brunos had become a ritual for me.

"Discophonic Sue! See you in a bit."

Sue was sixty-seven years old, but she got a kick out of it when I treated her like one of my "yon teenagers." She broke up laughing when I said it.

"Do me a favor. Can you stop at Isgro on the way over?"

Isgro's was a pastry shop at 10th and Christian.

"Not a problem."

I usually brought biscottis to satisfy Angelo's sweet tooth—or ricotta cheesecake—but with Holy Week a day or two away, I knew exactly what was on Sue's mind.

"St. Joseph's bread?" I asked.

"You're a doll!"

The amarigans called them "hot cross buns," but that was a fugazi term to Italians—completely fake and an unfortunate sign of Americanization.

"How many? One dozen? Two?"

Sue cupped her hand over the mouthpiece and yelled to Angelo in the living room. My mother did the same thing when she talked on the phone.

"Ange, one dozen or two?"

Sue must have loosened her grip on the mouthpiece, because I could hear Angelo speaking to her from a few feet away.

"Ange said three dozen. Michael's coming over."

The Brunos lived at 934 Snyder Avenue in the heart of South

Philadelphia. I arrived around 11 a.m., and we sat in their kitchen like we always did.

"Have another one," Sue said, nodding toward the St. Joseph's bread, and without waiting for me to answer, Angelo slid the cardboard box across the table. I reached in for seconds. It was drizzling, and a heavier rain was expected later on.

"What are you doing today?" Angelo asked.

After eight years, Memories was still the hottest club at the Shore. On Friday nights, I opened at nine o'clock sharp; our live radio broadcast started an hour later.

"I don't think I'm doing anything. I have to be at the club by seven or seven-thirty, that's all."

"Can you drive me to City Line Avenue?" Angelo asked. "I'm meeting with Nastasi."

Nick Nastasi was one of his lawyers, and they needed to review Angelo's testimony from the day before, when Angelo had appeared before the Senate Investigating Committee in Trenton, the capital of New Jersey.

"We gotta wait for Johnny Keys," Angelo said. "Then we can go."

"Johnny Keys" was John DeSimone, one of Angelo's associates. He knocked on the back door a few minutes later, and Sue let him in.

Angelo glanced at his watch. "You're late."

"I got stuck in traffic. Some prick was double-parked."

Angelo looked at him. He didn't appreciate language like that—especially in front of his wife. "Come on," he said, "we gotta go."

"Can't he have a cup of coffee?" Sue asked.

"All right. As long as he drinks it fast."

DeSimone drank the coffee as fast as he could, but he only had two or three sips before Angelo stood up from the table. Sue glanced anxiously at the St. Joseph's bread. She wanted DeSimone to have some, but it was out of the question now. Angelo read her expression and said, "Maybe later."

DeSimone laughed. "I'll come back for the St. Joseph's bread. I promise!"

"Who are you kiddin'?" Sue said, getting up to clear the table. "You won't be back here today."

"Sure I will. I'll take some home for Terry."

Sue turned back to Angelo. "What time you be home?"

"I don't know yet. I'll call you."

"What do you want for dinner?"

Angelo smiled sadly. With Sue, he had the patience of a saint. "Whatever Michael wants, I don't care." Michael was their son.

"It's Friday. No meat."

"Make fish then."

"The kids like my scungilli salad," Sue continued.

"That's good," Angelo said. "Make that."

Sue looked at him. "Angelo, you look so handsome in that suit."

Angelo was wearing a blue business suit, made by a tailor on Passyunk Avenue.

He patted Sue on the cheek and we left.

"Park over there," Angelo said, when we arrived at a shopping center on City Line Avenue. "I'm meeting him at Horn and Hardart's."

Johnny Keys and I sat at one table, and Angelo and Nastasi sat at another. We sat on opposite sides of the room, so that Angelo could speak freely. Nastasi was an associate of Jake Kossman, Angelo's lead attorney. Later, Kossman would represent me in the investigation that followed.

Johnny Keys and I had three cups of coffee apiece while waiting for Angelo.

"I gotta piss like a racehorse," Johnny Keys said, as Angelo and Nastasi stood up.

Nastasi gathered his papers and left, nodding to me on his way out the door. Then Angelo joined me at the table.

"Where's Johnny?" he asked.

"He's in the men's room," I said.

"He should have thought of that before."

When Johnny Keys emerged from the men's room, we headed out to my car. By then, it was after two o'clock.

"Drop me off at Virgilio's," Angelo said. "Take Johnny back to my house."

Virgilio's was owned by Phil Testa, another associate of Angelo's. When I dropped Angelo off, he said, "I'll see you on Monday for coffee." That was the last time I saw Angelo alive.

By the time Johnny Keys and I arrived at the Brunos' house, it was close to three o'clock, and I had plenty of time to drive down to Margate. When dropping someone off, it has always been my habit to wait until they get in the door before I drive away, or in this case, get into their car. But instead of walking to his car like I expected him to, DeSimone said, "I left my raincoat inside. I'll catch you later."

I hesitated.

"That's okay," he said. "You can take off."

"No, I'll wait."

DeSimone smiled, but there was an edge to it, and it didn't come off the way he wanted. "I'm telling you, it's okay!"

With that, he walked up the sidewalk to the Brunos' house, climbed the steps, and rang the bell for Sue to let him in. When Sue failed to answer, DeSimone started fumbling in his pockets for a key. I didn't know that he had a key for the Brunos' house, and it didn't look right to me. But at the time, it didn't look wrong enough for me to say anything.

When Johnny Keys saw me watching all of this, he scowled, as though he had used up all of his smiles for the day. "It's okay, I said. Take off!"

As I pulled away, I realized that DeSimone didn't have a raincoat when he came in that morning. I watched in my rearview mirror as he walked to the corner of 10th and Snyder and made a call from a pay phone.

Knowing what I know now, I wish I would have done something, although I'm not sure what I could have done. Angelo treated me like a son, but I was never privy to the business he conducted with his associates. If I came right out and said I didn't trust DeSimone—or if I advised Angelo to watch his back—I would have been out of line. It would have shocked Angelo if I had done that, and it almost certainly would have damaged our relationship. At the same time, though, it might have saved his life. Instead of violating Angelo's trust, I drove away without saying anything. (If a family member spoke out of turn, engaged in gossip, or talked behind someone's back, Angelo would always say, "Mind your own business," and whether or not that factored into my thinking, I can't really say—but I've often wondered if I could have altered the chain of events.)

My father was working the door as I prepared for my broadcast on WAYV. Like always, he had a couple of his associates with him, and I was free to do what I do best, which is play the music I love. For me, it was more than spinning records: it was touching people and keeping them young, whether they were out on the dance floor, listening to a car radio, or tuning in at home.

At 9:55 p.m.—five minutes until airtime—a Margate police officer pulled up in front of the club, lowered his window, and called my father over to his squad car.

"Tell the Geator they just killed Angelo Bruno."

"You gotta be kidding," my father said.

Looking back on it, my father's doubts were reasonable. After all, Angelo had always abhorred the use of weapons, and for more than twenty-five years, he had settled disputes in a peaceful way. If anyone believed in a civilized society, it was him. Even the newspapers referred to Angelo as "the Gentle Don."

Leaving Spanish Pete in charge at the door, my father came looking for me inside the club. I was already up on the stage. I had my headphones on for the sound check. "This is the Geator with the Heator, the Boss with the Hot Sauce, the rebel jock who rocks the ol' tick tock. . . ."

"Take those off," my father said.

"What?"

"Take those fucking things off!"

I still couldn't hear him, but the look on his face communicated the urgency. I removed my headphones. "What?"

"They said Angelo Bruno was killed."

I stared at him. My first reaction was that it was a joke.

"Dad, that's impossible. I dropped him off at three o'clock."

"Some cop came by. I'm just telling you what he told me."

Just then, the phone rang. We had it hooked up so that it rang in two places, the office and the bar.

I turned back to my father. "Get that, would you?"

My father walked over to the bar and answered the phone. I still didn't believe that Angelo was dead. The idea of someone killing him didn't seem real, even knowing what we knew about how he made his living.

When my father returned to the stage, he was obviously upset.

"You better pick up the phone," he said. "There's a lot of noise on the other end. I think it's Sue."

"Okay. I'll take it in the office." I was due on the air in two minutes.

When I held the phone to my ear, I heard sirens on the other end of the line and Sue Bruno screaming hysterically. Although I had learned Italian from my grandparents, and was still able to speak it, I could barely understand her. *"Angelo e mort! Angelo e mort! Vene qua!"* And then I heard Michael speaking to her soothingly and hanging up the phone.

As soon as the broadcast was over, I jumped on the Atlantic City Expressway, listening to reports of Angelo's death as I returned to South Philadelphia. I knew that I would be subjecting myself to unwanted attention in the media, and that I would be placing myself in the crosshairs of a federal investigation. But even if I was risking everything that I had achieved, there was never any question of letting the family down. And so, my day ended exactly where it started—at the Brunos' kitchen table. Angelo's troubles were over, but mine had just begun.

ELEVEN: Trouble with the Law

S nyder Avenue was blocked off when I got there at two in the morning. The police had put up barricades, and I couldn't get to the Brunos' house.

I parked three blocks away, walked down Jackson Street, and called the Brunos from a payphone. I talked to Michael, and he got Rose, the next-door neighbor, to open the gate in her backyard.

The Brunos had gathered in the kitchen. Making my way through Rose's yard, I entered their house without being seen. Sue had been sedated. Lena, Peter Maggio, and Ralph Puppo were there also, along with Michael's wife, Zaria, and their children, Maria and Susan.

After the shooting, all kinds of people converged on the scene. Helicopters were flying overhead. It looked like a scene from a movie.

For the Brunos, however, it was all too real. Their patriarch was dead, and his body was in the passenger seat of John Stanfa's car. His head was leaning on the headrest, his mouth was open, and there was a gunshot wound behind his right ear. The crowd was staring at Angelo's body. Angelo had always had a respectful relationship with the police, and the family was devastated that they left him out on the street like that.

I stayed with the family for the entire weekend, sneaking out the back way once or twice to go to my apartment, shower, and get a change of clothes. Isgro's, Ralph's, Dante and Luigi's, and other South Philadelphia restaurants sent trays over out of respect for Angelo. Even though everyone was in a state of shock, the family was relatively calm, and Michael seemed to take over, as Angelo would have in a situation like that.

Willie Jacovini, Sr. came over with his sons to make arrangements for the funeral. They owned the Pennsylvania Burial Company on South Broad Street and had been friends with Angelo for years. After talking with the Jacovinis, Michael walked over to me and said, "Please, we need you at the funeral. We don't want this to become a media event. My father was a private person."

The viewing was scheduled for Monday with the funeral mass on Tuesday morning at the Epiphany on Jackson Street. I didn't hesitate. "Michael, don't be concerned about it. You have my word." In the back of my mind, I knew what I was getting myself into with law enforcement and the media, but loyalty was something I learned from growing up on the streets.

Needless to say, I knew what Michael was thinking. He didn't want the funeral to become a circus. As an entertainer, I knew most of the people in the media, and I had spent enough time with Angelo to recognize the law enforcement types that were watching him at the house.

On the night of the viewing, I stood in the lobby of the Pennsylvania Burial Company with the pallbearers. There were lines around the block. I had a strong sense of who was there to pay their respects, and who was there to sneak in a camera or tape recorder. Members of the press tried to sneak in, hiding their cameras in trench coats, but I blocked them at the door. "You can't go in there," I said. "These people are in mourning." They would walk away and take photographs of the crowd that had gathered outside of the funeral home and the people lining up to enter.

Larry Fields, the *Daily News* columnist who had fallen asleep at the Sinatra show, was trying to get in. He had always been kind to Angelo in the paper, painting a sympathetic portrait without taking shots. When he approached the lobby, I said, "Lar', I really can't let you in." But knowing that he had been fair to Angelo, I told him that I would see what I could do. I walked into the viewing area, where Michael was greeting mourners, and said, "Michael, Larry Fields is here. He would like to pay his respects."

"What do you think? Is he okay?"

"I think he is. He's always been nice to your father in the paper."

I went back to Fields and said, "Larry, you can pay your respects, but you gotta promise that you won't put it in the paper." He gave me his word—and kept it—and he was the only member of the media that was ever allowed to enter.

After the viewing, I went to the Saloon with Peter Jacovini and some of the other guys from the funeral home. I had barely eaten all weekend. I had no appetite and just picked at the food. But now I was exhausted and knew I had to eat something. Afterward, I went home and got some sleep.

The funeral was the next day. I stood on the steps of the Epiphany and made sure that only friends and family were allowed into the requiem mass, and I did the same thing at the cemetery as the news helicopters flew overhead. The pictures that appeared in the paper were taken from across the street. I wouldn't let any of the photographers get close. With that said, my picture was taken more times than I could count, and there was nothing I could do about it. Until then, my association with the Bruno family had never been made public; now the press was all over the story, insinuating that I was more involved with Angelo than I actually was.

Looking back, if I had to do it over again—and knew what I know now—I might have said, "Michael, I would prefer that we handle the funeral differently." That's what I should have said for my own self-preservation. The reality is, I loved the Brunos and was acting on loyalty alone. When Michael asked for my help, I never gave it a second thought. (Later, Michael tried to give me money. I said, "I don't want any money, Michael. I did this out of love for your dad and your family.")

After the funeral, the press hounded me. I wanted to get away, and when I mentioned it to Olga, she said, "How 'bout Puerto Rico?"

"Let me talk to Michael and Sue first to see if they need me."

When I spoke to Sue about it, she said, "You should go. It's the best thing you can do." Michael agreed, and I told Olga that I would get the plane tickets.

"I already have them," she said. That was Olga. Without my knowledge, she made the reservations and bought the tickets. None of the women I had been involved with had ever done anything like that for me. I was always the one to pick up the tab. It wasn't the money that impressed me; it was the fact that she took it upon herself to make it happen. We went to Puerto Rico and made love all weekend long. All of a sudden, I found myself falling in love with her. She was the first woman since Pattie that I felt that way about.

We stayed at the Caribe Hilton. Olga had no idea that it was one of my favorite hotels. I had taken Pattie and the girls there in happier times and had gone there by myself just to get away. That's where

Donny Kirshner reached me when he was interested in acquiring the rights to "Expressway to Your Heart."

When it was time for us to check out of the hotel, I went down to pay the bill, but the clerk told me that it was already taken care of. I stared at him. "Who took care of it?"

He checked his records and said, "Olga Rivera Pagan."

As far as I knew, Olga's last name was Siegel from a previous marriage. When I got back to the room, I said, "Olga, what's your real name?"

She laughed. "Rivera's my maiden name. Pagan was my daughter's father. He was my first husband."

"Who's Siegel?"

Olga looked at me. I could tell that she was uncomfortable. "That's my American name," she said, and I didn't press the issue.

After Olga and I returned to Philadelphia, I got a call from Frank Rizzo. His second term as mayor had ended two months before. "Can you come up to the house? I'd like to see you."

When I got to his home in Germantown, he and Carmella invited me in. Frank said, "I want you to give our condolences to the Bruno family. And I want you to bring them this." He handed me a large gold chalice in a beautiful velvet bag. "Let Sue know that we share her grief."

When I took the chalice to Sue, I told her that it was from the Rizzo family, and that they were deeply saddened by Angelo's death. Sue removed the chalice from the bag, and said, "It's beautiful, but what am I going to do with it?"

"I have an idea."

Years before, I had attended a midnight mass at the Assumption B.V.M. at 12th and Spring Garden. This was one of the few churches that had a midnight mass. Its congregation was mostly black and Asian, and the parish was extremely poor. That night, the priest mentioned that their raffle hadn't raised enough money. I left the mass and went to the Variety Club in the Bellevue. I asked the bartender, Benny, to let me use the phone. I called the rectory and told the man who answered that I had attended the mass, and that the priest had mentioned the problem they had with the raffle. He said, "I'm the priest," and introduced himself as Father McDermott. I asked him how much he needed, and the next day I sent over a check.

Father McDermott never forgot that, and we became friends. One time, when Sammy was in town, Father McDermott asked if we would attend a commemoration ceremony for a new wing they had built at the school. When the Father announced that Sammy Davis was going to be there with the Geator, the entire street was packed. Sammy and I stood on the roof as Father McDermott blessed the new building.

Remembering that, I said, "Sue, there's a very poor parish on Spring Garden Street. I'm sure they could use this chalice for mass."

Sue said, "Please give it to them."

I took the chalice and knocked on the rectory door. Unfortunately, Father McDermott was almost blind by that time. I had to tell him who I was. He recognized my voice immediately. "Jerry, please come in."

"Father," I said, "I have a gift for you," never telling him that it had been intended for Angelo Bruno's widow. He never knew.

Once things settled down, Michael rented a summer home in Ventnor. He wanted his mom to get away from Snyder Avenue, and he and the family would be there on the weekends. Angelo's sisters and the Maggios would also visit during the week, and Sue would always have company.

After Angelo's death, I began to spend more time in New York, hanging out with some of the guys who came into Memories during the summertime, including Biff Halloran, Joe DeKama, Rocco Maselli, Carlos Colona, and Charlie Cumella, who had his own table at Reo's every Thursday night. If I had to stay overnight, I would stay at the Doral Hotel at 49th and Lexington. Dusty Mormando owned the bar at the Doral, and Rocco Maselli, who was known as "the Jeweler of the Stars," had his jewelry store there. Sinatra, Robert De Niro, Lauren Bacall, and other celebrities who stayed at the Waldorf-Astoria across the street would buy jewelry from him. I would also have dinner with my old friend Victor Potamkin. Victor was from Philadelphia and owned a chain of Cadillac dealerships, not only in this country but also in London.

Joe DeKama did business in New York when he worked for Faberge, commuting from his home in Jersey. When he found an apartment at 30 West Lincoln Center, he asked Biff Halloran and me if we would like to go in on it with him. With as much time as I was spending in New York, I thought it was a great idea. The rent was $2,100, and we divided it three ways. We would hang out with my pal Jilly at his joint and would go to Regine's, the 21 Club, and Danny Stradella's new restaurant. Stradella had originally owned Danny's Hideaway, where I would go whenever Sammy was in town. We would have dinner with Johnny Carson, Elizabeth Taylor, and Baby Jane Holzer.

In the afternoon, we would hang out at Rocco's jewelry store. Harry Guardino would also come in. He was doing a musical called *Woman of the Year* with Lauren Bacall, and for a brief period of time became romantically involved with her. Whenever Olga was in town, she would join us.

I turned forty on July 3, 1980—four months after Angelo died. Like always, I planned to celebrate my birthday with a party at Memories in Margate. The party would be open to the public, and I would still do my show. This time, however, Olga threw a surprise party at the club, inviting Dick Clark, Jilly Rizzo, Harry Guardino, Rocco Maselli, Charlie Cumella, and some of my other friends from New York. Dick was performing at one of the casinos that weekend, and he came to the party with his third wife, Kari.

When I walked into the club, I was completely shocked. I had no idea how Olga had managed to get all of my friends there without me knowing, but she pulled it off. No one had ever done that for me, and again she picked up the tab.

That summer, I would check on Sue Bruno and have coffee at the house they rented in Ventnor. I had a place a few blocks away and would drive over to the Brunos' whenever I could. One day, as I pulled up in my Cadillac Eldorado, Sue, Lena, and Jean Angela were sitting on the porch. When Lena saw my car, she said, "Oh, my God, you're the person that has the black car with the silver top!"

I said, "Lena, what are you talking about?"

"Since Angelo's death, I've been seeing a psychic. She told me about a young man that Angelo loved. She didn't know his name, but she said he drives a black car with a silver top. That's you!"

I didn't know what to say. Then, all of a sudden, I remembered the night a few years before when Ruby put me on the phone with a psychic.

Lena said, "I can't tell you what she said to me. You have to call her. Tell her that you're the young man in the black Cadillac that she spoke about."

The psychic's name was Elizabeth Dolan. When I called her, she spoke in a thick Irish brogue. She didn't know my name, but said, "I live in Upper Darby. Why don't you come over and visit?"

Elizabeth was elderly. She lived in a poor neighborhood. Her apartment was on the second floor of a house. When I sat down, she said, "I saw a vision of Angelo smiling as you walked in here."

Normally, I wouldn't have believed something like that, but Elizabeth was sincere about what she was saying.

"How do you know that?" I asked.

"I've been blessed with a certain gift."

She went on to say that she was Catholic and had been born with a "veil," referring to a thin membrane that sometimes covers the face of a newborn. The medical term for it is "caul." It isn't a serious condition, and there are those who believe that it's a sign of greatness or spirituality.

"After Angelo's death," she continued, "you were in danger for a brief period of time, but the danger has passed. Now you're facing another difficulty. You're going to have a lot of problems with the law, but they're going to find absolutely nothing wrong." She stated it emphatically in her Irish brogue.

I stared at her. If the situation at the Winner's Circle was any indication, she knew what she was talking about. I never gave her my name. All she knew was that I was the young man in the Cadillac.

"You shouldn't worry about these problems," she concluded. "In the end, you will persevere."

When I got up to leave, I took a hundred dollars out of my wallet.

"No, I don't take money."

"Please," I said. "Take it." I put the money on her coffee table and left.

The next time I saw Lena, she said, "Did she tell you that you were in danger?"

"Yeah. She also told me about law enforcement."

"I couldn't tell you that. She had to tell you herself."

Ever since the surprise party, I found myself falling deeper in love with Olga. Toward the end of the summer, she rented a house in Ocean City for her family and would sneak over to my place in Ventnor and stay with me every chance she got.

One night, Memories was packed, and I was on stage doing my radio show. I could see the customers as they came and went. I noticed an older gentleman who walked in and sat at the side bar. He had white hair and a suit and tie, which was unusual for summertime.

An hour later, Olga walked in. The side bar was a few feet from the stage, and Olga always sat there when she came to the club. I noticed the older man walk over to her. They started to talk, and all of a sudden, Olga left without waving to me or saying good-bye. I didn't know what to make of it.

After the older man walked over to me, he said, "Can I see you? I'd like to talk to you."

I said, "I'm doing a radio show. You'll have to wait till I'm finished."

After the show, I went over to him and said, "Let's go into my office."

We went into the office and he said, "Do you know who I am?"

"I have no idea."

"I'm Abe Siegel, Olga's husband."

I was dumbfounded. I didn't want to blow my cool, so I said, "I didn't know she was married."

"I'm the guy that finances her modeling school and beauty line. I pay all the bills for her apartment in Willow Grove, and I even pay for the limo. Because of my business, I live in Fort Lee, but I visit her whenever I can."

"What's that got to do with me?"

"Are you having an affair with my wife?"

"Mr. Siegel, Olga supplies the models for my TV show."

All of a sudden, he broke down. "She does this all the time. I can't handle it any more."

When he said that, I was saddened, and I answered him honestly. "I didn't know she was married. You don't have to worry. It's not my style to get involved with a married woman."

We shook hands, and he left.

After we closed the club that night, I went back to my house in Ventnor. I was still in shock, and I felt a sadness that I had never experienced before. I was in love with Olga, but I truly had no idea that she was married. One of the things that confused me about her was the fact that she was always picking up tabs and living in high style. Now I realized that Abe was supporting her lifestyle.

About five in the morning, the phone rang. It was Olga.

I said nothing.

"What did that man say to you?"

"Olga, why didn't you tell me you're married?"

"We're separated. I'm not married."

"What do you mean you're not married? Just because you live in Willow Grove and he's in Fort Lee, it doesn't mean you're not married. Getting involved with a married woman is not my scene." And I hung up.

It killed me to find out that she was married, and I was lonely without her. I started to hang out more and more in New York. I would call Victor Potamkin and we would get together for dinner with some of our friends there. Afterward, we would go to Regine's, and I would head on back to Philly or stay at the apartment in New York.

At the end of the summer, Olga called me in the middle of the night. "I want you to know that I'm divorcing Abe. I want to see you."

We met the next day. She showed me the divorce papers, and it began all over again. Olga moved in with me. She had all of her expensive furniture from Willow Grove moved over to my apartment.

The months that we lived together were terrific. She would get up early in the morning, go to her modeling school, and meet me at night for dinner. It was a peaceful time for us.

By that time, my father's lifestyle had caught up with him, and he was having problems with his heart. I spoke with Victor, and he made arrangements for my father to see one of the top guys at Mt. Sinai Hospital in New York. Olga drove with me to the appointment. Out of nowhere, when the three of us were in the car, she said she had to move out of my apartment. She told me she needed to be closer to her office, and the ride to Willow Grove was too much. I was shocked. She had never given me any indication that she needed to move out.

My father, who always liked Olga, didn't say a word until we got to the doctor's office. He knew all about Abe Siegel, and when we were alone in the examination room, he looked at me and said, "You better wise up." That was the same thing my mother said when I fell in love with Pattie.

"What are you talking about?"

"She's full of shit."

Olga wound up moving out and taking her furniture. I got an interior decorator to redecorate my apartment. As far as I was concerned, we both had to move on. I would see her whenever I could, but it wasn't the same. I kept hearing my father's words—"You better wise up." The lovemaking was always hot, but I felt an emptiness in my heart. Somehow, I knew that it wouldn't last.

Olga had once told me that no one had ever made love to her like that, and now I wondered if our relationship had been strictly sexual and if we had ever loved each other at all. But no matter how I looked at it, I knew that I had gotten hooked.

I have always believed that there are two parts of a man—his head, which I call "Sam," and his prick, which I call "Harry." Harry gets Sam in trouble all the time. With a woman, "Katrina" is the head and "Regina" is the vagina. My Harry has always gotten me in trouble. He's sexually attracted to Regina, and nothing is going to stop him. For a woman, it's different. Regina doesn't make a move until Katrina tells her to. With me, Harry doesn't listen to Sam. Sam says, "You're gonna get me in trouble," and Harry tells Sam, "Go to sleep. Don't worry about it. Let me handle this." Harry goes to work, and when he's done his business, he says to Sam, "You handle it from here." Sam says, "Wait a minute. You got me involved!" Katrina and Regina are simpatico—they're in sync with each other—but Harry and Sam are constantly at odds.

Men often talk about their conquests sexually, but I've often gotten in trouble with sex. It's like I'm the one who was conquered, and not the woman at all. Maybe it was like that with Olga. I had always thought that we were in love, but maybe she didn't love me like I loved her. If that was the case, our relationship wasn't what I thought it was. It was painful for me, but it didn't stop me from seeing her.

By then, the district attorney's office had started a grand jury investigation into Angelo's death. Arthur Shuman was the Assistant DA under Ed Rendell, who would later become governor of Pennsylvania. Before long, I was subpoenaed.

I asked Emmitt Fitzpatrick to represent me. His tenure as the District Attorney had ended, and he was in private practice. "I can't be with you when you go before the grand jury," he said, "but I'll be in an anteroom. If you don't understand some of the questions, you can excuse yourself and come out and talk to me." I had no need to do that because I answered all of the questions honestly and had nothing to fear.

After I gave my testimony, I was excused, but before Emmitt and I could leave, Arthur Shuman caught up with us in the hall. "We have one more question to ask you." I went back before the panel, and he said, "Do you still see Mrs. Bruno?"

"Absolutely," I said.

"What is the purpose of your visit?"

"I have coffee with her."

I realized that they had been tailing me, and that they wanted to see if I would perjure myself with my answer. They knew I had coffee with her. That's how devious they were, but it was nothing compared to what came next. Officer Leaf was just the beginning. The moment I exposed myself by assisting the Brunos, I became a target of law enforcement for more than a decade. That's how long it took them to puzzle over the one question that they couldn't get a handle on: How could someone like me be so close to Angelo Bruno and not be involved in his business? They never realized that the Brunos had replaced the family I had lost when Pattie kicked me out. I really knew nothing about Angelo's business dealings. At the same time, though, I knew how it must have looked to law enforcement.

With two of our daughters out of the house, the place on Overbrook Avenue was getting too big for Pattie to handle. She didn't need that much space for Stacy, Deserie, and herself, and she decided to move to Atlantic City. Pattie didn't have any friends or family there, but she wanted to get away from Philadelphia and start a new life.

"The house is in both our names," she said. "I think we should put it up for sale."

We ended up selling the place for $100,000. That was double what we originally paid, but it wasn't a lot of money for twenty-two rooms in 1981. If the house had been on the other side of City Line Avenue, we would have gotten a lot more. Unfortunately, like with other major cities, there was a racial element to the housing market. When Pattie and I first moved into the house on Overbrook Avenue, the neighborhood was mostly Jewish; now it was turning black. The houses were still beautifully maintained, and our neighbors were hard-working people, but not everyone is as colorblind as they should be. (I had run my first dance at the Har Zion Synagogue at 54th and Wynnefield Avenue. It wasn't a synagogue any more; it was a day care center. They had moved their congregation to the "whiter" side of City Line Avenue.)

"I'll take the $100,000 and buy a smaller place at the shore," Pattie said. "We'll put it in both our names."

"No, that's your house. We'll put it under your name."

I wasn't living on Overbrook Avenue, but I took care of my responsibilities as if I never left, paying all of the bills, giving Pattie whatever she needed, and making sure the kids got a good education. Pattie and I have never had any problems about money, and I'm still providing for her to this day.

Even though it was all bullshit, the Winner's Circle incident came back to haunt me. Norman Hiemie, a former Camden County judge from Lewis Katz's office, had submitted me for the pre-trial intervention program, but a year later, I still hadn't heard if they accepted my plea. In the back of my mind, I always had a feeling that New Jersey law enforcement would try to go after me. My fears came true. After Angelo's death, I was rejected for the pre-trial program and indicted. I went to Emmitt, and he told me that he wasn't a member of the bar in Jersey, but he suggested that I get Charlie Nugent to represent me. Charlie was a friend of his, and a former U.S. Attorney. He was a big Irishman. His daughter would eventually become a top-notch lawyer, and his son would follow in Charlie's footsteps by becoming a U.S. Attorney himself.

Even though I was indicted, I wasn't going to let it change my lifestyle or my friendships with people from South Philadelphia. I continued to see Sue and her family.

One day, I was having lunch at the Nostalgia Room with Frankie D'Alfonso. The Nostalgia Room was formerly D'Alfonso's Funeral Parlor and had been sold to Frank Palumbo as a part of his vast complex. You could go from the Nostalgia Room to the C.R. Club to Palumbo's. There was a flower shop a few doors away. Frankie turned it into an office and lived on top of it—thus the nickname, "Frankie Flowers."

I had known Frankie for years. He was the head of the Italian Civic

Association and ran the 9th Street Italian Festival every year. I did the festival with Jimmy Roselli and Lou Monte. Lou was a favorite because of his hits "Pepino, the Italian Mouse" and "Lazy Mary." I was having lunch with Frankie and Lou Monte when Phil Testa walked in. Frankie invited him to join us. As we were talking, I noticed three guys at the other end of the bar. They were wearing suits and had law enforcement written all over them. I didn't know if they were following Phil or having lunch. One of them kept looking at me. After a minute or two, I made eye contact with him, and he motioned for me to come over. When I got up, Frankie said, "Where you goin'?"

"I'll be right back. There's a guy I wanna say hello to."

When I got to the bar, the guy who motioned me over said, "Do you know who I am?"

"I think I do, Mr. Best."

"How do you know who I am?"

"About a year ago, I was in Jake Kossman's office, and he got a call from *The Joel Spivak Show*. They wanted him to be a guest." Spivak had a morning show on Channel 10, and they were having a panel discussion on organized crime. "It was you, a member of the Organized Crime Squad in Philadelphia, Frank Friel, and U.S. Attorney Greg McGarrity. I'm the guy who drove Jake to the studio. You were representing the FBI in the Philadelphia region."

"I didn't know you were there," Best said, "but let me tell you why I called you over. I admire what you did for the Bruno family. It was very courageous."

"Thank you, Mr. Best. I appreciate you telling me that."

"Angelo was our friend, too. But I also have to tell you that you have a high profile now. There's gonna be a lot of heat on you."

When I went back to the table, Frankie said, "Who was that guy?"

I laughed and said, "The head of the FBI in this district."

Testa and D'Alfonso almost fell off their chairs.

"How do you know he's the head of the FBI?"

"He was on *The Joel Spivak Show* with Jake Kossman. I took Jake up to do the show."

"What the fuck did he want from you?" Frankie asked.

"Nothin'. He just told me I was gonna get a lot of heat."

Testa laughed and said, "Don't worry about it. You'll get used to it."

Afterward, I started to think about what Edgar Best meant when he said that Angelo was their friend. For twenty-five years, Angelo had kept the peace, maintaining an unspoken alliance with law enforcement. Loansharking, running numbers, working the unions; these were all non-violent crimes that didn't embarrass anybody. Dumping bodies in the street was another matter. As I thought about it, I remembered an incident that happened after I had coffee with Angelo one day. He asked if I would take him to the vending company at 8th and Christian. I always saw surveillance cars outside his home, but that day, as we walked to my car, two men approached us. Angelo said, "Keep on walking. I'll meet you in the middle of the block."

When he finished talking with them, he said, "Let's take a ride to 10th and Moyamensing. I want to see the skinny fella."

The "skinny fella" was Frank Sindone. I dropped Angelo off and waited for him outside. When he came out, he didn't say a word, and I took him to the vending company and went about my business. Two days later, when I was having coffee with the Brunos again, the same two guys were standing at the corner. Angelo walked over to them while I waited in my car. I never asked questions, but after Edgar Best's remarks, I came to understand that whenever the FBI had a problem, they would need Angelo to straighten it out before anybody got hurt. Angelo kept a lid on everything.

Even before the Rizzos gave the chalice to Sue, I knew how much respect law enforcement had for Angelo. The situation with Edgar Best was another example of it, and if you've ever read books on the FBI, you would realize that J. Edgar Hoover always denied that there was a Mafia.

I got my Eldorado from Henry Paul Cadillac on Frankford Avenue. One day, I took it in for service. When the technician reached into the glove compartment for my registration, he saw the gun I kept there, along with my permit to carry it. Trying to be helpful, he put them under the seat of the loaner, but failed to mention it to me. I was working in Jersey at the time, at a club called Prospectors.

When I got out of Prospectors that night, a Cherry Hill police car pulled me over. An officer got out of the car and walked over to me. It was Larry Leaf. I found out later that another cop had been tailing me, and had given Leaf a heads up on where I was. Apparently, harassing Jerry Blavat was official police business.

"Get outta the car," Leaf said.

"What did you stop me for?"

"Just get outta the car. We want to search it."

I got out of the car and let them search it. A minute or two later, Leaf found the gun. "What's this?" he said.

"I have a permit to carry it."

"I can see that. The permit's for Pennsylvania."

"This is a loaner. My car's being serviced. The mechanic must have put it under the seat."

"Yeah? Tell it to the judge. We're impounding the car."

Leaf kept the gun, the permit, and the car. I had to get Angelo Bruno's grandson, Mark Puppo, to pick me up. The next day, I called Henry Paul Cadillac and explained what happened. The mechanic felt horrible about it, but it wasn't his fault.

I was charged with illegal possession of a handgun. Charlie Nugent represented me again, and said, "Let's go to the law library in Camden."

We went to the library, looking up cases on illegal search and seizure. When I had my day in court, the judge interrupted Larry Leaf's testimony.

"Why did you stop him?" the judge asked.

"He was speeding. When we pulled him over, he reached under his seat."

I knew that Leaf hated me, but from that point on, I realized that he would stop at nothing in an attempt to make things difficult. I wouldn't have had any reason to reach under the seat. As far as I knew, the gun was still in the glove compartment of the Eldorado. Leaf was lying under oath.

"You saw him going under the seat," the judge said, "and you searched the car. But there wasn't any probable cause."

"Your honor, I thought I was in danger."

"Why? He's a well-known radio personality. He wasn't leaving the scene of a crime. You stopped him for a moving violation—you didn't stop him on a gun charge. You needed a search warrant," the judge concluded, and he threw out the case.

In 1972, when I bought Memories in Margate, the cigarette machines that were already there were put in by John's Vending. Raymond Martorano ran the company, and Angelo was listed as a salesman. In order to get their machines into a stop, the vending company would offer an advance of anywhere from $2,500 to $5,000, and then they would make their money back from the sale of the cigarettes. In the end, the front money was all the club owner would ever get.

When Angelo was alive, I would have a serviceman from Stan Harris Vending come down to service the machines. Now that Angelo was gone, it was a different story. My machines were old and antiquated, and I wasn't getting any service. Phil Testa had taken over all of Angelo's stops in the vending business, and I bumped into him one night at Dante and Luigi's. I told him that I was having problems with the machines.

He said, "Why don't you buy two new machines? You'll get the cigarettes from us and keep the profit."

"That's great."

"I'll tell you what. I'm gonna call Raymond and tell him to get you two machines that you'll pay for. We'll supply the cigarettes, and if you do have problems, I'll make sure that somebody from Stan Harris services you."

Two days later, I called Raymond. He had already spoken to Testa. He said, "I don't want to talk on the phone. I'm having dinner at Melitis at 8th and Catharine. Why don't you come down?"

"I can't stay long. I have a date with Olga. We have reservations at Bookbinders."

"I understand. You'll have a drink, and then you'll go on your way."

When Olga and I got to Melitis, Raymond was standing at the bar with his wife, Evelyn; Steve Bouras and his date; an ex-policeman who worked for Bouras; and the girl the ex-policeman was with. While I spoke with Raymond, Olga talked with the girls. As usual, with her accent, good looks, and laughter, Olga mesmerized them. I made the arrangements with Raymond and was set to go. "Olga," I said, "are you ready?"

Before she could answer, Evelyn said, "No, don't leave—have dinner with us! We love her!"

"Ev, we've got reservations at Bookbinders."

Raymond said, "Just sit down for a bit."

"All right. We'll sit, maybe have an appetizer, then we gotta go."

As soon as we sat down, two guys with ski masks rushed into the restaurant and started firing. The next thing I knew, Olga, Evelyn, and the ex-cop's date were under the table. Olga was screaming. When I looked around, I saw that Bouras and his girlfriend were slumped over. They weren't moving. It happened that fast.

Raymond said, "You better get outta here." Olga was shaking. As I pulled her to her feet, you could hear all kinds of sirens. I didn't want to go out the front door. Instead, we went through the kitchen, leaving my car where I parked it. Police cars were all over the place.

I walked with Olga through an alleyway and on to 4th and Bainbridge. We went into a bar that had a patio in the back. I sat Olga down and went to the bar to order a drink. The TV was on, and the shooting was all over the news. They were reporting that the police were looking for Raymond Martorano and Jerry Blavat, and that they had impounded my car. They referred to Bouras as a reputed mob figure and said that he and his girlfriend were dead.

I called Emmitt Fitzpatrick. He already knew what happened. He said, "Get in a cab as fast as you can and come to my home in Merion. You and Olga will spend the night here. I'm gonna call the Roundhouse and tell them that I'll turn you in in the morning."

It was amazing how quiet Olga became in the cab. She just stared out the window. It seemed to me that she was still in shock. (Throughout the years, people have asked me about my reaction in that situation. To be honest, it happened so fast that I didn't have time to think about it. I realize now that my guardian angel had been looking over me.)

The next morning, Emmitt took me to the Roundhouse at 8th and Race. My car was parked outside. Emmitt was with me as the detectives conducted the interview. They wanted to know what I was doing at Melitis. I told them about the cigarette machines and my conversation with Raymond.

"I didn't even plan to go there," I said. "I had reservations at Bookbinders."

They took notes on everything I said. After an hour or so, they let me go. Two days later, when I went to Bookbinders, the owner, Johnny Taxin, told me that the detectives had come in. They asked if I had made a reservation and checked the reservation book and saw that I did.

After Angelo's death and the Bouras murder, my reputation was badly damaged. With all of the bad press I was getting, Zvi Shubin and Gene McCurdy decided that I was the wrong guy to do a five-day-a-week show, and they canceled the Saturday night show from the 22 Karat Club. Instead of Jerry Blavat, the daily show was hosted by Eddie Bruce, who today has his own orchestra. The show was called *Dancing on Air*, and within months, it became a local success and aired nationally on the USA Network. My loyalty to the Bruno family would haunt me for years to come. (If I were an employee of Channel 17—and under contract—the station would have fired me as soon as my name was associated with Angelo's in the press. I would have had the same kind of morals clause that got Bob Horn fired from *Bandstand* in the 50s. I was an independent producer, which enabled me to hang on a little longer with my show on Channel 17.)

After Angelo's death, Phil Testa took over the local mob, and Nicky Scarfo became his underboss. For a year, there were no more killings. Eventually, there was a conspiracy within Phil's family, and a nail bomb killed him on his front porch. People like Harry "the Hunchback" Riccobene got into the act—along with his brother, Sonny—and all hell broke loose in the streets of South Philadelphia. Angelo had been in charge for more than twenty years, solving his problems in a peaceful manner; those days were over.

One morning, as I was walking out of the Society Hill Towers, a black car pulled up in front of the building. Three guys got out and threw me in the back of the car. I didn't know who they were until one of them turned around and showed me a badge.

I didn't say a word as they took me to the station at 24th and Wolf and put me in a cell. I was locked up for about an hour when the head of the Organized Crime Squad, Frank Wallace, walked in. He said, "I want you to give your friends a message."

"I don't know what you're talking about," I told him.

"Well, you'll find out."

I didn't say anything. I waited for him to continue.

"When your friend was alive and our friend was Police Commissioner," he said, referring to Angelo Bruno and Frank Rizzo, "we never had any problems. But now you're embarrassing us. There are too many bodies in the street. Give your friends a message that we're going to come down on them, okay? Now get outta here." As it turned out, this wasn't an idle threat. From that point on, local, state, and federal law enforcement stepped up their efforts to prosecute members of the Philadelphia crime family.

One night, after Nicky Scarfo became the boss, his nephew, Phil Leonetti, got into a situation at Memories. He smacked a girl, and I threw him out of the club. Naturally, he beefed about it to Nicky. Nicky asked me to meet him at his home on Georgia Avenue.

"How come you threw him outta the club?" he asked.

"Nicky, he smacked a girl around! I've got enough heat on me already."

Nicky said, "I'll keep him out."

Ever since then, Phil Leonetti had a hard-on for me.

After the incident with Steve Bouras, people in the industry started to make jokes. The punchline was, "Don't have dinner with Jerry Blavat," and it gave my competitors an opportunity to knock me every chance they got.

When we opened Memories for the season, the notoriety actually helped. We were packed, and I opened the club seven nights a week. My father was living at the shore. He looked after the place while I went back and forth to Philly to do my one-nighters. One afternoon, he called me, and I could tell that he was upset. By then, his heart problem had gotten worse, and my dear friend, Dr. Bernie Siegel, was taking care of him along with Dr. Pennock. They had put in a pacemaker because of his irregular heartbeat.

My father went on to tell me that the New Jersey State Police had raided the club. They went behind all of the bars and opened every drawer, checking the cash registers and liquor. "I tried to stop them," he said, "but they pushed me aside."

"Dad, don't say another word. I'm gonna call you right back."

I immediately reached out for an Atlantic City attorney named Harold Garber. He handed me over to Gary Mangel, a lawyer who worked in his office. Mangel called my father, but by that time, the State Police had already handed him a subpoena and left the club. As soon as I hung up with Mangel, I drove down to the shore and met with him.

The subpoena was from the ABC—Alcoholic Beverage Control— and it was signed by their chief inspector, Grant Cuzzupe. He demanded to see all of my financial records from the past eight years, dating back to my acquisition of Memories in Margate. He wanted them within ten days at their offices in Bellmawr, New Jersey.

I told Gary Mangel, "There's no way I can get all this together in ten days."

"We'll go down for the interview, and we'll give them whatever you have."

When we arrived at their offices, I met Grant Cuzzupe for the first time, not realizing that he would become my nemesis for almost a decade. Like Javert, the obsessive police inspector in *Les Miserables*, Cuzzupe was blinded by the desire to ruin my career. He wanted to know how I bought the club, where I got the money, and what the nightly receipts were. He demanded the income tax returns from all of my enterprises, including Celebrity Showcase, which manages Jerry Blavat to this day. In addition, he wanted my personal income tax records and Pattie's, implying that he would yank my liquor license if I didn't get my financial records to him in a timely manner.

When I asked Gary Mangel if he could do that, he said, "Yes, he can, if you don't cooperate with him. Your liquor license is a privilege. It's like a driver's license. It's regulated by the State Police." I realized that they didn't need a judge to issue a subpoena for what they wanted. They had the power. You had to give them everything they asked for. For the entire summer, I was back and forth to their offices. Later, I found out that they were under the impression that Angelo had given me the money to buy Memories, and that I was a front for his activities. They were in for a surprise.

Central Penn Bank had all of my deposit slips on microfiche, and we were able to prove that I bought Memories with my own money. The one thing that the ABC failed to realize was that I had always earned at least $125,000 a year since the very beginning. They couldn't grasp the reality that I had made big money as a kid. All of the record hops, television shows, and royalties had added up from the time I was twenty years old, and $125,000 a year went a lot farther than it does now.

At the end of the summer, things got worse. The IRS and the Feds started an investigation, subpoenaing my accountant, my bookkeeper, my bar manager, and eventually, Olga. I had to get lawyers for everyone so there wouldn't be a conflict. I had Emmitt Fitzpatrick as my primary attorney, and my accountant, Bruno Fedele, had an attorney of his own;

my sister-in-law, Nanny Scotese, needed an attorney, and so did Olga. Nanny was working as my bookkeeper.

When the Feds started their investigation, I called Elizabeth Dolan. A year or two before, I never would have consulted a psychic, but I needed a little reassurance, even if it came from an unlikely source.

When I sat down with Elizabeth, she told me that she was aware of the investigation, but that I had nothing to worry about. Once again, they wouldn't find any wrongdoing. "They can pound sand," she said. I left her house feeling relieved and ready for the struggles ahead.

Bruno Fedele recommended a fella named Dan Hewitt to represent Nanny. He was a young lawyer out of Reading. His father was a well-respected federal judge. When Nanny and I met with Hewitt, I explained what was happening. Hewitt said, "There won't be a grand jury. We're going to request an in-house conference with the U.S. Attorney. None of your people should go before a grand jury." An in-house conference is similar to a deposition. You're under oath, but it's not as intimidating as a grand jury. The grand jury comes later, if the Feds feel that they have probable cause with your testimony.

I didn't know if the Feds would go for that, but when they found out who Nanny's lawyer was, they granted Hewitt's request. When he went in to the U.S. Attorney's office and they began their questioning, Hewitt discovered that they were using all of the financial information that I had turned over to Grant Cuzzupe.

Jake Kossman, who was advising the attorneys I hired, suggested a lawyer from his office to represent Olga. His name was Carmen Nasuti, and he was a former U.S. Attorney. To this day, Carmen and I have remained very close, along with his law partner, Jeff Miller.

I realize now that the investigations were fueled by the mean-spiritedness of Grant Cuzzupe and the misconceptions that he and the others had about my relationship with Angelo. If it wasn't for Memories and my one-nighters, I don't know how my career could have survived. But with all of the publicity, the clubs were packed, and I was still doing my radio show.

When it came to their perception of me, the New Jersey State Police had it all wrong. As far as they were concerned, I was a member of Angelo Bruno's crime family; that was a figment of their imagination. In South Philadelphia, however, the perception of me was real. To them, I was a stand-up guy.

Unfortunately, the investigation took a heavy toll on my father. He was never the same after the ABC busted into Memories. One Saturday night, on Easter weekend, Spanish Pete was about to take my father home. I said, "Dad, I'll call you tomorrow when I get back to Philly." When I spoke to him on Sunday, he told me that he was taking a lady friend to the Melrose Diner, and that he was going to spend the night with her. That Monday morning at six o'clock, when I was in my apartment with Olga, Methodist Hospital called and asked if I was Jerry Blavat. "We would like you to come down to the hospital."

"Is it my father?"

"We would like you to come to the hospital. We can't discuss it on the phone." As soon as she said it, I knew that my father had died.

I called my sister, Roberta, in Reading. When I rushed to the hospital, they confirmed what I already knew. Roberta arrived a few hours later. She was sobbing.

My father was still in his hospital room, and when they let us in, his expression was peaceful. It comforted me to see him like that, but Roberta was extremely upset. She demanded to know what happened, and suggested that they conduct an autopsy. I said, "Roberta, look how peaceful he is. You don't need an autopsy. You can see that he died of a heart attack." Unfortunately for the Feds, we buried my father a few days later, and they never had a chance to subpoena him.

The investigation lasted close to a year. Olga was the last person they subpoenaed. She testified at an in-house conference with Carmen Nasuti representing her. Two days later, Carmen called me and said, "They've concluded that there is no evidence of any wrongdoing."

A week later, Grant Cuzzupe called me at my apartment. He demanded to see me, saying he needed additional information. "You need to come to my office immediately."

"Inspector, that's impossible. I worked until four in the morning last night. I've given you all of the records you wanted. If you want to see me, I'll meet you at the diner at 2nd and Market."

"Be there in a half hour," he said, hanging up the phone.

When I got to the Continental Diner, Cuzzupe was having a cup of coffee at the counter. As soon as I sat down, he asked me about a check that I had made out to Dorchester.

"If you would have checked your records," I said, "you would have found out that they're one of our liquor suppliers."

If Cuzzupe was going to get me out of bed for something like that, he was even more of a prick than I thought. I said, "By the way, do you know that the Feds have dropped their investigation? Apparently, all the records you asked for with no subpoena power, you handed over to the Feds, and they concluded that there's no case here." His mouth fell open. Up to that point, he had no idea that I knew about him turning my records over to the Feds.

"We'll see about that."

I turned to the waitress. "Give me his check."

"Don't you dare!" Cuzzupe said.

"Fine," I answered, and walked out the door.

That was the end of the ABC and federal investigations.

Because of the success of Memories and the radio show at the shore, I called my friend Ed Hurst. Together with other investors, Hurst had bought WKIX in Trenton. I told him that I had an idea that would be perfect for the station—a one-hour radio show called *Lunchtime with the Geator.* He thought it was a great idea and set up a meeting with his program director, a good old boy from down south named Terry Watts. Watts and I hit it off immediately, and in the early 80s I went on the air Monday through Friday from 12 to 1 p.m. The show was a smash, and WKIX replayed it every night from midnight to 1 a.m.

Between the radio show from Memories and the daily show in Trenton, we created enough noise that Bruce Holberg contacted me. Holberg had just become the general manager of Power 99-FM and WFIL-AM, which were owned by Linn Broadcasting. He wanted to bring back the glory days of WFIL. I met with him and his program director, Jay Myers, and they asked if I would re-create *For Lovers Only* from 11 p.m. to midnight.

When I worked the clubs, I would tape the show from their studios; when I wasn't working, I would do the show live. *For Lovers Only* became successful, and Bruce decided to put me on from 6 to 8 p.m. At that point, I no longer needed the Trenton show and discontinued it, leaving me with my daily show on WFIL and my weekend shows from Memories. On Friday nights during the fall and winter, I would do the show from the Betsy Ross Inn on WFIL. My friend Biff Halloran owned the Betsy Ross Inn, along with the Halloran Hotel in New York. Halloran was originally from Philadelphia.

WFIL had a morning guy named Joey Reynolds. Reynolds was too wild for his own good, and Bruce Holberg couldn't control him. Eventually, Reynolds got fired for some of the remarks he made on the air, and when Bruce looked around for a replacement, he asked me what I thought about Humble Harvey Miller. Miller had gotten me started at the Ice House nearly 30 years before.

After leaving WIBG, Harvey became one of the biggest disc jockeys in Los Angeles, working the night shift on WKHJ. He had married his wife, Mary, on the East Coast, and they had gone to California together. Unfortunately, word got out that she was sleeping with other guys while he was on the air. One night, Harvey taped his show and caught Mary off-guard. She was in bed with a guy, and in a wild rage, Harvey took out a gun and shot her.

Harvey was convicted of manslaughter and spent ten years in a California prison, getting released in 1980. He worked at a series of radio stations in Los Angeles and Seattle before Holberg considered the possibility of hiring him to replace Reynolds. Like Joe Niagara, Harvey Miller was one of the best format jockeys in the country, and when Holberg asked me about him, I said, "I think you should give him a shot." Holberg went along with it, and Harvey Miller was back on Philadelphia radio again.

For a brief period of time, Harvey was sensational on 'FIL, but he missed Los Angeles. One night, he came into the studio when I was doing the show and told me that he was unhappy. A week later, he packed his bags and moved back to L.A. He did it without telling anyone, including the management of 'FIL, and he never worked on the East Coast again.

When WFIL and Power 99 were sold, I received a phone call from Mike Martaer and Gus DeJohn. Gus was the sales manager for SUNY 101-FM and WPGR-AM. 'PGR was a daytimer. It would only broadcast from daybreak to sunset. Hy Lit and Don Cannon were two of the jocks. Martaer and DeJohn asked if I would go on following Hy. They would allow me to program my own show and promote my personal appearances. I said, "I have no problem with it, guys, but I think you better check with some of your jockeys."

Martaer called a meeting with me and all of his jocks. He told them that he wanted me to be a part of the station, and that he didn't want anyone to be petty about it. I went on following Hy. After twenty years, he realized that I wasn't any competition to him. He had his audience, and I had mine.

When Biff Halloran sold the Betsy Ross Inn, the Degenhardt family approached me. They were in the catering business and had recently purchased Schillig's restaurant on the Black Horse Pike. Seeing the success I had at Memories and the Betsy Ross, they wanted to rename the place Degenhardt's and create a Memories-type operation.

We made a deal in which the Degenhardts would pay me a weekly fee for my radio spots, and whenever I would appear, I would get the door receipts.

Just when things were going well, we got a subpoena from the State Investigating Committee (SIC) in New Jersey. Their general counsel was Ileana Saros. Carmen Nasuti accompanied me to an in-house conference at her office. I was sworn in and answered her questions under oath. She had a stack of papers in front of her, and I recognized it as the material that Grant Cuzzupe had brought with him from Alcoholic Beverage Control. To my amazement, Cuzzupe was no longer with the ABC—he was with the SIC.

Saros had pictures of me with Angelo, and she asked if I knew him. "Certainly I knew him." Then she showed me police photographs of Angelo's viewing, photographs from newspaper reports, and surveillance photos from Memories in Margate.

"Did you ever have any involvement in his businesses?"

"No."

"Do you know anything about his businesses?"

"Not at all."

When we left the hearing, Carmen said, "I don't think you have anything to worry about. You didn't perjure yourself—you told them the truth."

The prosecutor didn't realize that the people she was asking about shared the same kind of upbringing I had. We grew up in a culture of openness and generosity. On Christmas, everybody came over to the house. My grandmother made ravioli for Judge Panetta across the street and for neighbors up the block. The law never understood the ties that bind the people of South Philadelphia. The tradition might be dying now, but it was going strong when I was a kid, and that's the way I was raised.

Just because I walk into a restaurant with a priest doesn't mean I'm a member of the clergy. And if I associate with Walter Annenberg, it doesn't mean I'm in the same league; it just means that we enjoy each other's company. If you're my friend, you're my friend. That's what life is all about. Now if you do something improper that jeopardizes me, that's another story. It means you're not my friend at all.

Six months later, when I walked into Degenhardt's, Grant Cuzzupe was waiting for me. He said, "I want to ask you some questions. I have a subpoena, but I don't have to issue it."

I said, "What questions?"

He wanted to know what my involvement was with the Degenhardts. I said, "There's no involvement. I work here as a performer. They pay for the radio advertisements, and when I appear here, I get the door receipts."

As he got up to leave—the prick that he was—he still handed me a subpoena. This time, I was required to testify in a televised hearing in Trenton. The SIC was investigating the infiltration of organized crime into the bars, restaurants, and nightclubs of South Jersey. I immediately called Carmen, and we went to see Eddie Jacobs at his office. Jacobs recommended that I get Al DeCotiis to represent me. At one time, DeCotiis had been general counsel to the governor of New Jersey.

Eddie explained to Al that I had previously gone before the SIC and answered all of their questions. Instead of calling me in again, Eddie suggested that they should refer to my previous testimony. Al agreed, but when he proposed it to Saros, she refused to do it that way. Although they were going to refer to my previous testimony and ask the same questions, they insisted that I appear.

Bill Lunsten—a lawyer from Al DeCotiis's firm—accompanied me to the hearing. As soon as I walked into the chambers, I saw the television cameras, and it was obvious that their primary objective was to embarrass me. Saros showed me the same pictures that she had shown me in the previous hearing, and repeated the same questions. It was a waste of time, and it really pissed me off.

As I answered her questions, I remembered something that Emmitt

Fitzpatrick had told me about asserting my constitutional rights. When I finally had enough, I looked at Saros and said, "I am asserting my Third, Fourth, and Fifth Amendment rights as a United States citizen. I refuse to answer any further questions, and I am leaving right now." I got up and walked out of the hearing. That night, it was all over the news that Jerry Blavat took the Fifth and refused to answer any questions. I wasn't concerned because I knew the whole thing was bullshit. They were grandstanding at the taxpayers' expense.

Two months later, the State Police raided Degenhardt's. When I arrived for my Friday night show, the parking lot was crawling with police cars. I went around to the side of the building and walked into the kitchen. Skip Degenhardt told me that Grant Cuzzupe was in his office and wanted to question me. They had already asked Skip about his relationship with me, and his two brothers—Bill and Frank—were still in the office with Cuzzupe. When I got there, Cuzzupe asked the Degenhardts to leave, which seemed a little strange to me. I had nothing to hide, and I didn't think the Degenhardts had anything to hide either. As a result, my antenna was up.

When they started to question me, I said, "Fellas, I'm not gonna answer any questions unless my lawyer's here."

"You don't need a lawyer," Cuzzupe said.

"If you don't allow me to call my lawyer, I'm walking outta here right now."

"Call your lawyer."

I called Peter Brusco from Eddie Jacobs' office. He got on the phone and told them that I wasn't answering any questions unless he was present. With that, they left.

Several weeks later, the Degenhardts got a letter stating that they were in violation of the ABC regulations. The regulations stipulated that they had to control every aspect of their operation, including cover charges at the door. They had to collect the money and give me a check in the same amount every week. The letter also stated that they were going to be fined. I told the Degenhardts that I had no problem with whatever they wanted to do. We agreed on a figure of $1,500 per night whenever I appeared.

Along with the fine they received, the letter from the ABC created a problem for them. The Degenhardts were a hard-working German family, and they were scared. When the attendance started to drop, they reneged on my salary, and that was the end of the Memories-type operation at Degenhardt's.

I'm sure there are people who misinterpret my decision to invoke my constitutional rights at the SIC hearing. It's not always an admission of guilt. I had simply had enough, and I refused to let the Grant Cuzzupes of the world break my balls any more. In the end, the Feds knew that I was 100 percent clean; local law enforcement respected me because I never created any problems for them. Most of the other clubs had fights that spilled out into the street; Memories wasn't like that. There were never any incidents at Memories that required the police to be called in. To this day, Memories has a reputation for being one of the best-run clubs in South Jersey, but for years, Grant Cuzzupe and the New Jersey State Police continued to harass me.

I remember a night when two undercover ABC agents came into Memories. The place was packed. One of my fans brought her twenty-year-old daughter into the club. Before I knew it, the agents called me offstage and took me over to the girl. She had a glass in her hand, and her mother was sitting next to her.

One of the agents turned to me and said, "You're in violation. You're serving alcohol to minors."

The mother said, "That's my daughter. She's not drinking alcohol. It's ginger ale."

With that, the agent took a sip of the ginger ale. As soon as he tasted it, he realized that the mother was telling the truth. Apparently, he and his partner were embarrassed, because they left the club without saying another word.

On one of my trips to New York, I was sitting in Rocco Maselli's jewelry store when Robert De Niro walked in. He went into Rocco's office, and a few minutes later, they came out.

"Geator, I want you to meet somebody," Rocco said. "This is Robert De Niro."

I greeted him like I would greet anyone else. "My man—you're the greatest!"

We shook hands, and De Niro said, "I'm doing a movie called *Once Upon a Time in America*. I like your looks. Why don't you come down to Tribeca tomorrow and do a reading for me and the director?"

"That sounds great."

When he left, I said to Rocco. "What's this all about?"

"He knows you're from Philly, and that you know Little Nicky."

Once Upon a Time in America was about the Jewish mob. I found out later that De Niro was offering me a part because he wanted to arrange a meeting with Meyer Lansky. He knew that Little Nicky Scarfo had access to Lansky.

"If you can set that up," Rocco said, "this guy's going to be very grateful to you."

Nicky was not only a regular at Memories in Margate, but when I owned Memories West in Philly, he also would stop by whenever he was in town. Years before—after my Friday night dances at Chez Vous—I had taken my dad, Nat, Pepsi, and Uncle Doo-Doo to Piccolo's Little 500 at 11th and Christian. Nicky's uncles owned Piccolo's, and Nicky was the bartender there.

The next day, I went to Tribeca. De Niro was there with the director, Sergio Leone, who made his name doing "spaghetti westerns." An assistant director gave me two pages of the script. They wanted me to read the part of a lawyer. I was in and out in less than twenty minutes. When I finished, De Niro was noncommittal. He said, "Somebody will get in touch with you."

Later that night, I had a drink with Rocco. "I spoke to De Niro," he said. "He really wants to meet Lansky. If you can call Little Nicky, he would really appreciate it."

I said, "Rocco, I'm not gonna do that."

As fate would have it, Little Nicky came into Memories the following weekend. I was curious about what his reaction would be if I told him about De Niro's request. Nicky laughed and said, "Forget about it."

A few days later, I got a call from one of the assistant directors. They wanted me for a different role in the movie. The scene I was supposed to be in was going to be filmed in Italy. A week before I was supposed to leave, I was dancing on stage at Memories when I felt a sharp pain in my side. A young doctor by the name of Larry Anastasia was in the audience. He and his partner, Dennis Piccone, had an office in Margate.

I said, "Lar', can you come back to my office? I wanna show you something."

When he examined me, Anastasia said, "You've got a hernia. You gotta get that repaired. It's not gonna go away."

I had already been operated on for a hernia, and now I had another one. I'm not the kind of person that procrastinates when I have a medical problem; I'd rather get it corrected immediately. I said, "Lar', who's the best guy for this?"

"Dr. Powers in Philadelphia. I'll give you his number."

The cast and crew of the movie were already in Italy. They had been filming for a couple of weeks. When I went to see Dr. Powers, he told me that he could fix the hernia and assured me that it would never come back. I told him that I needed it done right away, and he scheduled the surgery for two days later at Doctor's Hospital in Bala Cynwyd. Fortunately, the operation was a success, but my role in *Once Upon a Time in America* would never be. They got somebody else to play the part.

In addition to the friends I had in New York, I was always running into celebrities or people I knew. One night, I was at Bici's with Seymour Stein, the president of Sire Records. Sire had Madonna, k.d. lang, the Talking Heads, and other top-selling artists. When I looked across the dining room, I saw Bette Davis sitting at a table in her wheelchair. This was after she had her stroke. I turned to Seymour and said, "I just want to say hello to her."

When I got to Davis's table, I said, "Miss Davis, please allow me to introduce myself. I did a movie with your ex-husband, Gary Merrill. I've always admired you. My name is Jerry Blavat, the Geator."

Davis looked up at me and said, "So you're the fucking Geator that Gary used to talk about!"

"I don't know if he said good things about me or not," I answered, and Davis laughed.

"I know who you are!"

Another time, I was meeting Sidney and Caroline Kimmel at Cipriani's in the Sherry-Netherland Hotel. Sidney was from Philadelphia, and I had known Caroline since her marriage to my dear friend, Leonard Tose, the former owner of the Philadelphia Eagles. Caroline was a flight attendant for TWA, and Leonard was smitten the minute he saw her on a flight from Los Angeles to Philadelphia. When the Eagles won the NFC championship in 1980—and made it to the Super Bowl—I did their victory party. I brought Patti LaBelle with me, and she got pissed off because the Eagles players were making too much noise when she was singing. Patti stopped right in the middle of a song, and said, "Hey, man, I'm here to sing. You guys might be the champs, but you better listen to me!" Patti is something else.

Caroline was one of the classiest ladies you would ever want to meet. She was not only beautiful, but she also had a certain style. After she and Leonard divorced, Caroline got their house in Ventnor, and she and her girlfriends would frequent Memories. One of her friends was a flight attendant named Jane. Jane would stay with Caroline, along with Marla Maples. The house was known as "the love nest." Donald Trump used to sneak into Memories to hook up with Marla. At the time, he was still married to Ivana. (I got involved with Jane briefly. She spent a weekend with me at the Society Hill Towers.)

Caroline was a good friend of Frank and Barbara Sinatra. Later, she married her second husband, Jack Davis, the president of Resorts. Jilly and I attended the wedding at Rita Rome's home in Philadelphia. The other guests included the actress, Janet Leigh, and I ended up spinning records at the reception.

A year later, Jilly and I were invited to the Davis's anniversary party at Le Club, a private club in New York. A former Philadelphian owned it, and you never knew whom you would see there. On the night of the anniversary party, Senator Ted Kennedy was sitting at the bar.

When Caroline married Sidney Kimmel in 1999, I did the wedding at their home in Palm Beach; after that, we saw each other whenever we could. To this day, they are two of my closest friends.

As it turned out, I got to Cipriani's before they did; when I was waiting for them to arrive, I saw a woman who looked familiar. I called the bartender over. "Who is that?"

"That's Patricia Neal," he said. "She lives in the building."

Neal was one of my favorite actresses, having starred in *The Fountainhead*, *The Day the Earth Stood Still*, and *Hud*, where she played Paul Newman's lover. While shooting *The Fountainhead*, Neal had an affair with Gary Cooper, but Cooper was Catholic and refused to divorce his wife. In the aftermath, Neal had a nervous breakdown.

"She comes down almost every night," the bartender said, "and sits by herself."

"Do me a favor. Give me her tab."

The Kimmels and I were eating when the bartender told Patricia Neal that her check was already taken care of.

"Who did that?" she asked.

"The man who's sitting with the Kimmels."

A few minutes later, our waiter came over and said that Patricia Neal wanted to speak with me. When I walked over to her table, she said, "Who are you?"

"I'm just a fellow who really appreciates the great talent you have and the wonderful movies you're made."

"But why would you pick up my check?"

"It's a sign of gratitude for the wonderful years of enjoyment you've given to so many people."

"That's very kind of you, young man."

Even with the advent of the casinos, Memories was still the place to be seen. Whenever anyone was in town—Dionne Warwick, Harry Guardino, Jack Carter, Frankie Valli, Jilly, Sammy, or Sinatra—my mother would cook for them. I had a private garden behind the club, and they used to sneak in the back and munch on my mother's ravioli, sausage and peppers, manicotti, and pasta fagiole. Sinatra would never come over—we would send the food to his hotel. (When Donald Trump wanted to see Marla Maples, he would sneak in the back way also.)

Sinatra raved about my mother's ravioli and peppers and eggs. I'll never forget the night that he had a private dinner party at the Golden Nugget. He asked if my mother could make the ravioli. She made two gigantic trays of ravioli, sausage, and meatballs, and I brought it down to the Golden Nugget. When I got to the private dining room, Jilly had a seat for me next to Frank. For some reason, Frank's wife, Barbara, wasn't there that night. Merrill Kelem was there, along with Bobby Palermo. Bobby was previously married to Skinny's daughter, Paula Jane, and he and Merrill were Frank's private bodyguards when he appeared in Atlantic City.

When Frank tasted the ravioli, he put his fork down and turned to me. It looked like he was choked up. He said, "Matchstick, your mother's a saint. This cooking reminds me of the way my mother used to cook. My mom was the only one that would criticize me. If she did-n't like one of my shows, she would say, 'You sounded like a bum tonight.'" Years before, his mother, Dolly, had died in a plane crash on her way to his show in Vegas. I'll never forget the look in his eyes that night, as he tasted my mother's cooking.

One night, when I was doing a radio show at Memories, Susan Seidelman came to the club with her English husband, Jonathan Brett. She was about to direct *Desperately Seeking Susan* starring Aidan Quinn, Rosanna Arquette, and a hot new talent who was rapidly climbing the charts—Madonna. Susan loved the way I did the radio show with my mix and my rap. She said that she had a scene on the boardwalk where Madonna and Rosanna Arquette were talking. The Madonna character was listening to a transistor radio, and Seidelman thought that I would be perfect for the voice of the disc jockey. They recorded my voiceover at a studio in New York, showing me some of the dailies to give me an idea of the disc jockey's pacing. It took an hour or two, and afterward I went back to Philadelphia and forgot about it. They still had another six weeks of shooting, and the editing would take months.

At the time, I never realized that my old friend Freddy DeMann was managing Madonna. We hadn't seen each other since the 6os. When Freddy saw the daily rushes of the boardwalk scene and heard my voice, he said, "Holy shit! Is that the Geator?" Seidelman had no idea that Freddy and I knew each other, and when Freddy asked how she found me, she said, "I grew up in Philadelphia. He's doing radio there, and he owns Memories in Margate."

The next thing I knew, Freddy called me, and from that moment on, we renewed our friendship. Whenever he and his wife, Candy, were in New York, Olga and I would get together with them; Olga and I even flew out to L.A. to attend the Bat Mitzvah of their daughter. To this day, Freddy is one of my closest friends. (Every once in a while, I still get a royalty check for *Desperately Seeking Susan*. I framed one of them and put it on my wall. It's a check for $5.)

When Olga and I were vacationing in Mexico, I got a call from Freddy. "I've got an idea," he said. "You should be doing national radio."

Freddy played tennis with Norm Pattiz, the founder of Westwood One, and ran the idea past him. Like everybody else in radio, Pattiz knew me from the trade papers, and he thought it was a great idea. Freddy said, "Instead of going back to Philly right away, fly into L.A. I want you to meet Norm."

When I sat down with Freddy and Norm, we came up with an idea for a weekly show called *Jukebox Saturday Night.* Pattiz was excited, and so was I. We shook hands and Freddy said, "Great. We got a deal."

When I got back to Philly, Pattiz had his promotion and programming department get in touch with me. We were far enough along that Westwood reported it in the trade papers, and the *Daily News* did an article about it. In the 60s, I had gone national with a syndicated television show, and now it was about to happen again with radio.

A week after the *Daily News* article appeared, Freddy called and said, "I gotta see you. Can you fly out here?" I realized that he didn't want to talk on the phone.

Freddy and I met at the Café Roma in Beverly Hills. Olga and Candy came along, but before we even sat down, Freddy said, "Let's you and I take a walk." I knew it was serious if he didn't want to talk in front of the girls.

When we got outside, he said, "The deal's off."

"What do you mean? The trades reported that we had a deal."

"Pattiz got a letter saying, 'How can you hire Jerry Blavat? He's an associate of organized crime.'"

"Freddy, you know that's bullshit."

"I know—and I told Norm. He said, 'Look, I've got a public company. I can't afford to go there.'"

That was it—the deal was off. The opportunity to have a syndicated radio show came and went just like that. Even with that setback, I created my own network called Geator Gold Radio in Pennsylvania and New Jersey. It may not be as big as a national radio show, but that's cool because I still have the freedom to play the music I love.

In the off-season, Memories was open on Friday and Saturday nights, and I would drive back to Philly. One night before we closed, Olga called and said she was coming down with her sister, Lisa. They were going to the casino and wanted to stop by, but they never showed. I got a message from one of the bartenders that Olga had called and was still at the casino. The message said that she would reach out for me the next day.

For some reason, as I drove back to Philly, my antennas went up. Instead of going to my apartment, I went back to Olga's in Willow Grove. It was seven in the morning. When I got there, the door was unlocked. I walked in and her daughter was sleeping on the couch. She woke up when I came in, and I asked if her mom was home yet. She said, "No, she's still down the shore."

I said, "Okay, I'm gonna wait for her in the bedroom."

A half hour later, I heard voices. Olga wasn't alone; Abe was with her. Olga stormed into the bedroom, screaming, "What are you doing here? You're not supposed to be here!"

"Is Abe with you? I thought you were divorcing this guy. Where's he at?"

"No, please don't—he's got a bad heart!"

Abe had locked himself in the bathroom.

"Please leave," Olga said.

"Olga, I want you outta my fuckin' life. Forget we ever met."

It was the last straw. Lonely or not, it was over, and I got on with my life. One night, when I was at the Elan at the Warwick Hotel, I bumped into Monti Rock. He said, "Hey, did you hear? Olga moved to Texas." I said nothing, but felt an emptiness.

Out of the blue, around Christmastime in the middle of the night, I got a call from Olga. She told me that she loved me and that she had finally divorced Abe. For a moment, I said nothing, and she went on to say that she wanted to see me.

Deep down inside, I still had feelings for her. Whenever I could, I would fly down to Houston on the weekends, meeting her at the Marriott Hotel at the Intercontinental Airport. I would fly back to Philly on Sunday night. Occasionally, Olga would visit her sister in Philly and spend the weekend at my apartment. One time, it seemed like something was bugging her. I couldn't figure it out. The lovemaking was great, but something wasn't kosher. When I took her to the airport, she told me that she had to go to Puerto Rico for a couple of weeks, and that she would call me when she got back. Her mother wasn't feeling well.

A week later, I got a call from an older woman who spoke in broken English. I could barely understand her. All I heard was "Olga." I said, "Who is this?"

"Mamacita, Olga's mother. Olga getting married!"

I was shocked. I didn't say a word.

"Don't let her do this!"

Now it all made sense. There was nothing I could say. I just hung up the phone.

Two days later, Olga called. She was her old self again. "Darling, I miss you. I can't come up for a few weeks. I have business to tend to."

Without missing a beat, I said, "How come I haven't gotten an invitation?"

There was silence at the other end of the phone, and then she freaked out. "You crazy sonofabitch, what are you talking about?"

"Your mother told me. What kind of game are you playing?"

"You won't marry me. This man is very rich."

"Olga, good luck and good-bye. It was a wonderful journey."

As much as I may have loved her, I knew in my heart that it would never work out.

A few weeks later, I was staying at Turnberry with Biff Halloran. Biff was a partner in the Jockey Club with Jack Penrod, who owned Penrod's nightclub. Turnberry and the Jockey Club were two of the hottest "in" spots in Florida. While I was at Turnberry, I bumped into my old friend Ewart Abner. Abner was no longer with Vee-Jay Records.

I said, "Ab, what are you doing here?"

"I'm managing Stevie Wonder. He did the soundtrack for *The Woman in Red*. We're having a press party at the Fontainebleau. Why don't you come over? I'll send a car for you."

"Ab, I've got my own car."

When I got there that night, there were hundreds of media people at the party. I spotted Abner and started talking with him. Stevie was doing an interview a few feet away. All of a sudden, he heard my voice and said, "Is that the Geator?" I walked over and hugged him. We hadn't seen each other since my TV show in 1966, and I was really amazed that he recognized my voice after all those years.

Another time, Freddy DeMann and I went to the Columbus Club, a popular spot for writers and actors in New York. When we walked in, Bobby McGowan was there. He was a friend of mine from back home. McGowan had managed Julia Roberts at the beginning of her career, and at one point, had been engaged to Kim Delaney, a young actress from the Roxborough section of Philadelphia.

McGowan was sitting with Joe Pantoliano. I had known Joe since the filming of *Eddie and the Cruisers* in Jersey. Pantoliano said, "Guess what, Geat? I'm doing a movie on you!"

"You are?"

When he saw how shocked I was, he said, "They never contacted you?"

"I don't know anything about that."

Freddy didn't say anything, but I knew that he was picking up on it.

"I even have a tape of you," Pantoliano said. "The producers sent it to me. They want me to get your delivery." He went on to tell me that the writer was from Philadelphia. His name was Mark Rosenthal, and he had cowritten *The Jewel of the Nile*.

"Who's producing it?" Freddy asked.

"Orion."

When we left the club, Freddy said, "Orion distributed *Desperately Seeking Susan*. When I get back to L.A., I'm gonna get the script."

Freddy called Orion, and they said, "No, the story's not about Jerry Blavat, it's about Dick Clark."

"Can we get a script?"

"We don't know if we can give you a script."

Freddy took me to a high-powered law firm in L.A. They got a copy of the script, and when Freddy read it, he called me. "This is about you!" he said.

The plot revolved around a teenage dance show and its host, Perry Parker. Because the movie was being shot in Philadelphia, the firm in L.A. couldn't institute the lawsuit in California. When I told Carmen Nasuti that I needed a local firm, we met with Jake Kossman. Jake laughed and said, "Who would make a picture about you?"

Carmen said, "Jake, I read the script. The lawsuit has merit."

Jake took me to Dilworth, Paxton, and Kalish. When they got the discovery materials from the firm in L.A., the case was so strong that they took it on consignment. They assigned it to David Patinsky, an entertainment lawyer who co-produced *Peggy Sue Got Married*.

When Patinsky contacted the producers of *The In Crowd*, they still insisted that it wasn't about me. After we filed legal papers, we received a print of the movie, and it made our case even stronger. The producers screened a preview of the movie in Philadelphia, and Jonathan Takiff of the *Daily News* did a four-page article on it, including a series of photographs from my show *The Discophonic Scene*. The photographs demonstrated the obvious resemblance of the Perry Parker character to me. When Joe Pantoliano said that the producers had shown him a tape so that he could get my delivery, he wasn't kidding. He even dressed like me in the movie, with a V-neck sweater, khaki pants, and chukka boots. If there was any doubt at all that the producers of *The In Crowd* ripped me off, Takiff's article took care of it. Once we threatened them with an injunction, they were forced to settle. Otherwise, *The In Crowd* would have never seen the light of day.

Years later, when Mark Rosenthal was asked about it, he said, "We were afraid to approach Blavat. If he didn't like the script, he might have gotten the unions to stop us from filming." If Rosenthal had come to me in the first place, I could have served as a technical advisor, but my relationship with Angelo Bruno scared them off.

When Susan Seidelman was casting the movie, *Cookie*, she came to see me at Memories. "I have a part for you," she said.

"What do you want me to play?"

"A lawyer. What are you laughing about?"

"That's one of the parts I tested for when De Niro was doing *Once Upon a Time In America*."

Two weeks before I was scheduled to do the filming, Susan told me that the producers wanted Jerry Lewis to play the lawyer. "Your read was perfect," she said, "But Jerry Lewis is a bigger name, and they need that star power."

"Don't worry about it. I understand."

"But I want you to be in the movie. You can play the disc jockey."

Pater Falk played a mob boss in *Cookie*. His character just got out of jail, and they were throwing a party for him at the Riviera in Coney Island. The disc jockey was spinning records at the party. After Susan pointed out my mark—the spot where she wanted me to stand—I walked over to it and waited for the other actors. Jerry Lewis was sitting a few feet away. He had a toy poodle in his lap. When the assistant director said, "Mr. Lewis, would you kindly get on your mark?" he walked over.

"Let's run through this," Susan said, and we started to do the scene. They weren't filming; they were working on the camera angles. All of a sudden, Lewis turned to me and said, "I don't want you to stand on that mark. I want you to stand where I am." He wasn't happy with the camera angle and wanted my mark instead!

I said, "This is where the director put me."

"I wanna switch with you."

Knowing that he had a reputation for being difficult, I said, "Mr. Lewis, if you want me to move, talk to the director. If she tells me to move, I will." With that, he walked off the set, and Susan shot the scene with somebody else standing on his mark.

I found out later that Lewis was aware that Seidelman had wanted me to play the lawyer originally, and that was one of the reasons that he gave me a hard time. In the end, though, it didn't matter because my scene with Lewis got edited out. I only appeared in *Cookie* briefly. The audience barely caught a glimpse of me, but they heard my voice throughout the party scene as I did my rap as the disc jockey. When it was all said and done, Lewis's part was very small, and having him in the movie didn't do anything for *Cookie* at the box office. Despite his "star power," the movie flopped.

As the decade came to a close, I had Memories, two radio shows, and one-nighters throughout the region. Whether Grant Cuzzupe liked it or not, I was back in business again.

TWELVE: Beyond Teens

O ne day, when I was doing my show on WPGR, the receptionist came into the studio and told me that Victor Potamkin had called. After I finished my show, I called Victor back, and he invited me to have dinner with him the following night. He was going to the 21 Club in New York with George Burns and Dr. Norman Orentreich. Norm was Victor's dermatologist. He was a prominent physician whose claim to fame was hair plugs.

I said, "Vic, thanks for the invite, but I'm on the air until six o'clock."

This was August 14, 1989. I didn't realize that the next day was the Feast of the Assumption, a holy day of obligation if you're Catholic.

The next morning, I got dressed and went to a twelve o'clock mass at Old St. Joseph's. The church was in my parish in the Old City section of Philadelphia. When the mass was over, I visited the Blessed Mother at the side altar and said a prayer.

Normally, I wouldn't get dressed up when I did my radio show, but that day, I went to the station without getting changed. Realizing that, I decided to call Vic and see if the invite was still on. He said, "Absolutely. Why don't you hop on the 6:25 Metroliner? I'll send my driver. We'll wait for you at the 21 Club."

When I arrived, Victor was sitting at a table with Burns, Orentreich, and Orentreich's head nurse, Margie. We had a lot of laughs, and everybody had a great time.

If you've ever been to the 21 Club, you know that it's dimly lit. Every so often, I took my watch off and held it up to the light. I needed to get back to Philly, and I had reservations on the last Metroliner at eleven o'clock. After we had a few drinks, I took my watch off again.

Dr. Orentreich was sitting next to me. He said, "Let me see that." I handed him my watch, and he said, "No, let me see your wrist."

My watch was covering a mole, and as soon as I held out my wrist, Dr. Orentreich asked me how long the mole had been there. I said,

"Doc, I don't really know."

"I need to see you in my office tomorrow morning at 7:30."

The entire table fell silent.

"I gotta get back to Philadelphia tonight. I have a show to do tomorrow."

Victor had an apartment at the Park Regency. "Listen," he said, "you'll stay at my place tonight. Norm'll see you early in the morning, and my driver will take you to the train station afterward. You'll be back in plenty of time for your show."

"Vic, I didn't bring a change of clothes. As a matter of fact, if I didn't go to church today, I wouldn't be here tonight."

George Burns was listening to this as he puffed on his cigar. He took the cigar out of his mouth and said, "Putz! This guy wants to see you tomorrow? I've been trying to get an appointment with him for six months!"

George wasn't exaggerating. Orentreich's patients were among the elite of the entertainment world—Elizabeth Taylor, Liza Minnelli, Frank Sinatra—and it was almost impossible to get an appointment.

Victor said, "George, at your age, what are you worried about?"

Everybody broke up laughing—except Margie. "Get here tomorrow morning," she said, "and we'll get you in and out."

"I'll tell you what. I'm gonna go home tonight. I'll take the first train out tomorrow."

I got up early the next day and took the Metroliner to New York. Victor's driver picked me up at Penn Station and took me to Dr. Orentreich's office. The office was packed, and Margie took me through a side door. When Dr. Orentreich walked into the examining room, he was wearing a white lab coat.

"Take your shirt off," he said, and he told Margie to bring him an anesthetic. She came back with a syringe and a small bottle of lidocaine. Dr. Orentreich examined my back and found two more moles that he didn't like. He injected the lidocaine and told me that he would be back in ten minutes. By then, my back would be numb.

When it was all said and done, he removed a total of three moles, including the one on my wrist. "You're all done," he said. "I'm not worried about the ones I removed from your back, but I'm concerned about the one on your wrist. It looks like melanoma."

I had never heard that term, so I didn't know how to react.

"I think I got it all out," he continued. "Go back to Philly. I'll call you tomorrow."

When I got back to the radio station, it was almost time for my show, and Jere Sullivan saw the bandage on my arm. Jere was the program director of WPGR and SUNY 104.5. He said, "What happened to you?"

When I told him about my doctor's appointment, he said, "Norman Orentreich? How'd you get an appointment with him? He's the most famous dermatologist in New York City!"

"I got it through my friend, Victor Potamkin."

"What did Orentreich say?"

"I might have melanoma."

"You know that's serious? In six months, that could be fatal!"

Until then, I had no idea how serious the situation was. I was a street kid from South Philadelphia. What did I know about melanoma?

That night, after my radio show, I appeared at the Coliseum. I had a couple of drinks afterward and got home around two-thirty. The next morning, I couldn't get out of bed. I called Dr. Orentreich immediately, and told him that I was dizzy and nauseous.

He said, "When you left, did Marge give you a prescription for the anesthesia?"

"No."

"Did you have anything to drink?"

"I had a few drinks after work."

"Well, that and anesthesia will do it. This is what I want you to do. Take some Excedrin and stay in bed for a few hours. After that, you'll be okay."

"All right, doc. Thanks."

"I'm glad you called. I spoke with the lab. They confirmed the melanoma. As I told you, I think I got it all, but I want you to follow up with Clark Ramsey at the University of Pennsylvania. He's the head of the dermatology department and one of the top lesion specialists in the country. Let's try and reach him right now."

I held the line while Margie placed the call. It turned out that Clark Ramsey was vacationing in Europe, and out of respect for Dr. Orentreich, he responded to the phone call. It seemed like I was on hold forever. Two days before, I was on top of the world, having fought my way back from the state and federal investigations, but now—if Dr. Orentreich hadn't removed all of the cancer—there was a chance that after a year it might be a different story.

When Dr. Ramsey came to the phone, Norman said, "I have Jerry Blavat on the line. I removed three moles, and one of them is a grade two melanoma. When will you be back in the country?"

"In ten days," Ramsey said. "I'll get him right in."

When Ramsey returned from Europe, he checked me out from head to toe. He had a number of colleagues with him, and it was awkward for me. It was the first time that I was completely naked in front of so many people. My wrist was still bandaged from two weeks before. "You look clean," Ramsey said, "but just to be sure, I'd like to go in a little deeper than Norm did on that arm."

Because of the heart condition I've had since I was a kid, I consulted Dr. Pennock. He had been my cardiologist for years, and I had sent my father to him also. "What they gotta do is block you for this operation," he said, referring to a specific kind of anesthesia. "There's nothing wrong with Penn, but I want it done at Hahnemann. We have all of your records here. We'll get Dr. Orentreich to send his report."

Dr. Pennock made the arrangements for Dr. Shinya, the head surgeon at Hahnemann Hospital, to perform the surgery. Dr. Shinya ended up removing my lymph nodes, which were swollen, and cutting deeper into the tissue of my wrist. The surgery required skin grafts from my thigh to replace the skin they removed. When it was all done, I looked like I had been hit by a car. My arm was bandaged from my wrist to my shoulder, and my leg was bandaged from my knee to my groin.

Not only was my guardian angel watching over me, but in my mind the Blessed Mother saved my life. If I hadn't gone to church that day, I would have never had dinner in New York, and I probably wouldn't be here today. As it turned out, all of the follow-up reports were clean, and I've been cancer-free ever since. (I was recently inducted as a Friar, and before the ceremony, I stopped by the 21 Club to see how it looked after all these years. Sure enough, nothing had changed. I saw the same table where they discovered my melanoma, and the same dim lighting.)

My melanoma scare was a sobering reminder that none of us are invincible, and that I wasn't as indestructible as I thought. It got me thinking about the people who were still coming to my dances after all those years. Most of them had been with me since they were teenagers at the Dixon House; even now, they still come up to me at Memories in Margate and other venues to thank me for keeping the music alive. The truth is, I'm the one who should be thankful. They're aren't "yon teens" any more—I call them "beyond teens"—but they're doing just as much for me as I'm doing for them.

In the 60s, the kids looked up to me because I understood what they were going through. I had gone through it myself, and they treated me like I was one of them. It's the same way now. Many of the people who come to see me have health problems of their own, and we still relate to each other. I dance with them, I joke with them, and it enables them to relive their youth. For two hours, I bring them back to a better time in our world; I relive my youth through them. I'm seventy years old, but I still feel like I did when I first started out. As a result, my philosophy has never changed: Youth is a gift of nature; age is a work of art.

There's no secret to my success. It comes from hard work, the love I have for the music, and the respect I have for my audience. The fact is, they've been a blessing to me for all these years. We're growing old together, but we remain young at heart, and that's why I tell them, "Keep on rockin'. You only rock once." (When we were kids, we all wanted to be older. Now, as we grow old, we want to stay young.)

Even though Dr. Pennock was my cardiologist, we were close friends and would have dinner together. One night in 1989, we were at South Street Souvlaki. Pennock was a ladies' man. Whenever he saw an attractive woman, he would start a conversation. That night, a woman with long black hair was sitting at a table next to us. She was wearing a short skirt and writing in a looseleaf notebook. Pennock turned to her and said, "Do you know who this guy is?"

That was Pennock. The woman looked up and said, "I have no idea."

"You must not be from around here. It's Jerry Blavat."

She wasn't impressed. Pennock asked her about herself, and she told us that she worked for a nonprofit organization called The Cure Drive. When she found out that Pennock was a cardiologist, the conversation got more involved. Pennock asked what her name was, and she said Keely Stahl. Not only was she a knockout physically, but she was also bright and articulate.

As we were about to leave, I called the waiter over and said, "Give me her check." I printed my name and phone number on a page of her notebook, and wrote, "To the future Mrs. Blavat: Give me call." I told the waiter not to say anything until we left the restaurant.

Later that night, when I was in bed, the phone rang. It was Keely. Apparently, she was intrigued by my boldness. "Why did you pick up my check? You don't even know who I am."

I said, "I just loved your short skirt and long legs. You're a beautiful woman. What are you doing now?"

"I'm just finishing my meeting."

"Why don't you come over for a drink?"

She came over that night, and before she left, at 3:30 in the morning, I told her to listen to my radio show the next day. She tuned in at 1 p.m. sharp, and I dedicated "At Last" by Etta James to her, and we've been together ever since. (I finally realized that you have to let "Sam" fall in love before "Harry." Keely put it all together for me, and Sam and Harry are living happily ever after.)

My melanoma reinforced the fact that time was passing, and that we were increasingly susceptible to issues with our health. As it turned out, Sammy Davis was about to experience a medical problem of his own.

Sammy and I had gotten closer over the years. From the time that I first met him on *Bandstand* to his appearances on my television show to the good times we had whenever we got together, it was like we were family; it was extremely upsetting to me when he was diagnosed with throat cancer. Sammy had already survived a car accident that cost him his left eye in 1954 and cirrhosis of the liver that forced him to curtail his drinking in 1982, but in 1989 he would face his biggest challenge.

I was staying at Sammy's house on Summit Drive when Liza started rehearsing with Sammy and Frank. Dean Martin was on the original bill, but he and Frank had a falling out, and Liza replaced him. Their tour was called the "Ultimate Event." The first stop was the Fox Theatre in Detroit, and then they came to the Spectrum in Philadelphia. They had two dates in Philly. Sammy called me the night before he arrived. It was a Sunday night. He was staying at the Four Seasons with Liza. Frank was staying at the Waldorf and flew in to do the show.

Sammy asked if I could close down a restaurant after the Monday night show. He wanted to have a little get-together with Frank, Liza, members of the band, and Sammy's entourage. My mother would do the cooking. I made the arrangements with Ristorante Galleria at 5th and Passyunk, which was owned by my friend Carlo. My mother spent the whole day cooking on Monday. She made sausage, meatballs, ravioli, pasta fagiole, and all of their other favorites.

Sammy invited my mom to the Monday night show and arranged for her to sit next to the Annenbergs. When I went to Sammy's dressing room, he told me that Frank was upset because he couldn't join us. The Annenbergs had invited him to Bookbinders after the show, but he asked if my mother could get her ravioli to Bookbinders. The policeman who picked up Frank earlier in the day drove me over to Ristorante Galleria, waited for me while I put together the trays for Frank, and took me over to Bookbinders, where I gave the trays to Johnny Taxin and told him that they were for Frank and the Annenbergs.

After the show, a police escort took us to Ristorante Galleria. The place was closed except for us. Twenty minutes after we sat down, Carlo told me that I had a phone call. Carlo spoke with an Italian accent, and it was hard to understand him, but he managed to communicate the fact that the person on the phone was upset. When I picked up the phone, it was Jilly. He said, "Where are you? Where are Sammy and Liza?"

"We're at Ristorante Galleria."

"You guys better get over here right away. The old man is livid. Where are the raviolis?"

When I got back to the table, I told Sammy that Frank was pissed off. Sammy said, "Come on—we better go to Bookbinders." Sammy, Liza, and I excused ourselves, jumped into my Mercedes, and went to Bookbinders, which was just a couple blocks away. When we got there, the place was dead. Frank, Barbara, and the Annenbergs were sitting in the President's Room. Jilly and the Taxins were sitting at the bar. Jilly said, "You better find out what happened with the raviolis."

"Jilly, I delivered them hours ago."

I turned to Johnny, and said, "John, the raviolis are in the kitchen!" Johnny and I walked into the kitchen, and there they were. The three aluminum trays were sitting on the table where I left them. We put the ravioli in the oven and served them while Sammy and Liza joined Frank at the table. Around one-thirty in the morning, a limousine took Frank and Barbara to the airport; the Annenbergs went home; and Sammy, Liza, and I went back to Ristorante Galleria, where we continued to party.

A day later, after their stay in Philly, Sammy called me and said, "You gotta do me a favor. I left a $3,000 video camera in my room at the Four Seasons. They're holding it for me. Can you bring it to me tonight?" The next stop on their tour was the Nassau Coliseum on Long Island, and after the show, they were going to Rocky Lee's, one of Frank's favorite hangouts in New York. I picked up the camera and drove to New York, meeting them at Rocky Lee's around two o'clock in the morning. Like Bookbinders, the place was empty. Frank, Jilly, Sammy, and Sammy's security guard, Brian Dellow, were sitting at a table. Frank seemed mellow that night. The conversation turned to the tour and how successful it was. In the middle of the conversation, Frank turned to us and said, "You know, the day I stop performing is the day that it's all over for me." I never forgot that, because Frank performed until the day that he got sick.

In December, Sammy and Frank appeared at the Golden Nugget in Atlantic City. It was the time that they celebrated their birthdays together. Sammy's was on the 8th and Frank's was on the 12th. Liza had another engagement. Sammy called and invited me to the birthday party they were planning. He had always admired a diamond bracelet that Olga had given me, and I decided to call the jewelers who designed it. Nick Balestra, Sr. was an old friend of mine, and now that he had passed away, his sons were running the business. When I showed Nick Jr. the bracelet, he told me that it would take him a couple of weeks to duplicate it. I told him that I needed it immediately, and after calling New York for the materials, Nick Jr. got it done in a couple days.

Sammy also asked if my mother could cook something for the party. Sinatra always loved the homemade dough that she would make, wrapping peppers and eggs and baking them in the oven. She made twelve loaves in all, and when I arrived, I handed them over to the maître d'. Sammy walked over and hugged me. Lenny Perna, an old friend of mine from South Philly, was playing the playing piano at the party. I said, "I have something for you, Sam," and I slipped him the jewelry case from Balestra's. As soon as he saw the bracelet, he said, "I can't believe that you got this for me." He started showing it off to everybody, and said, "Come on, you gotta sit with us."

I sat with Sammy, Altovise, Jilly, Frank, and Barbara. After a while, Frank said, "Matchstick, did your mom make the peppers and eggs?" I signaled to the maître d', who came out with Frank's favorite. Barbara told everyone at the table how much they loved my mother's cooking, and how much they enjoyed the packages I sent them. Every Christmas, I would send them homemade macaroni from Talluto's in Norristown, and they would serve them to their guests during the holidays. It was the last time that we all sat together, and it was a special night.

In addition to the "Ultimate Event," Sammy had previous commitments in Las Vegas. He called me one day and told me that he was going back into the studio to record again, and asked if I had any ideas about material that would be suitable for him. I immediately remembered some of the songs that Teddy Randazzo had written for Little Anthony and the Imperials—"The Wonder of It All," "Lost without You," "Cry My Eyes Out," and "It's Not the Same." They were great songs, and in my mind, they would fit Sammy's vocal style. I made a tape and flew out to Vegas.

Sammy was at the Hilton. He was opening up as a favor to Jerry Lewis. He looked frail to me, much frailer than I had ever seen them. When he listened to the tapes, he flipped over them. He also told me about a movie that he was doing with Gregory Hines. The movie was about legendary tap dancers. It featured the Nicholas Brothers and a young tapper named Savion Glover.

Sammy invited me to come down to Florida, where he and Frank were performing during Super Bowl weekend. We all stayed at a hotel in Coconut Grove. Altovise wasn't there, and I remember being with Sammy in a dressing room before the show. He was coughing a lot. I thought he was just clearing his throat. When he went on stage, we watched him on the monitors in the dressing room. I could see that he was taking out a handkerchief in between songs and coughing into it. When he came back to the dressing room before the grand finale, I said, "Sam, what's wrong?"

He looked at me and said, "I think I've got a problem."

"What are you gonna do about it?"

"I've got one more engagement at Harrah's in Reno. When I get back to L.A., I'm gonna get a complete physical."

"Can you get out of the engagement?"

"It's only a three-day engagement. It's from an old contract, and Bill Harrah's always been good to me."

When it came to performing and remembering old friends, nothing ever stood in Sammy's way. He was the epitome of show business. To him, the audience was the most important thing. He knew they were paying good money and they were there to be entertained. Unless you were on your deathbed, you got up and did just that. It wasn't about how you felt or how sick you were. The fans were there to see you, and you had to perform. Sammy and a few others taught me that early on. That's the world I came from. It was the world of show business—not the world of disc jockeys—and in all the years that I've been performing, I can honestly say that I've never missed a date.

Before I went back to Philly, Sammy told me that they were going to have the premiere of *Tap* in New York City, and that his engagement at Harrah's would prevent him from being there. He asked if I would take Altovise in his place. Liza was also planning to attend. At that time, she was married to a young sculptor, Mark Gero, but her date for the evening was the famous clothing designer, Halston. Altovise was staying at the Waldorf. I picked her up in a limousine, and we went to Liza's apartment on East 69th Street.

After the premiere, there was a party at Roseland. Besides the old tappers, one of the highlights of the movie was a scene where Etta James performed "Baby, What You Want Me to Do?" an old Jimmy Reed song that always knocked me out. Lo and behold, when we walked into Roseland, Etta was onstage, doing it live.

When we left the party, Liza invited us up to her apartment, where she showed us some of the original sketches that Andy Warhol had done of her and her mother, Judy Garland. Again, it was a night that I'll never forget.

After the engagement at Harrah's, Sammy went back to L.A. His doctors told him that he had a tumor. After all of the tests to determine its size, they informed him that it was small enough for them to remove it.

Sammy's life as a performer was singing, dancing, and doing impressions. He asked if there was another solution. They told him that they could use radiation, but that they couldn't guarantee the outcome. Because the surgery could have damaged his vocal chords, Sammy opted for the radiation. Later, Brian Dellow told me what Sammy had said: "If I lose my pipes, I'm not sure I want to live."

Sammy was admitted to Cedars of Sinai hospital. Shirley Rhodes, who was Sammy's manager at the time, called and told me what was happening. Her husband, George—Sammy's musical conductor—had died of a heart attack in 1985, and after his death, Shirley took over management from Sy Marsh.

Sammy was in the hospital for several weeks while they gave him radiation, and I tried to visit as frequently as I could. Because of the time difference, I would fly out on the first plane on Sunday morning, spend half the day with Sammy, and get back to Philly by late evening. On one of my visits, he told me about a state-of-the-art video camera that Sony had developed. It taped, recorded, and played back instantly, but it wasn't on the market yet. When I got back to Philly, I called the Hi-Fi House, the biggest Sony distributor on the East Coast, and they got the camera for me in a matter of days. I called Shirley and told her that I was coming out to L.A. to surprise Sammy. By then, Sammy was at the house on Summit Drive, and it seemed like the radiation treatments had worked.

When I arrived, Altovise told me that Sammy was resting, and I sat in the kitchen with Murphy Bennett. Sammy came downstairs a little while later, and I couldn't believe how weak he looked. I hugged him and gave him the camera. He looked at it and smiled.

"You've always been there for anything I've ever needed," he said. I felt very sad and lonely when I left him to go back to Philly.

A week later, Shirley called me and said that the United Negro College Fund was doing a salute to Sammy for his 60 years in show business. George Schlatter was producing it on television. He was the guy who did *Laugh-In*. Shirley said that Sammy wanted me to be there with the family. I flew out and sat with Shirley, Murphy Bennett, and Bernard, Sammy's valet. Sinatra, Clint Eastwood, Michael Jackson, Goldie Hawn, and other giants of show business saluted Sammy. Sammy and Altovise sat on stage while they performed and made their remarks. Eddie Murphy was the emcee, and Charlie O'Donnell—my old friend from the *Bandstand* days—was the announcer. (O'Donnell was also the announcer on the Pat Sajak-Vanna White show, *Wheel of Fortune*.)

Magic Johnson presented Sammy with a basketball, and after Gregory Hines performed, Sammy threw Gregory the ball. As frail as he was, Sammy got up and tapped with Gregory, and it brought the house down.

After the show, everyone went over to his home, including Michael Jackson, Whitney Houston, and Clint Eastwood. His mom, Babe Sanchez, was there, and the place was packed. I sat with Sammy at the bar out of everybody's way, which I had done many times. Before long, Sammy told me that he was tired and wanted to disappear without saying goodnight. He didn't want to interrupt the party. I told him that I was going back to Philly the next day, and he mentioned that he was going to Chicago to do a TV movie for CBS with Eddie Murphy.

Unfortunately, while shooting the movie in Chicago, Sammy caught a cold, and eventually the cancer returned. By May, word was out in the press. Family and friends were visiting him at home. After visiting him, Jerry Lewis announced that Sammy was dying, and that he was comatose and weighed less than 90 pounds. Once that became public, there were TV cameras and newspaper reporters from all over parked outside of Sammy's home. Needless to say, everyone around Sammy was upset with Lewis for his remarks to the press.

On Thursday, May 10, Brian Dellow called me and said, "If you want to say good-bye to Sammy, you better get out here right away. He's not expected to live through the weekend."

I was devastated, and before I left to see my friend for the last time, I decided to call Cardinal Krol, one of my old neighbors from Overbrook Avenue. When his secretary came to the phone, I explained that my friend Sammy Davis was dying, and that I wanted to bring holy water when I flew out to L.A. The secretary put me through to one of the priests at the Cardinal's residence, and the priest said he would talk to the Cardinal and call me back. The next thing I knew, I received a call that Cardinal Krol had a small bottle of holy water from Lourdes. As every Catholic knows, Our Lady appeared there miraculously in 1858, and Catholics have been making pilgrimages to Lourdes ever since. A stream of water flowed from the rock where she appeared, and it still flows to this day. That was the holy water I brought to Sammy.

I flew out on Friday morning and went straight to Sammy's home. Shirley, Brian, Altovise, and Sammy's mother were all there, along with his ex-wife, May Britt, and the daughter they had together, Tracy. May was just as beautiful as I remembered. Tracy's husband was at Sammy's bedside also, along with Mark and Jeff—Sammy's adopted kids. They had converted Sammy's huge office into a waiting room, and had taken an additional space and converted it into a bedroom. When I arrived, there were TV cameras all over the place, and visitors were told to enter by the back of the house or the garage entrance. Brian had his own security at the gates. Liza had already been there, and so had Frank. When I walked into the house, Robert Blake, the actor who played Baretta, was up in Sammy's room. He and Sammy had become very close over the years, and Sammy had recorded the theme song for *Baretta*, "Keep Your Eye on the Sparrow." Blake was so emotional that he had to be removed from Sammy's bedside. He was sobbing, and kept whispering over and over again, "You can't go, you can't go. I don't know what I'm gonna do without you."

Steve Blauner—Bobby Darin's manager—was there. Sammy had been one of Darin's biggest supporters, and he was the one who recognized Darin's extraordinary talent. When Darin did the album *That's All*, which included "Mack the Knife," "Beyond the Sea," "I'll Remember April," and "Softly as in a Morning Sunrise," it skyrocketed Darin into superstardom. No other rock and roll star had ever recorded songs like that.

When I arrived, Sammy was off life support. He was in a fetal position on the bed. His throat was bandaged where the cancer had eaten away the flesh, and there was a strong odor in the room. Every so often, they used a spray bottle to dispense perfume. Sammy's male nurse replaced the bandage periodically, and when I gave him the holy water, he placed it directly on the bandage before he wrapped Sammy.

No one was cooking at the house, and I told Altovise that I was going to have food delivered by Poponi's, an Italian restaurant in Brentwood. Poponi's was always Sammy's favorite. For some reason, when the food arrived, it reminded me of Angelo's death a decade before, when Ralph's, Dante and Luigi's, and other South Philly restaurants sent food over. It was almost like a flashback for me. Late at night, I would sneak out through the garage to get back to the Beverly Hills

Hotel. I could have stayed at the house, but Sammy's family was there, and I wanted to respect their privacy.

By Monday, nobody could believe that Sammy was still alive. He had been off life support for days. As far as the doctors were concerned, the ordeal should have been over. In my mind, I attributed it to the holy water. The crowd of reporters continued to grow on the street outside.

Come Tuesday, I explained to Shirley, Brian, and Altovise that I had to get back to Philly. Wednesday was Keely's birthday, and I was scheduled to do the Thrill Show on Thursday afternoon at the Spectrum. Natalie Cole was the headliner. I said, "I'll fly out tomorrow morning, and I'll come back Friday."

That night, I went back to the Beverly Hills Hotel and booked the first flight out in the morning. I got up at 5 the next day, and before going to the airport, snuck back into the house to say good-bye. When I went up to Sammy's room, Altovise was sleeping on the couch, and the nurse was sleeping a few feet away. Mark was there, and so were Brian and Shirley. When I bent down to kiss Sammy good-bye, I noticed that the line on the heart monitor was flat, and that there weren't any fluids in the bags he was hooked up to. Gently, I walked over to Altovise and whispered, "Sammy's passed."

The reaction was amazing. There was no panic. Sammy's death was expected, and it had a calming effect on the family. Everyone felt a sense of relief that his suffering was over. I went out of the room as his family paid their last respects. The question was, how were we going to get Sammy's body out of there without the press being aware of it? The family didn't want any pictures taken of an ambulance retrieving the body. Everyone looked for an answer.

I said to Shirley, "I think I have it. This service that delivers flowers every day—why don't you tell them that there are too many flowers here? Tell them to bring an empty truck. They can drive through the gates and go to the garage like they normally do. We can take Sammy's body out with the flowers."

Everyone agreed, and an hour later, the truck pulled up to the back of the house. After the nurse put Sammy in the body bag, we carried him out to the truck along with the flowers. As the truck drove away, the press had no idea that Sammy was on his way to the funeral home.

Most of the funeral arrangements had already been made, and

Shirley took care of the rest of them before she started the long process of calling Sammy's friends. There were hundreds of calls to make. (When Frank died in 1998, there were terrible pictures of him in the tabloids, including photographs of him on a stretcher. But fortunately, there was never a picture of Sammy in the last days of his life. He died with his dignity intact.)

I knew that the funeral would become a Hollywood spectacular with cameras everywhere and show business people coming out of the woodwork. I explained to Shirley that I really didn't want to be there. "There's no need for me to be a part of this thing." Shirley understood, and the family knew where I was coming from. I was about to turn fifty, and Sammy was gone.

On the plane back to Philly, I couldn't stop thinking of Sammy—how he loved my mother's cooking, and how he would always come over to the house on Overbrook Avenue and shoot pool with me in my basement. We would listen to music on my jukebox and watch old Warner Brothers movies on my projector. At one point, after I cooked for him, he started calling me, "My man, pots and pans!" and became a gourmet cook himself. When he was on the road, he would bring his own pots and pans and cook for everybody in his hotel room at four in the morning. I remembered how he would call me every time he appeared at the Latin and ask if I would go to Foo Foo's in West Philadelphia and get him his "mammajamma" sandwiches, and how he threw a punch at me in his dressing room one night to see how I'd react. He was about to make a TV movie called *The Trackers* with Ernest Borgnine. He told me that he wanted me in the movie and would call me before production. The call did come, but the producers used Noah Beery Jr. for my role. (When I got home, *Philadelphia* magazine profiled me in their June issue, and the photograph that accompanied the article told the story of how I felt. There are very few pictures of me where I don't have a smile on my face, but that was one of them. Sammy's death left a void that I feel to this day.)

As I look back on my life, everything that was important started with a new decade. In the 60s, I got married and went on radio for the first time. Going into the 70s, I let my television contract expire after making *Cycad* the previous summer. Angelo died in 1980, I met Keely in 1989, and Sammy died on Keely's birthday, May 16, 1990. My first show at the Kimmel Center was in 2001, and I've been doing shows there ever since, ushering in 2010 with *Jerry Blavat's Legends of Rock and Roll*. Whenever I look at it like that, with the significant events of my life occurring at regular intervals, it's almost like the decades of the rosary.

In the fall of 1990, I got involved with television again. WCAU had acquired *Live with Regis and Kathie Lee* and had scheduled an agency party to promote their fall lineup. Steve Cohen was the general manager, and Bernie Webber was the head of their promotion department. Webber had been one of my original dancers, and as a surprise—as part of the entertainment for the party—he asked me to recreate a ten-minute portion of *The Discophonic Scene*. Once again, I danced on a podium, interacted with the dancers, and introduced my guests. The segment featured Martha Reeves and the Vandellas. They did "Heat Wave," and I did my rap over the intro. The agency people flipped over the segment, and the party was a huge success.

After the party, Steve Cohen congratulated me. I said, "Why don't we recreate *The Discophonic Scene* as a special on a Saturday night?"

"Great idea. Let's talk about it later."

When I met with Steve and his program director, Dan Sitarski, I told them that I would like to produce the show in conjunction with WCAU. I knew how great their production people were from when I worked there. I said that I wanted to use their guys, and that I would pick up the above-the-line costs. I knew I had the money because of my settlement from *The In Crowd*.

I brought in La Toya Jackson, Frankie Avalon, Danny and the Juniors, and Harold Melvin and the Blue Notes. When the show was finished, I went to see my old friend Mel Korn, who had sponsored the original *Discophonic Scene* with Mountain Dew and Pepsi. When we aired it for Mel, he flipped, and Pepsi became the principal sponsor. Even though the Saturday night show was a commercial success, Steve told me that WCAU didn't have a time slot to continue it on a weekly basis.

Because of the excitement we generated, I approached Channel 57. Carol Healy was the program director and knew what we had done at 'CAU. She set up a meeting with the general manager, Bob O'Connor. I made the same deal that I made with 'CAU. Channel 57 supplied the technicians, the editing, and their facilities, and I picked up the costs of producing it.

I built a set that duplicated a radio station and interviewed some of the biggest names in rock and roll—Frankie Valli, Jerry Lee Lewis, Jerry Butler, Brenda Lee, Chuck Berry, and Chubby Checker. At that time, I was doing a Sunday night gig at the Aztec Club on Delaware Avenue. My concept was to tape the dancers at the Aztec separately and insert the interviews into the show. When all of the editing was done, it was like a radio show on television. We aired it on Saturday nights from 7:30 to 8, right after *Star Search* with Ed McMahon, and then repeated the telecast between 12:30 and 1. The show was called *On the Air with the Geator*. I went on to do 26 episodes, and they were completely sold out. (I still have the episodes on DVD in my office. They're called *The Lost Episodes*, and the back cover says, "They came, they saw, they grooved.")

During that time, an oldies war broke out in Philadelphia. Four major radio stations were converting to oldies formats. The jockeys from 'PGR left. I was offered a job at one of the new oldies stations also, but I was happy where I was. I had the freedom to play the music I wanted to play for my audience. At the same time, the ratings at Sunny 104.5 were dropping. Pyramid Broadcasting brought in new management, getting rid of Mike Martaer and Gus DeJohn. They replaced them with Jeff Spector and Phil Siglione. Spector became the general manager of both stations—'PGR and 104.5—and Siglione became the sales manager for both. Pyramid was based in Boston, and these two guys had turned one of their stations around when it was struggling. During our conversations, it became obvious that the AM station was not their concern, and that they were trying to turn the FM station around. They changed the name from Sunny 104.5 to Star 104.5. It was only a matter of time before Don Cannon, the program director of 104.5, would lock horns with the new management and leave to join WOGL.

Jeff Spector came to me one day and said, "We don't have any more money to budget for the AM. We're thinking of simulcasting the AM with the FM."

I told him that it would be a total disaster. As the ratings showed in "time spent listening," we were among the top five in the Philadelphia market, and the 'PGR audience would be devastated if they didn't hear their music.

At first, Spector took my advice, but six months later, he said, "Look, we're gonna have to simulcast."

"Why don't you sell the AM?" I asked. "I would like to put together a group of investors to buy it."

He contacted Richard Balsbaugh, the owner of Pyramid Broadcasting, and got back to me a few days later. Balsbaugh is a good guy. Even today, he still comes to see me when I do my shows down the shore.

Spector said, "We're looking for a million-two."

I went to my friend Sam Rappaport, the Center City real estate owner who had helped me with Memories West. Sam was a multi-millionaire, and he was well-connected.

"Sam, they want a million-two."

"Nah," he said, "you negotiate."

Sam got involved. For the next few weeks, there was no movement on the part of Pyramid, but when they found out that Sam owned the building they were broadcasting out of in Pittsburgh, things changed in a hurry. Sam offered them a reduced rent if they would make a deal for us to purchase 'PGR for $800,000. They went for it.

Sam asked if I had $80,000, which he would put in escrow while he looked for other investors. At that time, he was going through a bitter divorce. He was involved with a young Russian attorney named Marina Katz, and the lawyer representing him in the divorce was Bob Daniels. He put Marina Katz, Bob Daniels, Bob Rovner, and Tony Coradetti together as investors. Each of them came up with $80,000.

When I was at WFIL, a kid named Eric Farber was working as a sales rep for Power 99. Farber expressed interest in becoming an investor but didn't have that kind of money. He could only come up with $50,000, but I thought that his radio experience made him the perfect guy to run the station. Sam met with Farber, and he also became an investor.

Sam asked me, "What should we call the corporation?"

I thought for a minute, and said, "Sam, all the investors are stars in their respective fields. Let's call it All-Star Radio."

The next step was for us to file the papers to incorporate, which meant that all of the stockholders had to be listed; then we would submit an application to the FCC. While the papers were being drawn up, Sam got a call from Bob Rovner. "We have to divulge the members of the corporation," Rovner said. Once again, my friendship with Angelo got in the way. Rovner was concerned that my presence would hold up the sale.

Sam called and told me the situation. "You're not gonna be a stock-holder, but you'll have a contract as the program director for as long as All-Star Radio owns the station. If and when the station is sold, you'll get your $80,000 back, as will the other partners, and you'll receive an equal share." Trusting Sam, and not wanting to hold up the sale, I signed the papers, and the deal went through. I was now a part-owner of WPGR, which we called Geator Gold Radio. This was the first step in the creation of the Geator Gold Radio Network.

The station struggled from the very beginning, experiencing severe financial problems, and unfortunately, Sam had to replace Eric Farber. I suggested Tom Primavera. Primavera was an older guy who had worked for Jack Downey on WCAU Radio. Primavera became the gen-eral manager. He was a nice man, but he wasn't energetic enough to turn things around.

For the first few years, Sam kept the station afloat, reaching into his own pocket whenever we couldn't make payroll. In 1993, however—after paying off the bank note—Sam became ill. I took him to Hahnemann Hospital, where they diagnosed his illness as lymphoma. At first, I would take him for his treatments, but after the cancer weak-ened him, he made arrangements to get the treatments at his home in Bucks County.

Sam's health steadily declined. It was affecting his business and holdings, and through no fault of his own, he could no longer support the station. I knew that something had to be done, and that we would have to fend for ourselves.

During that time, I received a phone call from my old friend James Brown, who told me that Georgie Woods was unhappy at WHAT. In the heyday of rock and roll, Georgie was the #1 jockey on 'DAS, but he was now doing a talk show. James said, "He hates the talk show. Do you have a place for him on your station?" I explained that I really had no money, but with a name like Georgie's, I was sure I could work some-thing out. "If I give him the morning show," I said, "I know I can sell it. I'll give him 25% of the sales plus $200 a week."

"Give him a call," James replied. "Make sure he doesn't do any bullshit." I didn't know what he meant, but I found out soon enough.

When I brought Georgie Woods to WPGR, he joined a lineup that included me, a young kid named Armand Colianni, and another kid named Andy Volvo. Because the station was a "daytimer," we were on until 8:15 at night in the summer, and I put one of our interns on the air after me. His name was Jason Sklar, and he loved the music. Sally Starr, a local personality, did a morning show for us. I had worked with Sally at Channel 6, and we were friends. Sally had a kids show in the 50s and 60s, and an entire generation of Philadelphians knew her as "our gal Sal." With local legends like Georgie Woods and Sally Starr, we were able to make some noise.

I hired an African-American woman named Sharon Powell. Powell was thirty-two years old. She had come to me for a sales job, but I couldn't offer her a salary; I could only offer her a straight commission on whatever sales she made. Powell had a pleasant voice, and in addition to selling, I gave her a fee for doing commercials.

We had applied to the FCC to go full-time, and had gotten the approval to broadcast at a lower frequency at night. I decided to develop a show like *The Lovers Hour*—but with a female host. I thought that Sharon Powell's voice would be perfect. Instead of putting her on the air under her own name, I called her "Lady Love," after the Lou Rawls song, and I had her play soulful R&B. I wanted her persona to have a sensual aspect—like Lou's voice—and I instructed her to sound mellow. We worked on her delivery, and by the time the show went on the air, it really sounded good.

Unfortunately, Georgie Woods wasn't making it as a morning jock. He had lost his rhythm and timing and was talking too much. I had to do something. Powell's show had taken off, and my idea was to switch her and Georgie around. I would put "Lady Love" on in the morning and Georgie on at night. Apparently, Georgie found out before I could talk to him, and it caused a problem. At first, I was unaware that there was a problem brewing, but eventually it came to my attention. I've always believed in being straight up with people and never pulling any punches. I met with Georgie and told him what I was looking to do, but I knew that it didn't sit well with him.

I had other problems with the station. All of the bills were going to Sam's office, but now Sam was sick. One morning, I was in the dentist's chair at Dr. Matarazzo's when Armand Colianni called. He said that the electric company was there, and that they were going to shut off the power. Sam had never paid the bill. I talked to the guy from the electric company, and he told me that we owed $20,000 for the last two months. I explained that I knew nothing about the bill.

As luck would have it, the guy was a fan. He said, "I'll give you twenty-four hours. I'll tell them that I couldn't get in to find the box, but the bill's gotta be paid."

At that time, Sam had a partner in some of his real estate ventures, Richard Basciano. Richard and I had become friends through Sam, and to this day, he's one of the most honorable men that I have ever met in my life. When Sam was ill—and his empire was about to collapse—Richard helped him out financially.

Sam wasn't in any kind of shape to help with the electric company. I called Richard and said, "Rich, you're the only guy I can turn to." I explained the situation, and he immediately offered to lend me the $20,000. I said, "It's not for me, it's for the station. The stockholders have to know that you're laying out the money as a loan." If Richard Basciano hadn't lent us the money, WPGR would have gone down the tubes.

Shortly before Sam died, he named Richard as the executor of his estate. It was the smartest thing he could have done. Richard ended up saving the estate and keeping it whole for the Rappaport family. Sam's estate was losing value at an alarming rate, but Richard came through for the Rappaports, just like he did for the station.

When I told Richard how bad the situation was at WPGR, he called for a meeting of the stockholders. He told them about the problems with the cash flow, and suggested that they all throw in another $20,000. None of them had anything to do with the station. After making their initial investment, they left the running of it up to Sam; now, they had no intention of investing any more money.

After the meeting, I spoke with Bob O'Connor. He had always been interested in radio, and now that Paramount was buying Channel 57 and bringing in new management, I knew that he would love to get involved with buying 'PGR. I told Richard, and when Bob told him how lucrative radio could be, Richard decided to become an investor for his kids. He called for another meeting of the stockholders, and said, "If you don't intend to provide additional support to the station, why don't you sell it to Jerry? He has investors, and they'll give you 20% on your initial investment. All of you are successful in your careers," Richard continued, "but this is Jerry's livelihood."

"We'll think about it."

At the next meeting, they agreed to sell the station to a new group of investors. Bob O'Connor and his lawyer drew up a letter of intent, and the stockholders signed it. Bob Rovner—one of the original investors—congratulated me. In my mind, Bob O'Connor, Richard Basciano, and I were on our way to owning WPGR.

Sometime later, Bob O'Connor called me and said, "Do you realize that there's an ad in *Broadcast Magazine* for a station in the Philadelphia market?" As it turned out, Rovner had placed the ad and had told the stockholders that there was a potential buyer for $1.1 million. O'Connor couldn't believe what Rovner and the others had done. He said, "What they're doing is unconscionable."

I called Rovner and said, "Bob, you guys signed a letter of intent."

"Don't worry about it. You're gonna get your money."

"It's not a question of money—this is my profession. What you're doing is not honorable. You made a deal," I said. "I've got an agreement. I'm the program director for as long as All-Star Radio owns it."

"We'll fight you. Sam had no right signing that paper with you."

One morning, before I went to the station, Andy Volvo called me. He said that the press had gathered outside, and that they were waiting for me to come in. I had been hit with a sexual harassment suit from Sharon Powell. "Did you see the *Daily News*?" Volvo asked. "You're all over the front page."

As I drove to the station, I couldn't help suspecting that the stockholders might have fabricated it to discredit me. I knew it was all bullshit—just like the Grant Cuzzupe mess the decade before—but it was a serious charge that could damage my reputation.

The *Allentown Morning Call* picked up on it, and so did the *New York Daily News*. The headline in the *Morning Call* said, "Geator Feels the Heater: Philly Radio Personality Faces Sex Harassment Charges." The article ran on February 25, 1995, and the first paragraph went like this: "Philadelphia radio and music personality Jerry 'the Geator' Blavat has been charged with sexual harassment by a disc jockey at his radio station whose on-air name is 'Lady Love.' A lawsuit filed in U.S. District Court accused Blavat of making repeated sexual advances toward the woman, whose real name is Sharon Powell-Ross of Philadelphia. Oldies station WPGR-AM originally hired Powell-Ross as a saleswoman, but in April 1993, Blavat, the station's program director, asked her to host a 70s music radio show with a romantic emphasis."

Now I was fighting two injustices at once—getting double-crossed by my former partners on the sale of the radio station, and getting hit with a lawsuit by a young woman I was trying to help.

I had nothing to hide, and when I got to the station, I told the press that I would issue a statement. By then, I had called Carmen Nasuti, and he stood next to me as I spoke to the reporters. I told them that I had run teenage dances for years, with thousands of kids in attendance, and that their parents had put their trust in me. "I've never been accused of anything improper," I said. "At this point in my life, why would I even think about doing that?"

Powell accused me of calling her during her show and making sexual advances on the phone. I told the press that I had developed the Lady Love persona, and that I only called Powell when she was straying from it on the air, or when she was playing the wrong music.

Because the accusation was made by an African-American woman, I wanted an African-American lawyer. I called my friend Kenny Gamble, who recommended that I use Ron White. White and I went into federal court, and Judge Jules Dasell threw out the case, ruling that it shouldn't have been filed there in the first place. It wasn't a federal matter. Powell and her lawyers re-filed the case in Municipal Court, and Carmen Nasuti recommended that I get Alan Epstein to handle my defense. Once again, the case was thrown out.

After the sexual harassment suit hit the newspapers, Sharon Powell never showed up for work again, and neither did Georgie Woods. Looking back on it, I'm not sure it was a coincidence. There was so much going on after Sam's death that it was hard to keep track of it all, but I was always a little suspicious of the fact that Georgie had talked to Powell about the switching of their schedules. The stockholders might have fabricated the lawsuit, and Georgie Woods might have been instrumental in it as well.

Meanwhile, we initiated a lawsuit to stop the sale of the station. We hired Dave Lazar, a young lawyer from Pittsburgh, and held up the sale in the local courts. When the stockholders took the case to the State Supreme Court, however, we were overruled. Not only did they prevail in the Supreme Court, but they also refused to give me back my initial investment. Richard Basciano couldn't believe what the stockholders were doing. He told them, "You guys should be ashamed of yourselves. This is Jerry's career. You're trying to destroy him. It's not right, and he's not going away."

The sale of the station went through, and the new owner converted it to a talk radio format, allowing me to remove all of my music and equipment. Now that Richard was the executor of Sam's estate, I told him that I needed a place to broadcast. He talked to the Rappaport family, and out of gratitude for what I had done for Sam when he was sick, they agreed to rent me a property on the 600 block of Market Street at a reduced rate. I have done my broadcasts from there ever since. (As if I needed any more reminders of the legal system, the James A. Byrne federal courthouse is right across the street.)

Now, I needed a station to broadcast over. My old friend Pat Delsey was the new owner of WCAM in Camden. I told him that I wanted to buy time, and he gave me three hours a day Monday through Friday. I took all of the sponsors I had on Geator Gold and started all over again.

I was absolutely relentless when it came to getting my money from the stockholders. It took time, but with Richard Basciano's backing, I finally prevailed. In the end, they not only gave me my initial investment back but the same portion of the proceeds that they received from the sale of the station and the property.

I went on to broadcast on WPAZ in Pottstown and WBCB in Bucks County, but when Pat Delsey sold WCAM—and the new owners converted it to an all-Spanish format—I needed another outlet. After the sale of WPGR, Sally Starr did a show on 92.1 in Jersey, and she told me that I should talk with Carl Hemple, the general manager. I bought time from 5 to 7 p.m. Monday through Friday, and I've been on 92.1 ever since.

Over the years, I have continued to expand the Geator Gold Network. In addition to WPAZ, WBCB, and Cruisin' 92.1, I can be heard on KOOL 98.3 (Linwood, NJ), 104.9-FM (Lehigh Valley, PA), 88.1-FM (Harrisburg, PA), and 90.5-FM (Baltimore, MD), doing live remotes from Memories in Margate, the SugarHouse Casino, Chickie's and Pete's, and a number of other clubs. When it comes to the advertisers, whoever buys Blavat, buys Blavat; they don't buy the station. The advertisers don't care what station I'm on, because they know I have a following; some of them have followed me around as the stations have come and gone. Jefferson Hospital is an example of that, and so are Geno's Steaks, Gary Barbera Dodge, Chickie's and Pete's, and Yuengling Beer. It goes back to my earliest days on radio and television, and the importance I place on keeping the advertisers happy. When they sign on with me as a sponsor, they know that I'll produce. I have the track record to prove it.

In November 1998, Sidney and Caroline Kimmel invited me to attend the groundbreaking ceremony for the Kimmel Center in Philadelphia. The building was more than a performing arts center; it was destined to become a cornerstone of the Avenue of the Arts project on South Broad Street. Sidney took me aside and said, "You should think about doing some shows here." Shortly after that, a letter from Stephanie Naidoff, the president of the Kimmel Center, arrived at my office. Naidoff thought it was a great idea, and she invited me to meet with John Fernandez, her programming director. The meeting went well, and Fernandez went on to schedule me for three shows in the first year of the Kimmel Center, which opened in December, 2001. This venue turned out to be the perfect place for me to present some of the most influential artists of early rock and roll.

During this time, my mother was living by herself in Broomall. She was going blind, having been diagnosed with acute macular degeneration, and even though she had great neighbors and friends who watched over her, Roberta and I became concerned that she might fall in the middle of the night. Roberta was living in Reading, and I was in Center City. After much convincing and coaxing, we moved my mother to St. Mary's at 5th and Locust, just a few blocks away from my apartment. The mercy nuns were there to watch over her. Unfortunately, after eight months, her conditioned worsened, and she developed dementia. When that happened, she needed a greater level of care than the sisters were able to provide.

Roberta and I spoke to Sue Bruno's doctor, Dr. Mingrone, and he moved my mother to Liberty Court at 17th and Lombard. I would ride my bike over every day like I did when she was at St. Mary's, and I would make tapes of all her favorite music from the 40s and 50s, asking the nurses to play it for her when I wasn't there.

One night, about two in the morning, one of the nurses called and said that my mom had fallen out of bed. They rushed her to Jefferson Hospital, and when I got there, I found out that she had a broken hip.

Dr. Rothman performed the surgery, and though he was able to repair my mother's hip, she lapsed into a coma. Every so often, she would regain consciousness, but between that, the dementia, and the blindness, the doctors recommended that we place her in hospice care. My daughter, Stacy, flew in from California, and whenever Roberta, Keely or I couldn't be there, Stacy would stay with my mother.

My mother's failing health coincided with the opening of the Kimmel Center, and one Saturday, I was invited to attend the opening ceremony. I left my mother's side to attend, and Roberta and Stacy stayed with my mom. Sidney Kimmel sang a song with Paul Anka that day, but it was hard for me to concentrate with my mother in such bad shape.

Despite that she was off life support, my mother refused to give up. She was a fighter, and she continued to hang on. For more than a week, she was in and out of the coma. The nurses were amazed that she was still alive, and when I asked them about it, they said, "It's not her time."

After they said that to me, I would always whisper in my mother's ear and tell her how much I loved her. One day, I said, "Mom, you know I love you, but it's time for you to go."

Amazingly, she opened her eyes and answered as clear as a bell. "But who will watch over you when I'm not here?"

Roberta was sitting a few feet away. I said, "Mom, don't worry about me. I'm fine. I have your strength."

My mother didn't say anything. "You have to go," I continued. "Roberta and I will be with you one day." She smiled, closed her eyes, and passed away a few minutes later.

My mother was the strongest woman I have ever known. Even though she regretted the fact that we had struggled financially, she never talked about it when Roberta and I were kids; she never let on how devastated she was by the death of my half-sister, Lou Anne. Even when my grandparents died, she thought of others before she thought of herself. Knowing that she was the youngest—and that her brothers resented her for being named the executor of the estate—she relinquished that role to my Uncle Jimmy. My strength comes from my mother; my street sense comes from my dad.

With the passing of my mother, I've never had any regrets. In my heart, I always tried to do the right thing by her; even though she may not be with me physically, her spirit is with me to this day.

A month later, I put on my first show at the Kimmel Center, presenting artists from my world—Lloyd Price, Jerry Butler, the Starlights, the Skyliners, the Duprees, Lenny Welch, the Impressions, Ben E. King, the Drifters, Jay Black and the Americans, and Johnny Maestro and the Brooklyn Bridge. I backed all of the artists with a 22-piece orchestra, and that's what makes my Kimmel Center shows unique. No one ever presented these groups with an orchestra that size. They would normally carry a rhythm section and a couple of horns.

The Kimmel Center shows have been a tremendous success. Local celebrities have packed Verizon Hall, along with the fans that have been with me for years. The first show drew people like Ron White, Congressman Bob Brady, and Police Commissioner Sylvester Johnson, and movers and shakers have been attending the shows ever since.

By then, Ron White and I had become close friends. Along with Kenny Gamble, he was responsible for getting John Street elected. Unfortunately, by the end of his first term as mayor, Street had lost a lot of his popularity. Now, he was running for a second term against Sam Katz, a respected businessman who was ahead of Street in the polls. Street complained to Ron that the leaders of the Jewish community were supporting Katz and contributing major dollars. He mentioned that Sidney Kimmel had contributed a large amount of money to Katz's campaign and little to his own. Street reminded Ron that he had helped to get the Kimmel Center built when he was the president of City Council.

"Wait a minute," Ron said. "The Geator knows Sidney Kimmel!"

"The Geator? Who's that?"

"You never heard of the Geator? That's Jerry Blavat! He's an icon with the white people. He was Sammy Davis's best man. He knew Sinatra and all those guys."

"You think he can get Sinatra to campaign for me?"

Ron broke up laughing. "Man, don't you know that cat's been dead since 1998?"

At that time, no one knew that the FBI was listening to the entire conversation. They were investigating the Street administration, members of his staff, and Ron White's involvement with the mayor.

Shortly after that, Ron called and said that Street wanted to see me. I met Ron at a conference room in City Hall, and Street walked in a few minutes later. Ron said, "Mr. Mayor, this is the Geator, Jerry Blavat."

Street shook my hand and asked for suggestions on how he should campaign. Until then, he was spending most of his time in the black neighborhoods.

"This is a city that's made up of neighborhoods," I said. "I think you should campaign in all of them. Let the people know that you're going to respond to the needs of their community."

"That's a good suggestion," he said, and then he paused for a moment. "I understand you're friends with Sidney Kimmel."

"I know Mr. Kimmel."

Street reiterated what he had done as president of City Council, and repeated his complaint about Sidney's campaign contributions.

"Mr. Mayor, I'm not involved in Mr. Kimmel's business or politics, but I've always known him to be a very fair man. He's done wonderful things for the City of Philadelphia. Why don't you write him a letter and explain just what you said to me?"

Ron asked, "Have you done that?"

"No," Street said.

"I think you should."

As I walked out of the meeting, I realized that Street wasn't really interested in my suggestions about the campaign.

A week later, KYW broke the story that Mayor Street's office had been bugged, and that Ron White was under federal investigation for his dealings with the Street administration. Shortly after that, Ron was indicted, and I received a call from Erin Einhorn, an investigative reporter at the *Daily News*.

"Are you friends with Ron White?" she asked.

"Absolutely. He was my lawyer."

"Has the FBI contacted you?"

"Why should they contact me?"

"No reason. I'm just curious."

The Daily News had petitioned the courts and gotten a copy of the FBI tapes. The conversations between Ron White and John Street were in the newspapers, including their discussion of my friendships with Sammy, Frank, and Sidney.

Although Street wasn't the target of the investigation, it actually helped him. He picked up a groundswell of support from a large segment of the population, which felt that he had been treated unfairly. He seemed like a victim, and I believe that's one of the reasons that he was elected to a second term.

Shortly after that, Ron and I had dinner together. He complained that his stomach was bothering him, and that he couldn't keep his food down. I called my doctor and friend, A. J. DiMarino, the head of gastroenterology at Jefferson Hospital. They took all kinds of tests, and the diagnosis came back as pancreatic cancer, a disease that progresses rapidly. A. J. recommended Dr. Ernest Rosato, the head surgeon at Jefferson, and one Friday, I accompanied Ron and his family to the consultation.

Rosato recommended a Whipple procedure. He explained that it was a long operation in which the head of the pancreas, a portion of the bile duct, and the gall bladder are removed. The operation was risky, but it had been successful. It was the best option that Ron had.

Rosato said, "We can do it immediately. We'll bring you in first thing Monday morning. No one will know about it."

At that point, Ron agreed, and as we walked out, Rosato said, "If you change your mind, call me at my home Sunday."

On Sunday morning, Ron called me. He said, "Geator, I've been thinking about this. Even if the procedure is successful, I'm not gonna be able to fight this indictment while recuperating."

Unfortunately, without the operation, Ron White died three months later. I gave a eulogy and served as a pallbearer at his funeral. (Although Ron was spared the agony of a trial—and Mayor Street survived to serve a second term—Corey Kemp, a former city treasurer, is now serving a ten-year prison sentence for political corruption.)

Because of the success of the Kimmel Center shows, the head of the Philadelphia Mural Arts Program, Jane Golden, approached me. She wanted to commission a mural to recognize entertainers from South

Philadelphia, including myself. Golden asked if I could suggest the other entertainers they should honor. I mentioned Frankie Avalon, Chubby Checker, Bobby Rydell, Al Martino, and Jimmy Darren. The mural was called *The Sounds of Philadelphia*, and it recognized all of the entertainers I suggested, except for Jimmy Darren. For some reason, they decided to substitute Eddie Fisher, who wasn't a rock and roll guy at all.

The Philadelphia Mural Arts program partnered with WXPN—the FM station owned by the University of Pennsylvania—to commission an artist named Peter Pagast. Pagast did a great job, and a few months later, the mural went up at 9th and Wharton, across from Gino's Steaks. I got Al, Frankie, and Chubby to attend the dedication, and we all spoke. The mayor's office presented us with a proclamation, and Congressman Bob Brady honored us as well. Roger LaMay, the general manager of WXPN, attended the event. I talked about my passion for the music and how proud my mother would have been. These were the same blocks that she walked on 9th Street when she went shopping.

At the time the mural went up, I was doing a show on WPEN, but they were about to convert the station to an all-sports format. Many of the listeners felt abandoned, and I knew that there was a need for our music. Although I had never met Roger before, I was aware that he had been the general manager at Fox 29 before taking over WXPN. I was impressed with the eclectic nature of WXPN's programming, and I decided to call him. When I told him that none of the local stations would be playing oldies once WPEN completed the conversion to sports, he agreed that there might be a void in the Philadelphia market.

"I love what you guys do," I told him. "I think my music would be a perfect fit, and I'm not looking to get paid."

"I'll tell you what. Make me a tape, and I'll sit down with the program director."

I immediately went into my studio and cut a ten-minute sampling of what I called *The Geator's Rock and Roll / Rhythm and Blues Express*. It featured the giants of the industry—the producers, the writers, the labels—and through the miracle of the mind, I took listeners to the great musical Meccas of the United States, including New Orleans, Chicago, and L.A. I sent a messenger over with the tape, and Roger called the next day. "Wow," he said, "you really work fast. I'll call you in a week."

A week later, he called me and said, "Can you come over to the station? I want you to meet Bruce Warren, our program director." I hopped on my bike and rode to their studios at 30th and Walnut. When I got there, Warren told me that he loved what I did. "I think it would be a great fit. We'll give you from 6 to 7 every Saturday night and see what happens."

When the show went on, the reviews were amazing. Local columnists commented on how ingenious it was for WXPN to hire the Geator, and in *Philadelphia* magazine's "Best of Philly" issue in 2006, WXPN was singled out for the best move by a radio station.

My show immediately follows *The Many Moods of Ben Vaughn*, which Ben tapes on the West Coast. Although he has lived in Los Angeles since the mid-90s, Ben grew up in the Philadelphia area and got hooked on rock and roll when his uncle gave him a Duane Eddy record. He went on to form the Ben Vaughn Trio, which got rave reviews in *Rolling Stone* and elsewhere, before embarking on a solo career and composing music for TV and feature films. Ben paid me the ultimate compliment when he said, "I grew up listening to him. He has his own AM radio station and he still plays old records and talks a mile a minute and pounds his desk with his fist and screams. He's amazing. He's my hero. I started listening to him on AM radio when I was 8 or 9 years old, and he played the craziest shit. My dad was just appalled."

Radio will never be the same. What I did will never happen again. Top 40 thinking eventually brought down AM radio, and now it's bringing down FM.

It has led to the demise of disc jockeys with originality. In my opinion, that's why talk radio is so big today, because it gives the listener an opportunity to be a part of the discussion. I've always made my money via advertisers and the personal appearances that arise out of my radio shows; I've resisted format and sacrificed a salary in order to play my music and bring the audience into my world.

Music is my life, and most of the people who tried to change me are no longer in radio. They're either dead or doing something else. My advice to young people who want to get into radio is to hook up with a college station that will give them the freedom to create their own persona. If they become successful with it, they shouldn't let anyone take it away. It's actually good advice in any field of endeavor.

A few years ago, after my show on Friday at Memories, I left a little early and drove back to Philly. My daughter, Deserie, called me from the club. "Dad," she said, "you'll never guess who's here."

"Who?"

"Olga! She's here with her sister. She wants to talk to you."

By that time, it was already over. I was with Keely and truly in love with her, but I was curious to see what happened with Olga's life.

After Deserie put her on the phone, Olga told me that she had come to see me. I explained that I was on my way back to Philly and that I was going to stop in at the Pen and Pencil, a private after-hours club frequented by the press and people in the hospitality business. I told Olga that she could meet me there if she was coming back in town.

Olga came over with her sister, Lisa, and their driver. It was about three in the morning. She still was beautiful, but she seemed lonely.

"Lisa sends me all of your clippings and tells me how well you're doing."

I laughed and said, "Let me ask you a question. How many times you married now?"

Olga broke up laughing. "You crazy sonofabitch. You're still the same. I'm divorced again and living in Florida. Where are you living?"

"Still at the Towers."

"Can we spend some time together?"

"Olga, I'm in love with someone else. She's been sharing my life for several years. Let's just cherish the good times we had together."

That was it. I never heard from her again until I had the hole in my heart repaired in 2006. Dan Gross of the *Daily News* reported my surgery in his column, and Lisa sent Olga the clipping. When she called, I told her that everything was fine, thanked her for calling, and said goodbye; I thought for a moment, isn't it strange that when the right one comes along, all of the hurt and disappointment of the past fades away.

In January 2007, the Kimmels invited me to a ceremony commemorating the 150th anniversary of the Academy of Music. Prince Charles and Camilla Parker Bowles were in attendance, along with Mrs. Annenberg, who arranged for the royal couple to be there. Mayor Street, Governor Rendell, and other dignitaries were invited. Rod Stewart was scheduled to perform with the Philadelphia Orchestra.

Prior to the concert, the orchestra's biggest contributors were invited to meet the royal couple in a private room. The invited guests were divided into two groups, with the men on one side and the women on the other. As Prince Charles and Camilla arrived, they would make their way along each of the two reception lines, with Prince Charles greeting the men and Camilla greeting the women. Their secretaries would stand next to them and make the introductions.

The guests were instructed to remain silent unless Prince Charles greeted them, and they were told to address him as "Your Royal Highness." Prince Charles would spend a few seconds with a guest and then move on to the next person. As he made his way down the reception line, Prince Charles spent several minutes with Governor Rendell and Sidney Kimmel, but only a second or two with most of the other guests.

When Prince Charles approached me, his secretary said, "Your Royal Highness, may I present the Geator, Jerry Blavat."

Prince Charles stopped in amazement, and asked, "What's a Geator?"

I chuckled and said, "I do radio and television, Your Royal Highness, but I gotta tell you a great story. I once had the pleasure of meeting your uncle, Lord Mountbatten."

"You did?"

"Yes. When I worked for Ambassador Annenberg in 1969, I was invited to the Variety Club International when they honored him and Maureen O'Hara. I danced up the red carpet like I did on my television show."

His face lit up. "You know," he said, "my uncle was a terrific dancer. He must have gotten a royal kick out of that!"

Everyone was staring at us. Finally, Prince Charles said, "You're a fine chap," and moved on to the next person.

After the reception, the guests were invited to take their seats in Academy Hall. Caroline Kimmel was holding a full-length mink coat and asked if I would hold it for her until after the concert. I said, "I'll take it and wait for you guys backstage."

When the concert ended, Dodie Hamilton, the Pearlmans, and other big contributors greeted Mrs. Annenberg backstage. Unfortunately, Mrs. Annenberg was not in the best of health. Walter had died in 2002 at the age of 94, and Leonore was close to ninety herself. As she made her way to the private waiting room, she had an attendant with her, and she was using a walker to get around. The small group of contributors introduced themselves to her, and she thanked them. I was standing with the Kimmels and Constantine Papadakis, the president of Drexel University, when Mrs. Annenberg approached me.

I said, "Hello, Mrs. Annenberg. I'm Jerry Blavat, the Geator."

She grabbed my hand excitedly. "Oh, my God—Geator! If only Walter were here to see you! I have such fond memories of your mother cooking for us at your home. Those were wonderful nights for the ambassador and me. Is your family well? Please give them my best." Turning to the Kimmels, she said, "Did you know that this man did the coming-out party for my daughter, Libby?"

Everyone was amazed. These people had given millions of dollars to the Academy of Music, and Mrs. Annenberg was appreciative, but here she was, recalling the happiest days of our friendship.

As I look back on that night, I realize how much joy my mother brought into the lives of others. She devoted herself to her children—raising us without my dad—and I could have gone the wrong way if she hadn't taught me right from wrong. With my mother's influence—and a guardian angel watching over me—I've been able to stay on the right path.

It's funny how things turn out. Pattie is still living in the house I bought her at the shore. She shares it with Rita. Rita still acts as though she's Kathi's mother, even though she's her aunt.

I have four wonderful kids. They are my heart. As my hand has five fingers, each different, so are my kids—but they all belong to my hand. I've always wanted them to have the freedom that I had to find something in their lives that would make them happy.

Kathi turned out to be a terrific mother herself. She's given us two beautiful granddaughters—Samantha and Christine—and Deserie has given us a grandchild, too, a fantastic kid named Joey. At one point, when Kathi and Deserie were talking, Kathi said, "You know, if it wasn't for daddy, I wouldn't have turned out the way I did. He made sure I was disciplined. I attribute the way I raised my kids to the way that daddy raised me."

My daughter, Gerry, is a go-getter; she works for a major educational publisher. I like to think that some of my business sense rubbed off on her, along with my ability to sell, but whatever she's achieved, she's achieved on her own.

Stacy works in real estate in California and looks at the world through the eyes of a butterfly. She thinks that everyone is beautiful. Stacy has two boys.

My sister, Roberta, still lives in Reading. She has a wonderful family of her own, and we still remain close.

Keely has been with me for over twenty years, and we have a special relationship. She allows me the freedom to pursue my career and understands how important my audience is to me.

People ask me, "You've been married for fifty years and separated for thirty of 'em. How come you didn't divorce Pattie?" The idea of getting a divorce bothered me because of my religion, and I always wanted to keep the family structure together. Maybe it was because I didn't have that as a kid growing up.

My mother was the most important person in my life. She had the biggest influence on me, and she set the standards that I live by. My motto has always been, "Do unto others," and I've tried to teach my kids that, bringing them up with love and respect and knowing that, even though Pattie and I have been separated, they still have a mother and father who think alike when it comes to them.

From the very beginning, I've always wanted to make people happy. That's my goal every time I take the stage. When you make people happy, word gets around, and if you're sincere, they know. As a result, whatever success I have, I owe it to the people who appreciate the energy and honesty in my performance.

Even when I do my shows at the Kimmel Center, I revert back to the show business philosophy—look good, entertain, make people feel good. When I come out on stage, I wear ten or fifteen different outfits before I introduce the next act. When I'm at a social affair, I dress to the T. That's my father's influence and the influence of the older people that I admired. When I'm on my bike, riding around town or going to the station, I'm in my street clothes like a workingman.

People say I'm a pretty good businessman. I don't know about that. I never based my career on business. I always wanted to be free to do what I wanted to do and create other avenues to reach my audience. Compilation albums, CDs, T-shirts—it all goes back to being creative and reaching people. Whether I'm doing radio or TV or promoting a show, that's my nature, and if you come to any of the shows, you'll see that the audience is very much involved. Money has never been the important thing. I've always felt that man makes money; money doesn't make the man. If you're happy with what you do, you'll make money.

I'm not ashamed of anything I've done or any of the friends I've made. I will repeat again from the old school: Loyalty and respect are more important to me than anything else; even though some of my competitors have tried to use my friendships to knock me out of the box, it didn't matter.

I've had many highlights in my life, including the recent honor of having a street named after me in Wildwood and my induction into the broadcaster's wing of the Rock and Roll Hall of Fame. Another highlight was an award I received in Washington, DC.

Along with Arnold Schwarzenegger, the trumpeter Wynton Marsalis, and several others, I was recognized for my influence on young people. The ceremony was held at a Civil War-era livery stable that had been historically preserved. Over 2,000 people attended, including President Bush. In my acceptance speech, I spoke about the importance of education to the youth of this country, and how I overcame the adversity of coming from a broken home. "In my opinion, the most precious gift that we have in this country is our young, and besides education, the most important thing we can give them is guidance and a spiritual awareness of a greater being."

I ended my speech by saying that I grew up in a place where not only your parents but also your neighbors watched over you to make sure you did the right thing, and where people worked for a living and took care of their families. These were my early influences. I lived in a time when people had innocence and passion, and when they found their dream, they had the balls to see it through. Nobody gives you anything in life; you have to find your way. When I was finished, Tom Daschle, the Democratic senator, told me that I should run for public office. Trent Lott, who was standing next to me, said, "Only if he runs as a Republican."

As this chapter comes to an end, I look back on my life and realize that the loneliness I had as a child and the love my mother gave me have brought me to where I am. There was always music growing up, and there's always music as I grow older. My love for the Native

Americans comes from the freedom they had to do the things that made them happy. They shared the bounty of the hunt with their people. I share my life and music with my audience. I remember the holidays in the neighborhood when everybody would share, and I realize that I'm a product of that environment.

I grew up in a world of show business with class and style. The audience meant everything, and when they spent money to see you, you had to entertain them. My philosophy has never changed. I never made money from radio or TV; these vehicles have given me the exposure that I needed. My success comes from my audience. They're the ones who have supported my family and me all these years, and I consider them my second family. Trends may come and go, but the fans have always been there. (When they were young, they would come to me with their problems, and some of them still do.)

I'm often asked, "Don't you ever get tired?" My answer is always the same. Do you ever get tired of seeing people smile? Happiness is contagious.

Radio stations change formats today like you change suits. It's all about the dollar. Most of them play music that they think the public wants to hear, but they really have no idea. Music is universal; it's timeless; it doesn't have to be put into a category. I can take you anywhere and everywhere with my music, as long as it's good. As I've said my entire career, I play it from the heart, not a research chart. It's not only my music that's a part of me, but also the philosophy of a world that I came from, and that's what I share with my audience.

I remember Larry Kane once asked me on a TV interview about my friendships with some of the great show business people like Rickles and Sinatra and Sammy. He wanted to know how they allowed me to be so close to them. The answer was simple. They knew that I respected their privacy, loved their talent, and wanted nothing from them but to be a friend; they knew that if they needed me, I was always there.

Unfortunately, though, I learned at a very early age that success brings false friends, jealousy, envy, greed, and eventually, hate. But then again, it only happens when you're successful, and you learn how to handle it. I've also learned that when someone extends their hand in friendship, you shake it, but if somebody comes at you with their fist, you protect yourself. As I look back, I realize now that my father may have taught me about the streets, but my mother taught me love.

In closing, I might be the last guy on radio in America that has the freedom to do what I do. Again, I've never considered myself a disc jockey. I'm an entertainer, and I know now—going back to my child-hood—that I've always thought differently than others. Everyone has a dream, and I followed mine.

Maybe my friend, Frankie Avalon, summed it up best on the Lynn Doyle TV show. He said, "I've been around them all—radio guys, TV guys, Dick Clark, everybody. Nobody does what the Geator does. He's one of a kind. He holds an audience in the palm of his hand."

The other day, someone asked me what I was up to. It was a guy from the old neighborhood. We have known each other forever. "Me?" I said. "It's the same since I was thirteen. Working every day, doing what I've always loved to do, and hoping to make a difference in people's lives." He smiled and went on his way.

INDEX

A

ABC (Alcohol Beverage Control), 289–93, 297–98
ABC (network), 59, 96–97, 137, 189, 195, 211
Abner, Ewart, 154, 155–56, 157, 306
Adams, Don, 77, 124
Adler, Lou, 149
Alan Freed Christmas Show, 81, 84–85, 89–90
Albert, Shelly, 254
Alberts, Al, 175, 217
Ales, Barney, 145
Allen, Dick "Richie," xxiii, xxviii, 217
Allison, Steve, 64
All-Star Radio, 327–31, 333
American Bandstand, 36
    see also *Bandstand*
"And the Angels Sing," 107
Anka, Paul, 85, 91, 335
Annenberg, Leonore, 200–203, 213–14, 341, 342
Annenberg, Libby, 200–202
Annenberg, Mo, 213
Annenberg, Walter, xvii, 59, 64, 66, 201–3, 205–6, 212–14, 229, 250, 296, 316–17, 342
Apple, Dave, 146, 172
Aquaroli, Sammy "Sammy La La," 49–50, 62, 108
Arquette, Rosanna, 303
Astaire, Fred, 222
"At the Hop," 80, 97, 101, 105
Aunt Millie, 253–54
Aunt Mim, iii, 36
Avalon, Frankie, 88, 108, 125, 325, 339, 347
Avena, Sal, 260–61, 262

B

Bacall, Lauren, 276
Bacharach, Burt, 151, 153
"Back to School (One More Time)," 160
Baker, LaVern, 85
Ballard, Hank, 115, 234, 236, 243
Balsbaugh, Richard, 327
Bandstand, ix, x, xi, 36–38, 40, 46–47, 58–60, 53–54, 58–61, 206
Bankhead, Tallulah, 124
Banks, Billy, 162–63, 164–65, 167
Banks, Dolly, 162–63, 164–65, 167, 168, 180, 187–89
Barone, Kathi, 109, 111–12, 119–20, 203, 250, 343
Barone, Mino, 110
Barrie, Karl, 225
Bartlett, Richard, xxviii, 206, 214–15, 216-17, 219
Basciano, Richard, 330–31, 333
Bassey, Shirley, 210–11
Battles, Don, 107, 210, 247
Beasley, Frank, 175–76
Beatles, 168
Bee Gees, 257
Beery, Noah, Jr., 324
Bell, Freddie, 80
Benedictine, Sister, 33–34
Ben-Hur, 197–98
Bennett, Murphy, 225, 320
Bennett, Ronnie, 141
Bennett, Tony, 46, 48

Bennick, Bernie, 106, 172
Berns, Bert, 151–52
Bernstein, Elmer, 171
Berry, Chuck, 97, 195, 237–40, 241-42, 243, 326
Best, Edgar, 283–84
Bill Haley and His Comets, 46
Billy and Lillie, 97
Bishop, Joey, 207, 222, 252
Bishop Neumann, 89–90, 92, 106
Black, Jay, 336
Blaine, Jerry, 159–60
Blake, Robert, 222, 322
Blanc, Victor, 67
Blauner, Steve, 322
Blavat, Deserie, 182, 203, 250, 281, 341, 343
Blavat, Geraldine, xvi, 137, 203, 250, 261-62, 343–44
Blavat, Louis, i, vii, xxvii, xxx, 17–26, 29–31, 53-55, 61, 68, 160–162, 193, 269, 279-80, 289, 292
Blavat, Lucille Rosa Capuano, I, ii, iii, iv, v, vii, viii, xxviii, 18–23, 26–29, 56, 69–70, 119, 121, 164, 183, 203, 224–25, 253–54, 302–3, 316, 317, 318, 334–36, 343
Blavat, Pattie Scotese, xvi, xxiii, xxix, 107, 109–12, 116–119, 142–43, 157, 209, 217, 225, 228, 244– 50, 281–82, 343
Blavat, Roberta, vi, 22, 25, 29, 31–33, 35, 48, 292, 334–35, 344
Blavat, Stacy, 138, 203, 250, 264, 281, 335, 344
Blocker, Dan, 217, 218–19
Bonds, Gary U.S., 203
Bono, Sonny, 195, 204
Boone, Pat, 40–41, 207
Borgnine, Ernest, 324
Bouras, Steve, 286–87, 289
Bowles, Camilla Parker, 341–42
Boyd, Stephen, 197–98
Bracken, Jimmy, 153–54
Brady, Bob, xxxii, 336, 339
Breen, Julian, 255–56
Brett, Jonathan, 303
Brill Building, 101–2, 245
Brisson, Frederick, 217
British Invasion, 168–69
Britt, May, 322
Brooksheir, Tom, 184
Brown, James, xviii, xix, 180, 195, 328–29
Brown, Larry, 64
Bruce, Lenny, 163–64
Bruno, Angelo, xxix, 26, 63, 248, 251–52, 256–57, 265–70, 271–73, 280–81, 283–84, 290–91
Bruno, Maria, 271
Bruno, Michael, 267, 270, 271, 271–73, 275
Bruno, Sue, 26, 248–49, 256, 265–67, 268, 269–70, 271, 273, 274–75, 276, 281
Bruno, Susan, 271
Bruno, Zaria, 271
Brusco, Peter, 297
Bryant, Bruce, 173, 192
Buckley Broadcasting, 254–55
Buddy Holly and the Crickets, 91

Burke, Father, 89–90
Burke, Norman, 139
Burns, George, 310–11
Burton, Richard, 197
Bush, George W., 345
Butler, Jerry, 153, 326, 336
"By Love Possessed," 170–71

C

Cadumo, Ed, 43–44
Calliope, 217–18
Cameo-Parkway Records, 74, 98, 105, 114–15
Cannon, Don, 294, 326
Cannon, Freddie, 154
Capuano, Alfonso, 121
Capuano, Annie, ii, viii
Capuano, Philomena, viii, 18–20
Capuccio, Tony, 233–34, 235
Caputo, Charles "Chubby," 110–11
Carlo's Satellite Lounge, 223–24
Carson, Johnny, 276
Carter, Calvin, 153
Carter, Jack, 302
Carter, Vivian, 153–54
Celebrity Room, 76-77, 165
Chambers, Roland, 195
Channel 6, 137, 191–92, 194–95, 195, 197, 202, 204, 207, 217–18, 220, 328
Channel 10, 172–73, 175, 178, 183, 184–85, 192, 283
Channel 12, 172
Channel 17, 165, 258, 288
Channel 57, 325, 330
Charles, Prince, 341–42
Checker, Chubby, xiv, 105, 115, 116, 203, 234, 326, 339
Cher, 195, 204
Chess, Leonard, 232–33
Chess, Phil, 232–33
Chipitz, Harry, 172, 193
Christian, Johnny "Mahoody," 66–69
Churchill, Savannah, 124
Churchill, Winston, 214
Cini, Alfred. see Martino, Al
Clara Ward Singers, 180
Clark, Barbara, 105
Clark, Dick, xxvi, 59–61, 80–81, 95–98, 102, 105– 6, 137–40, 141–44, 160, 162, 172, 192–93, 204, 206, 226, 276
Clark, Kari, xxvi, 276
Clark, Loretta, 142, 143, 172
Clipp, Roger, 193–94, 204, 212
Clovers, 236
Cohen, Larry, 193
Cohen, Myron, 77
Cohen, Steve, 325
Cole, Natalie, 323
Colianni, Armand, 329, 330
Colona, Carlos, 275
Coltabianco, Henry, 105
Como, Perry, 151
Conway, Joe, 186–87
Cookie, 308–9
Cooper, Gary, 301
Copacabana, 98–100
Coradetti, Tony, 327
Corletto, Fred, 205–6, 229, 235
Cornell, Don, 48

Costa, Don, 73, 222
Cox, Father, 89–90, 106
Crane, Gene, 174
Crawford, Bob, 205
Crawford, Joan, xxiv, 125, 178–79, 198, 208
Crewe, Bob, 154–55, 155–56, 157, 203
Crimson Records, 193, 199–200
Crisconi, John P., 123, 229
Cronkite, Walter, 167
Crumlish, Jim, 186
Cumella, Charlie, 275, 276
Curtis, Buzz, 193
Curtis, Tony, 222
Cuzzupe, Grant, 289–90, 291, 292– 93, 295, 296, 297
Cycad, xxviii, 214–15, 218–20

D

D'Alfonso, Frankie, 282, 283
D'Amato, Paul "Skinny," 143, 144, 238
D'Amato, Willy, 143
Damone, Vic, 221
Dancing on Air, 288
Daniels, Bob, 327
Danny and the Juniors, 80–82, 83–84, 89, 90– 95, 97, 101, 106, 125, 325
Darin, Bobby, 89, 98–99, 148–49, 322
Darren, Jimmy, 89, 125, 339
Dasell, Jules, 332
David, Hal, 151
David, Mack, 151
Davis, Altovise Gore, 318, 319, 320, 322, 323
Davis, Bette, 214, 222, 300
Davis, Jack, 301
Davis, Jeff, 322
Davis, Mark, 322, 323
Davis, Sammy, Jr., xxi, xxv, xxvi, xxvii, 46, 96, 180, 197, 203, 207–209, 215–16, 224–227, 244, 247, 252, 257, 302, 315–24, 346
Davis, Tracy, 322
Day, Frankie, 106
Day, Laraine, 144
De Niro, Robert, 298–99
DeCastro Sisters, 74
DeCotiis, Al, 296
Dee, Sandra, 149
Degenhardt family, 295, 296–98
DeJohn, Gus, 294, 326
Delaney, Kim, 306
DelColla, Mike, 235, 242
Dellow, Brian, 225, 317, 320, 321, 322, 323
Delsey, Pat, 231, 233, 333
DeMann, Candy, 303, 304
DeMann, Freddy, xxxi, 159–60, 164, 303–4, 306–7
DeMille, Cecil B., 198
Denny, Michael, 125
DePaul, Peter, 211
DeSimone, John "Johnny Keys," 266– 68
Desperately Seeking Susan, 303
DeVito, Tommy, 157
Dick Clark Saturday Night Beechnut Show, 95, 96–97
The Dick Clark Show, 226
Diddley, Bo, 243
Diller, Phyllis, 210–11, 217
DiMarino, A.J., 338
Dion, 195
Dion and the Belmonts, 52, 103, 243
DiPietro, Arlene, 140

The Discophonic Scene, xii, xiii, xiv, xviii, xix, xx, xxii, 172–75, 184–85, 89, 307, 325
The Discophonic Scene '79, 258
Discophonic Style Shops, 177
Dixon, Luther, 151
Dixon House, 114–16
Doc Stark and the Night Riders, 74
Dolan, Elizabeth, 277, 291
Dolenz, Micky, 195
Domino, Fats, 79, 180, 243
Donahue, Sam, 91
Donahue, Tom, 233
Donovan, Ward, 211
"Don't Make Me Over," 151–52
D'Ortona, Paul, 125, 206, 208–9, 235
Douglas, Genevieve, 225–26
Douglas, Mike, 211–12, 225–26, 227
Downey, Jack, 243, 328
Doyle, Lynn, 347
Drexelbrook Country Club, 141–42
Drifters, 234, 236, 243, 336
Driscoll, Danny, 159
Duke, Billy, 106
Dulcinea, 209–10, 221
Duncan, Peter, 172
Dunleavy, Donald, 233–34, 235
Duprees, 159, 336
Durgom, Bullets, 219
Durocher, Leo, 144

E

Eastwood, Clint, 197, 320–21
Edelstein, Jackie, 250
Einhorn, Erin, 337–38
Elbow Room, 233
Elman, Ziggy, 107
Emery, Ralph, 93
Epstein, Alan, 332
Erie Social Club, 76
Ertegun, Ahmet, 203
Eskin, Howard, 244
Esko Brothers, 226
Evans, Ernest, 105
Everly Brothers, 91, 195
"Every Day of the Week," 146
"Expressway to Your Heart," 193, 199

F

Fabian, 245
Facenda, John, 184, 206
Falk, Peter, 308
Farber, Eric, 327–28
Fedele, Bruno, 228, 290–91
Feld, Irvin, 90
Feller, Frank X., 128, 184
Ferrer, José, 210
Fields, Larry, 250–51, 272
Fields, Marty, 233
Finfer, Harry, 47, 48, 104, 112, 141, 158–59
Finfer, Sylvia, 48
"Fingertips," 145
Fisher, Eddie, 339
Fisher, Irv, 250
Fisher and Marks, 92
Fitzpatrick, Emmitt, xxix, 67, 68, 250, 254, 280– 81, 282, 287, 290, 296– 97
Flamingos, 79
Foley, Red, 94
Ford, Frank, 206
Four Chimes, 36
Four Seasons, 154, 157, 191, 243
Four Tops, 180, 191

Francis, Connie, 89, 124, 195, 217, 221
Frankie Lymon and the Teenagers, 85
Franklin, Aretha, 195
Frawley, Jim, 196, 208
Freddie Bell and the Bellboys, 80
Freed, Alan, 84–86, 102
Friel, Frank, 283
Frunzi, George, 134
Funicello, Annette, xii, 124–25

G

Gamble, Kenny, 139, 193, 332, 336
Garber, Harold, 289
Garland, Judy, 319
Gaudio, Bob, 156, 157
Gaye, Marvin, 155, 181, 195
Gaynor, Gloria, 258
Geator and the Geatormen, 207, 220, 223, 226, 234
Geator Gold Network, 333–34
Geator Gold Radio, 304, 328–31, 333
The Geator's Den, 133
The Geator's Rock and Roll/Rhythm and Blues Express, 339
Gentile, Johnny "Shammy," 114
Geofreddo, Mikey "Golf," 122
Gero, Mark, 319
Giardello, Joey, 125
Gillespie, Dizzy, 163
Gleason, Jackie, 174, 192
Glickstein, Benny, 21–22
Glover, Savion, 318
Gola, Tom, 254
Gold, Joseph, 225
Golden, Jane, 338–39
Goldner, George, 102, 169
Gone and End Label, 102
Good, Jack, 189–90
Goodman, Dodie, xiii
Gordy, Berry, 145, 181, 203
Gore, Altovise, 225–26
Gormé, Eydie, 189, 222, 257
Goulet, Robert, 210
Grady, Joe, 172
Grant, Joe, 225
Graziano, Rocky, 124–25, 217
The Greatest Rock and Roll Reunion of Them All, 243–44
Greco, Buddy, 222
Green, Stan, 151
Greenberg, Florence, 151–53, 155
Greenburg, James, 261
Greene, Jerry, 158, 170, 199
Greene, Lorne, 217
Greene, Shecky, 211
Greengrass, Ken, 189, 190
Greshler, Abby, 219
Griffith, Andy, 252
Gross, Dan, 341
Guardino, Harry, 276, 302
Gunnella, Lou Anne, 121, 335
Gunnella, Matty, 69–70, 82, 121, 183, 250

H

Halloran, Biff, 275, 293–94, 295, 306
Halston, 319
Hamilton, Dodie, 342
Hampton, Lionel, 143
Hank Ballard and the Midnighters, 115, 243
Harold Melvin and the Blue Notes, 325
Harrah, Bill, 219
Harrison, George, 181
Hawkins, Jay, 243

Hawn, Goldie, 320
Healy, Carol, 325
Henderson, Jocko, 41, 85–86, 103–4, 130, 138, 169
Henry, Pat, 143–44, 251
Heston, Charlton, 34, 197–98
Hewitt, Dan, 291
Hibbs, Bud, 123–24, 129, 130, 135, 137, 165
Hiemie, Norman, 282
Hines, Gregory, 318, 321
Hobson, Sonny, 187
Holberg, Bruce, 293–94
Holiday, Billie, 73
Hollander, Al, 173–74, 184–85, 192
Holzer, Baby Jane, 276
Honickman, Harold, 176
Hook, Jack, 85–86, 169
Hope, Bob, 204, 210
Horn, Ann, 48, 191
Horn, Bob, x, 24, 36, 38–41, 47–48, 53–54, 57–75, 97–98, 104, 191, 206
Horn, Marianne, 48
Horn, Peter, 48, 58
Horn, Pinkie, 48
Houston, Cissy, 151
Houston, Whitney, 151, 321
Howe, Buddy, 201
Huff, Leon, 139, 193
Huggins, Edie, 206
Hunt, Tommy, 151
Hurst, Ed, 171–72, 173, 293
Hyland, Brian, 124

I
Ianelli, Terry, 253
Ierardi, Pete, 172
Iglesias, Julio, xxv
Impressions, 336
The In Crowd, 307, 325
Ingui, Richie, 200
Isley, Ronnie, 153
Isley Brothers, 152–53
"Itsy Bitsy Teenie Weenie Yellow Polka-Dot Bikini," 124

J
Jackson, Chuck, 152
Jackson, La Toya, 325
Jackson, Michael, 320–21
Jacobs, Eddie, 296
Jacovini, Peter, 272
Jacovini, Willie, Sr., 271–72
Jagger, Mick, 181
"Jam Up," 174
James, Etta, 319
James, Joni, 46, 74, 77, 89
James, Rick, 258
Jamie-Guyden, 159, 170
Jerry Blavat Presents Frankie Lymon's Greatest Hits, 169–70
The Jerry Blavat School of Radio and Television, 206, 214
The Jerry Blavat Show, 192, 204
Jerry's Place, 194–95, 199, 204, 207, 208, 217–18
Johnny Maestro and the Brooklyn Bridge, 336
Johnson, Lyndon Baines, 167
Johnson, Magic, 321
Johnson, Perry, 257
Johnson, Sylvester, 336
Jones, Carolyn, 197
Jones, Davy, 195–96

Jones, Quincy, 197, 225
Jones, Tom, 192, 193, 194, 211, 212
Joplin, Janis, 152, 196
Justis, Bill, 97

K
Kane, Larry, 346
Katz, Harry Jay, 229
Katz, Lefty, 210
Katz, Lewis, 262
Katz, Sam, 336
KC and the Sunshine Band, 257
Keating, Jim, 243
Keiter, Les, 206
Kelem, Merrill, 302
Kemp, Corey, 338
Kennedy, Jackie, 116
Kennedy, John F., 167
Kennedy, Joseph, 213
Kennedy, Ted, 301
Kenton, Stan, 163
Kilgore, Theola, 155
KILT, 69, 71
Kimmel, Caroline, xxx, 300–302, 334, 341, 342–43
Kimmel, Sidney, xxx, 300–302, 334, 335, 336–37, 341–43
Kimmel Center, 334, 335, 336
King, Alan, 246
King, Ben E., 243, 336
Kirshner, Donnie, 148–49, 195, 199–200, 206, 274
Klein, Janice, 172
Klein, Lew, 172–73, 193, 200–201, 202, 212
Knox, Buddy, 85
Koehler, George, 60–61, 191–92, 193, 194, 212, 217–18
Korn, Mel, 175–76, 178–79, 190, 191, 229, 325
Kossman, Jake, 267, 283, 291, 307
Krol, Cardinal, 203, 321

L
LaBelle, Patti, 194–95, 300–301
Laine, Frankie, 229
Lamar, Jack, 103, 123, 231
LaMay, Roger, 339–40
Lansky, Meyer, 299
Laurie Records, 52, 102
Lawford, Peter, 213
Lawrence, Steve, 189, 222, 257
Lazar, DaVe, 333
Leaf, Larry, 260–61, 281, 284–85
Lee, Brenda, 326
Lee Andrews and the Hearts, 236
Leigh, Janet, 301
Leonard, Jack E., 77, 144
Leone, Sergio, 299
Leonetti, Phil, 289
Lerner, Dorothy, 165
Lerner, Sam, 165
Levy, Morris, 85–86, 154–55, 155, 169–70, 226
Lewis, Jerry, 213, 308–9, 318, 321
Lewis, Jerry Lee, 142–43, 326
Lindsay, Mark, 204
Lipschutz, Louis, 67
Lipsius, Clara, 112
Lipsius, Harold, 48, 50, 104, 112, 141, 159, 170-71, 173, 182, 185, 205
Lipton, Peggy, 197
Lit, Hy, 135, 137, 140, 186, 254–55, 256, 294–95
Lit Brothers, xix, 176–78

Little Anthony and the Imperials, 103, 236
Little Caesar and the Romans, 103
Little Richard, xx, 79, 85, 180, 195, 240, 242
Litvak, Bernard, 177
Live with Regis and Kathie Lee, 325
Longstretch, Thacher, 235
Lopez, Trini, 203
Lorne, Greene, 217, 218
Lost Nite Records, 158, 170, 200
Lott, Trent, 345
The Lovers Hour, 147, 165, 170
Lowe, Bernie, 73–74, 105, 106, 114, 146, 160, 193
Lowe, Roz, 172
Lunsten, Bill, 296
Lymon, Frankie, 169–70
Lynn, Barbara, 158–59

M
Madara, Johnny, 80
Madonna, 164, 303
Maestro, Johnny, 336
Maffei, Frankie, 84, 92–93
Maggio, Lena, 249, 271, 276, 277
Maggio, Peter, 249, 271
Magid, Larry, 243–44
Mammarella, Tony, 38–39, 47, 58–59, 80
Mangel, Gary, 289–90
Mann, Esther, 172
Mann, Gloria, 81, 92
Mann, Kal, 146, 160, 172
Maples, Marla, 301, 302
Mara, Emmitt, 130, 133, 137
Marciano, Rocky, 124
Marcucci, Bobby, 139
Marhsall, William, 198
Mark, Sid, 163–64, 167, 206
The Mark of Jazz, 16
Marks, Guy, 144
Marlowe, Mickey, 79–80
Marra, Vince, 215–16
Marsalis, Wynton, 345
Marsh, Sy, 226, 227
Marshak, Larry, 243, 245
Martaer, Mike, 294–95, 326
Martha Reeves and the Vandellas, 325
Martin, Dean, 315
Martin, Deana, 196
Martinelli, Alex, 108–9, 111, 114, 160, 193, 236
Martino, Al, xiii, 226–27, 339
Martino, Pat, 106
Martorano, Evelyn, 286
Martorano, Raymond "Long John," 251, 285–87
Maselli, Rocco, 275, 276, 298–99
Massi, Nick, 157
Matalucci, Phil, 234
McAdams, Ed, 137–38
McBrown, Johnny, 93
McCourt, Mike, 237–40, 241, 246
McCurdy, Gene, 212, 217, 258, 288
McDermott, Father, 274–75
McFadden, Ray, 149
McGarrity, Greg, 283
McGinnis, Joe, 206
McGowan, Bobby, 306
McGuire, Phyllis, 144
Meaux, Huey, 158–59
Melvin, Harold, 325
Memories, 235–37, 289, 298
Memories West, 252–55

Mercer, Johnny, 107
Merrill, Gary, 214–15, 217, 222, 300
Michaels, Howie, 193
The Mike Douglas Show, 207, 211–12, 226, 227
Miller, Debbie, 172–73
Miller, Harvey, 128, 133, 294
Miller, Jeff, 291
Miller, Mary, 294
Miller, Stanton, 247
Mingrone, Dr., 334
Minnelli, Liza, xxv, 311, 315–17, 319, 322
Mitchell, Bob, 233
The Mod Squad, 197
Monk, Thelonius, 163
The Monkees, 195–96, 206–7, 218
Monte, Lou, 283
Morgan, Jaye P., 46, 73–74
Morley, Cozy, 92
Mother's Club, 192–93
Mountain Dew, 175–77
Mountbatten, Lord, 214, 342
Mummers' Parade, 35–36
Munez, Ricardo, 125, 126, 230
Murphy, Eddie, 320, 321

N

Nabors, Jim, 252
Nader, Richard, 236–37
Naidoff, Stephanie, 334
Nardi, Joe, 229–30, 231–33
Nastasi, Nick, 266–67
Nasuti, Carmen, 291, 292, 295, 296, 307, 332
Neal, Patricia, 301–2
Nelson, Father, 132
Nesmith, Michael, 195
Newman, Eddie, 236
Newman, Paul, 216–17
Newmar, Julie, 252
Niagara, Joe, 112–13, 128, 171, 254, 294
Nicholas Brothers, 318
Nicholson, Jack, 207
Nixon, Richard, 212
Noga, Helen, 141
Novenson, Joe, 192
Nugent, Charlie, 282, 285
Nutter, Michael, xxxii

O

O'Brien, John, 67–68
O'Connor, Bob, 325, 330
O'Donnell, Charlie, 172, 204, 320–21
O'Hara, Maureen, 214
Once Upon a Time in America, 299–300
Orentreich, Norman, 310–13

P

Pagan, Olga Rivera. *see* Siegel, Olga
Pagano, Teddy, 256–57
Pagast, Peter, 339
Page, Patti, 46, 48, 74, 77, 84
Palermo, Bobby, 302
Paley, Bill, 174
Palumbo, Frank, 78, 107, 282
Panetta, Judge, 295
Pantoliano, Joe, 306–8
Papadakis, Constantine, 342
Pappas, Nick, 221
Parker, Charlie, 73
Parker, Perry, 307
"Party Lights," 139
Pasternak, Joe, 221
Patinsky, David, 307

Pattiz, Norm, 303–4
payola investigation, 102–3, 134–35
Peaches and Herb, 258
Pearlman, Al, 205, 254, 342
Pendergrass, Teddy, 258
Pennock, Dr., 313, 314
Penrod, Jack, 306
Pepsi, 175–77, 178–79, 325
Perna, Lenny, 317
Perry, Rita, 119
Peters, H.G., 214–15, 217, 218–20
Philadelphia Mural Arts Program, 338–39
Pierce, Al, 135
Pina, Dom, 122–24, 129
Pitney, Gene, 195
Platters, 236
Podell, Jules, 98
Pollini, Father, 89–90
Poni-Tails, 91
Poppa Daly's, 71
Potamkin, Victor, 275, 279, 310–12
Powell, Sharon, 329, 331–32
Powell, Teddy, 145
Powers, Dr., 300
Prestillo, Danny, 258–59
Price, Lloyd, 336
Puppo, Jean Angela, 63, 248–49, 276
Puppo, Mark, 285
Puppo, Orlando, 63
Puppo, Ralph, 63, 248–49, 271

R

Ramsey, Clark, 312–13
Randazzo, Teddy, 318
Rapp, Billy, 101
Rapp, Danny, 84, 91, 94–95
Rappaport, Sam, 251–53, 256, 262, 327–28, 329–30, 333
Rawls, Lou, 181, 204
Ray, Johnnie, 46–47, 48
Rayburn, Margie, 91
Record Museum, 135, 158, 170, 171, 200
Reeves, Martha, 325
Rendell, Ed, 280, 341–42
Revere, Paul, 204
Reynolds, Joey, 294
Rhodes, George, 225, 320
Rhodes, Shirley, 225, 320, 322, 323–24
Riccobene, Harry "the Hunchback," 288
Riccobene, Sonny, 288
Rich, Robert, 185
Rickles, Don, 76–77, 79, 96, 143, 215, 346
Ridarelli, Robert, 106
Ridgley, Tommy, 174
Righteous Brothers, 236
Rizzo, Carmella, 274
Rizzo, Frank, xxvi, 205–6, 234–35, 243, 245, 254, 274
Rizzo, Jilly, xxv, 217, 245–46, 276, 301, 302, 316– 17, 318
Robinson, Edward G., 227
Robinson, Harold B., 51–52
Robinson, Matt, 172
Rock, Monti, 263, 305
Rock and Roll Hall of Fame, xxxii, 345
Rockettes, 93
Rogers, Timmy, 160
Roker, Wally, 152
Rolling Stones, 168, 181
Rome, Rita, 301
Ronettes, 180, 234, 243

Rooney, Mickey, 217
Rosato, Ernest, 338
Rose, "Slim," 158
Roselli, Mimmy, 283
Rosen, Abe, 205, 234
Rosenthal, Mark, 307–8
Rothman, Dr., 335
Roulette Records, 154, 226
Rourke, Mickey, xxv
Rovner, Bob, 327–28, 331
Russell, Bert. *see* Berns, Bert
Russell, Rosalind, 217
Rydell, Bobby, xxvi, 106, 204, 217, 339

S

Saloman, Lee, 189
Salters, Lee, 250–51
Sanchez, Elvera "Babe," 224–25, 321, 322
Saros, Ileana, 295, 296–97
The Savage, 198
Savitt, Buddy, 195
Scardilli, Joe, 232
Scarfo, Nicky, 288–89, 299
Scarpati, Joe, 108
Scepter Records, 151, 152, 155
Schlatter, George, 320
Schwartz, Roy, 103, 104–5, 140
Schwarzenegger, Arnold, 345
Scotese, Annette "Nanny," 107–8, 111, 291
Scotese, Pat, 111, 118–19, 120
Scotese, Pattie. *see* Blavat, Pattie Scotese
Scotese, Phyllis, 107–9, 111, 160
Scotese, Rita, 107–9, 111, 193, 246, 343
Scotese, Rosemary "Scottie," 108, 110–11
Scott, Herb, 149
Segall, Nat, 24, 48, 53, 73–76, 80–82, 91, 96, 123–24, 131–33, 137, 143, 146, 149–50, 154–55, 157–58, 164, 170, 173, 185, 188–190, 190–91, 193, 199–200, 212, 223, 227–28, 242–43
Segall, Sam, 242
Seidelman, Susan, 303, 308–9
sexual harassment suit, 331–32
Shapiro, Kenny, 262
Shapiro, Shep, 165
Shapp, Milton, 214
Shawn, Dick, 77
"Sherry," 155–56, 157
Shindig, 189–90
Shinya, Dr., 313
Shomus, Thomas, 250
Shore, Dave, 78
Shore, Dinah, 252
Shubin, Zvi, 258, 288
Shuman, Arthur, 280–81
Siegel, Abe, 277–78, 305
Siegel, Bernie, 291
Siegel, Olga, xxxi, 263–64, 273, 274, 276, 277– 80, 286–87, 290–91, 292, 303, 304–6, 341
Sills, Lester, 141
Silverman, Al, 184–85
Sinatra, Barbara, 301, 302, 316, 318
Sinatra, Frank, xxv, 79, 96, 143–44, 197, 216– 217, 246, 250–51, 257, 301, 302, 311, 315–17, 318, 320, 322, 324, 346
Sindone, Frank, 284
Singer, Artie, 80–81, 105–6
Singer, Matty "the Humdinger," 104, 193

The Singing Nuns, xxiv
Sinkow, Barry, 244
Skinny Annie, 24, 30
Skyliners, 243, 336
Slate Brothers, 79
Slay, Frank, 154
Slotkin, Herb, 105
Smith, Joe, 144
Solomon, Morton, 254–55
Sonny and Cher, 195, 204
Soul Survivors, 193, 200
Sound and Teen, 73–74, 199
Spagnola, Frankie, 60
Specter, Arlen, 203
Specter, Joan, 203
Spector, Jeff, 326–27
Spector, Phil, 140–41, 203
Spector, Ronnie, 236–37, 243
Spelling, Aaron, 197
Spivak, Joel, 283
Stahl, Keely, xxxi, 314–15, 324, 335, 341, 344
Stallone, Sylvester, 252
Stanfa, John, 271
Starr, Sally, 329, 333
State Investigating Committee (SIC), 295–96, 298
Steele, Alfred, 178
Stein, Seymour, 300
Steinberg, David, 200
Steve and Eydie, 257
Stevens, Jerry, 128, 171
Stevens, Len, 164–65, 257
Stewart, Rod, 341
Stewart, Sandy, 80, 81
Stradella, Danny, 276
Straight Arrow, 27, 28
Straigis, Roy, 195
Street, John, 336–38, 341
Sullivan, Arlene, 140
Sullivan, Ed, 174
Summer, Donna, 257, 258
Summertime on the Pier, 171–72, 173
Supremes, xii, 180, 204
Sussell, Allen, 47, 48, 50–51, 52, 104, 107
Swan Records, 98, 102, 154

T

Taino, Ricky, 106
Takiff, Jonathan, 307–8
Tap, 319
Tarsia, Joe, 139
"Tasty to Me," 226
Tate, James, 205–6, 214, 229, 235
Tavares, 258
Taxin, Johnny, 287, 316
Taylor, Elizabeth, 197, 276, 311
Tendler, Lou, 76–78
Terranova, Joe "Joe Terry," 84, 92–93, 94, 97
Testa, Phil, 267, 283, 286, 288
"This Is My Prayer," 155, 157
This Is Tom Jones, 211
Thomas, Mitch, 41, 103–4, 107, 130, 172
Tillman, Bertha, 155
Tilton, Martha, 107
Tork, Peter, 195
Tose, Leonard, 300
Townsend, Ed, 155
Treniers, 79
Treyz, Oliver, 204
Triangle Publications, 192, 193
Trump, Donald, 301, 302

Turner, Ike, xxiii
Turner, Tina, xxiii
"The Twist," 105, 115–16
"Twist and Shout," 152–53
Tymes, 194

U

Uncle Carmen, 25–26, 36
Uncle Jimmy, iii, 25, 34, 36, 336
Uncle Joe, 25, 26
Uncle Sam, 48
Uncle Vito, 25

V

Vaden, Bud, 194, 212
Valdera, Felix, 107
Valino, Joe, 89
Valli, Frankie, xviii, 154, 156, 157, 191, 195, 203, 209, 236–37, 245–46, 247, 302, 326
Van Buren, Steve, 113
Vanaman, Al, 173, 180
Vaughn, Ben, 340
Vee-Jay Records, 153–54, 157
Venus Lounge, 123–24, 129
Verrelli, Vince, 250
Vignola, Louis, 119
Village People, 257
Vines, Lee, 61–62
Vinton, Bobby, 195

W

WADO, 138
"Wall of Sound," 141
Wallace, Frank, 288
Wallace, Mike, 250–51
Walsh, George, 212, 217
Walters, Barbara, 78
Walters, Lou, 78
Warhol, Andy, 319
Warner Brothers Severn Arts, 184–85, 191
Warren, Bruce, 340
Warwick, Dee Dee, 151
Warwick, Dionne, 151–53, 181, 222, 225, 302
WCAM, 103, 123–31, 133, 135, 137, 140, 146, 149, 158, 163, 165, 229–33
WCAU, 173–75, 180, 185, 187–88, 243, 257, 325, 328
WDAS, 41, 85, 102–5, 137, 138, 146, 163, 164, 166, 186, 188, 232–33, 257, 328
Webber, Bernie, 212, 325
Weiner, Warren, 178–79
Weinstein, Jared, 158, 170, 193, 199
Weir, Chuckie, 254
Welch, Lenny, 336
Welles, Orson, 198
Wells, Mary, 234, 236
West, Adam, 210
West, Judi, 210
Wexler, Jerry, 171, 203
Wexler, Larry, 255–56
WFIL, 46, 59–62, 172, 192–93, 198, 207, 211–12, 217–18, 229, 258, 293–94, 327
WHAT, 71, 85, 102–5, 146, 162–66, 180, 186–89, 232, 328
White, Dave, 80, 84, 91, 97
White, Ron, 332, 336–38
WIBG, 102–3, 104, 128, 131, 133, 135, 139, 140, 146–47, 153, 154, 162, 184, 186–88, 229, 254–55
Wildwood, 49–50, 78–79

Williams, Kay, 104, 130
Willis, Bill "Kilocycle Pete," 150, 167
Wilson, George, 188–89
Wilson, Jackie, 195, 243
Winkler, Henry, 244
Wissert, Joe, 154, 155, 156–57, 170
WKHJ, 294
WMID, 138, 149
Wonder, Stevie, 145–46, 180, 306
Woods, Georgie, 41, 50, 104, 121, 130, 163, 171, 175, 206, 328–29, 332
WPAZ, 149, 333
WPEN, 64, 131, 233, 255–56, 339
WPGR, 294, 326–32, 333
Wright, Bill, Sr., 128, 171, 254
WTTM, 149
WVLT, 165
Wyler, William, 197–98

Y

"You Belong to Me," 159
"You'll Lose a Good Thing," 158–59
Young, George, 195
Youngman, Henry, 77

Z

Zann, Dave, 242
Zurzolo, Al, 260, 261

There Are No Spies

BOOKS BY BILL GRANGER

THE NOVEMBER MAN NOVELS

The November Man
Schism
The Shattered Eye
The British Cross
The Zurich Numbers
Hemingway's Notebook
There Are No Spies

CHICAGO POLICE STORIES

Public Murders
Priestly Murders
Newspaper Murders

Sweeps
Queen's Crossing
Time for Frankie Coolin

NONFICTION

Chicago Pieces
Fighting Jane (with Lori Granger)
The Magic Feather (with Lori Granger)

BILL GRANGER

There Are No Spies

WARNER BOOKS

A Warner Communications Company

W A Warner Communications Company

Printed in the United States of America
First Printing: November 1986
10 9 8 7 6 5 4 3 2 1

Designed by Giorgetta Bell McRee

Library of Congress Cataloging-in-Publication Data

Granger, Bill.
  There are no spies.

  I. Title.
PS3557.R256T44 1986   813'.54   86-40040
ISBN 0-446-38049-0

*This book is for
Herman Kogan,
a ferocious editor
and writer in Chicago,
who once told a young
man that he should
write books.*

If you think we are worked by strings,
Like a Japanese marionette,
You don't understand these things:
It is simply Court etiquette.
Perhaps you suppose this throng
Can't keep it up all day long?
If that's your idea, you're wrong.

—*W.S. Gilbert*

NOTE

This book reflects a struggle going on in the world of intelligence between those who deny the usefulness of agents, contractors, case officers and all the other personnel involved in the business of espionage and those who defend the worth of HUMINT (human intelligence and analysis) in the face of the technological revolution.

The *New York Times* gathered estimates by intelligence officials who agree that 85 percent of all information gained by the various U.S. intelligence agencies comes from ELINT (electronic signal intelligence), SIGINT (signal intelligence), PHOTINT (photo intelligence), RADINT (radar intelligence) and all the "hardware" sources, opposed to the information gained by spies (HUMINT).

Intelligence analyst Walter Laqueur noted in *A World of Secrets* that "the need for HUMINT has not decreased, but it has become fashionable to denigrate the importance of human assets because technical means are politically and intellectually more comfortable. On the other hand, the opportunities for hostile intelligence agents operating in democratic societies are incomparably greater than for their Western counterparts."

In 1985, there was a furious exchange of spies between East and West before the Reagan–Gorbachev summit. In every case of a mole's "defection" to his true side, another agent in the field was picked up by the side sinned against. In one bizarre case, a Soviet KGB agent who "defected" West later "redefected" to the Soviet

embassy in Washington, claiming he had been kidnapped. Central Intelligence Agency denied his claims. In 1986, a Chinese double agent buried inside CIA claimed he had worked for China for two decades to improve relations between the countries and not for monetary gain—though he had to take the money to convince the Chinese he was a legitimate traitor. He committed suicide, according to official reports, by putting a plastic bag over his head in his cell and voluntarily suffocating himself.

These things are all true; these things are all reflected in this book.

—Bill Granger

There Are No Spies

PROLOGUE
The Edge of the World

In a little while, she had to go away. There were assignments in the East, in the Philippines, then back to Washington . . . She gave him the itinerary, she fussed about him. It was a way of making love to him.

This was the other way. Rita moved beneath him and her belly bumped his belly. They were tangles of arms, they were tastes and smells; they mingled with each other. Devereaux was never so lost as when he made love to her. Never so abandoned. There were no cold places in him when he made love to her. He cried out like a lost child when he came. She held his shuddering body with legs, arms, hands, pressed him into her. She closed her eyes very tight to feel the wonder of this very common act they shared with nearly every other member of the species.

Let me be lost in you.

They shivered in pleasure in each other and then fell away like flowers thrown on a still pond. They never spoke when they made love; lovemaking was too true for words. He didn't trust words. Words lied. You could say anything.

And they both heard the telephone ringing from the next room, though it was in the middle of the morning, in Lausanne, at the edge of the world they had fled from . . .

1

ONE
Hanley's Discovery

"Tired," Hanley said on the third Tuesday in February. He repeated the word several times to himself, alone in his windowless cubicle that was the office of the director of operations. He blinked, looked around at the white walls of the cold, bare room, and said the word again. It was as though everything familiar to him had drained his life away.

He said the word again to Miss Smurtty in the outer office and by then he had his hat on. He shrugged into his overcoat as he walked along the hall to the elevator bank on the sixth floor. He repeated the word to the security policeman at the elevator bank. The policeman said nothing.

Hanley said the word like a man searching memory for words to a song at the edge of the mind.

He went home and it wasn't even noon yet.

He took to his bed.

Each morning thereafter, he called in by nine. He talked to the same woman in personnel and recorded his absence. He said he was ill because he felt so tired. He explained to the woman in personnel how tired he felt. And he stayed out sick the rest of the month of February. It was the first time in twenty-one years that Hanley had missed a day of work.

He was the good civil servant. As director of operations for R

Section, he had a love for the Section that transcended mere identification with a job or mission.

The tiredness colored all his thoughts. He would lie in bed at night and listen to the roar of traffic beneath his apartment windows. He lived on the third floor of a large apartment building at the juncture of Massachusetts and Wisconsin avenues in northwest Washington. The rooms were large and airy but all the light was gray because it was spring in Washington and always raining.

Hanley sat by the window in his apartment in the afternoons and looked down at the cars climbing up the hill from DuPont Circle and around the Naval Observatory grounds where the Vice President's white house sat in splendid isolation. Hanley thought too much. He thought about the Vice President having a better view and neighborhood to live in than the President trapped in the tangle of the central city. Hanley thought the traffic was very thick and very loud; it was like undergrowth around a neglected house. The weeds had grown and grown until one day there was nothing to be done but burn them off and tear the old house down and start again.

Hanley wept when he thought such things.

He had been growing more and more tired for weeks before he decided to take sick leave. Dr. Thompson's pills did not seem to help him but he took them with precise faithfulness. He was a man of habits. He was cold and thin and his voice was flat as the Nebraska plains he had come from.

He thought of the child he had been. He wept when he thought of himself.

Once in a while he thought he would have to get better. He was director of operations for R Section and that meant he was director of spies. The master of the marionettes. But he was ill now and the spies were being left to dance without direction. This couldn't go on. It mustn't go on.

On March 1, the doctor came.

Dr. Thompson was vetted twice a year. He had taken his annual lie detector test in January. He was thirty-four years old and very nearly incompetent, which is why he was only employable by a government agency. Before joining the Section, he had nearly been

3

stripped of his license to practice in his native Oregon because of some damned business involving surgery on a woman where the wrong organs had been removed. It had not been his fault.

Thompson carried a top secret clearance and had access to secrets to the level of N. He was a jolly young man with a pink face and a hearty, almost English manner. He slapped his hands together when he talked; he resembled Alec Guinness in early films.

Hanley allowed the prodding. It was government procedure. Thompson talked and poked and made Hanley cough; he tapped at his back and asked him to urinate into a jar and took a blood sample and talked about the Washington Redskins and laughed too much. Hanley endured it. He wanted not to feel so tired.

For no reason, Hanley began to weep. Thompson stared at him and asked him why he was crying. Hanley excused himself, went to the bathroom, wiped his eyes and looked at his thin, cold, old sallow face.

"Why are you crying?" he asked himself.

When the ordeal was over, Hanley buttoned his pajama shirt and slipped the gray bathrobe over his thin shoulders and resumed his seat in the large chair by the front windows.

There were books strewn on the floor around the chair. He had been reading Somerset Maugham. He had been reading autobiography disguised as fiction in which Maugham, who had been a British agent in the First War, describes himself as "Ashenden, the secret agent." And Ashenden takes a ferry one day across Lake Geneva, from France to neutral Switzerland, and . . .

Hanley had read the story over and over. He didn't understand why. He didn't understand why he was so tired.

"You need rest," Dr. Thompson said. "You need to get some sun, get some color into those cheeks. Stop moping about. You took the pills I prescribed?"

"They seem to make me more tired."

"They're supposed to relax you," Thompson said. "Listen to your doctor." Smiled. "Go to Florida. Get some sun. Plenty of sun down there. Shouldn't mope around here."

Hanley thought of Florida. He had never been there. He blinked and looked out the window at his city, a place he had used and

4

grown to love through use. They were going to tear down the café down on Fourteenth Street where he had gone to lunch every working day. Every working day of thirty-five years of work and they were going to tear it down.

He blinked and his vision was as wet as the rain-streaked windows. Thompson was talking to him. The voice droned.

Hanley thought of all the places he knew so intimately and had never seen. Like Number 2, Dhzerzhinski Square, Moscow. That ugly gray building—the headquarters of Committee for State Security. KGB. He knew it as an old enemy. It was nearly the same as knowing an old friend.

"What do you say to that?"

Hanley looked up and Thompson was beaming his professional beam.

"What do I say to what?"

"Hospitalization. A complete rest cure."

"No." Hanley's voice was quick. "No. If I'm sick, I'm sick. If I'm not sick, I don't need a hospital."

"You need rest."

"You can't get rest in a hospital."

Dr. Thompson frowned.

Hanley turned away, stared at the street below, stared at the traffic. The goddamn traffic. The noise pounded at his thoughts day and night. No wonder he was tired. Where were all those people going to? Did they live in their cars?

Hanley blinked and felt his eyes moisten again. He had never noticed the traffic before. His thoughts seemed to go in circles. What had he been thinking of—he had to get well, get back to Operations, see to the delicate business of Nutcracker.

He thought of Nutcracker.

He thought of the toy nutcracker from Germany he had owned as a child. Given to him one Christmas by a long-ago great-aunt. A child's toy. Fierce and bristling in guard's uniform, with a mustache and horrible large teeth.

He smiled as suddenly as he wept. He felt warm. He wanted Thompson to go away. The warmth of memory filled him. He had to get back to Section, back to seeing what was wrong with Nut-

5

cracker. Director of spies. To play the great game as he saw it in his mind.

". . . medication," Thompson concluded.

Hanley nodded, said nothing. He took the prescription sheet and looked at it. He waited for Thompson to leave.

Yackley listened to Thompson, asked him two questions and dismissed him.

It was the same afternoon. It had stopped raining. The sky was full of clouds and warm winds billowed along Fourteenth Street, cracking the flags on government buildings. Yackley's office on the sixth floor of the south Department of Agriculture building had a large window that looked across the street at the dour Bureau of Engraving building.

Yackley was not pleased by anything Thompson told him about Hanley.

Yackley was director of R Section. Hanley worked for him. Hanley was letting the Section down.

Yackley stood at his window, looked down at his view, and thought about his Section. He was a political appointment from the early Reagan days. He was an attorney, a Republican, wealthy enough to work for the government. He took a Level Four polygraph examination once a year to maintain his Ultra clearance. He had access to level X in security and in the computer system called Tinkertoy.

Yackley was called the New Man by his derisive subordinates, including Hanley. They thought he was an ass; he knew that. He had replaced Rear Admiral Galloway (USN Retired) as head of Section because Galloway had stubbed his toes badly in some Section business in Florida. Galloway had been the Old Man.

Thompson had told him: "He won't go."

"Damn. He won't go. Did you talk to him?"

"He wasn't listening to me."

"This was important, *Doctor*." Yackley had put heavy emphasis on the last word, as though he didn't believe it. He could have saved the sarcasm; Thompson was immune.

He would have to do something else.

Yackley felt nervous when he had to do something. Something on his own. Maybe he needed advice. Maybe he should consult his "rabbi." Maybe he didn't have to act right away.

The thoughts flung themselves one after the other through his mind. Yackley went back to his rosewood desk and sat down in the $455 leather swivel chair. He swiveled and put his hands behind his head to aid thought. He frowned. He thought about Hanley and the goddamn agent Devereaux and the business in Florida in which Galloway had stubbed his toes and been fired. It had been Hanley's doing. And Devereaux's. Hanley wanted to be head of Section. That's what Yackley thought from time to time: A goddamned civil servant wanted to be head of Section.

Scheming. Hanley was scheming and it was all against Yackley because Hanley hated Yackley's success. Yackley had issued a directive saying that, in order to "downtrim" the budget of Section, "cutbacks were needed in every sector" and that the effort would succeed only "if we all realize we are in this boat together and help pull each other's oars."

There had been any number of obscene drawings on Section bathroom walls showing Yackley pulling the oars of others.

It wasn't funny. And Hanley—that was something Hanley would have dreamed up. To undermine his authority.

So Yackley had tapped Hanley for six months. Home and away. The taps were designed by the National Security Agency, which is the "hardware" supplier to the other intelligence services, including R Section. The taps were perfected and installed by Richfield, the Section's own ELINT man and resident "hardware" genius. As well as the supreme loyalist.

Yackley squinted at the words of the transcript of the taps. Damned good thing he had tapped Hanley; should have done it years before.

February 21, time: 1:02 A.M. Electronic count indicates the telephone number is: Country—Switzerland; City—Lausanne; Number 28-23-56.

HANLEY: Hello?

(Silence for five seconds.)

HANLEY: Hello? Hello?

(Silence for two seconds.)

HANLEY: Hello? Someone say something.

VOICE: What do you want?

HANLEY: There's a problem and I think I am beginning to understand it and I have to tell someone. I've discovered—

VOICE: I don't care. I'm not in the trade. (Pause.) There is no November.

HANLEY: That's just it. No November. There are no spies. I think I can tell you. I need to tell you. And did you know that your duplicate November is on his way to Moscow?

(Silence for five seconds.)

HANLEY: Hello?

VOICE: I'm not in the trade, Hanley. That was our agreement. I don't exist. November is some man running away from a wet contract.

HANLEY: A wet contract from Moscow. And now the man you tagged November is running right into the arms of the Opposition. Why is that?

VOICE: I don't care. Don't call me anymore.

(Broken connection.)

February 23, time: 1:13 A.M. Electronic count indicates the same country, city and telephone number as previous conversation.

HANLEY: Hello?

VOICE: I'm not interested in talking to you.

HANLEY: Listen. For just one minute. I've got to tell someone this, I've got to talk it out to someone who understands. Who understands what's going on in Section. Someone who isn't in Section anymore.

VOICE: Are you drunk, Hanley? Has the one-martini lunch finally gotten out of control after all these years?

HANLEY: (garbled) has to be at the highest levels. Do you understand?

VOICE: I am not in the trade. That was our agreement.

(Garbled)

HANLEY: The pills. I stopped taking them and I don't feel as bad.

Are the pills . . . something wrong? I sleep all the time and then I wake up and I can't sleep. I never knew there was so much traffic, all day and night, you can't sleep. Where are all those people going?

VOICE: Home. You go home too.

HANLEY: I am home.

VOICE: Then have a drink and go to sleep.

HANLEY: My lunch. They are going to tear down the place on Fourteenth Street. I went there every day of my life. A martini straight up and a cheeseburger with raw onion. One martini. I knew all the people there. And Mr. Sianis said to me, "Mr. Hanley, I have to sell the place because they are going to put up a trade center."

VOICE: Why are you calling me? Leave me alone. Everything is over.

HANLEY: Damnit. You never leave the service. You know that. You're in for life. And I've told you that.

VOICE: November is going to Moscow. You said it. November does not exist.

HANLEY: (portion missing) the secret, the point of the thing, when it comes down to it, it might just be that simple.

VOICE: What are you talking about?

HANLEY: I read Somerset Maugham over and over. *Ashenden.* About the secret agent in World War I, he reminded me that you were in Lausanne and that you probably took the same ferry boats between France and Switzerland that he did. All those years ago. When it was accepted finally. The need for spies. Reilley. Maugham. The people in BritIntell— I thought about you when I read those stories. Because of the location. You took that ferry.

VOICE: Yes.

HANLEY: I am not insane. I am not going insane. I am tired and I have time to think about things. I mean, sanity is understanding where your feet are planted, isn't it? But I'm off my feet, I don't have perspective anymore.

VOICE: Seek professional help.

HANLEY: Sarcasm. You have to help—

VOICE: —no.

9

HANLEY: (interrupted) secret. I think of one thing and think of another. I had a nutcracker when I was a child and—

VOICE: Goodbye, Hanley.

HANLEY: Wait. There are no spies. That's what it means. There are no spies at all. But that's not true. That's the one thing I realize now. That's not true.

(Disconnect)

February 28, time: 10:13 A.M. (Incoming call; location uncertain.)

HANLEY: Hello? Hello?

LYDIA NEUMANN: This is Lydia Neumann, Hanley. You're still ill. I wanted to see how you were. Can I get you anything? I'm worried about you and we need you in Section.

HANLEY: So we can pull our oars.

NEUMANN: (Laughter)

HANLEY: I need rest, that's all I need.

NEUMANN: Should I come over?

HANLEY: . . . sleep at night. Traffic. Where are those people all rushing to?

NEUMANN: Have you seen a doctor? Not Thompson. Don't use Thompson.

HANLEY: Thompson? He doesn't know a damned thing. I understand his little game. Pills. I know all the secrets, you know, Mrs. Neumann. I know everything. You let me fool myself but you were on to the secret as well, weren't you? This is a game in a computer and you're the master of Tinkertoy. The mistress of Tinkertoy. So I'll ask you: Where is my Nutcracker?

NEUMANN: Hanley? Hanley? Are you all right?

HANLEY: My Nutcracker. New Man knows, New Man (Neumann?) knows—

NEUMANN: Hanley, I don't know what you're talking about.

HANLEY: Spies, Neumann. I am talking about the whole business of spies. Of moles and sleepers and agents who come awake, of doubles and triples, of dogs who bark and dogs who bite, covert and overt, going into black and black bag operations and the business of the trade. I am talking about goddamn bona fides and about

10

software and I am telling you, I am going to get to the bottom of the whole damned business.

NEUMANN: (garbled)

HANLEY: Oh, you believe that. I know you do. There are no spies. But I have my spies and you have a bunch of circuits. I have the spies. There are no spies?

NEUMANN: Hanley, my God—

(Disconnect)

Three telephone calls, except the call from a woman asking Hanley to subscribe to the *Washington Post*.

Yackley's frown was deep and sincere. His skin was burned brown by January's sun in St. Maarten; his eyes were blue and quite empty. But the frown spoke for his thoughts.

The room was lit by a single green-shaded banker's lamp. The soft light framed the two photographs on his desk. His wife smiled crookedly at the photographer; his daughter smiled at Daddy. If they only understood all the secrets he had and was privy to. If they only could understand the nasty business that had to be done.

There are no spies.

Hanley told Devereaux that. And he told Devereaux about Colonel Ready, tagged as November, now making his way to Moscow to try to arrange a defection. A damned mess, all of it. And what was the real November going to do now? Except plot with Hanley.

There are no spies. And the New Man knows.

Yackley considered the matter for a moment. He knew exactly what he was going to do; he was working up an argument in conscience to sanctify it. But it had to be done in any case, even if it was going to be dirty.

TWO
The *Finlandia* Incident

Alexa was quite beautiful in the way of a certain kind of young Russian woman. Her eyes were coal-dark and deep and it was difficult to describe their color. Her eyes were also set sharply in the paleness of her strong features. Despite the generous width of her mouth and her very high cheekbones that seemed to stretch her skin, despite her coal-black hair that severely defined the edges of her pale features, her eyes held you. Her merest glance compelled you to stare at her, at her eyes, in total fascination.

Her eyes were her only drawback, from a professional point of view.

She might be able to change the color of her hair or disguise her slender figure by flattening her full breasts or by stooping to seem shorter or older than she was. But she could never disguise those eyes.

Alexa turned from the bar in the warm green room on the third deck of the *Finlandia* and gazed across the room at the man she was going to kill.

The trouble with Alexa's usefulness as an intelligence agent for the Committee for State Security was that she was very good at those assignments that called for action—immediate, brutal, violent—and very bad at those assignments that called for mere intelligence gathering.

She was intelligent; but she was too visible. She was very beautiful and she was noticed wherever she went. Her Moscow accent was slight when she spoke English; her Moscow manners might have made many people mistake her for a New Yorker or a Parisian. She had the right mixture of rudeness and grace.

But it was no good having your informant fall in love with you or having your network of agents desire you sexually. Or have the watchers from the other side find it too agreeable to watch you. And suspect you, even as they fell in love with you. Besides, she could never change her eyes.

She stared at the man with graying hair who sat at the wide window, gazing into the gloomy night of the Baltic Sea. Alexa was the death-giver. It was not so bad, it was over so quickly, it was part of a large game. She never felt bad afterward. In fact, she had felt bad just once, when her victim had lived.

Two years ago. She was sent up through the Soviet embassy in Mexico City, which was the usual route of spies working on the West Coast of the United States. In that area south of San Francisco called Silicon Valley—where they made computers and invented wonderful things—she had seduced a somewhat shy, certainly amoral security guard who was twenty-four years old and made $7.23 an hour guarding the great secrets of M-Guide Computer Laboratories in Palo Alto.

His name was Tony. Poor Tony. He was now in the very harsh maximum security prison at Marion in southern Illinois. He was kept in a narrow cell most of the time and his only recreation was reading and working with weights. She felt bad afterward not because she had loved Tony at all—that had been business—but because she thought of herself caught in a cell for the rest of her life. She pitied herself. It would have been a merciful thing to kill Tony. She had considered it, the night he put his face between her legs and she had the Walther PPK under the pillow and she thought about it because Tony was very close to being caught. But he had pleased her and she had been merciful. Too bad for Tony.

Better to die like the man at the window in the bar. She studied his face, his lean chin, his glittering eyes. Dead man, she thought.

13

The *Finlandia* slid down the open sea passage between the islands that are flung out in a stream east from Stockholm, almost to the coast of Finland. In the bright moon of the starry night, here and there, above the snow, poked roofs or sticks of summer homes on the islands. The islands were the perpetual retreats of middle-class Swedes in summer; the islands, some no more than an acre or two in size, promised summer even now at the end of the long Scandinavian winter.

The *Finlandia* was a huge ship, the largest car ferry in the world. She might have been an ocean liner but was trapped in the dull passage every day between Stockholm and Helsinki. She always passed at night because the trip took exactly thirteen hours. It was midnight and the ship was halfway to the lights of Helsinki.

The man at the table was Colonel Ready. He had been chased for 400 days. He had killed three "contractors" sent by KGB. He had disappeared in Copenhagen five months ago and despite the large network of Soviet agents working in that city he had not been found.

Until he surfaced four weeks ago. With messages to the Soviet courier. He wanted to sell secrets; he wanted to sell himself. After all, the KGB knew he was an agent of R Section called November. He had many secrets.

The bartender was in love with her. He was a large blond Swede and he spoke good English. He thought his good looks impressed her. When she treated him with reserve, even coldly, he adored her. Her eyes always lied; her eyes always told of passion and unbelievable lust. The coldness of her manner only framed the passion promised in her eyes.

"Please, another drink for you?" he said, not sure of himself, fawning. He was too large and handsome to fawn.

"Perhaps," Alexa said, as though deciding. "Yes, I think," she said, deciding, giving him one small smile as a reward. "Glenfiddich." She had her preferences: single-malt Scotch whisky; and the Walther PPK, a very small automatic with a deadly accurate field of fire at short range. She worked in very close because she was not afraid of killing or feeling any passion at the act of giving death.

14

It was just as well that Alexa was so good in the matter of wet contracts.

She had been contracted to November four days ago. There had been confusion for a long time inside KGB over who November was. He was supposed to be the man who kidnapped KGB agent Dmitri Denisov six years ago in Florida; who had wrecked the IRA plan to kill Lord Slough in his boat off the Irish coast; who had caused enough troubles and embarrassment—all outside the rules of the trade understood by both sides—that Gorki had "contracted" him. He had to be killed. Which is why he wanted to come to the Moscow side. Gorki said it was too late. Gorki said November—who was this man, Colonel Ready—had to be killed because he could not be trusted.

Alexa thought of Gorki, head of the Resolutions Committee. Her mentor. A gnome with yellow skin and sandpaper hands. He had used her; the only man who had truly used her. When he was finished with her—in the dacha, long ago—she belonged to him. He knew that and never made great demands on her again. She was a painted wooden doll upon his shelf. He had opened her and found the doll within and the doll within the third doll and so on. He had gone to her core. She had shuddered at his touch and needed it. She had danced naked for him.

Gorki was not his name. Alexa was not her name. They were named by computers and codebooks. They were puppets, all of them. But some puppets danced naked for the others.

Alexa had been at Moscow University when KGB approached her. She had been afraid at first and then curious. What if she ended up in the translation pool that worked in one of the buildings adjacent to KGB headquarters in Dhzerzhinski Square? She knew what the pool was. She would be plucked from the pool as though she were a piece of fruit, by some KGB major to serve as his mistress, to feed his ego and maleness, to be discreet so that when he had to escort his plain, quite fat official wife she would understand and say nothing. She would be taken to Paris by him but not to the Black Sea because the Black Sea was for the family. She didn't want that to happen to her, not at all. And it had not happened. She

15

had been placed inside the Resolutions Committee and her superior, who was not permitted to make love to her, an obnoxious man named Mikhail, had said of her: "Women cannot kill, except in fury."

She had proven him wrong in a brilliant bit of business in Finland. She had attracted the attention of Gorki.

She thought of Gorki now and shivered as she drank the Scotch. The Scotch flooded her with warmth. Her loins were warmed. Gorki commanded her.

And she was very good at what she did.

Which is why he had full confidence in her to wet contract the annoying American agent called November.

November had limped and left a trail until he disappeared in Copenhagen. Then he made contact with the Soviet courier chief in Copenhagen. His code name was Stern. He played November along until he got instructions. They came from Gorki. The wet contract was still in force, Gorki said. Tell November we will negotiate with him—but in neutral Finland. Give him money to get to Finland. Tell him the running is over. And I will send Alexa to intercept him and to kill him once and for all.

November had no choice but to believe them.

Alexa had flown to Stockholm for the intercept at eight in the morning. She had spent the day in the splendor of the Birger Jarl, which was a warm hotel. In the afternoon, she took a walking tour through the narrow old streets of the Gamla Stan, the island of Stockholm that contains the oldest parts of the city. She had never been in Stockholm and found it charming. She bought a pair of leather boots at a shop in the Old Town. The clerk had very dark hair and an innocent face. He knelt before her to put the boots on her legs. She had felt the warmth build in her then and nearly considered it. But there was business to take care of. She had no doubt the clerk would have obeyed.

She had not seen boots like the ones she purchased even in the special stores in Moscow. They fit her well. Everything she wore fit her well. She always got a second-hand copy of *Vogue* each month from the Paris courier. She dressed in fashion.

The *Finlandia* had sailed at six from the grimly modern terminal

16

on the southeast coast of the city. The terminal was as sullen and cheerless as a bus station and she had sat at a table in the cafeteria, eating a stale cheese sandwich, watching November enter the place, look around, wait in line with the others. She had boarded the ship at the last moment.

She had watched him at dinner in the vast dining room. She would have preferred to dine alone but agreed to be seated with a middle-aged woman from Malmo who spoke no English. They smiled to each other with the wary grace that only women display when meeting other and unknown women. The woman from Malmo certainly saw how much more beautiful and better dressed Alexa was.

The dining room had been cheerful, full of small lights and small tables and a quiet orchestra at one end. Everything was made very intense by the presence of the Baltic Sea all around them. We are alone in the world, Alexa had thought with pleasure.

The American agent dined alone across the room.

Their eyes met once and held.

He had not smiled at her.

He did not turn his eyes away. It was she who broke contact.

She had followed him after dinner. He had gone on deck, he had visited one of the smaller bars, he had looked in the duty-free shops. She followed him and he knew it; it was what she had wanted him to know. The advantage was hers.

He was handsome in a rugged sense. Perhaps he believed she followed him because she desired him.

There was a trick to killing him on this ship, in the middle of the night, in the middle of the winter of the Baltic Sea.

Alexa would use the obvious approach and he would stop it; he was smart enough to have eluded Moscow for 400 days of running, so he would see the obvious. But the obvious way sometimes worked when a man had grown lonely or careless or dejected or had been lulled into the belief that Alexa merely wanted to go to bed with him.

Alexa had backups. When the obvious did not work, the backups would.

She decided to cross the room.

17

She carried her glass and sat down across from him in the overstuffed chair. She put her glass on the table and stared into his blue eyes. He was smiling at her.

He wore a ragged red beard now, perhaps to cover the scar that was on his cheek. He looked a little different from the descriptions given her, but then, anyone on the run for more than a year undergoes changes.

She let her eyes lie to him. Her eyes, she knew, glittered with lust. But Alexa was calm, without any feeling at all. She stared at him and let her eyes do the trick. Then she said, in precise English: "I have seen you and I want to go to your cabin and make love to you. Tonight. Now. Or you may come to my cabin."

"All right," he said. Just like that.

They did not speak or touch again until they reached his cabin door. He turned the key in the lock. The carpeted passageway was empty. He smiled at her with perfect white teeth. There were pain wrinkles at the corners of his eyes. He had lost weight in 400 days of running. She thought he might be thin beneath the loose shirt and that his ribs would press out against his skin. But it wouldn't come to that, Alexa thought.

He kissed her very suddenly at the door to the room and reached for her purse with one motion.

He pushed her away a little.

It was in the purse and they both knew it and it seemed to relax the tension between them.

He produced the shining Walther PPK and unsnapped the safety and pointed it at her. She wore a short fur jacket and a black silk blouse and a dark wool skirt that came to the top of her boots. The darkness of her clothing accentuated her paleness. She wore no jewelry and her lips were painted lightly. Her eyes were wide and deep and November stared into them. She was smiling.

"You know who I am. I wanted you to know so that there would be no trouble—"

"You're a little obvious," he said.

There, Alexa thought. There. That made it better.

"Come in," November said.

18

"All right."

She smiled—a properly small smile of acknowledgment of his superior instincts in this matter—and brushed past him through the narrow cabin opening into the room. There was a single bed made up. There was a small dresser and a porthole. In the front was a shower and a toilet.

"Strip," he said.

She turned and he smiled at her.

"Please," she began.

"Strip," he said. And he smiled.

She took off her coat.

She looked hesitant.

He was grinning at her. He put the pistol on the purse on the dresser.

"You want help? I could take off your clothes for you. Not as carefully as you might do it."

"I am KGB," she said.

"I know exactly what you are. Right now, you're a woman and I want you. I saw you get on the ship, I saw you at dinner, I guessed we would meet. Do you think I'm crazy? I know there's going to be a setup along the way. You're the setup; but if I overcome it—overcome you—they'll have to talk to me. I'll have you and then we will talk some and then maybe I won't kill you," he said.

Gorki had emphasized the brutality of the man and his cunning. He had lectured her about him. Alexa had taken precautions.

She began to unbutton her blouse. She undressed slowly, watching his eyes watching her.

November stood still, fully dressed, watching her, smiling.

She took off her blouse. Her brassiere fastened in front. She opened her brassiere and her large breasts sank a little against her slender frame.

She sat down then, on the only chair in the room, and removed her boots.

She reached beneath her dark skirt to remove her nylons. She blushed now because it seemed a good idea to her. "Really," she said.

19

"Come now. Only a few more things."

She blushed furiously. She reached for the top of her panties and panty hose.

The weapon contained two plastic bullets encased in a plastic firing device that was eighty-nine millimeters in length. She pulled down her hose and panties and the device, between her legs, fastened by the elastic of the panties, was in the palm of her left hand.

The device—it could scarcely be called a pistol because the principles were not the same, all the firing parts were electronic—popped loudly once and there was a sudden and large dirty hole in the middle of his forehead.

It was over that quickly. It amazed both of them.

He was quite dead, though it takes the brain some moments to realize that the flicker of images in mind and eye are terminated, rather like a reel of film still spinning after the screen has gone blank.

There was no need to fire a second time—there were only two charges in the plastic device—but Alexa was a woman of carefulness. It was why she had risen in a bureaucracy that might be described as not very progressive in the matter of respect for the talents of women.

The second opening in the skull came very near the first. Alexa was a professional and played a top game.

She had to step aside to let his body fall between her and the bed.

She went through his pockets. He had a few notes of Swedish money on him; also a Danish passport and a credit card issued by a Danish bank; also a passbook with a canceled account from Credite Suisse in Geneva.

She opened his shirt out of curiosity. He had a very nice chest, she thought. If there had been time to arrange the matter differently . . . well.

She dressed again. She put the device in her purse. As a precaution, Alexa buried the Walther under his mattress.

She lifted the body onto the bed and covered it with blankets and buried a pillow over the face so that the holes could not be seen clearly.

She went to the door and opened it carefully and looked up and down the empty corridor. She flicked off the lights in the room. The engines of the ship chugged serenely below decks. The night was clear and the waters of the Baltic Sea were gentle and shining beneath the full moon.

THREE
Breach of Security

It was the fourth of March. The day was filled with sun and blustery winds down the broad avenue that connects the White House with Capitol Hill. In the dark corner office of Frank L. Yackley, there were four chairs around the big rosewood desk. The illumination in the room had not improved. The light from the green-shaded banker's lamp made the faces of the four arrayed around the desk dark and indistinct. Frank L. Yackley's face seemed large and unreal, as though he might be the Wizard of Oz. It was the effect he desired.

"The problem is Hanley," Yackley said.

Lydia Neumann felt the chill again in the pit of her stomach. She counted as Hanley's closest friend in the Section, though "friend" might be too strong from her point of view and "friend" might be too weak from Hanley's. Hanley had no friends and pretended not to want them. He trusted Lydia Neumann as he trusted no one else. He had been a bachelor all his life, he was sexually indifferent; he was a bore, in fact. But Lydia Neumann with her raspy voice and Ma Joad manner had liked him in the way that some people favor the runt of a litter of farm dogs.

But she knew there was a problem as well. She squirmed in her chair and the leather squeaked protest.

"He needs help," Yackley continued in his careful voice, slowly

rubbing the side of one hand up and down the palm of another, as though playing his hands.

There was no sound in the room. The other chairs were occupied by the director of signals, the director of translations and analysis, the director of research. Lydia Neumann, the only woman at this level, was director of the computer analysis division. Since her duties overlapped those of Franz Douglas in TransAn (slang for translations and analysis), they were rivals in the fabric of the bureaucracy. Naturally, Franz Douglas would oppose Neumann on the matter of Hanley. It was the way things worked.

"We are all aware of his illness. We are also aware of his extraordinary response to Mrs. Neumann's call of . . . sympathy. I have talked to him as well. I am afraid that Mr. Hanley has suffered some severe shock."

That was a giveaway, Lydia Neumann thought. She narrowed her eyes. *Mr.* Hanley. He was getting the setup.

She was a large woman and huddled for a moment in her even larger loose sweater, her hands on the lap of her cotton dress. She might have posed as a farmwoman from another era. She was a Midwesterner as Hanley was; perhaps that explained their attraction to each other.

"I am not competent medically to make a judgment," he continued. "I have sent for Dr. Thompson to make a report."

"He said Hanley needed rest," Lydia Neumann said. "He's been overburdened."

"Yes, Mrs. Neumann," Yackley said. "But there is rest and there is rest."

"I don't understand—"

"Neither do I. I consulted with Dr. Thompson, who agrees with me that some evaluation needs to be made of Mr. Hanley. Perhaps at a different level than that afforded by Dr. Thompson. Who is, after all, concerned with the ills of the body."

"The mind," said Franz Douglas. "There's something in what you say."

"Acted peculiar," chimed in Claymore Richfield, director of research, a white-gowned scientific sort who never noticed anyone

or anything. He had developed a large budget because he agreed with everyone in the Section and then went off and created miracles. Like the wire of the innocent copper bracelet worn by field officers and used to garrote the unsuspecting. Like Marcom One, which not only analyzed photographs from the spy satellites but automatically coordinated them in computer memory so that the face of the Soviet Union from ninety-seven miles up was captured fresh from morning until night by photos that could sense the change of traffic lights in Moscow. Claymore Richfield was not of this world, Hanley once observed; he did not see things on a human scale but as a god might. Hanley had imparted this observation to Lydia Neumann once as they got drunk at the Christmas party held in the translation pool. "Intelligence is a mountain to be climbed," Hanley had intoned. "It is not a mountain to be descended to."

The fifth person in the room, Seymour Blyfeld, was director of signals and the upper-level liaison with NSA. He didn't count.

"Whether there is or not, we are faced with difficult decisions," said Yackley, quietly picking up the consensus. "The trouble with Hanley is that he has Ultra clearance, he can be very dangerous to us, to the Section, to the country. He has secrets."

"He's not a traitor. You're not calling him that," Lydia Neumann said. "He's ill—"

"I am not diagnosing him, Mrs. Neumann," said Yackley in a stiff voice, grinding the walnut words into powder. "I am suggesting that there must be an evaluation. A psychological evaluation."

"From which he won't return," she said in a stubborn voice. "No one ever gets a clean bill of health in a psychological evaluation—"

"And no one is ever recommended for one unless there is something wrong with him," Franz Douglas said in his thin, snippy voice.

"We have a problem, Mrs. Neumann. In the past three years, FBI has uncovered thirty-two traitors, thirty-two spies who have—"

"FBI? What does that have to do with us—"

"Traitors," said Yackley. "What if it were proven by one of our dear sister agencies—let us not name the agency, let us just

assume it is one of our Competition—that the director of operations division was not only off his head but that he was babbling secrets to outsiders?''

"Has that happened?" Lydia Neumann said.

"Yes. He has made contact with a former agent. A former agent who no longer exists. He is babbling over an open line—"

"How do you know this?"

"Because the line has been tapped for six months. At my directive," Yackley said. Richfield looked innocent.

Lydia Neumann's face went red. "What about us? Are we tapped as well?"

Yackley smiled at that. "It wouldn't do to tell you if you were, would it?"

"I wouldn't mind being tapped," said Franz Douglas. "I have nothing to hide."

Mrs. Neumann ignored him. "Who is the agent? The ex-agent? What did he say?"

"That's not really your concern, Mrs. Neumann."

"What secrets did he—"

"Mrs. Neumann. I have called this meeting for the purpose of gaining a consensus for a course of action in the matter of Mr. Hanley. I think the course of action is obvious. I will recommend to the director of National Security that Mr. Hanley be examined at the facility at St. Catherine's."

Mrs. Neumann knew. She felt the ice grow as a real thing in her belly, press against the warm skin from the inside and freeze it, grow up into her chest and make the breath come short.

"That's wrong," Mrs. Neumann said at last, choking.

"It is the only solution of the moment," Yackley said. "St. Catherine's is secure. St. Catherine's is a perfectly respectable private institution with a government contract and they have served us well over twenty-five years. The Claretian Sisters—"

"This is not about the nuns, that man has some say in this, some rights—"

"Mrs. Neumann, this is a matter of grave national security. Mr. Hanley is a sick man, he needs treatment." The voice had stopped

grinding walnuts. There was the balm of healing. Yackley looked at the photograph of his wife on his desk for a moment, at the crooked, good-natured grin. He smiled at his wife. He smiled at them all. He felt a string of reassuring clichés coming on. "This is a matter of security at every level of government, at the level of secrecy in our private agencies. The government has become a sieve intelligence-wise. There are Soviet agents on the prowl—"

"And we know it," Lydia Neumann said in her barking whisper. "We know everything."

"Only God knows everything," said Claymore Richfield in his vague and scientific way, as though he might be on intimate terms with the Almighty. "We *guess* we know."

"We know who they are. They know who we are. We trade our agents from time to time. A long time ago, we had a field agent, he said there was so little worth knowing and so many people bent on finding it that it mixed us up. We had too much information."

She thought of an agent called November, long buried now in dead files.

"I'm not going to let the Langley Firm or the Sisters make us dance to their tune. I am not going to be embarrassed by discovering the first Section agent who has gone over to the Opposition," Yackley said. He was using the voice he used on Capitol Hill during the budget hearings in the clubby privacy of the ornate Senate Conference Room.

"So this is about politics, not about Hanley's mental health—"

"It is about reality."

"Hanley didn't give up his human rights when he joined the Section. And I add he joined it a long time ago, before any of us."

"This is not a matter of depriving him of his rights," Yackley said. With patience. "It is a matter of helping him. Of restoring him. Of finding the best way to treat him."

"But he's committed no crime—"

"Indiscretions—"

"But how can you order an evaluation, a psychiatric evaluation—"

"—done all the time—"

"But he's not crazy—"

"—we're not talking about crazy. The word is meaningless. People aren't crazy, people have psychological problems they have to become aware of to solve—"

"—Hanley has the right—"

"That's it, Mrs. Neumann." Yackley never spoke in a loud voice. The room was jarred to silence. Yackley's face was as round as that of a wizard; he thundered and spoke fire:

"It is done. It is going to be done. Hanley is a security risk until further notice. He is a problem. We are going to resolve our own problems. Until I make a further decision, I will take over active directorship of operations, pending selection of a successor. To Hanley. The rest of you remain at your posts, carry on as before. We are all going to have to bend to the oars to make this work. The loss of Hanley diminishes us."

Franz Douglas said, "We understand, sir."

Claymore Richfield mumbled assent. Richfield was working on an equation that might be able to link CompAn with Translations, eliminating an entire division inside the Section. It was fantastic, and it was being worked out right now on a sheet of paper during a long and tedious meeting in the office of the director. Richfield never looked up, even when the others filed out of the room in silence. Yackley left him alone because it was obvious that Richfield was lost in thought, on another plane. Not of this world, as poor old Hanley had said once.

FOUR
Once in a Blue Moon

She was not allowed back into the Soviet Union.

The message had been left for her at the dock by a seaman in a dark-blue pea coat and stocking cap and full blue-black beard. The message puzzled her. There was a dead man on the *Finlandia* who would be found in time. Alexa had wanted to be back in Moscow in time for dinner.

She took a taxi to the Presidentti Hotel in the center of Helsinki, near the bus depot and down the street from the red granite walls of the imposing Central Railroad Station. There was a train every day from Helsinki to Leningrad. The journey took eight hours because of the procedures at the border crossing. It was the route that Lenin had taken in 1917 to return to the Soviet Union and lead the Revolution.

Alexa waited in the lobby for a long time. She amused herself by playing the slot machines and watching the herds of Japanese tourists check in after their numbing flight over the polar cap from Tokyo. They all appeared to be dressed in thin clothes with cameras and a need to bunch together, chattering like birds.

She drank Scotch at the bar. It was very expensive. After a while, an American began to talk to her but he was rather old and portly and she pretended to be French. It worked because she knew Americans never spoke foreign languages.

At noon, the contact arrived. He was a man called Alexei. She had worked with him once before and he had presumed too much based on the similarities of their code names.

He was a large, bluff man and carried the accents of Georgia. Like all Georgians, he was rather brutal, loud and crude, and Alexa worked around him carefully until she was in a position to explain her independence from him and his good will. He had been reprimanded, that last time, by Gorki himself.

They sat in the inner lobby of the hotel. It was a place of dark woods and square architecture and large spaces.

He had to have a drink. He sipped the chilled Stolichnaya like a thirsty man.

Alexa watched him drink with her deep, dark, glittering eyes and noted it. That would be useful sometime as well. Everything was useful to a careful woman.

"It is too late," he began.

"Everything went all right," she said. The responses must be kept at a minimum.

"All wrong," Alexei said. He had thick eyebrows that bridged his nose and hostile blue-gray eyes and the overwhelming smell of cologne of the sort smuggled into Moscow in attaché cases.

Alexa had never worn perfume. Her body was clean and pure. She drank a little Scotch whisky at times and, at dinner, wine. She ate vegetables. She did not smoke. Her breath was sweet. Her body smelled like fields of flowers and she thought the smell of her body was more beautiful—even to herself—than the appearance of it.

She waited, attentive, her hands on her lap, her legs slightly apart because it was amusing to sit in such a way and no less comfortable to her.

"You have taken care of the wrong man."

"No," she said. "I was certain."

"I have information from the Committee. They could not reach you on the ship. In any case, it doesn't matter."

"What doesn't matter?"

"You killed a man named Ready." He pronounced the name with a long *e* sound and spoke it again. "He was not November."

29

"I killed November—"

"Like a blue moon," Alexei said suddenly and she saw that he was smiling. "Gorki is embarrassed."

"What embarrassment?"

"The wrong man. There were two men called November. One was the shadow of the other. But the man we were to have killed was not the man on the *Finlandia*. He was another man. Your task, my dear, is not over."

"I am not at fault—"

"You know how it is," Alexei said, still smiling. "Everyone must share responsibility."

"I was sent to fulfill a contract. I fulfilled a contract."

Her voice was absolutely clear and chill, chips of arctic snow on a tundra at the edge of the world. It was without mercy. It had no anger in it because she could hide anger. Or fear. Or desire. She was very good at what she did.

"Like a blue moon," said Alexei. "You were in London Station? The English have a saying for this, it is very amusing. It is the second moon that comes in a month. Two full moons in one calendar month. It is called the blue moon and because it is rare, the English—they call this rare thing, 'once in a blue moon.' It is rare. But it happens all the time in nature."

"I don't know English expressions. I prefer the sayings of my own country. There is no more rich language than Russian." She was annoyed by the situation. "Besides, why do they call the moon blue? Does it become blue? Of course not. I am Russian; speak Russian."

"Russian spoken by a Muscovite," Alexei said with sarcasm.

"Certainly," she said. She might have been a Parisienne or New Yorker, she might have been a Chinese Mandarin or a London chartered accountant forced to share a first-class coach from Victoria with two Irish businessmen.

"Two moons of November," Alexei said in a voice of poured gravel. "So the other one. It begins for you now. A long journey. You find him and resolve him."

"Another contract," she said in a dull voice. She felt tired. She

had felt tired after killing the man in the compartment of the *Finlandia*. It was her reaction to death. "All right. Who is he and where is he?"

"That is a problem," Alexei said. He was enjoying this. "The details are very few. A man with gray hair."

"Like the man I killed—"

"Yes. But he was not the man. A man with gray eyes. A man last seen twenty-six months ago in Zurich—"

"That's no information at all," she said, moving the iceberg of her voice. "This cannot be serious."

"I do not understand this matter." Alexei suddenly confessed it. "There will be more information. Into your mission, they tell me. Information along the way, that is the expression used. You are to go to Zurich first, there will be more information—"

"This is absurd, like a children's game—"

"In two days time. The problem is with the information. I have an instinct. They are developing the information as you travel. They want you very close to the target when they have it certain."

"Like the spy satellites," she said.

"Yes. I suppose that is where we must now borrow our imagery from. Spy satellites. Is that what we are, my dear Alexa? This matter with two Novembers—why does it come up now? Why didn't we know this before? I don't understand it at all."

Of course not.

"Money," he said, handing her a packet. She opened the packet. There were Swiss francs, dozens of pieces of the colorful bits of paper engraved with stalwart drawings of stern Swiss heroes. The largest objects on Swiss bank notes are the numbers; the numbers can never be misunderstood.

"All right," she said with a little note of defeat. It seemed fantastic to her; and wasteful. "I will need a weapon."

"At the time," he said. "Now, you have two days. Enjoy yourself. You will stay here tonight?"

"I don't know—"

"Please, I would take you to dinner—"

"No. I don't think so."

31

"My dear cousin," he began.

"We are not related," she said, rising out of the soft chair to lift herself from her note of defeat and tiredness. "I told you that a long time ago."

"Please, cannot we be friends?"

"Of course. We are comrades," she said. "But I have much to do. I have to leave you now, Alexei."

"One more message. From Gorki. He said that this one, this second November, was as dangerous as the first. Perhaps more dangerous because he has survived so long."

"I am not afraid of anything," she said.

"He said that I should tell you this," Alexei said.

"Thank you, Alexei," she said. She turned. The American was at the bar, staring at her. Because she was beautiful and she knew men had to stare at her, it had not annoyed her for a long time.

She smiled a smile of pity at Alexei, who had scrambled to his feet to be polite. It was so difficult. "Comrade," she said. She took his hand. She let him kiss her on the mouth as he had wanted to do and felt his large hand on her back, pressing her body to him as he kissed her. She endured it for a moment. Then she broke the contact with a slight body movement and she was free. She really pitied them sometimes.

FIVE
St. Catherine's

Hanley offered no resistance although they came prepared for resistance. It was a matter of following standard procedure. They placed the restraints on his thin, gray body and took him downstairs on a stretcher. He complained loudly about the treatment. So the second one, who rode in the back, gave him a heavy dose of sedation. He slept as he left the city he had lived in for thirty-five years.

The ambulance screamed its way through the heavy afternoon traffic. The ambulance prowled through the maze of traffic northwest along Wisconsin Avenue, to Old Georgetown Road where it turned west, along the road to the Beltway. The ambulance was orange and white and the lights on the roof were orange, red and white. Across the hood was painted the word "ambulance" written backward, presumably for terrified drivers ahead who would glance in their mirrors and see a beast of a vehicle approaching with lights and flashing headlamps and not be able to guess that it was an ambulance.

Hanley slept in the early March afternoon. The trees were forming buds along both sides of the parkway. The buds stood out like embroidery on the bare limbs. The clouds floated as brightly as sailing boats in warm waters. The wind was blowsy and voluptuous. The first garlic was growing in the shade of the forest; and the first

blades of grass. There were mushrooms springing up in the soft soil beneath the elm trees.

The ambulance siren was turned off ten miles north of the capital. The lights continued to flash. The interstate journey continued for nearly two hours, through Hagerstown and the little towns once strung like garlands along the old National Route, which had been Route 40, now replaced by the prosaic Interstate 70 that forgot everything the old towns could have taught the new road.

Hanley saw none of these things. He had a long and strange dream he could never recall, except for the feeling of being lost in the dream, of being so lost to the world that he could never find home again.

The ambulance turned off at Hancock and then the journey was slowed down by fog in the deep valleys that begin west of Hancock. At the top of the road entering the second valley the ambulance began its wail again and the scream echoed back and forth across the valley. The people in the small city at the bottom of the valley who were on the street, feeling their way through the fog rolling down the hills, knew that sound.

Someone was going up to St. Catherine's.

Sister Mary Domitilla had taken her adopted religious name from a Roman woman who lived in the fourth century, was martyred for her faith, and became the patron saint of cemeteries. In 1968, it was decided at the Vatican in Rome that the saint had never existed. It was a blow to Sister Mary Domitilla at the time but she had learned to live with it. She had a round face and sharp faith. Her hands were always clean and she had no protruding fingernails—she clipped them nearly every night, so that the edges of her fingers were always sore. She offered the small, useless pain to God.

Sister Mary Domitilla waited at the entrance. Mr. Woods was usually on the gate, but for special cases he was replaced by Finch, the government agent. Finch operated the gates, and the ambulance, its siren now muted, slid through on wet gravel.

"I have the key to Ward Seven," she said to the driver. She got

into the passenger side of the front seat. She glanced back at the man on the stretcher.

"Violent?" she said.

"He put up a fight," the driver said. He slipped the GMC ambulance into drive and came around the turning circle, the tires crunching the gravel.

"Is he all right?" she said.

"Yes. He's all right."

"Did you give him?"

"Yes."

"He'll be dopey."

"We gave him less this time. The last one. Whew." He sighed, remembering the last time.

"Sister Duncan is there."

"That's good. He'll sleep it off. He's all right," the driver said.

Ward Seven was detached from the pile of old red brick buildings that formed St. Catherine's. Ward Seven was built of cinder blocks and had very small windows. It was two stories high and there were bars on the windows because the patients were violent. That's what everyone in the town in the valley believed, when they thought about St. Catherine's at all. St. Catherine's had always been in the valley and always apart from it; it had been there so long that people in the town could remember when it was called the Insane Asylum. That was before a more humane time.

The buildings of St. Catherine's were done in a neoclassical style popular at the end of the nineteenth century. There was a small church called "the chapel." Ward Seven was located at the rear of the property, near the electrified fence that ran through Parson Woods. The ward was isolated in another way as well. There was a fence within the fence, so that there was a space between the outer electrified fence and the inner, nonelectrified fence. This was useful on days when there were visitors to St. Catherine's. The power to the fence was shut off and three Dobermans ran in the alley between the fences instead.

Sister Mary Domitilla fed the Dobermans. She called one Victor, after a childhood dog; the second was Spot, after a childhood book;

the third was St. Francis of Assisi, after a saint whose reputation had fared better than her namesake's.

Hanley awoke in darkness, sweating. He was in a bed like a hospital bed. He wore a hospital gown, open in the back. He felt uncomfortable and he had a headache. He realized his feet were manacled to the sides of the bed. His eyes were wide in the darkness.

The room was furnished like a motel, save for the bed. There was a pressed-wood dresser done in walnut veneer with a mirror. There was a straight chair. Above the desk was a portrait of sunny Spain complete with Man of La Mancha with pike. On the opposite wall was a couch. It depressed Hanley to see the couch; wherever he was, they expected him to remain here for a time. Above the couch was another bit of factory art, this time a watery portrait of a Paris street.

He saw clearly in the darkness. The door to his room was closed but there was a light that came from a built-in neon tube above the Paris scene and ran the extent of the wall. The tubing was shaded but it gave enough light for someone to check on the guest in the hospital bed from the square of window in the door.

There was a thin small window high on the third wall to Hanley's left. It was protected by three vertical and two horizontal steel rods that might be considered bars.

The headache overwhelmed him for a moment with nausea. He blinked, gagged, held his breath. The nausea passed. He waited and let the sweat drop down his face, blinding his eyes with salt.

He blinked at the harshness of his body sweat.

He felt very dry. He found he could move his hands. He reached for a table lamp to his left and turned it on.

On the table was a remote control device for a television set. He glanced up and saw the set was on a platform between the wall to his left and the wall opposite that carried the bad painting of Paris. He turned on the set. The set crackled for a moment in darkness and then flicked on. It was the David Letterman Show. So that's what time it was.

He flicked through the channel selector to get some idea of where

he was. The network program flipped to a movie, flipped to a second movie, flipped to a religious program, flipped to a station off the air. No identification. He might be in any place in America; he was lost.

He remembered the two men now. One with rimless glasses and the other with a blue stubble of beard. It was important to remember what they looked like. The trained operative in the field was an observer of insignificant details.

The trained operative.

All of it a charade. Meaningless. There are no spies at all.

Hanley groaned and turned off the television set. The image of Victor Mature evaporated. The peculiar sickness came over him again. It was a sense of déjà vu with a physical reaction in his stomach; it put his brain out of control. He sweated. His body felt cold. He closed his eyes to get out of it. His brain stopped, filled with light, then colors, then triangles built within other triangles. He opened his eyes. He shivered.

He thought of November. And he saw an image of a nutcracker, the one he had owned as a boy, the nutcracker with outrageous teeth set in that fierce mouth. *The better to bite you with, my dear*.

He had to reach November.

He stretched out his hand and felt a water pitcher on the table next to the bed. The pitcher was made of plastic; so was the glass. He sniffed the water in the glass before he drank it. It tasted like water to him. He was very thirsty and drank another glass; and then another.

He could not move his ankles. They had cuffed him. He tried to move against the restraints.

They couldn't do this to him.

He wept again.

When he was through crying, he looked at the table again. There was a call button on it. Also, a plastic toilet used in hospital situations.

He would not stand for it.

If spies ceased to exist, nothing mattered. Then why torture him like this?

Nutcracker, he thought. He had to keep Nutcracker in his brain and tell them nothing. He had to reach November.

But his mind was drifting again. He was a child. He was back in Nebraska and he could smell the earth. It was summer and he stood in a Fourth of July cornfield with the stalks knee-high all around him. The corn smelled sweet and tempting; it even smelled of growth in the rich field. The child saw the bees above the stalks where they kept their nests. All was alive, all was nature, all was part of one single great sense that was seeing and hearing and smelling and touching. The touch of corn silks tickled his palm. The farmhouse was white. A red Ford pickup truck with flared fenders stood in the soft brown earth of the long drive that wound up to the house from the country road. The child saw and heard the world in that moment and understood perfectly.

Hanley wept.

SIX
Dead Agent in Lausanne

Lausanne is a wonderful city. It is in the French-speaking part of Switzerland, beneath the mountains, above the shores of Lac Leman, which is also called Lake Geneva in honor of its principal city at the southwest corner of the lake. It sprawls up the hills on several terraces. The lower town is connected to the upper by a system of funiculars (called the Metro) and elevators. Lausanne is an easy place to live in. There seem to be no strikes, no graffiti, no intolerance, no rudeness, no hustle (though enough commerce to satisfy all who wish to be satisfied by commercial transactions), no crime, no cuisine. They serve the same *poissons* from the lake in Lausanne that they serve 7.5 miles across the lake in Evian, in France, and they are satisfying without being as good. Everything in Lausanne is old shoe. It is a city with a university and a cathedral, some good restaurants and some solid hotels, some intrigue (though not as much anymore as one might think), and a place where a man named November shed his identity as an American field officer with R Section and went to ground.

His name was Devereaux. It was his surname when he had not been in the Section. It did not matter what his Christian name might have been.

He did not know, on the fifth of March, that a woman called Alexa was on her way to Switzerland to kill him.

He did not know that the man who had been his control for nineteen years in R Section—a cold and close-pursed man with a flat voice and bare manners named Hanley—was residing in the violent wing of a private hospital that once had been called an insane asylum.

He did not know about Ready. He did not know that KGB and an agent named Alexa had killed the agent mistakenly called November.

Four hundred days before, he had laid a careful trail to move the wet contract against him to a man named Colonel Ready. He had reason to hate Ready, enough to kill him. Ready had been his enemy. Ready had raped Rita Macklin. Devereaux had cut his Achilles tendon and tagged him November in the eyes of Moscow and the world of spies and sent him limping down the trail, trying to get away from the killers sent after him. It was the cruelest thing Devereaux had thought to do; and it still did not make up for his violation of Rita Macklin.

In the long list of things he did not know, the last item—the death of Ready—might have amused him. It was what he had wanted: to be retired, to acquire anonymity at the edge of the world of spies, to go to "sleep" in the terms of the old trade. November was dead; long live the man who had been the real November.

It was a curious thing that he had never questioned the wet contract put out against him. KGB had its reasons. He had been an agent who had played outside the rules of the game. Hanley had once pointed that out. Hanley had once said, "There are procedures to be followed."

Devereaux had replied. Usually, he said nothing because he thought Hanley was a fool, a petty bureaucrat to be endured and not trusted. But he had replied once: "There are no procedures to be followed; there are no limitations; there are no rules."

"But that is chaos," Hanley had said.

And Devereaux said nothing more.

Devereaux had retired because he could force Section to let him go to sleep.

Three people knew of his existence: Hanley, Mrs. Neumann and

Yackley. They had to know, to make the scheme work. They had disinformed files and reports on Colonel Ready to make it seem he was really November. The reports and files had fooled the KGB into shifting its focus on Ready. Ready could protest but he did not have anything but the truth on his side and the truth was rarely enough.

And the three in Section would keep the secret because they had to.

That was what Devereaux believed on the fifth of March.

He was a man alone. He had always been.

He had been a child of the streets in Chicago and had killed a gang member when he was twelve. He had grown tired of the trade long before he could leave it. He had never wanted a thing in his life except Asia—except the view of blood-red suns over morning paddies and farmers squatting in their pajamas to tell stories to one another. He had loved the idea of the East and joined Section to find the East and, because of the trade, lost the East forever. After that, he had found Rita Macklin.

She was thirteen years younger than Devereaux. She had red hair and green eyes and a face of openness that was beautiful. She was very tough because she thought she was tough. She spoke the beautiful lilting accent shared by some people in Wisconsin and Minnesota. There was a song about her presence that always made people smile.

Devereaux had met her; used her; slept with her; left her. And all the time, he fell in love with her more deeply than he had loved anything or anyone else in the world. Because of her—because it was possible—he had quit the trade and gone to sleep at the edge of the world.

They lived together in Lausanne. They slept together. They went everywhere together and shared silences with each other. When she was away on her long assignments in far places, he was truly alone: The cold thing in him came back as before. When she was away, he was transformed back into what he had been.

He walked the crooked streets of Lausanne every day and saw everything and filled his mind with the images of the trained

spy. He saw too much, as a spy will if he becomes good at the trade.

He walked down the hills of the city to the train station where he bought the newspapers every day from the same kiosk just inside the entrance. He was there nearly every day at ten in the morning —though he had not noticed he was now a man of fixed habits.

He was tall, rugged, with deceptively large shoulders and flat, large fingers. His square face, creased with care lines, suggested the cold thing inside him. His hair was gray mixed with dark brown. He wore an old corduroy jacket most days now and shoved his hands deep into the pockets when he walked. His gray eyes watched and watched and saw too much; and saw nothing because the world held no consequences when you were withdrawn from it.

He bought *Le Monde*, the *Herald-Tribune*, the European *Wall Street Journal*. Sometimes, because it was so well written, he bought *Libération*. He thought he should interest himself in the world for the sake of Rita Macklin and for the child they had taken in, Philippe.

It was hard work. He was a man of silences who preferred the world to be a separate place. He read books that others might find gloomy, the kind of works of philosophy that are never fashionable. He felt solace in them. He had not expected much from existence for a long time. And then Rita had changed that. So he read newspapers to learn about the world.

Philippe was the third member of the ménage. He was black and very tall for his age, which was now thirteen. He attended boarding school near Lugano, by the Italian border. He loved snow and he knew how to ski. He said he wished to be a sailor when he grew up—but he said it in the way of boys who are being boyish to please their fathers.

Devereaux had taken him off the island of St. Michel at the last moment, almost by instinct, as the boy stood in the waters and pleaded to leave that place of hell. It had been another business in another time. Rita had understood that gesture, though no one else would have. Philippe did not love Devereaux because Devereaux did not expect love, not even from Rita Macklin. It was enough to love her.

Rita was now in the Philippines. There was an election to cover, a riot and an assassination. It was an old story but Rita told him that all the stories were old ones. "Everything has been written before," she said.

"Shakespeare's advantage," Devereaux had replied.

"Yes. Something like that. A cliché is only something well said in the first place."

He had been alone for three weeks; she would leave the Philippines for America then, to see her mother in the city of Eau Claire, in Wisconsin; and then to Washington, to see Mac, her old editor at the newsmagazine; and then back to Paris. They would meet again in Paris in four weeks time.

He sat in the bar of the Continental Hotel and drank Kronenbourg poured into a cold glass and tried to understand the world according to *Le Monde*. It seemed that France was at the center of this world, just as it seemed the United States was at the center of the world portrayed in the *Herald-Tribune*.

Devereaux said once to Rita Macklin that Switzerland was never at the center of the world. It was a good place to be.

He spent his days like this: Walking, reading, seeing as much as he could, playing chess with the old man in Ouchy who came down to the chess pavilion on good days. They moved the large pieces around and walked on the board and considered all the moves and problems from the perspective of almost being participants. The old man said that he and Devereaux were the two best in the world because they had so much time to practice.

Devereaux wondered if he could do this for the rest of his life. He had buried himself by making someone else assume his identity. He was safe, detached from R Section. He read and read and read, absorbing the worlds of Montaigne and Kierkegaard and Hegel. He read Dickens all the time because it represented a world more real to him than the one he was in.

On Sundays, he would drive down to the school near Lugano and take Philippe out for the day. They might go to Italy and they might, in good weather, rent a sailboat on Lac Leman and sail down to Vevey and to the castle at Chillon. The man and the boy did not

speak much to each other. It was all right; they both understood the value of silence.

Besides, they both felt the absence of Rita on those Sundays when she was away. She warmed them both, a cold black child who had seen murder and war and a cold white man who had made murder and war. They felt damned unless she was with them.

"Encore, s'il vous plaît," Devereaux said to the woman behind the bar. It was just noon on the fifth of March.

She was a pleasant-faced Swiss with small eyes and an intent expression. She thought she had a nose that was too large but she was wrong. She thought that Monsieur Devereaux, who came to the little café nearly every day, might be a professor at the university. He was always reading.

She opened a bottle of Kronenbourg and poured it into the new cold glass. He liked chilled glasses and cold things. He had requested the chilled glass and she had been pleased to refrigerate his glasses for him.

Devereaux sighed, put down the very funny column by William Safire in the *Herald-Tribune*, and tasted the new beer. It was sweet and bitter at the same time, the way beer can be when it is very cold and very welcome.

He saw his face in the mirror behind the bar. He had been lost in newspaper words and had tried to forget about Hanley. Something had jarred him to think of Hanley again. So he had called Hanley yesterday and Hanley was gone. Gone.

He called Hanley at home. He had never been to Hanley's home but he knew all the numbers he needed to know. He had called and the telephone rang briefly and then an operator interrupted to explain, with a recorded voice, that the telephone number had been disconnected. Disconnected with no forwarding number.

Hanley was gone; where had Hanley gone?

Devereaux tasted the beer again. He stared at nothing at all and tried to picture Hanley in his mind and hear again the disjointed words of those two telephone calls, the first when he and Rita were making love, the second when she was gone.

Claudette, who was the girl behind the wide oak bar, gazed at M. Devereaux and thought she might be in love with him. Why not? Didn't he come every day to see her? Didn't he give her extravagant tips? Exactly as a lover might do. He was shy; he wanted her attention. She was so ready to please him. Dear man.

"That's just it. No November. There are no spies. I think I can tell you. I need to tell you. And did you know that your November is on his way to Moscow?"

Warning. Or threat?

Rita had sprawled in bed, in afterlove, her nakedness warm and open, her body ajar. She had stared at him as he listened to Hanley that night, listened to the mad words: Warning. Threat. It didn't matter.

And then Hanley spoke of a nutcracker and that made no more sense and Hanley was truly mad, Devereaux had thought. Nearly two weeks before.

Now, in the *Herald-Tribune*, he saw a little essay on the editorial page, arguing that the day of the spy was passed, that electronic devices had made the work of spies irrelevant. He had smiled as he read it and then he had thought of Hanley. He had decided to call Hanley. And Hanley was gone.

Devereaux felt a peculiar chill growing inside the coldness already inside him. Rita Macklin was a million miles away. He felt the prickle on the back of his neck that signified awareness and the presence of danger. And yet, what was all around him but this dull life and the girl behind the bar with the small, secret smile?

Devereaux did not trust R Section or Hanley. It was a matter of survival. It was a wise course.

He frowned. Claudette saw the frown and frowned in sympathy, worried for the professor. She hurried along the polished oak bar to him and asked him, in French, if everything was all right.

He tried a smile. He said yes. He looked away, back to his newspaper.

So shy, Claudette thought. She blushed. She felt warm, thinking of him. It didn't matter even if he was married. It didn't matter. All right, she thought: Take me. He needs comfort and I am com-

fortable. I will make no demands; I earn my own way, I can do as I please. She thought of him holding her and his weight pressing down on her the length of her body, pressing her breasts and opening her legs. So close together.

Devereaux stared at the paper and only thought: There was Hanley, Mrs. Neumann, who had buried the files, and Yackley. But had any of them told the others? Was Hanley saying that Colonel Ready convinced Moscow to come after him again? Spies were terrible at keeping secrets. Secrets were meant to be broken and exposed.

There are no spies.

Could it mean: There are no secrets?

Hanley was dull, stable and the most predictable man in the world. Was he drawing Devereaux back into the trade with riddles and puzzles? It was childish and very much like Hanley.

Claudette decided she would surrender herself on the first night because the professor was too shy to be flirted with. He had to know he did not have to be shy. She would be the bold one.

She offered him a bowl of pretzels.

He was startled. He looked up at Claudette. She was young and fair and her eyes were empty and shining. He said no in a polite way and shut her out of mind.

But she hovered now. "Another beer?"

No. No. No.

He rose from the chairlike stool with back and arms and put down a note that was probably too much to leave as a tip.

She thanked him and tried to put meaning into her voice. She smiled at him. She had beautiful teeth.

He tried another smile on her. He used smiles like disguises. He nodded and took his papers and walked out of the café.

March was chill and damp and bright. Clouds brooded above the snowfields in the mountains. The lake at Ouchy below was choppy and bright. The day was a promise of warmth which, after a long winter, was good enough. It was a day to be with friends and find warm places to drink in and find laughter. Devereaux only knew the old man from Ouchy who played chess as though it were war.

All the Swiss men played at war all their lives. And they only took those things seriously that were not war.

He wondered if Hanley had a new game.

He walked up the steep streets to the upper town and was lost in thought and the exertion of the climb. He walked along the Rue Mon Repos and failed to see as clearly as he was trained to see. He was so preoccupied with thoughts of Hanley that the two men in the Saab who followed him had no trouble at all.

SEVEN
Dr. Goddard

Hanley was not given clothing. He understood the technique. Everyone in intelligence knew the technique and used it. The naked prisoner is like the naked patient or the naked captive: They are all rendered defenseless by their nakedness.

Hanley sat on the vinyl side chair in the examining room. His naked bottom pressed against the vinyl. He wondered if it was cleaned with disinfectant after each use.

It was the first full day of his captivity. They had given him oatmeal with prunes for breakfast. He had wanted to gag.

And no coffee.

"Coffee isn't good for you," chirped the nun who had brought his tray.

"Where is this place? Why am I—"

"When you see the doctor," she said, smiling and flitting about the room like a nervous bird. She said "doctor" as though saying "God."

He sat on the vinyl chair and stared at the man at the empty desk. He guessed there was a tape recorder set up somewhere. On the cheerful blue wall behind the desk was a very bad print of a painting by Modigliani in which a reclining woman is represented in bright colors. Hanley did not like modern art. Hanley did not like sitting on a vinyl chair wearing a ridiculous hospital gown. He wasn't sick;

he was tired. He had felt frightened and confused last night; now he felt anger.

"My name is Dr. Goddard," began the man with the salt-and-pepper beard and the guileless brown eyes. He had large hands and clasped them on top of the desk. He spoke in a voice that was made for a lecture hall. He smiled at Hanley.

"Doctor of what? And where am I? And why was I brought here?"

"This is St. Catherine's," said Dr. Goddard, still smiling. His glasses were brown and round and owlish. He seemed to have all the time in the world. "This is a hospital. Do you remember anything?"

"I remember two goons who came to my apartment and showed me some papers. I said there had to be a mistake but that I would go with them. And then one of them wanted to put me in a strait-jacket, for God's sake. What is this place, a nut house?"

"Unfortunate word," said Dr. Goddard. The voice was a pipe organ played by Lawrence Welk.

"You don't have any right—"

"Mr. Hanley. I assure you we have every right. You understand this is a matter of both national security and your wellness."

Hanley blinked. "What did you say?"

"Mr. Hanley. St. Catherine's is equipped with all the best medical equipment. We intend to examine you thoroughly for physical causes of your . . . depression. But I think this will go deeper than mere physical causes."

"What are you talking about?"

"What are the causes of depression?" said Dr. Goddard as though speaking to a classful of students. "Many. A chemical imbalance is certainly involved. Perhaps some trauma that has created a subtle neurological impairment. Perhaps—"

"Who are you, Dr. Goddard? What kind of a doctor are you?"

"I'm a psychiatrist, Mr. Hanley. As you suspected." He smiled with good humor. "There. I'm not so frightening, am I?"

"I'm not afraid of you," Hanley said. "But you can't keep me in a place against my will."

49

Dr. Goddard said nothing.

Hanley stood up. "I want my clothes—"

"The hospital gown is appropriate when—"

"I want my goddamn clothes," Hanley said.

And Dr. Goddard did a strange thing. He took out a can of Mace from his white cotton jacket and sprayed Hanley in the eyes.

Hanley was in his fifties. It had been forty years since he had been assaulted physically. He understood the uses of assault, he understood terror. But in that moment, he was hurtled back more than forty years to when he was a child. Suddenly he was falling, his eyes stung by the liquid, the burning creeping over his face. He cried out in pain. And no one came to him.

The pain and burning lasted a long time and he thought he made a fool of himself, writhing helplessly on the floor, his senses distorted by the pain and the suffocating powerlessness. His hospital gown was opened; he realized his backside was naked to anyone who might see him. He didn't care in that moment. He wanted the pain in his eyes to end.

Dr. Goddard gave him a damp towelette. He wiped at his face.

"You're not harmed," Dr. Goddard said. His voice was Bach playing variations on the fugue.

"Why did you do that? How dare you—"

"Mr. Hanley. I am the doctor," Dr. Goddard said.

"You're a goddamn sadist. Is this a prison? Who sent you?"

"You were referred by your superior officer," said Dr. Goddard.

"What are you talking about?"

"I know all about you. I have access to your 201 file, profile chart, skills index rating, your entire dossier. I know all about you. I don't want you to see me as the enemy."

Hanley had staggered to his feet.

"Sit down," Dr. Goddard said in that voice lurching into the third Brandenburg Concerto. The notes progressed relentlessly. It was enough to drive a person crazy.

Hanley sat. His bare behind was cold on the cold vinyl seat. He shivered. He felt humiliated, as though he might be a child again, forced into some ridiculous position because of something he knew

was not his fault. It had not happened to him this way since he was in the sixth grade, nearly a lifetime ago.

"We are here to help you," began the voice, sounding the theme. "You have altered your behavior severely in the last six months and your superior is concerned for your mental balance. You have become moody and distant—"

"I was tired," Hanley began.

Dr. Goddard stared at him. When the room was silent again, he resumed:

"Tiredness is a symptom of a greater problem. Your problem, in all likelihood, is not physical. It is deeper than that."

"Why?" said Hanley.

"Why what?"

"Why is it deeper than that?"

"Aberrant behavior can be a symptom of many things. It can be a cry for help," Dr. Goddard said.

Hanley shrank with chill.

Dr. Goddard continued. "Fortunately, our knowledge of the mind has made wonderful advances in the past thirty years. We now understand and can categorize behavior that would have defied categorization only a generation ago. We have a powerful range of psychological drugs—a chemotherapy—that we feel, and I think you will find we are as good as our word, can help restore you to normality and to a vigorous life again. Perhaps not as before; but to return you eventually to a useful participation . . ."

Eventually was such a terrible word, Hanley thought. The words went on and on. He realized he was shivering. He wanted to say he was cold, sitting in this ridiculous and humiliating hospital gown, listening to this nonsense. It was coming clear to him.

He began to cry as the doctor droned. He had found tears easy these past weeks and months. The tears released many feelings in him. The tears made him feel weak and relieved to be helpless.

Dr. Goddard stopped speaking.

He saw the tears stream down Hanley's pale, drawn cheeks.

He understood tears. They were useful as part of the "grieving"

51

process in which the patient understands his status as a patient, understands there is something wrong with him, understands Doctor is there to help him. Dr. Goddard did not smile outwardly because he did not want to appear to mock the grieving process. Or to stop it at the moment.

EIGHT
Hitters

Claudette was behind the bar at ten in the morning. It was too early for respectable Swiss to come in for a drink but she needed the extra hour to clean the bar. The place always smelled sour in the morning. She would open the window in the back and leave the front door open, even in cold weather, to let the place air out and remove the odor of stale tobacco and spilled beer.

The two men walked in at nine minutes after ten. Claudette was so intent on washing the glasses that she did not notice them until they sat down at the bar.

"Hello, dear," said the first one. He was large and had flat fingers on his large hands. He rested his hands on the bar. "Anyone else around here?"

Claudette stared at his lizard brown eyes for a moment and then shook her head.

The second one was thin and quite hairless. He did not have eyebrows. He looked as though he might have been ill—except his very black eyes glittered with life. His face was tanned, which was unusual enough for Claudette to notice it.

They both spoke French but with strong accents.

"No one is in back?"

"No. Not at this hour. The owner doesn't come until the lunch hour. If you want to see the owner—"

"No, that's all right. You're the one we wanted to talk to."

53

Claudette was bent over the sink as she spoke with them, washing glasses. Now she stopped. She straightened up and wiped her hands on a damp towel on the bar. She stared at the large man and then at the hairless man and waited.

"We want to ask you about the man who comes in here at lunch almost every day."

"We have our regular patrons—"

"Look, we mean the man who comes in here, sits right here at the bar every day. You know who we mean."

She stared at the big one as though she knew. She said nothing.

"Are you sure no one is in back?"

"Yes."

"You're all alone here, then?"

"Yes."

"I see," said the big one.

"All alone," said the hairless one. They didn't look at each other. They were staring at Claudette very hard.

Claudette was afraid of them. "What can I do for you?"

"Do for us? We told you."

"Yeah. We were talking about the American who comes in here every day. Around lunchtime."

"The one who reads the papers."

"Gets all the American papers to read."

"You know who we mean."

"You don't get that many Americans up in this neighborhood, not in winter."

She knew who they meant.

"You got a tongue, don't you, dear?"

"I'll bet she knows who we mean," said the big one. He wasn't smiling.

They were silent for a moment. The silence was like a pause planned in a symphony.

The big one said, "You see, we want to know where he lives. You know where he lives?"

"No. I don't know."

"But you know who we mean, don't you?"

"I—"

"Don't lie. I mean that. The last thing you want to do is to lie."

"Yeah," said the hairless one. "The thing is, we have to find out where he lives because we've got something to deliver to him. You know what we mean, something special for him. Only we know he drinks here but we don't know where he lives and his name isn't in the telephone book."

"No. He has an unlisted number."

"It's too bad," said the hairless one.

"Please," said Claudette. Her voice sounded very thin to her. She tried again. "Please, I don't know what you're talking about."

"Is that right?"

The big one got up then and came around the bar. He ambled like a walking bear. He was almost too large for the back way behind the bar.

"You are not permitted—" began Claudette, her Swiss sense of order horrified by this breach.

He picked up a bottle of Johnnie Walker Red Label Scotch whisky, opened it, and began to pour it into the sink. She took a step forward and the hairless one reached across the bar to grab her arm.

"You see, dear," said the big one. "We are permitted just about anything we want. So when we ask you where the American is, the one with gray hair who reads all the papers, you should tell us where he lives."

"Definitely," said the hairless one. He had small hands that held her arm like pliers.

"See what I mean? Anything we want to do."

"Anything," said the hairless one.

"Please," said Claudette. "I don't know. I honestly don't know where the professor lives—"

"Professor? Professor?"

The hairless one smiled and twisted the skin beneath his grip.

Claudette winced with pain. The bar was dark. She noticed they had closed the front door when they entered.

"I like that," said the big one. "You think he's a professor of something because he spends all his time reading? Ha. He was a professor."

"A long time ago."

"But he hasn't been in a classroom for a long time."

"And he needs a refresher course."

"He needs a review of old lessons."

"We were sent out to teach him a few things."

"It's too bad you don't know where he lives. It would make things simpler."

"Yes," said the hairless one. Her skin had a burning sensation beneath his hand. He let her go and her arm was ugly and red.

"Well, we'll go now."

She stared at both of them.

"One thing, dear. I don't think you would want to tell him we were here looking for him. I mean, this is to be a surprise. Understand?"

"Yes. We don't want you to tell him a thing."

"Because if you tell him we were here, we'll be coming back here."

"Definitely," said the hairless one.

Devereaux sat at the bar, watching Claudette move anxiously up and down the bar, serving beer and wine and schnapps while the owner pulled out plates full of steak *haché* smothered in onions and gravy, prepared in the minuscule kitchen at the rear.

The owner had not noticed the missing bottle of Scotch. He would in the afternoon, she knew, and he would question not Claudette but Monique. Monique would be innocent but Claudette felt, at that moment, too afraid to intervene in the coming storm. She hurried; she was clumsy; she broke two glasses and the owner scowled at her.

When she served the professor, she did not look at him. This was not usual.

Monsieur le professeur.

The dinner hour progressed and everyone could have seen that Claudette was upset; save that no one engaged in the hurried business of eating chopped steak and onions and potato salad in a little dark café had the time to observe Claudette's distress.

Devereaux ordered a second bottle of chilled Kronenbourg.

She pulled the green bottle out of the cooler and opened it and took him a fresh glass chilled in ice, the way he preferred it.

"Merci, Claudette," he said. He had never spoken her name before. She blushed for a moment.

Devereaux stared at her for a grave moment.

"Is there something wrong, Claudette?" he said at last. The voice was low like morning fog. It was remarkable: In six months, he had not exchanged two dozen words with her. He had never called her by her name, though she had offered it from the beginning.

She thought he was concerned. She was touched. Her fantasy of herself and her professor returned, burning to the surface. It pleased her that he was concerned and made her brave.

Devereaux was not concerned. He was observing her as he observed all his surroundings, trying to spy what was unusual. He would walk down a street and refocus his gaze automatically every few seconds: First street, then walk, then buildings, then mailbox, then lamp post, then car, then street . . . It was the technique learned painfully over the years. It had to do with survival. In a way, it served to slow down the sense of life rushing past. With the senses focused intently on the surroundings, the mind worked on the unconscious and semiconscious problems that were presented.

"I am a little upset, monsieur," she said.

He said nothing.

"Monsieur, it concerns you—" she blurted.

He almost smiled.

But then she spoke slowly about two men who had entered the café at nine minutes after ten in the morning and who had frightened her. She tried to remember what they said and the professor's gray eyes did not leave her face. She felt like a schoolgirl under his gaze. She told him everything; it was important to hold nothing back.

She told him the last part, about not telling Devereaux any of these things. His eyes gazed into hers as she told it, and it seemed to her that he must understand how brave she was, how uncaring for her own safety.

Devereaux wanted to know what they looked like and she told them. She had been too frightened of the large man to notice much

about him. But she remembered details about the hairless man. Devereaux began to construct an image of him.

He listened to the woman's trembling voice for a long time, and when she had finished her story he took her through it again, questioning her to extract every bit of information. As she talked the instincts rose in him and made his face tingle.

He thought he had accepted the idea of impermanence but he had not; he was unprepared for what Claudette said about the two men. They were emissaries from the world he had hoped to leave behind. It was too bad: He saw Rita and the boy, Philippe, and he saw himself as though all three were framed in an old photograph kept in an album as a souvenir.

It was probably over now.

And while these melancholy feelings came in waves over his consciousness, another part of his mind was deciding where to run and how to run.

He felt as he sometimes had felt on fall mornings in the old place in the Virginia mountains, when the air was crisp and dry and the leaves in the forest on the hill crackled with the alert movement of animals. He felt aware of all things around him. It was what he had been trained for.

"It's all right, Claudette," he said at last.

"*Monsieur le professeur*, I am afraid. For you, not for me." This was true, she felt. The steadiness of his gaze and the concern she read in his eyes had warmed her.

"There is nothing to be frightened of—"

"If they come back—"

"They won't come back," Devereaux said. "If they know this place, they could watch for me easily enough. They had some other reason for saying what they said to you."

"I don't understand," she said.

"Neither do I." He tried a smile. "But it's going to be all right."

"What will you do?"

"Go away for a while, Claudette. But I'll be back."

As he stood up he saw that she knew he was lying to her in that moment, and it made him feel a peculiar emotion, one he could not

place at first. Yes, he realized: It was sadness. This café, even Claudette's presence in it, had become one of his touchstones, though he had not consciously attempted to create touchstones in a foreign land. It was weakness to need such things. Was he becoming weak? Did he need the ritual of morning newspapers, this café, the old man who played chess on the pavilion outside Ouchy?

He left a ten-franc note and Claudette thought to say something else, something to draw them together. But there was nothing to say.

Devereaux was in the street, standing for a moment framed in the door of the café. The day was brilliant. The sun was high and there was a warm breath of wind from the French side of the lake. The sun glinted on the perpetual snowfields in the high reaches of the mountains.

There was no need to return to the apartment. Whatever had to be arranged could be arranged from another place. He considered the pistol sealed in plastic and strapped to the underside of the toilet tank lid. He would find another weapon. He had his passport, his bankbook.

He walked down the hillside to the Avenue de la Gare and went into the first branch of the Credit Suisse and withdrew 10,000 Swiss francs. Because he wanted the money in denominations of 100 francs, there were 100 bills and the wad was thick enough to split in two—half in his inside jacket pocket, the other half in the lower "cargo" pocket of his denim trousers.

While he made these preparations for flight, he tried to see what was unusual around him. He had lived long enough in Lausanne to find the oddities in the colorful scenes on the street.

There were old women in black coats hurrying to do their shopping and men in brown caps, smoking curved pipes, and businessmen with their coats open to the warm breeze, walking with the light step of their younger days. What did not fit this scene?

And he saw the two men sitting in the Saab down the street, watching the life surge around them.

Two men at noon on a weekday in a car bearing the license plates of Bern. This was Vaud; they were far from home. They were sitting

in an expensive Swedish car in the middle of the day on a side street, waiting for someone. They had to be waiting for someone. In a rental car most likely. Businessmen from abroad.

They seemed to be parked just on the periphery of his activity.

He thought about the crude warning given Claudette in the café. It was stupid, almost self-defeating. It invited him to flee, which was what he was doing.

Why?

KGB, like the other espionage services and some terrorist organizations, passed through Switzerland easily on their way to activities in the north and—more likely—the south of Europe. But incidents of terror in Switzerland were rare enough to be nonexistent. The reason was simple: Switzerland was a compact, orderly country with a fierce military tradition and an absolutely cold-blooded approach to dealing with terror. It was not acceptable, not negotiable and, in the long run, not worth the effort on the part of terrorists. Devereaux considered all this information in a split second, as a computer might, except that the mind worked faster when it was trained to consider information with both thought and feeling.

Devereaux crossed the broad avenue to the long, red stone train station. A white-gloved policeman held up his hand against the traffic.

Devereaux stopped at the kiosk where he usually bought the papers and chose the current copy of the *Economist*. Exactly as a potential railroad passenger might, choosing a magazine to kill the time on the train. He paid and turned around and saw the Saab parked illegally at the curb by the Continental Hotel across the way. He walked into the train station, across the concourse, to the ticket windows. He stood in line behind two schoolgirls who were talking to each other between giggles. When he reached the window, he bought the ticket for Zurich. He stood with the ticket a moment and looked in a glass window of a confectionary shop inside the terminal. He saw the two men at the entrance of the station.

Devereaux crossed the concourse to the platforms. The train for Geneva was just pulling into the first platform. It didn't matter: They had seen him buy the ticket, they had observed him walk to the platform. They would draw the right conclusion.

He climbed aboard.

The train waited.

He went to one of the windows and watched.

The two men stepped onto the platform and they stared at the train, at the very car where Devereaux waited. They looked at each other and then looked up and down the platform. At the last moment, they started across the concrete platform toward the waiting train.

Perhaps they had miscalculated and thought he would flee by auto.

Devereaux opened the door at the end of the car and dropped from the train onto the platform as the electrified express to Geneva quickly picked up speed. A conductor at the far end of the platform frowned at Devereaux. He walked over and shook his finger and told him about the dangers of jumping from a moving train. Devereaux had broken the rules in a country of rules.

Devereaux crossed the platform slowly, watching the train swing out east of the city in the tangle of tracks. He entered the concourse and looked around. There were the usual crowds of midday travelers. The trains were swift and frequent so that all classes and ages took the trains as a matter of course. Devereaux tried to see if there was anything different he could find in this crowd around him. There had been two men. Perhaps there were more. He was a patient watcher, falling easily back into the habits of a trade he had sought to quit more than once. The habits couldn't die—they merely became rusty through disuse.

Outside the station, the sun was still blindingly bright. The passersby were shedding themselves of heavy morning coats and scarves and soaking up the sun and the warm southern breeze. There was a cheerful feeling on the Avenue de la Gare.

He crossed the street to the abandoned Saab and opened the door. He saw the keys in the ignition. He reached in the glove compartment and took out a rental agreement between a M. Pelletier and a Swiss rental car company at the airport at Geneva. So they had flown into Geneva, picked up a car with Bern registration, and gone directly to Lausanne. They had arrived yesterday.

They had known exactly where to find him. He had eluded them. But it had been much too easy.

61

He felt the vague chill that he had learned to live with in the years in the old trade. He had the feeling of watching and being watched. He looked around. A policeman approached with a sour look and told him to move the car.

Devereaux started the engine. Devereaux turned left on the east side of the station, went under the viaduct and down the road that parallels the Metro to Ouchy at the bottom of the hill. It would be better to get out of the tangle of Lausanne, to find an open road and see who might be on it.

A gray Renault pulled from its parking spot in front of the McDonald's and followed the Saab down the steep hill toward Ouchy and the lakeshore.

Devereaux drove quickly enough to see if anyone kept up with him.

The gray Renault leaped ahead of a slow-moving bus and pushed between a dull limousine and a truck turning into a service drive. There was no one between Devereaux and the Renault.

They wanted him to flee.

They wanted him to leave Switzerland. They wanted to isolate him, he thought. There had to be a killing field where he could be hunted in the open. Switzerland was never a good place to trap a spy.

He turned at Ouchy and followed the line of the highway toward Vevey and Chillon. The highway rose into the hills above these coastal towns, suspended on pilings driven deep into the rocky hillside. All along the highways were disguised pillboxes, arms depots and rocks set in such a way as to cause a rockslide across the roadway at a signal. The Swiss perpetually boobytrap their country in preparation for a war that has not come in five centuries.

Devereaux pushed the Saab now, screaming through the gears, pushing the tachometer to the red line with each gear, shifting down hard, driving the engine to its limits. He was pushing 150 kilometers and the Renault was keeping pace.

The midday traffic was thin. Travelers were taking their dinner breaks. The countryside was empty and full of peace. The road was rising into the hills above the lake. Down on the lake, the ferry boats plowed through the waters.

Devereaux thought there might be two men in the Renault but the light was so brilliant that it made a mirror of the windshield behind him.

The light blinded both drivers. He thought of what he would do then.

He had no weapon but the car and his own knowledge of the roads around the lake.

There was a small road that tumbled down the mountain from the main highway toward Chillon. The road was made for slower transport in a slower age. He tried to remember exactly what he knew of the road. And then he remembered.

If they wanted him to flee, they would expect him to be running as fast as he could.

The Saab growled and whined as he pulled off the main road and onto the smaller road down the mountain. He pushed the gears down, taming the engine, feeling the tires catch at the asphalt and hold it despite the sway of centrifugal force. He pushed into a slow slide around a long and lazy curve and then pushed the car into a screaming acceleration down a short stretch of straight ground. He glanced behind him once in the rear-view mirror and saw the Renault. Was it ten seconds behind? Was there enough time?

The Saab whined through a second, sharp turn around a boulder and Devereaux slammed the brakes with brutal force, so that the rear end of the car bucked and the tires squealed as the car lurched sideways toward the edge of a cliff at the margin of the road. The car nearly turned around. Below was a farmer's field with the earth waiting for a plow.

Devereaux was out of the car in a moment and across the road to the rocks.

Two seconds later, the Renault surged around the blind turn and slammed into the left side and rear end of the Saab.

There had been two men.

One hurtled through the windshield, over the Saab, and over the cliff to the broken field below.

The second hit his head hard against the crumpled steering post.

The Saab and Renault ground into each other in slow motion. There was no fire.

Bits of metal exploded against the rocks around Devereaux where he crouched in a ditch. Below the road was the old castle sitting in the waters of Lac Leman. It was the place where Byron had come and meditated on the prisoner held there twelve years and written a poem. It was peaceful and of another world.

Devereaux ran to the door of the Renault. The driver was unconscious or dead. He could not open the crumpled door. The window was broken. Devereaux used his elbow to break more glass, to get a way into the car. Devereaux reached through the window and felt into the pocket of the driver. He pulled out the pistol. It was an ordinary Walther PPK with a short barrel and six hollow-point bullets seated in the clip. He shoved the pistol in his pocket.

The wallet was inside the vest pocket.

He opened the wallet and found a sheaf of French banknotes and a photograph of a young man and a young woman and an American Express card made out to Jonathan DeVole.

And a second card.

Devereaux stared at the second card.

It was plastic, cut hard and brittle exactly like an ordinary credit card.

Except it was gray. Without numbers or letters on it. The card was perfectly smooth and unmarked.

Devereaux saw that his hand was closing over the card as though to swallow it and make it disappear. It was as though his hand were separate from his body.

Devereaux knew the card.

It was familiar to him when he had worked for the R Section in a life he had abandoned.

The card was accepted at 120 machines located throughout the world, identifying the cardholder as a member of the operations division of R Section, a very secret intelligence agency of the United States.

Hanley's division.

NINE
Alexa Beneath the Stars

Alexa waited until dark to enter the apartment building. It was small and there was a concierge but Alexa had taken care of that—the concierge was distracted from her apartment on the ground floor by a boy who threw a brick through one of the ground-floor windows and then ran down the Rue de la Concorde Suisse. It was not so difficult to find vandals, even in Lausanne, if they were well paid.

She climbed to the third floor and went to the apartment at the end of the hall. She had waited outside the building all day, sitting in the Volkswagen at the end of the block, watching for any sign of life at all.

The information had come with unexpected precision and it was timely.

The agent named November—the second moon of November—had been observed twenty-four hours previously in this apartment, in this building. It had been determined by the resident extra at Geneva that he had been living there for nearly two years.

Why was everything so precise, so exact? And yet, Alexa had a strange feeling that this was all too easy. What was it about, exactly?

She wore a black sweater that had a high collar; she wore black cotton trousers and black running shoes. Her jacket was a variation of a sailor's pea coat. Her long black hair was tied up. She wore no makeup at all and her pale features were small and frail.

The lock was not so simple but she found the way in after a few moments with a pick and tumbler setter which electronically felt for the tumblers and tripped them.

The apartment was dark as it had been all day. It was still, save for the ticking of an electronic clock on the wall of the kitchen. The clock was quartz, the ticking was added to fake the sound of a real clock.

She went into all the rooms. She opened the closets. They did not have many clothes, the agent and his mistress.

There were no photographs. There was a sense of impermanence to the apartment.

She saw that the Panasonic answering machine was on but that there had been no calls. The red call button was not blinking.

She found a chair near the window where she could watch in the shadows down the length of the Rue de la Concorde Suisse.

He did not own a car but rented them often from the Avis garage next to the Lausanne train station.

He had not rented a car in a week. He was usually back in the apartment by eight. The mistress was gone, the resident extra in Geneva had no information on her. But he had so much other information that it amazed Alexa.

Alexa frowned in the darkness. This was not usual. She had spent two days in Zurich waiting for contact. She had not expected to be given much information—but when the contact was made she had received a cornucopia of detail. If they knew so much about this man, why had they not taken care of the matter before this, before the bungled business on the *Finlandia*?

Alexa removed the Uzi from her purse. It was made in France, fitted with a silencer, and it had eighteen shots. It was sufficient to tear a living man's body in half.

The final arrangements were her own. It was a form of self-protection. After all, if she were to survive, it must be on her own terms. KGB ran her on a very loose leash; it was necessary to the business at hand.

The quartz clock in the kitchen ticked with a false sound. The bright day had turned to clear night. There was a full moon and she could see the street clearly.

When she had been a child, living in the flats along the Lenin Prospekt in Moscow with her mother, her brother and her youngest sister—her father had been a colonel in the Soviet army and had spent long periods in command of troops on the Sino-Soviet border seven thousand miles to the east—she had thought once to count all the stars and end the mystery about the endless number of stars in the heavens. She was nine or ten and had a very precise mind and nature, however naive. She reasoned with her mother this way:

The stars we see cannot be infinite because the scope of heaven we see is not infinite. So it is possible to count all the stars you can see from Moscow.

Her mother, who was intelligent and who had been beautiful when she was young, said it was impossible because the sky changed each night as the earth revolved around the sun.

Alexa had said it was still possible. On one night, a determined person in Moscow (such as herself) could count all the stars visible from an apartment on the Lenin Prospekt. It could be done in winter, on a clear, cold night, when the night stretched from the middle of the afternoon to the middle of the next morning.

Her mother had seemed amused and would not argue with her. She was a child.

Alexa thought of a child growing inside her body. It would be a splendid idea. But not now. Not for a while yet. The child would be magnificent. It would be a boy.

She had waited until winter to count the stars and when winter came she was older and wiser and she knew it was foolish to want to limit the number of stars by counting them. It was better to ignore them. Or accept the word of the scientists who did such things.

Still.

What if she had counted all the stars on a clear winter's night in Moscow, from horizon to horizon? What would the number have been, all the stars seen with the naked eye? Would it have been possible at all?

She saw both men at the same time.

They approached from opposite corners, where the Rue de la Concorde Suisse ends in a terraced wall above the streets below that lead to the Cathedral.

They were on foot and there could be no car behind them because the walkway along the wall was a mere pedestrian path.

She watched them approach the building from opposite sides of the street.

She knew they were coming to this place and she felt trapped. Why had she been trapped?

For the first time, she felt a sense of guilt. Was there something in the past, something she had done or said that would have forced her Committee to list her for a ''wet contract''? A contract to be carried out as far away from Moscow Center as possible?

But she had made no mistake. The careful child who wanted to count all the stars above Moscow had made no mistake. What had Alexei said in Helsinki? The mistakes had to be blamed on someone.

She rose from the chair and looked down at the two men on opposite sides of the street. They were staring up at the darkened window where Alexa stood. They glanced at each other and she thought one of them shrugged.

They entered the building, one at a time.

The street was nearly fifty feet below. There was a balcony outside the window. At the end of the hall, there was a fire escape. She hesitated. She felt terribly confused.

When she decided, it was too late.

She went to the door and reached for the handle and heard steps in the hall.

She waited at the door, the length of the Uzi pistol extended away from her body.

There were no voices, only steps in the hall. Then one of them knocked on the door.

The three waited, two outside, Alexa inside.

The dark made all sounds more intense. The clock in the kitchen seemed to reverberate with sound.

They had trouble with the lock, just as she had. They opened the door cautiously.

Alexa fired through the door. The Uzi thumped and bucked in her hand. The door splintered and she heard them cry in pain and surprise. She expected them to push into the room. Instead, the second one retreated back into the hall.

That would be messy.

She sprayed six shots into the hall, firing from right to left as she filled the frame of the door, straddling the man on the floor dying between her legs.

The flash of her pistol was met with the *whump* of another pistol, fitted with a silencer.

They've killed the concierge, she thought dreamily in that moment of action. It was so messy and they didn't care, as though they wanted this to be done quickly or not at all. She thought they must be in a hurry and that puzzled her. All these thoughts crammed the moment needed to spray the darkened hallway with death from the Uzi.

The second one fell heavily and then she realized the first one was alive because he stirred against her feet. She lowered the pistol to finish him off—and stopped.

She knelt and turned him over.

The bullet had grazed his head, he was bleeding heavily, he might even live. His eyes were open wide but he did not seem to be conscious.

She reached into his pocket and found money. She pushed the bills into her own pocket. She stared at him in the moonlight and saw a man completely bald. He didn't even have eyebrows. She knelt and cradled his head and spoke to him harshly in the voice of the Moscow agent, the voice of death that is without sex or promise—only a threat:

"Why do you come to kill me?"

But the hairless one only stared wildly at her, frightened into unconsciousness or mere inability to speak.

She went through his pockets, all of them, turning over his body roughly to go through his pants. Nothing at all.

She went to the second one in the hall. One of the shots had caught him full in the face and now there was no face left. Brains were splattered against the wall behind the body.

Without distaste, she knelt again and pushed her hands patiently through his clothing.

There was a wallet at least.

She opened the wallet and saw the bills.

There was nothing else.

Two contractors, she thought. Not even someone from Moscow Center but contractors hired on the broad assassins' market in Europe. They might even be Swiss.

But Switzerland was a dangerous country to act so boldly in. They had not been careful at all. They had come into a peaceful neighborhood in the old city and they had surely killed the concierge to gain access to this apartment.

It occurred to Alexa then they had not come to kill her at all. But to kill the same man she had been sent to kill. She felt anxious. She smelled the beginning of death in the hall. It was the warm and sweet smell of the slaughterhouse and killing ground.

She stepped over the body in the hall and went back into the apartment. She looked around her, took her purse from the chair and glanced down again at Rue de la Concorde Suisse. The lights of Lausanne, low and few, spread down the hill. The sky was full of stars, too many to count because one no longer could believe in counting stars.

TEN
Breach of Security

The assistant national security advisor was the less formal contact between the executive branch and the various intelligence agencies that operated under the umbrella of the Director of Central Intelligence. These included R Section.

Yackley had not been kept waiting. The assistant advisor was not a rude man. His name was Weinstein and he was more intelligent than most of the people he had to deal with.

His office on the sixth floor of the Executive Office Building—the ornate hunk of Victorian architecture that squats between Seventeenth Avenue and West Executive Place, just off the White House lawn—was the office of a transient. There were no photographs on the rather plain government-issue metal desk; there was not the requisite couch or even two upholstered chairs set off to the side for informal tête-á-têtes. Everything in the office seemed careless and temporary. There were cardboard boxes and a battered Selectric II typewriter on a rickety metal typing stand. The assistant advisor might have been his own aide-de-camp. He projected a sense of energy, of wearing shirts two days in a row, and of being a bachelor who probably did not eat very well. He wore horn-rimmed glasses that made his thin face seem thinner. He was forty-one years old and looked thirty.

"Hi, Frank," he said, as his secretary led Yackley into the office. "Get you something? Coke or coffee or something?"

"No thanks, Perry," Yackley said. He felt uncomfortable with the informality yet thrilled by the intimacy. Everyone did. The administration projected a sense of order, tuxedos and gray business suits. Perry Weinstein might have been a holdover from the Carter administration. Save that his accent was West Coast and his politics were the kind satisfying to readers of *National Review*.

Yackley sat down in one of two side chairs pulled up to Perry Weinstein's desk.

"We have a problem," he began in that way of his that indicated a long recitation of the facts. Yackley was a careful man who carefully screened his own words before uttering them.

"I know. How is Hanley?"

"It's too early. He's still being tested—"

"It's a shame. The best sort of bureaucrat—no strong partisan stance, devotion to duty beyond and above. I think I met him the first time when I moved in. Two years ago. A strong 201 file—"

"You read his 201?" Yackley seemed amazed. It was such a pedestrian thing to do. There must have been 150 bureaucrats at Hanley's level in the intelligence establishment, counting all the agencies.

Weinstein nodded. There was no color in his face. His eyes were light blue. Everything about him spoke of innocence, of straight-forwardness. Naturally, everyone was suspicious of that.

"I've read everyone's," Weinstein admitted with a smile and a blush. "Two years. It doesn't seem that long. I'm still not moved in."

Yackley said nothing to that.

"Well, what's it about?"

"You saw the transcripts I sent over. When Hanley tried to make contact with this former agent—"

"Sleeper named November," said Weinstein. Perfect memory. Mind like a steel trap. Never misses a trick. Every cliché in the large book kept in Washington applied to Weinstein. And Yackley, a master of clichés, was just the man to apply them.

"November's come awake again," said Yackley. He spoke the words with care and precision. He said, "There were two incidents

in two days. We sent two agents—contractors—to make contact with Devereaux, to see what his game was. I indicated in my memo that I was disturbed about Hanley. Lest there was a breach of security. I'm afraid we have troubles—''

Weinstein waited. There was no judgment on his face. He might have been waiting for a bus.

"Devereaux apparently killed both men. On a mountain road outside of Lausanne. The details are incomplete and we have a stationmaster from Zurich down there—''

"It would seem better to have sent someone from Geneva or even France. I suppose a German speaker will seem odd in Lausanne.''

Perry Weinstein said this softly and quickly, also without judgment. But Yackley blushed. "He was the easiest man—''

"It doesn't matter," Weinstein said. His voice said that it did.

"Then there were two more men killed. This time in Devereaux's apartment in Lausanne.''

"And who were they?''

"We don't have the faintest idea. Except that it's obvious that Devereaux is on some sort of rampage. I mean, we sent two agents to make inquiries—and they're killed and—''

"How killed?''

"He arranged an auto accident. I don't have details. He was in a car on a road, apparently the car driven by our two chasers was—''

"This seems botched, doesn't it, Frank?''

Yackley felt acute embarrassment. There was silence. Weinstein stood behind his desk, his hand fiddling with some papers. The desk was littered with papers, some of them secret. Behind Yackley was the window that opened to a view of the White House. The White House occupied a bucolic space in the middle of crowded Washington with its littered streets full of hurrying office workers and the shuddering roars of planes bombarding the suburbs from National Airport. Life and noise and layers of society pretending other layers did not exist—and in the middle of it all, the quaint White House with the porticos and plain windows and the gentle lawn where the children gathered to roll Easter eggs with the President.

Only the ugly concrete bunkers at the edges of the lawns reminded you of the absurd importance of it all.

"Yes. I was concerned from the beginning, I was in a hurry to see if there had been a breach. I think there has been—"

"How? Your tapes don't show anything."

"Hanley had other ways to reach Devereaux—"

"Why Devereaux? I mean, what is the importance of this agent except that he doesn't exist anymore?" Weinstein softened all the hard words. You might have missed them if you weren't listening closely.

"He killed two men. Chasers from Section."

"Oh, yes, the chasers," Weinstein said. "What was it the chasers were going to do when they contacted Devereaux?"

Yackley winced. "I didn't send them. Hanley—"

Weinstein ignored that. "Wasn't this a bit drastic? Why not send down your stationmaster from Zurich?"

"Hanley must have ordered the chasers. Before he . . . went away. It was done without my knowledge. But they existed, they were sent from Section. Hanley must have—"

Weinstein seemed to consider this, fixing his pale eyes on a spot somewhere above Yackley's head. "Hanley," he said. "Hanley is very ill, I think you said?"

Yackley cleared his throat. "He is being tested," he said. "It's not possible to discuss the thing with him now . . . At least I don't know if we . . ."

Weinstein's eyes focused full on Yackley's face then. "I see," he said.

Yackley seemed confused and reached for a metaphor to help him: "I would have preferred to let sleeping agents lie; I wouldn't want to disturb the fabric."

The mixed metaphor amused Weinstein. He let the trace of a smile float across his pale, soft features. He pushed the horn-rimmed glasses up his long nose until they reached the bridge.

"Well, what about Devereaux? Where is he? After his murderous rampage?"

Yackley looked up sharply. Was Weinstein mocking him?

74

He wanted to use just the right words. He thought he found them: "We don't know."

"I see."

Struggled on: "As far as I can tell, from signal section, the Swiss are puzzled as well. And they've got a lot more men looking for him."

"Devereaux makes trouble, doesn't he?"

"Yes."

"Disturbed," Weinstein said.

"Crazy," Yackley said.

"Outside the rules."

"Not a team player."

Weinstein blinked. "This isn't polo, Frank."

"I meant—"

"Hanley tells him about Nutcracker. What about Nutcracker, Frank? You said it was important. What is in that old man's mind?"

"We're trying to find out—"

"And why did he say to Devereaux 'There are no spies'? Tell me that, Frank."

"I . . . I." But there were things Frank Yackley did not know. Or did not seem to know.

"Code? Was he making a joke out of it? Like the graffiti in your washrooms over at D.A.?"

Yackley was amazed that Weinstein knew about the oars on the walls. He had had the walls scrubbed clean in two days. Weinstein really was on top of things.

"I wish you had come to me earlier," Weinstein said. "Before all this mess with Hanley. When you first had suspicions about Hanley."

That was a warning, Yackley thought. "I don't see what else I could have done. It was so unusual. Nutcracker was such a strange idea."

"No one denies that," Weinstein said. He turned from Yackley to the window and clasped his hands behind his back. The White House below was bright under a bright March sky. Washington was warm with the approach of spring. The coming season seemed to

move visibly from day to day. The blossoms would be blooming soon on the Japanese cherry trees that surrounded the tidal basin south of the White House.

"Why has Devereaux gone crazy?" Perry Weinstein said in a soft voice, still facing the window.

"I don't know."

"Hanley. And Devereaux."

"Hanley isn't crazy. I think he's been under a strain, I think—"

"You think security may have been breached—"

"I think it is my duty—"

"Yes, of course." Perry Weinstein turned around and faced Yackley, who fidgeted in the small side chair. "So what do we do about our long-sleeping agent?"

"That's what I want to know."

"You want a sanction, is that it?"

"I . . . I don't know. I really don't know," Yackley said, dancing away from the word.

"There is no sanction," Weinstein said. "The term does not exist. It cannot be authorized. It isn't in law or in case studies. It is illegal to sanction anyone, let alone a former employee of the government. It is impossible to authorize a sanction." The words were delivered without tone, softly, as though a child in first grade, without understanding, were reciting the Pledge of Allegiance.

Yackley waited.

"What do you suppose he will do?"

"Go to the Opposition," Yackley said. "He has committed himself. He killed our chasers."

"You really think so?"

"I think so. It is my best guesstimate," Yackley said. "I have asked Mrs. Neumann for the full file, 201 and appendages. Here it is." He handed the file in the folder to Weinstein but Weinstein did not take it. "Put it on the desk," Weinstein said, staring at Yackley with curious eyes.

Yackley let the file drop onto the papers already littering the desk.

"You want a judgment." Weinstein did not say it as a question.

"Yes."

"All right."

"The sooner the better."

"I understand."

"It's important . . . that—"

"That it be handled inside the Section, you mean? Not by NSA? Not by CIA?" Weinstein's voice, for the first time, took a tone that might be considered mocking. "Yes, I figured out why you wanted to see me. The buck stops here. It was the only true thing Harry Truman ever said. And then I doubt he said it in the first place." Perry Weinstein smiled. He took Yackley's hand though it had not been extended. "I'll get back to you by morning," he said. His eyes were cloudy now.

ELEVEN
Hanley's Game

It was March 11. Hanley had been held for a week and a half. He had learned to adjust to life at St. Catherine's.

Sister Mary Domitilla thought his progress was absolutely wonderful. She began to include Mr. Hanley in her prayers and in her sacrifices, including the sacrifice that involved the pain of cutting her nails severely almost every night. Her fingers were always raw and she refused to put salve on them.

Spring was not ready to come to the valley. There had been snow the previous morning and the valley was enveloped in whiteness from the streets of the old town all the way up the hill to the St. Catherine's grounds. The four-wheel-drive vehicles marched through the hilly streets and people with ordinary cars did the best they could. They were all accustomed to hills and slick streets and the sense of isolation in endless winter.

Hanley was given clothing as a gift for good behavior on his sixth day. The clothing consisted of blue denims and a blue shirt marked with his name above the left pocket. He looked like a prisoner.

They ate in their own ward at night but there was a time, between three and five, when they went to the enclosure between the two fences for exercise. They could run along the enclosure or they could just stand around and breathe the clear, damp air of the valley. Hanley chose to run. Dr. Goddard said he was pleased because his response to the situation was "appropriate."

The truth was, Goddard was puzzled.

The dose of HL-4 prescribed for Hanley from the first day was enough to render him harmless, perfectly docile, drowsy and enfeebled. Hanley was certainly more compliant than he had been— but why should he show such extraordinary energy in the afternoons in the yard between the electrified fence and the inner fence?

The electricity was never shut off for these afternoon excursions but the killing voltage was turned down. Now and again, one of the patients would make a bolt for the fence and touch it and be knocked down by the force of the electrical charge.

Hanley had been given a battery of examinations that showed he was in reasonable health for a man of his age. Dr. Goddard, in his second interview, said the absence of any physical cause of Hanley's illness proved Dr. Goddard's thesis that Hanley suffered from depression. The depression was induced by a chemical imbalance, Dr. Goddard said, as well as a "cross-wired burnout" in the brain.

Hanley had blinked at that.

"The brain is like a computer," Goddard said. "The information it can process is controlled by the raw data fed to it. But computers can go haywire. That's why computer owners have service contracts. That's why you have government health insurance—it's your service contract, in a sense."

Hanley was given pills twice a day, at the morning and evening meals. He and the other patients stood in line at the nurse's station outside the mess hall and docilely received the pills prescribed by Dr. Goddard. These were issued by the nurse on duty. In the morning, it was Sister Duncan, a simple soul of pressed habit and acne-infested features who could not be more than twenty, Hanley thought. In the evening, it was Nurse Cox, a formidable beast in a nurse's white pants suit. The difference in their techniques helped Hanley's game.

Both issued the pill and waited for the patient to swallow it.

There was a technique of slipping the pill under one's tongue and throwing the paper cup of water back on the tongue and making a swallowing noise. The nurse then was to examine the mouth, to see that the pill had been actually swallowed. The patient opened wide and made an "ah" sound and then lifted his tongue, first on

one side and then the other, to show that the pill was not being concealed.

Fortunately, Sister Duncan hated to look into people's mouths. She was still a nurse in training and she thought there might be matters of human anatomy she might be able to avoid in the future: Men's sex organs, blood and bedpans.

Hanley could not fool Nurse Cox. He didn't even try.

And so, during the days, his strength increased and the nausea and sense of profound depression only returned at night, when the evening pill took effect. He slept badly because of the pill; he would awake at three in the morning, sweating, shivering, wondering where he was.

He knew he would never ask Dr. Goddard about the pills he was forced to take. Dr. Goddard did not invite questions because he had all the answers. Dr. Goddard, Hanley thought, knew exactly what the pills were doing, to Hanley and to the other patients.

They were a sad lot.

Kaplan had been the third-ranking officer inside the Internal Revenue Service until it was revealed he was the self-ordained founder of the Church of Tax Rebellion, a nonprofit enterprise in Falls Church, Virginia. Kaplan had not paid income tax for fifteen years—and somehow this fact had escaped the computers which constantly cross-checked the tax forms for those in IRS to make certain the collectors were collecting from themselves as well. Poor Kaplan: If it had been a simple matter of fraud, it would not have been so bad. But his scheme was perfectly legal, according to at least six experts in the department. There was the matter of freedom of religion, even for IRS employees. It was important to cure Kaplan of his delusion that the Lord had not meant that one should render to Caesar anything more substantial than a Bronx cheer.

Kaplan, Hanley thought, was crazy. And then he learned that Kaplan had been in the place for two years. He had disintegrated in mind and body in that time. He scarcely weighed more than a hundred pounds. He spent his days reciting scriptural verses and summarized rulings from Tax Court.

Hanley thought he would not last as long as Kaplan.

There were no women, save the nuns and Nurse Cox, in Ward

Seven. Hanley had inquired about that and been told that women were treated at St. Trinian's in Ohio.

There's a network of these places, Hanley thought with horror then. And he had been unaware of them.

It was the second Sunday of his incarceration. The model patients from Ward Seven were taken to the chapel for the "Patients' Mass" at nine in the morning. The chapel was segregated at this mass and no outsiders were allowed. There were no services of other denominations. Kaplan conducted his own services in his room inside Ward Seven but he had only three converts who joined him for the ceremonies involved. He tore up symbolic 1040 forms (actually, since he was not permitted forms, sheets of writing paper with "1040" inscribed on them) and distributed them to the members. They ate them.

On Saturdays and Sundays, Sister Duncan handled the administration of the morning and evening pills. Hanley, by Sunday morning, began to feel much better. The poison of the pills was having less effect on his body.

It was cool and damp and the clouds clung low in the valley. At two in the afternoon, the patients—except those locked in their rooms for various infractions of the rules of St. Catherine's—were permitted visitors.

Hanley was surprised to see them.

There were Leo and Lydia Neumann, emerging from a large, dirt-streaked gray Oldsmobile, crossing the gravel path that crunched beneath their feet.

He felt so grateful that he realized he might weep. He could not weep. It was more than a sign of weakness now; it was a sign of craziness.

On Sunday afternoon, they were allowed to walk on the grounds beyond the double fence. On Sunday, a special effort was made by staff and patients to show the normality of the surroundings and the institution.

Hanley led them down the path through a grove of elms. Buds decorated the thin branches of the elms. It would be spring, even if there was snow on the valley floor.

Leo Neumann was not in government service. He was a me-

chanical engineer and he cut his wife's hair, which is why it was short and spiky and looked terrible. Leo Neumann was a man unaware of his faults; everything he did was a matter of love or self-respect. Cutting his wife's hair every three weeks was love and Lydia Neumann understood that and accepted it. Leo Neumann knew what his wife did and never said a word about it. They couldn't talk about their jobs in any case: Lydia did not understand engineering and Leo was horrified by computers.

The gravel path circled back, almost to the double fences, and they did not speak beyond greetings. At the fences, Hanley paused and gazed at the path between the fences where he was confined with the others in Ward Seven on their daily outings during the week.

"You seem a lot better," said Lydia Neumann.

Hanley turned and looked at her. "Do I?"

"Your old self," said Leo Neumann. He had met Hanley only once.

"I was wrong," Lydia said. She stared at Hanley with the gaze of a mother examining a sick child. "I argued against sending you here."

"You were not wrong," Hanley said. He looked at Leo. "Can I speak to you for a moment, Mrs. Neumann?"

Mrs. Neumann and Hanley left Leo. They strolled a little further along the double fence, looking in at the path between the fences. When he thought they were alone, Hanley said:

"I was depressed. It began last summer, during all the spy exchanges. I started to examine them. I used computers to set up scenarios."

"I know," she said.

"Of course you know. But not the results. Not the results. The computer logic—I think I've learned it well enough to understand that the logic is not really logic but a way out of a puzzle once the puzzle is described."

"Something like that," Lydia Neumann said. "It has as much morality as you give to the puzzle."

"Morality was not a factor," Hanley said. He stared at the double

fences. "We're confined there, between the fences, during the week. The outer fence is electrified. When the juice is turned down, they let the dogs run between the fences at night. Three Dobermans."

Lydia Neumann said nothing. Her face was white. Hanley saw her hand was clenched. She stared at the path between the fences.

"They're killing me," Hanley said. Quietly.

"No—"

"The pills come morning and night. On Saturday, I get rid of the pills. I feel much better today. Tomorrow, it's back to the pills. This is called HL-4. Can you find out what HL-4 is?"

And he handed her one of the morning pills, wrapped in Kleenex. She stared at it in her hand and then slipped it into her pocket.

"I have to get out of here," Hanley said. "The first day here, the psychiatrist in charge, Dr. Goddard, he sprayed me with Mace when I asked for my clothes—"

"You were kept naked?"

"In one of those hospital gowns."

"This is horrible," Lydia Neumann said.

"Most of these places are, I think now," Hanley said. His voice was very soft. "I called Devereaux. Twice, I think, when I was ill—"

"But you were ill, you really were ill—"

"I must have been. It seems like a long time ago. Like thinking of yourself as a child. I really must have been ill."

"You called him. I thought that's who it was. When Yackley had the conference. On what to do with you—"

"And you stuck up for me." Hanley's eyes were wet. "Don't mistake my tears, Mrs. Neumann. I'm not crazy. I'm really not crazy. I feel so broken down. Tears are the last refuge of the weak—"

"Cut it out, man," Lydia Neumann said. "I don't think you're crazy. You were sick. You called Devereaux—"

"Mrs. Neumann. I need an outside contractor. I wanted Devereaux to . . . come back into the trade for a while. I have to find out something—"

"What?"

83

"The computer analyzed the spy transactions of last summer. Before the summit. First there were two men from the West German intelligence agency who defected East. Then the Brits picked up the mole in Copenhagen and revealed he had been turned for three years. Then CIA picked up that Soviet in Rome. And then he defects back to the Soviet embassy in D.C. There was also the Chinese agent in Seoul and the two ROKs uncovered in Peking. Trumpets and flourishes. So I went through our own network. Who belongs to us and who, on our side, belongs to them? And how do we know which is which?"

Lydia Neumann blinked. Hanley seemed so intense. He was staring at the path between the two fences. Hanley's face was pale and his eyes were dull. He seemed very tired.

"I wondered if there were any spies at all," he said.

"What are you talking about?"

"We go into budget crunch and the people at NSA can show figures—what they are based on, I don't know—they can show figures that show eighty-five to ninety percent of all intelligence is done by machine. Satellites, computers, bugs. Raw data. The listening post at Cheltenham, at Taipei. The goddamn space shuttle overflies the Soviet Union and Eastern Bloc on every second mission. It all comes down to coming down to the mountain. I was convinced of it."

Tears again. Mrs. Neumann looked away while Hanley found a handkerchief and used it.

"Yackley was on me day and night. Cutbacks in stationmasters, networks . . . my God, he thought it was all just so much meat cut off the bone. It wasn't that. And then there was Nutcracker—"

He stopped, frightened.

"What are you talking about?"

"Nothing. Nothing at all. Forget that. It was over long ago." Frightened. He gazed at Mrs. Neumann. "I played with the computer and there were all these coincidences in which we got their spies to defect to us and our spies defected at the same time, almost as part of a game. Musical chairs. But aren't there real spies?"

She said, "You should know that."

"But Yackley doesn't believe in them."

"Yackley is a fool," she said.

"Yackley does not believe in spies. He says there are no spies any more than there are elves or leprechauns. There are only intelligence agents on each side analyzing computer materials, making value judgments . . ."

"Hanley, get hold of yourself."

He was crying again.

"Pawns. He said they are pawns. The game moves in feints and little gestures. I said he was wrong. I would prove it. I could have proved it—"

"Proved what?"

He looked through his tears at her. She wanted to understand, he thought.

And he knew he didn't trust her at all.

"They know our secrets, the Opposition," he said. "We know their secrets. That's all it is, two sides equal, starting from scratch just to stay even. But what if they had advantages over us that we didn't have?"

"What are you talking about?"

Hanley looked puzzled. He put his handkerchief away. "I called November, I wanted him to understand. At least, he said he was outside the game. Maybe everyone was in it together. Even you?"

Mrs. Neumann bit her lip.

"I have to get out of here," Hanley said. He looked at the path between the fences. "Dr. Goddard keeps saying 'eventually' as though he knew it was never going to happen. Eventually can mean when I die. I have to get out of here."

"What do you want me to do?"

He stared at her. "Whatever you do, don't pray for me. I have a nun here. She prays for me. It is sufficient. I couldn't stand any more prayers."

"Hanley—"

"Get me out of here," Hanley said in a low and terrible voice. "I need to get away, get away from the drugs and routine. I have to think about—" He almost said something and stopped. "I have to think."

"I'll talk to the New Man, to Yackley—"

"No, Mrs. Neumann." Very cold, very much like the old Hanley who had not been ill. "You will not talk to that man. I've talked to you too much. Do you want my secrets? Try my test: Do not talk to Yackley. You are going to have to help me get out of here."

"I can't."

"November," he said.

She shrank from his grasp and the name. "He's buried, dead in files."

"Asleep," Hanley said.

"Buried," she said.

"Wake him." His eyes glittered. "But you're afraid, aren't you? You don't want him to wake up, do you? My God, is it all true?"

"Is what true?"

But he had turned. He began to run back toward the ward. She started after him. She stopped, listened to his footsteps. Poor frightened man, she thought.

Perhaps the horrible best thing to do for Hanley was to keep him here.

Right between the fences.

TWELVE
Moscow Is Waiting

Not all of the intelligence operations of KGB are headquartered in the dreary building on Dhzerzhinski Square, which the other intelligence services call Moscow Center. The Committee for External Observation and Resolution, for example, is located in a long and windowless building two miles east of the square.

The man who was called Gorki (by the same computer that named Alexa) sat in his office at the end of a long hall. There was a reception area at the end of the hall and three closed doors. One of the doors led to Gorki; a second led to a supply room; the room beyond the third door was not spoken of by anyone.

Gorki's office was wrapped in darkness made more acute by the fluorescent lamp on his desk. Everything in the office had been chosen as a prop, save for the giant General Electric air conditioner built into the wall. The building was something of an embarrassment. It had taken too long to construct, it was gloomy (even by Russian standards), and the marble corridors had been stripped at last because the great slabs of marble kept falling off the walls. A party undersecretary had been injured shortly after the building opened by a piece of marble that separated from the wall. The stripped marble was now used as flooring in the various dachas of high Party officials around Moscow.

Gorki's office was decorated with the portraits of three men:

Lenin, Felix Dhzerzhinski, the founder of the secret police, and Gorbachev. He had no other ornaments. He was a spare man with Eurasian features and small, quick eyes that seemed to glitter in the light of the single lamp in the room. His skin was parchment and it was yellow with age and liver disease.

The man across from him was an agent called Alexei, a man of little consequence from the Helsinki station.

Alexei was sweating profusely though the office was very cool in the way a tomb is cool.

Gorki did not smile or speak; he sat very still for a long time. He took a file folder and dropped it on the desk and indicated with a nod of his head that Alexei was to retrieve it. The desk was very wide and Alexei, sitting in an overstuffed chair in the cramped room in front of the large desk, had to rise awkwardly and reach across the desk for the file folder. When he sat down heavily, he was sweating all the more. He had to squint to see the photographs.

"She killed these men," Gorki began.

"I don't understand. I don't understand any of this," said Alexei. He really didn't understand. He stared at the faces. There were four photographs. They were grouped in twos by paper clips. The first man was shown as he appeared for his official photograph (updated each year—the Russians have great faith in the power of photographs to identify people). The second had a man with his face blown away.

"It's the same man?" said Alexei.

"Of course."

The second grouping featured a hairless man staring at a camera. The "after" picture showed him on a slab in a morgue, his eyes open, a large wound on the side of his head.

"She killed them? Alexa?"

"Alexa. She was informed at Zurich they would accompany her on her . . . assignment. The contract on this second November. November." Gorki closed his eyes a moment. When he opened them again, they were liquid and on fire. "Will no one get rid of November for me? Does he subvert every agent? Does he have nine lives?"

Alexei said nothing. The questions were not to be answered.

"Alexa was our most formidable agent in her specialty. What has happened to her? She goes to Lausanne and she betrays us. Why?"

"How were they killed?"

"She had gone to the apartment of the agent. The American we had told her was the second November—"

"The blue moon," Alexei said.

Gorki blinked. "I beg your pardon?"

"I was—" Alexei blushed. "It was nothing, Director."

Gorki resumed in the same sandpaper voice. "I want to question you as I will question our stationmaster in Zurich. I want to be absolutely certain that Alexa understood the contract and what was expected of her. The two agents she murdered in that apartment—I say 'murdered' because it was nothing more than that—I want to know exactly how this came about. There was an old woman also killed. The police in Switzerland are not very happy. The missions in Geneva and Zurich have been shut down in part until the matter is over—"

"How do you know she killed them? It might have been this November."

"The police are looking for this woman. There was a child she hired to distract the concierge, to gain entry to the apartment in the first place. It appears she ambushed Yuri and Vladimir—the agents, I can use their names now, they are dead. November is gone, Alexa is gone. What does that suggest to you?"

"Comrade Director," Alexei began. "I don't know what to make of it. I told her to go to Zurich. To wait for her instructions. You have talked to our Zurich stationmaster—"

"Not yet. He is sent for. He filed a long dispatch and he is flying into Moscow this afternoon from Zurich." Gorki projected a sense of self-pity: Alexei knew this would be marked against him; something like this had to have blame affixed. It was nearly a repeat of what had happened to the agent Denisov who had been sent into the United States once, to Florida, who had been turned by November and induced to defect . . . And now Alexa. "I cannot emphasize too strongly the displeasure felt by the Committee—"

"My deepest sympathies, Comrade," said Alexei, who under-

stood that the focus of scrutiny was on Gorki and that Gorki wished to shift it to another. But not Alexei. Alexei had been in Helsinki. Alexei knew nothing. Alexei was quite certain he could not be blamed.

Gorki had spent the morning with the Secretary of the Fourth Directorate. It had not been a good morning. A new administration in the Soviet Union was cleaning house in all areas, including the area called Committee for State Security. There were, nominally, 300,000 agents who qualified to call themselves KGB. But some were nothing more than timekeepers in factories that consistently fell below quota or where the level of theft was unusually high. Simple policemen and nothing more. The business of intelligence-gathering and disinformation dissemination and the business of agents like Alexa—they were handled by a select group, carefully screened, given long profile tests and psychological examinations. How could Alexa have gone crazy?

It was the perpetual question of the Secretary of the Fourth Directorate, who had pounded his desk again and again, until the little toy railroad engine on the desk danced to the edge and fell off and broke. It did not improve the Secretary's humor. There were break-downs in security at every level. Just this winter, the second man in San Francisco station in the United States had been seduced into defection by a homosexual CIA agent. A homosexual! the Secretary had stormed. Why did our profiles not screen out the homosexuals?

Gorki could not explain that the homosexual agent had been sent to San Francisco in the first place to seduce other homosexuals in positions of power inside Silicon Valley. The world of spies, Gorki thought, was a mirror constantly reflecting different images—but always the mirror image of itself.

What was real? The mirror or the thing beyond the mirror?

Alexa was an embarrassment particularly because November had been presumed dead once and then presumed to be another man— a man named Ready who was still unidentified in the morgue in Helsinki. Was it so simple to fool a bureaucracy? the Secretary had asked with sarcasm as he put the pieces of the broken toy train into his center drawer.

Gorki had no answer that would satisfy either of them. He interrupted his thoughts to speak: "You and Alexa worked together. A long time ago."

"Yes, Comrade Director," said Alexei. "I reminded her of this when I saw her in Helsinki. I can assure you, the meeting was brief. I had many matters—"

"You were reprimanded—"

"I can assure you, we met in the open, in the lobby of the Presidentti hotel. I told her the assignment as I knew it and she caught the afternoon plane to Zurich." He reached into his pocket for a notebook. "Flight 21, Finnair to Zurich, it left at 14:22 hours—"

"Yes," said Gorki. "We know." He sounded disappointed. He sounded tired. Where would he be able to begin?

The red light on the telephone console flashed on.

He picked up the receiver and said nothing.

He replaced it without a word. He looked across at Alexei.

"Go back to the hotel, Alexei. We'll send for you—"

"Comrade Director—"

Gorki looked at him sharply.

Alexei blushed, struggled to rise, and squeezed out of the chair. He went to the door in the dark room and looked back for a moment. If only there was something he could say.

But he opened the door in silence, stepped outside and closed it. The secretary in the bare, depressing foyer with its linoleum floor and blank white walls stared at him. Alexei saw that a light on her telephone console was flashing. There was a call waiting for Gorki and he wished to take it alone; it was probably from the Zurich stationmaster, kept in another anteroom, waiting to tell Gorki that the problem of Alexa had been the fault of the man in Helsinki, that he must have fouled the message in some way. Alexei felt very sorry for himself as he crossed the bare reception room with its straight wooden chairs lined along one wall. He said something to the secretary, apologized, took his coat from the rack, and opened the door that led to the hall.

Gorki picked up the telephone again.

He heard the voice of his secretary. She said the call was waiting on the third line, the one protected from listening devices by the expedient of a black box that emitted radio signals to jam the line. It was not as efficient and marvelous as the electronic scrambler system used by the Americans but it worked well enough. He dialed to line three and waited.

The line crackled and then was silent. Then he spoke in a whisper: "Moscow is waiting."

They were the usual code words.

The voice at the other end of the line finished the obligatory salutation: "Everything must go ahead."

So. The code was complete.

Gorki realized he felt immense dread in that moment. He gripped the receiver tightly.

He knew the voice on the line. There was no mistake.

It was Alexa.

THIRTEEN
Captain Boll

Devereaux walked into the apartment building on the Rue de la Concorde Suisse. It was a bright morning, three days of hiding after the incident on the road to Chillon. He had taken the time of retreat to try to think his way through all that had happened. Twice he had visited Philippe in the school the boy attended. Philippe had understood about everything Devereaux told him. To see the understanding in Philippe's clear blue eyes—which were set hot and shining in that brown face—was to see a clear reflection of his own thoughts.

He did not try to telephone Rita Macklin in the troubled Philippines. There was no way to explain to her what he would do next.

They had had a conversation once upon a time and it had never reached a resolution.

In the conversation, Rita said, "Would you try to go back? Into the old trade?"

In the conversation—which they both believed they had never actually taken part in—Devereaux replied, "I would never go back. That's what we went through all that for. That's why we can be together."

Rita said, "But if you had to go back. To survive?"

"I wouldn't do it. But if I had to go back, to survive, what would it do to us? I mean, what would you do then?" Because they both

knew the linchpin that held them together was that he was quit of the old trade.

It was a conversation that always stopped at that point—if it ever took place in reality or only in their separate thoughts. It had to stop there. Neither of them wanted to know the end of the conversation.

Devereaux turned in at the gate and crossed the walk lined with tulips to the door. He expected what he found there.

He opened the door to the lobby and the large policeman in bulky blue seemed to have been studying him through the glass. The Swiss are not subtle about their weapons. The policeman had already produced an automatic weapon—it looked to Devereaux like a variation on the Uzi—and had it pointed at Devereaux when he entered the lobby. The policeman had some words and Devereaux gave him some others.

The journey to the police station was framed in silence. Devereaux had made all the necessary calls abroad from the hotel in Lugano, during the three days of his hiding.

The police station of Lausanne smelled exactly like all the other police stations in the world. There was sweat, a certain musty sense of hopelessness, and the smell of despair that is mated with the sounds of iron doors closing shut very hard.

Captain Boll was on the second floor and his room was spare. The window faced south, toward the lake, and you could even see the lake through the trees. The trees were gaining foliage quickly in the warm sun and thickening above the red rooftops on the terraces below.

Captain Boll was even bulkier than the policeman who had been waiting in the apartment building. He did not wear a uniform and he seemed put out. His eyes were small, not particularly shrewd, and his brows beetled together above a long, wide nose that betrayed some liking for Swiss wines.

Boll indicated a hard chair in the middle of the room—directly in front of the large, bare desk. Devereaux sat down and waited. His face was wreathed in wrinkles and calm. His eyes were steady

and cool. He felt ready—which was not the same as feeling in charge. To do something was to exist. He had begun the process.

Boll said his name and Devereaux waited.

"This is about murder. Three people killed in your building. Two of them outside your apartment."

Devereaux said nothing. Words were not really expected, he thought. Captain Boll had something to say.

But Boll surprised him by waiting as well, his hands flat and placid as rowboats on the desktop.

"I was in Lugano," Devereaux began. "Three days. Visiting my son."

"I know that," Captain Boll said, surprising him for a second time. "It was convenient to be in Lugano, wasn't it?"

"I don't know what you're talking about."

"The policeman said you didn't seem surprised to be arrested."

"I am rarely surprised. Or perhaps my innocence reassures me," Devereaux said.

"You aren't accused of anything."

"Of course I am," he said.

Silence again. There was a wonderful warm breeze from the south that brought smells of the lake and the trees through the window. The bare room warmed with the sun. The two men waited. The silence was complete.

Captain Boll sighed. He got up and went to the window and looked down at the housetops. "I should be sailing today. It's early but it is running good and no one is in the lake," Captain Boll said. His voice was surprisingly soft, Devereaux thought. Devereaux was on guard now because the soft voice did not seem to fit the big man or the situation they were talking about.

"You are an American agent." Boll turned as he said it.

"Was," Devereaux began.

"Peterson," said Captain Boll.

"That's one of the names," Devereaux said, giving ground a little the way a fisherman feeds the line after the hook goes in.

"How did this killing concern you?"

"I don't know."

95

"But it did concern you?"

"It must have," Devereaux said. "There would be too much coincidence to suppose it didn't."

"You are retired. From your . . . profession?"

"Yes."

"You are much too young."

"I am much too tired to continue."

Boll smiled. The smile might have meant anything.

"The same with me. But I have not grown rich enough yet to sail every day."

"I was in Lugano," Devereaux said.

"Yes. And the woman at the brasserie, Claudette Longtemps, she said two men came for you the day before. They questioned her and threatened her. Very nasty people. They were killed. But you were in Lugano. So. Did you have someone kill them?"

"No," Devereaux said.

"A woman, perhaps?"

For the moment, puzzlement crossed Devereaux's face. That made Boll frown. Was he such a good actor?

"A woman, M. Devereaux?" said Captain Boll.

"I don't understand." The words came out simply, like the truth.

"A half hour before this horrible thing, a woman—a woman who was noticed with great interest by so many men in the area that their descriptions make me believe she is quite beautiful—hired one of our young thugs in Lausanne to break the window of the lobby of the building in the Rue de la Concorde Suisse. The woman wanted to draw the concierge from the lobby briefly enough to pass into the building. To go to your rooms, M. Devereaux."

"What description?"

"It is not your wife, M. Devereaux. We have had a good long time to check on everything. Your wife is a journalist?"

"Yes. She is not my wife," he added, automatically trying to separate Rita from this though he knew that was not possible.

"She is in Manila. She booked Swissair. She left a wide trail."

Devereaux twisted in the chair. He realized it was designed in such a way that it would never be comfortable, like one of those

modern stools but attempted from time to time by famous architects which never work out.

"Rita is a journalist, nothing more. I came to Switzerland to live, to be on the edge of things and not in them anymore."

"Do you think I'm a policeman, monsieur? I am something more than that. The Swiss are prepared for nearly everything, monsieur. That is our nature. That is why nearly nothing ever happens. And then something like this. Do you have an idea of what has happened?"

Devereaux waited for a long moment to pass between them. He spoke in a monotone. He knew the tone of voice that would satisfy both of them.

"The woman, whoever the woman was, went to the apartment to kill me. The two men, whoever the men were, went to the apartment for the same purpose. Apparently, neither of them was aware of the other."

"And the woman killed all three—"

"No. Not the concierge. She wouldn't have hired whoever she hired to lure the concierge out of the building just to end up killing her."

"Yes," said Captain Boll. "What I thought as well." And he stared at Devereaux for a long time. "They want to kill you."

"It would seem so," Devereaux said.

"Are you so cool to face death?"

"I did not invite it," Devereaux said.

"What will you do?"

"Not impose on the hospitality of the Swiss in this matter. I am going back."

"Is this so?"

"Yes."

"Then why come back here to face me?"

"Because it had to be done this way."

Boll was perplexed. He crossed again to the window and looked down enviously at the long finger of the lake that stretched to the mountains.

"When it's done, I'll tell you," Devereaux said.

"And if I kept you here?"

"For what reason?" Devereaux said.

"We found a pistol taped in the toilet in the apartment. Is it your pistol?"

"No," Devereaux said. "It was planted there."

Boll turned. "You lie to me."

"Perhaps."

"This is not some joke. You should not have involved an innocent person. Like Claudette Longtemps. She was very shaken, I can tell you, to identify those two men in the morgue. She thought they had killed you. I had to assure her that you were alive. You live with one woman and you have a black child—God knows where you got him—and you have this young girl from the countryside who is so much in love with you. I tell you, you disgust me."

Devereaux waited.

"Damn you, man," Boll said and came around the desk and struck Devereaux very hard on the face. When he drew back his hand, there was blood at the corner of Devereaux's lips. The blood trickled down, dropped on the dark fabric of the corduroy jacket. Devereaux did not move. He looked at Boll. His eyes were mild and waiting, as though Boll had to finish some private game he was involved in.

"I could lock you up a good long time."

"That's one way to do it," Devereaux said. Now the voice was flat, without any tone at all. The gray eyes were steady.

"That would suit you?"

"I can take it, if that's what you mean. If I were in your prison, it would be up to you to keep me safe. You believe the woman came to kill me. You didn't get her, so she will try again. Or others will try again. If you want to make this a Swiss matter, then I'll oblige you by going to prison."

Boll thought about that.

There were birds in the trees and both men could hear them clearly.

"And if I expel you—"

"On what grounds?"

"I can find grounds."

"I have an attorney retained in Geneva. There are laws in Switzerland."

"You are a guest of the country and you abuse the country's hospitality."

"It was not me, Herr Boll," said Devereaux. "I will leave the country. I'll resolve this—this is an American matter. In a little while, when it's resolved, then you'll know what happened."

"Are you so sure you won't be killed?" Boll smiled.

"Not at all." Devereaux waited. "If that happens, then it's resolved. If I'm not killed, it's resolved. But it has to be finished. You choose where it will be finished—in Switzerland or not here."

"And your son? Or whatever he is, the black child?"

"He's in school. The lawyer has his trust. If things happen . . . then he's taken care of. He's fourteen. He understands."

"And Rita Macklin? Will you arrange for her as well?"

But Devereaux had run out of words. The conversation with Rita—the one in mind—always ended at this point. He had broken free twice; twice he had been dragged back.

He didn't know. Any more than Boll.

FOURTEEN
Among the Insane

Hanley was falling into himself.

He had been in Ward Seven for three weeks and each day grew more indistinct in mind and memory. Was today Wednesday or was it the day before? Was it spring? Was it this year or last?

In lucid moments, he knew that it was the medicine. There were pills in the morning and at night and there were pills as part of therapy and there were pills to ease the pain and to encourage sleep and to end anxiety and to modify behavior. He felt drugged all the time and yet the dependency was restful to him. He needed it.

Hanley began to speak to himself for company. He knew they didn't care. They were very tolerant of the gentle patients and he was a gentle patient. He was learning all the lessons they wanted him to learn.

He sat at the window in his room and looked through the bars and watched the inmates walk to and fro in the exercise area. They were insane, he knew; at least, most of them. He was not so certain about Mr. Carpenter, who had been in the place for six months and who said he had been an assistant security chief at NASA and that he had been placed in St. Catherine's after he had made certain allegations about the safety of the shuttle program. Like Hanley, he had been a bachelor. The place was full of bachelors, divorced men and homosexual men. That was an oddity, Hanley thought in

lucid moments. Hanley knew that he had few lucid moments now. It was why he sat at the window and spoke to himself; he thought the sound of his own voice might keep some sanity in the broken bowl of his mind.

He felt an almost physical sense of losing control. He felt spastic at times, as though his limbs might begin to work or shiver without his instructions. He finally mentioned this phenomenon to Sister Duncan, who relayed the information to Dr. Goddard, who talked to Hanley in a chummy way and changed Hanley's daily dosage of drugs. The condition worsened.

Hanley said aloud, "It feels as if my body has become very small and the world has become very large. Not as though I am a child but that I am much much smaller. As though I am shrinking. Is that why they call psychologists shrinks?"

He smiled at that. A smile was not such a rare thing anymore. Much in the world amused him; at least, the part of the world that did not frighten him.

He thought of Washington, D.C., and it seemed to him a long time ago. Not so much a place but a memory of something that had once been an important experience to him.

It was absurd now, in his present state, to believe he had been a director of espionage. Espionage was such a ludicrous idea. Look around: What would a spy have to do with a place like this? That world must be as insane as this one, he thought with great satisfaction.

He had bananas and corn flakes for breakfast. The taste of the food lingered in memory. When he had been a child, he had eaten cold cereal and fruit for breakfast.

Tears came to his eyes. He thought of the child he had been. He thought of that often now in the dim days of faltering images. The child he had been was gangly, alone on a farm with elderly parents, a watcher who was slow to speak. When he was a child, he would awaken each morning to go to the window in hopes there was some change in the endless, flat Nebraska landscape. The only change was weather. There was snow and blistering summer heat and, in the fall, a brief and beautiful time of color that was melancholy

101

even to an eleven-year-old boy. He wept and watched out the window. The day was warm and bright, almost sultry. The spring came like a woman waiting for sex. There was a perfume that haunted the world. The day was lascivious, almost wanton. Hanley thought of a woman—once, a woman in memory—and open legs on a narrow bed, a woman with the smell of sex on her lips.

Hanley realized he was aroused again. Sometimes, now, he was aroused five or six times a day. The experience was not pleasant finally because the arousal—and his masturbation—had eventually chafed his penis. He had not masturbated since he was a child. Arousal was pain. He thought he should tell someone but there was only Sister Duncan, who would blush, and Dr. Goddard, who would give him more medicine.

Am I sick? he thought. He watched Carpenter walk around and around the yard with large, angry strides. How did Carpenter resist?

Resist, he thought, turning the word over and over in mind until it almost tumbled out of mind.

He blinked.

He was still aroused and he could smell the perfume of spring all around him. He touched himself and felt pain. Pain and pleasure; arousal and sleepiness; memory and failing images all around. He blinked his eyes. They were wet.

"Mr. Hanley."

He removed his hand, turned, saw Sister Mary Domitilla, a large nun shaped like a cookie. She was smiling and sweet-faced and it frightened Hanley because he did not think she was a sweet woman. He blinked and the wetness was almost gone. He said nothing.

"How are you today, Mr. Hanley?"

"I'm fine," he said. His voice was low and flat and not accustomed to being used. "I'm fine today. I'm better today, feeling better."

If you did not feel better, they gave you medicine to help you to feel better.

They were going to give Carpenter electroshock treatments in a week. Of course, they didn't say that but everyone knew that was

what Mr. Carpenter's condition indicated. He was on the schedule to report to Room 9 for "therapy" sessions next week. No one spoke of Room 9 because the people who came out of Room 9 were altered. They did not seem to be the same person.

"Mr. Hanley? Mr. Hanley? Are you with us today, Mr. Hanley?"

"Oh. Yes. Yes I am." He got up from the straight chair by the window. He smiled at Sister Mary Domitilla. They all wanted you to smile; it was the first rule of Ward Seven. Smile and the world smiles with you.

"You have a visitor, Mr. Hanley," said Sister Domitilla in the manner of one giving a child an unearned treat. "I want to be certain that you're up to seeing him."

"Who am I seeing?" Hanley said. "Yes, yes. I'm up to seeing him." He felt a nervous shiver of anticipation.

"You'll see soon enough," said Sister Domitilla. "Come with me."

He followed her out of the room. Her dark habit flowed down the hallway, accompanied by the clattering of the large rosary she wore at her belt. She was not as tall as Hanley and she was fat. She spoke in a musical voice in a way that most women have not spoken for years. Her voice had the notes of a toy xylophone.

Hanley shuffled behind. He wore bedroom slippers most of the time. They seemed more comfortable than shoes. What was the point of shoes? Or wearing trousers? He wore his pajamas and the hospital robe—it was gray and carried the insignia "St. Catherine's" above a small cross—and he hadn't brushed his hair for days. His hair was turning white, what was left of it.

"In there," said Sister Domitilla. She stopped by an unmarked door. She nodded to the door. Hanley opened the door.

He blinked.

The man who sat on the edge of the table in the small, windowless room was lean and edgy and wore glasses. Hanley felt certain he knew him but he could not place him for a moment. The puzzlement crossed his features and made him frown.

"Perry Weinstein," the man said, to jog memory. "You remember me?"

"Perry Weinstein," Hanley repeated. "You're the assistant national security advisor." There, it clicked into place just like that.

"Yes," Perry said. He paused and studied Hanley's face. "You all right?"

"Yes. I'm fine." And Hanley smiled the smile they all expected.

"Are you sure?"

"Yes," said Hanley.

"I'd like to talk to you," Perry said.

"Yes. Yes, let's talk."

"Could we go outside? Take a walk?"

"Yes. If you want."

"Do you want to dress?"

"I am dressed."

"I mean . . . well, it doesn't matter."

"No, not at all. I'm fine, I tell you."

"Is something wrong?"

"No, not at all."

They walked out of the room, down the hall, out into the yard. Into the open front yard, not the yard behind the building where the others walked. Dr. Goddard glanced out his window at them and frowned. It wasn't a good thing, to see Dr. Goddard frown. Dr. Goddard only frowned when he had a problem.

The air assaulted Hanley. He shivered and Perry Weinstein said: "Are you cold?"

"No, not at all. I'm fine." Could he explain that the air was a woman's perfume and the smell of trees and buds growing on bare branches and the smell of the earth itself aroused him? He could bury his face in the earth and lick it. He thought of that and he was embarrassed again and fastened his robe tightly around him. He walked painfully along.

Perry Weinstein said nothing for a long time. They walked down the gravel drive toward the other buildings. Toward the gate. Hanley saw the gate and thought about it. Beyond the gate was the valley and beyond the valley was the world.

"There are no spies," Perry Weinstein said. He said it in an offhand voice, as though saying it was a fine day.

Hanley blinked and said nothing. They stopped walking. Perry pointed to a green bench and said, "Let's sit down."

They sat down. Hanley folded his hands over his crotch to hide his erection from the other man. He felt foolish and embarrassed. He blushed and stared at the gravel and then, once, looked up and saw the gate down the path.

"Why did you say that?"

"Why did I say what?"

" 'There are no spies.' "

"Did I say that?"

"You said it in a telephone conversation. Do you remember?"

"My memory . . . is failing. I remember events of thirty or forty or fifty years ago quite clearly but I forget so much. I think I might be going blind. Not outside but inside."

"Are you on medication?"

"Don't you know?" Hanley said in a quick, sly voice.

"I don't know. I came up here to see you."

"What day is today?"

"Tuesday."

"There are no visitors on Tuesday. Visitors come on Sunday after the last mass."

"What do they do to you here, Hanley?"

"What do you mean?"

"What do they do to you here?"

"Don't you know?"

"I don't know."

"You should know." And there was a sudden and unexplainable sob in his voice. "Yackley sent me here. You should know."

Perry Weinstein studied the older man through his horn-rimmed glasses. His eyes were mild and quick. He slowly rubbed the bridge of his nose, back and forth.

"There are no spies," Perry Weinstein said.

"Yes. That's true. And all of what we do means nothing. It is pointless, fruitless, hopeless. The Section means nothing. We are to spy upon the spies. Well, there are no spies, are there?" And Hanley smiled and was crying.

105

"Of course there are spies," Weinstein said. His voice was cold. "You don't know?"

"Know what?"

"Perhaps you don't have a need-to-know."

"Cut that bullshit, Hanley." Weinstein came close to his face. "Why is November in Moscow?"

"Is he in Moscow?"

"You said he was—"

"I wanted to warn him," Hanley began quickly.

"Warn who?"

"November." Hanley waited. "November was in Denmark, he was going to Moscow, he had put out feelers to Moscow Center. He wanted to go over. I had to tell November—"

"The real November," Weinstein said.

"Of course. He was sleeping. I had to tell him to come awake. The words were all wrong. I realize that. I wanted to tell him that none of it mattered, there were no spies in any case—"

"That's crazy talk," Perry Weinstein said. "Why are you talking crazy?"

"Burke in Romania. They had him on a string for three years and pulled him in and traded him for Rostenkowski who we had. We had Rostenkowski in Paris for four years. Three for four." Hanley smiled.

"Are you crazy, then?"

"No, I'm not crazy. It is difficult to explain," Hanley said. "I was tired, it was the shock of it all, I suppose. I wasn't crazy. Every day I went to the same bar on Fourteenth Street and they closed it down. So I had to find a new place. I started to eat in the cafeteria. Can you imagine doing that? The food was awful."

"It has to be awful up to GS 13; then it improves," Weinstein said. And he smiled at Hanley.

Hanley realized he was smiling back. A tight and typical Hanley smile, the smile of the bureaucrat who does not wish to be amused about jokes concerning the bureaucracy. The smile that Hanley had not smiled in Ward Seven in the three weeks he had been there; or three months; or three years. Eventually.

The smiles faded.

"Tell me about the two Novembers," Perry Weinstein said.

Hanley shrugged in his robe, as though to recede into it. The air was still and very cold for the time of year. When he spoke, his breath was puffed.

"Do you have a need-to-know?"

Perry Weinstein nodded. His face was grave.

Hanley thought about it for a long time. The spring seemed too sultry to him; he did not realize it was cold. The spring caressed him. The woman of the season blew into his ear and licked inside his ear and it made him shiver; another person would have thought it was cold. He could smell perfume and the peculiar touch of a woman's fingers running up and down his arm. The woman in the season put her wet tongue into his ear and he shivered because she promised so many pleasures to him.

Hanley blinked. The reverie disappeared. The tongue and woman and smell were gone. He stared at Weinstein. "What did you say?"

"Tell me about November. Tell me what is wrong with Section," Weinstein said.

"Wrong with Section," Hanley said.

Weinstein waited. He was a listener.

"I have thought, for a long time, that someone inside Section does not mean us well. Does not mean well to Section."

"Tell me," Weinstein said.

"Nutcracker was taken from me. My nutcracker is gone," he said. "I was given it and it was mine. My sister took it."

"What about Section?"

"I see teeth and that face that will kill you to see you. It was my nutcracker," Hanley said. He began to cry.

"I can get your nutcracker back to you," Perry Weinstein said.

"No. You're telling me that but you can't. It was lost a long time ago."

"Tell me about the Section. Tell me what's wrong with Section."

"Is it safe to tell you?"

Weinstein waited.

"I tried to tell November. He wouldn't listen to me. I think he knows, though."

"Knows what?"

107

"That there is something wrong. With Section." Hanley felt the cold around him, pressing on his pale skin. "I need to tell someone."

"Tell me," said Perry Weinstein.

And Hanley began then, in a slow voice, to tell him everything he could remember.

FIFTEEN
Assignment

The cities of the Eastern Bloc are dark at night. There is light but just enough. In the center of old Prague was a red star, illuminated at night, revolving slowly around and around. From the top story of the restaurant in the Intercontinental Hotel—the only modern hotel in Prague—the Soviet visitors and their women of the evening could view the red star revolving above the old church spires. Even above the spires of the old cathedral on the hill.

The restaurant was expensive and glittering. The wines served were from Hungary and Romania and were not very good. The cuisine was French with a heavy touch. Everything about the restaurant was a parody of poshness because parody is the only thing possible in such a society.

Alexa thought it was crude. She honestly loved Paris, for example, and all its excesses; she loved Moscow out of an inborn love for the ancient city that seemed part of her roots; but she saw the rest of the world for what it was. And Prague was a sad old city, neglected too long and full of sorrows buried in the ancient stones.

Perhaps Gorki would have understood. Gorki was a complex man and she was his protégée in the Resolutions Committee. She would have explained her feelings to him on any night but this one. She was too nervous.

He had seduced her in the beginning, as she expected, but had

never treated her as his mistress or even his property. Gorki was a detached man who sampled pleasures, never gorged on them.

She thought Gorki had sent men to have her killed. She wanted to understand why. He had seemed surprised to hear her voice when she telephoned.

Prague was a short plane ride from Moscow and from Zurich. They had agreed to meet there because Gorki did not want her to return to Moscow. Not yet.

Gorki put down his glass of brandy—French, not the Hungarian version offered on the menu—and looked across the white table-cloth. Her eyes had never left his face. He was a small man with the delicate manners of the Oriental Soviet. No one who worked for him knew his past and no one wanted to speak too much about it.

He stared at Alexa until she looked away, out the wall of windows.

"All organizations have their duplications," Gorki said in a quiet voice as though summarizing some lesson. "I have wanted this American agent dead for a long time. The two men you killed—by mistake, dear Alexa—were backup to you and the unfortunate agent in Helsinki failed to explain that to you."

"Why?" she said.

"Alexei claims no knowledge of the two men but the truth is quite different." He spoke Russian with patient clarity, as though each word had been painfully learned and was reluctantly released in speech.

"I could have been killed," she said.

"It was such a waste—"

"I still don't understand—"

"Nor I," interrupted Gorki. "But I understand this: November is still alive and that is not acceptable."

"So I go back to Lausanne," she began. She had eaten very little. She wore a dark dress with long sleeves that framed her pale features and made her skin seem more like porcelain. She watched Gorki as though she felt she had to be certain that he was telling her the truth; it was the first time she had felt suspicious.

"No. He has left Lausanne."

110

"What happened?"

"He left Lausanne. He left the country after four days. He talked to Swiss police. He went to London, we think. Today or tomorrow he flies to New York on the Concorde. We think. We have this information—"

"What are you going to do?" Alexa said. Her words were soft, but she stared at him very hard.

"You," said Gorki. His lynx eyes glittered at the table. The wine steward came and Gorki waved him away.

"You have watched him so closely, then why—"

"Because this is a delicate matter," Gorki began.

She saw that he was lying to her. Why was he lying? What part of what he said was a lie and what was the truth?

She felt the same coldness she had felt the first day in Zurich, after the killings, when she tried to decide what to do next. Her first thought had been to contact Moscow but she had elected to do nothing at first. The newspapers were full of information about the killings. She could not understand who the men had been. Even now. She did not believe Gorki at all; she had flown to Prague as though flying to a rendezvous with her own death.

"Who is November?"

"He was our mole in the R Section," began Gorki.

She waited, her disbelief suspended. Her long fingers held the edge of the white tablecloth as though holding on to reality.

"It is very complex. Seemingly, over the years, he had performed a number of actions against our interest but that was to be expected. He had to be useful. To them and to us. However, most importantly, we began to suspect two years ago that he had changed allegiances—that he had been found out and that he was being used now by R Section to feed us disinformation that we would believe, because we would believe him to be our man. Much as the British did with the German spy network in Britain in the Patriotic War."

She nodded; she knew the reference to World War II when British intelligence managed to triple every German agent in Britain, creating an entirely traitorous network of German spies working for the British and still feeding their German controls information.

"The important matter now is that he has to be dealt with. It was to be done in Switzerland, before he had any warning. Unfortunately, he has been warned now by the killings and by R Section itself. His cover is blown as far as we're concerned."

She waited and the cold feeling grew in her. Gorki spoke in a sharp whisper, the words glittered, he was constructing a story that seemed entirely plausible. And yet Alexa knew it was a lie, it had to be a lie from the beginning. And if it was a lie, then it meant Gorki wanted to eliminate her.

He wanted to kill her.

The thought fastened to her like a leech. She felt the blood draining from her face. She went very rigid and pale and cold in that moment. *He wanted to kill her.*

"You have had the training of an illegal agent and that is what you will become again," Gorki said, staring at his cognac. It seemed he did not want to look at her. "In the packet is identification. A French passport, papers, driver's license . . . all the paperwork. It seems better to travel to Montreal from Paris first and then shuttle to Washington. The Canadian entry is much easier."

"But our own people . . . in Washington—"

"This is not a matter for them. It is too delicate for more usual channels—"

She felt the words like blows; they were all lies. Gorki was isolating her and there was nothing she could do about it.

He had sent the killers in Lausanne not to kill the American but to kill her.

A rush of guilt overwhelmed her. It must be some flaw in her that exacted this punishment; some failure.

She was a woman of great beauty and cunning. In that shaken moment, she fell back on her resources.

She reached her hand across the white linen and touched the parchment fingers.

Gorki looked at her for a moment, as though he could not understand the gesture. He looked into Alexa's glittering eyes. Eyes that could not be disguised, he thought. Eyes that will always give her away.

Gorki smiled at her as though she might have been a child.

"My dear Alexa," Gorki said, removing his hand. "I fly back to Moscow in an hour. There is so little time. Believe me—" He spoke in a soft voice and then interrupted himself with silence. His eyes spoke regret. He smiled. "Perhaps—" Again, silence intervened. He rose and she saw he had left a packet on the table. Instructions and identification and money—the usual precautions.

But Alexa felt failure. Acute and cold. He was instructing her to follow a trail of lies to her own death. What was her failure?

And what was her alternative?

She shuddered. She looked up. Gorki was already threading his way through the tables, past the Party officials and their girlfriends, his thin frame silhouetted against the black window that looked out on blackened Prague. And the great red star turning slowly, slowly, above the church spires and the steeples.

SIXTEEN
Among Friends, Among Enemies

For a long time, the bulky man in dark cashmere coat and homburg hat walked along the seawall that jutted out into the Channel in Dover.

Dover was having a British spring with drab days and the threat of rain in the air. The Channel was choppy and gray, the way it always seemed to be. The great gulls groaned madly above the waves crashing into the seawall and the chimney pots of the town boiled up with curls of smoke. It was a day for hot tea and cold sandwiches and the huddled conversations of the public house. It was a day for dampness, wet wools and the red noses that come with sniffles and deep spring colds.

The bulky man in dark had his hands folded behind his back as he patrolled the seawall and felt a touch of spray now and again on his ruddy face. His eyes were mild as a saint's behind rimless glasses. He looked like a man of great kindnesses. He might have been one of those millionaires who gives all to the poor. In the case of Dmitri Ilyich Denisov, all those assumptions about him would have been wrong.

Once he had been an agent from Moscow; then, again, he had been made a reluctant defector to America. He was certainly a killer; he was certainly ruthless; he certainly broke laws as part of his new trade in the world of supplying those things to the world that the world wants but does not want to allow to be traded.

Denisov had once battled a nemesis named November, an American agent who had embarrassed him, nearly killed him, used him twice and who had also given him a complete set of Gilbert and Sullivan recordings to while away his days in American exile. Gilbert and Sullivan was the only thing that had kept Denisov's sanity in those terrible first days when the American questioned him over and over and he felt the deep sense of loss: He would never be in Russia again, nor walk Moscow streets, nor smell the home smells, nor sleep with his wife, nor hear his son and sister argue for the privilege of the morning bathroom. They were things he thought he would never miss and then, on a beach in Florida, an agent named November had arranged to deprive him of everything that defined his life.

It had happened a long time ago.

Now, out of the grayness, came the hideous roar of the beast that crosses the Channel. The Hovercraft was in the waters, propellers turning and the whoosh of air pounding the waters flat beneath it, the hull like a rubber inner tube inflated and absurd. The roaring of the beast grew and the Hovercraft seemed to lumber sideways toward the landing apron.

"Time," Denisov said aloud, in Russian. He had a pistol, as always, and he felt for it in the pocket of his large overcoat. He turned and walked back along the seawall and down the road to the terminal where the Hovercraft would crawl ashore, resembling some link in the chain of being turning from sea monster to creature of the land.

The Hovercraft was late, delayed on the French side as usual. Now they were going to build a railroad tunnel between France and England and the day of the ferries would soon be over. Denisov thought he would not miss it. He hated the Hovercraft and detested the slow ferries with their cafeterias full of dreadful English food. He made the crossing twenty times a year. He could afford to fly, naturally, but there were reasons to take the land-and-sea route.

He saw the other man enter the green customs line marked "Nothing to Declare." The man had only a small suitcase and he was stopped and told to open it. He did so. Denisov watched this and

115

smiled. They never could find a thing. It was the first thing you learned, no matter what side you were on. If clumsy assassins like the Palestinians could do it, how much better the professionals could be.

Like us, Denisov thought with something like affection. Of course, he would just as gladly have killed the other man if it had been to his advantage.

At the moment, he was curious.

Devereaux crossed into the glittering and cheaply modern terminal which was typical of so many bad buildings put up by the British in the 1960s and 1970s.

He fell in beside Denisov without a word and then passed him as though they were strangers. Everyone is careful in the trade. Was Denisov watched? Devereaux became a second set of eyes behind his back, to see who the watchers might be.

Denisov waited in the terminal, puzzled, looking for a face of a friend.

Disappointed, Denisov turned and walked out in the gray day full of spray and the cry of sea gulls. Devereaux was nowhere to be seen. Devereaux had gone around the building, waiting for Denisov's retreat.

The other passengers pushed to get on buses that would deliver them to the train station in Dover and the tedious ride up the tracks to London. The pushers were French, of course; the English can tell the rude continentals from their own people.

The green buses belched black smoke and rattled away from the curbing.

Denisov was halfway up the road to the public house with the sign of the flying fish.

No one behind; no one before. No unaccounted plain cars full of intent men who seem to be waiting for someone. No careless men in trenchcoats pretending to light cigarettes into the face of the channel winds.

And Devereaux followed. They both knew the way to play this particular game.

Denisov sat in a corner of the dark, dirty and quite somber public house with a pint of Bass ale before him and a copy of the *Wall*

Street Journal's European edition. There was a little time to kill before Devereaux joined him. He was a large, lethargic man, accustomed to waiting.

His eyes followed the lists of the stocks, up and down, searching for the acronyms of his holdings.

Devereaux sat down with a large glass of vodka, chilled with ice. The English had grown more relaxed about ice in the last few years; they had given it away in public houses with less reluctance and less sense that they were surrendering the Crown Jewels.

Denisov did not look up from the paper. "You seem unchanged by the years," he said in the voice that still contained a stubborn, thick accent. He spoke English very well because he loved the language (which is why he had loved the merry cynicism of Gilbert); but accent cannot always be lost, perhaps as a reminder to the speaker that he is still a stranger in a strange world.

"It's old home week talk now?" Devereaux said.

Denisov sighed. Tribune stock—listed Trbn—was up 1½. He folded the paper shut. "You have no time for sentiment. For cheers? For *l'chaim*?" Denisov smiled, lifted his glass, nodded and sipped.

Devereaux watched him. He was the careful agent now, not the careless man who had wandered through his days in Lausanne. He had been so careless because he had believed in his own myth, that he could shake the traces of the old trade.

He thought now all the time about that unfinished (perhaps unspoken) conversation he would have with Rita Macklin someday, if he survived this time.

"You are too serious," Denisov said. "Lighten yourself."

"Lighten up," Devereaux corrected.

"Yes," Denisov said. "Your message was insistent."

"I would not have interfered with your life unless I had to," Devereaux said. Denisov did not understand that this was going to be a serious matter after all.

"Of course." He said it with irony. "I thought you wanted my company."

"Two men are killed in Lausanne. The day before they are killed, they go to a place—a brasserie—and they terrorize a young Swiss girl with a stupid dialogue about how they are looking for me."

"I see. The girl—is she pretty?"

"She's young, which is better," Devereaux said.

Denisov stared at him without expression for a moment and then put a smile on his face. On purpose. He was an amiable bear, like the trained bear in the Soviet circus; and yet, a bear is a bear, with teeth and claws and strength and the instincts to kill when killing is necessary.

"So. These men." Denisov stared at his beer. "Do you owe them money? Perhaps they are brothers of the young girl and they wish her to stop seeing you. I think that you must be careful about who you go to bed with when you are in a foreign country." He smiled. "There are different customs."

"Yes. You'd know about that. The widow in California."

"I have so much to thank you for," Denisov said. The edge was bared. It was steel and cold and it killed. Denisov stared at Devereaux.

They had been spies against each other. And one day, when there was no other way, Devereaux had "defected" Denisov. Denisov had been trapped in America because Devereaux had made it so. He had lived on his hatred of Devereaux for three years—before Devereaux came to him in his hidden lair in California and decided to use him. Devereaux had let him free because it suited him to do so after Denisov had been used.

Once, in a car in Zurich, he had the chance to kill Devereaux. And he had hesitated. Why had he hesitated? He still hated him but he saw there was no hatred on the other side. Devereaux did not hate; therefore, Denisov thought, he could only use. Denisov was in the arms trade now and he was a rich man and he pitied Devereaux, who could only use. And who had scruples, in an odd way.

"So tell me about these men if you have to," Denisov said, shaking out of his thoughts.

"They go to my apartment the following day. They are killed there."

"By you."

"By a woman. A woman who kills in the professional way. There is a picture of her."

Captain Boll of the Swiss army had commissioned a drawing of the woman based on the description by the unfortunate young thug who had been hired to break a window in a building and lure the concierge out of it. He had been arraigned on various charges and he would go to prison for at least two years and he said the likeness was very good.

Denisov stared at the drawing for a moment.

There are some faces—even captured in an imprecise drawing —that are unforgettable.

He felt a strange stirring. He looked up. His face betrayed nothing. His hand framed the drawing on the table. Alexa.

"She might be beautiful," Denisov said.

"Yes."

"It is she who killed those men?"

"Yes."

"Why?"

"I think she came to kill me instead."

"I don't understand this."

Devereaux stared at the Russian in silence. Denisov was very good. The eyes hid everything. Denisov glanced again at the drawing. For a moment. But it was too long a time, Devereaux thought. And the hand on the table still framed the picture.

"Who is she?" Devereaux said.

"I don't know."

The silence shared the space between them.

"How are things?" Devereaux said.

"Well."

"Business is booming."

"Perhaps," Denisov said.

"Perhaps you are too busy."

"No." Carefully. "Not too busy." And his hand on the table around the drawing was still.

"I want to know about her—"

"You are the agent, not I."

"You're close to the trade," Devereaux said. "To old sources and new ones."

"Perhaps."

"I set you up. With Krueger."

"I am so grateful."

"I don't expect to pay in gratitude," Devereaux said.

"You have your sources, comrade," Denisov said. "Why do I become involved?"

Devereaux said, "I defected you in Florida because there was no choice. And I sprung you from your golden prison in California because I had to use you. You're free, Denisov, freer than you ever were in the old trade." He paused, the eyes gray and level and even mocking: "I need to know about her. About two other men. And I need to know about a nutcracker."

This was too much. Denisov started. His eyes widened. He knew too much to hide it this time. It was the last word he had expected the other man to utter.

And then Denisov smiled, a strange and dominating smile that broke in waves across the cold harsh presence of the other man.

"Nutcracker involves you?"

Devereaux stared at Denisov for a long time. "A man I once knew called me twice in Lausanne. Before these things happened. He babbled to me and I have been trying to remember the things he said. He talked about old spies and fictional spies and he sounded deranged."

"And he told you something about Nutcracker."

"He said he had a nutcracker when he was a child. It was such a strange thing to say. Even in the context. I thought about it then and now. I wanted to see what you knew. And you know, don't you, Russian?"

"I heard a rumor. In London three weeks ago. You know we have our gossips in the arms trade. Something is up. But no one knows what it is."

"But Nutcracker. It means something?"

"Why should I tell you anything?"

"What moves you, Russian?"

But Denisov saw. He smiled and it was genuine. "You are outside, are you not? That is what this is about. You are outside and

you cannot go back to R Section and ask them for help. Is that it? I feel so terrible for you, my friend. It is bad for you, is it not?" The smile was very good and wide and open. "Is someone to kill you and you cannot save yourself?" The syntax was breaking down. "I think it would be terrible to make your woman weep for you. But then, these things must happen."

"How much money?" Devereaux said.

"Let me enjoy myself for a minute," Denisov said. "It gives me pleasure to think you must need me. I owe you so much."

"Fifty thousand dollars," Devereaux said.

The smile faded. The blank face of the careful agent replaced it.

"There is an aerospace company in California. They are to award the contract. I mean, they will receive the contract for a certain plane. I think no one knows this now except your government. So for four thousand shares of stock, perhaps I will become even more a capitalist."

"That's insider trading, Denisov. It's against the law."

Denisov did not smile.

"You can't fix Wall Street," Devereaux said.

"There is no free dinner."

"Free lunch."

"Agreed," Denisov said.

"It will be done," Devereaux said. "Now tell me about Nutcracker."

"I know nothing. It was a phrase. A subcontractor in London who must think he knows everything but he knows nothing. He said there was chatter out of Cheltenham, the Americans were working on something called Nutcracker. That was all. Realignment of networks in Berlin. But it was chatter, even gossip, and you know that Cheltenham is a sieve. You cannot believe anything that comes from there."

Cheltenham was the mole-ridden listening post shared by the Americans and British in the English west country. Cheltenham eavesdropped on the radio "chatter" of the world and tried to make sense of all that it heard. Nutcracker was a name, something that had been dropped by computer or transatlantic phone or radio

transmitter—it was an odd name of some odd thing that had struck Denisov in memory and now, in this damp and dirty public house in Dover, had been retrieved by a retired American agent.

"And you know this one," Devereaux said. He was pointing at the picture.

"I do not think so."

"When will you tell me who she is?"

"Perhaps I must understand what this is. What this is about. So there is no danger for me," Denisov said. "I do not trust you too far."

"This does not concern you."

"I will see if that is true."

"She came to kill me. Who is she?"

"Perhaps I do not know yet. Perhaps in a little time, I will know."

"KGB," Devereaux said.

"Perhaps."

"And these are photographs of the men she killed."

They were morgue shots, obtained from Boll along with the drawing of the woman. One of the faces had been obliterated.

"I do not know them."

"I do. They were KGB. Resolutions Committee."

"They wore cards? Did they tell you before they died?"

"They were identified."

"And KGB kills KGB?"

Devereaux stared into the eyes of the saint. "Yes. Think about it: KGB kills KGB."

"And R Section?" Denisov tried a shy smile. "Does R Section kill its own?"

"Perhaps."

"Someone called you. In Lausanne. And then these things happen. Do you kill R Section, my friend? Is R Section to kill you?"

Devereaux said nothing.

"You speak madness," Denisov said. "You say nothing to me but your quiet is madness. You want me to say that KGB kills its own and that R Section kills its own? Speak, my friend, and tell me why I should play this mad game for you."

"For four thousand shares of stock," Devereaux said.

Denisov sighed. "My weakness. It is my only weakness."

"It's greed."

"I am a careful man."

"You stole from KGB when you worked the Resolutions Committee. You steal now. I don't care. I want to know about this woman. And about Nutcracker—"

"Four thousand shares. Must I trust you?"

"I will call Krueger and make the purchase through him. Is that satisfactory?"

Krueger was a man in Zurich who kept all the accounts and knew all the numbers and was an honest broker for every side because he was on no side but his own. Denisov nodded.

"He holds them until you deliver," Devereaux said.

"Good. Be careful. Always be careful and do not trust too much," Denisov said.

SEVENTEEN
Family

Leo said he didn't mind. Leo was an easygoing sort of man, which suited Lydia Neumann to a T.

They always drove in spring. Sometimes to Florida, sometimes to Canada for the last of the winter carnivals in places like Montreal and Quebec City. They brought their own weather with them, their mutual comforts, their sense of each other. It was hard to believe that after seventeen years of marriage they still wanted to be alone with each other. They had no children and yet they still expected children in the vague and rosy future.

They went to the Midwest this time because Lydia had to see the woman in Chicago.

"Besides," Leo had said, "I haven't been in Chicago since the navy. Took boot camp at Great Lakes. We went down to Chicago on Saturday and used to hang around the Walgreen drugstore in the Loop, right on State Street. Wait for the girls to come down and look for us. We had a lot of fun."

"Did you meet many girls, Leo?"

"Oh, some. I guess. I don't remember."

He did remember, of course. Lydia smiled fondly at her husband.

And yet she was not relaxed. She had to do this one thing. She probably should not even do this.

Leo was to spend the morning in the Loop, staring up at the tall

buildings as though he had never seen such wonders. The day was bright, crisp, full of crowds on the wide walks of Michigan Avenue. The old elevated trains rattled around the screeching curves of the Loop. Leo had a Polaroid camera and took lots of pictures of buildings, monuments, the Picasso statue and the Chagall Wall, and of pretty girls on Dearborn Street who reminded him of all the pretty girls he had known as a sailor a long time before.

Lydia Neumann entered the IBM Consumer Product Center precisely at 9:00 A.M. At 9:02, the attractive black woman, in businesslike attire from Saks Fifth Avenue down the street, crossed to her, smiled the automatic IBM smile, and took her to see the woman visible in the glass office beyond the carpeting.

"Hello."

The voice belonged to a breed of professional class raised in the last generation that has no regional inflection, no accent, no betrayal in voice of any background at all. The voice suited her surroundings and her looks. She was a white replica of the black woman with a different wardrobe. Her eyes were defined in a businesslike way by eyeliner—just enough—and her mouth by lipstick—not too much. Her clothes spoke of being a bit more expensive than one might expect from one so young. Her blouse was silk but not revealing. Her hair was mousey brown and broken up into swaths to reveal a $125 haircut.

Lydia Neumann patted her own spikes created by Leo every three weeks or so. She sat down and didn't smile and waited for the smile of the young woman to fade.

"How can I help you?" The voice was eager, formless, nearly a controlled squeal. It revealed nothing.

"My name is Neumann but you musn't mention that again," Lydia Neumann said. She felt the weight of what she was about to do. What did any of it have to do with her? And then she thought of Hanley.

"All right, Ms. Neumann." She was as uncluttered as her office. Her figure was slight and everything about her was what Mrs. Neumann hoped she would not find. Still, she had to try. It was all she could do.

"I work. In an agency. Of government."

She let the words sink in. They didn't. The young woman with the poised Mont Blanc pen and the unringed fingers and the recent Bahamian tan was not impressed because it meant nothing to her.

It was hopeless, Lydia Neumann thought.

And then she thought of Hanley and tried again.

Perhaps her face reflected some anger.

"He is all you have. And all he has," she said.

"I beg your pardon, Ms. Neumann?" At least she dropped the pen this time.

"Margot Kieker," she said, pronouncing the name of the young woman. "Your great-uncle I'm talking about."

The doll blinked.

It walks and talks, said Mrs. Neumann to herself.

"Uncle Hanley," said Margot Kieker.

"He has a first name—" began Lydia Neumann.

"It doesn't matter." For a moment, she caught the dull trace in the voice of the doll-face. The blue-rimmed eyes blinked, while precisely defined lashes met and separated. Her eyes were very blue, Lydia Neumann saw, clear and cloudless as though they had never seen any rainy days.

"We called him that. If anyone thought to speak of him. My grandmother . . . Ten years older than he was. Cancer. And then, my mother. My mother died six years ago."

Lydia Neumann waited.

"Do you think it runs in families?"

"What?"

"Cancer," said Margot Kieker.

"Yes," she said, to be cruel, to break through to the doll. But it wouldn't work.

"So do I. There's nothing to do about it," said Margot Kieker, the voice becoming soft, intimate. But not with Lydia Neumann. It was the voice of herself speaking to herself. Her eyes were seeing far away on a bright Monday morning in Chicago.

Then she snapped awake again and stared at Lydia. "Uncle Hanley. You work with him?"

"Yes."

"How is he?"

"He's in a hospital," began Mrs. Neumann. She had planned what she would say to this strange creature all the way out to Chicago. They had traveled a while through the panhandle of Maryland, through the mountains that enclose the narrow valleys in the west of the state. It was the part of the state that lies beneath the weight of Pennsylvania coal country. The part where Hanley was being held in a hospital of a special kind.

Lydia Neumann had checked on Hanley's question. The drugs he was given were very powerful psychoactive compounds and when she had asked a friend of hers to describe them—a man who knew the secrets of pharmaceuticals—he had been uncomfortable with the question. At last, he had explained that knowledge of such drugs constituted a breach of security in itself. He wouldn't say any more. He had worked in the secret drug experiments at Aberdeen Proving Ground in Maryland in the 1960s and he had managed to stay out of trouble by being discreet.

Lydia Neumann had felt terribly frightened. When she had gone back to see Hanley the following week, her fear had increased.

Hanley had been moved out of Ward Seven to Ward Zero. It was a ward not listed in the organizational charts of the mental hospital. He could receive no visitors. He was reported to be terribly ill and terribly depressed.

"Your great-uncle is in an asylum. Against his will. There have been no procedures to put him there. Nothing very legal, I think. And I think he is in terrible trouble unless you go to help him."

"But I haven't seen him since I was a baby. My mother never spoke of him. There was some slight. Some family business between my grandmother and him. They were brother and sister and—"

"You are his flesh." She said it as well as any preacher might have done. Mrs. Neumann, in her great raspy voice, said things of certainty with a certainty of expression that made no mistake about her beliefs. She was refreshing in that, even to someone as cynical as Hanley had been.

"Flesh," said Margot Kieker as though the word did not belong in this cool, gleaming room.

"Flesh and blood. It carries weight in law. You are his relative

and he has been committed against his will to an asylum. In Maryland. You have to get him out.''

''But. I don't understand. Is he insane?''

It was the question Mrs. Neumann had pondered as well. Like an unfinished conversation, there was no answer. Let that conversation wait for a time.

''No,'' she said, without believing it. ''The point is: He is very ill. He is very, very ill and I can't see him.''

''Are you his friend?'' she said.

''Yes,'' said Mrs. Neumann without thinking.

''Are you his lover?''

Mrs. Neumann laughed and both of them realized that laughter did not belong in this holy place full of holy things of a new age.

Margot Kieker tried on a smile approved by the company.

Mrs. Neumann responded. ''No, dear, not his lover. I am . . . his friend.'' To say the word again, deliberately, seemed strange to her. She had never been in Hanley's home and he had declined all invitations to visit her and Leo. Hanley was the solitary man, enjoying his solitary nature. Or, at least, accepting it as a priest accepts the restraints on friendship and love in his vocation.

''That's very nice of you to be concerned about him,'' Margot Kieker said. It was the sweet butter sentiment of the prairies. Then her lips snapped shut like a purse. The sentimental visit was over. The workday was beginning and Margot Kieker was fresh and starched.

''You're not interested in a computer then?''

Mrs. Neumann blinked.

Margot stared at her, the mouth poised to register an emotion—if appropriate.

''Yes, I am interested in computers,'' said Mrs. Neumann, saying too much to a stranger. She felt angry and embarrassed. She had gone out of her way to save her ''friend'' and it was nothing more to this creature than if she had gone across the street to buy a newspaper.

Mrs. Neumann opened a paper file and pushed it on the desk. It was a computer printout that told most of the story of Hanley's life.

''Do you know what this is?''

128

"A résumé?"

"It is a print of Hanley's 201 file. I've made some deletions because there are . . . matters that do not concern you. What concerns you is the bottom line, honey."

The "honey" was intended to shock but it sailed over Margot Kieker. She didn't even blink. She guided her eyes to the place on the printout indicated by Mrs. Neumann. She frowned.

"This isn't our company's computer. I've never seen that typeface in our training modules and—"

"Look at what it says, honey."

This time, the edge of a frown. Mrs. Neumann figured she could get through in six or seven weeks of intense confrontation. It must be the same as deprogramming a Jesus freak: The intellectual argument never counted because there was no intelligence involved.

"I don't understand," said Margot Kieker. And she licked her lip, slowly and unconsciously, reading the words.

"His government insurance policy, his own insurance policy, his benefits, and title to a vacant bit of land in New Jersey he had acquired. It is his will. Every agent"—she almost bit her lip— "every employee in our section is required to file the will in the 201 file."

Margot Kieker looked up. "Why leave this to me?"

"Family," said Lydia Neumann.

"But I don't even know him."

"Flesh and blood," Mrs. Neumann preached.

"But I don't understand," Margot Kieker said.

"No." Softly. "No." Defeated. "You don't, do you? But you are going to have to. Or are you some kind of a monster?"

EIGHTEEN
November Is Coming

Claymore Richfield, the director of research for R Section, gathered the signals (written on "yellow-for-caution" paper) and put them down neatly on Yackley's desk at 9:06 Eastern time Friday morning. He arranged the yellow three-by-five notices in such a pattern that they formed an outline of a Mercator map projection. The first signals—and sources—moved from the east to the west.

"He doesn't move at all unobtrusively, does he?" Yackley thought to say. He felt fear closing him in a bag. He stared hard at the photographs of his wife and daughter on the desk as though they might be obliterated at any moment.

"So it appears," Claymore Richfield said, tapping his stained front teeth with the eraser end of a Number 2 pencil. The tap had a beat—the exact beat of "Sweet Georgia Brown" in fact—but it just sounded like tap, tap, tap to Yackley. He looked up in annoyance at Richfield, who was staring out the window at the mass of the Bureau of Engraving across the street. Even old Engraving inspired Richfield: He had in mind a hard, holistic dollar to replace the paper dollar, just as various credit cards were now designed. The "hard dollar" would inspire public confidence in currency again, he reasoned, and make it more difficult to stash or make illegal transactions. A "hard dollar" would be harder to counterfeit as well. The people at Treasury were appalled by the idea.

"So it appears," Yackley repeated. "Does that mean the information isn't any good or does that mean we don't care enough to check on bona fides?"

"Not in this case," Claymore Richfield said. He had been pressed into temporary service as acting director of Computer and Analysis during Mrs. Neumann's absence.

"What do you mean?"

"There is unusual traffic. Some of it radio, radio computer, some of it routine filings. Devereaux left Switzerland openly on Tuesday, told the police his destination, used his own passport. He even contacted his lawyer. He made himself the talk of the town. On Wednesday, he appeared in London and used *Economic Review* facilities for all sorts of inquiries that are—at the moment—still secret. He paid for them in cash and ER has a policy about this sort of thing."

ER was the London-based research tank and resource center used by public and private intelligence agencies from countries on both sides of the Curtain.

"What could he be preparing for?"

"Perhaps nothing," Claymore Richfield said. "He's a good one, our November."

"He's not 'our' November. He's a goddamn renegade agent, he's killed two of our men—"

"Our chasers," corrected Richfield. "Casual laborers."

"Two of our men," repeated Yackley, trying to raise his voice a tone or two, to impress the other man. It was pointless. Claymore Richfield wore Levi's when he met the President at the White House. He was a loyalist to Yackley but a difficult one.

"Thursday, he flew into Toronto on Air Canada out of London. That's been the end of it. Of course, he used his own passport. We picked up all the routine entries out of Toronto—as usual—and there he was. Using 'Devereaux' even." Claymore Richfield smiled at that. "He's coming our way. He's in Washington by now."

"How do you know?"

"I don't. We can't sweep the hotel registers as easily as the French used to do. But he's here. I sent along a couple of boys

from Operations to do the police routine. For all I know, he's at the Watergate by now,'' Richfield said, referring to the famous hotel and office complex above Georgetown.

Yackley bit his lip and said nothing.

There were some things he felt he couldn't say to Richfield.

It was time to consult Perry Weinstein again. Quickly. About the matter of sanctions.

NINETEEN
Methods

Devereaux had been professor of Asian Studies at Columbia University in New York City when he had been recruited to R Section in 1966. The lure had been Asia. He would go to the land of blood-red morning suns and the eternal fog that hung over the endless rice paddies; he would go and squat down in the rich delta earth with peasants with wizened faces and flat and serene eyes and attempt to understand that part of him that yearned for Asia as for a lover. He would be an intelligence agent, of course, but that was the means; it was never the end.

The means became the ends. Then the means obliterated the ends. The Asian earth was pounded by death from skies, the paddies turned red with blood, the jungle crawled over all—over civilization, over conqueror and defeated, over the living and the dead. Over Devereaux. He had gone to Asia to find his soul; instead, he had lost it there.

Devereaux had learned to think during the years in school in which he had earned his doctorate in history. He had always known how to think on the level of the street: On the street, thought was part of instinct, part of conditioning. It is thought that makes the fighter choose the combination that breaks the defense of his opponent and lets him come inside and tear away the flailing arms

and land hammerblows on face and chest and belly until the weight of the other cannot stand any more; those who don't understand call it instinct, as though instinct were something that could not be developed as part of thought.

Devereaux knew the street and knew street thinking; he had just grown lazy in that regard in the idyllic months of Lausanne. He had allowed himself to be circled and nearly trapped.

The other part of thought was reason and the key was research. There was no other way around it. With a certain number of facts, a certain number of theories could be put together.

He had the facts now. Not all of them. It was not so difficult.

He sat in the glow of a single lamp in Hanley's living room. The apartment was unchanged from the day nearly three weeks before when two men had come to take Mr. Hanley away. They were described by the doorman and by the super in the building.

No. No one had seen Mr. Hanley again since they came to take him away in the ambulance. Yes, he had been home a lot; he had been ill. Yes, Mr. Hanley continued to pay rent on his apartment; probably part of some government insurance plan. No. No one had come to visit Mr. Hanley or his apartment after that first day. They mentioned the name on the ambulance that had taken Hanley away. He took down the name and looked it up.

The answers were so prosaic that they were undoubtedly true. Devereaux had very little difficulty in gaining entry to Hanley's flat. He had various badges and cards of authority; he had authorized papers to search the premises. Besides, people wanted someone to be in that flat again. It wasn't natural for a flat to be empty all this time. It just wasn't right.

Devereaux spent three hours in going through Hanley's life, scattered in the apartment, to find a clue. Not to his disappearance. That would be solved in time. But to Devereaux's part in it.

Once again he was the scholar on the trail of just a few facts. He was the student in study hall at the University of Chicago again. He was waiting as he pushed his way through graduate theses, through long-forgotten letters written by long-forgotten people, through books that had not been removed from the stacks for decades: He

was waiting for first the one fact and then the second and then the third to fall from the pages in patterns and for the patterns to be seen at last in his mind.

Sometimes the patterns had come very late at night, in the room he lived in on Ellis Avenue down the street from the university complex. Sometimes they came in thoughts before sleep; sometimes, the pattern fell out with morning coffee. But the pattern was always apparent at last because Devereaux had prepared his brain to receive it.

There were insurance policies set out on Hanley's desk. Hanley had a desk as plain as the desk in his office. His whole apartment was furnished with plain and useful furniture, without regard for elegance, grace, even beauty. Perhaps all the furniture had been left here by a previous tenant; it had that feeling of anonymity, like the man himself.

The perfect spy.

Devereaux smiled. He read the policies and noted the name of the beneficiary: Margot Kieker.

The policies were laid on his desk because Hanley was thinking about death. In that sense, his telephone calls to Devereaux had been honest. And if he had not been in his apartment for three weeks—and had been off the job for weeks before that—then Hanley had not set the operation against him.

But who had? And for what purpose?

There was so little of Hanley in the apartment with pearl-gray walls and mournful tall windows and dark furniture and large bare rooms.

Save a single sheet of paper found in a spring-locked false panel beneath the last drawer on the right side of his desk. Devereaux would have missed it. He had shifted his weight in the brown leather chair at the desk and accidentally kicked at the drawer and the panel had dropped. After it dropped, he began to dismantle the desk and the other furniture in the room. He did the job as quietly as he could. He broke apart the desk and the bureau in the bedroom.

But there was only the single sheet of paper.

It was standard 16-pound typing paper, white, 8½ by 11 inches.

135

In ink, at the top, was written a single word in block letters, as though Hanley decided on the word as a title for an essay. (He could not be sure it was Hanley's handwriting; he had never seen it.)

NUTCRACKER

Below the single word were other words, lined up neatly flush left but in a slightly smaller handwriting:

> January
> New Moon
> Equinox
> June
> August
> Vernal
> Winter

And below that, in a handwriting that might have been added later:

> November?

The words fell out into his mind, formed patterns like falling leaves, fell wildly against the void of blackness. He waited for thought. He waited for the meaning of the words. He waited calmly in the light of a single lamp in the apartment. And after a time, he folded the paper, put it in his jacket. He turned out the lamp, closed the door and left the building.

There were two approaches. They had been taught this at the training school in Maryland where he became an agent a long time before. The first approach is always best: To effect some sort of bluff of officialdom when approaching another for information. Most people are intimidated by those who appear to be officials or in charge, even if they are actually trained in the same business. No one wants unnecessary trouble.

The approach wasn't going to work.

The young man in steel-rimmed glasses had a wise, mocking look to him and Devereaux waited while he read through the bona fides Devereaux had purchased in London. He wasn't going to buy any of it.

The ambulance garage was on Sixth Street N.E., in a shabby section of Washington just east of Union Station. The garage was made of brick. It was one story high and the few windows carried bars on them. The windows were darkened by soot. The entrance of the garage was barred by a large Doberman pinscher, who set up a racket when Devereaux entered.

The man in the steel-rimmed glasses was not alone. He wore a white uniform and his shirt was open enough to reveal most of a pale, muscular chest. He had the easy grace of an athlete as he walked across the oil-stained floor. Devereaux waited in front of the barking dog.

"Come on, Tiger," the young man said at last, waiting until the last moment to restrain the dog. "Go on over there, Tiger."

Devereaux said who he was and why he had come. The young man looked at the papers and looked at Devereaux and looked at the dog. The second man, larger and softer, was in a sort of office at the back of the garage. There were sixteen bays in the garage, four occupied by ambulances, three by private cars and one by a brand-new black Cadillac hearse.

"For the ones you don't get to the hospital," Devereaux said.

The young man looked up, annoyed, turned, saw the point of the joke. He grinned without pleasure. "Yeah. Something like that. You don't leave anyone in the place where he dies."

Devereaux was thinking about the dog. It was a shame. Because the kid wasn't going to buy it the easy way. And Devereaux didn't have all that much time.

Devereaux shifted on his feet and the dog sensed the shift and gurgled a growl. But the young man kept reading.

"I don't get it," he said. "So what do you want?"

"I want to see some of your records over the past two months. Delivery schedules, you might say."

"I'm not sure I can do that," the young man said.

"What's your name?"

"Sellers," he said. "What's your name?"

Cocky.

"It's on my identification."

"I never heard of identification like this."

"Maybe you've never had an insurance inspector come around before."

"We have insurance guys—"

"We're the guys who check up on insurance guys." The line had worked in the apartment, of course, because the people there wanted to believe in him. But Sellers knew. And it was too bad.

"Come on back to the office," said Sellers. "Let's talk to Jerry."

Devereaux had not expected that.

It was late afternoon. Sunlight tried to fight its way through the dark windows but it was a losing battle. Caged lights hanging from the ceiling provided the only illumination.

The office was three stairs up at the back of the garage.

The walls were bright yellow and covered with graffiti and calendars. Miss National Hardware Convention held a wrench in one hand and showed her bottom.

The desks were butted into one wall and littered with bits of paper. There was grease on the chairs. Jerry was taller than Devereaux but his eyes looked a shade slower.

And the dog was outside. That was just as well. Not that it would have mattered.

Devereaux figured they would have made a call by now.

He walked into the room ahead of Sellers and when Sellers was nearly through the door, Devereaux turned suddenly and flung him at the second man.

But Sellers was braced. He only stumbled. Jerry pulled out a pistol.

Just a shade slow in the eyes.

Devereaux fired up and the bullet caught him flat in the throat. It was a small-caliber pistol—the Colt Python .357 Magnum was in the custody of the Swiss army captain named Boll—but it was good enough.

138

The dog was barking like mad and flinging itself against the door.

Sellers was deafened by the explosion. He turned and stared at Devereaux. His blue eyes were very wide. Jerry slid down the wall.

"I don't have any time," Devereaux said.

"We don't keep the records here."

"Sure you do."

"I'm telling you—"

"When you do a job for an agency, you keep one copy of the records." It was said like a dead man was not in the same room.

"I don't know what you're talking about."

Devereaux said, "Take off your glasses."

Sellers removed his wire-rims carefully.

"Give them to me."

Sellers handed them to Devereaux, who stood with the pistol in hand.

Devereaux dropped them. He stepped on them and broke them.

"Glass," Devereaux said. "I thought everyone used plastic."

"I've got another pair," Sellers said. He almost smirked. He was tough enough, Devereaux thought. No one was tough enough to stand up forever but the tough ones could wait you out. Especially if they had made a phone call and they were waiting for reinforcements.

Devereaux put the pistol in his pocket. There just wasn't enough time.

"Come on," he said.

"Tiger is waiting," Sellers said.

"And I don't want to kill the dog," Devereaux said. "You see the way it is."

The voice was reasoned and Sellers saw the way it was. He'd get this guy, there was no question of that. But there had to be a little room to do it. And the guy sure had dropped Jerry. Jesus Christ, he'd dropped Jerry without even thinking about it.

There are slums in Washington very nearly as bad as those in cities like New York or Chicago. They are the best places in the country to conduct business without interference from people in authority.

Or people who might be looking for you.

It is true that most urban slums are inhabited by blacks and that the presence of two white men—like the two white men who now entered the house on Eleventh Street N.E.—might appear odd to the neighbors. But one of the men—the man with the graying hair and the hard face—that man had already turned the right color. He was green. He had green and it came up front. And he was Syndicate, there was no doubt about that. You can tell the Syndicate because those boys look right through the back of your head. So don't mess with the man—this was the advice of Junius Falkner to his nephew—don't mess with the man, let him have the room he wants, just you go 'bout your business and you say none to him. Even if the other white man was blindfolded.

It was not what Sellers had expected at all.

Devereaux tore off the blindfold. The room was illuminated by three lamps fed off a single outlet. The single outlet looked like an octopus with streams of wires running from the core. There was a television set and a linoleum floor and a single bed with a swayback mattress covered with dirty sheets. There was a second mattress on the linoleum itself. There was a wooden table, painted green, and three chairs. Rooms like this always have three chairs. The single window was bolted with burglar bars and there were roaches above the sink on the far wall. The far wall was only eleven feet from the entry door.

The room smelled of neglect, dirt and fear.

Sellers thought, for the first time, that the fear might be coming from him.

The gray man indicated one of the straight chairs. Sellers sat down. He was still blinded. He blinked and his eyes teared.

"I suppose you can't see very well. Do you want me to describe the room?"

Devereaux's voice was flat but it was not heavy. It was the voice of a doctor asking a patient how he felt and not really caring because the doctor already knew the diagnosis.

"Where the hell are we?"

"Where people don't look for other people."

140

"But we're still in the District?"

"Perhaps."

"Man, you made me ride around in a trunk. That's shit, you know, man?"

"Sellers. What do you do?"

"I drive an ambulance."

"That isn't what I asked you."

"I drive an ambulance."

Devereaux hit him very hard, probably as hard as he had been struck by Captain Boll on that warm spring morning in Lausanne police station. The difference was that Devereux had expected the blow; the room was bright; Devereaux knew where he stood with Boll . . . there were so many differences. And this blow came down hard on the bridge of Sellers' nose and broke it. They both heard the crack.

Sellers made a fuss. The blood broke down both nostrils and he tasted his own blood and his eyes teared because of the pain. He held his face, and when he tried to get up Devereaux shoved him back down on the chair at the table. He finally began to sob. When you taste your own blood, the reality of the situation penetrates.

Devereaux waited without a word for a long time. Sellers was such a small part of whatever it was that was happening. He was the corner of a package that had come unraveled and had to be worked loose before you could get to the rest of the wrapping.

Devereaux's code name had been the last name on the sheet of paper in Hanley's desk. Why the question mark? And what did the other names mean? They were obviously the names of other R Section agents—but why were they listed together? And what was Nutcracker?

The questions nagged while he waited for Sellers to think through the pain. The questions made Devereaux impatient.

He pulled Sellers' oily black hair up until Sellers almost had to rise out of the chair.

"Oh, Christ," he screamed.

And Devereaux banged his face on the edge of the table again, breaking again that which had already been broken.

Sellers passed out.

When he awoke, he was on the floor, bathed in blood, and the swimming image of the other man remained. It was as horrible as the endless nightmare he had once floated through during a long and terrible acid trip.

"All right," he said. "Jesus, man, don't do that again, I can't even breathe, I'm breathing my own blood."

"Who do you work for? What do you do?" It was the quiet voice.

"I work for Mr. Ivers. I swear to God about that. I just work for a guy named Ivers who comes around every day and he tells me what to do. Sometimes it's a straight pickup. You know, an old lady in a nursing home finally stops straining the family budget and we pick her up—old ladies are light, you know, like birds—and we take them to the funeral home. Sometimes we do funeral work. You know, a pinch. All over the place."

"This isn't getting me anywhere," Devereaux said. His voice was very soft and it frightened Sellers to hear it.

"All right. All right, man, lay off, will you? Sometimes. Sometimes we get a pickup order."

"What's a pickup order?"

"Special stuff. It's a government order. Got stamps on it. You know, all that tiny print and them pictures of eagles on them."

"Where do they come from?"

"Orders from all over. Orders from Defense, orders from Treasury. You'd be surprised."

"And what are the orders?"

"Man, I don't want to get in trouble, you know?"

Devereaux said, "If you tell me everything I want to know, and it's the truth, then I won't kill you. If you don't tell me everything, or you try to lie to me, then I will kill you but it will take a long time. And in the end, you'll still tell me everything I want to know."

"Who are you, man?" Sellers was sniffling because of the blood and the fluids in his mouth and nose. His sinuses hurt; that was the least of it.

"The last man you ever wanted to see," Devereaux said.

142

They waited. The building was full of sounds. There were children running in the halls, shouting and threatening; there were television sets full of canned laughter.

"We get pickup orders. They use our service. We take them where we're supposed to take them."

"Where's that?"

"Couple of places. There's a place in Virginia, down near Roanoke, called the U.S. Center for Disease Isolation Control and Rehabilitation. That's for ones that got contagious diseases, you know. The ones you don't send to Atlanta. We got to wear masks and rubber gloves when we handle them. We don't get many of them but I don't like those cases."

"And who are these people?"

"I don't know."

They waited.

"I really swear to God I don't know. I mean, I got guesses, but I don't know."

"Go ahead and guess."

"Man, it's plain, isn't it? They fucked up with the government, man, didn't they? You got to get rid of people sometimes. I mean, nobody says that to me but what the fuck do you think it would be about? You gotta be a genius to see that or what?"

Silence. This time the waiting was exhausted. There was no menace to it.

"Tell me about the other places," Devereaux said. In another part of the building, someone was listening to a very loud rendition of "The Bill Cosby Show." The children were laughing. A warm spring night in the capital of the United States.

"St. Catherine's. That's out beyond Hancock in Maryland? You know where—"

But Devereaux knew suddenly. He was listening but he knew. The R Section had its training base in the rugged mountains of western Maryland, the same line of Appalachians that ran down from Pennsylvania and the deep mining valleys, down through the panhandle, down into Virginia and North Carolina and eastern Tennessee. He had heard vague rumors then about government contracts

with various hospitals, to take care of mentally unhinged agents. And now, their directors.

Places that were secure.

Places that were under control.

Hanley was a director.

There are no spies. Hanley's words suddenly surged into consciousness from wherever it had been buried and floated like a leaf.

"You went to a building about five or six weeks ago. It was in northwest Washington. There was a pickup. A man about fifty-five or sixty, man was bald, had big eyes. A man with blue eyes." He began the careful description of Hanley, creating the photograph from memory.

Sellers waited again. "Is that what this is about?"

"Yes," Devereaux said.

"This is about that one old man?"

"Who gave the order? And where did it come from?"

"Mr. Ivers. Like always."

"Where did it come from?"

"I don't remember that."

"You see. That's where you fail me. You fail to tell me exactly what I want to know."

He saw the other man rise. He felt the pressure of Devereaux's foot on his left hand.

"No, man," Sellers said.

"Where did it come from?"

"All right. Let me think. Just give me a damned minute, will you? Let me think about it."

He closed his eyes and tried to see the order.

He opened his eyes.

"Okay."

"Okay," Devereaux repeated.

"I didn't remember because I never heard of it before. Is that okay?"

"All right."

"Department of Agriculture," said Sellers. "Isn't that a kick? How the hell does the Department of Agriculture have any secrets? Can you figure that out for me?"

"What section in the Department of Agriculture?"

"Man, gimme a break. I don't read the whole damned thing. It goes on for pages. You know, name and judgment and all that jazz. I just look at the place I'm supposed to take him and if I'm gonna need to use restraints. We had to use restraints."

"I suppose you did," Devereaux said. It was broken. At least the part of it that would involve Sellers. The problem was what to do with Sellers.

Sellers lay on the floor, blinded and gagging on his own blood. He never realized that Devereaux was deciding his life in that moment of silence. Sellers thought it had all been settled.

Devereaux counted on his own survival—alone—once. And there was now that unfinished conversation in mind with Rita Macklin. She would say:

And you want to go back to that?

And he would say:

I protect myself. I make decisions for my own survival.

And she would say:

The good agent. (He knew her tone of voice.) Well, maybe it's not good enough for me. No, not good enough at all.

They found Sellers on Saturday afternoon, locked in the trunk of a Budget rent-a-car parked in the crowded lot at National Airport, in the spaces reserved for Congressmen.

He was really upset and very frightened when they found him.

TWENTY
Death Comes to the Taxman

Kaplan died shortly after dawn on Saturday.

Hanley had been unaware of his death, though they shared the same room.

Kaplan had made a noise, started, been still.

Kaplan was the tax accountant who worked for IRS and had devised the Church of Tax Rebellion, also incorporated as the Church of Jesus Christ, Taxpayer. The death of the prophet went unnoticed for two hours.

Hanley had awakened suddenly at seven and pressed the button. The button was all-important. It was his last link to life. He was sinking away, into himself; he would be dead in a little while.

His arms were scrawny and his eyes bulged.

He did not read or watch television.

He would stare in the darkness at night; and into the light during the day. He would see nothing. His eyes seemed to react very badly to the things around him. He knew smells: The smell of Sister Domitilla, the smell of Dr. Goddard. He heard voices but they were from far away.

There was the voice of his sister Mildred. And his mother. And the voice, very deep and very slow and very certain, of his father.

There was the voice of the Reverend Millard Van der Rohe in the pulpit of the plain wooden Presbyterian church on Sunday. The

smell of dust on summer afternoons coming through the plain windows. Women with paper fans from a funeral home fanning themselves. The sweat breaking in stains across their broad backs. Men sitting as solemn as the church, listening to the words of the Lord.

And sometimes, he heard the Lord as well.

The Lord explained things to him in such a simple and wonderful way that Hanley felt glad.

He freely confessed his sins to the Lord and the Lord was as kind as the face of his mother. The Lord reached for his hand and took it and made it warm. The Lord spoke of green valleys.

Hanley became aware again.

They were closing the curtain that divided Mr. Kaplan's bed from his own in the small white room. The room did not have a couch. No one in the room was expected to stay for a long while. There were no restraints. No one needed them. Age restrained; illness restrained; the weakness that comes at the end restrained.

Hanley waited for them to feed him. He felt like a baby again and that was comfortable. In a little while, he would go to the Lord, who had the face of his mother. The Lord smelled of his mother's smells. The Lord comforted him. He would lie down in green pastures. There was a summer storm coming across the meadows and he was a child in the pasture, watching the magnificent approach of the high black thunderclouds eating up the blue sky, tumbling up and up with power and majesty and glory.

He had never felt so close to God.

TWENTY-ONE
Not Monsters

William said she did the right thing. Of course, she called him by his nickname but when she thought of him, she thought of him as William.

William was a software programmer and he wore very white shirts to work every day.

They had met at one of those little group parties that form after computer conventions. She had been attracted to him by his stern face, his light brown hair and the expanse of white covering his chest. He seemed very serious and sincere. They had shared Virgin Marys together and made a date that first meeting.

They both liked music in the little clubs on Lincoln Avenue. They both lived in the Lincoln Park neighborhood and cared for plants that insisted on dying anyway. William had a cat named Samantha which Margot Kieker thought was real cute, and it was rather touching in William to have a cat at all. The cat didn't like Margot. She was used to that. At least William liked her.

He had theories about the seriousness of the world. He didn't like black people very much because he had never met very many of them; but he wasn't prejudiced at all. He once voted Democratic and then stopped voting until Reagan. He was twenty-eight and he owned a condo and a BMW.

William said Margot did not owe a thing to some distant relative she barely remembered. Someone named ''Uncle Hanley.''

For two days, she carefully cleaned her apartment, thought about William, sold $32,000 in hardware and software for the new PC line of computers, played her complete file of Boston Pops records and thought about an old man named Hanley.

Lydia Neumann met her at 8:30 in the coffee shop of the Blackstone Hotel, where the Neumanns were staying. Leo was up and about already but he was not involved in this; it was better to keep it separate. Leo and Lydia had a lot of separate compartments and that kept them together.

Margot Kieker was drinking a Coke. Actually, a Diet Coke. And carefully applying strawberry jam to her whole wheat toast.

Lydia Neumann sat down heavily and saw no change in Margot Kieker. The hair was precise, the makeup muted, the face unlined, the eyes unclouded. No worry, no sleepless nights, no fears of tomorrow. The future was perfectly assured. Lydia Neumann felt disgust for the creature in front of her. And yet, there was curiosity as well.

"You don't understand me," began Margot without looking up from her toast. She was saying words that were unpleasant and she never wished to be unpleasant. There had been unpleasantness last night when she had explained to William what she was going to do. Well, that was unpleasantness enough to last for one week.

"This really is too much," Lydia Neumann said in her best voice. It was the voice of her Aunt Millie. It defined the world with a series of boldly drawn lines. "Do all conversations you have begin with yourself?"

Margot looked up. "I beg your pardon?" She was really puzzled. Lydia frowned, let it go.

"You don't like me," Margot said. She had given it a lot of thought. "You don't understand me though. That's what I meant. It took me awhile. You have to be careful, someone like me. I mean, I have to be careful."

"I can see that," Lydia Neumann said.

"You don't even understand. You think I can't think about things or that I don't know what I am or what my limits are. But I do. Everyone does. Everyone my age does. We know there are rules

and rules and rules and God help us if we don't learn all the rules the way we're supposed to.''

It was the first bitterness in her voice, the first crack of the facade.

"Do you know how many people would give their life for a job like mine?''

"And how many have,'' Mrs. Neumann said. Her throaty whisper made Margot shudder.

"I worked very hard. I think you have to understand that. I'm not pretty but I can look pretty. And I am willing to work very hard, even if I have to work harder than others just to stay up. You came into my life two mornings ago and you talk about flesh and blood and you expect me to enter into a very complex thing for the sake of someone I haven't even laid eyes on for more than twenty years. And you called me a monster.''

Lydia Neumann stared at her.

"I am not a monster,'' Margot Kieker said. "I am alone in the world and I am making my way by myself. I close the door of my apartment at night and it is my apartment—that's a good thing—but that's all I have. It reminds me that anything I have and anything I am still means I am alone. That doesn't seem to mean much to you. You said you were traveling with your husband. And naturally, you work for the government. No one in the government has to worry too much about working too hard.''

"Don't bet on it, honey.''

"Why do you patronize me?''

Yes, Lydia Neumann thought with a start: Why was she hostile to this pathetic creature with her too small nose and wide eyes?

Because of Hanley, came her own answer. This was Hanley's legacy, all he had in the world to leave his world to. It made her mad. She and Leo might go to the end of their lives without children and there would be no legacy but it didn't matter to them.

They were not alone. Until they died.

"Why did you call me?'' Lydia Neumann said.

"You left your number. At the hotel that day. You said you would be here until today. I wanted you to go back but then, last night, I realized that I couldn't let that poor man, whoever he is, just die.''

150

"Whoever he is is your great-uncle."

"Some stranger who came to the house once. Do you know my mother was thirty-seven when she died? Breast cancer. I'm twenty-eight. My grandmother was fifty-one. The same thing. Do you know what I think about at night alone? Just the thought of being alone. I never smoked, I don't drink, I take care of myself. I had a mammogram last month. Every year. The doctor said that in view of my history, it might be a better idea for me to have my breasts removed surgically before any sign of disease appeared."

She said this in her mechanical, computer voice. It was the only voice she had. It was borrowed, without accents and with rounded consonants to sound like vowels. She was crying when she said these things.

Lydia Neumann stared at her.

Margot wiped her eye with a handkerchief of white linen. The handkerchief had her initials sewn in blue. William had given her the handkerchiefs at Christmas; it was the last gift she had expected.

"I can arrange this for you," Mrs. Neumann said.

Margot looked up.

"With your company, your supervisor. It'll only take a few hours; a few telephone calls. It won't appear to be what this is about at all. I am quite well known in some very upper circles in the wonderful world of computer science," said Lydia Neumann. She touched Margot's pale, ringless hands. "Leave it to me."

151

TWENTY-TWO
The Gossip of Berlin

Denisov learned enough in three days to understand the direction of things. He merely didn't understand the sources.

He had tapped the informal network of private intelligence operatives (called "casuals" and "contractors" in some jargon); he had caught the thrust of Alexa's trail. It was dangerous for Alexa. She was "going into black" in the citadel of the West to kill an American agent. "Going into black" was to go illegal, off the charts, into enemy lands, into illegal jobs that no one would vouch for.

Why was it so obvious?

Denisov was a careful man and he was appalled at the carelessness of the information sources he tapped. Everyone seemed to know about Alexa's mission; everyone seemed to agree that it was going to be very dangerous. It was as though information were suddenly free and intelligence had become a sieve. There was so much that so many knew that it was like a story agreed upon before the telling by both sides.

The last source had been Griegel, the "wise old man of Berlin." Griegel was— How could you explain him? He was the go-between and lived quite undisturbed in his three rooms on the top floor of an ornate old residence off the Unter den Linden. He was an old man who had always been old, who smoked American Chesterfield cigarettes in a long black holder.

Griegel was alone now. His wife had died two years ago, about the time that Denisov had finally met him through Krueger in Zurich.

Griegel was one of the honest go-betweens. What information he had was given to him. He offered no bona fides because none could be given. He fulfilled the role of an international neighborhood gossip. He lived undisturbed 1.4 miles east of the Berlin Wall at the point of the Soviet War Memorial.

"Birds of peace," said Griegel, pointing with his cigarette holder at the pigeons wheeling in the bright spring air. "East or West. All the same to them."

The trite sentiment was expected. Griegel was a man who liked company. He held on to the company of others by delaying the inevitable moment when he would have to reveal all of substance that he knew. Like many gossips, the facts were less important than the talk; he kept stoking the talk with prods of unimportant comments.

The two men sat at a table by the balcony and looked down. At the corner of the narrow street, they could see a few of the famous linden trees for which the great Berlin street is named.

Denisov said nothing. He watched the street.

"The next summit meeting is to be in Berlin," Griegel said. He had the sharp accents of the Berliner and Denisov raised his hand in protest—his German was too slow.

"Would you prefer English then? Or Russian?" Griegel smiled. "Unfortunately, I cannot speak Russian very well. This makes it difficult when they want to tell me things." And he smiled. He had the wizened flat German eyes of the kind seen on some old men, with Oriental corners and merriment that is kin to mischief.

"I came to see you," Denisov began because the old man would not start the conversation. "I am not concerned with the summit meeting. I am concerned with my own business."

"And what is your business now?"

"I am in trade. Commercial trade."

"Ah," Griegel said. He smiled at the shadows on the street. "What do you sell?"

"The things that people need," Denisov said.

"Ah," Griegel said again, catching his breath and bobbing his head as though he understood.

153

"Why does the community speak so openly of intelligence? Of exchanges?" Denisov began again.

"The community," Griegel said. "The community lives on gossip."

"And you are the greatest gossip of all," Denisov said.

Griegel cackled. He ended his laughter with a fit of coughing and placed a new Chesterfield cigarette in his holder.

"The summit interests me," Griegel said. "It is such an important thing. And to have it here, in Berlin. There is talk these days about the summit and the air is filled with hope." He puffed the cigarette. "Hope like pigeons who are the symbols of peace, flying freely over poor Berlin. Holy doves."

Denisov frowned. "Flying rats," he said. He would prefer the conversation to end within a week or two. He shifted his bulk uncomfortably at the table. Even the saintly eyes seemed irritated. He had done his work in Europe, tapping into old sources and networks, feeling his way around the dark room of espionage without bumping into any unexpected pieces of furniture.

There are rarely facts found in such a search; Denisov had merely discovered a sentiment, a feeling of change to come. Griegel was useful because he was a parrot—he repeated the lies told him exactly as they had been stated in the first place. A useful parrot, used by both sides and by independents—like Denisov.

"How can you say such things about birds? They are God's creatures, even in this godless state," Griegel said. He was smiling still. "You are such a cynic, friend. Reality should not cloud your vision." The smoke drifted out the window. The old man sat in a wooden chair beside a wooden table butted against the iron balustrade that formed a small, crude balcony. He never moved from the chair. The street—narrow and in shadows—was his world. Up and down the street they came to the gossip of Berlin.

The old man sighed. He took the cigarette out of the holder and threw it out the window. He stared at the holder for a moment and then put it down.

"All right," he said.

Denisov said, "What about Switzerland?"

It was automatic, like pressing the button on a jukebox. Griegel played the record triggered by the words.

"They talk about action in Switzerland," he said. His eyes glazed over. "Soviet agent, one of the best, goes mad and kills two of her comrades. It was a quarrel, they say. She has fled to the West, they say."

"She."

"She," Griegel said.

Denisov put the money on the table. Not overvalued East German marks but Swiss francs. Hard money. The amount never varied, was never haggled over. The information retrieved from the old man was all alike to him, like so many songs on so many recordings.

"Who controls her?"

Griegel blinked; again, the eyes seemed glassy, as though he were drugged. When he spoke, the voice was automatic: "They say there is an old man in Moscow who is old and diseased and who wishes to live forever. Although, in a way, he is already immortal because his name lives forever."

"What about him? Is he in control?"

"In control? Who can say about that old man who wants to live forever." Griegel frowned. The wrong record was chosen. "Who can say." The frown deepened. "Some say the old man will go."

Go. Defect.

"Alexa," Denisov tried. He was operating in darkness. What buttons had to be pushed to retrieve information?

"She went to kill a man in Switzerland and killed her own comrades." He was silent; it was all.

Denisov was sweating though it was a cool day. The sweat broke on his forehead and beaded and fell down his face.

"November."

Griegel closed his eyes. The machine of memory whirred. He opened his eyes and saw nothing. "November is dead," he said.

"November in Switzerland."

"There is no November. November is dead," Griegel said.

"Who did Alexa go to kill?"

"Alexa killed two comrades in Switzerland. She went mad."

155

Denisov wiped at his face because the sweat stung his eyes. Outside, the rumble of Berlin filled the air. Pigeons fluttered above the low buildings and thought about East and West and where to eat next. The Wall was a good deal safer these days for pigeons because it was difficult to recruit soliders to man the Wall and some of the watchtowers contained machine guns and cardboard cutouts of soldiers. The pigeons knew these things.

Devereaux had wanted information. Had wanted Denisov—for a considerable price—to tap into the "community" of shadows that existed in Europe—the soldiers of fortune, the mercenary agents, the contractors and private intelligence sources, the arms dealers who knew many things about many countries. He had tapped, probed, prodded: And all he had was this vague feeling of momentous events yet to come.

"Who is the old man in Moscow?"

Griegel snapped out of the trance. He smiled. "Who can say?"

"Her control?"

"Who can say?"

"Gorki," Denisov said. The man in control in Resolutions Committee was always code-named Gorki. Was it the same man who had controlled Denisov long ago? But it had to be: He controlled Alexa, he had controlled Denisov when Denisov had been in the trade.

Denisov watched Griegel.

Griegel closed his eyes.

Denisov wiped at his face again.

"Gorki," Griegel said. And opened his eyes. He smiled at Denisov. "That reminds me of an absurd thing. It is too absurd."

"What is it?"

"A nutcracker. A wooden nutcracker."

"A nutcracker?"

Griegel blinked. He was back in the present. "Did you remember the case of the Soviet agent who defected to the West in Italy and then redefected back into the Soviet embassy right in Washington in the United States?" He laughed in a dry voice. "Do you ever wonder that perhaps it is all a great game and that none of the players understands it?"

"What is Nutcracker?" Denisov said. His voice rose.

And Griegel went into a trance again and this time, the voice was dull and slow:

"Nutcracker is an operation which involves the suspension of certain long-held beliefs: Nutcracker assumes the truth of the game. The truth of the game, which cannot be admitted, is simple: There are no spies. The game exists for its own sake."

Griegel shuddered and seemed to fall asleep in the wooden chair. His mouth gaped. His hands were slack on his lap. Was it a trance? Or was it a game played within a game, a little show for Denisov's money?

Denisov sat still for a long time, trying to catch his breath. His face felt flushed to the touch of his cold hand. He thought of Alexa then and he was almost feverish.

He had known her, of course.

He had slept with her.

They had been under control of Gorki, together, in Finland. She was Gorki's pet, it was obvious. She deferred to Gorki when they spoke of the man. Denisov had never been under illusions—about the trade, about Gorki, about the system he served. Denisov had been faithful in his way but he saw the true believer shining in Alexa's eyes and it had made him wary for a long time. They had business to do in Finland and it was a dirty job and she had been good enough and Denisov had been better. Denisov had shown her certain ways of doing things that had impressed her.

He was not a beautiful man and he was large and his manners were too shy. He was not at all in appearance what he really was, in his heart, in his mind. Alexa had been like the others—like his old wife even, whom he remembered less and less—she had seen only the external Denisov at first, the clumsy and amiable bear. But then, in the business in Finland, when he had been quite ruthless, she had seen the power and sureness in him and she had loved the power of him and he had taken her as simply as a man takes a streetwalker.

He had slept with her. He made love as never before. When it was over, the smell of her filled his memory. Back in Moscow, in

the small and noisy flat, he had made love to his old wife after the assignment and he still remembered the smell of Alexa. He had made ferocious love, hard and cruel, demanding. He had moved over his old wife and felt her under him, her big belly and sagging breasts, and with his eyes closed and the smell of Alexa in memory, he was making love to Alexa again in Helsinki, before they had parted. He closed his eyes in Moscow and remembered the smell of Alexa beneath him, the firm, straining belly that pushed against his belly until he had to explode, again and again, into her.

The breasts were firm, and he had felt suspended above Alexa and felt her long, cat's tongue drag across the flesh of his throat and reach his ear and lick into it like a saucer of milk. His head exploded and this strong woman beneath him—he had been thinking of Alexa—moved and moved and he grasped her buttocks, her back, every beautiful part of her perfect body . . .

He was sweating in the coolness of morning in the shadowed street in Berlin. He remembered: He had opened his eyes in the darkness when he made love to Alexa and she had been watching him. He was above her and her body was moving beneath him but she was watching him with an apartness that frightened him.

Griegel's voice intruded.

"No. Nothing," Denisov replied, though he had not heard what the other man had said. He closed his reverie and looked around him.

"Quite beautiful," Griegel jeered. The Berliner always attempts humor, even when it is most inappropriate.

"I was thinking about Nutcracker."

"Ah, she's cracked a few nuts in her time," said Griegel. The English pun startled Denisov. It was something he wished he had the skill to say. Even the puns of Gilbert had to be studied and had to be explained for Denisov.

His head filled with music then. He rose.

He nodded in a correct German way at the old man at the table and saw, from his height, the East German agents in the street below. Berlin was not so difficult and neither was Prague; the past that had been an agent named Denisov had been obliterated long since. No one looked for him anymore or even suspected he existed.

* * *

If you think we are worked by strings,
Like a Japanese marionette,
You don't understand these things:
It is simply Court etiquette—

The music pounded as he pounded down the stairs, round and round the balconied marble stairs. What was the reason for so much music?

But Griegel had made a pun.

The pun had given him Gilbert and Sullivan's wonderful tunes.

He saw the players again of the old D'Oyly Carte company before it disbanded in London. He saw them go round and round with the music. He saw the strutting English actors in Japanese costumes and the strains of the opening of *The Mikado.*

He was on the street, hurrying along to his car parked illegally at the corner of Unter den Linden. He would be in West Berlin in ten minutes; he could be in Washington in ten hours.

Did this matter affect him?

Yes.

He saw it clearly now. And the danger to Alexa, the danger so palpable that he was certain he could see her dead in the streets.

It was a price worth paying, to save her. To have her gratitude.

He saw the images and rushed past the security forces in their trenchcoats loitering in dark doorways.

When he reached the car, he had a ticket.

And he thought—in one blinding moment—he had the key to Nutcracker. If only he could keep it in his head.

TWENTY-THREE
Reports

You are a busy little fellow, Yackley thought.

The reports were coming on a regular basis now. They had picked up on him at the border when he crossed from Ontario into upstate New York at Niagara Falls. But the report from U.S. Border Patrol had not been correlated into Devereaux's running file (NOVRET) until Sunday morning. He had been granted two days of mischief.

There had not been any luck involved in finding Sellers in the trunk of the car at National Airport. The arrogant bastard had parked the car in one of the stalls designated for use by Congress and staff. Obviously, it would have been found as soon as a Congressman complained about someone using a privileged space.

By then, someone thought to secure Hanley's apartment. It was too late. The place had been wrecked. Devereaux must have gone there sometime Friday.

The problems were multiplying as well. Mrs. Neumann had apparently pulled a copy of Hanley's 201 file. That was discovered Thursday night by Claymore Richfield, who hadn't even been looking for it. She had left a trail in the computer and she had been gone on leave for four days. She would be back Monday. There would be questions to be answered Monday.

Yackley felt the Section was falling away from him and that

Devereaux was suddenly on the periphery of every action, waiting for Yackley's move. Yackley knew he was the target.

There was a name in the 201 file—the will section. Margot Kieker, whoever she was. They had run that through the National Credit Center in Virginia and the information was thin. She lived in Chicago, she was a salesperson for IBM—she sold computers.

Computers, for Christ's sake.

Two agents from the Section hit the sales center in Chicago on Thursday. They were told that Ms. Kieker had been called to Washington. They said it like that, very proudly: She had been called to Washington by the director of a top secret computer design program and would be gone for several weeks. It was quite an honor for everyone in the sales center.

Yackley read through the reports, fingered them as though they might speak. He glanced at the photographs on his desk. His wife still smiled at him as she always did, even in life. She thought none of it was terribly serious. He had tried to impress upon her the changes going on in government, the changes going on in the business of intelligence. He was on the cutting edge of those changes. He always used terms like *cutting edge* in trying to explain to Beverly. She would have none of it. She made apple pies from scratch and read *USA Today* and thought baseball was boring and wore cotton dresses during the week. She didn't understand a damned thing. If she hadn't supported him through law school, he would have felt he owed her nothing.

The reality of the White House is always so much less. A thousand books and movies have given the public the image of a great manor with a full staircase that reaches and reaches upward to a heavenly second floor. The Oval Office—which had begun life as the presidential library—is a gigantic room in image; in reality, it is very much of the eighteenth century, small and cozy and able to be heated by a single fireplace.

Perry Weinstein considered the vulnerability of the place every time he crossed the underground corridor to the White House proper from the Executive Office Building.

161

He was coatless with his tie askew. His glasses had been patched that morning with a paper clip inserted at the place the screw fell out. He looked like a man on fire. His eyes were wide with interest in some idea percolating inside him and when he talked, he brushed at his rep tie with nervous fingers, as though the fire had spilled ashes on him.

The man on the other side of the narrow desk was Reed. Reed was about four or five in the hierarchy, if anyone paid attention to numbers like that. In fact, a good-sized forest was felled each week to print just such speculation.

Reed was Eastern, which was unusual; he was old money but he made more of it in new ways; even though his funds were in blind trusts, it didn't matter because what was good for Quentin Reed was good for the U.S.A.

"We need some orchestra music for this one," Reed was saying. The room was modern, dull, white, windowless and devoid of charm—exactly like Reed.

"We've worked OT," Perry Weinstein said. It was not his style at all. Clichés fell by the bushelful in this administration. Jargon clogged the corridors of power. Everyone had slang or invented it. Yackley was probably chosen to head R Section because of his inability to speak in anything but clichés.

"Play me some," Reed continued. He assumed a pose of power that required him to lean back in his swivel chair and feign defenselessness.

"I'm coordinating with Section, Langley, Puzzle—" He stopped. Was it too much jargon? But Reed nodded as though he understood. "We have a scenario ready for a road show three weeks before the Pow-Wow."

Pow-Wow was Summit; the leaders of the United States and the Soviet Union were scheduled to meet in one month's time in Berlin—in both sections of the city to symbolize a new beginning to peace. Peace was full of new beginnings.

"Two years ago, we started our exchange program," Perry said. He lapsed out of jargon, to Reed's annoyance:

"We picked up their agent in Italy and the Brits picked up one

162

in the Isles; they defected two West Germans into the East. I think we rattled our sabers effectively. It set the tone.''

"But the one from Italy—what's his name—that was badly handled by Langley. He redefected into the Soviet embassy right on Mass Ave.''

Perry let that one go. Reed sighed, shifted the swivel, tapped his fingertips together to make certain they were still there, and continued:

"I don't want a fuck-up like that this time. That's why you're in place on coordinating this thing. And I don't want to see the Red Machine come back as quickly.''

"I've tried to explain to you, Quent,'' Perry Weinstein said, brushing at his rep tie again. "We can't absolutely control the Opposition. All we can do is hold our own.''

"I'd like to see a better scenario than that.''

"It can't be guaranteed,'' Perry said, his voice on edge. "We have identified nine agents, all very top drawer, very KGB and GRU upper echelon. Including, I might add, the director of the Resolutions Committee.''

Quentin stared at him. The eyes had no comprehension.

"His code name is Gorki. He's an old man, he made contact with us in the last eighteen months through the CIA. He wants to come over to our house. He has some health problems and he needs us. I think it's less a matter of ideology than just wanting to live longer.''

"I like this—''

"It's timed for the summit exchange.''

"I like this very much, Perr.''

"We have our little Indians all lined up. There's a cipher clerk in SovEm in Rome, there's an East German intelligence director in Potsdam, there's—''

"More and more,'' enthused Reed, cutting off the litany. "How do we begin?''

"The best one is a Resolutions courier named Alexa. Really attractive. I thought you'd like this.'' And he slipped the photograph out of his pocket and dropped it on Quentin Reed's empty desk top.

Extraordinary face, without any doubt. The eyes held you.

But the body. The sheer, voluptuous nakedness of that body. She stood quite naturally, not posing at all, not hiding anything either. Reed felt an urge and hid it by slamming his body forward into the kneehole of the desk and plunking his elbows on the desk top. The picture required several more seconds of careful study.

"This girl is naked," said Quentin Reed.

"Her name is Alexa. Rather, her real name is Natasha Podgorny Alexkoff. But she's Alexa, which is a good name for a killer. She seduced that security guard in Silicon Valley a few years ago. She's been active. Considered their best 'Resolutions' courier."

"And she's here?"

"Reasonable supposition. She crossed the Canadian border into Niagara Falls three hours ago."

"We have her?"

"Not yet. It's better to bait your trap. You see, she's sort of a gift to us. From Gorki. The old man who's coming across on Summit eve."

"That's one helluva gift," Reed said. His tongue licked at his dry lips. He had gray eyes to match his suit, and right now he felt he could take on this Alexa-Whatever. It was only ten in the morning and he was thinking about the bedroom. Hell, the top of his desk.

Perry Weinstein appreciated the spectacle of Quentin Reed. Reed was looking at the photograph of Alexa and could not see the contempt in Perry's eyes.

After a salacious moment of silence, Perry spoke again: "Gorki took that. He had her. About five years ago, in his dacha."

"But what does she do? Besides this, I mean?"

"She kills," Perry Weinstein said.

The cold word fell between them. Perry dropped the photograph on the desk top. "What does that mean?"

"It means she kills. She's a courier. That's their slang for Resolutions agent. She killed a man on a ferry in Helsinki two weeks ago. She killed three people in Lausanne a week ago. She kills people, that's what she does."

Perry repeated the word because of the effect it was having on

Quentin Reed. The spirit was drooping. The gray eyes became old again. The hands left the desk top. The photograph was an orphan.

"I can't believe it."

"Yes. Apparently, that's one of the reasons she's effective. So many can't."

"Why is . . . why has she come here?"

"We guess she's here to kill somebody." Perry Weinstein said it without emphasis and watched the effect on Quentin Reed.

"My God, this doesn't involve the President, does it?"

"No. That would be so unlikely, so crude, so—"

"It wasn't so goddamned unlikely when they put those assassins on the Pope, was it?"

"We are monitoring her constantly."

"Why not just pick her up?"

"We'd like to see what she has in mind."

"How did you get this photograph, Perr? How do we know about her?"

"That's why we have spies, Quent," Perry Weinstein said.

"Spies? Spooks?" Quentin smiled. "Are you going to give me that booga-booga stuff? You're coordinating Changeover, aren't you?"

"Joke, Quent."

"Changeover. I think the budget director outdid himself. Save five bill over five years."

Perry nodded. Changeover was the newest idea in intelligence since the invention of invisible ink. Cost analysts had figured out that information gained through fixed investment enterprises—satellites, computers, machine analysis—was far more cost efficient than information gained by agents in the field. The agents would be cut back over five years to avoid the sort of bloodletting that had crippled CIA during the Carter administration.

"But what about this dish of Russian ice cream? Tell me about her."

"There's nothing to tell—so far. She's a gift from our man in Moscow Center. She's already cut off from her control, she's flying blind. She has some sort of S&D here—"

165

"S&D?"

"Search and destroy, Quent," said Perr.

"Right."

Silence.

The jargon machine was on hold. The room was silent. Being this close to the most powerful man in the country—he was 150 steps away at the moment, sitting in the Oval Office, reading briefing papers for tonight's live press conference—awed them both, awed everyone. The reality of the presidency was borne by the sense of awe.

"I think this is going to put the President in a strong position. At the summit."

"It did at the first one. We had spies and they had spies and there were defections all over the place. They started it with that couple pulled out of West Germany. And we aced the game with the agents in Italy and Britain. We won the battle of the magazine covers."

"It was like war," Quentin agreed.

"A lot of war is trading prisoners," Perry said.

"Is that what's going to happen?"

"I don't know. You can't always predict the Opposition."

"I thought we could," Quentin said. "Isn't that why we have intelligence services and why we finance estimates?"

Perry cleared his throat. He got up.

"I'm fifteen minutes behind as usual," he said to Quentin, who had not moved at the desk. He reached for the photograph.

"Don't you have a copy?"

Perry smiled.

He left the picture of the naked Soviet courier on the desk.

TWENTY-FOUR
Stranger in the House

The car was streaked with dirt and road salt. The suitcases in the trunk were crammed with dirty clothes. Ends of vacations always look like this. The car growled up to the garage door in the last of the afternoon light—the muffler had been pierced by a rock on the road somewhere in Pennsylvania.

The garage door opened automatically and the car crept into its space.

Leo Neumann turned the key in the ignition and the engine dieseled into silence with a few sputtering coughs. For a moment, no one said anything. There had not been many words in the last five hours, in the last 150 miles.

Lydia Neumann sighed and reached for the door handle and pulled herself out.

Margot Kieker took it as a clue. She pushed at her handle, was confused a moment, and then found the right lever. The rear door opened with a groan.

"I'll bring the bags in," Leo said.

"Leave them for a moment. Let's open the house. I could use a beer," Lydia Neumann said. She really meant it. Her voice was more hoarse than usual; she had been fighting a cold. And now this. This thing that had happened in the morning, at St. Catherine's.

* * *

A great fuss. Sister Mary Domitilla had to consult with Sister Duncan, and then Dr. Goddard himself had come into the matter. But the matter had been settled by Finch, a small-faced man with large ears and a way of talking through his nose that made everyone around him want to offer him a handkerchief.

Finch was clearly in charge, though no one deferred to him. He was like a janitor in a corporation who has executive pretensions. He had to interrupt conversations to be heard.

But he was heard.

It didn't matter about Miss Kieker being next of kin or not next of kin. Yes, she had proof. Yes, she had rights. Get a lawyer, Finch said at one point. It didn't matter. Not to Finch and not to the good ladies who ran St. Catherine's.

No one could see Mr. Hanley.

Not at all. Not at this time. Not at all.

But Margot Kieker was his only living relative.

Mr. Hanley is in a bad way, miss.

But I want to see my great-uncle—

You wouldn't want to see him the way he is now, miss.

Finch went on and on, reasonable and wheedling and talking wetly through his nose. His little eyes shifted back and forth across the globes of white and watched the faces of Leo and Lydia Neumann.

They were all travelers, all tired by the eight-hundred-mile journey from Chicago.

And somehow, Mrs. Neumann had expected this. She had expected it because she had this very bad feeling about what was really going on in St. Catherine's.

They entered the house like burglars. As though they did not belong there. Then Mrs. Neumann shook herself out of the gloom. She went from room to room, turning on the lights. She turned on all the lights. The house looked so unlovely because it had been closed for nine days and everything in it was too perfect. She and Leo had lived there for twelve years and it fit them to a T.

Because Mrs. Neumann led the way, lighting the house, she saw him first.

He was not at all changed. She almost smiled. She knew him, had known him; and then the absurdity of it struck her. He had intruded on her house.

"What do you want?"

He said nothing. He sat on a plain wooden chair near the front window. His hands were on his knees, he sat very still. He put his finger to his lips and looked up at the chandelier.

Leo came in then. He didn't know the man. He reached for a poker at the fireplace and took a step.

"Leo," Lydia said in annoyance. He paused.

"Put the poker down," Mrs. Neumann said. "He's not here to do anyone harm." She looked carefully at Devereaux. "Are you here to harm anyone?"

Devereaux shook his head no. It was like a game. They were real; Devereaux was the ghost. The spook who sat by the door. Devereaux got up then and walked to the telephone on the side table and pointed to it. Mrs. Neumann watched him. Devereaux looked at her. She nodded. She understood. The other two merely gaped. It was like a game suddenly going on between two people in a crowded room that involved no one else.

Leo Neumann put down the poker into the holder next to the brick fireplace. Margot Kieker stood at the door, uncertain about what to do with her hands. She stared and would have been surprised at how young she looked. There was a natural grace to her, beneath the clumsy artifice, and it was clear in that moment.

Mrs. Neumann pointed to a door. They crossed the room. The door led to the paneled basement. Devereaux smiled to her and she flicked on the light at the top of the stairs. They went down to the basement, the two of them.

Basements are secure, packed with earth and surrounded by a moat of concrete. Even the sophisticated listening devices trained on houses are not made to work efficiently on basements.

There was a telephone in the basement room and Devereaux unplugged it from the wall. And then Mrs. Neumann spoke to him:

"Do you know what has happened to Hanley?"

"Yes," Devereaux said. "Part of it."

"He called you, didn't he?"

"Yes."

"His telephone was tapped. He told us that. He implied all our telephones might be tapped—"

"They probably are," Devereaux said.

"You get accustomed to this, in the field. I am not accustomed to this. I understand secrets; I do not understand spying. Not on your own people. Not on Hanley."

Lydia Neumann went to the stairs and called up. "Go on, Leo. Get the cases out of the trunk, show Margot the spare room, will you? And get her towels?"

Leo said, "You just said—"

"Please, Leo," Lydia Neumann said.

They even ate in the basement, for the sake of their visitor.

Devereaux and Lydia Neumann sat at a cardtable at the south end of the basement, in the direction of the highway. There was a reason for that as well.

All was secure. The room was paneled and dominated by a large felt-green pool table with carved legs. It had been a gift from her to her husband six Christmases ago. He had expressed a vague interest in the game which he had played in his youth. Now they used it to store things on.

Lydia Neumann thought about security: Devereaux was an agent in the field, retired, and Yackley said he had killed two chasers in Lausanne. Lydia Neumann had thought about that for a long time, as she prepared a dinner of sandwiches and cole slaw and beer in the kitchen. They ate in silence—for a while. Margot Kieker came out of herself enough to talk about her mother and what life had been like in the Nebraska of her growing up, so different from Hanley's Nebraska.

Devereaux had watched her during the meal.

There is a way a man can watch a woman which does not frighten her. It is a watching that implies interest, even attraction, but it is not dominating. It implies that the man is watching out of some respect, some physical attraction, and he is attentive to the words of the other.

Devereaux had the trick of watching like that. It can be acquired and practiced, like all tricks.

Lydia Neumann would glance at him from time to time and then at Margot and then at Leo, who was enjoying the mystery of it all.

No, there was something wrong with security that put Hanley away, that denies him visitors; something wrong with the way things were going inside Section. She said this to Devereaux. It was a matter of making a judgment about Devereaux.

They sat at the cardtable with the flimsy top and rickety metal legs and she began her story which began about six months before, when the new budget message came down from the National Security Council. There was to be an increased emphasis in the coming years on electronic intelligence gathering. And a think tank study —coming from one of the vaguely conservative institutions—had concluded that the weakest link in the chain of intelligence security was the case officer.

"Machines don't lie," Lydia Neumann rasped. "Machines cannot do anything but tell the truth."

Devereaux stared at her a moment. "Is that true?"

"No, of course not. 'Garbage in, garbage out.' But if they think it's true, it's true. Yackley had everyone in and we talked about Section, about how much a field agent costs us. A half million a year in Section. Do you believe that?"

"As much as I believe in thirty-seven-thousand-dollar coffee pots," Devereaux said.

"The point is, it got to Hanley. I mean, it was his division they were talking about."

"Operations."

"The director of spies, chief spook. They were talking about heavy cutbacks over the next five years. Not the kind of bloodbath that Stansfield Turner did at CIA, but the same sort of cutback. He was supposed to start a list and—"

Devereaux started. Just for a moment, he betrayed himself. Lydia Neumann saw it.

A list of names of agents.

"It got to Hanley, as I said," she said in a hoarse voice. "Poor Hanley."

"What got to him? You mean, he had a breakdown?"

"Of course. That's why he was committed to St. Catherine's. Except it gets worse and worse. I'm afraid. I'm afraid he's going to die."

"Yes," Devereaux said. "I didn't understand it. I thought it was Hanley. But it wasn't Hanley at all. That means he's going to die."

Mrs. Neumann blinked, stared. Devereaux's voice had not changed at all; the pronouncement was routine. It was a matter of life and death all along and now the verdict was death.

"What is it?"

" 'There are no spies.' I remember he said that to me. His line was tapped. He was babbling and I thought he was drunk. Perhaps he was drunk; perhaps he was drugged."

"Drugged?"

"He complained about the doctor. About medicine. I didn't quite understand it because I thought he was drunk at the time. Two men came after me in Switzerland. Chasers from Section."

"Yackley said you killed them."

Devereaux almost shrugged. His eyes never wavered. "There was an accident on a country road. The point was: They were chasers. I was asleep. Let sleeping agents lie. That's always a good policy."

"What is going on?"

"What is Nutcracker?" Devereaux said.

She stared at him.

"Is there an operation? Is there something called Nutcracker?"

"No. I'm not aware—I would be aware of it if it existed in Section."

"Perhaps," he said.

"Damnit, I would be aware of it—"

"If it existed in Section," he said. The voice was quiet. The furnace thumped on and the fan began to send surges of warm air through the vents. They felt the chill first and then the waves of warm air. The house was absolutely silent, save for the sounds of the furnace.

"Why did Yackley have Hanley committed?" Devereaux said.

"I don't know. He said it was on the advice of the houseman. Dr. Thompson. But Thompson is a fool; I mean, he's not a shrink even. Hanley went home in February. He told everyone he was tired."

"He was on medication."

It was not a question.

"I don't know," she said.

"He was on medication. It explains what he was saying to me." He paused, thought of something else. "Who runs Operations now? On a day-to-day?"

"Yackley. I mean, there are the sub-directors. A lot of it is automatic."

He said nothing. He seemed to be looking beyond her. "They're killing him," he said. Then he paused. "Perhaps I should prepare him for his death." And smiled.

TWENTY-FIVE
Watcher

Alexa adjusted her length in the car. The car was large, larger even than a Ziv, but she had been waiting for four hours.

Her muscles ached across her back beneath the silken shirt. She wore very dark slacks stuffed into the tall leather boots she had purchased in Stockholm. The day that she had gone to kill November; it seemed a million days ago.

The night had stars.

She stared at the stars and felt pity for the child from Moscow who had wanted to count the stars and contain heaven.

She felt pity for herself. As she had been, as she was.

She felt pity for her own fear. She was bereft, alone in the West, adrift in a foreign place she would never escape from.

Even after she killed the target tonight.

He was contained in this suburban house that was grander than Gorki's dacha outside Moscow. The Americans lived like such profligates. Every home was an estate. Yet she saw the people in Washington, in the city, at night: They came with cardboard for warmth and also newspapers and they bedded down under the bridges and in alcoves of doorways, in alleys where there was some warmth. She had contempt for Americans and their ways.

And fear for herself.

The target was at hand and there was nothing more to be done.

She had delayed the inevitable too long. She had not wanted to decide her own fate while deciding the life of another. Gorki had abandoned her and done it cruelly. He had not transferred her, not posted her abroad to another assignment, not banished her from Moscow. He had decided she would die. She was sure of it and could not understand the wrath of the man who had been God to her.

She had danced for him.

She had been naked for him.

Not for any favor from him. Because he had so much power in him and she had been attracted to the power in him. It was a palpable thing to her.

Four times in two days—four times in forty-eight hours exactly —she had seen Devereaux. He was the target; the second November that came once in a blue moon. And when she killed him, as she would do tonight, she would have killed herself. Somehow, this was implied in the assignment. There would be no escape or there would be a botched escape; in any case, she would die when November died.

Once every six hours, she contacted the source at a phone with a New York City area code. The voice assured her this last time that the target was in this suburban house in Bethesda, Maryland. The voice was always right. He knew everything, Alexa realized: He really knew.

Which made it so sinister.

This was a script, she thought. This was a play with Alexa as an actress in a role assigned long before to her. It was all made easy for her. Which meant that it was all a trap—a death for November, a death for Alexa.

Gorki had ruled her passions but not her mind. Gorki thought he could pat her hand at a table in a restaurant in Prague and tell her that everything was all right. That she would believe him.

She was not a fool. Not even when she had danced naked on the Afghan rug that night, before the crackling fire, the fire lighting up her loins and her breasts and making her skin a tawny color. Not a fool when she had heard music that was unplayed and danced to

175

it, intoxicated by drugs shared and the wine and all the making of love that had gone before. Danced in bare feet on the Afghan rug and showed him her power to arouse him. But in that mad moment, she had not been a fool. Not that.

Gorki treated her so. But what choice did she have now. To perform the assignment, she would die; to not do the job, she would betray her commission. And die as well.

She was strong; she had power because she was beautiful and men desired her. Also, because she controlled herself and those around her. She was aware of everything around her and she was cunning and intelligent.

And Gorki was so much more.

Power was the aphrodisiac.

He had commanded her as easily as a child commands its doll.

Now he commanded her death.

The moment she killed November, she was dead.

His death carried her own inside him.

She blinked. Her eyes had made tears and that had made her eyes irresistible.

She sat in the darkness, under bare trees, beneath stars. She sat in a rented car with a borrowed pistol on her lap. She sat very alone and still. Her shoulders ached. Beyond those yellow-lighted windows were homes of strangers where strangers were warm, familiar with each other, at some sort of peace, even for a moment. Alexa let tears fall on her perfect, taut cheeks because she was so cold and alone.

And then he was there.

On the steps of the house she had watched.

She put her hand on the pistol. Her long fingers crept over case, housing, trigger guard, trigger—they were like snakes creeping over stones. She held her breath—not that he could hear her.

November.

He was bright against the darkness because of the street lamp. His jacket was light blue, his sweater was black. He wore tan trousers.

He was a large man and he paused at the curb to look around

176

him. He stared right into the darkness where she was hidden. It didn't matter; he didn't see her.

It was important to take care of him away from the house of spies where he had spent Sunday afternoon.

His image flashed beneath the street lamp.

Tall, long legs, a certain strength in the way he walked. It was the way a lion stalks in the veld.

She blinked her eyes to blink away the tears. She was aware her life was coming to an end very soon, even as his life was ending.

She pushed the car into ''drive'' and let it slide forward into the street. She turned toward Wisconsin Avenue at the end of the street.

She came abreast of him.

Was he a hundred feet away? It would not be difficult.

She rolled down the window.

Because Alexa was careful, she wanted all the advantages. Let him step toward her on this quiet street.

''Can you help me?''

So small a voice. Her mother said she was given the gift of a small voice in a beautiful face. A strong woman's deception.

''Can you help me, please? I am lost, I think.''

He stopped. Turned.

Stared at her.

She brought the pistol up beneath the window.

And he smiled at her.

What man would not smile at a beautiful woman in distress?

From that moment, doubt ceased. There was no thought of Gorki. She must obey because obedience was the way taught to a courier in the Resolutions Committee.

Take a step toward me.

And another.

She spoke to the target without words.

It will be very easy for you, dear one. She crooned to the target in her mind.

She had once stroked poor Tony's hair. His face was between her thighs and he pleased her and she thought to blow his head off in that moment. Poor Tony.

But he did not move, the one on the sidewalk.

She brought the pistol up and rested it on the sill of the window.

He was halfturned toward her now, almost in profile.

"Be careful, Alexa," he said. In very soft English. "They want to kill you as well. When you kill me."

The English words had no emotion but a sort of wonder to them. Her hand trembled. The pistol shook.

"Please," she said. In English.

What did she want to say?

She had to kill him.

"Please."

But he was gone, between the buildings opposite, into absolute darkness beneath the stars. The street was empty.

She was crying.

He knew. He knew her, knew the danger she had felt. It was like another man knowing your secret belief that you were going to die soon. It confirmed everything.

And all her courage was gone.

TWENTY-SIX
Spies

Devereaux grinned when he saw the sign on the door.

But he removed the pistol from his belt anyway. He unlocked the safety—he detested automatics but it was the only reliable piece he could acquire quickly on the hot market—and he went to the door.

On the knob, a "Do Not Disturb" sign printed in four languages —presumably for the benefit of the staff, rather than the room resident—hung like a signal flag.

It was Devereaux's room.

He had not hung out any sign at all.

He turned the key and opened the door with a slight kick from his right foot. It is exactly the way it is taught in all the training classes. The pistol surveys the room from right to left as the door swings inward.

Except it was on a chain and the chain held.

"Who is it?"

Devereaux did not put the pistol away but he held it loosely at his side. "Come on," he said.

Denisov opened the door. His shirt was open, revealing an expanse of chest and curly black hairs. A bottle of vodka and a small ice bucket sat on the sideboard.

"Make yourself at home," Devereaux said. He entered the room.

179

"I didn't want you to shoot me if I fell asleep," Denisov said in his heavy accent. He was in good humor.

"I didn't expect you until tomorrow."

"The work was satisfactory." He frowned. "As far as it went. You were right about a few things. Do you know the woman is here? Is waiting to kill you?"

Devereaux took off his corduroy jacket and threw it on one of the double beds. He went to the window and looked out at the winking red lights set in the obelisk of the Washington Monument. The lights looked like eyes and the Monument resembled—at night—a hooded Klansman.

He had his back to Denisov and he replaced his pistol in his belt. Denisov smiled. "But you can see me in the glass, is that it?"

"Of course."

"Good. Do not trust too much."

"No. That wouldn't do for either of us."

"The woman is here."

"I know."

"You know this? You have seen her?"

"At least three times. I saw her tonight. I think she was finally going to kill me. She's very confused." He said it mildly. "I told her to be careful; I said they wanted her dead."

"Then you did nothing?"

"She caught me the first time. In the morning. Yesterday morning. She was in a car and I was careless. I guess I have learned to retire from the old trade too well." He turned back to face Denisov. "Smirnoff vodka?"

"Actually, I had great trouble. I ask for Russian vodka. I ask for Polish vodka even. The man in the store said he refused to carry Communist vodka. As though vodka had a political party. He says I have an accent and he accused me of being a goddamn Russian spy."

"But you are."

"Not anymore. Thanks to you." He paused again. "I was in Berlin."

"You saw Griegel. How is Griegel?"

180

"As boring as ever. He said there is a control inside Moscow Center who wants to defect. Do you know who it is?"

"Gorki," Devereaux said.

Denisov frowned. He didn't like this at all. He was tired as well. The Concorde from London had utterly exhausted him. "Perhaps I should not ask you questions. Perhaps you know all the answers."

"Perhaps," Devereaux said.

Denisov poured some vodka into a water glass. Devereaux removed the Saran Wrap seal over a second glass, sniffed it, and dropped in some ice. He took the bottle from Denisov. They sat down. The hotel room was like a thousand others strung around the world and they were like the thousand others who hung their trousers on hangers and washed their shirts in the basin and set chairs against the door at night and always left a light burning and kept the television set on to an empty channel to produce a certain, soothing amount of "white noise." The white noise protected against eavesdropping and the chair on the door against surprises.

"She surprised me in the morning," Devereaux said. "She could have taken me out then. I was an open target, the street was empty."

"She is cautious," Denisov said.

"I don't know. But she's thinking about the setup. She was set up in Lausanne. And I just wanted to tip her a little. If I know her name and what the business is about, it will scare her. I think it will. Maybe you can stay on her and find out who she's dealing with."

"Yes. That would not be so unpleasant. She is beautiful. But what do I do when I discover . . . her associates?"

"I don't know."

"You fail at the end, comrade. You fail when I ask you for the last answer. Why do you always fail at the end?"

"Because I don't know."

"Take her in," Denisov said. "It is not so bad."

"Yes. You read the *Wall Street Journal* now."

"It is not so bad," Denisov said. "But even freedom cannot replace memory. An exile is an exile, no matter how great the freedom of the exile." He said, "Perhaps you will survive this

181

matter. I think you will. You have lives like cats." He drank his vodka neat and harsh in the Russian manner.

"She's afraid of us as well," Devereaux agreed.

"Yes. We have proof positive in KGB that CIA agents eat defectors and flush their remains away in sewers."

"We have such proof as well," Devereaux said. They had automatically assumed their old sides for the sake of speech. It was easy to be against; it was familiar, like friendship. But it was easier than friendship.

"I knew Alexa," Denisov said.

"I thought you did."

"I betrayed nothing."

"Yes. That's why I thought you knew her. You saw her picture and you weren't even struck by her. By how she looked. You're not so much of a saint as that."

Denisov blinked behind the saintly rimless glasses. "I think of how to save her."

"For yourself."

"I knew her. In Finland. There was a business there and we worked together."

Devereaux said nothing. To say anything would be wrong. He wanted Denisov to think about the business at hand.

"I came to settle with Hanley. And Hanley is the key to this thing. If he's alive."

"You have killed him?"

Devereaux told him about Hanley then, as though there were no secrets between them. The spy withholds; it is part of training. He withholds from control, from his friends, from his co-workers, from his network. A spy's reserve is knowledge that is not shared. And yet there was so much they did not know that everything Devereaux had learned seemed no more than two or three interlocking pieces of a puzzle.

The two men talked into the middle of the night and the words opened into other words.

At three in the morning, Devereaux got up suddenly and went to the window again and looked down at the utterly silent, utterly empty streets of the city.

"Why do we know all this?"

Denisov stared at the back of the other man. He considered the question. He stared at the empty bottle of vodka they had shared.

"Because we are professionals," Denisov said.

Devereaux did not turn to look at him. "Because it doesn't matter. This is a scenario. A long and involved scenario and the answers are all written down long before it started."

"Yes." Slowly. "I thought about that too. But this Hanley, this man is in an insane asylum which—"

"—which is where we put our actors who refuse to play their parts," Devereaux said. "What is Nutcracker?"

And Denisov started so violently that Devereaux thought he would fall off the straight chair.

"The word was used. By Herr Griegel in Berlin when I saw him. An operation. But it seemed to connect to nothing at all, I nearly forgot it. What is it?"

"I don't know. No one knows. Except that I think Hanley knows. Or he knew. Somehow, Hanley had to be taken care of and it was the easiest way to do it. He had to be put in a secure place where he could be examined to see what he knew, whom he had told—"

"You, my friend," Denisov said.

They both saw it in that moment.

"He called me. He was raving or drunk but he called me twice and his telephone was tapped and someone was afraid that I shared Hanley's secret. Whatever the secret was . . ."

"Except that you didn't. When you came back, when you started searching Hanley's rooms—they knew you didn't know a thing about—"

"About the only thing worth knowing, Russian," Devereaux said. "We are caught up in words and secrets and agents dancing around one another and it doesn't mean a thing, none of it. The only thing worth knowing is what Hanley knows. Or what he guessed. And they've kept him alive long enough to find out what that was and to find out if I knew any more than Hanley did."

For the first time, Devereaux's face clouded.

He closed his eyes, heard Hanley's words, heard his responses.

Yes. There was enough. To make someone think that he and Hanley knew more about something than they did. He had been involved because of a mistake; because someone misinterpreted the raving conversation recorded on tape on a tapped phone line.

"You can go back to sleep now, my friend," Denisov said.

"But it doesn't explain Alexa—"

"There was a man killed on the *Finlandia* who has not been identified. He was November."

Devereaux waited.

"Was there a second November?" Denisov asked.

"You didn't tell me this before—"

"Alexa took care of him. Two Novembers. Once in a blue moon, that is what Alexei said. It was the only unfortunate part of my journey. You see, it was necessary to retrace her steps and they led back to Helsinki and I had to see our stationmaster there. His name was Viktor. I had known him from days in the chess union, in Moscow, after I came out of Madrid embassy. His code name was Alexei."

"Tell me about the other November."

"On a boat in the Baltic. You know it, the *Finlandia*. A November with a scar on his face and gray hair who was to defect. Do you understand this?"

Devereaux betrayed nothing. He thought of Colonel Ready. So they had caught him at last. He had tagged Ready with the code name and his own identity so that the wet contract on him would be shifted to the other man. Somehow, the Opposition had finally understood that Ready was not Devereaux. And that meant that someone in Section had told the Opposition. Only Section knew the truth—and only the top people in Section. So there was a mole and he was in Section. Or she. And he thought very suddenly and painfully of Mrs. Neumann and of Alexa waiting outside Mrs. Neumann's house.

Denisov frowned at the silence. But if Devereaux would not talk, the silence would last forever. Denisov frowned again, like a misunderstood child. "I had to finish Alexei."

"Don't you ever call it by what it is?" Devereaux said.

"No. It's only business. Killing is not business, it is some mad act. When you finish something, you are only taking care of business. Alexei must not know about me, not enough to tell anyone again." Denisov frowned a third time, then erased the thought from memory. "But I learned about Gorki. Why does he know so much about you? Why can he follow your movements so easily? I tell you, we don't have that capability. Not in the U.S.A."

"No," Devereaux said. "I wish we had another bottle."

"So do I. But the night is not so long from here now, is it?"

Devereaux was struck by that. Denisov had become entangled again in intricate English construction but it was appropriate. *The night is not so long from here now.* Whatever was going to happen, whatever had been set up, would happen quickly.

"You don't have the capability and neither would we. No one predicts everything so easily except in spy novels. All the satellites and agents in the world only give us a clue, not the whole story. But someone has the whole story. About me. About Alexa."

"Who is it?"

"The man who tapped the phones. The man who listened to Hanley's conversation with me and decided I was dangerous."

Denisov did not speak. His hands were flat on the creases of his trousers. When he breathed again, his breath came in a whiney rush. "You have a mole in Section."

"More than that," Devereaux said.

"What is more?"

"Hanley knew. Somehow, Hanley had it figured out. Not all of it but parts of it. There is something called Nutcracker and it worried Hanley. Maybe it sent him off the deep end. I don't know."

"But Hanley. You know what you will do?"

"Yes. Part of it. No one knows everything."

"Except God," Denisov said. It was the voice of ikons and incense; even a rational man, even a man such as Denisov, had these moments of automatic piety, gained from childhood.

"Except God," Devereaux said. "So let us pray tomorrow for guidance."

And Denisov was shocked to see that the other man was smiling.

TWENTY-SEVEN
Father Peterson
Brings Salvation

They left a little before five in the morning. This was due less to the need to get an early start than the fact that Devereaux and Denisov felt there was too little night left for sleep.

Devereaux had made preparations.

In the small black bag were vials and vestments, the working tools of the Roman Catholic priest. He showered for a long time—the water restored him in a way that the vodka could not—and then he called Lydia Neumann's home. She didn't answer. The signal was not verbal: Three rings. Silence. Three rings.

Denisov was shocked.

Devereaux put on the clerical collar and fastened it with a stud. He slipped on the black blouse that ties in the back. He slipped on the black coat. He took the .32 Baretta police special, checked the action, and slipped it under the blouse into the belt of his black trousers. He looked at Denisov and smiled.

"I don't like this at all," Denisov said.

"You've become superstitious in old age," Devereaux said. "I'm going to leave by the back entry. The car is in the parking garage. I don't suppose she's stayed awake all night watching it, especially since she can get information whenever she wants from our mole. Only this time, I really want a couple of hours. I'll shake any tail but you've got to cover the rear door."

"What is the gain again, exactly?"

"A chance to play the old game," Devereaux said.

"Substantially more than that."

"Seventy-five thousand."

"I'll leave you a poor man."

"I don't intend to take it out of my account," Devereaux said.

"No. I didn't think so."

He was not followed. Even spies sleep. Denisov had followed him out of the hotel and watched the back door while Devereaux took the rental car out of the garage.

Devereaux pulled into the driveway in Bethesda and the garage door opened and he slipped the long gray Buick into the second, empty parking space. It was typical of Leo Neumann not to have allowed junk to clutter up the second space.

He turned the ignition. The car fell silent. He had liked the idea of a Buick; a priest's car.

They waited at the kitchen. There were no lights on in the house. Dull dawn crept across the fog and lit the field behind the house.

Margot Kieker was as ready as she ever was. Her eyes were made up in that careful way that can be jarring at six in the morning. Her palms were wet and cold and she held them pressed together. She didn't quite believe all this was happening to her and that she had allowed it to happen.

But, in a strange way, she felt just fine.

He talked to her in a soft voice, explaining what they would do as though it were nothing at all.

"I only want to locate him. When I find him, I'll do the act and then we leave. That's all. I just want to know where he is. I can get him out myself."

"But what if they won't let you in?"

"I'm a priest. He's dying."

"But what if they say he isn't dying?"

"Don't worry about that."

Of course, Devereaux had thought about that since the night before, from the moment he had studied the girl at the supper table.

187

He had acquired the clerical garb from a religious supply house in the afternoon and the plan had been to replace the regular priest who said mass on Sunday in the chapel inside the grounds. Once inside, he would have improvised.

Using the girl seemed safer. Especially for Hanley.

Mrs. Neumann spoke as softly as the morning.

"The problem with what you want me to do is that it alerts whoever it is that—"

"The mole," Devereaux said. "It has to be a mole in Section."

"Yackley," she said.

"Perhaps. Perhaps it is Richfield—he would have initiated the actual hardware part of the tap on Hanley's phone. He would have seen the transcript. It doesn't matter. Whoever it is has had it his own way and you have to flush him. Maybe Nutcracker will do that—"

The fog on the road made the going slower than expected. It was nearly 8:30 when they descended into the steep valley in western Maryland and then took the old road up to the south rim, where St. Catherine's stood.

Two and a half hours in a car can create a suggestion of intimacy between passengers.

Devereaux drove without much thought. Sunday morning was without traffic and the white fog that clung to the hills, to the meadowlands below the roadway, to the road itself—all hushed the outside world so that it ceased to exist.

"What is my great-uncle like?" She had tried once.

Devereaux glanced at her. She was on the edge of fear, like a doe in autumn at the edge of an Interstate Highway, deciding whether to cross. Her eyes were wide but steady. She had guts, Mrs. Neumann said. Maybe Mrs. Neumann understood these things well enough.

She was dressed in light blue, in a soft business suit that permitted a frilly blouse instead of an old school tie. The blouse had no color and it allowed the color of her face to define her face. She had a round face that might grow rounder with age. Her eyes were good

188

and when she stared straight at you, you had to respond in the same way. She was good at silences.

"I didn't really know Hanley," Devereaux said at last.

"You worked with him."

"In a sense."

"You don't anymore."

"No."

"Why do this? For him?"

"It's for me."

"What did you do?"

"I worked for the government. At jobs." It wasn't enough. "Estimates. Field work. Department of Agriculture."

"No," she said.

Devereaux glanced again at her. The Buick clambered over the rise and there was a long, blind descent into white fog. Above them, the sun was trying to burn it off.

"No what?"

"This Department of Agriculture stuff. And Mrs. Neumann said that too. This isn't about the price of soybeans."

"In a sense, everything is. About the price of soybeans," Devereaux said. But with gentleness.

"I ought to be told," she said.

He thought about it.

There was no more speech for two miles. And then:

"Your uncle is an intelligence officer. A director. In an agency that you have never heard of."

"Like the CIA?"

"Like the CIA."

"But I thought that was all there was."

"No. There are others. And he knows a good number of things. And secrets. So, I suppose, he was committed here for his own good and the good of keeping his secrets secret."

"But that's not right," she said. "I mean, I'm not being naive. But what's the point of doing things wrong for all the right reasons?"

Because that is the way things are done, Devereaux thought. Because there is no morality in this, any of this; that morality is

189

something for afterward, the sermons and soda water that follow the frenzy of the game. The politicians who preach about the amoral code of the intelligence establishment don't believe in what they say but like to hear themselves say it. The morality comes at the end of the game; when it is won.

No, not won.

Merely not lost.

Devereaux drove and said none of these things. The fog pressed against the car and intensified the silence.

"Why would he leave everything he had to me?"

"Because you were all he had."

"That's really pitiful, isn't it? Someone he doesn't even know? All he had."

And Devereaux thought of Rita Macklin. There was a conversation they were going to have to have. They both knew the form of the conversation but they never let it play out to the end because the end might really be too bad. What would Rita Macklin think of the morality in this? About rooting out a mole inside R Section for the love of government and country?

She would see through that.

When they had the conversation, they would have to be honest at least. He could never fool her anymore; that's what made it so good to be with her. Pretense was down and the careful agent could be careless. It was just that good between them.

He rehearsed in his mind: I had to do this. To save myself, to find out what had happened—

And she would say: What will you do now? It's not enough to go back, is it? You're going to have to stay inside, aren't you? Everything we arranged—it's not enough.

And he would say:

What?

What exactly would he say?

The silences in the car lasted the rest of the morning.

Finch looked at the priest. He saw the nuns on the steps already.

"Look, Father, this is a restricted area here, we are talking about the government—"

"I am a priest. I understand you have a dying man here, and his niece has called me."

"We don't have a religious preference on his card and—"

"He's a Catholic," Margot Kieker said. "Sister, Sister!" She shouted to the fat nun who waddled over. She saw the nun had cuts on the ends of her fingers and she wondered why.

Finch thought: Terrific.

"Sister, my uncle is dying and I want him to have the last rites. Extreme unction. Father Peterson was his priest, his friend, I had to ask him—"

"I hadn't seen Mr. Hanley for months, I thought he was out of the country, if only I had known—" Devereaux dithered. He stared hard at Finch and thought about how much Finch knew about anything going on around here.

They were at the main house and the morning fog was still thick and white around them. They might have been ghosts in a Scandinavian film.

Sister Domitilla looked confused. She looked at Finch—a man lately attached to the establishment by the government—and then at Sister Gabriella. "I don't want . . . I don't want to be responsible for denying the last rites to Mr. Hanley." She bit her lip. "Why can't they see him, Mr. Finch?"

"There are orders—"

"There is God's order which is greater," Sister Domitilla blurted, surprised by her eloquence. She had felt very badly about Mr. Hanley. He had deteriorated so quickly, especially in the last week after Dr. Goddard began the electroshock treatments. The treatments were designed to help "resettle" the random electrical patterns in the brain. Hanley was sliding now; he would be dead in a matter of days.

"Look, I don't take orders from anyone but Mr. Ivers—"

Devereaux looked up at mention of the name. Who the hell was Ivers? It was the same name Sellers had mentioned.

"Mr. Finch," Devereaux said. "I am a priest. I want to help my old friend in his last moments—if these are his last moments. You can come with me. I am a man of secrets, as you are, as poor Hanley was." He paused, looking at Margot. "This poor creature

191

is worried about her family. I am worried about my friend. But God is worried about his soul.''

Devereaux's eyes were mild and he nodded solemnly to Sister Domitilla, who looked as though she might fall on her knees in prayer at any moment. Instead, she did something else.

"Come with me, Father, child," she said. "And don't interfere with me, Mr. Finch. This is St. Catherine's and I am in charge here and not you. You take care of security and Dr. Goddard will take care of the medical ills but I will take care of souls. Even the least of these, the most demented, is a creature of God.''

"Let me see what's in the bag——''

It was all right, Devereaux thought, as Finch sniffed at the vials and replaced the tops, as he felt in the purple confessional stole for a hidden pocket. It was going to be all right.

Hanley had awakened after dawn and the room was vague in the watery morning light and he thought he might be dead at last. And then he had managed to focus well enough to see the crucifix on the opposite wall, above the place where Kaplan had died.

He felt unusually clear. He had felt this way for days. Ever since the beginning of the electroshock treatment. He was quite certain that he had been in this room all his life. He was now six or seven years old. Kaplan had been an old man. For some reason, he was supposed to die very soon, though he was quite young. His mother was due to visit him any day now. He was in Christ Community Hospital in Omaha and they were going to remove his appendix in a little while. They explained to him that it would hurt afterward but it would hurt much less than the hurt he suffered now. He had tried to explain yesterday—to Dr. Goddard—that he was feeling no pain at all. But Dr. Goddard only smiled at him.

He smiled when the door opened.

It was his sister, Mildred.

"Hello, Mildred," he said.

His sister seemed strange. As though she had something to say and didn't know how to say it. That was Mildred. The quiet one. And what was wrong with her eyes?

"Mildred? Is there something wrong with your eyes?"

"What?"

"It looks like someone has given you a black eye," Hanley said.

"He thinks you're his sister," said a nun.

Of course this was his sister. Who did she think it was? He was six years old and he was having an operation tomorrow.

"Hello, old friend," said a man.

He stared at the man over him.

He blinked and could swear he knew that man. He saw that man and part of him knew him. The man was a reverend.

"Reverend Van der Rohe," said Hanley. "You came all the way to Omaha for me? Am I going to die?"

"No. You're not going to die, old friend."

"I was good. I missed Sunday school that one time but I was really sick, I wasn't just playing hooky."

"Go ahead with it," said another man. He was at the back of the room. "The guy's crackers."

"Mr. Finch," said the nun.

He had not seen a nun until he was twelve. He was certain of that. So how old was he? He couldn't be seeing nuns now. He was only five or six. No, at the time of the operation, he was seven. A terrible pain in his belly, they had been at the state fair, which is how he came to be in Christ Community Hospital. He didn't know anyone. They were so kind.

Hanley blinked.

"Mill? Are you there?"

"It's me, it's Margot."

"I don't know Margot," Hanley said. He thought of a name on something. What? A form of some sort? Margot Kieker. But this person was Mill. Mildred Hanley. She would marry Frank Knudsen and have a daughter named Melissa and up and die. Cancer. So young. It broke your heart. And then Melissa died. And then there was Margot. Now, was this Margot?

Hanley's eyes went wide in that moment and the priest leaned close to him.

"Make an act of contrition, my friend—"

193

Close. So close. He could see the gray eyes above him, feel the sense of power so close to him. He knew that face, he knew the sense of power. The face grinned hideously.

Like a nutcracker.

"Devereaux."

The name echoed in conscience. What does the brain know?

"Devereaux. I wanted you to come. I called you, damn you! I needed you!"

And the priest did a strange thing. He rolled on the floor and he came up with a pistol in his hand and the man at the door fired into the room.

Can you imagine a reverend shooting a pistol? There were more shots and the room shook.

The fat nun fell down. There was blood and Margot was pulling his arm. It hurt. Was it really Margot?

He was dragged to the floor, atop the woman who looked so much like Millie.

"Get out, get out, get out," she said, making a litany of the same words.

And he thought he really understood.

There was more firing and the man in the doorway screamed. He screamed and screamed. It was probably one of the patients. They were always screaming. He had to get out of here.

He had to get out of here.

He was up and it was absurd because he was nearly naked, he shouldn't appear this way in front of his sister. Once, in a bedroom in the old farmhouse, two children of intense loneliness, brother and sister, surrounded by emptiness, filled in by only each other: He had opened her blouse to see her breasts and she had let him and that was all they had done but they had been deeply ashamed for a long time and been bound to each other by the secret.

One man was dead. He was a small man with small eyes and there was the reverend standing at the door and Margot Millie was pushing him—

They were on the grounds and it felt good to be in the air. Hanley blinked at the ghostly fog and inhaled the air and felt lightheaded

and nearly fell. The girl held him around the waist. He was so weak and it was cold in the milky-white morning.

Shouts and sounds and sounds of ghosts in the fog.

There were shots again.

Dr. Goddard was on the steps and he had a shotgun.

They heard the blast. The sound of the shotgun firing filled the dense air and exploded so that it hurt their ears. Hanley fell again, this time dragging the girl to the ground. He was so sorry.

"I want to apologize, Mill—"

"Come on, goddamnit!" the girl said with such savage zest that Hanley scrambled up eagerly. She shoved him in the back of the gray car and he felt the seat close to his face and the car was moving, there were shots and the side glass above his head was splattered by gunfire. The glass fell on him. The car shot through the closed gates, driving them off their hinges.

Hanley felt the razor cut of glass on his cheek. He opened his eyes. He sat up. The girl was next to him. He glanced around. The driver was the same; the girl was the same; he was in a car and it was plunging down into a valley and the fog grew around them.

"My face. I cut my face," he said. His voice sounded numb and strange to him.

In the rear-view mirror, he saw the face of the driver.

"Devereaux," he said. "Devereaux."

The driver glanced in the mirror once. He saw the gray eyes. He knew the face, the eyes, the voice of that man.

"November," he said.

It felt such release to say that.

"November came back," he said.

195

TWENTY-EIGHT
Damage Control

L ydia Neumann sat in her office. Her fingers were poised above the cream-colored keys. The screen was blank save for a flashing green cursor.

The floor was nearly deserted because this was Sunday and her office was in the suite at the west end of the floor where R Section hierarchy had their private rooms and private showers and executive washrooms. Her presence was sometimes inconvenient, especially in managing executive washroom privileges, but there was nothing to be done: She was a woman, and she had risen very high indeed in Section.

The door to her office was open, as always. The office did not have a window; she was the only one of the four division directors without a window. But it was the most cheerful office of the four. There was a sampler on one wall, above the computer screens, that advised: "Garbage In, Garbage Out." It had been a gift from some of the staff in division when she made the grade; it was a little joke the women shared and the men in the other divisions would never understand.

Lydia Neumann sat at the keyboard like Stravinsky. She summoned Tinkertoy to life on her screen.

She knew Tinkertoy so well.

Tinkertoy was the computer system used in R Section. It was

named for the child's building toy. Link by link by link. The endless links fit numberless pieces of information together. Tinkertoy reconstructed the universe every millisecond as information poured into the computer from a thousand sources. Each bit of information was not merely added—it was indexed, categorized, fitted with other bits of information. Tinkertoy contained all the secrets of the spies, living and dead.

Tinkertoy was secure. It required a voice print, face print, fingerprint and heat print.

When Tinkertoy's monitor flashed: "READY," she began.

She approached the information she wanted in three ways. Each approach was cautious and it allowed her time to retreat.

In each approach, she signed on at her level but then changed level of access by inserting the correct "add-on" code. This was only possible to her because she had designed the system with the safeguards. Even locked doors in secret buildings have to have keys and, generally, the lowliest worker in the building—the cleanup man—is given all the keys.

In each of the three approaches, she added on at a higher and higher level, to see how high the level of the secret of Nutcracker was kept.

She did not see Claymore Richfield walk into the room.

"Back on it already, Mrs. Neumann?"

She struck "BLACK," the key that cleansed the screen. She was annoyed; she would have to start over. She turned to Richfield.

Richfield lounged in his jeans and sweater at the door.

"I hope I kept everything in order."

"I hope you did, Clay," Mrs. Neumann said.

"I wouldn't expect you back until tomorrow."

"Yes. I wouldn't have expected to be here."

"Problem?"

"No problem."

Claymore Richfield smiled. He was one of Yackley's loyalists. Why shouldn't he be? He had a free hand and free budget. His only complaints came when field agents rejected one of his devices. He had a James Bond idea for an exploding briefcase that had cost the

197

hands of one of the field agents in Japan. He had complained the Japanese agent did not know how to use it properly and that the briefcase was perfectly safe. The agent in Japan had sued R Section for $4 million.

"I kept things tidy," Claymore said.

"Yes."

There was no encouragement to further conversation.

She waited at the keyboard.

"Well." Richfield seemed put out. "I suppose I'll be going."

"Yes," Mrs. Neumann said.

"Nice to have you back," he said.

"Nice to be back," she said.

When he was gone, she closed the door. She went back to the screen. She tapped Tinkertoy to life again.

At the fourth approach, in the fourth add-on level of security, she moved very far and it was frightening. She existed in a world of secrets, those kept and those stolen. Secrets have their own familiarity, like the furniture in a room you know well. But to stumble in the dark in a strange room and not to know where the room is or when there will be light to see the way makes for fear.

She nearly stopped. She was in a country without maps.

For a moment, she paused. She thought of Hanley in St. Catherine's. She thought of Margot Kieker, overcoming her own fears and uncertainties.

She thought of November, in clerical collar. And that made her smile and she plunged in.

The computer was very quick to respond this time. The numbers tumbled out.

NUTCRACKER:

CODE 9, PRIORITY ULTRA:

NUTCRACKER: 22 APR: DIRECTOR GORKI RESOLUTIONS COMMITTEE;

EXCHANGE OF PERSONNEL: JANUARY, NEWMOON, EQUINOX, JUNE, AUGUST, VERNAL, WINTER; EXCHANGE: ALEXA, ANDROMEDA, SATURN, MERCURY, HEBRIDES, GORKI.

KEY: GORKI FLUTTER ONE; ALEXA IN BLACK: ANDROM-

EDA TO GREEKSTATIONFIVE; KEY: VERNAL IN BLACK; WIN-
TER IN GREEKSTATIONFOUR; JANUARYX; NOVEMBERX.''

She used a Number 2 pencil to write down all she saw on the fluttering green screen. The screen held the message, waited patiently.

She understood it only a little but it would take too long—perhaps be too dangerous—to press the file inward for CLEARSPEAK. CONDSPEAK (for condensed version, the version on screen) would have to serve.

But serve whom?

Noon on Sunday. The fog was gone from the capital. The streets were wet and warm under the sun. The churches spoke songs and the bell tolled in the National Cathedral. From his apartment a block away, Hanley had often listened to that bell. But Hanley had not been in that place all this spring.

The gray Mercedes sloshed through puddles along Massachusetts Avenue. The car followed the gentle circle beneath the U.S. Naval Observatory and down across Rock Creek Park and down into the bowels of power. At DuPont Circle, the automobile leaned slightly into the curve and continued south along Connecticut Avenue toward the White House and the Executive Office Building.

The driver was a GS 9, cleared to Top Secret level for no other reason than that he drove an assistant national security advisor named Perry Weinstein.

Yackley had been on the phone at eleven. He had been contacted by Claymore Richfield, who had gone back through Tinkertoy after Mrs. Neumann left the DA building. Richfield had been merely curious and he had no way of understanding a damned thing that was going on. But Richfield was now a dangerous man.

Damnit. This was what you had to work with.

Perry Weinstein, in the back seat of the Mercedes, still had not repaired his horn-rimmed glasses. He wore a jogging suit that had never been sweated in. He sat back in the Mercedes and closed his eyes and tried to think.

It had only been thirty hours to Nutcracker, Yackley had shouted.

It was April 18, the feast of Pentecost. Every move had been put in place. All the agents to be defected East were in place; Gorki had kept his bargain as well. But, perhaps, that was the way it was supposed to be. You didn't bargain with the devil.

Yackley, on the phone to Perry, had been very close to hysteria.

Hanley was snatched. By someone. Dr. Goddard said a nun was dead, as well as the security director, Randolph Finch. There had been two of them: A priest and a young woman.

Yackley had been babbling when Weinstein hung up the phone on him and made a second call. There was a scramble going on right now inside Operations Wing 3 of FBI. "The Sisters," as usual, didn't have a clue but they were the domestic intelligence agency and when it came to tracking people inside the citadel, they were the best at the game. So the FBI director kept explaining to the National Security Director who passed on his budget recommendations to the White House.

Now prove it, Perry Weinstein thought. Find Hanley and his abductors and do it in twenty-four hours.

He had allowed too much rope for Yackley. Yackley, in the end, was too stupid to know what to do with it. Weinstein had even had to prod the boob on electroshock treatment. Hanley was lingering too long; it was quite possible he could be legally rescued from St. Catherine's before he died. At least let his memory die.

He never said it in those terms to Yackley, of course.

Perry Weinstein was so careful and so close and it was not going to end badly. He had worked out a careful bargaining. Yackley had been assured he would have five enemy agents to show for the work and he would be more secure than ever. Even when this administration came to an end, Yackley would be included at the highest levels in the next administration—whatever the party. Perry Weinstein was a pragmatist and he promised practical things to people like Yackley.

And he would bring out Gorki. That was the key to the whole exchange. The master spy, the director of the Committee for External Observation and Resolutions—the Resolutions Committee of KGB. Gorki would come, kicking and screaming, because Gorki

was the prize that Weinstein needed to make himself a "made" man in intelligence, one of the litmus tests to apply to others again.

And now some goddamn double-cross at the lowest level was being worked and two killers had snatched Hanley from St. Catherine's.

And a busybody named Lydia Neumann had somehow uncovered the digest of Nutcracker. She was being taken care of now.

The telephone was ringing when Weinstein entered his office. He popped buttons on the console and put on the speaker phone. He crossed to the window, hands in jacket, and stared down at the White House while he listened.

"Two chasers were put on Alexa ninety minutes ago," said the voice. There was a laconic charm to it. Ivers was the fixer from NSA; he had been part of Nutcracker from the beginning. Not that Ivers understood what Nutcracker was really all about. He was a good, loyal, conspiratorial and limited man of action; his part in Nutcracker was just large enough to hold his interest.

"Where is she?"

"She is due to call in by one. We'll hold her this time, trace the call—"

"It'll be a pay phone—"

"That's in the movies, sir. We can trace anyone. Anytime. From any place." Ivers was sure and that amused Perry Weinstein. He pushed the glasses up his nose and smiled at the White House. The President was at Camp David. In a little while, the helicopter would clatter in and the ghouls from the networks would gather and wait for some word from the Main Man and the helicopter blades would keep rotating until the President had crossed to the south portico and entered the White House.

In two weeks, there would be the summit in May. But first, a crossing of swords called Nutcracker. A skirmish with spies and defectors.

Ivers rang off.

Dickerson at FBI was next. The Sisters had already found the abandoned Buick in Hancock. A second car had been stolen in that

small town in western Maryland. "They're heading back this way," Dickerson said.

What a genius, Weinstein thought. "Do you have helicopter surveillance?"

"Yes sir, but it's a limited advantage today. The fog is really thick out on the Panhandle, I—"

"Roadblocks?"

"Yes sir, this is Division A emergency, we are moving—"

He rattled on in that dry disguise-my-accent voice. He offered reassurance like a telephone company salesman.

When the domestic business was done, Perry Weinstein moved to the other phone. It was colored red and it was safe and the numbers that it dialed were also safe.

He picked up the phone, waited, decided on the first block to be pushed over. Nutcracker was commencing in the morning because every block was in place now and the whole edifice could be tumbled.

Alexa had not slept at all.

She had followed the taxicab containing November all the way back to the hotel. Wisconsin Avenue was bright and unsuitable for the sort of direct hit she intended. And then the hotel had been wrong as well. She had lost him at the elevators and she suspected he had doubled back behind her. Watergate was so complex.

She had failed again. Everything else was an excuse.

She had not eaten for two days. She felt sick to her stomach all the time. She thought her breath smelled foul, for the first time in her life.

She dressed carefully, as always, but there was no joy in it. She was a woman who had delighted in all her senses, in feeling and smelling and touching. She was imbued with self-love but she never thought it was excessive. There had been much to love about herself.

How quickly it broke down, she thought.

A gesture from an old man with yellow skin in Moscow and suddenly she was a puppet on the stage with its strings cut. She had no action. She could not even save herself.

She pitied herself. And that was why she had not slept. That and

the words of the man she had come to kill. So flat and soft in the darkness. He had known her. He had told her she was in danger.

She stood on Pennsylvania Avenue and the street was empty because it was Sunday and she looked at the White House. She thought it should be more impressive, like the Kremlin. She thought she would kill the second November today and then kill herself. It would be far better than to be arrested by the Americans and put in cells for the rest of her life.

She dropped coins in the pay telephone and made the call to New York City.

The phone was picked up at the other end. There was no other sound.

She identified herself.

"You had opportunities. Why didn't you take them?" The voice spoke English; it was without any accent.

"I could not ensure my own way out," she said. She spoke as brutally as the voice. "Each time, there were difficulties. He knows me. He called me by name last night."

There was silence. She had silenced the pitiless voice for a moment. It was almost a moment of triumph.

"Is this true?"

The question was not meant to be answered.

"Do you have him?" Alexa said. "It doesn't matter now. I know what I will do. I will fulfill the mission." She closed her eyes and felt faint. She tried to think of the heroic posters thrown up in Moscow each May Day and in the fall, in celebration of the October Revolution. Men and women marched on banners hundreds of feet long, striding with Lenin toward the Revolution. But she did not feel heroic. Only sick and alone in this foreign, savage country. She would do her duty this last time.

"Yes. This time, without fail. Even at risk to yourself."

"Where is he?"

"There is a house on P Street," the voice began. "Go to the house on P Street and when you reach it, wait inside. The key is under the mat at the door. Wait there for instructions." He gave her the address on P Street Northeast.

She felt very afraid in that moment, more afraid than at any time since Helsinki when the agent there had directed her to "the second November in Switzerland."

"What will happen to me there?"

"Happen to you?" The voice seemed on the point of taking on coloration. But the voice paused and resumed in the same bland tone. "Nothing, Alexa. It is for instructions. This time, there will not be failure. There is no time for failure now."

And the line was broken.

She replaced the light-green telephone receiver. She looked around her. What a queer city of low buildings and Greek columns and shabby streets full of slums. There were trees everywhere and yet there did not seem to be gaiety to the city at all. She felt a sullen undercurrent around her. She was accustomed to the same thing in Moscow: But there was vitality in Moscow that came from within, from secrets kept locked in secrets.

Alexa thought there was no vitality in Washington on this Sunday afternoon. She felt alone and abandoned in the West.

She stared around her. Her eyes carried down to her soul. They were shining and black and dangerous. Her eyes could not be disguised and she would not die like a victim. If they meant to kill her, they would have to engage her.

She felt the pistol in her pocket.

She saw Lenin on the wall hangings, striding toward the Revolution.

She even felt the first stirrings of hunger.

TWENTY-NINE
Flight and Refuge

"Why are we going back?" Margot said.

"The best place to hide is a city," Devereaux said. "Is he all right?"

"He's shaking."

"Give him my coat."

"You killed that nun?"

"Give him the coat, Margot." Softly, firmly.

"You killed her and that man—"

"Give him the coat."

She draped the coat around Hanley.

They heard the helicopter again. The copter swept low over the road but there was nothing to see. The fog was blinding. It was an act of desperation to fly in fog like this.

Devereaux drove very fast and very hard. His eyes were so fixed on the road—on the billows of fog—that it was painful to refocus them. The fog seemed to roll at the windshield. It was worse than it had been that morning. The day was warm and the ground wet. He rolled down the window and could smell the springtime all around, all hidden.

"His face is bleeding."

"Is it bad?"

"I don't know."

"For Christ's sake, Margot, wipe the blood away and see how badly he's hurt."

She shivered. She wiped the blood from Hanley's cheek and saw the wound. "No, it's not bad," she said. "You killed two people."

The copter blades sounded very close. That was the trouble with fog. It affected hearing as well as vision. It enclosed everything.

Devereaux had not intended to rescue Hanley that Sunday morning. He never thought that Hanley would recognize him. Or, if he did, that he would have been enough in his senses to keep quiet. It had been a surveillance, to see where they kept Hanley and how hard it would be to get him out.

Now it was a mess. There was no time left at all. Hanley must hold the key to whatever was going on in Section. But what help could he be?

The police car passed them and Devereaux saw the taillights wink in the rear-view window. Turning around. It was a good idea to get back to Washington but this was a terrible road for it.

"Hold him, Margot," Devereaux said. "And get down."

She slid down in the seat and the car came very near behind them. The Mars lights were flashing. Devereaux slowed down as though to stop. The police car slowed down. The helicopter surged overhead.

Radio contact, he thought.

Nothing to do. He pushed the gas pedal and the Buick roared ahead and the reaction time from the patrol car was just a moment slow. There was no time to do anything else.

The Buick was going fifty miles an hour into blind fog. Devereaux could barely see the yellow line on the two-lane road; it was the yellow line that guided him. If he couldn't see the yellow line at all, they were finished.

Margot's voice was too loud: "My God, you can't drive this fast!"

He didn't answer. He held the wheel hard.

The cops had guts. They were following his taillights, scarcely thirty feet behind.

More guts than brains, Devereaux thought. He slammed the brakes,

turning the wheels left to the wrong side of the road, and then rode the shoulder, controlling the skid.

The police car crashed into the right rear bumper and careened into a grove of trees that led down a gentle slope to a secondary road below. Devereaux never stopped. He pushed into the fog and Margot got up and looked around and guessed what had happened.

"This is insane, you're making me . . . an accomplice to . . . this is killing . . . you killed a nun!"

"Shut up, Margot," he said, never looking at her. "Hold him," he said.

"This man is dying," she said.

"He can die later," Devereaux said. The voice had no pity in it at all.

They made it to the edge of the city in a stolen car, swiped from a church parking lot in Fredericksburg. For a moment, Margot had forgotten her fear because she had been fascinated by the technology of stealing a car without keys in it.

In Bethesda, Devereaux said, "Change cars again."

"Are you insane? Are you just insane?"

"Margot, there are people after us. They are using helicopters. Just do what I say and don't ask me any more questions."

The car was a Rambler with the keys in it. It had patches of rust on the body and the tired look of a car that no one makes anymore. He pulled up the stolen Pontiac and got out. He helped Margot lift Hanley into the back of the Rambler.

The dude came out of the liquor store into the lot and watched them. He was in his twenties and looked scuffed at the toes. He had a worn leather jacket and he wasn't wearing a shirt.

"Hey, buddy," he said in an easy voice. "My car."

"I was just taking it," Devereaux said.

The kid grinned. "Why don't you steal something worthwhile? This is a shitbox."

Devereaux smiled. "I could buy it from you."

"Then I'd be stealing from you."

"Do you have scruples about that?"

207

"No. Do what you gotta do, you know? Been driving that old sucker all winter, though. Got me through. Have some affection for it."

"Are both of you crazy?" Margot was in the car now.

"Tell you what," Devereaux said. "I'll give you a hundred for it and I'll return it later. Just renting it."

"Ain't worth a hundred. Why don't you go to Avis?"

"What do you say?"

"Sure. That's what I say. Just give me a lift, will you? You going into the District? Drop me off down by the Huddle House over the line, will you?"

The Rambler coughed across the District line on Wisconsin Avenue shortly after two in the afternoon. The kid's name was Dave Mason and he told Devereaux to watch for the cop who always waited behind the supermarket on the south side of the line for speeders who wanted to push over the twenty-five-mile-an-hour limit.

Devereaux eased it down and was passed by a BMW. A better prospect. The D.C. police car shot out into Wisconsin Avenue with Mars lights flashing. They passed the BMW pulled over to the side of the road two blocks later.

"You got some idea where you're going?" Dave said. It was just a friendly voice. He smiled at Margot in the back seat.

"Some," Devereaux said.

"Ain't nothing to me, man. But I would like to get the car back."

"You'll get it back or I'll have one built just like it."

"Rust and all," said Dave. He smiled. He popped a beer out of the sack. "You want a beer, lady?"

"No," Margot Kieker said. None of this was real. It wasn't happening.

"You drop me off up ahead," said Dave. "I can hoof it."

"You working, Dave?"

"Not much. Do a little housepainting. Things are slow. Everyone with a job to offer wants you to work for two dollars an hour and clean out the toilets in your spare time."

"Gimme the address," Devereaux said.

Dave wrote it down on the paper sack and tore off a piece of the sack. He gave it to Devereaux. He looked him right in the eye and Devereaux stared back at him. Dave smiled. "Damn. You're gonna bring it back, ain't you?"

"Bet on it," Devereaux said.

The house was in Georgetown and it had occurred to Devereaux as they entered Hagerstown, an hour before.

The house was narrow and tall and elegant, with polished bricks and gleaming black iron. The roof was flat and ornamented with a copper facade. The Rambler seemed out of its class parked in front of the house. The Rambler would have to go. But first, there was the matter of Hanley. And the girl.

Margot had asked him after they dropped off Dave, "Why would he trust you?"

"He doesn't."

"He gave you the car."

"I gave him a hundred dollars."

"I don't understand. He didn't call the police or—"

"Why would he do that?"

"You were stealing his car."

"No one would steal a car like this."

"You would."

"Margot." Softer now. "You have too much belief in rules. There aren't any rules."

"Then it's chaos. No rules means it's chaos."

Yes, Devereaux thought.

That exactly described it.

He opened the door of the car. His arms felt heavy. His back was knotted with lumps of tension. He would have to shake all his muscles awake again.

He went first, up the three stone steps. The street was empty but it could be full of people if the sun came out.

He knocked at the ornate brass plate. The door opened and it was an old woman.

"Dr. Quarles."

"It's Sunday," said the old woman.

"Tell him it's Mr. Devereaux."

The old woman frowned and slammed the door. He waited. The afternoon was full of sweet smells and the fog. The wonderful fog that had covered their tracks all the way into Washington. Even the best agent needs luck; he had not expected the fog at all.

The door opened. Quarles stared at him. Quarles had large eyes and a red nose and his eyebrows exploded on a broad forehead. His hair was wild, long and combed in the absent manner of men who have better things to do than worry about how they look. He resembled an Old Testament prophet or John L. Lewis.

"What do you want?"

"I've brought you a patient."

"Just as well. I don't make house calls," Dr. Quarles said. He opened the door wide and stared at the car. "My God, I didn't know they still made those things."

"They don't."

"Well, get it out of here. You're driving down property values. Put it on M Street and let it roll down the hill and into the river."

Devereaux nodded at the car and Margot Kieker opened the rear door.

"Well, she's young enough. Knock her up?"

Then they saw the second man, emerging painfully, half-consciously, from the back seat.

"Goddamnit. He's wearing a hospital gown," Dr. Quarles said and he took a step down and then another and reached Hanley before Margot sank under the burden of the man.

Quarles was large and strong. He had the arms of a Welsh miner, which his father had been, and the manner of a Welsh preacher, which his father had opposed. Quarles had no time for foolish people or foolish notions. He was immensely successful. Seventeen years before, in Vietnam, he had been captured by a file of Viet Cong. Seventeen years before, he had been rescued—not for himself but for the sake of someone else captured that day. The second prisoner had been important for some reason of state. For some reason of

210

state—neither Devereaux nor Quarles ever knew it—Devereaux had saved Dr. Quarles' life. It was a matter of a debt that could never be repaid and both of them knew it. And both knew that Devereaux was ruthless enough to exploit it.

Quarles picked up Hanley the way a child will pick up a bird with a broken wing. He carried him into the house.

He put Hanley down in an examining room, on a table covered with a leatherlike surface. He grasped his wrist, held his fingers to his throat, did all the things doctors do quickly.

"He ought to be in a hospital."

"That's where he has been."

"Why did you take him out?"

"Because they were killing him."

"Who is he?"

"It doesn't matter; you don't need to know."

"Need to know?" Quarles turned the face of the prophet on him. "Like that, is it, Mr. Devereaux? You'll roast in hell someday."

"But not right now."

"You wicked man and your wicked ways. Still playing at the game? Why don't you grow up and act your age and get into something important?"

"It's too late for that," Devereaux said. "What can you do for him?"

"What did they do to him, is more like it?"

"It was a mental institution—"

"A goddamn looney bin? You took this wretch out of a nut house? Well, you're not so far gone after all, you grave-robbing son of a bitch. Good for you."

Margot Kieker blanched but this wasn't the worst she had seen this day. She stood by her great-uncle, on the other side of the table, holding his hand because she didn't know what to do with her own hands. She was so amazed with herself—with her calm, with her actions—that she felt in a perpetual state of shock.

"Who's this? Your moll?"

"His niece."

"Niece my foot. I see Congressmen with their nieces prowling

211

the joints on M Street. Those are nieces. This looks like a girl to me.'' He had such an odd manner of speech—as though he had learned to talk by reading old books—and the cause was precisely that: He had been nearly dumb until he was ten because he could not see very well and no one in that village in Wales understood it. He had taught himself to read by closing one eye and reading with the other.

Devereaux said, ''There isn't much time.''

''What? For him? He'll make it by the look of him. Just needs some beef. Heartbeat's slow but regular, pulse is— But then, why am I explaining this to you? I'm the goddamn doctor. If I say something, it's so.''

Devereaux seemed to ignore the tone of voice, the glowering face, the posturing and theatrical gestures. He went to the window and looked out of the examining room at the street. ''Bring him around,'' Devereaux said.

''What is this about?''

''Do you have a medical directory?''

The book listed surgeons in Washington, D.C., and environs and their specialities.

Devereaux found the name he was looking for. ''I'll be back in a little while,'' he said.

''Where's your shirt, man?''

''It's a long story.''

''And you don't have time to tell it.''

Devereaux buttoned the black coat over his collarless clerical shirt. He had no more time to waste with Quarles. Quarles owed him because of his own sense of debt; Devereaux would not have felt the same way. But if Quarles owed him, then let Quarles satisfy his conscience by paying the debt.

THIRTY
The House on P Street

Alexa saw the man in the house on P Street. He was at the window. Alexa stood across the street and felt for the pistol in her pocket.

She thought she would shoot the man in the window. Then she would wait six more hours to see what the reaction would be when she called the number in New York.

Action was better than worry, she thought. If this was a trap, it would not matter. And if this was a mistake—well, then, she was being condemned for some mistake she could not even understand.

She drew the pistol out of her coat pocket and unsnapped the safety and drew the target in line.

And felt the muzzle on her neck.

"Don't even turn."

Said in bad Russian. But she understood.

He reached for her pistol and took it from her cold hand and pushed her ahead of him across the street and into the house.

There were three men. It was as she imagined it would be. She felt something like relief. She had been on a tightrope for so long. At least, this was the end.

The first man said it was necessary to handcuff her. For reasons of security. He said it as an explanation, which comforted her. He spoke fluent Russian but he was obviously not a Russian.

213

They cuffed her hands in front of her. The cuffs were attached by very thick and very heavy links of metal.

They searched her.

One of the men derived some pleasure from this. They removed her underpants and explored her body. They wanted to humiliate her; she understood that; she understood the techniques, all of them. It was preliminary to what would follow.

She hoped death would be easy. She had never dwelt on inflicting pain for its own sake or for her pleasure. She killed because she was a soldier in a war and that was what she was supposed to do.

Until the matter of the second November.

It had been a trap, all of it, and she had waited for the trap to be sprung on her with the timid courage of an animal that understands its impending doom.

They told her to sit down at last in a straight chair next to a wooden table in a room at the back of the house. One of the men went out. The second man sat at the table. The third man went to the window and looked out.

The first man—he was stocky, with rigid blue eyes and very blond hair—said, "We are United States agents."

"CIA," she said.

"Perhaps," the blond man said.

That confused her. She opened her eyes very wide and he seemed to stare straight into her, as though she had no secrets and no defenses. She felt the cuffs on her wrists. She was strong and she felt outraged—despite her training, despite her understanding, the search had touched an outrage in her—and she pressed her lips together very tightly. She had no intention of resistance, except in that moment of outrage. She had seen resistance shown by other prisoners and how that resistance was gradually broken down.

"My name is Ivers," the blond man said. "But how much do you know of this already?"

Again, she felt disoriented. She blinked and stared at him and tried to understand. She spoke in English now:

"I want to tell you what you want to know. I know that I am

trapped in this. I have no way out. I realize all of this and I want to cooperate with you. My government has . . . abandoned me. I do not understand. But I do not want pain.''

The one at the window said, ''She doesn't want pain. You hear that?''

''I heard that,'' said Ivers. It seemed to give him pleasure to think about that. He said to the one at the window, ''Why don't you go out and get some sandwiches. Some coffee and sandwiches.''

''Oh,'' said the one at the window. ''I get it.''

Alexa stared at Ivers.

''All right,'' he said. The second one went out the door. ''What do you know about Nutcracker?'' It was what he had been told to say. Ivers was the fixer, the errand boy. He understood his status and it didn't bother him. No one else knew how important he was. Or who he reported to.

She stared at him without speaking. It was the wrong response. He got up from the chair and came around the table slowly. He hit her on the face. He hit her five times. The blows were open handed and his hands were large and when they cracked her skin, the pain filled her head and clouded her vision. When the blows were done, the pain burned across her skin and filled her thoughts. She was crying but it was not self-pity; it was because of the pain. The tears came involuntarily.

''All right,'' Ivers said. He went back to his chair and sat down. ''What do you know about Nutcracker, and who else was involved? Why didn't you do your contract, Alexa?''

''I don't understand you.''

''Really? You don't really understand me? Dear, this is not a game. We have a loose cannon out there and it's up to you to help us haul it in.''

''Please. Mr. Ivers. I will tell you. Please, I will tell you everything. I can tell you about the business in Finland five years ago, I can—''

''I'm not interested in ancient history. I want to know about November. Are you two in this?''

She felt she was sitting in the company of a madman.

215

"You didn't take out November. You were supposed to take out November. You had chances. Was he part of the deal?"

"I was to resolve him. Yes. But I did not resolve him because I saw this was a trap. If I resolve him, then I am trapped worse than if I am a spy. Yes, I am an agent."

"Oh, God, dear, we know that," Ivers almost laughed. "Everyone's known that. That's a given. You're a spy, he's a spy, everyone's a spy. So you tell me, dear, tell me if November was part of this scheme with you and . . . and who else? That's what we have to know, dear. Who else?"

She sat very still. She was locked in a room, in handcuffs, and she was speaking to a madman. Her head was ringing with pain. She felt isolated and alone and afraid. She could smell the fear in her breath.

"This is the way it is," Ivers said. "You are a Soviet agent in the United States. You were involved in the seduction of a security guard in California a couple of years ago. That's a felony, dear. You have no diplomatic status. We could lock you up for the rest of your life."

"No," she said. "No." Softer.

"And think of pain, dear," Ivers said. "I have no aversion to that. I like my work. I do jobs for people and I do them well and I said, 'You can leave her to me, I can take care of her.' I saw your photograph. Very nice, all those photographs that Gorki took of you."

The photographs.

On a spring morning six years ago.

So inventive. Why would she agree to such a thing? Because he was Gorki and there was power in the glittering lizard eyes and the yellow skin was parchment to the touch and, in those moments with him, alone, he controlled her utterly.

And now he had abandoned her.

And thrown her to people like this man.

"Now, let's try this again," Ivers said.

The door opened.

Ivers looked up. It was too soon for sandwiches. Didn't the idiot understand anything?

Denisov said, "Will you take the handcuffs off?" The voice was as mild as a vicar speaking of children and flowers. The eyes swam behind rimless glasses and the right gloved hand held a Walther PPK.

"Who are you? This is government—"

"Shut up, please. Take the handcuffs off."

Ivers reached for the key.

"Slowly."

Alexa stared at him. He said to her, in Russian, "Why do you let yourself be trapped by dull people?"

She said nothing.

The wrists were freed and she felt for her face with her right hand. She felt the bruise.

"Who has sent you?" she said in Russian.

"I have come out of gallantry," he said. The approximate English could not explain the degree of mockery built into what he said in Russian.

"This is a fucking double-cross," Ivers said in plain English, without any subtlety at all.

"Perhaps," Denisov said in English. "Alexa, will you put him in the restraints? Behind his back, please?"

"There is no escape," she said.

"There is always escape. We are in America. There is always another way."

"I don't understand," she said.

"No. No one does at all. But that is the beginning of understanding, to admit you are ignorant." And Denisov smiled at his own cleverness.

Ivers learned to talk in a motel room outside of Arlington, Virginia, on a Sunday afternoon. It was amazing, Alexa thought. Denisov appeared so mild and the means were so brutal and direct. Ivers was eager to talk after only a few hours. Alexa thought it was the sense of patience that Denisov brought to the task; also, the sense that it did not pleasure him, any of it. Denisov was so powerful and controlled.

Alexa thought she was falling in love.

THIRTY-ONE
Hanley's Secret

Devereaux found Dr. Thompson and Dr. Thompson agreed, after a lengthy explanation, and persuasion of short duration, to talk about part of Hanley's treatment. He was not so jolly when it was over. Dr. Thompson was left alive because Devereaux could not think of any reason to kill him.

The city of Washington was sunk into the calm of its usual Sunday.

The President had returned from Camp David in the mountains. He had an extraordinary ability to rest completely in a short period of time. He had shouted out answers to the hordes of photographers and newsmen awaiting his arrival by helicopter on the White House lawn. He had waved at them in that characteristic way and shrugged off those questions he did not wish to hear. The helicopter blades kept whirling until the President was inside the White House.

Across the city and into the suburbs, people dozed in front of their television sets, read the remains of the Sunday *Washington Post*, dined on sandwiches made with leftovers from the big dinner meal, sank into the torpor of the day.

Nothing was happening in the city. Even the police stations were unusually quiet. There was a small mattress fire reported on Eastern Avenue shortly after seven but no one was hurt and it was

218

quickly doused. Washington was calm; therefore, the world was sleeping.

Hanley spoke rationally at 9:00 P.M. He recognized Devereaux. He was able to understand the questions.

Quarles had said this might happen. Hanley was weak but the passages of clarity were frequent. The doctor had summoned Devereaux from downstairs.

Dr. Quarles, unchanged in appearance from the afternoon, sat at the foot of the bed in the spare room at the top of the narrow house. He said, "The body is free of drugs but there's been abuse. Definitely. They gave him tranquilizers in the last week but there's nothing active now."

Hanley said, "They gave me electroshock treatments." He remembered it so well. His voice was weak but the train of thought was clear.

He had been fed twice. The portions were small but the soup was very rich. The liquid had warmed him. He felt vague and weak, as one does at the end of an illness that fevers the brain.

"They were killing you."

"Yes," Hanley said. "I didn't expect that. Not that part of it. I thought they just wanted to get me out of the way. I really didn't think this was going to come to murder." The thought of murder —his own murder at the hands of others—was compelling to him.

Quarles stood up. "Time now for shop talk, is it? The evil you do is never worth the good it brings."

Devereaux said nothing.

Hanley watched Devereaux's face.

Quarles wanted some reaction and there was none. "Goddamnit. There should be rules."

"But there aren't. There never were," Devereaux said. It was the first time he had responded to the doctor's rages and sermons.

Quarles stared at him with the face of Moses for a moment. And then he opened the door, stepped out, and closed it. They heard his heavy tread on the stairs.

"I don't know how long I'll be rational," Hanley said. Very

soft. "I think they've done some damage to my mind. I was quite rational in the last week. I was dying and weak and I was trying to think of a way to get out of that place. Or at least, tell someone."

"Why didn't you tell Mrs. Neumann when she came?"

"I wanted to. You see, the drugs, they had this effect on me. They must have drugged me all along."

"You were given medication by Dr. Thompson. When you were still functioning in Section," Devereaux said. And he told him everything Thompson had finally told him.

"So that explained . . ." Hanley trailed off. "I was trying to figure it out. And I thought about you and decided you must have been part of it, part of the trade. Or maybe, because I was drugged, I thought of you."

"You were reading Somerset Maugham. You were reading *Ashenden*. All set in Lausanne and Ouchy and across Lake Geneva."

Hanley blinked. "Yes. That's it."

"It was a mistake about me. I wasn't supposed to be awakened. They tapped your phone and they made a mistake."

"There's a mole. In Section," Hanley said.

"Yes."

"You understand that?"

"Yes."

"I felt it for the last nine months. It's been terrible. It could have been anyone. It could have been Mrs. Neumann. My God, even her. I suspected her. I thought the day she called up, she called me at home, I thought she was setting me up. I suspected everyone. I was paranoid. We lost two agents—two damned good men and their whole networks—in three months last fall. They defected. Can you believe that? The networks were blown up. All that work wasted. All those lives . . . They defected to the goddamn Soviet Union." Hanley tried to sit up. He was exercised and his face flushed.

Devereaux held up his hand.

Hanley coughed. "And now I've got a goddamn cold," he said. He never swore. He was a man of propriety. "I feel like a fool."

"There are no spies," Devereaux said.

Hanley blinked. There was a silence that could be felt in the room. The house was shuttered for the night. Margot Kieker slept on a cot in the basement room. The whole house had been squeezed to find room for the three visitors. The housekeeper said nothing to any of them, as though it might be quite normal for three strangers to drop in on Dr. Quarles in the middle of a Sunday and stay for the night.

"I said that. I said that on a goddamn open line."

"What does it mean?"

"Yackley. Yackley said it to me. He attributed it to Richfield, our mad scientist. Richfield was very gung ho on this retrenchment program that was coming down from Administration. We had too many agencies, too many spies. It was involved."

"A lot of bureaucratic infighting," Devereaux said. "The same old thing. It had to be more than that."

Hanley's eyes brightened. "More. A lot more than that." The dry voice was drier still but the flat Nebraska accent emerged with clarity.

"Richfield was trying to sell Yackley on the idea of cutting back Operations, that the work of agents was now largely redundant because we had so many surveillance devices, computers, satellites . . . all the hardware. Yackley liked the argument. He used it against me. The cost could be shown so clearly as savings. I mean, he wanted to eliminate a bunch of agents to start, as an experiment, to see if the operation would suffer—"

"Who?"

Hanley frowned. "One of the things . . . specific memory. It's harder to fix times. This morning I woke up and I thought I was six or seven years old, the time I was in hospital with appendicitis in Omaha—"

But Devereaux had opened a sheet of paper. He read: "January. New Moon. Equinox. June. August. Vernal. Winter."

Hanley said nothing for a moment. "Yes. The names. The agents."

"They're all in the field—"

"Yes. No chasers or safehousekeepers. All watchers and stationmasters. They had networks. My God, I couldn't explain to

221

Yackley that he wasn't talking about seven men. He was talking about hundreds of men. The links . . ."

"I know," Devereaux said.

"It wasn't a matter of protecting our investment alone. It was all that work thrown away. And what good is the hardware without software? I mean, we get soft goods all the time from the Opposition. The hardware bona fides it for us. And the other way around. The satellite spies movement outside of Vladivostok. What's the good of knowing the SIGINT without knowing what the motive is? Software. Human contact. HUMINT. That's what you need. But the hardware doesn't have life or soul or judgment. It isn't human. You can't make it all on hardware, can you?"

"What did you do?"

"I didn't know what to do. I thought something was wrong. Yackley was positively demented on the subject. You'd think he was brainwashed."

"Yackley struck me as a man waiting for some stronger brain than his to tell him what to do. They call him a team player."

Hanley plucked at the cover for a moment. He was waiting but Devereaux said nothing more. Devereaux had made the contact with Denisov at five. It was the fallback point, derived from an old show business routine. Denisov called the lobby of the hotel and asked if there had been any messages for him. Then Devereaux called and used the same name and asked for messages. He then left a message for anyone who would call him. Denisov called again, asked for the name he had used before, and picked up the message Devereux had left. They made contact and the final message was: Ivers had talked.

"Damnit, man, what is going on?"

"What is Nutcracker?"

Hanley said the unexpected: "It was set up a year ago. We were collating information inside Operations. This was strictly Operations, Mrs. Neumann's division wasn't in on it at all. It was strictly software, strictly HUMINT."

"Go ahead."

"The idea came about because of what happened at the first summit. You remember the exchange of agents? It was all just

coincidence. I thought it was coincidence at the time. I really wasn't paranoid."

Devereaux said, "In the trade, that might just be reality."

"But the idea took on some urgency." Hanley was going back over memory. "I mean, there was all this talk about cutting back Operations. Cutting back software. Field agents and Number Four men and stationmasters and housekeepers and garbagemen. Even chasers. My God, you need chasers."

"My experience with chasers hasn't been all that pleasant. Section chasers," Devereaux said.

Hanley looked at the patterns on the wall. "A woman designed this room."

"The clever spy," Devereaux said.

Hanley said, "Sarcasm." Devereaux felt better at that. It was a trace of the old Hanley and not this weak man sitting up in bed in front of him.

"I'm so damned tired," Hanley said.

They waited for each other.

"Nutcracker. The idea was to find and identify three or four men from the Opposition. That wasn't so difficult. What we were going to do was to turn them. And if they wouldn't turn, we were going to muddy them up so that Opposition wouldn't know if they had been turned or not. We decided early on it would be in Europe exclusively, because that's where the Summit was going to be held."

"Berlin."

"Exactly."

"This was for politics?"

"For survival. Of Operations. Operations is the heart of the Section. Operations is HUMINT. Besides, it was legitimate."

"We're supposed to gather intelligence, not play 'I Spy,' " Devereaux said.

"We're supposed to survive. That's the first rule of every game."

"This is crazy," Devereaux said. Nutcracker didn't turn out to be what he expected.

"It got crazier."

"How?"

"It was downholded."

"What happened?"

"I had my own file in Tinkertoy. On Nutcracker. Yackley didn't know about it, Neumann didn't know. Well, I thought Neumann didn't know; she's a smart cookie. I had the file to keep track of my own reports . . . we were moving along, setting up our targets, we had made contact with one . . ."

Devereaux waited. Hanley seemed to be seeing something beyond the room. He plucked absently again at the covers. His eyes were wet. There might be tears at times, Dr. Quarles had said. The body reacts in strange ways to the manipulation of the mind. Give him time, give him rest.

"In January, I came in one morning and I had . . . I had been feeling bad. I had seen Dr. Thompson a few times. He gave me pills. Iron pills or something. I don't know. At least, I thought they were." His voice was small. "I came in this morning in January. It snowed. You know what snow is to Washington. The office was half deserted. My God, people are babies."

Silence again. And then the distant voice resumed. "I went into Tinkertoy for the Nutcracker file. And Tinkertoy stopped me. 'Access denied.' It was my goddamn file. And I am the director of Operations. It was my file and my plan and it had been taken from me. I felt . . . so strange. I felt like I had gone through the Looking Glass. I had to know what happened. I went to Yackley and he looked at me like I was crazy.

" 'What are you talking about,' he said. 'I never heard of Nutcracker.' Of course, it was true. I mean, it was my operation. I hadn't shared it with anyone. I had used discretionary funds. I made it a secret and now someone had taken it away from me. I couldn't figure it out. It was making me . . . well, what happened to me? Did I go crazy or not?"

"I don't know," Devereaux said. "I'm not a shrink."

"They were going to kill me," Hanley said with wonder. "The first day at St. Catherine's, that bastard Goddard sprayed me. With Mace. He sprayed me in the goddamn face. That dirty son-of-a-bitch."

"You can get him later," Devereaux said. "Why did you write

this? Why did you write Nutcracker and then list all our own agents? And my name?''

Hanley stared at the paper as though he had never seen it before. And then there was recognition.

"I was home. I was on fire all the time and so tired. I couldn't think what had happened to Nutcracker. It existed in Tinkertoy and I had no access to it. But if I went to Mrs. Neumann, what if it turned out that she was part of this . . . this thing that was happening in Section. She was the computer wizard. Maybe she wanted to destroy Nutcracker before it started. Hardware, she's in hardware. Software is old-fashioned. 'There are no spies.' It kept going around and around in my head. Everyone was against me. I went to Yackley a second time and then I thought that maybe Yackley was part of whatever it was that was going on.''

"There is no file above you, is there?''

"My level, you mean? Yes. The Security file, the level of the National Security Advisor. And the President's file.''

Devereaux said, "Why did you list the names of your own agents?''

"Because we had lost men and I got the idea—I got the idea that the Opposition was pulling a Nutcracker on me. On the Section. On our side. It just came to me like that. I thought I was crazy but there it was. It was logical. Maybe they—the other side—they were working against the Section. They could have access to my Nutcracker scenario and use it against me. Against the Section. They could let it go along and then, when the time was ready, turn it inside out.''

"You called me,'' Devereaux said. His gray eyes shifted focus. He was remembering as much as he could. The room was as still as a confessional. "You said something about the highest levels. When you called me.''

"I was babbling.''

"But what were you babbling about?''

Hanley squinted, picked at the coverlet again and again. He sighed and tried to remember. It was so difficult to remember things. "I was out of my head most of the time. It was like being on fire.''

"Remember,'' Devereaux said.

"The highest levels. The highest levels. It was like an itch inside my brain and I couldn't reach it. That's why I was writing down ideas. Like Nutcracker. That's it. The highest levels. I couldn't get through my computer to Nutcracker and that meant it was taken from me at the highest levels. But that didn't make any sense."

"Unless there is a mole," Devereaux said.

"A mole in Section." Hanley seemed to visibly collapse into the sheets. "A mole in Section." The horror of it clouded his face. He closed his eyes and felt like weeping again. He had said it before as though in a dream. And now, there was no dream. When he opened his eyes, they were wet. He loved Section. He had given his life to Section as you give your life to a bride or a cause or anything you love. The director of operations had become defined over the years by his job: He was the puppetmaster and, yet, it made him a puppet himself. And now the thought: There was a mole in Section and it would all come down and the play would be over, the stage cleared.

"Who committed you?" Devereaux said.

"Yackley."

"And supported him?"

"Richfield."

"And visited you at St. Catherine's?"

"Mrs. Neumann."

"Who else?"

"Perry Weinstein."

"Did Yackley ever come?"

"No."

"Yackley," Devereaux said, turning the name over in thought. "Yackley tapped your phone. Yackley knew you had called me. So Yackley must have sent the chasers after me."

"Yackley," Hanley said. "Are you sure?"

"In a little while," Devereaux said. "I need some things from you. Promises. And some money. Oh, and four thousand shares of stock."

"What are you talking about?"

"Expenses," Devereaux said. He tried a smile. "The only serious thing ever worth talking about to an employer."

"But you're not an employee anymore, Devereaux," Hanley said. He said it very softly.

"Yes. That's what I prefer." He listened to himself as if he might be detecting a lie. But then, that's what words were for. "I might come back. On active duty roster. But let everyone know so there are no more mistakes, no more independent contracts against me from the other side."

"Why?"

"Protection. If I come back, then Section is behind me." He said the words without any feeling in them.

He had given up his trade because he did not love it anymore and because he loved Rita Macklin. He had thought all along what he could say to her if he went back into the trade, back into the cold. The conversation in mind never had a conclusion but now, in a little while, it would have to be played out for real.

"I was set, I was anonymous, I was asleep. Only three people knew in Section—you, Mrs. Neumann, Yackley. And then one day, a Soviet courier kills Colonel Ready and it is neat and finished. Except someone told the Opposition they had killed the wrong man. That the real November was alive in Lausanne. So they sent a hitter down and two other hitters and pretty soon, it was like a comic opera. Every move that everyone made was orchestrated; everyone knew everything about everyone else. They couldn't have such good information unless it came from us. Came from you."

"I'm not a traitor—"

"I came back to kill you, Hanley," Devereaux said.

They let the silence support the words.

"You have to carry me on the books," Devereaux began again.

"But you won't come back."

"No. Not in the way you think. That's the way it has to be. I need my bona fides back. The badge and the gun." Said with bitterness. "You can't quit. You told me that when you called. You said you can never quit."

Hanley closed his eyes. He was weak but without pain. It was not an unpleasant feeling.

"I was so tired. At the end. Maybe I did have a breakdown. It was hopeless. If I went to the security advisor, what could I tell

him but the raving suspicions of a paranoid? And if I did nothing, the Section was finished.''

"The Section may be finished in any case.''

"I gave my life to the Section.''

"You nearly did.''

"Who was it? Who is the mole?''

"In a little while,'' Devereaux said. "Mrs. Neumann was arrested at two. Right in the Department of Agriculture building. She must have penetrated Nutcracker. It must be very close, whatever it is.''

"My own plan turned against me. But how are they going to do it? And why did you trust Mrs. Neumann?''

"Because I had to.''

"You put her at risk.''

"Yes.''

"She's a woman.''

And Devereaux smiled at that. "Are you a male chauvinist then?''

"That woman saved my life.''

"Be quiet. She's in Section. What do you think they're going to do with her? Execute her? They took her to Fort Meade.''

"My God, I can't stop whatever it is that is happening because I don't know what is happening. And no one knows.''

"So think about it.''

"I can't. I'm too tired.''

"You were pushed about agents. Too many agents. The talk in Europe is about a major Soviet coming out. It's too much talk, too open. Gorki in Resolutions Committee—Denisov's old boss. It doesn't make any sense.''

"Why?''

"Because everything is made so easy. Everyone knows everything about everyone else. 'There are no spies.' Who told you that?''

"Yackley,'' Hanley said.

"There are no spies,'' Devereaux repeated. "So what does the loss of a few spies mean? If they really don't exist. If we know all their secrets anyway?''

"But what is Nutcracker turned into? What's going to happen?'' Hanley said. His voice was dry.

"I think I know." Devereaux stared through Hanley, through the walls of the room, to a schematic in his mind reflected on a blank screen. Like a sheet of white paper with names on it.

"I think I know," Devereaux said.

And began to tell him everything that would be done.

THIRTY-TWO
Nutcracker

The operation called Nutcracker commenced thirteen hours after Hanley began to explain the procedures to Devereaux. Nutcracker had been too imminent to stop.

The Soviet agent identified as Andromeda was drugged and slipped into the western zone of Berlin at 1945 hours. When he was awakened, in an American hospital in Frankfurt, he demanded to know what was going on. Two officers of the Defense Intelligence Agency said he was Andromeda, a Soviet agent who had just "defected" to the West. One of the agents was a little smug about that. It had been so slick a maneuver, without any trouble at all. The man called Andromeda said over and over that he was a Lutheran minister in Potsdam. No one believed him. Not at first.

At the same time but in a different time zone—1845 Greenwich Mean Time—the Soviet agent identified as Hebrides was picked up by two SIS men from BritIntell and hustled to the safehouse outside London off the Great Western Road that leads to Oxford. Hebrides was clearly bona fided; his description had been confirmed by Washington. He was questioned, rather harshly, about his network. He explained, just as harshly, that one did not treat a British subject and the second tenor in the Warwick Light Opera Company in this manner. The SIS men were not very gentle and the CIA men looked the other way.

In three hours, Saturn and Mercury fell into the orbit of the West as well, the first in Tokyo, the second in San Francisco.

Nutcracker appeared to be functioning smoothly. Everyone was pleased. Quentin Reed phoned Perry Weinstein twice with a happy tone in his cultivated voice.

But Perry Weinstein was not so happy.

There were problems, all sorts of problems.

But nothing to tell Quent about.

There had been a definite fuck-up in Athens. The agent there for R Section, codenamed "Winter," reported to Athens police an attempt to kidnap him as he sat in Plokas Café on the sidewalk in Constitution Square. Only the chance that he had been dining that day with four business associates—all heavily armed—foiled the plot. Two men were dead.

By midmorning in Washington, D.C., the word from Athens was that the two dead men were Soviet commercial attachés with the embassy in the Greek capital.

Weinstein broke a pencil as he heard the report from Yackley by phone. Yackley was quite happy about it. Yackley did not understand.

Weinstein dropped the broken pencil in his wastebasket.

By noon, the watcher in Helsinki for R Section told police there his apartment had been broken into and ransacked.

Again, the R Section agent had not been harmed. Yackley had phoned Weinstein with that bit of news as well and now he was not happy, merely puzzled.

Weinstein saw what was happening.

He thought about it as he stared out his window at the White House. There was still a way to salvage things, he thought. If only—

He reached for the phone and pressed the button to connect him with Yackley.

Yackley could still be used.

Weinstein heard the phone ring and ring and ring. And then Yackley's secretary was on the line, explaining that Mr. Yackley was at lunch at an undisclosed location and expected to be out of the office until late in the afternoon.

231

"I don't believe this," Weinstein shouted. He never shouted. "I don't believe that idiot is out to lunch! What the hell does he think is going on?"

But the woman at the other end of the line said nothing and Weinstein slammed down the receiver so hard that the phone jumped on the desk. The white room was suddenly wrapped in silence.

What was going on?

Perry Weinstein considered himself a man of intelligence and calculation but there was a third part to him in that moment. He could not identify it. It began in his stomach and made him nauseous and built up through his organs until it reached his throat and made him dry and hoarse.

It was fear. For the first time, he felt afraid of what was going to happen.

He crossed the quiet room to the outer office.

His secretary was gone; well, it was lunch hour. He stared at her desk and at the two television monitors connected with the security lobby.

He pulled his eyes away and started back into his own office and stopped.

He turned again.

On the black-and-white screen focused on events at the security desk he saw the man cross the lobby and flash an identification to the guard. The guard put the ID card into a machine and looked at the machine and at the man before him.

Weinstein knew the card. It would be gray and featureless, like a blank and unused credit card. The machine would read the message buried inside the card, between the twin layers of smooth plastic bonded together.

He stared at the monitor screen and the man looked at the camera.

He knew that face.

His mind swept memory, clicking over files implanted in brain tissue, connected to life with electrical impulses.

He knew the face from a 201 file he had read carefully before beginning everything that was now happening.

Perry Weinstein retreated into his own office and went to the

THERE ARE NO SPIES

desk. He opened the upper right drawer and removed the old, heavy .45 caliber Colt army automatic. It was the type designed at the turn of the century to kill a horse—literally, because there was still a cavalry in those days. It was replaced in service now by a light Italian handgun. Weinstein had a fondness for weapons and for antiquities. He was a very good shot and no one in the building knew he had a weapon in his drawer. It would not have been allowed, this close to the White House across the street.

He sat down at his desk and waited. He waited for a telephone call to break the silence, to tell him the fortunes of Nutcracker were reversed. He didn't see how the blame could come back to him in any case.

But the door to his office opened anyway.

Perry Weinstein almost smiled in relief. The pistol in his hand was very heavy and felt good to him. He held it up so the other man could see the pistol clearly.

"Bang bang," Perry Weinstein said.

"You're dead," Devereaux said and stepped into the room. His presence filled the room. Weinstein held the pistol easily in his big right hand. He propped his elbow on the desk top to steady the grip.

"Bang bang," Perry Weinstein said again, like a child who finds himself very clever.

Devereaux waited by the door.

"The TV monitor. I was in the outer office and I saw you in the security lobby," Weinstein said.

"It doesn't matter."

"Why?"

"Nutcracker is off. Dead in the water."

"November," Weinstein said. His eyes glittered in the dull light of the room. "Our man November."

Devereaux stood very still.

"Come into the room a little more," Weinstein said.

Devereaux took a step.

Weinstein waved the barrel of the pistol in welcome.

Devereaux stood before the desk.

Weinstein came around the desk carefully. "I am very good with

pistols. Very good. In case you think I'm one of those desk-bound bureaucrats who doesn't really know anything about anything.''

He pressed the pistol against Devereaux's head, behind the left ear. The barrel felt cold on the scalp. Devereaux said, ''In the belt, left side.''

Weinstein reached and removed the pistol from the clip.

''Hands on head,'' he said. He pointed to a straight chair by the north wall. Devereaux went to the chair and sat down. Weinstein pushed the chair back on the rear legs so that it balanced Devereaux back against the wall. ''Is that comfortable?'' he said.

Devereaux did not speak.

Weinstein went back to the desk and sat on the edge of the desk. He stared at Devereaux with owlish curiosity. His eyeglasses were still held together by a paper clip. He had a rugged and tired look to him. It really had been a lot of work and now it was over.

Devereaux said, ''You should have let sleeping agents lie.''

''I couldn't do that,'' Weinstein said.

''I was curious about Hanley's calls. But it was only curiosity.''

''I couldn't be sure of that. It was difficult for me to maneuver.'' He said this with a slow, funereal cadence. He wanted someone as smart as himself to understand.

He went on: ''I was succeeding. In getting Hanley out of the way. In another year, I would have R Section stripped down, discredited.''

''How long have you worked for them?''

'' 'The other side,' you mean?'' Weinstein smiled. ''It's old-fashioned to think in those terms, don't you think? There is only one side: Stability. A sense of order. Real peace. The enemy is the terrorists and they're nothing more than nuisances. Who cares greatly that eight or nine people are killed in a Rome airport? I mean, beyond the eight or nine and their families? There is death like that every day, in every city of the world. No. There's no 'other side' anymore; just as there are no spies anymore.''

For the first time, Devereaux smiled. He seemed at ease and that annoyed Weinstein. ''You're the author of that nonsense.''

''Yackley is my messenger, my agent. Yackley is an empty mind

waiting to be filled. I gave a talk, actually, at Yale three years ago, before this assignment. I was trying to make an intellectual point that is true in practice. Eighty-five to ninety percent of our intelligence is hardware. It comes from things. It comes from satellites, skyspies, automatic listening devices. ELINT. PHOTINT. SIGINT. You know. There is so much information we can't process it all. The information is like a constant avalanche that just never ends, never runs out of snow, never fills the valley below. On and on, year after year. There is too damned much intelligence and we are drowning in it. So what is the use of agents in the field? Are they going to steal the drawings of the Nordam Bombsight? Or a copy of the Enigma Machine? My God, no one grows up. HUMINT is passé." He became agitated and got up, walked around his desk, dropped the .45 heavily on the desk top. He sat down and Devereaux was very still.

"This is modern times. There are no spies and spies are not only a drain upon the resources of the government—an argument, November, that flies well in budget-making circles—but a positive detriment. Spies generate spies. We spy on one another like kids. We misinterpret information because we are limited in intelligence; we hold up important analysis of real intelligence because we have our doubts or we are fed disinformation by our opposite numbers . . ."

"And then, there are times when there are moles in government and it takes a spy to catch a spy."

Devereaux's words were not expected and the room was quiet now. The man at the desk with the gun stared at Devereaux with something like hatred.

"You caught me? I caught you," Weinstein said. "You're a renegade to Section. You crashed a crazy old man out of St. Catherine's. You killed a nun—or it looks that way. And you killed a state policeman pursuing you. He died in the crash."

"He was driving too fast for conditions."

"You are a killer. You are out of control."

"I am licensed again." Very softly. "In the old trade."

"Goddamnit. I can kill you right now and get a medal for it."

"Why work for them?"

"Work for them? Those midgets? I saw a way clear to do some good. Don't tell me you believe in that nonsense about recruitment in college and years of quiet dedication to the cause? I was in Czechoslovakia five years ago on a fellowship and I made the contact, not them. I told them I would do what I could. To make the world a saner place."

"How kind of you."

"I didn't even want any money but I had to take money or they wouldn't have believed me. I wanted to contribute to understanding."

"You're crazy, Weinstein."

"No. You are. And Hanley. Spies and spymasters. I was handed R Section practically as a gift by that idiot Yackley. He was a climber and a star-fucker. He wanted me to see what a good job he did. Liked to call me Perry just as if we worked out at the same club together. What a complete asshole."

"Most of them are," Devereaux said.

"Yes. None more so than Hanley. I wanted to get rid of Hanley but you can't just kill people, you know. Not at that level. I convinced Yackley, who convinced Dr. Thompson that Hanley needed calming down. Some sort of tranquilizer. Thompson is to medicine what Typhoid Mary was to cooking. Hanley was being blocked, going through some sort of career crisis—he doubted himself. And then, when I took Nutcracker away from him, he went off the edge. It was a clever enough bit of business, I think. I wasn't even suspected."

"What is Nutcracker?"

"Didn't Hanley tell you?"

"But that isn't what it is—"

Weinstein smiled. "You don't know. So you haven't blocked it after all. Nutcracker isn't finished, is it?"

"Only the parts I could understand. About the other side snatching our agents. Part of our pre-summit maneuvering in the field—we get a defector/spy and they get two—"

"That can't be." Weinstein picked up the pistol again and sighted

Devereaux along the barrel. "That can't be." The voice was soft. "There are four hundred and fifty-three agents in field. They can't all be notified that quickly. I wasn't concerned when you escaped with Hanley that you could figure this out right away. And notify all the agents. You couldn't do it."

"No. You're right."

"Then what did you do?"

"I guessed which ones were the targets."

Weinstein blinked.

He felt his finger become very heavy on the trigger.

"You guessed?"

Devereaux waited.

"You *guessed? You don't guess! This isn't a matter of guesswork.*"

"But it is. That's what it always is. All the information doesn't mean anything unless you can guess what the missing pieces are."

"How could you guess?"

"Hanley had a list of names. Of agents. Scheduled for early retirement to trim the budget. They seemed most logical. And it would be enough to begin wrecking the Section—"

"I gave Gorki all the information. I told him about you—that you were sleeping. I told him to take care of you. And that damned idiot Yackley had already sent out two Section chasers to talk to you. So we ended up with four dead agents in Switzerland. What a mess. What a stinking mess that was."

"You gave Gorki all the information. It was so good. He knew where to send Alexa. He wanted to get rid of Alexa."

"I know. She was an embarrassment to him. The old fool had photographs of her naked and dancing. Pictures of them together. Stolen New Year's Eve from his dacha. He has his enemies in the bureaucracy as we do. I had word that he was coming out when the matter was over. Voluntarily or not. My little reward. After November was dead and the R Section spies were defected, Gorki was coming out. He was tired and old and he had enemies."

"Which side were you on?"

"I didn't care about Gorki, except that I could get credit for his

defection. R Section was going to be ruined by Nutcracker. Let CIA get credit, NSA, the Brits for pulling in some low-level Soviet flotsam . . . Gorki set that up as one of his bona fides, to show he was going ahead with the program. The grand prize was Gorki himself from Resolutions Committee. I would arrange the meeting myself—''

"You're a fool, Weinstein. Gorki gave you crap."

"They were low-level agents—"

"Gorki gave you a Protestant minister and an opera singer. He targeted innocents and turned them over to half a dozen intelligence agencies. Gorki isn't coming out. And Gorki was going to take credit for bringing in all the R Section people you were willing to betray. Gorki—whoever Gorki is—is a survivor. He got rid of Alexa—he was going to have her killed in Switzerland and put the blame on me—but it didn't matter if she killed me first and then you got her. In any case, she was no longer a problem to the man in Moscow. She wasn't going back to the Soviet Union to cause him trouble just by being alive. An old man learns to survive in a bureaucracy just because he's practiced all the tricks."

"We would have her. Ivers. It was pressure on him—"

"You're a fool in the long run, aren't you, Perry?" Devereaux's eyes seemed to glitter in the strong afternoon light. "I was asleep in Switzerland, dead to the world." For a moment, the two men were silent, considering the image of a sleeping agent, buried in a country at the edge of the world of spies. "You goddamn fool," Devereaux said at last. "I was on that ship in the Baltic as far as Gorki knew—and then you let your contact know that I'm still alive in Switzerland, the real agent named November, because Hanley had called me, because Yackley had tapped his line, because you saw the transcript and saw that I had heard something about a nutcracker. One wrong conclusion and all the rest comes tumbling down and you had to believe that your masters would get Gorki out of Moscow, one way or another. Gorki must have a sense of humor, whoever he is. He played you the fool for so long you still don't understand that's what you are."

"Shut up," Perry Weinstein said. His voice hissed and a vein in his neck seemed enlarged. "Shut the fuck up."

"And I would have stayed asleep in Switzerland but you sent those chasers after me—"

"Yackley did. To talk to you. They were only sent to talk to you and you killed them and—"

"Killing and killing and everything came down because of it. Because you made so many smart moves that you couldn't move at all. And you forced me to come back into the cold, into the trade."

"There is no cold," Weinstein said. "Don't you understand a goddamn thing I tried to tell you? Are you as stupid as the rest of them?"

Devereaux dropped his hands on his lap. He was smiling.

A damned smile. A damned smug smile. Weinstein picked up the pistol and came around the desk. "Nothing matters," he said, regaining a tone he had lost in the last minute. "You're dead. The real November is dead. And I'll be more careful in the future. A little setback along the way. I can assure you that Hanley is finished in Section and that's a victory—one less HUMINT believer. And we'll put a new man in for Neumann in CompAn and—"

"You won't survive," Devereaux said. He said it so certainly that Perry Weinstein paused. The pistol was fixed in front of him, pointed at Devereaux's face.

"I'll survive you. It's time to kill. End of the game, end of words."

He held the pistol in exactly the right grip, with the legs in a stance, the pistol in the right hand and the left hand around the right wrist to support its weight. Everything was exactly right.

Except for Devereaux's size. A petty miscalculation. His legs were longer than they seemed.

Devereaux's right foot reached the barrel just as Weinstein fired.

The shot singed his hairline and there was blood on Devereaux's scalp. He went down because the kick pushed him back off balance. His legs went flying. He rolled and Perry Weinstein brought the pistol down and fired again.

The shot destroyed a foot of plaster.

Devereaux braced, kicked out with both feet, making his legs points of a projectile. His feet slammed into Weinstein's left side.

The pain crushed the breath out of Weinstein and the third shot went into the ceiling.

Devereaux was up again, seeming to spring up like a halfback from a tangle of bodies on the football field. He grasped the gun hand and the gun exploded a fourth time.

Devereaux brought Weinstein's wrist down hard on the edge of the desk and Perry gripped the trigger in pain and a fifth and sixth shot went off.

Devereaux cracked his wrist.

The pain went white, right up to Weinstein's eyes.

Devereaux moved in close, chopped at the damaged left side.

Weinstein was big and strong but very slow. He was taller than Devereaux. He grabbed the smaller man's face in his left claw and tore it. There was blood on the cheeks.

Devereaux stepped back.

Weinstein pushed him very hard with his whole body and exploded his body against the north wall. Devereaux hit the wall hard. He went to one knee.

The second pistol—a very light Walther—was on the desk top. Weinstein reached for it and the pain of his broken right wrist paralyzed him.

Devereaux pushed off the wall and slammed again into Weinstein, pushing his body against the desk.

Weinstein had the pistol in his left hand—not his shooting hand. He brought it around and the trigger wouldn't pull. The safety was on. It was enough.

Devereaux hit him with a very heavy right hand square in the face, breaking his jaw and sending his glasses broken and sprawling across the desk top.

Perry blinked with pain that engulfed him like fear. It rose in his belly and reached for his throat and blinded his eyes.

The room was all sounds without speech. The shots lingered in echoes that nearly deafened both of them. They grunted with pain and effort. Weinstein brought the pistol down hard against Devereaux's head and he went down.

Weinstein stood over the body for a moment.

240

He pointed the pistol at Devereaux's head and unclicked the safety. He went to the outer door and stood there and looked at the twin monitors on the desk.

And then he saw it.

Terror crept over his broken features. The eyes were wide. He saw the horror of it.

It was there, on the monitor, the second screen.

A picture of the room he stood in. A picture of Devereaux on the floor by the desk. The monitor had been turned to the room. Someone had put a goddamn spy camera in his private room. Recording everything he had said to Devereaux. He looked up at the ceiling and still could not see the camera that had recorded everything.

And now they were coming, all of them coming. He saw them in the lobby on the other monitor. He heard the machinery of the elevator whirring beyond his outer office.

It was so damned clever of them.

But there was one way to escape.

He put the barrel of the Walther PPK in his mouth and squeezed the trigger easily. The trigger, unchecked by the safety, slid back to the guard.

He didn't hear the shot at all.

THIRTY-THREE
Exiles

They sat in one of those coffee shops on Third Avenue in New York City that are full of old men and bored waitresses. The couple sat quietly in the corner. They ate and drank and talked. They talked Russian. It was good to talk Russian, for both of them.

They became lovers, as well.

Alexa disappeared from the game, just as Denisov had and by the same way of escape—through Section. She was a good defector but she knew so little about anything except killing. Gorki had gotten rid of her—the photographs had been stolen from his dacha at Christmas and Gorki knew that his enemies intended to use them against him—and yet he had betrayed very little because Alexa knew very little. She was a disappointment to the Section but not to Denisov.

Denisov had cut off two of Ivers' fingers before Ivers learned to talk. To tell Denisov about his various errands for Perry Weinstein. Ivers had exceeded his authority and Ivers was in disgrace; worse, he was going to prison. The thought of prison terrified Alexa when Denisov explained what would happen to Ivers.

But Alexa had been drawn to Denisov that night in the room in the motel outside Alexandria. He had been utterly cold, ruthless, and without any compassion at all. He was cruel without pleasure.

It had given her great pleasure to see his power over Ivers.

She had slept with him. She had made love to him with great skill. She had done so many things to please him and he had come awake to her. She needed him so desperately because he was like her in this damned and strange and hostile world. She felt sadness because Russia was denied them and all the Moscow nights she had yearned for as a child—when she had wanted to count the stars— were over. She needed Denisov, the Russian words, the shared remembrances. If Denisov left her, she would be utterly alone and she could not stand that.

And Denisov, sitting across from her, his eyes mild and kindly behind the rimless glasses, understood her need. It very nearly frightened him.

THIRTY-FOUR
Conversation Finished

Rita Macklin unsnapped her seat belt when the plane hit the runway with a thump. The airlines all caution you not to do this. Old travelers always do.

She was so damned tired of traveling. The story hadn't been in the Far East at all.

She reached under her seat for the travel bag that had been home, office, comforter and dresser for four weeks. She thought she wanted a bath and then about three or four days of sleep. But she had only a day here and then it was back to Europe.

Back to him.

Because she was thinking of him being in a place that was not here in the bright and sterile concourse of Dulles Airport, she didn't see him at first. And then she realized what it must have meant, his being here. She felt a coldness rise inside her.

She crossed the terminal to him.

She stood apart from him for a moment. She was so damned tired and she didn't look her best. Her short red hair was mussed and she hadn't worried about lipstick. Her wide green eyes took him in. Nothing ever changed in him, she thought.

"Where are we going?" she said.

"I got you a room."

"All right."

It was all they said. They had too much to say to each other. He wanted to touch her. He took her bag instead and led her to the waiting car.

"Are you back?" she said, getting in the car. Her voice was dull, tired.

"Yes. In a way."

"That's the end of it," she said.

"I want to talk to you," he said.

And she did not answer him.

Rita Macklin slept in the afternoon and into the evening. When she woke up, in the darkened bedroom, she was alone. She stumbled to the bath and took a long shower to ease the coldness that pressed between her shoulders. She held her sharply etched face up to the shower and let the water stream down on her. The water did not warm her.

She dressed in her "press conference" clothes. The skirt was washable—everything was washable and unwrinkleable—and so was the blouse. They were blue. He liked the way she looked in blue, though he never said these things to her.

She wasn't angry with him. She was just saddened.

She put on earrings. She brushed her hair. Her body was tanned by the Oriental sun. He had spoiled everything by being here, in Washington. She had wanted him so much. Not words, not tears, just touch and tasting. To be next to him when they slept. To have his arm draped over her shoulders. To burrow into him. To go to sleep with the smell of him next to her and awake and lick him awake. My God, she just had wanted him and not words and this stupid conversation that was going to have to be finished.

The note on the desk said he was sitting in the lounge off the lobby.

"Why?"

"Because they woke me up. Killers. Come to kill me in Switzerland. It was just a mistake. They made an error in judgment."

"I want a beer," she said.

She sat next to him at the end of the long, weekday-empty bar. It was nearly nine at night. She was wide awake.

He started at the beginning and told her everything. She didn't ask any questions. She drank beer and listened and after a while she looked at him.

"What about the girl?"

"Margot? She went back to Chicago."

"You used her," she said.

He waited.

"You're good at using people."

"When there's no other way."

"But do you know what everything means, everything you told me?"

"Yes."

"Nothing," she said. "It doesn't mean a damned thing. All that maneuvering, all the dirty tricks and betrayals and murders and all this booga-booga spy stuff you pretend you don't love . . . it comes out not meaning a damned thing. I go halfway around the world and I hear the same leaders, the same revolutionaries, all the same words. The rhetoric never changes, the stupid lurching from one disaster to another. There isn't enough suffering to satisfy humanity. Death isn't horrible enough, there have to be varieties of death. Babies cry but it's not enough—we have to drop napalm on them to increase their tears. Someone I never heard of who's a ninth-rate bureaucrat becomes a Soviet agent and then gets found out by our man November—hurrah, hurrah!—and blows his face off and what the hell does it mean? Tell me one thing it means."

But he was silent. He watched her. He watched her eyes and saw pain at the corners of her pretty green eyes.

"Everything that happened didn't mean a damned thing to the world," she said at last.

Silence was a bond. They were the only people at the bar. She finished her beer and stared at the glass, at the foam coating the inside of the empty tumbler. She thought about the first time together, when she had slept with him in that old motel room on Clearwater Beach. He had slept with her only to use her and when

she knew it, it wasn't enough to leave him. Use me. I'll do anything for you, Devereaux. You bastard.

Damnit, she thought. Why was there always pain between them?

"Is it finished? I mean, is it finished?"

"I can't finish it," he said.

"I thought you could do anything."

"I thought I could. I thought I could say no and walk away from it. With you."

"Make it finished," she said.

"I can't. Not anymore. Not in the way I wanted. The way we wanted it."

"Make it finished," she said again.

"I can't force you to agree to anything. I told you everything. I told you the truth."

"Is that right? Did you tell me everything? Did you tell me you love it? Tell me that. Tell me you love it. The trade, the business, whatever you call it. The spy who goes into the cold because it's the only thing that amuses him. Tell me." Her voice was bitter and her eyes were wet. "Tell me you love it."

"No."

Waiting. Quiet.

"I'm good at the trade, that's part of satisfaction, I suppose." He saw his face reflected in the mirror behind the bar. "No. I don't love it."

"Do you love any goddamn thing in the world?"

"You."

"What about Philippe? You saved his life. You took him off that island. What about that little boy?"

"No. I don't love Philippe."

"You cold son-of-a-bitch."

"I pitied him." He would not touch her. She had to understand him and the truth of things without tricks. "Perhaps I pitied myself. When I saw him. When I heard him plead. Pity is not such a small thing, Rita." He wanted to touch her, to smell her. But this conversation had to be finished now; it had been suspended between them for too long. "Pity is a good thing to feel as well."

"But you don't have pity for me."

He thought it was over then. He felt sick because the words were too brittle.

"I would have done anything for you," Rita said.

She got up. She stared at him as though fixing him in memory.

Her green eyes turned to liquid emeralds. And they were cold as gems. "Anything."

She turned from him and walked out of the lounge on the lush red carpet. Her steps were quiet and then she was gone, into the lobby.

The sickness overwhelmed him for a moment and then he saw his face again, in the mirror. He stared at the empty eyes.

He got up and dropped money on the bar.

He walked out of the lounge and saw her. She was heading toward the elevator bank. The lobby was bright with people who spoke in loud voices.

She waited for the elevator and he was behind her. She turned. She looked at him. The emerald eyes were still wet and the coldness in them was gone.

"More talk?" she said. "More facing the truth?"

"No more talk."

"We finished the conversation. I always knew we would have to come to the end of it," she said.

"No. It's not over."

"What's left?"

"I don't have arguments. Or words. I tried to show you."

"What?"

"I love you." He tried to say it right. The words were magic to him but they were so common to others. Everyone loved everyone else. No one else ever understood that Devereaux had not loved another creature in his life. He had existed on pity until he met Rita Macklin. But not pity for himself; it was the thing that kept him apart from the world. He could pity life and keep the cold thing inside himself to make him apart from everything he did or said.

"Don't I get to be happy?" she said. "Don't you?"

"No guarantees."

"There ought to be rules of behavior. There really ought to be."

And she stroked his face then with one lazy gesture of her hand. Her hand touched his face as though it were no part of her words, her eyes, her thoughts. Her fingers raked gently across his cheek. "But there are no rules, are there?"

"No," he said.

"Dev." The hand lingered on his shoulder. The elevator door opened. The cage was empty. The bright lobby full of loud people was around them; they were alone in the middle of her gesture. He felt the weight of her hand on his shoulder and his hand touched her hand then, covering it, holding it. They crossed into the cage and the door closed on them and they were alone. He held her hand.

It was the end of a conversation that had been unfinished for too long.

THIRTY-FIVE
Rambler

There was a tail car and a police car and then this thing. A 1973 Rambler.

Dave stared out the window of the rooming house and then rushed to the door and down the stairs. He paused on the first landing. What the hell was this about? If it came down to it, he could deny he owned the thing. But they had his name on the registration and the plates and—

He opened the door and crossed the sidewalk. It was a warm day in May.

The man in the tail car got out while the driver got out of the Rambler. The driver didn't seem too happy.

"David Mason?"

"What's this about?"

"Are you David Mason?"

"Yeah."

"This is your car."

"Maybe."

"It is your car."

"All right, it's my car."

"We found it."

"So, you found it."

"We're bringing it back to you."

"What are you, the tooth fairy?"

"Yeah, I'm the tooth fairy." He seemed bored. "Look, this is your car and here it is. Also, here's the bonus."

"What are you talking about?"

"The bonus for use of the car. Twenty-two cents a mile and forty-two dollars per diem. It comes to four hundred twelve dollars thirty-one cents." He produced a pen. "Just sign."

"Sign what?"

"Expense account form."

"What are you talking about?"

"Government. Got any objections to four hundred twelve dollars thirty-one cents?"

"Not one."

"Man who rented the car from you."

Dave caught on. "Yeah. What about him?"

"He works with us. Our . . . section."

"Yeah. What do you do?"

"We're spies," the man said.

"Is that right?"

"Yes."

"Okay, you're spies."

The man held the paper while he signed. He took back his pen and popped it into his shirt pocket. He looked at Dave as though he didn't like what he saw.

"Boss says I got to ask you."

"Ask me what?"

"You want a job with us?"

"You're spies, right?"

"That's right."

"James Bond? Cloak and dagger?"

"Yeah. And we all wear trenchcoats." In fact, he was wearing a trenchcoat, even though it must have been 85 degrees.

"Sure," Dave said.

"Sure what?"

"Sure, I'll take a job."

"Come on, then," the man said.

And that was that.

THIRTY-SIX
Mrs. Neumann

By June, Hanley was back, a little thinner but still back. He was examined by three psychologists who said his mind was perfectly sound. Of course, if the Section had wanted to prove the other argument, it had three psychologists ready to testify that Hanley was deranged.

St. Catherine's federal subsidy was withdrawn because of certain abuses noted in a report filed with the budget office and the General Accounting Office.

Not noted in the report was the fate of Dr. Goddard. Hanley knew the signature. Dr. Goddard had been found with his throat slit. Hanley thought about it—and then put it from his mind. There was work to do. Operations was still . . . well, operational. Nothing had changed. Yackley was out of course, but quietly. Same with Richfield and the other division directors. The new boss of R Section was quite ruthless in the matter of personnel. Hanley understood that and appreciated it. Who could have appreciated Mrs. Neumann better than Hanley?

Even Quentin Reed, who had escaped any blame in the Weinstein affair, thought it was terrific. As he told the National Security Advisor, "What could be better? A computer whiz to put software on the right track and at the same time score points in the FBM derby?" It meant: Female, black, minority.

The National Security Advisor had trouble with that—with all of Quentin's jargon—but he understood the gist of it. Mrs. Neumann was the right sex for a change. And she'd ride herd on Operations too.

THIRTY-SEVEN
Sleeper

The tourists were in Copenhagen. It was summer and the air was filled with their English chatter. They all seemed to speak English.

They came by the trainloads into the quaint dark station in the center of Copenhagen, across from the Tivoli Gardens. They filled the streets and shops. They came in surging gaggles, they filled the sidewalks, they bought everything, and the Danes smiled with good humor at them.

The English language sounded good to the man at the table in the café on Vesterbrogade, west of the train station. The café was not a usual tourist place, but now and then a couple wandered in and spoke loud English and it felt good to hear it. The Carlsberg was very cold and he drank quite a bit of it every afternoon, reading the papers in the way of an exile with a lot of time on his hands. He had been waiting all winter and spring for the time to be spent, to watch the trail, to see who might still be on it.

He spoke Danish fairly well. They knew he was a foreigner of course but they appreciated him all the more for taking the trouble to learn that difficult language.

He read the *Herald-Tribune* and the *Wall Street Journal*'s European edition. He read the *Journal de Geneve*, the French-language paper from Switzerland.

He was interested in Switzerland very much.

He was not an unattractive man. He had the scar, of course, across his cheek, from ear to the edge of his mouth. And he had the limp, inflicted on him one night by a gray-haired man whose name was Devereaux. He had taken a long time to overcome the perpetual pain in his ankle. Devereaux had cut his Achilles tendon. At least the pain reminded the red-haired man every day of whom he hated more than his own life.

He thought about Alexa sometimes. She had killed poor Nils on the *Finlandia*, Poor Nils.

Nils was a find. Nils had been attracted to him in one of those cellar clubs in Copenhagen where the smoke is very thick and the beer is cold and everyone talks too loud. They had sat at a booth together and shared secrets. Or Nils had shared secrets.

They were so much alike. They had reddish hair, both of them. Nils wore a beard and Ready was clean-shaven. He could not have grown a beard because of the scar.

They had shared their bodies with each other. Nils was fascinated by Ready. Ready always had that power—over men and women. He used Nils and Nils understood he was being used and accepted the position. It was a position of deference and some might have thought it was degrading. Nils attended to Ready's words and whims.

And then, as Ready listened at the trail for the sounds of those who followed him, he thought of the idea. Of using Nils to end the trail for once and all. To involve Nils in the job of being a spy. Ready's spy. Ready's goat. It would work because everyone would believe in it so thoroughly. It was too absurd not to work. Nils became Ready because he would do the things Ready wanted him to do; he would meet the agent on the *Finlandia*; he would seduce the agent and tell Ready about the seduction.

Except, of course, he would never live to tell a soul. The Soviets must have thought Ready very stupid to believe they would give him a second chance.

The trail was cold now. Ready slept and no one knew he was alive at all.

So, mostly, in the long lingering summer afternoons of Copen-

hagen where there is a smell of fish on the sea breezes and the chatter of tourists in the narrow streets and wide plazas, Ready thought about new things. About Devereaux and his girl. About the time to come when Ready would be awake again. And what he would have to do to Devereaux and to his woman to make up for all he had suffered.

THIRTY-EIGHT
November

"Is this what being a spy is about? It's not so bad."

"There are no spies," Devereaux said.

Rita was bare-breasted because this was a very upper-class French resort called the Baie des Anges—the Bay of Angels—down the Riviera from Nice. The resort was formed by a series of enormous buildings curved around a very small harbor full of very large boats. The buildings resembled ocean liners with stepped decks. It was all very exclusive and monstrously expensive and he had taken her hand one afternoon, led her to a plane, led her here. She looked around her, to make certain all the other women had not suddenly slipped on their halter tops. All was well; breasts were naked. She wore a small red bikini bottom. Devereaux stretched on the chaise next to her; he had his eyes closed.

"I said this is a pretty good life."

"It's all right," he said. The sun was very warm and they were both dark now.

"I feel odd. Not wearing a top."

"You'd feel odder if you did."

"You like to look at naked women, don't you?"

"Yes," he said.

She closed her eyes for a long time and felt the sun on her breasts. With her eyes closed, she said, "Do you think it will be like this for a while? I mean, don't we get a breather?"

"Sure," he said. "This is the breather."

"But things always turn out bad in the end."

"There are no happy endings. I knew someone in New York once who wanted to believe in happy endings. It was the saddest thing you ever saw." And he smiled at her.

Rita waited for a while, feeling the sun on her body.

"This is the way it had to be." She frowned when she said it. She wasn't talking about this. She was talking about the matter they didn't really talk about anymore.

"I don't know," he said.

"Everything you told me. Everything you didn't tell me. It was supposed to save R Section. And nothing happened at all."

"Nothing." His voice was lazy in the sun. The babble around them was full of French voices and the occasional German grunt. The Mediterranean Sea beyond the pool was blue, deeper blue than it had ever been before.

"It turned out to be meaningless."

"If Perry Weinstein had remained, it wouldn't have been. Perry was moving up the ladder. He was that close to real power. This was a skirmish in the war. It could have been more than that. If Weinstein had won it."

"De Big Cold War. What is it, exactly, De Big Cold War?" She used an Amos 'n' Andy accent.

"Skirmishes. Little battles. It doesn't mean very much."

"People died."

"Yes."

"People always die." She was smiling at him because she was mocking him. It was what he might have said. His eyes were closed but he returned her smile. The smile came in her voice.

"It's a condition of life," he said.

"You're a philosopher."

"I wish I could promise you happy endings."

She said, "Would you like to go up to our rooms and make love?"

"You mean in the middle of the day?"

"Yes," she said.

He stood up and waited for her. She put on her top to walk back to the buildings. It was all so beautiful.

"You never want it to end," she said.

He said nothing.

They held hands as they walked back, among the half-naked bodies all around the pool. They looked exactly like what they were. Friends and lovers.

Begun at Baie des Anges, France
Finished at Chicago

ABOUT THE AUTHOR

An award-winning novelist and reporter, Bill Granger began his extraordinary career in 1963 when, while still in college, he joined the staff of United Press International. He later worked for the *Chicago Tribune*, writing about crime, cops and politics, and covered such events as the race riots of the late 1960s and the 1968 Democratic National Convention. In 1969 he joined the staff of the *Chicago Sun-Times*, where he won an Associated Press award for his story of a participant in the My Lai Massacre.

He began his literary career in 1978 with *The November Man*, the book that became an international sensation and introduced the cool American spy who later gave rise to a whole series. His second novel, *Public Murders*, a Chicago police procedural, won the Edgar Award from the Mystery Writers of America in 1981.

In all, Bill Granger has published seven ''November Man'' novels, four ''Chicago'' police mysteries, two nonfiction books written with his wife, and three other novels. In 1980 he began weekly columns in the *Chicago Tribune* on everyday life (he was voted best Illinois columnist by UPI) which were collected in the book *Chicago Pieces*. His books have been translated into ten languages.

Bill Granger lives in Chicago with his wife and son.